A STUDY OF THE MODERN DRAMA

By BARRETT H. CLARK

A STUDY OF THE MODERN DRAMA
EUROPEAN THEORIES OF THE DRAMA
CONTEMPORARY FRENCH DRAMATISTS
HOW TO PRODUCE AMATEUR PLAYS
EUGENE O'NEILL, THE MAN AND HIS PLAYS
AN HOUR OF AMERICAN DRAMA
PROFESSOR CLARK

BOOKS TRANSLATED AND EDITED:

The Labyrinth, by Hervieu (with L. MacClintock); *Three Modern Plays from the French; Four Plays of the Free Theater; Four Plays by Emile Augier; Lovers,* etc., by Donnay; Curel's *A False Saint;* Hyacinthe-Loyson's *The Apostle;* Sardou's *Patrie;* Brieux' *Artists' Families; The Fourteenth of July and Danton, The People's Theater,* and *The Wolves,* by Rolland; *Mother Nature,* etc., by Vanzype; *The House That Died,* by Bordeaux; *The World's Best Plays,* etc., 54 vols.; *World Drama,* 2 vols.

BOOKS EDITED, WITH PREFACES:

Masterpieces of Modern Spanish Drama; Jurgen and the Censor (with Sidney Howard and E. H. Bierstadt); *The Appleton Book of Short Plays,* 2 series (with Kenyon Nicholson); *The American Scene* (with Kenyon Nicholson); *Representative One Act Plays by British and Irish Authors; Great Short Stories of the World* (with M. Lieber); *Great Short Novels of the World; Great Short Biographies of the World; The Judge* by Gorky (with M. Zakrevsky); *The Story of a Novel,* etc., by Gorky (with M. Zakrevsky); *One Act Plays* (with T. R. Cook); *A Bibliography of the Works of Eugene O'Neill* (with Ralph Sanborn).

PAMPHLETS:

Œdipus or Pollyanna; Speak the Speech; Maxwell Anderson; Paul Green; West of Broadway; The Blush of Shame; The Modern Drama; Theater Under Your Hat.

A STUDY OF THE MODERN DRAMA

A Handbook for the Study and Appreciation of Typical Plays, European, English, and American, of the Last Three-Quarters of a Century

BY

BARRETT H. CLARK

REVISED EDITION

D. APPLETON-CENTURY COMPANY

INCORPORATED

NEW YORK LONDON

1940

PRINTED IN THE UNITED STATES OF AMERICA

CONTENTS

WHAT THIS BOOK IS AND HOW TO USE IT

This latest revised edition of *A Study of the Modern Drama* is the result of a long series of revisions which I have made beginning, in my high school days, when I was asked to draw up a syllabus for a study club that was embarking upon the little-charted sea of "modern drama." That was shortly before the World War, when we in this country were reading and discussing Ibsen and other Europeans, and when, away from Broadway, we had just begun to realize that if we wanted a legitimate theater of our own we had to make it. Side by side with the early "Little Theaters" we established occasional study groups, most of them a bit too earnest in their determination to read messages and themes into works that were often quite innocent of anything but the author's intention to create effective drama.

One thing of importance came out of our study courses—in spite of an inordinate amount of affected purposefulness—and that is the knowledge that a great deal could be learned and enjoyed merely by reading printed plays. When, therefore, our own native playwrights came into their own, from 1920 onwards, they found a by no means restricted audience, all over the land, ready to accept their work, and a little later, in the colleges and universities and the Little Theaters, ready to produce it. Out of the earnest little groups came part of a national audience that was willing to watch and listen intelligently to plays that grew out of an intelligent attitude toward life, without which no adult writer can hope to do his best work.

My occasional typed study outlines were brought together and revised early in 1914, and published in a volume as *The Continental Drama of Today,* which was supplemented a year later by *The British and American Drama of Today.* With minor revisions these two volumes were used as text and reference books until

1925, when they were entirely superseded by what amounted to a new book, expanded, supplemented by a great deal of new material, and rearranged under the title of *A Study of the Modern Drama*. Three years later this was again somewhat revised and expanded. And now, ten years later, I offer the 1938 edition.

Although this new book has scarcely a line in it that was used in the earliest of its incarnations, the idea on which it is based remains almost unchanged. The following passages, quoted from various earlier editions, are today its justification:

A Study of the Modern Drama is a handbook for use in connection with the reading of a representative group of some of the most important plays of several outstanding dramatists of modern times. The period covered is, roughly speaking, the epoch from the early days of Ibsen's activity to the present time.

It should be clearly understood that the phrase "present time" does not mean this year, or last. I need hardly say that a certain perspective was necessary in compiling a book of this kind. Since the first edition appeared in 1925, our native American drama, for instance, has developed to such an extent that most of the playwrights included in my American section are no longer to be regarded as strictly contemporary. But the time has not yet come for giving certain of the younger writers as much space as is given to such relatively "early" writers as Thomas or Fitch.

The book is a guide and to a certain extent a history of a "movement" extending all over Europe and America which, so far as we are now able to determine, is destined to be regarded as one of the most fruitful and interesting in the entire history of the drama. To classify each type of play and to trace every stream that contributes to the vast ocean of modern drama would be not only an unwise attempt, but an impossibility. It is my aim simply to set before the reader a summary of the lives and achievements of some sixty of the dramatists who have shaped the modern drama form, and, what is more to the point, arouse his interest and curiosity about them.

These particular dramatists are chosen because of the significance of their contributions to the art of the drama. Plays are written to be acted, and if our study of these plays is based on the assumption that they are read and not witnessed in a theater, it is only because most of them are no longer produced. But most plays—many critics to the contrary notwithstanding—lose little or nothing in the reading, and some are even more effective between the covers of a book than they are behind the footlights.

A Study of the Modern Drama is a handbook of inductive study. Each play is considered as an independent work, and such problems and questions of art or technique as are suggested by it are treated as they arise. There are many books on dramatic technique and theory in which laws and rules are laid down with more or less rigidity. But each artist, as we know, usually makes his own rules and laws.

In this elementary work it is my aim to suggest rather than to teach; to stimulate interest and provoke discussion rather than to dissect; to analyze particular works only in order to determine what the dramatist has done and why he did it, and not to hold him to account for failing to follow the rules. Until the drama is dead it will not be possible to classify our knowledge and formulate immutable laws; that is why I prefer to adopt my pseudo-Socratic method of asking questions. My readers, I presume, have not yet learned all there is to know. Nor have I.

A play is intended to give pleasure as a reflection, a summary, an interpretation, of life and character, a presentment of man; its form is determined first by the individual temperament of the artist and only secondarily by the material conditions and limitations of the stage. But as great artists are proverbially rare, we find the majority of dramatists largely guided by practical considerations of technique. It is therefore well, in any study of technique, to consider not only the exceptions but the rules. The *essence* of every play defies analysis, and we are therefore forced to discuss for the most part the means rather than the content. But this is a matter of no little importance and value.

In compiling my bibliographies and reading lists I have of course called for assistance upon many persons. I am grateful, first, to several of the authors themselves, who have gone over my text and checked those sections which they were best able to answer for. I refer here specifically to Maxim Gorky, Sir Arthur Pinero, Henry Arthur Jones, John Masefield, Elizabeth Baker, W. S. Maugham, Sir James Barrie, St. John Ervine, Lord Dunsany, John Galsworthy, Augustus Thomas, and David Pinski. John Garrett Underhill has rendered valuable assistance in connection with the Spanish section; Isaac Goldberg has secured for me otherwise inaccessible material on the Yiddish playwrights; Samuel A. Eliot, Jr., Nicholas Nadassy, Montrose J. Moses, Thomas H. Dickinson, Lander MacClintock, Alexander Kaun, Winifred Katzin, F. W. Chandler, and Edwin Björkman, have likewise given me authoritative information on many matters.

The work of revision of the play and reference lists and other bibliographical matter for this 1938 edition has to a great extent been done by Miss Sonya Fogel, of the Drama Book Shop of New York City, that fountain-head of information to which all of us go when we want to know what plays are published, and what books on the theater and drama to consult. Miss Marjorie Seligman, also of the Drama Book Shop, has added many helpful suggestions.

The new material in this latest edition of the book does not follow the exact pattern of the earlier editions: instead of adding new sections on a few playwrights from each country, I have appended two short sections, one on the United States and one on Soviet Russia. The reason for this is that the period originally covered by the book has ended, and any attempt to bring it up to date would result in the sort of patchwork that could only confuse. A proper perspective on the theater world of the 1930's will be necessary before any such attempt should be made. Besides, the theater world during the past decade is an entirely different thing from what it was when this book was first planned, even from what it was when it was revised in 1928. Speaking very generally, and from evidence which is necessarily incomplete and not wholly reliable, Germany and Italy have contributed nothing of any importance to the theater, unless we can include under those countries the work of their exiled writers. Spain, for a variety of reasons, Holland and Belgium, and the Scandinavian countries are either marking time, or else producing no playwrights of sufficient interest to catch and hold our attention; England and Ireland—except for three or four writers—have added nothing of outstanding importance.

This leaves only our own country and Russia, on each of which I have added a short chapter.

B. H. C.

THE NORWEGIAN DRAMA

THE NORWEGIAN DRAMA

Ibsen and Björnson are the outstanding figures in the Norwegian theater. All of Ibsen's plays and most of Björnson's are now translated into English. Before the middle of the last century there were few dramatists, and these few not of great importance. The contemporaries and followers of Ibsen and Björnson are naturally rather overshadowed by these pioneers, but such men as Gunnar Heiberg, Vetle Visle, Gabriel Finne, Anders Stilloff, and Knut Hamsun, have all made interesting contributions to the Norwegian theater. Heiberg is known to readers of English as the author of "The Balcony" and "The Tragedy of Love." One of his best known plays, not yet translated, is "King Midas." Hamsun, the novelist, has in "Queen Tamara" and "In the Grip of Life" (this last has just been translated) shown that he can handle a dramatic theme in a skillful manner. Alvide Prydz, Alexander Kielland, Sigurd (son of Henrik) Ibsen, and Arne Norrevang, among the minor figures, are represented in translation by one play each. There is no one book covering the Norwegian drama. However, in most of the studies of Ibsen and Björnson, certain other dramatists are occasionally referred to.

Henrik Ibsen

Henrik Ibsen was born at Skien, Norway, in 1828. He spent some years at the small town of Grimstad as apprentice to an apothecary, and in 1850 entered the University of Christiania. It was at this time that he began writing plays, poetic dramas on historical and legendary subjects more or less in the pseudoclassical style of the day. After traveling in Denmark and Germany, he became director of the Bergen Theater, where he remained for five years. He then went to Christiania as manager of the theater, a position which he left in 1862, becoming "æsthetic adviser" to still another theater. In 1864 he went to Italy and Germany. Ten years later he returned to his native land for a short period, after which he took up his residence in Germany, remaining there until

1891. From that time until his death in 1906 he lived in Christiania.

As a dramatist Ibsen owes not a little to the French playwrights Emile Augier and Alexandre Dumas *fils*, from whom he learned valuable lessons in dramatic technique, but he eventually evolved a method all his own which has exercised incalculable influence upon practically all the dramatists who have written since his time. He was able by means of his skill as an artist to state in dramatic form a number of social problems and conditions of especial interest and significance to his generation. He took the French "Well-made Play," made it more flexible than it had ever been, and adapted it to his own artistic requirements.

Ibsen's international reputation is due, however, not so much to his technical achievements as to his popularization in play form of the social problem. His fierce individualism, his fearless proclamation of a rigid standard of ethics, his defiance of social prejudice and hatred of hypocrisy, have given him a reputation as a philosopher which he little deserves. He was first and last a dramatist, who chose his subjects (in his later and better known plays, at least) from the life of his time. True, he was interested in ethical problems, and he recognized the tremendous forces at work upon modern society, but these he perceived to be dramatic themes susceptible of effective treatment in plays: he was not so much interested in converting his audience as he was in moving them by arousing their emotions. It is as an artist, and not as a thinker, that he takes rank as the greatest dramatist of modern times.

Plays

"Catilina" (1850)
"The Warrior's Barrow" (1854)
"Lady Inger of Ostrat" (1855)
"The Feast at Solhoug" (1856)
"Olaf Liljekrans" (1857)
"The Vikings at Helgeland" (1858)
"Love's Comedy" (1862)
"The Pretenders" (1864)
"Brand" (1866)
"Peer Gynt" (1867)
"The League of Youth" (1869)
"Emperor and Galilean" (1873)
"The Pillars of Society" (1877)
"A Doll's House" (1879)
"Ghosts" (1881)
"An Enemy of the People" (1882)
"The Wild Duck" (1884)
"Rosmersholm" (1886)
"The Lady from the Sea" (1888)
"Hedda Gabler" (1890)
"The Master Builder" (1892)
"Little Eyolf" (1894)
"John Gabriel Borkman" (1894)
"When We Dead Awaken" (1899)

Editions.—The Collected Works of Henrik Ibsen, edited by William Archer, 11 vols. (N. Y. 1907), includes translations by Archer and others of all but three of the plays. These three ("Catiline," "The

Warrior's Barrow," and "Olaf Liljekrans") are translated with introduction by A. Orbeck, as *Early Plays* (N. Y. 1921); *The Pillars of Society and Other Plays,* edited with introduction by Havelock Ellis (N. Y. no date), includes "The Pillars of Society," translated by William Archer, "Ghosts," by H. F. Lord and William Archer, "An Enemy of Society," by Mrs. E. M. Aveling; *A Doll's House and Two Other Plays,* translated with introduction by R. F. Sharp (N. Y. 1910), includes "A Doll's House," "The Wild Duck," and "The Lady From the Sea"; *Ghosts and Two Other Plays,* trans., with introduction by the same (N. Y. 1911), includes "Ghosts," "An Enemy of the People," and "The Warriors at Helgeland"; *The Pretenders and Two Other Plays,* trans. with introduction by the same (N. Y. 1913), includes "The Pretenders," "Pillars of Society," and "Rosmersholm"; *Lady Inger of Ostrat and Other Plays,* trans. with introduction by the same (N. Y. 1915), includes "Lady Inger of Ostrat," "Love's Comedy," and "The League of Youth"; *Prose Dramas,* edited by William Archer, trans. by the same and others, 5 vols. (London and N. Y. 1890-1891), includes "A Doll's House," "The League of Youth," "Pillars of Society," "Ghosts," "An Enemy of the People," "Lady Inger of Ostrat," "Emperor and Galilean," "Rosmersholm," "The Lady From the Sea," and "Hedda Gabler." *A Doll's House and Other Plays* (no translators named, N. Y. no date), includes "A Doll's House," "Ghosts," and "An Enemy of the People"; *The Master Builder and Other Plays* (no translators named, N. Y. 1918) with preface by H. L. Mencken, includes "Hedda Gabler," "Pillars of Society," and "The Master Builder"; *The Wild Duck and Other Plays* (no translators named, N. Y. no date), includes "The Wild Duck," "Rosmersholm," and "The League of Youth."

Separate Plays.—"Love's Comedy," trans. by C. H. Herford (London, 1890); "Brand," trans. by W. Wilson (London, 1891); by F. E. Garrett (London, 1894, and later, 1911, in *Lyrics and Poems from Ibsen*); by C. H. Herford (N. Y. 1894); by R. F. Sharp (N. Y. 1915); by J. M. Olkerman (Portland, Ore. 1912); "Peer Gynt," by W. and C. Archer (London, no date); by R. E. Roberts (N. Y. 1914), and anonymously as *The Richard Mansfield Acting Version* (Chicago, 1906); by M. M. Dawson (Boston, 1916); by R. F. Sharp (N. Y. 1916) and by G. Hult (N. Y. 1933); "The Young Men's League" ["The League of Youth"] by H. Carstarphen (Boston, 1900); "The Emperor and the Galilean," by C. Ray (London, 1876); "Pillars of Society," by William Archer (Boston, n. d.); "Nora," by T. Weber (London, 1880); same title, by H. F. Lord (London, 1882); and same as "The Doll's House" (N. Y. 1889); by William Archer (Boston, n.d.); and, with preface, by H. L. Mencken (Boston, 1908); "An Enemy of Society," by William Archer (Boston, n. d.); "Ghosts," by William Archer (Boston, n. d.) and edited by G. H. Leverton (N. Y. 1937); "The Wild Duck," by Mrs. E. M. Aveling (Boston, n. d.); by Mrs. F. E. Archer (London, 1905); "Hedda Gabler," by Edmund Gosse (Boston, n. d. and N. Y. 1891); "Rosmersholm," by L. N. Parker (Boston, 1889); by M. Carmichael (Boston, n. d.); "The Lady from the Sea," by Mrs. E. M. Aveling (N. Y. 1910); by Mrs. F. E. Archer (Boston, n. d.); "The Master Builder," by Edmund Gosse and

William Archer (Boston, no date); "Little Eyolf," by William Archer (Chicago, 1894); with preface, by H. L. Mencken (Boston, 1908); "John Gabriel Borkman," by William Archer (Chicago, 1897); "When We Dead Awaken," by William Archer (Chicago, 1900).

Reprints in Collections and Anthologies.—"A Doll's House" (Archer translation), in Matthews' *Chief European Dramatists* (Boston, 1916), in Hubbell and Beaty's *Introduction to Drama* (N. Y. 1927) and in Clark's *World Drama* (N. Y. 1933); "An Enemy of the People," in Stauffer's *Progress of Drama Through the Centuries* (N. Y. 1927); "The Wild Duck" (Mrs. Archer translation), in Moses' *Representative Continental Dramas* (Boston, 1924). *Plays by Henrik Ibsen* (N. Y. 1927), edited by F. W. Chandler, contains "A Doll's House," "The Wild Duck," "Hedda Gabler," and "The Master Builder."

References

Henrik Jaeger, *Henrik Ibsen: A Critical Biography* (Chicago, 1890); H. H. Boyesen, *A Commentary on the Writings of Henrik Ibsen* (N. Y. 1894); Georg Brandes, *Henrik Ibsen—Björnstjerne Björnson. Critical Studies* (N. Y. 1899); Philip H. Wicksteed, *Four Lectures on Henrik Ibsen* (London, 1892); Edmund Gosse, *Henrik Ibsen* (N. Y. 1908); Haldane McFall, *Ibsen, the Man, his Art and his Significance* (N. Y. and San Francisco, 1907); Ellen Key, *The Torpedo Under the Ark,* translated by M. B. Borthwick (Chicago, 1912); Jeannette Lee, *The Ibsen Secret* (N. Y. 1907); R. E. Roberts, *Henrik Ibsen* (N. Y. 1912); George Bernard Shaw, *The Quintessence of Ibsenism* (N. Y. 1915); Montrose J. Moses, *Henrik Ibsen* (N. Y. 1908); Henry Rose, *Henrik Ibsen: Poet, Mystic and Moralist* (London, 1913); Otto Heller, *Henrik Ibsen, Plays and Problems* (Boston, 1912); Miriam Alice Franc, *Ibsen in England* (Boston, 1919); William Henri Eller, *Ibsen in Germany* (Boston, 1918); D. Merezhkovski, *The Life Work of Henrik Ibsen* (London, 1915); Y. Lavrin, *Ibsen and His Creation* (London, 1921); A. E. Zucker, *Ibsen the Master Builder* (N. Y. 1929); H. J. Weigand, *The Modern Ibsen* (N. Y. 1925); H. Koht, *The Life of Ibsen* (N. Y. 1931). See also *Letters of Henrik Ibsen* (N. Y. 1905); *Speeches and New Letters* [*by*] *Henrik Ibsen* (Boston, 1910); and *From Ibsen's Workshop, Notes, Scenarios, and Drafts of the Modern Plays,* trans. by A. G. Chater (N. Y. 1911); J. Ten Eyck Firkins, *Henrik Ibsen* (N. Y. 1924); Havelock Ellis, *The New Spirit* (N. Y. no date); F. W. Chandler, *Aspects of Modern Drama* (N. Y. 1914) and *Modern Continental Playwrights* (N. Y. 1931); Ludwig Lewisohn, *The Modern Drama* (N. Y. 1915); Bernard Shaw, *Dramatic Opinions and Essays* (N. Y. 1907); James Huneker, *Iconoclasts* (N. Y. 1905), *Egoists* (N. Y. 1909); Arthur Symons, *Figures of Several Centuries* (N. Y. 1916); Georg Brandes, *Creative Spirits of the 19th Century* (N. Y. 1923); B. Matthews, *Inquiries and Opinions* (N. Y. 1907); A. B. Walkley, *Playhouse Impressions* (London, 1892); Wm. Archer, *The Theatrical World,* 5 vols. (London, 1894-1898), *Study and Stage* (London, 1899), *Playmaking* (Boston, 1912); J. T. Grein, *Dramatic Criticism,* III London,

1902); C. J. B. Burchardt, *Norwegian Life and Literature* (London, 1920); W. P. Eaton, *At the New Theater and Others* (Boston, 1910); Norman Hapgood, *The Stage in America* (N. Y. 1901); Edwin Muir, *Latitudes* (N. Y. 1924); Edmund Gosse, *Northern Studies* (London, 1890); W. M. Payne, *Little Leaders* (Chicago, 1902); Allan Monkhouse, *Books and Plays* (London, 1894); Edward Dowden, *Essays, Modern and Elizabethan* (London, 1910); Archibald Henderson, *European Dramatists* (N. Y. 1926), and *The Changing Drama* (Cincinnati, 1919); Alexander Woollcott, *Mrs. Fiske* (N. Y. 1917); C. H. Caffin, *The Appreciation of the Drama* (N. Y. 1908).

THE PRETENDERS

Historical drama in 5 acts (1864). Texts: translation by William Archer in *Collected Works* (N. Y. 1907); and by R. F. Sharp, in *The Pretenders and Two Other Plays* (N. Y. 1913).

Although this play is based upon facts and incidents taken from early Norse history, a great deal has been added by the dramatist, in particular the elaborate motivation of the leading characters. "The Pretenders" marks a great advance over "The Vikings at Helgeland." The personages are more strikingly individualized and the story more subtly developed. The play is one of Ibsen's most highly effective dramatic achievements.

1. "The Pretenders" is largely a play about two men, Skule and Hakon: Skule, the king by actual right, and Hakon the king "by confidence." The poet has taken an old story and by the introduction of a modern theme, modified the simple saga-tale.

Bishop Nicholas says to Skule: "The right is his [Hakon's], for he is the fortunate one; 'tis even the summit of fortune, to have the right. But by what right has Hakon the right, and not you?" This is the underlying theme; it is this problem (primarily a philosophical problem) which attracted the dramatist, first as a practical maker of stage plays seeking theatrical effects, but also as a thinking human being. He is always concerned with matters of right and wrong; but this, you will note, is without doubt because such questions are essentially *of the theater,* and not because Ibsen was either a philosopher or a professor of ethics. Morals are the basis of society, and society is the subject that interests him.

Observe how the atmosphere is created in the opening scene. The setting, the crowds in the street, the incident of the ordeal, are elements that serve to prepare the audience for the ensuing action.

2. As in practically all plays, a scene of less tension follows one of storm and stress; note how the scene between Lady Ragnhild and Margrete releases the tension created in the preceding scene. Note also how the conversation between these two contains a good deal of exposition. This colloquy gives the audience the information that is necessary for the understanding of what is to follow.

Notice how scenes are contrasted one with the other throughout the play.

3. The scene just referred to—between Lady Ragnhild and Margrete—contains a good deal of repetition (see pp. 132, 133).[1] Repetition is used in order that the audience may not miss an important point. The French playwright Scribe is said to have repeated all his important points three times in the first act, and it is safe to say that all successful playwrights have acted on the principle that to state a fact once is not sufficient. Says the Spanish dramatist Benavente: "Everything that is of importance to the proper understanding of a play must be repeated at least three times during the course of the action. The first time half of the audience will understand it; the second time the other half will understand it. Only at the third repetition may we be sure that everybody understands it, except, of course, deaf persons and some critics." Does Ibsen repeat his point three times "during the course of the action"? Notice how Pinero emphasizes "points" in "Mid-Channel."

4. Most plays do not actually begin the moment the curtain rises; it is necessary to allow the audience a few minutes' leisure before introducing the chief characters and telling something of the past. In most plays it is easy to detect just where the action begins. Where in "The Pretenders" does the exposition stop and the story proper, or action, begin?

---

[1] In the second volume of the *Collected Works.*

5. One of the canonical, though often broken, "laws" of play-writing is, Never keep a secret from the audience. The dramatist usually hints early in the play as to what is going to occur. In Pinero's "Mid-Channel" Zoe Blundell says, "You'll see, when I put an end to myself, it will be in the winter time." In Galsworthy's "Justice" Falder says to Ruth, "It *is* too late" [to stay, that is]. These are examples of foreshadowing, or giving the audience some inkling of what is to come. Bishop Nicholas, in "The Pretenders," says, "Ever on your guard, good Dagfinn—ever on your guard." Find other examples of foreshadowing in "The Pretenders."

6. Every first act—and every other save the last—must as a rule arouse the interest of the audience in the fate of the characters; few acts can stand independently. It is usually toward the end of the act that an indication of the future course of events is found. They are in the nature of a "Continued in our next" notice, and serve as binding links in the story.

At the end of the second act of Björnson's "Gauntlet" (first version), Christenson says, "Then it is to be war?—Well, I fancy I know a thing or two about war," and goes out. That speech and the manner in which it is delivered, arouse the interest of the audience, and stimulate their curiosity to see what will happen in the following act. Another example is at the end of the first act of Wilde's "Lady Windermere's Fan," where Lady Windermere declares her intention of striking Mrs. Erlynne in the face if she comes to the reception. In "The Pretenders," Hakon says, "At last, then, I am King of Norway," and Earl Skule replies, "But I rule the realm." If it were not for this disquieting remark, the first act might almost stand as a complete one-act play. It is the presence of such speeches that gives continuity to a play.

7. Find the "bridging-over" sections in the subsequent acts.

Peer Gynt

A play in 5 acts (1867). Texts: translation by W. and C. Archer (London, no date); same in *Collected Works* (N. Y.

1907); by R. F. Sharp (N. Y. 1916); by R. E. Roberts (N. Y. 1914).

"Peer Gynt" is primarily a dramatic poem; a play, that is, not intended to be acted, and according to one "school" of criticism, not a play at all. To this question we shall return in the pages that follow. In a letter written shortly after "Peer Gynt" was published, Ibsen wrote: "I learn that the book created much excitement in Norway. . . . Why can they not read the book as a poem? For as such I wrote it. The satirical passages are tolerably isolated. But if the Norwegians of the present time recognize themselves, as it would appear they do, in the character of Peer Gynt, that is the good people's own affair."

1. Certain ideas, themes, motifs, are constantly recurring throughout Ibsen's plays; among these one of the most persistent is the idea of heredity. Worked out at length in "Ghosts," it is to be found as well in "A Doll's House" and "Peer Gynt." It is made clear that Peer owes much in his character to his mother and a great deal to his father; this we learn from Ase herself in one of the early scenes between her and her son. Despite the fact that Ibsen was in no sense of the word a scientist, and that his conclusions on heredity are open to question, his theme is essentially dramatic. Peer is consequently seen to be not altogether responsible for his acts: his is a being more or less shaped by the temperaments of his parents, and we naturally ask ourselves: How far is he to be held accountable for what he does and says? The same question may be asked about Nora Helmer. As for Oswald Alving, in "Ghosts," Ibsen manifestly depicted him as a totally irresponsible person. Character, for the most part, determines plot, whether in a novel or a play; that is, if the artist knows his business. Given a certain human being, he will act only in accordance with what we know of him. Are Peer's actions logical? Do they "follow" from what we know of him as a person?

2. Ibsen's later plays are regarded as models of technical "economy." The so-called "social plays," from "The League of Youth" to "Hedda Gabler," develop from first to last as

swiftly and logically as the subject permits. But it is not only in these prose plays that Ibsen reveals his craft. Take the first few pages of "Peer Gynt," and observe with what art the background is spread out: the first eleven pages (*Collected Works*) are sufficient (*a*) to create the romantic atmosphere in which the action is to take place; (*b*) to introduce the chief personage and show his dominant characteristics; (*c*) to make known nearly all of the past that is necessary for the understanding of the play; (*d*) to give some inkling of Peer's fate. These preliminaries are so skillfully introduced, so unobtrusively insinuated, that the reader scarcely realizes he is being told facts that he must know. Compare with this the opening of "Hedda Gabler," where the exposition is much more compact, perhaps too much so; in that play it is doubtful whether the audience can assimilate all that is offered, because practically every word is of the first importance. In "Peer Gynt" there is sufficient matter of extraneous interest—such as the intrinsic beauty of the lines and the situation itself—to attract the reader or auditor, so that he will pay strict attention to all that is said and done. In the exposition of "Hedda Gabler," what actually happens is of comparatively little interest. Take any play, read the first few pages, and see how much the author has told, noting carefully whether it is attractively served, as it were, or merely thrown at him haphazard.

3. Read "Peer Gynt" through as a story, a poem, a fantasy; do not the first time seek any explanation of hidden meanings and symbols. The work is a satire on human nature; and even if it is occasionally obscure, try to enter into its spirit, which is everywhere manifest. It is, of course, interesting to know what the Boyg and the Button Moulder represent, but not absolutely necessary. Says Ibsen, in a letter: . . . "both there [in Norway] and in Denmark they have discovered much more satire in it than was intended by me." He then proceeds to ask why the play cannot be read simply for what it is, a dramatic poem.

4. Compare the exposition of "Peer Gynt" with that of "The

Pretenders" and of "Brand." Is it as dramatically effective as the expositions of these other works?

5. Ibsen rather proudly declared that if critics objected to his play on the ground that it was not poetry, they would have to change their conception of poetry to fit what he had written. But it is curious to note that when it came to a question of stage production he was careful not to ask his critics to change their conception of what a play ought to be. He constantly refers to "Peer Gynt" as a poem, and in a letter written some time after its publication, he says: "Of course it is impossible to stage 'Peer Gynt' except in an abbreviated form. . . . I shall be satisfied so long as the piece is reduced to a proper length; not to do this would spoil everything." And yet the play is often produced (in Germany) with few cuts. Is there any reason for cutting this play? Is there any reason for cutting any long play, provided it is interesting and dramatic? Some of Wagner's operas require from four to seven hours for their performance.

A Doll's House

Play in 4 acts (1879). Texts: translation by T. Weber under title of "Nora" (London, 1880); same title by H. F. Lord (London, 1882), later as "The Doll's House" (N. Y. 1889), by William Archer (Boston, no date); by H. L. Mencken (Boston, 1908). Archer translation reprinted in *Collected Works* (N. Y. 1907), in *Prose Dramas* (N. Y. 1890-1891), in Matthews' *Chief European Dramatists* (Boston, 1916), in Chandler's *Plays by Henrik Ibsen* (N. Y. 1927); Sharp translation in *A Doll's House and Two Other Plays* (N. Y. 1910); and anonymous translation in *A Doll's House and Other Plays* (N. Y. no date).

Ibsen's so-called "social dramas," written between 1867 and 1899, differ widely in style and spirit from his earlier plays. Most of them, the later especially, are dramatizations of the end of a situation, the events of which happened long before. These are aptly called "catastrophic" plays, because they are concerned almost exclusively with the end, or catastrophe. "Ghosts" is perhaps the best example of the type. When the curtain rises, everything but the inevitable result has already taken place. Ibsen is interested and actually concerned only with the end. "Ghosts" is the dramatization of an effect; the cause of the tragedy is over years before the play begins. "A Doll's House" is similar, because the audience sees only the termination of the story.

1. The gist of the play lies in the last half of the last act, in the conversation between Nora and Helmer. Ibsen said that the play was written for the sake of this scene. The first three acts and the first part of the fourth are, in fact, an elaborate sort of preparation. The exposition in the first act—the unfolding of Nora's previous history—serves as additional preparation. Therefore, when the momentous conversation takes place, the audience have well in mind the important events in the lives of the characters.

Technically, the "Doll's House" is one of Ibsen's best plays; it is clear, interesting, unified. No time is lost in letting the audience know what has gone before. We are curious to learn more, to see how Nora will extricate herself from her difficulties. Throughout, there is scarcely a superfluous word.

In studying this play—for that matter, any play—it would be well to reconstruct the story of what has happened before the rise of the curtain.

2. How does the conversation between Nora and Mrs. Linden advance the story in the first act? In other words, what is the purpose of Mrs. Linden?

3. It has been said that every line in a good play does one of two things, or both: advances the plot, or reveals character. What is the purpose of the scene between Rank, Nora, and Mrs. Linden in the first act? Of the scene with the children?

4. Do you see any good reason why Helmer should speak of Krogstad before his wife in the first act rather than in a later one; or indeed why he should speak of his dealings with Krogstad at all?

5. Early in the second act, Nora says to the maid who tells her that if she goes out she may catch cold: "Worse things might happen." Is this a good instance of foreshadowing? In the first two acts, are there better examples? If so, what are they?

6. What structural purpose is served by Rank's exposition of his views on heredity? In spite of what Ibsen's critics have said, Ibsen was too great an artist to risk spoiling a play by the insertion of extraneous material or ideas. No doubt Ibsen felt the truth of the words he put into the mouth of Rank, but was this the only reason he introduced the scene?

7. The play has sometimes been criticized on the ground that it was impossible for Nora to develop from a "doll" to a mature thinking woman within the three days allowed her by the author. Trace the process by which that development has progressed, and determine whether Ibsen was justified in making such a change.

8. Read the scene between Nora and Helmer in the last act and see how it has been prepared for during the earlier acts. It is certain that such reasoning power as is displayed by Nora must be motivated by the preceding action and events; otherwise we could not accept the dramatist's conclusions or believe Nora capable of saying what she does say, and at last of leaving her home and family.

Hedda Gabler

Play in 4 acts (1890). Texts: translation by Edmund Gosse (Boston, no date); same in *Prose Dramas* (N. Y. 1890-1891), and in *Collected Works* (N. Y. 1907); anonymously in *The Master Builder and Other Plays* (N. Y. 1918); re-print in Chandler's *Plays by Henrik Ibsen* (N. Y. 1927).

"Hedda Gabler" is an excellent specimen of modern dramaturgy, one that will repay close study. It is primarily the exposition of the character of a woman out of harmony with her surroundings. All the skill of the dramatist is brought to bear upon a complete revelation of her past life, her thoughts, and her acts.

1. The exposition is so deftly contrived that every word counts; in fact, the words "I don't believe they are stirring" at the very first, stimulate our curiosity. The first two pages are so full of information that the reader—not to mention the spectator in the theater—must pay the strictest attention, or miss what he should have well in mind. Up to George's en-

trance, we learn a good deal about him from the others: we shall see and hear him soon enough. His presence varies the scene a little, and by the time the audience know what he is like, they are ready for more information. Judge Brack is mentioned, then a little further movement is introduced; then more exposition, this time regarding the relations between Hedda and Miss Tesman. Little by little the details are accumulated, until we know practically everything that we need know. Then at last Hedda makes her appearance.

Study this introductory scene, and observe the way in which the past is formed into a background for the play proper; how each new personage is introduced, how each point is stressed. The moment these preliminaries are over, the action may begin. The "curtain" (or close) of the first act terminates the expository section.

2. In the second act the plot is set in motion and develops straight toward the climax. The climax is that point in a play at which the action reaches its culmination, the most critical stage in its development, after which the tension is relaxed, or unraveled. In Jones' "Liars," Lady Jessica says to Falkner (Act III), "Tell my husband the truth," and Falkner proceeds to do so. That is the climax; up to that point, the situations of most of the characters depended upon a network of lies, and when these are discovered and the truth learned, the tension is released. The audience has only to wait and see "how it all turns out." The rest of the play shows merely the result of the revelation. In "Hedda Gabler," the climax is Hedda's burning of the "child," Lövberg's MS.; that is the culminating point of those events, or crises, in her life with which Ibsen, either in the play, *or before it,* is concerned. From that point onward, we see only effects; never again does the action rise to so high a point. Hedda's death itself is simply the logical outcome of what has gone before, and that was foreshadowed in the first and succeeding acts.

3. "Hedda Gabler" is sometimes played as a comedy. True, the laughter is bitter, but the audience have, at excellent performances, considered not only George, but Hedda, comic

figures. Did Ibsen intend this? At the latest production of the play (New York, 1924) the actors (on the whole, capable and intelligent) played for laughs. At Hedda's suicide the audience roared. Was this right?

4. Why is the play called "Hedda *Gabler*" and not "Hedda *Tesman*"?

Björnstjerne Björnson

Björnstjerne Björnson was born in Kvikne, Norway, in 1832. His primary education was received in Molde. At the age of twenty, he entered the University of Christiania, where he made the acquaintance of Ibsen. His first book, *Synnöve Solbakken,* appeared in 1857. It was received with enthusiasm and has remained one of his most popular works. The following year Björnson assumed the directorship of the Bergen Theater where he produced some of his own plays. The next few years were devoted to travel, the writing of stories, plays, and poems, and to politics. During the years 1865-1867 he was in charge of a theater in Christiania, as well as editor of a newspaper, which he used to further his struggle for Norwegian political and literary independence. For practically the rest of his life, Björnson participated in the great political upheaval in Norway, where he was looked upon as a leader of the liberal party. In 1880 he came to America where, like so many other celebrities of later years, he delivered lectures. From 1881, when he returned to his native country, until 1910, when he died in Paris, he spent most of his time on his estate in the south of Norway. In 1903 he was awarded the Nobel Prize.

Though he was primarily a novelist and poet, Björnson was an important dramatist; he was the first to found a genuinely national drama in Norway, and among the earliest to employ the theater as a medium for the promulgation and discussion of social questions. It is rather as an innovator than a master craftsman that Björnson should be considered. He utilized the stage in order to preach his liberal doctrines, and not, as Ibsen did, because the stage was the inevitable place for him to express what was in him.

"Björnson," says the veteran critic Jaeger, "is as consistent in his glorification of the home and the family as is Ibsen in raising the personality, the individual, to the skies. . . . In the name of personal self-expression, Ibsen lets a wife leave her home to seek by herself a way toward clearness and independence; in the name of the home, Björnson brings an estranged married couple back into each other's arms."

PLAYS

"Between the Battles" (1856)
"Lame Hulda" (1858)
"King Sverre" (1861)
"Sigurd the Bad" ["Sigurd Slembe"] (1862)
"Mary Stuart in Scotland" (1864)
"The Newly-married Couple" (1865)
"Sigurd Jorsalfar" (1872)
"The Editor" (1874)
"A Bankruptcy" (1875)
"The King" (1877)
"Leonarda" (1879)
"The New System" (1879)
"A Gauntlet" (1883)
"Beyond Our Power, I" (1883)
"Geography and Love" (1885)
"Beyond Our Power, II" (1895)
"Paul Lange and Tora Parsberg" (1898)
"Laboremus" (1901)
"At Storhove" (1902)
"Dayland" (1904)
"When the New Wine Blooms" (1909)

Editions.—Plays by Björnstjerne Björnson, trans. with introduction by Edwin Björkman (N. Y. 1913), contains "The Gauntlet," first version, "Beyond Our Power, I," and "The New System"; 2nd series, trans. by the same (N. Y. 1914), contains "Love and Geography," "Beyond Human Might" ["Beyond Our Power, II"], and "Laboremus"; *Three Comedies by Björnstjerne Björnson,* trans. by R. F. Sharp (N. Y. 1912), contains "The Newly-married Couple," "Leonarda," and "A Gauntlet" (first version); *Three Dramas by Björnstjerne Björnson,* translated by the same (N. Y. no date), contains "The Editor," "The Bankrupt," and "The King."

Separate Plays.—"Sigurd Slembe," trans. by W. M. Payne (Chicago, 1910); "Mary Queen of Scots," by A. Sahlberg (Chicago, 1912); revised version, "A Gauntlet," by Osman Edwards in Vol. 17 of *The Drama* (London, 1903); "A Gauntlet," by H. L. Braekstad (London, 1890); as "A Glove," by T. Sogard (*Poet Lore,* Boston, 1892); "A Gauntlet," by Osman Edwards (London, 1894); "The Newly-married Couple," by S. and E. Hjerteid (London, 1870); by T. Soelfeldt (London, 1868); and as "A Lesson in Marriage," by Grace I. Colbron (N. Y. 1910); "Pastor Sang" ["Beyond Our Power, I"] by W. Wilson (London, 1893); "Beyond Our Power, I," by J. H. Paulding (*Poet Lore,* Boston, 1905); "Paul Lange and Tora Parsberg," by H. L. Braekstad (N. Y. 1899); "Leonarda," by G. I. Colbron (N. Y. 1911), and by D. L. Hanson (*Drama,* Chicago, 1911); "Laboremus," anonymously (London, 1901); "When the New Wine Blooms," by Lee M. Hollander (*Poet Lore,* Boston, 1911).

Reprints in Collections.—"Beyond Human Power, I" [*i.e.* "Beyond Our Power"] is included in Dickinson's *Chief Contemporary Drama-*

tists (Boston, 1915), translation by Lee M. Hollander. For bibliographical data regarding other editions and translations of the above plays see Phelps' *Essays on Modern Novelists* (N. Y. 1918), and *Modern Drama and Opera. Reading Lists on the Works of Various Authors,* Vol. II (Boston, 1915).

References

Georg Brandes, *Henrik Ibsen, Björnstjerne Björnson. Critical Studies* (N. Y. 1899), and *Creative Spirits of the 19th Century,* trans. by R. B. Anderson (N. Y. 1923); H. H. Boyesen, *Essays on Scandinavian Literature* (N. Y. 1911); W. M. Payne, *Björnstjerne Björnson, 1832-1910* (Chicago, 1910); Edwin Björkman, *Voices of To-morrow* (N. Y. 1913); F. W. Chandler, *Aspects of Modern Drama* (N. Y. 1914); Ashley Dukes, *Modern Dramatists* (Chicago, 1912); William Lyon Phelps, *Essays on Modern Novelists* (N. Y. 1918); Richard Burton, *Literary Likings* (Boston, 1899); A. T. Quiller-Couch, *Adventures in Criticism* (London, 1896).

A Gauntlet

Play in 3 acts (1883-1892). The following discussion is based mainly on the original version as the revised one is not easily accessible. Texts: translations by H. L. Braekstad (London, 1890); by Osman Edwards, revised version (London, 1894, and reprinted in *The Drama,* Vol. 17, London, 1903); by T. Sogard, as "A Glove" (*Poet Lore,* Boston, 1892); by Edwin Björkman in *Plays by Björnstjerne Björnson* (N. Y. 1913); and by R. F. Sharp, in *Three Comedies by Björnstjerne Björnson* (N. Y. 1912).

"A Gauntlet" is an exceedingly well-defined example of the thesis play. The dramatist wrote it in order to prove that a woman has a right to demand of her fiancé the same sexual purity that he demands of her. It is a plea for the abolition of the so-called "double standard." The fault with most thesis plays is that the thesis is of more interest to the playwright than the play: he must first establish his thesis, and this is generally secured at the expense of verisimilitude. He who uses the drama as a means of preaching can have little respect for it as a means of expressing beauty, which is the end of all art. The Björnson play is open to criticism because it is above all a plea, and not primarily a picture, a story, an entertainment. It is evident that the dramatist is deeply concerned over the idea he wishes to set forth, and occasionally allows his conscience as a social reformer to take precedence over his instincts as an artist. But sometimes the artist is able to coördinate the functions of dramatist and reformer, so that certain scenes in "A Gauntlet" are effective as "pure" drama. Brieux, another reformer, is, like Björnson, something of an artist even when he is most anxious to succeed as a critic of the evils of society. "The Red Robe" is good drama and good propaganda: the two seem to go hand in hand. Bernard Shaw, a far greater artist than either Björnson (the dramatist) or Brieux, is also at times able to allow his thesis to give way to art: "You Never Can Tell" happens to be a thesis play, but it is likewise a first-rate comedy.

1. "A Gauntlet" may be profitably compared with the "social" dramas of Ibsen. Now Ibsen is interested in ideas; he never wrote a play that was not in some sense an exposition of an idea or the expression of a philosophy, but he rarely if ever writes primarily in order to prove a thesis. Even "Ghosts," the most pointedly didactic of his works, is first a "show," and only secondarily a philosophical work. In the Björnson play every speech and every scene supports the central theme, every scene presents some phase of it, or else prepares the way for such a scene.[2] Bear these facts in mind as you read the play. Just where does Björnson do violence to the play *as drama* in order to teach his lesson?

2. A consideration of this work is rendered doubly interesting by comparing the two versions. The second act, as originally written, ends with Svava's throwing the glove in Alf's face, and Christensen's declaration of war. This climax is effective and it occurs where we might expect it to occur: at the end of the last act but one. The last act shows the result of Svava's challenge, and ends with her reconciliation with Alf. This seems fairly reasonable and human, but Björn-

---

[2] Ibsen is quoted by Prozor, his French translator, as follows: "If, in placing upon the stage certain persons whom I have known or seen, certain facts of which I have been a witness or which have been related to me, and, in throwing an atmosphere of poetry over it all, I happen to awaken a soul within them, various ideas will take root in the minds of the different characters: that is the point of departure. I cannot help it if in my own brain, as I write, various ideas come to me. That is merely accessory; the first principle of a play is action, life."

son's thesis suffers: if he wished to preach the doctrine of the single standard, he has weakened his argument by making his strong character ruin it. Feeling, doubtless, that this was a weakness, Björnson rewrote the play, strengthening his thesis. He closes the second act with Svava's enlightenment regarding her father's relations with Mrs. North. This is a sufficiently dramatic climax in itself, but in that it creates greater tension than the first version—because it leaves the outcome more doubtful—it is theatrically superior. The last act of the new version is therefore much better than that of the old, as the audience eagerly await the "big scene" between Svava and Alf. The throwing of the gauntlet is the end of the play, and we are no longer left in doubt as to Svava's feelings and the author's intention. Now the climax of the earlier play serves as the end, or "catastrophe" of the later. But there is a still more unusual feature: while the climax is effective in both versions, that of the first is the more so, although the catastrophe is comparatively weak; the climax in the second is adequate, and the catastrophe powerful and wholly convincing. As a rule, it is more difficult to sustain interest in the last act than in any other, so that, dramaturgically, the second version of this play is incomparably better than the original.

3. The problem of ending a play affords material for a good deal of speculation. All plays must end somehow. A picture ends where the frame begins, and a sonnet ends with the fourteenth line, yet the painter must leave us with the feeling that his picture is complete in itself, and the poet that his sonnet expresses just what he wished it to express, no more and no less. The play form is not so rigid nor so restricted as that of a picture or sonnet, and yet there are certain conventions that the *average* playwright must observe. For one thing, most audiences seem to like what is called a "happy ending." It would be more exact to say a conventional ending. Few audiences would care to see Hamlet marry Ophelia, because in the sort of tragedy Shakespeare wrote, the unhappy Prince is marked out from the first as a victim, and the pallid Ophelia is obviously not the sort of person who could settle

down to domesticity. But the dramatist who makes his plays out of the life of to-day finds it peculiarly difficult to bring his men and women to tragic ends unless, according to conventional standards, they have richly deserved their fate.

This was probably Björnson's problem in the "Gauntlet," just as it was with Pinero, whose play, "The Profligate," was changed to suit the taste of the public in 1889. "Its thesis," says A. B. Walkley (in *Frames of Mind*), was that "prenuptial chastity is equally incumbent on both parties to the marriage contract. . . . Curiously enough, the author offered alternative endings. . . . In the one Dunstan Renshaw obtai[illegible] [illegible]is girl-wife's forgiveness, in the other he committed suicide." Several years later (1915), we find the following words in a preface to the same author's play, "The Big Drum": " 'The Big Drum' is published exactly as it was written, and as it was originally performed. At its first representation, however, the audience was reported to have been saddened by its 'unhappy ending.' Pressure was forthwith put upon me to reconcile Philip and Ottoline at the finish, and at the third performance of the play the curtain fell upon the picture, violently and crudely brought about, of Ottoline in Philip's arms. I made the alteration against my principles and against my conscience, and yet not altogether unwillingly. For we live in depressing times. . . ." That was during the war.

Certain critics have blamed Eugene O'Neill for the way he ended "Anna Christie."[3] Some thousands of successful plays—especially English and American—have "happy" endings where the logic of the situation demanded unhappy endings. Find two or three instances and discuss them, comparing them with those of the "Gauntlet," "The Profligate" (the old edition prints both versions)[4], "The Big Drum," and "Anna Christie."

---

[3] For a detailed discussion of O'Neill's difficulties in ending this play see quotations from his letters in my book, *Eugene O'Neill* (N. Y., revised 1937).

[4] Also to be found in George P. Baker's *Dramatic Technique* (Boston, 1919).

THE DANISH DRAMA

THE DANISH DRAMA

Denmark, according to Edwin Björkman, was the first of the Scandinavian countries to have a drama of its own. The names of Holberg and Oehlenschlager are well known in the annals of European literature. The former flourished in the first half of the eighteenth century, the latter in the first half of the nineteenth.

Modern Danish drama began in the seventies with Edvard Brandes, a dramatist and critic whose plays are practically unknown in England and America. His most famous play, "A Visit," was performed in London, in a translation by William Archer, in the nineties. Many of the poets and novelists of the past two generations have written plays, some of them successful in the theater, but most of them isolated specimens of poetic rather than dramatic literature. Holger Drachmann, whose "Renaissance" has been translated, is not one of the professionals, though his plays have met with a certain success in his own country; Einer Christiansen is a writer of historical and fantastic pieces; Peter Nansen, the novelist, wrote at least one play, "Judith's Marriage," which definitely belongs to the theater. Otto Benzon, Fru Emma Gad, Gustav Esmann, Sven Lange, and Gustav Wied, have all won a place for themselves on the Danish stage. Wied is well known in Germany, while two of his plays are translated into English. John Masefield has made an English version of Hans Wiers-Jenssen's "Anne Pedersdotter."

Fortunately, two of the best plays of Hjalmar Bergström are accessible in English. One of these is made the basis of the following outline. Outside a few newspaper and magazine articles, there is very little material in English on the Danish theater or drama.

Hjalmar Bergström

Hjalmar Bergström was born at Copenhagen in 1868. The only child of parents in moderate circumstances, he was none the less enabled to indulge his taste for literature. His first attempt at playwriting was, according to Edwin Björkman, "some verses added to one of Oehlenschlager's tragedies," at the age of thirteen. He was an apt pupil both at school and at college. He specialized in psychology and modern philology and earned a living by tutoring. "In 1893 he obtained his degree of Ph.D. From that year until 1905 he taught in the Commercial High School at Copenhagen. At the same time he was assiduously busy with his pen." He wrote novels and short stories, but it was not until the appearance of his first play, "Ida's Wedding" in 1902, that he received general recognition as a writer of exceptional talent. Other plays followed in quick succession. In 1905 came "Lynggard & Co.," a mature work that was widely popular. "Karen Borneman," two years later, was forbidden by the censor; the case was carried to the Rigsdag, but not until a new administration was able to turn the tables on the old, was the play produced. Bergström died in 1914.

Bergström was one of the most promising of a group of young playwrights. Like most of his fellow countrymen who write for the theater, he was interested in the struggles of men and women in adjusting themselves to a social order for which they are temperamentally unfitted. Although he has treated aspects of many problems, he was not a writer of thesis plays. To Edwin Björkman, who has made known the work of this dramatist to readers of English, he wrote: "Having never worked in accordance with any program, I have not been led into preparing any formulas as to what poetry is or should be. In regard to this question I can only say what personal experience has taught me. . . . To me one of the main characteristics of all good art lies in its striving to make truth seem probable, and on its success at doing so its beauty is founded."

Plays

"Ida's Wedding" (1902)
"Mint Street 39" (1903)
"Lynggard & Co." (1905)
"Karen Borneman" (1907)
"The Golden Fleece" (1908)
"The Birthday Party" (1910)
"In the Swim" (1910)
"The Way to God" (1912)
"The Day of Trial" (1915)
"What People Talk Of" (1915)

("Thora van Deken," 1915, is dramatized from a novel of H. Pontoppidan.)

Editions.—Karen Borneman, Lynggard & Co., trans. with an introduction by Edwin Björkman (N. Y. 1913).

In an Anthology.—"The Birthday Party," trans. by Edwin Björkman, appears only in Moses' *Representative One-Act Plays by Continental Authors* (Boston, 1923).

Reference

Introduction to Björkman volume above mentioned.

Karen Borneman

Drama in 4 acts (1907). Text: translation by Edwin Björkman in *Karen Borneman, Lynggard & Co.* (N. Y. 1913).

"Karen Borneman" is a particularly interesting specimen of dramaturgy, although it happens at the same time to be an attack upon ideas and institutions. In this respect it is similar to many of Ibsen's later plays. It is for this reason that the play was forbidden at first by the censors. "In their eagerness to incriminate the author," says Mr. Björkman, "the defenders of the 'old' morality charged him with having made a grotesque caricature out of the figure standing as the main representative of that morality within the play—namely, Karen's father. . . . Yet it is only necessary to glance at the play itself in order to see that this figure has been drawn with the tenderest sympathy. . . . Justice is one of the chief characteristics of Mr. Bergström's dramatic vision."

1. This play exhibits one of the most interesting technical processes we have yet encountered. Whether it was altogether deliberate or not, is difficult to know. In watching or reading the play we feel, as scene succeeds scene, that we are present at a gradual process of unfolding. Of exposition in the ordinary sense there is little; the whole play is exposition. From beginning to end, it is little more than the uncovering of past history. It is as if one were sitting down before a group of persons and cross-examining them for hours. First one fact emerges, then another, until finally the entire past stands revealed. Only in the play, it is the situations, as well as the words, that tear away as it were the veils between present and past.

Now in showing this past, the dramatist does not tell more than a little at a time. First there is a chance remark about Gertrude, and then about Karen and the others. Here is one example of the playwright's method:

Professor. . . . But when I think of the other children—poor Gertrude excepted, of course—but all the rest have brought us nothing but happiness!

Mrs. Borneman (*with a smile*). And Peter?

Professor. I don't want to give another thought to that stupid affair of Peter's. He is so young, and Sophie was a dangerous girl to have in the house.

It is like a clever lawyer drawing out an unwilling witness, who starts by declaring his ignorance and ends by incriminating himself.

By the end of the first act we are, of course, interested to know what will happen next, but we are just as interested to hear more of the past. It has already begun to take shape. As a matter of fact, the past becomes in a way the future, precisely as in "On Trial," an American play that was told backward, each act preceding the other chronologically. Our curiosity is aroused: there are surely more family skeletons to discover, and everyone enjoys gossip. The second act *does* open up new vistas. We hear about Adolph and Henrik, and this gives Borneman an opportunity to speak at length about his theories, because these theories are at bottom the cause of all the trouble in the Borneman family. A moment later enter Dr. Schou, who adds more information to our store.

The climax comes at the end of the third act, but it is not a physical crisis, led up to by action witnessed on the stage; it comes simply as a revelation from Karen of her relations with Strandgaard. Borneman, hopelessly out of touch with the situation, threatens to "make matters right," but we know that he will only blunder.

Early in Act IV he says:

What can I have done—an old man like me—what can I have done! . . . Four children I have had to lay in their graves; one daughter is incurably insane—that's what I have had to live through, and yet I tell you, all of it was as nothing compared with the blow I have just received.

The past is now seen crushing the old man, as revelation after revelation is made to him. Observe how these revelations affect the characters of the play. In themselves they would be meaningless, like action in certain melodramas, introduced simply because it is thrilling. Borneman considers his tragedy a visitation from the Lord:

MRS. BORNEMAN. Then the fault must lie with me, as there have been two of us to bring up the children.

PROFESSOR. With you?

MRS. BORNEMAN. Yes.

PROFESSOR. What do you mean anyhow?

MRS. BORNEMAN. What *you* would call a good conscience in regard to that point—I don't have it. But I, nevertheless, acted in the belief of doing what was right.

Borneman has just said that there must be a reason *why* the Lord punishes him. Then comes Mrs. Borneman's revelation: "I *knew* that Karen was living with Strandgaard in Paris." One incident precipitates another, one speech calls forth its counterpart. It is learned shortly after that Mrs. Borneman had received a letter from Paris, which she did not show to her husband. He is dumbfounded, but notice what comes next—still more revelations, going back ten years:

MRS. BORNEMAN. Yes—there *was* a reason. For ten whole years I have gone here and kept it hidden from you. Every day of those years I have had to struggle in order to keep it to myself and spare you. But now I can no longer do so.—The reason was Gertrude's misfortune.

This reason is now explained in detail, and Mrs. Borneman gradually unfolds a world of reasons which explain the past that has been rising up and taking shape during the earlier acts.

Straight up to the end we have nothing but explanation and revelation, and yet there is not a moment's release in the tension.

2. The translator, in the introduction to the Bergström plays, speaks of the "tenderest sympathy with which the figure of the Professor is drawn." Now, the Professor is neither a caricature nor a monster, but it is a question whether he is drawn sympathetically. He is a bigot and it is difficult to depict any bigot (so long as he is intended to be one) with sympathy. With justice is perhaps a better way of phrasing it. In order to make his point, Karen's father must be the embodiment of everything that Karen is not; otherwise she

will not develop: it is through opposition that human beings (in life, as in plays) show their characteristics.

In making a point of this kind most dramatists (and novelists as well) are easily led astray by their theme; they load the dice, as it were, in favor of their heroes or heroines. In Meredith's *Richard Feverel,* Richard's father becomes at the end an impossible embodiment of the writer's idea of parental oppression. In plays it is still easier to lose sight of the human being the moment one acts upon the logic of the situation rather than the logic of humanity. Are there such fathers as Borneman? is the question we should ask. And not, What is it necessary that Borneman should do in order that the dramatist may drive home his point? This is not to say that Borneman is overdrawn. We simply raise the question.

3. Mrs. Borneman is a far subtler character than her husband. She shares, to a certain extent, the Professor's notions on morality and religion, and yet, in critical situations, she unaccountably relies on her own instincts. Is she consistent? Not to an abstract conception of logic, of course, but to herself? Do people do such things? We find her helping Karen secretly, concealing for ten years a matter she ought (presumably) to have told her husband, and yet (p. 66) when confronted with the problem of Strandgaard's presence in her own city, she says, "But what in the world *is* this, Kristen? Why, it's a thing—something we cannot even speak to Karen of."

And, finally, Karen herself. She is, in a way, the embodiment of the author's conception of the new morality, but she is at the same time a human being. Is she altogether convincing?

4. Read Bergström's "Lynggard & Co." What of the characters in this play? Is the thesis of greater interest than the persons?

THE SWEDISH DRAMA

THE SWEDISH DRAMA

Strindberg has naturally overshadowed, not only in his country but throughout the world, all the other dramatists of modern Sweden. His best-known plays have been translated into English and interpreted mainly through the efforts of Edwin Björkman, whose half dozen volumes of translated plays, together with their authoritative prefaces, have familiarized American and English readers with the best of Strindberg's dramatic work.

So far the plays of no other important Swedish dramatist, except Tor Hedberg, have been translated: Hjalmar Söderberg, Per Hallström and Hjalmar Bergman, are all playwrights of repute, known to us, however, only by name.

There is no book in English on the Swedish drama, and practically nothing in the general books on the drama except what relates to Strindberg.

August Strindberg

August Strindberg was born at Stockholm in 1849. At an early age he entered the University of Upsala, but was unable to support himself and continue his studies at the same time. He left, though in 1870 he managed to return and continue his studies. He then began writing plays, and in 1872 "Master Olof" was offered for production; it was, however, refused for six years by the managers. The play, when it finally appeared, is said to have inaugurated Sweden's dramatic renascence. Strindberg turned his hand to many things in these early years: he was schoolmaster, journalist, dramatist, writer of scientific and political treatises, and short stories. In 1883 he left Sweden and traveled in Denmark, Germany, France, and Italy, at the same time publishing volumes of stories, novels, and plays. The production of "The Father" in 1887 established his reputation as one of the most powerful dramatists of Europe. To the period inaugurated by "The Father" Strindberg's characteristically bitter plays belong. Five autobiographical novels of this time reveal the writer's restless intellectual activity. As a result of great intellectual strain and the painful proceedings incident to one of his divorces, Strindberg was forced to retire to a private sanitarium for over a year, but in 1897 he returned to his work and published a large number of plays. He also established his Intimate Theater at Stockholm, where his own plays were produced. In 1897 he returned to Sweden, where he remained until his death in 1912. He was married three times, each marriage ending in divorce.

Strindberg, judged by the majority of his works so far translated into English, is a dramatist endowed with a trenchant and searching power of analysis and a remarkable, if limited, insight into human nature; his chief plays are exact, though narrow, analyses of the feminine mind and soul. His own experience was so unfortunate that his bitterness takes the form of a wholesale indictment of the sex. In "The Father," "Miss Julia," "Creditors," and "Comrades," woman is seen as a savage and soulless being. His greatest power lies in the portrayal of character, and the conflicts of human minds; he delights in showing the superiority of one individual over another.

While Strindberg is best known by his naturalistic plays, his "final" period of activity produced many poetic fantasies of a far different sort: "The Bridal Crown," "The Dream Play," and "Swanwhite," are idealistic in tendency, and mark a radical departure from the dramatist's earlier philosophy of life.

Plays

"Hermione" (1869)
"The Outlaw" (1871)
"Master Olof" (1872)
"The Secret of the Guild" (1880)
"Sir Bengt's Lady" (1882)
"The Wanderings of Lucky-Per" (1883)
"The Father" (1887)
"Comrades" (1888)
"Miss Julia" (1888)
"Creditors" (1890)
"Pariah" (1890)
"Samum" (1890)
"The Stronger" (1890)
"The Keys of Heaven" (1892)
"The First Warning" (1893)
"Debit and Credit" (1893)
"Motherlove" (1893)
"Facing Death" (1893)
"Playing with Fire" (1897)
"The Link" (1897)
"To Damascus, I" (1898)
"To Damascus, II" (1898)
"There Are Crimes and Crimes" (1899)
"Christmas" (1899)
"Gustavus Vasa" (1899)
"Eric XIV" (1899)
"The Saga of the Folkungs" (1899)
"Gustavus Adolphus" (1900)
"The Dance of Death, I" (1901)
"The Dance of Death, II" (1901)
"Easter" (1901)
"Midsummer" (1901)
"Engelbreckt" (1901)

"Charles XII" (1901)
"The Bridal Crown" (1902)
"Swanwhite" (1902)
"The Dream Play" (1902)
"Gustavus III" (1903)
"Queen Christina" (1903)
"The Nightingale of Wittenberg" ["Martin Luther"] (1903)
"To Damascus, III" (1904)
"Storm" (1907)
"The Burned Lot" (1907)
"The Spook Sonata" (1907)
"The Pelican" (1907)
"The Slippers of Abu Casem" (1908)
"The Last Knight" (1908)
"The National Director" (1909)
"The Earl of Bjällbo" (1909)
"The Black Glove" (1909)
"The Great Highway" (1909)

Editions.—Plays by August Strindberg, trans. with preface by Edwin Björkman (N. Y. 1912), includes "The Dream Play," "The Link," and "The Dance of Death," I and II; 2nd series, trans. by the same (N. Y. 1913), includes "There Are Crimes and Crimes," "Miss Julia," "The Stronger," "Creditors," and "Pariah" [also Strindberg's Preface to "Miss Julia"]; 3rd series, trans. by the same (N. Y. 1913), includes "Swanwhite," "Simoom," [*i.e.* "Samum"], "Debit and Credit," "Advent," "The Thunderstorm," and "After the Fire" [*i.e.* "The Burned Lot"]; 4th series, trans. by the same (N. Y. 1916), includes "The Bridal Crown" [*i.e.* "The Crown Bride"], "The Spook Sonata," "The First Warning," and "Gustavus Vasa"; *Plays,* trans. by E. and W. Oland, Vol. I (Boston, 1912), includes "The Father," "Countess Julie" [*i.e.* "Miss Julia"], "The Outlaw," and "The Stronger"; Vol. II (Boston, 1912), includes "Comrades," "Facing Death," "Easter," and "Pariah"; Vol. III (Boston, 1914), includes "Swanwhite," "Advent," and "The Storm"; *Miss Julie and Other Plays* (N. Y. n. d.), includes also "Creditors," "The Stronger Woman," "Motherly Love," "Pariah," and "Simoon"; *Plays,* trans. by Edwin Björkman (N. Y. 1912), includes "Miss Julia," and "The Stronger"; *Plays by August Strindberg,* trans. by same (N. Y. 1912), includes "Creditors" and "Pariah"; *Paria, Simoom, Two Plays,* trans. by H. B. Samuel (London, 1914); *Lucky Peter's Travels,* etc. (London, 1931) includes also "The Father," "Lady Julia," "Playing with Fire," and "The Bond"; *Easter and Other Plays* (London, 1931) includes also "The Dance of Death," "The Ghost Sonata," and "A Dream Play."

Separate Plays.—"The Father," trans. by N. Erichsen (Boston, 1898); "Easter," by Velma S. Howard (Cincinnati, 1912); "Lucky Pehr" [*i.e.* "The Wanderings of Lucky-Per"], by the same (Cincinnati, 1912); "Master Olof" (N. Y. 1915); "Swanwhite," by F. J. Ziegler (Phila. 1909); "Mother Love," by same (Phila. 1910); "There Are Crimes and Crimes," trans. by Edwin Björkman (N. Y. 1912); "The Creditor" [*i.e.* "Creditors"], by F. J. Ziegler (Phila. 1910); by Mary Harned (*Poet Lore,* Boston, 1911); "Debit and Credit," by same (*Poet Lore,* Boston, 1906); "Facing Death," by E. and W. Oland (*The Dramatist,* Easton, 1911); "The Stronger," by F. J. Ziegler (*Poet Lore,* Boston, 1906), and by E. and W. Oland (*International,* N. Y. 1911); "Simoom" [*i.e.* "Samum"], by Mary Harned (*Poet Lore,* Boston, 1906), and by E. Björkman (*Smart Set,* N. Y. 1913); "The Outcast" [*i.e.* "Pariah"] by same (*Poet Lore,* Boston, 1906); "Julie [*i.e.* "Miss Julia"] by Arthur Swan (*Poet Lore,* Boston, 1911; same play as "Countess Julia," by Charles Recht (Philadelphia, 1912); "Advent," by Claud Field (Boston, no date).

Reprints in Collections and Anthologies.—"The Father" (Erichsen translation), in Dickinson's *Chief Contemporary Dramatists* (Boston, 1915); "The Creditor" (anonymous translation) in Shay and Loving's *Fifty Contemporary One-Act Plays* (Cincinnati, 1920); "The Stronger" (trans. by Charles Wangel) in Loving's *Ten-Minute Plays* (N. Y. 1923), in Lewis' *Contemporary One-Act Plays* (Björkman translation) (N. Y. 1922), and anonymously, as "The Stronger Woman" in Shay's *Treasury of Plays for Women* (Boston, 1923); "Simoom" (Harned translation), in Moses' *Representative One-Act Plays by Continental Authors* (Boston, 1923); "Motherly Love" [*i.e.* "Motherlove"], anonymously, in Shay's *Treasury of Plays for Women* (Boston, 1923).

References

L. Lind-af-Hageby, *August Strindberg* (N. Y. 1913); Gustaf Uddgren, *Strindberg the Man* (Boston, 1920); Archibald Henderson, *European Dramatists* (N. Y. 1926); Edwin Björkman, *Voices of To-morrow* (N. Y. 1913); Ashley Dukes, *Modern Dramatists* (Chicago, 1912), and *The Youngest Drama* (Chicago, 1924); James Huneker, *Iconoclasts* (N. Y. 1905); Ludwig Lewisohn, *The Modern Drama* (N. Y. 1915), and *The Drama and the Stage* (N. Y. 1922); Otto Heller, *Prophets of Dissent* (N. Y. 1918); F. W. Chandler, *Aspects of Modern Drama* (N. Y. 1914), and *Modern Continental Playwrights* (N. Y. 1931); G. A. Campbell, *Strindberg* (N. Y. 1933); V. J. McGill, *August Strindberg*, etc. (N. Y. 1930); T. H. Dickinson, *The Theater in a Changing Europe* (N. Y. 1937).

See also.—Various prefaces to the translated plays listed above, and Strindberg's "Author's Preface" to "Miss Julia," in *Plays*, 2nd series.

The Father

Play in 3 acts (1887). Texts: translation by N. Erichsen (Boston, 1898); reprint in Dickinson's *Chief Contemporary Dramatists* (Boston, 1915); by E. and W. Oland, in *Plays* (Boston, 1912), in *Lucky Peter's Travels*, etc. (London, 1931).

"The Father" was published in 1887, the year Antoine founded his Free Theater in Paris, where it was afterward produced. It was the first and one of the most widely known of his "naturalistic" dramas. It was largely through this play and its immediate successors that Strindberg's "European reputation as a modern dramatist and a woman-hater was established."

1. Though it was written in disregard of conventional forms, "The Father" is a well-constructed play. Its single

dominant idea is clearly conceived and succinctly stated. The dramatist sets to work immediately, without troubling to approach his subject by means of the usual preparations. Alexandre Dumas the Elder is said to have declared that drama is the art of preparations. Strindberg was too anxious to get to the heart of his story to bother with the elaborate foundations that Dumas would require. No time is lost in showing the ideas and habits of the husband, and then those of the wife—"the man-eater, the destroyer of all that is noble, consistent, progressive in man." He makes the husband a high-strung, nervous man, and the wife a fiendish abnormal woman; the dice are loaded to begin with. But, granted the characters, what they do is sufficiently natural to create the necessary illusion of reality.

The dialogue is economical; there are no long divagations, no elaborated scenes of self-exposition—as in the plays of Chekhov and Gorky: conversation and action combine to reveal character, or as much of it as the dramatist cares to show.

As you read the play, notice how little is irrelevant, how each word strengthens the unity of the piece.

2. The dramatist's purpose was twofold: to paint a picture of Laura, and to tell the story as rapidly as possible. A few deft touches, and Laura is before us in flesh and blood. In the first act we find the following dialogue:

LAURA. Then is it reasonable to think that one can see, by looking in a microscope, what is going on in another planet?

DOCTOR. Does he say he can do that?

LAURA. Yes, he says so.

DOCTOR. In a microscope?

LAURA. In a microscope, yes.

DOCTOR. This is serious, if it is so.

LAURA. If it is so! Then you have no belief in me, Doctor, and I am sitting here and confiding the family secret in you—

But when the Captain is questioned by the Doctor, it turns out that it was a spectroscope, not a microscope, he had been using. This is but one of the many examples of the manner in which Strindberg reveals character and develops his idea. Find other examples in "The Father," and see whether they advance the story, reveal character, or are merely of an incidental nature.

3. "The Father" is a psychological play; that is, the action grows directly out of a mental struggle—in this case, it is a struggle or duel of the sexes. The climax is therefore reached when one of the two contending minds, so to speak, dominates the other. This comes at the end of the second act, where Laura tells her husband that she possesses the means of putting him "under control," in order that she may educate their child "without listening to his advice": she has "his own letter to the doctor declaring himself to be insane." The Captain "looks at her in silence," while she tells him: "Now you have fulfilled your function as an unfortunately necessary father and breadwinner. You are not needed any longer and you must go. You must go since you have realized that my intellect is as strong as my will, and since you will not stay and acknowledge it." Then "The Captain goes to the table, takes the lighted lamp and throws it at Laura, who escapes backwards through the door." She has conquered, by driving her husband to insanity.

The last act shows the result of Laura's "duel," and carries to a logical conclusion her inhuman work.

4. You have, doubtless, in reading the play, been struck by its appalling people and what they do; you are not touched, or moved to pity any of the characters, unless it be the little daughter. The father, though he ought to be an object of compassion, is so brutal and uncompromising that we have little sympathy for him. We feel more horror than pity; that is because Strindberg has made his characters incarnations of their worst qualities; they are for the most part abnormal and neurasthenic, and as such do not appeal to us as average, healthy beings would. There is a certain relief when the Captain is taken away; we are sure he will be better off away from his wife—indeed, it is rather disappointing that Laura is not sent to a sanitarium. Had Strindberg shown her as a sym-

pathetic victim, his play would have been much more terrible, and less purely horrible.

Is this lack of sympathy due to the dramatist's distorted view of life, or because he was bent upon proving his point? This question cannot, perhaps, be satisfactorily answered, but an intelligent discussion of the matter will serve to throw light on Strindberg's methods.

5. An interesting parallel is suggested in Laura's quoted lines at the end of the second act, with one of the principal ideas in Bernard Shaw's "Man and Superman." What does Shaw's Tanner owe to Strindberg's Laura?

There Are Crimes and Crimes

Comedy in 4 acts (1899). Texts: translation by E. Björkman (N. Y. 1912); same in *Plays,* 2nd series (N. Y. 1913).

This "comedy" belongs to a later period in the mental development of Strindberg. In "The Father," the tone is one of fierce denunciation, in "There Are Crimes and Crimes" there is little of this, but rather a philosophic questioning of the meaning of existence. In his own words, "Light after darkness; new productivity, with recovered Faith, Hope, and Love—and with full, rock-firm Certitude." In this frame of mind, he set to work on a play which should teach, or rather expose, the working-out of a higher code of morals than that recognized in our ordinary court-room. The play shows that the greatest crimes are the spiritual crimes done against oneself, one's higher nature, and that the law has nothing to do with them. Such, at least, is the ethical question treated in the play.

1. Given so abstract a theme as the conscience of man struggling within its own coils, what is the best way to write a play illustrating it? To allow the personages in a play to talk about and around a theme, is obviously a makeshift. In a play we demand action. In this play, however, the author shows in terms of action the result of a mental attitude, and does not merely talk about it or permit his characters to do so. Maurice says (p. 24, Björkman translation), ". . . If we had to answer for our thoughts, who could then clear himself?" and, as if to

test this statement, Strindberg places Maurice in a position where his thoughts really do result in acts, and shows how he succeeds in clearing himself. That is the play.

2. By dividing each act into two scenes, the author evidently intends to create an atmosphere of verisimilitude. There is a rhythm, an ebb and flow in life which is often lacking even in good plays; but it is felt in this one largely by reason of the division of acts into scenes. At least it is suggested, as we find it suggested in Tolstoy's "Live Corpse."

This rhythmic quality is well defined in the quarrel scene at the end of the third act of Henry Arthur Jones' "Dolly Reforming Herself." There the action rises and falls, suggesting the ebb and flow of life.

3. It has been pointed out that every important event in a play is usually prepared for in advance. When (p. 49) the Abbé announces to Adolphe and Mme. Catherine that Marion is dead, the news comes as a shock to the audience. Is there any reason for this apparent violation of the above-stated law? Why should this news shock? Why should the audience not be given some hint? Are not such situations shocking in life? Then why should they not be so in the theater?

Find similar examples of such surprises in other plays.

4. One of the differences between this kind of play and the average American or English play may be observed by comparing the scene (pp. 49-52) where the Abbé and the Commissaire announce that the Parisian public are up in arms against Maurice for what they believe to be the murder of his daughter Marion, with a play of Clyde Fitch or Haddon Chambers. The Commissaire speaks for several minutes, and the Abbé adds to the story from time to time. This is really a modern instance of the method used by the ancient Greeks, in whose plays the messenger tells the tale of disaster that has happened off-stage. The American dramatist would make a more vivid and appealing scene, by concretely showing the wrath of the public. Edward Sheldon does this in the "big act" of "The Boss," where the townspeople are just outside the house of the chief character throwing stones through the window and

breaking the furniture in the room. This sort of thing is by no means confined to the American and English drama, for Ibsen's "Enemy of the People" and Hauptmann's "Weavers" contain similar scenes. Most modern dramatists would regard it as poor craftsmanship to lose an opportunity of showing a crowd in conflict with an individual.

In the work of half a dozen younger American dramatists, there is no compromise in conducting the story to its logical conclusion. In this respect the work of Eugene O'Neill, Paul Green, and Lynn Riggs, is quite as logical as that of any European dramatist. See O'Neill's "Desire Under the Elms," Green's "In Abraham's Bosom," and Riggs' "Big Lake."

5. Strindberg is a master of his art. When he violates some technical canon we may be sure that he has good reason for doing so. The third act in a four-act play is especially important. Few dramatists, having successfully conducted their story up to this point, can afford to risk losing the cumulative effect created in the preceding acts by failing to keep the action constantly going. The third act of this play opens with a dialogue, interrupted only by the news of Marion's death. This is an important incident, no doubt, yet it is the only one to break the long and discursive scene.

What reasons can you offer for Strindberg's unusual treatment of the scene?

THE RUSSIAN DRAMA

BEFORE THE REVOLUTION[1]

Some of the work of the well-known Russian dramatists is adequately translated. There are many versions of Chekhov's plays; several of Gorky's "Lower Depths," but not more than half of his other plays can be read in English; and not half of Andreyev's are accessible. All of Tolstoy's plays are procurable in several versions. There is a volume of three Artzybashev plays, and one other is published separately. Feodor Sologub's "Triumph of Death" appeared in the *Drama Magazine;* Shchedrin (Mikhail Saltuikov) is now known through a translation of his "Death of Pazukhin." Sergei Stepniak's "New Convert"—also translated—is chiefly valuable as a revolutionary document. A few of the curious short plays and one long play of Nicholas Evreinov are translated and one short play of the Ukrainian woman (Carissa Petrovna Kossatch), known as "Lesya Ukrainka." Shpazhinsky's *Madame Major* is also translated.

Professor Wiener's *Contemporary Drama of Russia* contains a full account of the modern drama up to the Revolution; Oliver M. Sayler's *Russian Theater* is a vivid series of pictures of the recent activities in the Russian theater; Alexander Bakshy's *Path of the Modern Russian Stage* is largely theoretical. George R. Noyes' *Masterpieces of the Russian Drama* is indispensable for its many translated texts and editorial matter. See also Huntley Carter's *New Spirit in the European Theater.*

LEO TOLSTOY

Leo [Lev] Nikolaievitch Tolstoy was born in 1828 at Yasnaya Polyana, Russia. Soon after the early death of his parents he was sent to live with relations. Later he entered the University of Kazan, and subsequently studied in the School of Eastern Languages and the law school. In 1847 he left the law school, tired of the life of comparative idleness and dissipation he was leading. After a few months at his home, he went to St. Petersburg with his brother, "carousing with Zigani dancers, and throwing all serious

[1] For *The Drama of Soviet Russia,* see page 427.

thoughts to the winds." In 1851 he joined the army in the Caucasus, whence he sent back vivid accounts of the battles in which he fought. The Czar was attracted by the *Tales From Sebastopol* and summoned Tolstoy to the capital. In 1857 he traveled abroad, in Germany, France, Italy, Switzerland, England, returning from time to time to Russia. In 1861 he was once more at Yasnaya Polyana; the next year he married. The remainder of his life was devoted to a consideration of a host of political, moral, and religious questions, upon which he wrote numerous tracts; besides these, he published novels, stories, economic and philosophical studies and plays. For political and religious reasons he was excommunicated from the Orthodox Church in 1901. In 1910 he died at Astapovo.

Tolstoy's best work is not to be found in his plays, but these offer remarkable pictures of Russian life. Tolstoy was not a professional playwright: he wrote his plays for special and private performances, and the requirements were not such as would be necessary in the case of plays intended for regular production. Tolstoy shares with other dramatists of his country their lack of the sense of "form" as is commonly understood in Western Europe: the Russians have purposely avoided what they considered the "tricks of the trade," preferring to lay greater stress on the delineation of character. The plays of Tolstoy, Chekhov, Gorky, and Andreyev are interesting primarily as studies in character and atmosphere.

Plays

"The Nihilist" (1863)
"The Infected Family" (1864)
"The Power of Darkness" (1886)
"The First Distiller" (1887)
"The Fruits of Culture" (1889)
"The Live Corpse" (1912)
"The Light Shines in Darkness" (1912)
"The Cause of It All" (1912)

Editions.—The Plays of Leo Tolstoy, trans., with preface, by Louise and Aylmer Maude (N. Y. 1919), includes "The Power of Darkness," "The First Distiller," "Fruits of Culture," "The Live Corpse," "The Cause of It All," and "The Light Shines in Darkness"; *The Dramatic Works of Lyof N. Tolstoi,* trans., with preface, by Nathan Haskell Dole (N. Y. 1923), includes "The Power of Darkness," "Fruits of Enlightenment," "The First Distiller," "The Live Corpse," "The Light Shines in Darkness," "The Root of All Evil" [*i.e.* "The Cause of It All"] and "The Wisdom of Children," a series of scenes, unfinished. *Redemption and Other Plays,* anonymous translations with preface by Arthur Hopkins (N. Y. 1919), includes the play mentioned [*i.e.* "The

Live Corpse"], "The Power of Darkness," and "The Fruits of Culture."

Separate Plays.—"The Dominion of Darkness," trans. anonymously (Chicago, 1890); "The Fruits of Culture," by G. Schumm (Boston, 1891); same anonymously, as "The Fruits of Enlightenment" (N. Y. 1891, and Boston, 1901); "The Living Corpse," by Mrs. E. M. Evarts (Philadelphia, 1912); the same, as "The Man Who Was Dead," anonymously, with "The Cause of It All" (N. Y. 1912); "The Light That Shines in Darkness," trans. anonymously (N. Y. 1912).

Most of the plays are included in various collected works. The *Dramatic Works* are included (all but posthumous plays) in Vol. XVIII of *The Complete Works,* edited by Wiener (Boston, 1904-05); "The Power of Darkness" and "The Fruits of Enlightenment," trans. by Wiener, are in volume, "The Death of Ivan Ilich," etc. (Boston, 1911); "The Light That Shines in Darkness," trans. anonymously, in volume, "Father Sergius" (London, 1911); "The Cause of It All" and "The Man Who Was Dead" [*i.e.* "The Live Corpse"], trans. anonymously, in volume, "The Forged Coupon," etc. (N. Y. 1911); *Plays,* in Pocket Edition, 14 vols. (N. Y. no date); and in *Novels,* etc., 24 vols. (N. Y. 1899*ff*); *Stories and Dramas* (N. Y. 1926) includes "The Nihilist," "The Contaminated Family," and two sketches, "Dramatic Scenes About the Pan," etc., and "Peter the Publican," trans. by various hands.

References

Paul Birukoff, *Leo Tolstoy, his Life and Work* (N. Y. 1906); Aylmer Maude, *The Life of Tolstoy,* 2 vols. (N. Y. 1910; also another book in one volume, by the same, N. Y. 1918); Nathan Haskell Dole, *The Life of Count Lyof N. Tolstoi* (N. Y. 1911); Count Ilya Tolstoy, *Reminiscences of Tolstoy,* translated by Geo. Calderon (N. Y. 1914); Romain Rolland, *Tolstoy,* translated by B. Miall (N. Y. 1911); George Rapall Noyes, *Tolstoy* (N. Y. 1918); Maxim Gorky, *Reminiscences of Leo Nikolaevich Tolstoy,* translated by S. S. Koteliansky and L. Woolf (N. Y. 1920); William Lyon Phelps, *Essays on Russian Novelists* (N. Y. 1911); Ashley Dukes, *Modern Dramatists* (Chicago, 1912); Havelock Ellis, *The New Spirit* (N. Y. no date); Oliver M. Sayler, *The Russian Theater* (N. Y. 1922); Leo Wiener, *The Contemporary Drama of Russia* (Boston, 1924); Otto Heller, *Prophets of Dissent* (N. Y. 1918); F. W. Chandler, *Aspects of Modern Drama* (N. Y. 1914); Norman Hapgood, *The Stage in America* (N. Y. 1901); Clayton Hamilton, *Seen on the Stage* (N. Y. 1920); M. J. Olgin, *A Guide to Russian Literature* (N. Y. 1920).

See also.—*The Diaries of Leo Tolstoy,* trans. by C. J. Hogarth and A. Sirnis (N. Y. 1917); *The Journal of Leo Tolstoy,* trans. by Rose Strunsky (N. Y. 1917); and prefaces to translations of plays listed above.

The Live Corpse

Play in 5 acts (Posthumous, 1912). Texts: translation, as "The Living Corpse," by Mrs. E. M. Evarts (Philadelphia, 1912); as "The Man Who Was Dead" anonymously (N. Y. 1912); as "Redemption," anonymously, in *Redemption and Other Plays* (N. Y. 1919); by L. and A. Maude, as "The Live Corpse," in *The Plays of Leo Tolstoy* (N. Y. 1919); by N. H. Dole, as the same, in *The Dramatic Works of Lyof N. Tolstoi* (N. Y. 1923).

"The Live Corpse," like all of Tolstoy's plays, was written for an immediate and special purpose: it is intended to arouse indignation over the Russian divorce laws. But besides being a purpose, or thesis, play, it happens to be a study in character and a presentment of a very interesting situation. Fedia is a human being, though he is at the same time a lay-figure around which the writer has woven his situations and expressed his opinions. "The Live Corpse," like most modern Russian plays, is structurally loose; not *necessarily* faulty, of course, but by comparison with the professional products of the authors of close-knit pieces, it seems casual, possibly even a little vague.

1. Although Tolstoy disregarded or was ignorant of the "laws" of the "well-made play," he is apparently ready to utilize the conventional exposition form. But he does not write a full act: the moment the exposition is over, the curtain drops and another scene begins. There are several such changes of scene throughout the play; the dramatist appears to have seen his story in flashes, to have written along until he had said all he wished to say, and then turned to another incident. The unity of the play consists in Fedia and what he does.

Do you think the play would have been better in three, or perhaps four, acts? What, if anything, is gained by throwing the story into a series of short scenes?

2. The end of the first act is no less dramatic, certainly, than if it had been carefully prepared for, as Pinero prepares for his "curtains." The emphatic "curtain" is not so popular nowadays as it used to be; many dramatists have, indeed, achieved striking emphasis in the unemphatic "curtain." Both

are conventions, but the latter is generally of a realistic character: life, we know, is as a rule unemphatic, it is only in crises that unsuspected identities are revealed and sudden reversals of fortune occur, and the writer of unemphatic act endings feels that "things just happen this way." Tolstoy's instinct, we feel, was right: he was not concerned with building a climactic play, but with showing the character and acts of Fedia and how these affected his family and friends.

But can you picture him in a conventionally "well-made play"? How would Sudermann have treated him? How would H. H. Davies?

It might almost be said that in this case the unemphatic ending becomes emphatic. This is a favorite device with Galsworthy. Compare the unemphatic "curtains" in "The Live Corpse" with those of "Justice."

3. Having determined that the theme of the play was to be an exposure of the evil aspects of the divorce laws, and since one of its chief points of interest was Fedia, the author seems to have cared little how his drama—as a work of art—proceeded. The action is abrupt, and in places a little tedious. Observe, for instance, that although in the second scene of the second act Fedia declares he will disappear in order to enable his wife to marry Victor, the resolution is neither carried out nor the action developed, until after the lapse of an entire act. Is this felt to be a structural weakness?

4. After all the circumstances are made clear, and the audience are fully acquainted with the characters, we may expect the "big scene." The last act, laid in the Magistrate's office, is where Tolstoy drives home his lesson, and makes his plea against the laws. The scene is good, because it seems natural; suspense is preserved and interest sustained until the catastrophe, which is Fedia's suicide.

Court scenes and cross-examinations are nearly always effective on the stage, as they are in life.

Emile Faguet, the French critic, says: "Mankind seeks in tragedy a pleasure which is born of the misfortunes of mankind."

Is Faguet justified in assuming that our pleasure in tragedy arises from seeing *other* people suffer? What is the nature of our pleasure, for instance, in "Hamlet"?

5. Suppose—and this happens now to be actually the case—that the situation which Tolstoy sought to improve, were materially improved, would this play still be effective? In other words, how deeply are we interested in the idea, irrespective of the drama?

6. Tolstoy, as we have said, was not a professional dramatist; his plays were written for private performance, or else frankly as experiments. Says Nathan Haskell Dole in his *Life of Count Tolstoy*: "In speaking of play-writing, Tolstoy remarked that it was sculptor's work, whereas in writing novels he worked with a brush and was free to add color and simplify; but the drama, according to him, had no shadows and half-tones: 'Everything must be clear-cut and in high relief. The incidents must be ready, fully ripened, and the whole difficulty lies in representing these fully matured moments, these ripened moods of the dramatis personæ.'"

Remarkably well put, especially when we remember that Tolstoy was used to broad canvases (*War and Peace,* for instance, with its four thick volumes!). But is he not mistaken in assuming that the play-form, being so much more limited *in time,* is for that reason limited in scope? The novelist must almost of necessity find the 12,000 to 18,000 words of a play a rather small field to work in, when he has been used to from 30,000 to 300,000!

Mr. Sidney Howard, reviewing a volume of one-act plays recently, wrote: "Art demands leisure, dramatic art no less than any other. Three hours is none too long." But for many novelists three hours is far too short, and the chief trouble with novelists who do venture into the theater is that three hours' time is felt to be far too short for what the dramatist had to "put over," and far too long for the way he did it.

The Spanish novelist-dramatist, Galdós, is said to have adopted a "novelistic" method in his plays. Has Tolstoy done so in "The Live Corpse"? Has he in his earlier plays, "The Power of Darkness" and "The Fruits of Culture"?

Maxim Gorky

Alexei Maximovitch Pyeshkov, known as "Maxim Gorky," was born at Nizhni-Novgorod, Russia, in 1868. As a child and youth he led an extraordinarily varied life, as baker, gardener, ship's cook, beggar, tramp. Until the publication of his first story in the early nineties he was a restless wanderer. His stories and novels, by which he first won international fame, are memorable for their vivid power, and because the writer was able to impart his own passionate love of life to his characters. These consist for the most part of the outcasts he had himself known so well. He was one of the first Russians to introduce the proletariat into fiction.

For years an active propagandist in the cause of liberty and revolution, he was forced to leave Russia early during the present century. After the establishment of the Soviet régime he assumed for a short period editorial charge of one of the official educational bureaus, but disagreeing with the government on political issues, he left Russia to reside in Germany, where he resumed his literary labors. Later he returned and took active part in the social and artistic life of the U. S. S. R.

Gorky's plays are primarily interesting because of the qualities that render his novels and stories significant: they are the by-products of a genius who must try all forms in order to find what best suits him. Like Andreyev, who once declared he had never written a play, Gorky is well aware that his dramas are not written with the conscious art that characterizes the products of "regular" playwrights. He once declared to me (1923): "I don't like my plays. . . . Bad! Very bad! I didn't know how to write. . . . All the plays are bad. . . . If I have written plays, it was because I had to write them, or thought I had to. . . ." He said he knew nothing about technique: "That's why my plays are so bad. . . . But if I had studied the theory of the drama they would have been much worse." Gorky is interested primarily in human beings; he cares little about the elaboration of a structural edifice. "When the artist," Gorky says, "can no longer contain himself, he produces a work of art. What precise form that will take seems to me a matter of small importance." Gorky died in Russia in 1936.

Plays

"The Middle Class" (1901)
"The Lower Depths" (1902)
"A Country House" (1903)
"Children of the Sun" (1905)
"Barbarians" (1905)
"Enemies" (1906)
"The Last Ones" (1908)
"Odd People" (1910)
"Vassa Zheleznova" (1910)
"Children" (1910)
"The Zykovs" (1914)
"The Old Man" ["The Judge"] (1915)
"The Counterfeit Coin" (1926)
"Yegor Bulichov and the Others" (1932)
"Dostigaev" (1934)

Editions.—"The Middle Class," translated as "The Smug Citizen," by Edwin Hopkins (*Poet Lore,* Boston, 1906); "The Lower Depths," by Laurence Irving (N. Y. 1912); as "In the Depths," by W. H. H. Chambers (*The Drama,* Vol. XVIII, London, 1906); as "The Lower Depths," by Jenny Coven, separately and in *Moscow Art Theater Plays* (N. Y. 1922); same as "A Night Shelter," by Edwin Hopkins (*Poet Lore,* Boston, 1905), and in book form, as "Submerged"; and as "At the Bottom," by W. L. Laurence (N. Y. 1930); "A Country House," as "Summer Folk," by Aline Delano (*Poet Lore,* Boston, 1905); "Children of the Sun," by A. T. Wolfe (*Poet Lore,* Boston, 1906); "The Judge," by Marie Zakrevsky and Barrett H. Clark (N. Y. 1924); "Yegor Bulichov and Others," trans. by A. Wixley, in *Four Soviet Plays* (N. Y. 1937); *Last Plays of Maxim Gorky* (N. Y. 1937), contains "Yegor Bulichov" and "Dostigaev."

Reprints in Collections and Anthologies.—"The Lower Depths" (Hopkins translation) in Dickinson's *Chief Contemporary Dramatists,* 2nd series (Boston, 1921), and (Coven translation) in *Moscow Art Theater Plays,* preface by O. M. Sayler (N. Y. 1922).

References

E. J. Dillon, *Maxim Gorky, His Life and Writings* (London, 1902); H. Ostwald, *Maxim Gorky* (N. Y. 1907); Ashley Dukes, *Modern Dramatists* (Chicago, 1912); James Huneker, *Iconoclasts* (N. Y. 1905); Arthur Symons, *Studies in Prose and Verse* (N. Y. 1904); Prince Kropotkin, *Ideals and Realities in Russian Literature* (N. Y. 1915); Serge Persky, *Contemporary Russian Novelists* (Boston, 1913); Oliver M. Sayler, *The Russian Theater* (N. Y. 1922); M. J. Olgin, *A Guide to Russian Literature* (N. Y. 1920); F. W. Chandler, *Aspects of Modern Drama* (N. Y. 1914) and *Modern Continental Playwrights* (N. Y. 1931); Ludwig Lewisohn, *The Drama and the Stage* (N. Y. 1922); C. Stanislavsky, *My Life in Art* (Boston, 1924); Alexander Kaun, *Leonid Andreyev* (N. Y. 1924); Leo Wiener, *The Contemporary Drama of Russia* (Boston, 1924); Prince D. S. Mirsky, *Contemporary Russian Literature* (N. Y. 1926). See also Gorky's essay on *The Modern Drama,* preface to "The Judge" (N. Y. 1924).

The Lower Depths

Play in 4 acts (1902). Texts: translation by Laurence Irving (N. Y. 1912); by Jenny Coven (N. Y. 1922), and in *Moscow Art*

all the agriculturals . . . and even the gentry—they live for the better man! Each thinks 'e's livin' fer 'imself, yet it turns out it's fer that better man. A 'undred years . . . and maybe longer, we 'as to go on livin' till the better man.

But, perhaps ironically, the Actor "he's hanged himself!" And the play ends with Satine's "Ah . . . he's spoiled the song . . . the fool!"

6. Luka is the one bright spot in the play; technically, he serves as a contrasting figure to the rest, while his prophetic optimism makes the hopeless misery of his fellow beings the more tragic. He is intensely "Russian" in his philosophic questioning of the meaning and purpose of life, and in his inordinate desire to philosophize. Like Turgenev's Rudin, he is forever theorizing, and that tendency is what has brought about his failure.

Compare Luka with the Stranger in Jerome K. Jerome's "Passing of the Third Floor Back," Manson in Charles Rann Kennedy's "Servant in the House," and Gottwald in Hauptmann's "Hannele."

7. In his essay on *The Modern Drama* printed in the English translation of "The Judge," Gorky says: "The characters of a drama should all act independently of the volition of the dramatist, in accordance with the law of their individual natures and social environment; they must follow the inspiration of their own destiny, and not that of any other destiny arbitrarily imposed upon them by the writer. They must, driven by their own inner impulses, create the incidents and episodes—tragic or comic—and direct the course of the play, being permitted to act in harmony with their own contradictory natures, interests, and passions. The author throughout should behave as a host at a party to which he has invited imaginary guests, without in any way interceding, no matter how one guest may worry or torment any other—be it physically or morally; and finally, it is his business cold-bloodedly to describe the manner in which they all behave."

An admirable statement, but Gorky, being human, has perceived that the dramatist is incapable of "playing the host." He adds: "Now as a matter of fact, I know no play written according to this theory in all European literature, and as for myself, I could never write one."

In "The Lower Depths" can you detect any traces of the dramatist's effort to play the perfect host? How "cold-bloodedly" does Gorky describe the manner in which his characters behave?

ANTON CHEKHOV

Anton Pavlovitch Chekhov was born at Taganrog, Russia, in 1860. In reply to a request for a biographical outline, he wrote the following letter five years before his death (quoted in Gerhardi's *Anton Chehov*), offering the necessary information:

"I, A. P. Chehov, was born on the 17th of January, 1860, at Taganrog. I was educated first in the Greek School . . . then in the Taganrog high school. In 1879 I entered Moscow University in the Faculty of Medicine. . . . I began in my first year to publish stories in the weekly journals and newspapers, and these literary pursuits had, early in the eighties, acquired a permanent professional character. In 1888 I took the Pushkin prize. In 1890 I travelled to the Island of Sahalin, to write afterwards a book upon our penal colony and prisons there. Not counting reviews, feuilletons, paragraphs, and all that I have written from day to day for the newspapers . . . I have, during my twenty years of literary work, published more than three hundred signatures of print, of short and long stories. I have also written plays for the stage.

"I have no doubt that the study of medicine has had an important influence on my literary work; it has considerably enlarged the sphere of my observation. . . . It has also been a guiding influence. . . ."

Several years before his death Chekhov was forced to live in the South, and it was there, in the Crimea, that he wrote his best plays. In 1904, the year of his death, when "The Cherry Orchard" was produced at the Moscow Art Theater, he was accorded a stirring ovation by the public. He had come to be regarded as one of the most highly gifted of all Russian dramatists. He died in a small village of the Black Forest.

In contrast with the more or less loosely constructed plays of his contemporaries, the best plays of Chekhov are tightly woven of the finest fabric. "Three Sisters," "The Cherry Orchard" and "The Seagull" are replete with the apparently aimless confusion of daily existence, but this seeming aimlessness is the result of the most delicate art. Chekhov was first a teller of tales, and to the drama he brought the same gifts that made him a great story-teller; his is an art of revolt because he deliberately avoids the prepared climaxes, the obvious struggles and superficial characterization of the ordinary play, and in their place he puts simply the men and women he knows. Chekhov first became known as a dramatist through the Moscow Art Theater (sometimes called the "Seagull" after Chekhov's play), where his dramatic works were produced under the skillful direction of Constantin Stanislavsky.

PLAYS

"On the High Road" (1885)
"The Swan Song" (1886)
"Ivanov" (1887)
"The Wood Demon" (1888)
"The Bear" (1888)
"The Proposal" (1889)
"Tatyana Ripin" (1889)
"The Tragedian in Spite of Himself" (1890)
"The Wedding" (1890)
"The Anniversary" (1892)
"The Seagull" (1896)
"Uncle Vanya" (1897)
"Three Sisters" (1901)
"The Cherry Orchard" (1903)
"The Tobacco Evil" (1922)
"That Worthless Fellow Platonov" (published 1930)

Editions.—Plays by Anton Tchekoff, translated by Marian Fell (N. Y. 1912), includes "Uncle Vanya," "Ivanov," "The Seagull," and "The Swan Song"; same, 2nd series, trans. by Julius West (N. Y. 1916), includes "On the High Road," "The Proposal," "The Wedding," "The Bear," "A Tragedian in Spite of Himself," "The Anniversary," "The Three Sisters," and "The Cherry Orchard"; *Three Sisters and Other Plays,* translated by Constance Garnett (N. Y. 1924), includes "Three Sisters," "Ivanov," "A Swan Song," "An Unwilling Martyr" [*i.e.* "The Tragedian in Spite of Himself"], "The Anniversary," "On the High Road," and "The Wedding"; *The Cherry Orchard and Other Plays,* trans. by same (N. Y. 1924), includes "The Cherry Orchard," "Uncle Vanya," "The Seagull," "The Bear," and "The Proposal"; *Two Plays by Tchekhoff,* trans. by George Calderon (N. Y. 1912), contains "The Seagull" and "The Cherry Orchard"; *Five Russian Plays,* trans. by C. E. Bechhofer (N. Y. 1916), contains "The Wedding" and "The Jubilee" [*i.e.* "The Anniversary"].

Separate Plays.—"The Seagull," by F. Eisemann (*Poet Lore,* Boston, 1913); "Tatyana Ripin," by S. S. Koteliansky (*London Mercury,* Oct., 1925); "The Cherry Garden" [*i.e.* "The Cherry Orchard"], trans. by M. S. Mandell (New Haven, 1908); "A Bear," by R. T. House (N. Y. 1909); same as "The Boor," trans. by Barrett H. Clark (N. Y. 1915), and in Hubbell and Beaty's *Introduction to Drama* (N. Y. 1927); "Jubilee" ["The Anniversary"], trans. by O. F. Murphy (*Poet Lore*, Boston, 1921), and "The Tragedian in Spite of Himself," by same (*Poet Lore*, Boston, 1922); "A Marriage Proposal," trans. by H. Baukhage and Barrett H. Clark (N. Y. 1912), and by W. H. H. Chambers (*Drama*, Vol. 18, London, 1903); "The Three Sisters," "The Cherry Orchard," and "Uncle Vanya," by Jenny Coven (N. Y. 1923), in *Moscow Art Theater Plays*, II (N. Y. 1923); "Ivanoff," by M. Fell (N. Y. 1923); "The Wood Demon," by S. S. Koteliansky (N. Y. 1926); "That Worthless Fellow Platonov," trans. by J. Cournos (N. Y. 1930).

Reprints in Anthologies.—"The Cherry Orchard" (Calderon trans.) in Dickinson's *Chief Contemporary Dramatists* (Boston, 1915); same (Garnett trans.) in Dickinson's *Continental Plays, I* (Boston, 1935); "The Tobacco Evil," trans. in *Theatre Arts Monthly* (N. Y. 1922); "The Seagull" (Calderon trans.) in Moses' *Representative Continental Dramas* (Boston, 1924); "The Boor" (Clark trans.) in Shay and Loving's *Fifty Contemporary One-Act Plays* (Cincinnati, 1920); same in Lewis' *Contemporary One-Act Plays* (N. Y. 1922); "A Marriage Proposal" (Baukhage and Clark trans.) in *Twelve Plays*, edited by E. Van B. Knickerbocker (N. Y. 1924), and in *The Atlantic Book of Junior Plays*, edited by C. S. Thomas (Boston, 1924); "The Swan Song" (Fell trans.) in *Short Plays by Representative Authors*, edited by Alice M. Smith (N. Y. 1922); "On the Highway," in Shay's *Twenty-five Short Plays* (N. Y. 1925).

References

S. S. Koteliansky and P. Tomlinson, *The Life and Letters of A. Tchekhov* (London, 1925); W. Gerhardi, *Anton Chehov* (N. Y. 1923); Leo Wiener, *The Contemporary Drama of Russia* (Boston, 1924); A Bakshy, *The Path of the Modern Russian Stage* (Boston, 1918); C. Stanislavsky, *My Life in Art* (Boston, 1924); Oliver M. Sayler, *The Russian Theater* (N. Y. 1922); Maurice Baring, *Landmarks in Russian Literature* (N. Y. 1910); Ashley Dukes, *Modern Dramatists* (Chicago, 1912), and *The Youngest Drama* (Chicago, 1924); M. J. Olgin *A Guide to Russian Literature* (N. Y. 1920); Maxim Gorky, A. Kuprin and I. Bunin, *Reminiscences of Anton Tchekhov* (N. Y. 1921); Serge Persky, *Contemporary Russian Novelists* (Boston, 1913); Arnold Bennett, *Books and Persons* (N. Y. 1917); J. M. Murry, *Aspects of Literature* (London, 1920); L. Shestov, *Anton Tchekhov and Other Essays* (Dublin, 1916); F. W. Chandler, *Aspects of Modern Drama* (N. Y. 1914) and *Modern Continental Playwrights* (N. Y. 1931); Elizabeth Drew, *Discovering Drama* (N. Y. 1937); K. Macgowan and R. E. Jones, *Continental Stagecraft* (N. Y. 1922); Prince S. D. Mirsky, *Contemporary Russian Literature* (N. Y. 1926); Princess Nina Andronikova Toumanova, *Anton Chekhov*, etc. (N. Y. 1937).

See also.—Letters of Anton Tchekhoff to His Family and Friends, translated by C. Garnett (N. Y. 1920); *Letters on the Short Story, the Drama, and Other Literary Topics*, by Anton Chekhov, trans. by L. S. Friedland (N. Y. 1924); *Note-Book of Anton Chekhov*, trans. by S. S. Koteliansky and L. Woolf (N. Y. 1922).

The Seagull

Play in 4 acts (1896). Texts: translation by George Calderon in *Two Plays by Tchekhof* (N. Y. 1912), and reprinted in Moses' *Representative Continental Dramas* (Boston, 1924); by F. Eisemann (*Poet Lore*, Boston, 1913); by Marian Fell in *Plays by Anton Tchekoff* (N. Y. 1912); by Constance Garnett in *The Cherry Orchard and Other Plays* (N. Y. 1924).

In Oliver M. Sayler's book, *The Russian Theater,* is the following quotation from the Russian critic Efros: "It would be idle to measure exactly whether Tchekoff did more for the Art Theater or the Art Theater did more for Tchekoff. At any rate, the Art Theater would not be what it is if it had not been for 'The Seagull' and 'Uncle Vanya' and the problems they brought to the stage and to the actors. It is equally true that were it not for the Art Theater, Tchekoff would not have written at least 'The Three Sisters' and 'The Cherry Orchard' in the form of dramas."

1. Chekhov's dialogue is of the utmost importance. If we applied to his plays Augustus Thomas' statement that the basis of every play is a good pantomime, they would be nothing at all. It has been well put that in this writer's work what is said is more important than what is done. Since this is so, we shall see how apparently careless he is in the matter of plot construction—but only *apparently* so. While it is true that the words of his characters are far more interesting than their deeds, the deeds are carefully prepared for and what action there is worked out.

"The Seagull" opens with a conversation between Masha and Medvedenko; it is clear that a play is about to be performed. We learn also a good deal about the personalities of the two speakers. Soon after, another pair arrive, Sorin and Treplef. There is more talk, interrupted presently by the entrance of other characters. The entire opening scenes are as casual as life itself; at least they seem so. Nothing happens until (Calderon edition, p. 34) Nina appears, acting in Treplef's play.

Toward the end of the act Masha says to Dorn: "Help me, or I shall commit some folly, I shall make havoc with my life.

. . . I can't hold out any longer. . . . I am in pain. No one knows my sufferings. . . . I am in love with Constantine." Here at last is the thread of interest which is necessary—even with Chekhov—to bridge the gap between the first and second acts.

2. Let us briefly consider Chekhov's plot—since we have used the word. Says Gerhardi (*Anton Chehov*): "When Chehov told Gorki that his play suffered from the conservatism of form . . . he was probably conscious of Gorki's failure to profit by Chehov's own notable contribution to literature—an expedient by means of which literature could succeed in being truly realistic; in other words, of a form that was actually indistinguishable from the context and yet was clearly manifest. How did he do it? Not by dispensing with plot, but by using a totally different kind of plot, the tissues of which, as in life, lie below the surface of events, and, unobtrusive, shape our destiny. Thus he all but overlooks the event-plot; more, he deliberately lets it be as casual as it is in real life." Chekhov has dramatized the "tissues" of life, which are not obvious or exciting in the theatrical sense; he has *dramatized* his characters rather than his plot: it is they who direct the scenic development of the tissues. In "The Cherry Orchard" there is rather less plot than in "The Seagull." Compare the two plays. Do you find in "The Seagull" any incident that seems to be not wholly the result of what the people do, say, feel, or think?

Turn now to Mr. Underhill's remarks on Benavente (p. 217). Is there any vital difference between this critic's theory of the Spanish dramatist's technique and Gerhardi's theory of Chekhov's? Further, is there any difference—except in degree—between the methods of both Benavente and Chekhov and, say, Eugene O'Neill, as exemplified in "The First Man"? Or, to take an instance from prose fiction, in Sinclair Lewis' "Babbitt"?

3. In the middle of the second act, the plot—if the slender series of more or less connected incidents may be so termed—is resumed in the scene between Treplef and Nina, and further

advanced in that between Trigorin and Nina. Interest is sustained and events foreshadowed in Trigorin's speech to Nina, regarding a subject for a possible story: "A girl—like yourself, say—lives from her childhood on the shores of a lake. She loves the lake like a seagull, and is happy and free like a seagull. But a man comes along by chance, and sees her and ruins her, like this seagull, just to amuse himself." A good example of foreshadowing. If the reader is at all familiar with the ways of dramatists, he will suspect a definite application of such a speech and eagerly await the outcome.

For other examples of foreshadowing, see those already mentioned in connection with "Hedda Gabler," and the first act of Strindberg's "There Are Crimes and Crimes."

4. The third act contains a good deal of action, though rather disjointed and "jerky"; the important part is the end, where Nina evidently becomes Trigorin's mistress. Observe that the scene was not "prepared" for in the conventional sense, that it merely happened. That it occurred at the end of the penultimate act may be ascribed to the author's intent. He recognizes the value of climax, but does not unduly emphasize it.

5. The last act contains the *dénouement,* the unraveling, the resolution: this is, however, not all. There is further characterization. In this respect it differs from the ordinary last act, which is concerned with the unwinding of the plot, and scarcely at all with new characterization. The catastrophe is of course the death of Constantine.

6. In considering this play—and Russian plays in general—there naturally arises the question of the relation between plot and character. How far can a dramatist interest his audience simply by presenting a number of people on the stage and "analyzing" them by making them tell their thoughts? How far can he interest his hearers by placing puppets before them in more or less interesting situations? And how well can he combine the two processes? Much depends on the audience, much on the effect that is sought; the dramatist who aims only at the delineation of character is practically sure to fail, as people do not and will not go to the theater for that sort of

thing. It is not a matter of theory, but of cold fact, that audiences will not, as a rule, sit for two or three hours in a theater in order to follow the dramatist who dissects character and does nothing else. True, it is almost impossible to reveal character in the theater without the aid of action, but Chekhov often comes very near doing so. The critic Efros, above quoted in Sayler's book, says: "The Art Theater deserves well from the Russian stage and Russian society for having destroyed Tchekoff's prejudice that he could not succeed in the drama."

Chekhov was first a writer of prose narrative and believed that he could not write a good play. In what respects is "The Seagull" undramatic? Read the same writer's "Cherry Orchard," and then his farces, "The Boor" and the "Marriage Proposal." The farces are clearly "of the theater"; but do you think the longer plays would be more effective had they been written as stories or novels?

Leonid Andreyev

Leonid Nikolayevitch Andreyev was born at Orel, Russia, in 1871. For a number of years he struggled to earn a livelihood as a lawyer. He began writing about 1900, when he secured a position on a newspaper. His first work was immediately successful, and attracted the attention of Gorky. The stories are tragic and bitter, but their power and insight entitle them to a place among the best modern fiction.

The plays of Andreyev show a wider range of subject-matter and a broader viewpoint than any of the Russian plays we have yet considered. Tolstoy deals with ordinary human beings, Gorky with those in the "lower depths," Chekhov with the middle and upper classes, but Andreyev, adopting a transcendental outlook, treats normal and abnormal people from a position of almost unearthly aloofness. In "Anathema" the characters are considered as mere puppets, the tools of higher and extra-terrestrial forces; in "To the Stars" they are placed, characteristically, on a high mountain—at the ends of the earth, one feels.

In the preface to his translation of Andreyev's "Samson in Chains," Herman Bernstein writes: " . . . when I interviewed

Leonid Andreyev on Russian life and Russian literature, particularly the Russian drama, he said: 'We have no real drama in Russia. Russia has not yet produced anything that could justly be called a great drama. . . .' I asked Andreyev: 'What do you consider your own plays . . . for instance?' 'They are not dramas —they are merely presentations in so many acts,' he answered. . . . 'I have not written any dramas as yet, but it is possible that I will write one later on.'"

In Andreyev the restless questioning of the meaning of life, the attempt to unveil the secret of the universe, and finally the pessimistic and almost hopeless philosophy of impotence in the face of unanswerable facts, which are characteristic of so large a part of modern Russian literature, find their most complete expression. Says Dr. Alexander Kaun, author of the latest and most exhaustive biography: "He has spent forty-eight years on this earth, years of restless seeking, of futile attempts at solving life's riddle, in vain efforts to reconcile contradictions, to find a pacifying and harmonizing synthesis."

Andreyev died in Finland during the summer of 1919.

PLAYS

"To the Stars" (1905)
"Savva" (1906)
"The Life of Man" (1906)
"Tsar Hunger" (1907)
"The Black Maskers" (1908)
"Days of Our Life" (1908)
"Love for Your Neighbor" (1908)
"The Bat" (1908)
"Anathema" (1909)
"Anfisa" (1909)
"Gaudeamus" (1910)
"The Ocean" (1911)
"The Pretty Sabine Women" (1912)
"Professor Storitsyn" (1912)
"Honor" (1912)
"Katherina Ivanovna" (1912)
"Thou Shalt Not Kill" (1913)
"Thought" (1914)
"An Event" (1914)
"The Parrot" (1914)
"King, Law, Liberty" (1914)
"Youth" (1914)
"He Who Gets Slapped" (1915)
"Dear Phantoms" (1916)
"Requiem" (1917)
"The Waltz of the Dogs" (1922)
"Samson Enchained" (1923)

Editions.—Plays by Leonid Andreyeff, trans. by C. L. Meader and F. N. Scott, with introductory essay by V. V. Brusyanin (N. Y. 1915), includes "The Black Maskers," "The Life of Man," and "The [Pretty] Sabine Women."

Separate Plays.—"Anathema," trans. by Herman Bernstein (N. Y. 1910); "He Who Gets Slapped," by Gregory Zilboorg (in *The Dial,* N. Y. March, 1921, and in book form with introduction, N. Y. 1922);

"An Incident" [*i.e.* "An Event"], by L. Pasvolsky (*Poet Lore*, Boston, 1916); "Katerina" [*i.e.* "Katherina Ivanovna"], with introduction by Herman Bernstein (N. Y. 1923); "King Hunger" [*i.e.* "Tsar Hunger"], by E. M. Kayden (*Poet Lore*, Boston, 1911); "Savva" and "The Life of Man" (together), trans. with introduction, by Thomas Seltzer (Boston, 1920), also by C. J. Hogarth (London, 1915); "Love of One's Neighbor" [*i.e.* "Love to Your Neighbor"], by Thomas Seltzer (*The Glebe*, N. Y. 1914); the same as "The Dear Departing," by T. West (London, 1916); "The Pretty Sabine Women," by Thomas Seltzer (*Drama*, Chicago, 1914); "Samson in Chains," with introduction by Herman Bernstein (N. Y. 1923); "To the Stars," by A. Goudiss (*Poet Lore*, Boston, 1907), and by M. Magnus (London, 1921); "The Waltz of the Dogs," by Herman Bernstein (N. Y. 1922); "The Sorrows of Belgium" [*i.e.* "War's Burden"], with introd. by Herman Bernstein (N. Y. 1915).

Reprints in Collections and Anthologies.—"The Life of Man" (Seltzer translation) in Moses' *Representative Continental Dramas* (Boston, 1924); "An Incident" (Pasvolsky translation) in Moses' *Representative One-Act Plays by Continental Authors* (Boston, 1923); "Love of One's Neighbor" (Seltzer translation) in Shay and Loving's *Fifty Contemporary One-Act Plays* (Cincinnati, 1920).

References

Alexander Kaun, *Leonid Andreyev, A Critical Study* (N. Y. 1924); Serge Persky, *Contemporary Russian Novelists* (Boston, 1913); M. J. Olgin, *A Guide to Russian Literature* (N. Y. 1920); William Lyon Phelps, *Essays on Russian Novelists* (N. Y. 1911); Ashley Dukes, *The Youngest Drama* (Chicago, 1924); Oliver M. Sayler, *The Russian Theater* (N. Y. 1922); Herman Bernstein, *With Master Minds* (N. Y. 1913); Stark Young, *The Flower in Drama* (N. Y. 1923); Leo Wiener, *The Contemporary Drama of Russia* (Boston, 1924); C. Stanislavsky, *My Life in Art* (Boston, 1924); Prince S. D. Mirsky, *Contemporary Russian Literature* (N. Y. 1926); V. Nemirovitch-Dantchenko, *My Life in the Russian Theater* (Boston, 1936).

Anathema

Tragedy in 7 scenes (1909). Text: translation by Herman Bernstein (N. Y. 1910).

In conception and treatment "Anathema" somewhat resembles Goethe's "Faust." The Prologue, laid in "a wild deserted place, the slope of a mountain rising to infinite heights," at once suggests a vast and overwhelming immensity. The apprehension of the infinity of mysterious space pervades the air and becomes a sort of background to the scene of human action.

1. This Prologue is a necessary division of the play; it is not merely a first act. Compare with it the Prologue to Goethe's

"Faust" and that to Echegaray's "Great Galeoto." Why is it called a Prologue and not Act I?[1]

2. We have noticed how the opening scenes of plays almost invariably present that part of the past which must be understood by the audience. But there is still another function to be fulfilled: the audience must understand the spirit of the play, they must be told something of the manner in which the subject is to be treated. In Björnson's "Leonarda," the heroine exchanges a few words, at the very opening of the play, with an old servant and lets the audience know something of the chief character, in whom they must interest themselves for the two hours' traffic of the stage. In "The Live Corpse" there is a similar scene. The dramatist must "get into the subject" before the audience loses interest. Since "Anathema" is to treat of that questioning of the ultimate purpose of life which is characteristic of the Russian mind, we must be prepared for this early in the play. On page 21, Sarah says, "Happiness! Who knows what is happiness? All people are equal before God, and yet one sells two cents' worth, while another sells thirty cents' worth . . . and no one knows why happiness is given to a person." Here is at least a brief statement of the theme that is to be developed.

3. It has already been said that the Russians excel in the portrayal of character, and we have seen how Chekhov's "Seagull" was written primarily for the sake of the characters. It is pertinent now to inquire into the nature of characterization.

In "Anathema," David is a good example; he is shown acting and speaking in accordance with what the audience know of him, in many moods and under varying circumstances. The long speech (pp. 52, 53) in which he tells of the death of his children and refuses to accept the four million rubles, is no more than what we expect of such a man; precisely

---

[1] In Dr. Kaun's *Leonid Andreyev,* Tolstoy is quoted as follows: "'I have read the prologue to Andreyev's "Anathema,"' he said. "'It is insane, perfectly insane! Absolute nonsense! A certain guardian, certain gates. . . . It is astonishing how the public likes this incomprehensibility. Nay, it demands such stuff, and searches for some special significance in it.'"

as Sarah's washing Rosa's face is in accordance with what we know of her. In the following acts, David shows other traits under the stress of other situations, and in the end he emerges a fully portrayed character, human and intensely alive.

It need scarcely be repeated that characterization in a play is a very different matter from characterization in a novel or short story. The dramatist may either make his character speak or act, or do both; he cannot, of course, describe him, unless he resorts to the device of writing long stage-directions which are, after all, intended rather for the reader than the actor.

The Russians in general care more for the delineation of character than do the Western Europeans and the Americans. The Russian is passionately interested in himself, his thoughts and emotions, and when Russians write plays they insist upon crowding them with people. It matters very little what the people do so long as we may know how they feel about themselves, about others, and about God. "The Lower Depths" is, by comparison with a Sacha Guitry piece, a series of static portraits; "The Seagull" is slow by comparison with Augustus Thomas' "Arizona," but this is because Gorky and Chekhov care not two pins for plot as we understand it, while Thomas and Guitry do.

4. Andreyev, like most Russians, writes with little regard for the accepted forms, yet with the true instinct of the artist, for his play is, on the whole, admirably built. Each act comprises a separate and clearly defined incident, and at the same time advances the action. The first act is concerned with the story of the inheritance, the second with that of the renunciation. Notice how each of the last three acts contains a unified phase of the story, and how each grows logically out of the preceding.

It is interesting to see, in this study of the Russians, how the rules of dramatic technique have been adhered to, perhaps unconsciously, by some of the more iconoclastic playwrights; it is an indication of the essential rightness of these "laws." Rightness, that is, in the light of what *has* been accomplished. Let us be careful not to lay down laws for the future.

5. Andreyev once wrote a *Letter on the Theater,* in which he ventured to maintain that action, as we understand the word, is not necessary in drama. He asks the question, "Is action in the accepted sense of movement and visible achievements on the stage, necessary to the theater?" He then proceeds to contrast two characters, Benvenuto Cellini and the philosopher Nietzsche, the one living in the midst of "escapes, murders, surprises, losses and unexpected discoveries, loves and enmities,"[1] the other one in whom "the real drama of his life begins just at the time when his life withdraws into the silence and inactivity of the study. It is there," he cries, "that we find . . . the tragical struggle, the break with Wagner, and the charming Zarathustra." The Russian's attitude, not unlike Maeterlinck's (see p. 163), is easy to understand: he is weary of the outworn tricks of the dramatic craftsmen with their "visible achievements on the stage"; he would have the dramatist delve deep into the recesses of the soul.

But is it true that because Nietzsche suffered more deeply than Cellini (granted the fact), he is therefore as suitable a subject for dramatic presentation on the stage? What Nietzsche *felt,* in order to be effective in the theater, must needs be translated into more or less "visible achievements." Nietzsche, sitting in his study, may suffer all the torments of hell without in the least appealing to our sympathies, whereas an incident dramatized out of Cellini's autobiography can hardly fail to hold any audience.

Still, Andreyev was *seeking* new subjects, and his natural distaste for all the "paraphernalia of tin swords" which clutters the stage is shared by many other modern playwrights. Andreyev might have discovered some way of rendering the great figure of Nietzsche dramatic.

---

[1] Edwin Justus Mayer recently wrote a play about Cellini. See "The Firebrand" (N. Y. 1925).

THE GERMAN DRAMA

THE GERMAN DRAMA

Gerhart Hauptmann is the dominating figure in the modern German theater. All his plays—with one or two exceptions—are well translated, with critical notes, into English. Sudermann, who is of vastly less importance, is known to English readers only through his best plays, nearly all of which have been adequately translated. Only half a dozen Wedekind plays have attracted translators, but these are sufficient for a preliminary study of his methods and ideas.

The great mass of German drama is little known outside Central Europe. A few plays of the historical and poetic type that flourished in the 80's were translated a score of years ago: Paul Heyse's "Mary of Magdala," and two or three works of Wildbrandt and Wildenbruch. The men of the 80's and 90's are represented by one or two plays each: Hartleben, Beyerlein, and Fulda. Halbe's "Youth" and "The Rosenhagens" are accessible to readers of English, and such works as Thoma's "Moral," Ernst's "Master Flachsmann," Hirschfeld's "Mothers," and Dreyer's "On Probation"; likewise two plays by Carl Hauptmann, one by the romantic Hardt, and one by Schönherr. The less well-known playwrights (Stramm, Rosmer, Nordau) have sometimes been chosen as representative of German drama, while such men as Holz and Schlaf and Eulenberg have been neglected. Of these latter nothing has been translated. Paul Ernst, Lothar Schmidt, and Eduard Stucken still await their translators. Of recent years the most notable addition to our quota of translated German plays is Winifred Katzin's *Eight European Plays,* which includes the work of Heinrich Mann, Karl Vollmoeller, Carl Sternheim, and Walter Harlan.

The most interesting of the younger men is Carl Sternheim, one of the rare writers of German comedy. Only one of his score of plays has been translated, and one adapted. The post-war dramatists are a large and active group: one or more plays of Kaiser, Werfel, Zweig, Frank, Wolf, Toller, and Hasenclever, are now accessible to English readers. Fritz von Unruh, Arnolt Bronnen, Paul Kornfeld, Hanns Johst, Anton Wildgans and the rest, are not translated. During the past few years, so far as can be determined, no playwright of any importance has been able to write in "Nazi" Germany.

The only book in English devoted entirely to the drama is Witkowski's standard but sketchy *German Drama of the Nineteenth Century*. Otto Heller's *Studies in Modern German Literature* is a study of Hauptmann, Sudermann, and a few others. Lewisohn's *Modern Drama* contains many chapters on the Germans, and of course most books of essays on the theater and drama include sections on the German playwrights. Macgowan's *Theater of To-morrow* and Macgowan and Jones' *Continental Stagecraft*, are full of references to the drama and the dramatists of post-war times; also Thomas H. Dickinson's *The Theater in a Changing Europe*.

Gerhart Hauptmann

Gerhart Hauptmann, the foremost living German dramatist and poet, was born at Obersalzbrunn, Silesia, in 1862. His early schooling was received in his native town and in Breslau. The youth wanted to become a sculptor, and attended art schools in Breslau and Jena, and at last in Italy. In 1885, after his first marriage, he settled in Berlin, where he joined the Free Stage group. In 1891 he returned to Silesia.

His first play, "Before Dawn," was produced by the Free Stage in 1889, and was hailed at the time as one of the first important examples of Naturalism in the German drama. Then came various plays, some of them Naturalistic and some poetic, the latter proving that the young poet was not to be limited by abstract formulas. "The Weavers" created a profound impression; it was the most ambitious play as yet written in the nineties. Hauptmann has written about thirty plays, including historical dramas, folk-plays, prose comedies, fairy plays, and festival pageants. His success in Germany and Austria has been enormous. He is by no means a "professional" playwright; he is not a "man of the theater." Like all true poets, he is always seeking new modes of expression, never, apparently, quite satisfied with any one. As poet and dramatist (and to a certain extent as novelist), he has exercised an influence over his contemporaries that cannot as yet be measured. He is one of the few dramatic poets who have survived from the period of Naturalism.

The Free Stage

The Free Stage Society was formed in Berlin in 1889. It was an imitation of Antoine's Free Theater, organized two years before. Among the founders were Otto Brahm, Maximilian Harden, Paul Schlenther, Julius and Heinrich Hart, and Theodor Wolff. The dramatists whose works were produced were the Naturalists Ibsen, Zola, Edmond de Goncourt, and Tolstoy, among the foreigners, and Hauptmann, Sudermann, Otto Erich Hartleben, Johannes Schlaf and Arno Holz among the Germans. Brahm was the director, and for years he offered sympathy, understanding, and encouragement to the young dramatists. After the close of the Free Stage, he became director of the Deutsches and later of the Lessing Theater. He died in 1913. Like the Free Theater of Antoine, the Free Stage soon accomplished the work it had come into existence to do, and after 1894 it became merged, to all intents and purposes, with the Deutsches Theater, of which Max Reinhardt later assumed the directorship.

Plays

"Before Dawn" (1889)
"The Festival of Peace" (1890)
"Lonely Lives" (1891)
"The Weavers" (1892)
"Colleague Crampton" (1892)
"The Beaver Coat" (1893)
"The Assumption of Hannele" (1893)
"Florian Geyer" (1894)
"Helios" (1896)
"The Sunken Bell" (1896)
"Elga" (1896)
"Pastoral" (1898)
"Drayman Henschel" (1898)
"Schluck and Jau" (1899)
"Michael Kramer" (1900)
"The Red Cock" (1901)
"Poor Heinrich" (1902)
"Rose Bernd" (1903)
"And Pippa Dances" (1906)
"The Maidens of Bischofsberg" (1907)
"Charlemagne's Hostage" (1908)
"Griselda" (1909)
"The Rats" (1911)
"Gabriel Schilling's Flight" (1912)
"The Festival Play" (1913)
"The Bow of Odysseus" (1914)
"Winter Ballad" (1917)
"The White Savior" (1920)
"Indipohdi" (1920)
"Peter Brauer" (1921)
"Veland" (1925)
"Dorothea Angermann" (1926)
"Witches' Ride" (1930)
"Spook" (1931)
"The Golden Harp" (1933)

Editions.—The Dramatic Works of Gerhart Hauptmann, 9 volumes, edited by Ludwig Lewisohn, trans. by same and others (N. Y. 1912-1929), includes all the plays up to and including "Veland."

Separate Editions.—"Before Dawn," trans. by Leonard Bloomfield (*Poet Lore,* Boston, 1909); "The Coming of Peace" [*i.e.* "The Festival of Peace"], by Janet Achurch and C. E. Wheeler (London, 1900), and same as "The Reconciliation," by R. T. House (*Poet Lore,* Boston, 1910); "Lonely Lives," by M. Morison (London, 1898); "The Weavers," by same (N. Y. 1911); "Hannele," by William Archer (London, 1894), by

C. H. Meltzer (N. Y. 1908), and as "The Assumption of Hannele," by G. S. Bryan (*Poet Lore,* Boston, 1909); "The Sunken Bell," by C. H. Meltzer (N. Y. 1899, reprinted, Garden City, 1914), and by Mary Harned (*Poet Lore,* Boston, 1898); "Fuhrmann Henschel," by Marian A. Redlich (Chicago, 1910); "Elga," by Mary Harned (*Poet Lore,* Boston, 1906); "And Pippa Dances,"by the same (*Poet Lore,* Boston, 1909).

Reprints in Collections and Anthologies.—"The Weavers" (Morison translation) in Dickinson's *Chief Contemporary Dramatists* (Boston, 1915) and *Continental Plays, I* (Boston, 1935); "The Sunken Bell" (Meltzer translation) in Moses' *Representative Continental Dramas* (Boston, 1924); "Hannele" (Archer translation) in *The Drama,* Vol. XII (London, 1906).

References

Karl Holl, *Gerhart Hauptmann, His Life and His Work, 1862-1912* (London, 1913); O. E. Lessing, *Masters in Modern German Literature* (Dresden, 1912); Otto Heller, *Studies in Modern German Literature* (Boston, 1905); James Huneker, *Iconoclasts* (N. Y. 1905); Ashley Dukes, *Modern Dramatists* (Chicago, 1912); Kuno Francke, *Glimpses of Modern German Culture* (N. Y. 1898), and *German Ideals of Today* (Boston, 1907); E. E. Hale, Jr., *Dramatists of Today* (N. Y. 1905); Ludwig Lewisohn, *The Modern Drama* (N. Y. 1915); Georg Witkowski, *The German Drama of the Nineteenth Century,* translation by L. E. Horning (N. Y. 1909); Alfred Stoeckius, *Naturalism in Recent German Drama* (N. Y. 1903); J. F. Coar, *Studies in German Literature in the Nineteenth Century* (N. Y. 1903); Archibald Henderson, *The Changing Drama* (Cincinnati, 1919); William Archer, *Playmaking* (Boston, 1912); J. T. Grein, *Premières of the Year* (London, 1900); *Dramatic Criticism* (London, 1899), and *Dramatic Criticism,* III (London, 1902); Norman Hapgood, *The Stage in America* (N. Y. 1901); H. M. Walbrook, *Nights at the Play* (London, 1911); F. W. Chandler, *Aspects of Modern Drama* (N. Y. 1914); Kenneth Macgowan and R. E. Jones, *Continental Stagecraft* (N. Y. 1922); Bernard Shaw, *Dramatic Opinions and Essays* (N. Y. 1907); Frank Harris, *Contemporary Portraits,* IV (N. Y. 1923); George Seibel, *Hauptmann and Sudermann* (Girard, Kan., 1925); F. W. Chandler, *Modern Continental Playwrights* (N. Y. 1931).

The Weavers

Play in 4 acts (1892). Texts: translation by Mary Morison (N. Y. 1911); same in the *Dramatic Works,* Vol. I (N. Y. 1912), and in Dickinson's *Chief Contemporary Dramatists* (Boston, 1915) and *Continental Plays,* I (Boston, 1935).

As an experiment in dramatic form, "The Weavers" is highly significant. Instead of a single "hero," the playwright has created a mob; this mob is therefore the protagonist—or chief character;

if individuals do emerge from the rank and file it is only for a short time. It is the weavers as a class that are ever before us, and the unity of the play lies in them and in them alone; they are only parts of a larger picture which takes shape as the story progresses.

1. "The Weavers" offers a certain novelty in form, as we have just pointed out: the play is not a close-knit unit. The first act is somewhat casual; it seems as though it might have begun almost anywhere, and that the curtain rises as if by accident. The past, it is assumed, has been very much like the present; there is little need of the usual sort of exposition. Here is simply a situation, presented without comment, the situation upon which the rest of the play is built. We, the audience, are not directly urged to engage our sympathies either for or against one side or the other.

There is scarcely a hint in this first act of what is to come in the second: it is practically a play in itself, a situation not necessarily demanding development. It does, however, *prepare* for the rest of the play, and although it is not a bid for our sympathy, it does elicit a certain amount of feeling on our part.

2. Act II is another picture, another situation. We are taken from the office of the Company into the homes of the weavers themselves. Two points should here be observed: first, the dramatist begins to develop certain characters, like Mother Baumert and Ansorge, but does not go very far, for this is a play about the weavers *in general,* and not about individuals. Second, the plot, such as it is, is here set in motion through the agency of Jaeger. But this is not allowed to divert the interest of the audience; it is rather brought in as an incident, not reaching great proportions until a large number of the weavers participate, later on. And when that happens, the plot and characters have an equal claim upon our attention. This act does look forward; it throws out tentacles of interest, for when Ansorge says, "We'll stand it no longer! We'll stand it no longer! Come what may," the audience know that trouble is ahead, and wish to see how it will all end.

3. The third act carries the plot forward, and offers another picture of the life of the weavers, this time a little less sordid than in the preceding acts. The change of scene is introduced primarily to give variety to the whole picture, and also to furnish a likely gathering place for the instigators of the rebellion. The end of the act brings the plot to a higher point of development, and increases the suspense; Hornig's words, "It'll not surprise me if this ends badly," are clearly prophetic, and prepare for the next act.

4. Between the third and fourth acts the rebellion has come to a head, and the weavers start on their warpath of depredation. The contrast in setting is again artistically sound. This time we have the luxurious home of the capitalist. Soon we are aware of the presence of the wild crowd outside, and know that the revolt is making headway. The entrance of Jaeger as a prisoner, his release by the mob, the evacuation of the house by its owners, the entrance of the weavers, the destruction of the rich furnishings, all supply first-rate dramatic action. The savage weavers, now beyond control, precipitate the climax of the play.

What more is expected? Clearly, the result of what has happened. Are the weavers to conquer?

5. The last act must terminate the rebellion, but the mere ending, the defeat of the strikers, is not sufficient to fill an entire act; there must be something more. Hauptmann has therefore introduced an incident. The "reactionary" weaver is accidentally shot. This is doubtless a dramatic device employed to emphasize the irony of fate. This bit of action is skillfully interwoven, and leaves us with a keen appreciation of the wrongs of the weavers, by reason of its vividness, and also because it is the last incident of the play. While it is true that up to the last act we sympathize with the weavers as a group, we are not permitted to place our sympathies with individuals: in "The Weavers" we are constantly reminded that the individual is only a down-trodden victim of greed. But is it possible to arouse sympathy for a group, a class, a nation? For example, we may read in a newspaper that five thousand people

are perishing in a famine, but until we see the mother dying in an effort to feed her child, or the father killing his family outright rather than see them starve—until we see these things with our own eyes—they are not likely to affect us very deeply.

Hannele

A dream-poem in 2 parts (1893). Texts: translation by William Archer (London, 1894); reprinted (*The Drama,* London, 1906, Vol. XII); by C. H. Meltzer (N. Y. 1908); by G. S. Bryan (*Poet Lore,* Boston, 1909); and (Meltzer translation) in the *Dramatic Works,* Vol. IV (N. Y. 1914).

"Hannele" is described by the author as a "dream-poem." Bearing in mind that description, as well as the text which is prefixed to the printed edition—"Suffer the little children to come unto Me, and forbid them not. For of such is the Kingdom of Heaven"—there should be no difficulty in approaching the play in the proper frame of mind.

1. The play deals with the "assumption" of Hannele Mattern; everything is therefore subsidiary to the character of and circumstances concerning the child. The poet's viewpoint, and consequently the technical devices by means of which he seeks to achieve his effects, are diametrically opposed to what we find in "The Weavers," where an entire community is the "hero."

Whereas in "The Weavers" no character was developed to the exclusion of the others, in "Hannele" there is nothing—no incident or character—which does not contribute to the development of the child.

2. It is unusual to write plays in two acts. Can you explain why this is? In the case of "Hannele," it is true, the story very naturally falls into two almost equal parts, the first showing the child's illness, the second her "assumption"; but do you think the story simply happened this way, or was it so arranged by the poet? In other words, did Hauptmann choose the two-act form and fit his story into it, or did the story demand the two acts? This is a question not so much of technique; it touches the problem of conception, which in the final analysis controls and determines the whole matter of technique.

Applying your knowledge of the principles of act division in the plays already considered, imagine "Hannele" in three acts, then four, then five. What is the most satisfactory of these arrangements, and why?

3. The patent purpose of the sordid scene that opens the play is to provide variety; by this means contrast between the squalor of the almshouse and the purity and innocence of the child's vision becomes the more striking. This contrast is most dramatic when Hannele first appears on the scene, Gottwald protecting her, while Hanke, Hete, and Seidel quarrel among themselves. And at the end of the play there is a contrast, a bold relief to the sordidness of Hannele's entire existence: the triumph of the poetic, the highest ideal of the purity of childhood, summed up in the Stranger's song.

4. In his *Playmaking* William Archer calls attention to the fact that "Hannele" is not concerned with "conflicting wills," and is yet a "moving drama." Archer mentions this in connection with his contention that Brunetière's "law" is not all-inclusive. Brunetière has in various articles maintained that conflict is the essence of drama, and in his *Critical Studies* he says that "the theater in general is nothing but the place for the development of the human will, attacking the obstacles opposed to it by destiny, fortune, or circumstances." In his *Law of the Drama* he further states that "what we ask of the theater is the spectacle of a *will* striving towards a goal, and conscious of the means which it employs." And again in the same essay,[1] "Is it action to move about? Certainly not, and there is no true action except that of a will conscious of itself, conscious, as I was saying, of the means which it employs for its fulfilment, one which adapts them to its goal, and all other forms of action are only imitations, counterfeits, or parodies. The material or the subject of a novel or of a play may therefore be the same at bottom; but they become drama or novel only by the manner in which they are treated; and the manner is not merely differ-

[1] See Brunetière's *The Law of the Drama* (N. Y. 1914); also, for reprint and bibliography, my *European Theories of the Drama* (N. Y., revised 1929).

ent, it is opposite." One more quotation (again from the *Critical Studies*): "Drama is a representation of the will of man in conflict with the mysterious powers or natural forces which limit and belittle us; it is one of us thrown living upon the stage, there to struggle against fatality, against social law, against one of his fellow-mortals, against himself, if need be, against the ambitions, the interests, the prejudices, the folly, the malevolence of those who surround him."

Now, Archer cannot accept this "law" as final. "The difficulty," he says, "about this definition is that, while it describes the matter of a good many dramas, it does not lay down any true differentia, any characteristic common to all true drama, and possessed by no other form of fiction. Many of the greatest plays in the world can with difficulty be brought under the formula. . . ." Where is the struggle, he asks, in the "Agamemnon," in the "Œdipus"? In "As You Like It," "Ghosts," and finally in "Hannele"?

If we accept Archer's statement about "Hannele," wherein is that play moving and dramatic? For it is certain that "Hannele" arouses interest and emotion as a theater play. In Germany and Austria it has held the stage for a generation. But, as a matter of fact, is Archer right? Is there no struggle, no conflict of wills in "Hannele"? And what of "Ghosts" and "As You Like It"? Brunetière postulates the will in conflict with natural forces, with fate, with society, etc. Is not the child struggling with death, with her environment, with the powers of evil—even though these are not personified? A struggle does not necessarily imply a physical fight. What is the struggle in "Ghosts" and "As You Like It"?

Supposing Brunetière's "law" is not universally applicable, does it make a particle of difference? It is clear that struggle is always interesting, and for that reason dramatists *usually* make it the basis of their plays; so do novelists, only the novel form offers a wider canvas and the novelist is not required to arouse the interest of his reader in the first five or ten minutes.

5. What is much more to the point in discussing "Hannele" is the question whether Hauptmann, in choosing the theater as

a means of telling the story of the little girl, has chosen the best method of doing so. Would the story have been better as a novel or short story than a play? Whether Hauptmann's play happens to fit into the ingenious hypothesis of the French critic or the modification suggested by Archer, is really of little consequence.

The Sunken Bell

Play in 4 acts (1896). Texts: translation by C. H. Meltzer (N. Y. 1899, and Garden City, 1914); by Mary Harned (*Poet Lore*, Boston, 1898); and (Meltzer translation) in the *Dramatic Works*, Vol. IV (N. Y. 1914).

"The Sunken Bell" is primarily poetic, though it is futile to declare it a poor play because it does not conform to the ordinary standards of playmaking. It is, like all of Hauptmann's work, the exemplification of a philosophy of life. "It is the tragedy," says Ludwig Lewisohn, "of the creative soul. . . ." It is the "drama of the creative thinker of our age. . . ."

1. The question of influences [2] is always interesting to discuss, although it is only too easy to lose one's self in the by-paths of comparative criticism. It is hardly necessary to state that every work of art—and particularly the early efforts of all artists—bear the impress to a greater or less extent of other works.

"Before Dawn" shows traces of Tolstoy, "Lonely Lives" and "The Sunken Bell" of Ibsen. The French critic, Maurice Huret, has well said that "Henrik Ibsen was at once a naturalist and a symbolist. . . . This combination, though apparently contradictory, is effected in perfect harmony, which is the result of the labor of supreme genius. Hauptmann was incapable of so great an effort." Instead of welding into a harmonic whole

[2] Two English critics, some ten or twelve years ago, called attention to certain similarities in Galsworthy's "Silver Box" and Hauptmann's "Weavers," and implied that the Englishman was indebted to the German. In a letter to a London newspaper Galsworthy stated that he had never read a line of Hauptmann, and that he had merely heard that "The Weavers" had something to do with a strike.

the diverse elements of realism and poetry in "The Sunken Bell"—as Ibsen did in "Peer Gynt"—he has employed a more primitive method: he places side by side scenes of everyday realism with scenes of fairy romance; much as Shakespeare did in the "Midsummer Night's Dream." Whether Hauptmann purposely adopted this method or was unable to effect a complete fusion of his materials, is not easy to determine, nor very much worth while discussing. We are moved by what he has done, and if we seek to analyze the way in which the poet has managed to move us, we are likely to come a little closer to the meaning of art. That is why it is worth while analyzing the methods of any artist.

2. The eternal question "What is a Play?" is likely to arise every time we see or read a drama that differs in any way from our (conscious or unconscious) standards of what a drama ought to be. It arose in the days when "The Sunken Bell" was new, and it may arise even nowadays in the minds of those who have neither read nor seen that play. There are critics who declare that "The Sunken Bell" is first-rate poetry (even though they cannot read a line of German) and sound philosophy, but "no play." Whether "The Sunken Bell" can be called a good play or not depends upon what standards we have adopted. In Clayton Hamilton's *Theory of the Theater* (1910) the author stated that a "play is a story devised to be presented by actors on a stage before an audience." He excluded from the category of plays works like "Pippa Passes" and "The Sunken Bell." And yet, the German play is "a story devised to be presented by actors on a stage before an audience." It has also been performed many thousands of times in hundreds of theaters, over a period of thirty years. Mr. Hamilton, writing fourteen years ago, was doubtless thinking of the "well-made" plays of the French school. "The Sunken Bell" is certainly a far cry from these. But, like every thinking critic, Mr. Hamilton has been forced to modify his ideas, and in his next book, *Studies in Stagecraft* (1914), his theory is more inclusive. He does not risk putting his definition into a sentence, but his remarks, scattered through an entire volume, constitute a definite theory,

of which the essence is simply this: "A dramatist must not only represent his truth in a manner that is satisfying to his own mind, but must also express it in a manner that shall be convincing to his audience. To achieve this delicate endeavor, a high degree of technical accomplishment is necessary, in terms of the particular method that the dramatist has chosen." The whole matter of technique is summed up in the expression "that shall be convincing to his audience." To-day Mr. Hamilton would probably not deny that "The Sunken Bell" is a play, for it has proved convincing to innumerable audiences.

William Archer, in *Playmaking,* is perhaps even more liberal in his interpretation of the word "dramatic." He begins by saying that "there are no rules for writing plays," and yet he goes on to say that the "only really valid definition of the dramatic is: Any representation of imaginary personages which is capable of interesting an average audience assembled in a theater."

Now, "The Sunken Bell," as we have already observed, is not a "well-made" play.[3] It has no neat pattern, no clean-cut outline. Nor is it a "good play" as Bernard Shaw's "Man and Superman" is good—a work that is not "well made." Hauptmann's play is good because of a combination of qualities—psychological interest, dramatic as distinguished from purely lyrical poetry, a fairly well-constructed plot, and an atmosphere of beauty as different from the formal neatness of a Pinero or a Sudermann play as it is possible to imagine.

3. "The Sunken Bell" is, among other things, a study in temperament, the so-called "artistic temperament." The poet is chiefly interested in the psychological development of the artist, Heinrich. We are told that he is a great artist, but the fact is not made clear to us. One German critic takes Haupt-

[3] So much has been written about the Scribe-Sardou type of play that it might be a good idea to read a few examples. I suggest: Sardou's "Divorçons!" (Chicago, no date), "The Black Pearl" (N. Y. 1916), and "Patrie!" (Garden City, 1915); Scribe's "Ladies' Battle" (N. Y. no date), and Augier and Sandeau's "M. Poirier's Son-in-Law" (N. Y. 1915).

mann to task because Heinrich does nothing to prove that he is what he is claimed to be. He states that the more eloquently Heinrich speaks the less are we inclined to believe in him, since most true artists express themselves best through the medium of their art. In the theater we must believe what we are told. A dramatist of necessity asks his audience to take certain things for granted—such as the lapse of time and the consequent foreshortening of events—and the audience, having accepted these premises, are ready to attend to what follows. In "The Sunken Bell," we must not doubt that Heinrich is a true artist—otherwise the play will have no meaning.

Among the numerous studies in temperament, compare those in D'Annunzio's "Gioconda," Hauptmann's "Michael Kramer," Porto-Riche's "Françoise' Luck," Bahr's "The Concert," and Zoë Akins' "Greatness." How do these authors make their artists convincing?

Hermann Sudermann

Hermann Sudermann was born at Matziken, East Prussia, in 1857. After attending school at Elbing and Tilsit he was apprenticed to a druggist at the age of fourteen. His university training was received at Königsberg and Berlin. Soon after graduation he began writing. His first important works were novels, one of which, *Dame Care,* has already taken rank as a modern classic. In 1889 his first play, "Honor," was produced by the Free Stage Society under the direction of Otto Brahm. It was very successful, and the young writer was acclaimed as one of the group of rebels which had gathered beneath Brahm's standard. But with his later plays it became apparent that he was not so radical as he seemed: he was an exceptionally clever craftsman and man of the theater. A follower of Ibsen, he adapted during the nineties a few of the more "daring" ideas of the day. Since 1900 he has steadily sunk in the estimation of his own countrymen, chiefly because the drama has developed beyond the point to which he helped to bring it, and also because his own plays of the past fifteen or twenty years are on the whole rather tame. During the war Sudermann fell into line with the Monarchists and exerted all his influence to plead the Prussian cause. Sudermann died in 1932.

Plays

"Honor" (1889)
"The Destruction of Sodom" (1891)
"Home" ["Magda"] (1893)
"The Battle of the Butterflies" (1894)
"Happiness in a Nook" (1895)
"Teja" (1896)
"Fritzchen" (1896)
"The Eternal Masculine" (1896)
"John the Baptist" (1898)
"The Three Heron's Feathers" (1899)
"St. John's Fires" (1900)
"The Joy of Living" (1902)
"Storm-Brother Socrates" (1903)
"Among the Stones" (1905)
"The Flower Boat" (1906)
"The Faraway Princess" (1907)
"Streaks of Light" (1907)
"Margot" (1907)
"The Last Visit" (1907)
"Children of the Strand" (1910)
"The Beggar of Syracuse" (1911)
"A Good Reputation" (1912)
"Claudius' Songs of Praise" (1914)
"The Woman Friend" (1916)
"The Well-Turned Corner" (1916)
"The Higher Life" (1916)
"The Raschoffs" (1919)

Editions.—Roses, trans. by Grace Frank (N. Y. 1909), includes "Streaks of Light," "Margot," "The Last Visit," and "The Faraway Princess"; *Morituri,* trans. by A. Alexander (N. Y. 1910), includes "Teja," "Fritzchen," and "The Eternal Masculine."

Separate Editions.—"Home" ["Magda"], trans. by C. E. A. Winslow (Boston, 1895, and reprinted, N. Y. no date); "Teja," by Mary Harned (*Poet Lore,* Boston, 1897); "John the Baptist," by Beatrice Marshall (N. Y. 1908), and as "Johannes," by Mary Harned (*Poet Lore,* Boston, 1899); "The Three Heron's Feathers," by H. T. Porter (*Poet Lore,* Boston, 1900); "The Fires of St. John," trans. and adapted by Charles Swickard (Boston, 1904), by C. and H. C. Porter (*Poet Lore,* Boston, 1904), and by G. E. Polk (Minneapolis, 1905); "The Joy of Living," by Edith Wharton (N. Y. 1903); "Honor," by H. R. Baukhage (N. Y. 1915); "The Faraway Princess," by A. Alexander (N. Y. no date).

Reprints in Collections and Anthologies.—"The Vale of Content" [*i.e.* "Happiness in a Nook"], in Dickinson's *Chief Contemporary Dramatists* (translation by W. E. Leonard, in this edition only) (Boston, 1915); "The Fires of St. John" (Swickard adaptation) in Moses' *Representative Continental Dramas* (Boston, 1924); "Teias" (Harned translation) in Moses' *Representative One-Act Plays by Continental Authors* (Boston, 1923); "The Faraway Princess" (Alexander translation) in Lewis' *Contemporary One-Act Plays* (N. Y. 1922); "John the Baptist" (Marshall translation) in *German Classics,* Vol. XVII (N. Y. 1914).

References

E. E. Hale, Jr., *Dramatists of Today* (N. Y. 1905); Ashley Dukes, *Modern Dramatists* (Chicago, 1912); Otto Heller, *Studies in Modern German Literature* (Boston, 1905); James Huneker, *Iconoclasts* (N. Y. 1905), and *Ivory Apes and Peacocks* (N. Y. 1915); Ludwig Lewisohn,

The Modern Drama (N. Y. 1915); William Lyon Phelps, *Essays on Modern Novelists* (N. Y. 1910); Bernard Shaw, *Dramatic Opinions and Essays,* 2 vols. (N. Y. 1907); G. Witkowski, *The German Drama of the Nineteenth Century,* translation by L. E. Horning (N. Y. 1909); F. W. Chandler, *Aspects of Modern Drama* (N. Y. 1914) and *Modern Continental Playwrights* (N. Y. 1931); J. F. Coar, *Studies in German Literature of the Nineteenth Century* (N. Y. 1903); Kuno Francke, *German Ideals of Today* (Boston, 1907); H. L. Mencken, *Prejudices,* 1st series (N. Y. 1919); J. T. Grein, *Premières of the Year* (London, 1900), *Dramatic Criticism* (London, 1899), and *Dramatic Criticism,* Vol. III (London, 1902); William Winter, *The Wallet of Time,* 2 vols. (N. Y. 1913); George Seibel, *Hauptmann and Sudermann* (Girard, Kan., 1925); J. W. Marriott, *Modern Drama* (London, no date).

MAGDA [HOME]

Play in 4 acts (1893). Text: translation by C. E. A. Winslow (Boston, 1895; reprints, N. Y. no date).

"Magda" is an exceptionally "well-made" play and a particularly interesting study in character. A generation ago it was regarded as an advanced sociological document. It has been played by the world's greatest actresses all over Europe and America.

1. The entire first act is expository, and is on the whole cleverly handled. The important characters are introduced, or as in the case of Magda herself, so constantly spoken of, that they are well known to us before they actually appear. The past history is unfolded, the atmosphere of home created, and the struggle between old and new (personified in the figures of Magda and Schwartze) foreshadowed.

The play actually starts, the wheels are set going, the moment (p. 45) Schwartze says to Heffterdingt, "Then God's will be done."

2. While the opening act prepares the scene of action, and hints at what is to come when the opposing forces shall meet, the second is taken up with Magda's homecoming and reception. It will also show us her decision to remain with the family. But in the scene between her and Heffterdingt there is more exposition. This scene is also preparatory. One thing more is accomplished by the scene: the stipulation that Magda shall not be questioned as to her past life. The family agree to this,

and all goes well—up to the very last page of the act, where Heffterdingt ("Struck by a new thought") says, ". . . Yes, I am sure she will confess everything herself." This line is sufficient to arouse our suspicions. Will she confess? And if she does, what will come of it?

3. The contrast between the old and new—between the old German idea of home and the new idea of individual development, begun in the first act—is continued throughout the play; in the first act, the spirit of the old was conveyed to us through conversation, in the second, it is set forth in the struggle between Schwartze and Magda, and in the third it is both discussed and exhibited in terms of action. Magda's playful banter, the little humorous touches in her scene with the servants, the wonderment of Franziska and Mrs. Schwartze, contribute to the central idea. In addition, the first few minutes of the third act form an interlude between the rising action of the second and the tension that is to increase later in the third. The scene between Magda and Marie (pp. 91-95) is a "bridging section" or connecting link between the "interlude," and the Heffterdingt-Magda and Schwartze-Magda colloquies, which are followed by further scenes of varying tension, through that between Magda and Von Keller, to the culminating point in the act, where Schwartze and his "erring" daughter go into the former's room, each one having "something to say" to the other.

4. So far, the end of each act has reached a climax emotionally higher than the beginning, and more tense than the end of the preceding. The first, second, and third acts have each culminated in a crisis; while the end of the third was the greatest crisis—fraught with the utmost importance to the chief characters—in the play. That was the beginning of the climax. But the actual climax occurs off-stage in the interval between the third and fourth acts. This is more dramatic than if the clash had occurred on the stage, because we see the beginning, imagine the struggle, are ignorant for a few moments of its outcome, and when the curtain rises on the last act, are still in suspense. In this way, there is no relaxation of pressure. The

climax, begun in one act, is carried over into the next, and does not end until Schwartze enters (p. 130), as we see, defeated.

Another example of this is in William C. De Mille's play, "The Woman." A cross-examination is begun at the end of the second act, the curtain falls, and when it rises on the last act, the examination is still in progress, though it is nearly at an end. The culminating point in "Magda," however, is not reached until a little later in the act.

From that point on, the action subsides quickly to the catastrophe, where (p. 155) it rises momentarily, and then falls to the "curtain."

5. In a recent interview (1923) Sudermann discussed with me certain of his theories on playwriting. He is of the opinion that the dramatist is eternally and necessarily guided by the material conditions imposed upon him by the theater, the actor, and the audience. He is no more than a product of his day and generation. "When I wrote my early plays," he said, "it was for the simple stationary stage. We had no revolving stages then, and to change a scene meant time, trouble, and expense. It was our problem how often *not* to change the set during a play, and to that fact I attribute whatever virtue of unity my plays may possess. It is easy to write a play in twenty scenes, the way the youngsters do nowadays, but the effect is not happy. When I wrote 'Honor' and the play you call 'Magda,' I had to get down to work and keep my plot from scattering. And I believe our plays were on the whole better than the plays that are being written now. Indeed, if I were beginning all over again I am quite sure I should not take advantage of the new scenic devices: I should write my plays as nearly as possible as I wrote them in the late eighties and early nineties."

But *does* the sort of unity that Sudermann referred to make a play better than what he declared to be a want of unity—the result, that is, of using many scenes instead of one act? Does unity depend upon the number of changes in scene? How many different scenes are there in "Hamlet"? The Greek writers of tragedy (with one or two exceptions) used only one scene.

Frank Wedekind

Frank Wedekind was born in Hanover, Germany, in 1864. He was forced to study law, though his natural inclination was for writing, which at an early age he found time to do. In Zurich, where he continued his studies, he came into contact with some of the "Moderns," among them Hauptmann and Strindberg. In 1888, after the death of his father, Wedekind went to Munich, and later visited London, Paris, and "all the centers of European culture, all the sinks of its perversity and crookedness. He squandered his money and his beliefs recklessly. In 1891 he returned again to Munich." A few years later he was imprisoned for *lèse majesté,* was soon released and became a vaudeville performer, and settled in Munich, after his marriage in 1908.

Always an active and eager spirit, he was for a short period on the editorial staff of *Simplicissimus,* he read Ibsen's plays in public, he composed and wrote songs which he sang in cabarets, and was a prominent member of the Uberbrettl movement. Later on, he formed a company for the purpose of producing his own plays, himself playing the chief rôles; he toured the country, literally imposing his work upon theatergoers. To-day, some years after his death, he is one of the idols of the latest "New" Germany. His plays are performed throughout Middle Europe.

Frank Wedekind was, despite his savage bitterness, an idealist. Samuel A. Eliot, Jr., in his preface to a volume of Wedekind's plays, quotes the dramatist's statement that "the reunion of holiness and beauty as the divine object of pious devotion is the purpose to which I offer my life: toward which, indeed, I have striven since earliest childhood." True this undoubtedly is, but it is no less true that Wedekind's business in the theater—particularly with such plays as "The Earth Spirit" and "Spring's Awakening" and "Such is Life"—was the exhibition of powerful dramatic shows. He died in 1918.

Plays

"The World of Youth" (1890)
"Spring's Awakening" (1891)
"Earth Spirit" (1895)
"Fritz Schwigerling" ["The Love Potion"] (1899)
"The Court Singer" (1900)
"The Marquis Von Keith" (1900)
"Mine-Haha" (1901)
"Pandora's Box" (1902)
"King Nicolo" ["Such is Life"] (1902)
"Hidalla" ["Karl Hetman"] (1904)
"The Dance of Death" ["Death and the Devil"] (1906)

"Music" (1907)
"Censorship" (1908)
"Oaha" (1908)
"The Philosopher's Stone" (1909)
"Solid in Every Saddle" (1910)
"Hunted by Every Hound" (1910)
"Washed in All Waters" (1910)
"Franziska" (1912)
"Castle Wetterstein" (1913)
"Samson" (1914)
"Bismarck" (1915)
"Herakles" (1917)
"The Fast Painter" (1920)

(Besides the above are two pantomime ballets, "The Fleas," written 1892, and "The Empress of Newfoundland," written 1897. "Earth Spirit" and "Pandora's Box" were later published in rewritten form under the title of "Lulu." "Castle Wetterstein" is a combination of the three one-act plays, "Solid in Every Saddle," "Hunted by Every Hound," and "Washed in All Waters." "Oaha" was later rewritten as "Till Eulenspiegel," and "The Dance of Death" as "The Solar Spectrum.")

Editions.—Tragedies of Sex, translated with introduction by Samuel A. Eliot, Jr. (N. Y. 1923) includes "Spring's Awakening," "Earth Spirit," "Pandora's Box," and "Damnation!" [*i.e.* "The Dance of Death"].

Separate Plays.—"The Heart of a Tenor" [*i.e.* "The Court Singer"], adapted by André Tridon (*Smart Set,* N. Y. 1913); "Such is Life" [*i.e.* "King Nicolo"], by F. J. Ziegler (Philadelphia, 1912); "The Awakening of Spring," by same (Philadelphia, 1910); "The Earth Spirit," by Samuel A. Eliot, Jr. (N. Y. 1915); "Pandora's Box," by same (N. Y. 1914); "The Virgin and the White Slaver" [*i.e.* "The Dance of Death"], by André Tridon (*International,* N. Y. 1913).

Reprints in Collections and Anthologies.—"The Tenor" (Tridon translation) in Shay and Loving's *Fifty Contemporary One-Act Plays* (Cincinnati, 1920); as "The Court Singer" (A. W. Boesche translation) in *German Classics,* XX (N. Y. 1914), and same in Moses' *Representative One-Act Plays by Continental Authors* (Boston, 1923); "Erdgeist" [*i.e.* "Earth Spirit"], by S. A. Eliot, in Dickinson's *Continental Plays, II* (Boston, 1935).

References

Percival Pollard, *Masks and Minstrels of New Germany* (Boston, 1911); Ashley Dukes, *Modern Dramatists* (Chicago, 1912), and *The Youngest Drama* (Chicago, 1924); H. B. Samuel, *Modernities* (N. Y. 1914); James Huneker, *Ivory Apes and Peacocks* (N. Y. 1915); Ludwig Lewisohn, *The Modern Drama* (N. Y. 1915); F. W. Chandler, *Aspects of Modern Drama* (N. Y. 1914); Isaac Goldberg, *The Drama of Transition* (Cincinnati, 1922); Thomas H. Dickinson, *The Theater in a Changing Europe* (N. Y. 1937); F. W. Chandler, *Modern Continental Playwrights* (N. Y 1931).

Spring's Awakening

A children's tragedy in 3 acts (1892). Texts: translation, as "The Awakening of Spring," by F. J. Ziegler (Philadelphia, 1910); by Samuel A. Eliot, Jr., in *Tragedies of Sex* (N. Y. 1923).

One of the very earliest of Wedekind's plays, "Spring's Awakening" has held the stage in Central Europe for over thirty years. Ostensibly a thesis play, it is actually—like every work of art—a presentment of life for the sake of life itself. " . . . While he has a moral, or rather an antimoral, purpose," says Mr. Eliot, " . . . his chief interest is in Melchior, Moritz and Wendla—the vividness and promise of the life awakening in them, the cruelty and tragedy of its extinguishment, for which the adult world must take full blame."

1. This play is designated "A Children's Tragedy," and Mr. Eliot declares that the playwright's chief interest was in the characters of the children. Can you determine, on the basis of the text, just why Wedekind, in spite of the fact that a so-called "lesson" is inescapable, should be more interested in his characters than in the theme? Or rather, *is* he? It cannot be too often repeated that every critical dictum, every "law" or axiom, should be challenged, and while I agree with Mr. Eliot, I was not able to do so until I had challenged the statement.

This book is written in order to stimulate thought, and not to convince students that any conclusions I or any one else may set forth are to be accepted as infallible.

Ninety-nine Anglo-Saxons out of every hundred, were they to read "Spring's Awakening," would probably regard it either as very immoral, or strikingly moral; that is, they would think of it not in terms of art, drama, or life, but of morality. Some critics think it too didactic; Mr. Eliot regards it primarily as a character study.

Form your own conclusions.

2. Wedekind had his own ideas about the construction of plays; or rather he wrote without caring in the least whether his dramas happened to be "well-made" or not. One feels that he had something in him that demanded expression, and his plays were the result of his impulses. Never do you feel the hand of the skilled craftsman. Gorky has said that the "source of all art is no more than the overflow of the soul with impressions of life. When the artist can no longer contain him-

self he produces his work of art. What precise form the work will take seems to me a matter of small importance. Sometimes it's a play, sometimes a novel, and sometimes a picture. If I have written plays it was more or less because I had to write them. . . ."

Do you think that "Spring's Awakening" is good drama? Not, perhaps, "good" as other plays are, but good in itself? In what technical respects does it differ from such plays as Dunsany's "Gods of the Mountain" and George M. Cohan's "Broadway Jones"?

3. This play was written before the monologue, or soliloquy, was supposed to have gone out of fashion. What of Scene VII in Act III, which consists solely of a single speech?

4. Why is the last act divided into many scenes?

5. Says Ashley Dukes (in *The Youngest Drama*): ". . . It is not a play for the stage; these broken scenes are a dramatic epic." Just what does he mean? That the play *ought* not to be acted, or cannot be acted? At one revival alone in a Berlin theater the play had a run of 390 performances, and there is not a city in Germany or Austria that has not seen one or more performances of it. I have seen the play twice, and I can say with assurance that few plays have exercised so profound an influence upon any audience.

Mr. Dukes' statement is the more surprising since he is one of a school of critics who believe that an unacted play is scarcely a play at all. In his brilliant and suggestive little book on *Drama,* he says: "Plays truly live in performance alone." To this notion I am diametrically opposed: in my suggestive if not brilliant pamphlet, *The Modern Drama,* I state: ". . . plays are usually written to be acted; but . . . many of the greatest plays in the world . . . have actually been produced on the stage only at one particular epoch and for only a few performances. According to these theorists it is only the comparatively few persons who happened to see the productions who were able to understand or enjoy them!" What do you think about it?

THE AUSTRIAN DRAMA

THE AUSTRIAN DRAMA

The Austrian theater has a long and honorable history, and though many Austrian-born writers have followed the traditions of Germany, there is still a very definite native flavor in the indigenous Austrian play.

The most important figures are three members of the "Jung Wien" movement: Hermann Bahr, Arthur Schnitzler, and Hugo von Hofmannsthal. All but a few of Schnitzler's plays are familiar to readers of English; Hofmannsthal's "Electra" is translated by Arthur Symons, and several others in less satisfactory versions are procurable; but of Bahr there are only two full-length plays available, and one of them is an adaptation. Stefan Zweig, one of the younger dramatists, is known to us through his philosophical play "Jeremiah."

Nearly all books and articles on the German drama in English include chapters on the Austrians.

HERMANN BAHR

Hermann Bahr was born at Linz on the Danube, Austria, in 1863. He arrived at Vienna as a student, where he was later to play so important a rôle, at the age of eighteen. Waxing too enthusiastic one day in praise of Richard Wagner, who had just died, the young man was expelled. Had it not been for this incident, he tells us, he would "now have been a good notary in Linz on the Danube." He then went to Berlin, making the acquaintance of the young literary lights and the older Socialists. He remained there from 1884 to 1887. "It was during that period that I found myself," he writes. There followed some years of travel in France, Spain, Morocco, and Russia. In 1892 he was drawn to Vienna again, where he edited the famous magazine, *Die Zeit*. It was his dream to establish an Austrian school of art, in literature, the drama, and the plastic arts. As critic, editor, dramatist, novelist, stage manager, he worked heart and soul for the realization of his dream, whether he happened to be in Austria or, as was oftener the case, abroad. He was the moving spirit of the "Jung Wien," or "Young Vienna," movement, whose earliest and most famous adherents were Hugo von Hofmannsthal, Schnitzler, Richard Beer-Hoffmann, and Peter Altenberg. His enthusiasm for youth and the aspirations of the young has never left him. During the winter of 1923 I saw him in Munich, and the greater part of our conversation consisted of his questions and my answers on the subject of the young writers of America.

Bahr was an exceptionally versatile writer. For years he was the professional appreciator of all that was sincere in the art of his day: he has written criticism for nearly forty years. As a playwright, however, he did more than any other to create the "Wiener Stück" type—the "Viennese Play." Only Schnitzler has surpassed him in the art of portraying the people of Vienna and in the craft of writing plays. Bahr died in 1934.

Plays

"The New Men" (1887)
"La Marquesa D'Amaëgui" (1888)
"The Great Sin" (1889)
"The Mother" (1891)
"The Domestic Woman" (1893)
"From the Suburb" [with C. Karlweis] (1893)
"The Mermaid" (1896)
"Juana" (1896)
"Tschaperl" (1897)
"Josephine" (1898)
"The Star" (1898)
"The Athlete" (1899)
"Viennese Women" (1900)
"Franzl" (1900)
"The Apostle" (1901)
"The Bogey Man" (1902)
"The Master" (1904)
"Sanna" (1904)
"The Saviors' Club" (1905)
"The Other Woman" (1906)
"The Poor Fool" (1906)
"The Faun" (1907)
"The Round Dance" (1907)
"The Yellow Nightingale" (1907)
"The Concert" (1909)
"The Children" (1911)
"The Little Dance" (1911)
"The Principle" (1912)
"The Phantom" (1913)
"The Complainer" (1914)
"The Gay Soap-Boiler" (1915)
"The Voice" (1917)
"The Monster" (1919)
"Light o' Marriage" (1920)

Editions.—"The Master," adapted by B. F. Glazer (Philadelphia, 1918); "The Concert," trans. by B. Q. Morgan, is published only in Dickinson's *Chief Contemporary Dramatists,* 2nd series (Boston, 1921).

Reference

Percival Pollard, *Masks and Minstrels of New Germany* (Boston, 1911).

The Concert

Comedy in 3 acts (1909). Text: translation by B. Q. Morgan in Dickinson's *Chief Contemporary Dramatists,* 2nd series (Boston, 1921).

"The Concert" is one of the very few comedies written in the German language, and Hermann Bahr's best play. It has been very popular throughout Germany and Austria and, in a slightly adapted version, in America, where it was acted by Leo Dietrichstein. This play, says Percival Pollard, "settled in the German countries the reputation from which Bahr had suffered all his career, of being, like most of the other Viennese, merely clever. . . . Now that in 'The Concert' he has shown such grip of vital human things . . . it should be useless for even his former detractors to deny him consideration."

1. It is impossible to go into the reasons why the German people have as yet produced few or no real comedies; the fact remains that outside three or four classics by Lessing, Kleist, and Freytag, German literature has no comedies. "The German literary laugh," says Meredith in his *Essay on Comedy,* is "infrequent, and rather monstrous—never a laugh of men and women in concert. It comes of unrefined, abstract fancy, grotesque or grim, or gross. . . . Spiritual laughter they have not yet attained to; sentimentalism waylays them in the flight." Of all the writers of plays in the present generation Carl Sternheim is, I think, the only one who can be characterized as a comic dramatist, and he is avowedly a follower of Molière, and a cosmopolitan Jew. But with the Austrians the case is different: Schnitzler and Bahr and Hofmannsthal have all written good comedies. The Austrian writes in German, but spiritually and intellectually he is at least half Latin.

"The Concert" is a true comedy. It is, like all of its kind, a play of character, in which the plot is of only subordinate interest. It is thin; it just manages to escape being trite, but that is of little consequence.

The device of turning the tables is very common: A. is miserly, and B. wants to teach him a lesson. B. therefore becomes miserly in turn and reforms (or fails to reform) A.

Hein is a philanderer, and in order to cure him of his philandering, his wife pretends to philander with the husband of the artist's latest flame. Can you think of any other plays in which a similar situation is used?

By the way, this play is called a comedy. Transfer the facts of the case to life itself. Would the situation be comic? The facts themselves are rather tragic: at least, such facts result in tragedy every day in the week. Bahr did, as a matter of record, use a friend of his, the poet and dramatist, Otto Erich Hartleben, as a model for the character of Hein. Frau Hartleben, a most extraordinary woman, had rather a hard time of it, though she continued to love her Erich to the end of his life, and Erich returned to her with unfailing regularity after each of his "concerts." How has the dramatist been able to treat potentially serious material and make it not only amusing, but essentially true to life? This is what most writers of comedy do. Find other examples and compare both material and treatment with "The Concert."

2. The early part of the first act is a flood of dialogue, out of which we gain only an occasional inkling of what is about to take place. What is the purpose of this?

Where does the action really get started?

3. Toward the end of Act I is the following dialogue:

MARIE (*going to the sofa and sitting down*). Yes, I have had that pleasure. (*Invites him to be seated.*) Please be seated.

JURA (*threatening her with his finger*). We shall see whether it is a pleasure. (*Looking through the room, perceiving the flowers; seriously.*) But you shouldn't do that. Have you no garden?

MARIE (*surprised*). Oh, yes. Why?

JURA. Then why don't you leave the flowers in the garden? Flowers belong in the garden.

MARIE. They are so beautiful, they make the whole room bright.

This is not thrown in as padding: it comes at a critical point in the act. What is its meaning?

4. Never Keep a Secret From Your Audience. A good rule—sometimes, and sometimes a bad one. There is a very

good reason in "The Concert" for not keeping it, and that is that we may enjoy seeing how the trick is to be worked. It would be possible to have Jura and Marie surprise Hein in the next act, and surprise the audience as well, but there is as much fun in preparing your own surprise (and that is really what the dramatist allows us to do) as in preparing a surprise for some one else. Jura says to Marie: "No, but to drive there and confront the two of them, without any weapons, and merely to say to them, quite simply: Why this concealment? You can have each other. Well, then the truth must come out, don't you think?" He proceeds to outline the possible results of the confrontation: what will he do, and what will she? It is we, the audience, who wish to know this, and we are meantime permitted to sympathize and plan with the plotters.

But suppose we were not let into the secret? What would be lost? What gained? Is there no validity in the contention that people are surprised in real life, and that in a situation such as we are allowed to witness in Act II we, as spectators, ought to feel the same shock that is felt by Hein and Delphina?

5. Elsewhere in this volume (p. 347) it is suggested that plots, like certain situations in life, have really no endings, and that the dramatist, who must perforce ring down his curtain after two or three hours, must end his story in a more or less summary and conventional manner. This is one of several reasons why so many plays go to pieces in the last act. Listen to this passage from Lessing's "Hamburg Dramaturgy": " . . . In another still worse tragedy where one of the principal characters died quite casually, a spectator asked his neighbor, 'But what did she die of?' 'Of what? Of the fifth act,' was the reply. In very truth the fifth act is an ugly evil disease that carries off many a one to whom the first four acts promised a longer life."

Tragedies, it is true, are ordinarily conceived as stories in which the principal character dies of something other than the fifth act: his death or ruin is the logical culmination of the situation. In "Ghosts" there is nothing more to be known once it is clear that Oswald is insane; and Hamlet is certainly of little interest to us after the fatal duel. But the writer of comedy is a portraitist, and he winds up his little show as best he may: to kill off the sitter at the end is not only unkind but useless; he still goes on living. In the American version of "The Concert" the actor tells the audience (ostensibly he is talking to the lady who played the part of his wife) that he will give "no more concerts." We are asked to believe that he has reformed, but we know he hasn't. Bahr knew better. He knew that reformation is not a matter of the last act, and he closed his play in this way:

HEIN (*closing his arms about her; mechanically*). My darling little Eva.

EVA (*shivering*). What are you doing? Gustav, Gustav! Don't, don't!

HEIN (*resignedly*). I must, I must.

And the curtain falls. And we know that Hein will go on philandering to the end of his days, or as long as any pretty woman will look at him.

ARTHUR SCHNITZLER

Arthur Schnitzler was born at Vienna in 1862. He was graduated from the University in that city in 1885, and afterwards devoted himself to the practice of medicine, and the writing of novels, short stories, and plays. He died in 1931.

Schnitzler's plays are the epitome of the highly cultivated social life of Vienna. They treat, gracefully and charmingly, of the young well-bred lover and his mistress, in an ever-changing succession. In some of the more characteristic plays—like "Anatol" and "Hands Around"—the subject is the breaking-off of the relation between the two, and in others the tragic or pathetic side is seen—as in "The Legacy" and "Light-o'-Love." With his quiet cynicism and reminiscent moodiness, he is "content to take as his theme only a few scenes from life, and even in those few scenes he recurs continually to a single passage." His philosophy of life might well be expressed in one of his own lines, "We all play parts, happy he who knows it."

PLAYS

"The Fairy Tale" (1893)
"Anatol" [One-Act Cycle] (1893)
"Light-o'-Love" (1895)
"Free Game" (1896)
"The Legacy" (1898)
"The Green Cockatoo" (1899)
"The Companion" (1899)
"Paracelsus" (1899)
"Beatrice's Veil" (1900)
"Living Hours" (1902)
"The Woman With the Dagger" (1902)
"The Last Masks" (1902)
"Literature" (1902)
"The Puppet Master" (1903)
"Hands Around" [One-Act Cycle] (1903)
"Brave Cassian" (1904)
"The Lonely Way" (1904)
"Intermezzo" (1905)
"The Call of Life" (1906)
"The Great Show" (1906)
"Countess Mizzi" (1909)
"Pierrette's Veil" [Pantomime] (1910)
"Young Medardus" (1910)
"The Vast Country" (1911)
"Professor Bernhardi" (1912)
"The Hour of Recognition" (1915)
"The Big Scene" (1915)
"The Festival of Bacchus" (1915)
"Fink and Fliederbusch" (1917)
"The Sisters" (1918)
"The Comedy of Seduction" (1924)
"The Christening" (1926)

Editions.—The Green Cockatoo and Other Plays, trans., with introduction, by H. B. Samuel (Chicago, no date), includes "The Green Cockatoo," "The Mate" [*i.e.* "The Companion"], and "Paracelsus"; *The Lonely Way, Intermezzo, Countess Mizzie,* trans., with introduction, by Edwin Björkman (N. Y. 1915), includes the plays mentioned; *Anatol, Living Hours, The Green Cockatoo,* trans. by Grace I. Colbron (N. Y. 1917), includes the seven scenes of "Anatol," "The Green Cockatoo," "Living Hours," "The Lady With the Dagger," "Last Masks," and "Literature"; *Comedies of Words,* trans. by Pierre Loving (Cincinnati, 1917), includes "The Hour of Recognition," "The Big Scene," "The Festival of Bacchus" [these three originally published as *Comedies of Words*], "Literature," and "His Helpmate" [*i.e.* "The Companion"]; *Reigen* [*i.e.* "Hands Around"] *and Other Plays,* trans. by M. Mannes and G. I. Colbron (N. Y. 1933), includes also "The Affairs of Anatol," "Living Hours" and "The Green Cockatoo."

Separate Plays.—"Anatol" [7 one-act scenes] trans. by Granville Barker (N. Y. 1911); two episodes of same, "A Christmas Present" and "An Episode" (*International,* N. Y. 1911); "Light-o'-Love," trans. by B. Q. Morgan (*Drama,* Chicago, 1912), and as "Playing With Love," by P. M. Shand (London, 1914); "Free Game," by P. H. Grummann (*Poet Lore,* Boston, 1913); "The Duke and the Actress" [*i.e.* "The Green Cockatoo"], by H. Weysz (*Poet Lore,* Boston, 1910); "The Festival of Bacchus," by Pierre Loving (*International,* N. Y. 1916); "The Lady With the Dagger," by H. T. Porter (*Poet Lore,* Boston, 1904); "The Woman With the Dagger," by H. B. Samuel (*Fortnightly,* London, 1909); "Living Hours," by H. T. Porter (*Poet Lore,* Boston, 1906); "Living Hours" [including that play, "The Woman With the Dagger," "The Last Masks," and "Literature"], by P. H. Grummann (*Poet Lore,* Boston, 1913); "The Legacy," by Mary L. Stephenson (*Poet Lore,* Boston, 1911); "His Helpmeet" [*i.e.* "The Companion"], by Pierre Loving (*International,* N. Y. 1915); "Hands Around" [one-act cycle], by F. L. Glaser (N. Y. 1920); "The Hour of Recognition," by Pierre Loving (*International,* N. Y. 1916); "Professor Bernhardi" [adapted], by E. Pohli (San Francisco, 1913) and trans. by L. Borell and R. Adam (London, 1936); "Gallant Cassian," by A. L. Gowans (London, 1914), and by M. A. Jagendorf (*Poet Lore,* Boston, 1922); "Literature," by Pierre Loving (*International,* N. Y. 1915); "The Vast Domain" [*i.e.* "The Vast Country"], by E. Woticky and A. Caro (*Poet Lore,* Boston, 1923).

Reprints in Collections and Anthologies.—"Living Hours" (Colbron translation) in Dickinson's *Chief Contemporary Dramatists, II* (Boston, 1921), and in Loving's *Ten-Minute Plays* (trans. by Porter Davitts) (N. Y. 1923); "Countess Mizzie" (Björkman trans.) in Moses' *Representative One-Act Plays by Continental Authors* (Boston, 1923); "The Lonely Way" (Björkman translation) in Moses' *Representative Continental Dramas* (Boston, 1924); "Literature" (Loving translation) in Shay and Loving's *Fifty Contemporary One-Act Plays* (Cincinnati, 1920), and (Coleman translation) in Vol. XX, *German Classics* (N. Y. 1914); "The Green Cockatoo" (H. B. Samuel trans.) in Vol. XX of *German Classics* (N. Y. 1914) and, by E. van der Veer, in Leverton's *Plays for the College Theater* (N. Y. 1929); "The Festival of Bacchus" (Loving trans.) in Shay's *Twenty-five Short Plays* (*International*) (N. Y. 1925); one of the "Anatol" scenes as "Questioning the Irrevocable," by W. H. H. Chambers in *The Drama,* XII (London, 1906); "Light-o'-Love," trans. by B. Q. Morgan, in T. H. Dickinson's *Continental Plays, I* (Boston, 1935).

References

Percival Pollard, *Masks and Minstrels of New Germany* (Boston, 1911); Ashley Dukes, *Modern Dramatists* (Chicago, 1912), and *The Youngest Drama* (Chicago, 1924); Archibald Henderson, *The Changing Drama* (Cincinnati, 1919); James Huneker, *Ivory Apes and Peacocks* (N. Y. 1915); Ludwig Lewisohn, *The Modern Drama* (N. Y. 1915); H. B. Samuel, *Modernities* (N. Y. 1914); F. W. Chandler, *Aspects of Modern Drama* (N. Y. 1914); Pierre Loving, *Revolt in German Drama* (Girard, Kan., 1925); F. W. Chandler, *Modern Continental Playwrights* (N. Y. 1931).

Light-o'-Love

Play in 3 acts (1895). Texts: translation by B. Q. Morgan (*Drama,* Chicago, 1912) and in Dickinson's *Continental Plays, I* (Boston, 1935); by P. M. Shand, as "Playing With Love" (London, 1914).

"Light-o'-Love" has continuously held the stage in Germany and Austria since its first appearance, and even under the changed circumstances since the War it continues an old favorite with the playgoing public. It is a rare combination of Viennese sentiment and a serious study of modern life.

1. Schnitzler is a master of the one-act play form.[1] He understands its technique as few other playwrights understand it; but at the same time he can handle the full-length play with great skill. In this drama he has combined the qualities that make notable his one-acters, with a remarkable sense of plot structure.

If you compare the light and graceful treatment of the same theme in the "Anatol" cycle, with the no less graceful but serious treatment in the present play, you will see Schnitzler's methods well exemplified. In "Anatol" the man is the central figure; for him the continual change is picturesque, perhaps lingeringly sad, but never tragic; in "Light-o'-Love" the man takes the affair too seriously, and is killed, while the heroine goes off, presumably to kill herself.

2. Bright and witty dialogue is one of the chief charms in this play. Dialogue is naturally a very important element in drama. The best dialogue reveals character, and advances the plot, creates atmosphere, and is interesting and attractive in itself. At the same time, it should not be so brilliant as to overshadow the play, nor so subtle or involved as to overtax the mental powers of the audience. Such plays as Wilde's "Lady Windermere's Fan" and "A Woman of No Importance" suffer a little from their wit, while Donnay's "Return From Jerusalem" is far too detailed and expository throughout to interest an average American or English audience; though a French audience, better accustomed to listen to plays in which conversation predominates, will listen with rapt attention. The first act of "Light-o'-Love" is a model of good dialogue. From the entrance of Christine to the end of the act, the conversation *seems* as easy and natural as in life. Actually, it is not; it is a very compressed and carefully selected arrangement of seem-

[1] For a fuller discussion of the one-act play see pp. 245-246. For typical specimens of Schnitzler's one-acters, read "The Green Cockatoo," "Living Hours," and "Literature."

ingly natural speeches, each carrying a point that advances the story, reveals character, or else is a necessary connecting link between such speeches.

Henry Bataille, himself a master of the art of dialogue, writes regarding "Style in the Drama":

> The so-called style of the theater is true to life neither in appearance nor in actuality; it is neither conversation nor the language of the emotions. . . . It is a sort of written language, with a syntax such as that employed in the novel, . . . it is the natural outcome, pure and simple, of the situation or the characters. These expose everything, even their ideas, to the public. This is the essence of convention. . . . The art of dialogue is a moulding of the observation of nature; that must ever be kept in view.

3. What about the duel? Now, a duel—to those of us who know about such things only through novels and plays—is pretty hard to take seriously, and in this play it is imperative that we believe in its seriousness. Does the use of such a device weaken the appeal? This is not simply a question of duels, but of every device of its kind which happens to be foreign to certain audiences. If we do not *care* what happens to the characters, then the play fails, and often the introduction of a strange code of ethics (like the code of honor which necessitates a duel) may alienate the sympathies of persons who care nothing about duels.

In an essay of Oliver Goldsmith (quoted by Ashley Dukes), we find this passage: "A friend of mine, who was sitting unmoved at one of these sentimental pieces, was asked how he could be so indifferent. 'Why, truly,' says he, 'as the Hero is but a Tradesman, it is indifferent to me whether he be turned out of his Counting-house on Fish-street Hill, since he will still have enough left to open shop in St. Giles's.' "

Are we "indifferent" because the action centers about a duel? (See "Hamlet," Act V.)

4. Compare this long play with one of Schnitzler's one-act plays—"Literature," or "The Green Cockatoo."

Drama (N. Y. 1915); F. W. Chandler, *Aspects of Modern Drama* (N. Y. 1914); Mrs. Patrick Campbell, *My Life and Some Letters* (N. Y. 1922); William Winter, *The Wallet of Time,* 2 vols. (N. Y. 1913).

Electra

Tragedy in 1 act (1904). Text: translation by Arthur Symons (N. Y. 1908).

"Electra," distinguished though it is as poetry, is none the less a drama of passion. "The poet's aim," writes Ludwig Lewisohn, "is to get behind those [*i.e.* the great Greek] dramatists to the wild human origins of the myths with which they deal, to the fierce and primitive and noble folk that must have antedated the Greece of immortal marbles and Sophoclean choruses. . . . What Hofmannsthal has most powerfully laid hold upon is the idea of fate . . . as the immediate spiritual experience of an entire world."

1. The poet has chosen to put his ideas into what seems to be an ancient mold, and the result is perhaps a little bewildering. Does he intend to present in "Electra" merely a Greek play, or does he wish to use the Greek form as a frame in which to portray modern characters? These questions raise a doubt as to the advisability of pouring new wine into old bottles, for it cannot be denied that in this play there is little of the Greek spirit of Sophocles, and that the modern thought and characterization of Hofmannsthal suffer from the alien form into which they have been put. If the poet intended to produce merely a translation of Sophocles, he has of course failed. If he wished to give a characterization of an abnormal modern woman—which he has done—has he chosen the wrong medium?

On the other hand, how far is "Electra" Greek? Compare it with the "Electra" of Sophocles and that of Euripides. What similarity, if any, exists? The question, then, arises, Why did the Austrian poet use even the names of the famous Greeks, and why did he not rather write a drama of passion that was *altogether* alien in spirit and form from the ancient originals?

2. Hofmannsthal has made of Electra a modern and abnormally overwrought woman; he has substituted for the spiritual

motive of revenge (in the Greek play) a personal and almost pathological hatred. But, supposing for the sake of argument, that the modern dramatist has not selected the best form in which to present his theme or sing his poetry, how well has he accomplished the task he has set himself? That, after all, is the important consideration.

3. We know that the dynamic element in drama is a vigorous element, eternally striving for supremacy. But we also know that great drama is and always has been—from the time of Æschylus down to the present—an amalgamation of the dynamic and (shall we say?) "static" elements, and we are therefore a trifle suspicious of every effort toward the predominance of one element over the other. The 19th Century witnessed many such efforts, and each time great drama disappeared during the process. There is a constant danger that action—whether it masquerades as thesis-play or play-of-ideas, problem play or drama of intrigue, or simply as the vehicle of a virtuoso playing with an anecdote—may prevail over the subtle and difficult but indispensable combination of dynamic and "static," the inseparable oneness of plastic form and action. (From Hofmannsthal's article on Eugene O'Neill, 1923.)

Reduced to its essence, Hofmannsthal's statement is simply a formula in which he demands a well-balanced combination of action and character. Determine, so far as possible, what is "dynamic" and what "static" in "Electra"? It is not an easy task, for every living work of art, like every human being, defies *complete* analysis.

And now turn to Hofmannsthal's examples of "static" and "dynamic" (in the article on O'Neill):

Sardou, the heir of Scribe, created a type of play the ingredients of which were entirely dynamic; action took the place of all else; and for twenty years Sardou dominated the stages of Europe, while his followers—the Sudermanns, the Bernsteins, the Pineros—have continued to dominate it to the admiration of the middle classes. . . . This was the type of play in which the personages were never guilty of any "irrational" exhibition of character: They were the fixed units in a sharply outlined plot, manipulated by the skilled hand of the playwright, and they passed their lives in rooms hermetically sealed against the breath of mortals.

Sardou declared that his type of play expressed "Life through movement," while his opponents—the Naturalists—claimed that "movement through life" should be the aim of the artist. Hauptmann, for instance, at first identified with the Naturalists, doubtless swung back too far from the Sardou formula. Hofmannsthal continues:

> It may be that this is the reason why the plays of . . . Hauptmann are not popular outside Germany; for a large part of the German public is ready and able to listen to plays in which the "static" element is predominant. . . . Hauptmann's plays are the exact antithesis of the plays of Eugene O'Neill. Where Mr. O'Neill reveals the first burst of his emotions in powerful, clean-cut pictures that seem almost like simple ballads in our complex world, Hauptmann applies himself to making his characters plastic.

Hofmannsthal is, of course, about as different from O'Neill as one dramatist can be from another. Have they anything in common? How far are his strictures on the American justified?

4. For a further discussion of Hofmannsthal's article and O'Neill's plays, see my recent book, *Eugene O'Neill.*

THE HUNGARIAN DRAMA

THE HUNGARIAN DRAMA

The modern Hungarian drama is known to us in America and England chiefly through the work of Molnar, Lengyel and half a dozen others whose plays have been adapted for stage production. A few of Molnar's plays have recently appeared in translation, but of Lengyel only "Typhoon"—and that adapted—is accessible to English readers; of Ernst Vajda only "Fata Morgana," of Lajos Biro only two one-acters, and of Ernö Szep only a slight one-act comedy. Imre Földes, author of "Over the Phone," is not accessible in book form but Ferencz Herzeg's "Seven Sisters" has recently been translated. Several other talented writers should be mentioned, none of whose plays are published in English: Milan Füst, Dezsö Szomory, Imre Liptai, Sandor Hevesi (director of the National Theater), Imre Farkas, Andor Garvay, and Andor Gabor.

There is practically nothing in English—besides a few stray periodical articles—on the modern drama in Hungary.

Ferenc Molnar

Ferenc, better known as "Franz," Molnar was born in Budapest in 1878, "the son," according to his translator, "of a wealthy Jewish merchant. He graduated from the Universities of Geneva and Budapest. His literary career was begun as a journalist at the age of eighteen. He wrote short sketches and humorous dialogues of such beauty and charm that he became a national figure almost at once, and the circulation of his newspaper increased until it was foremost in Budapest. Then he married Margaret Vaszi, the daughter of his editor, herself a journalist of note. Two years later he was divorced from her, and subsequently he married an actress who had played rôles in his own plays."

A writer of novels and short stories and a prolific dramatist, Molnar is to-day one of the most important literary figures in Hungary. He is known abroad almost exclusively as the author of six or eight fantastic and poetic plays. The Hungarian drama—known to us by translations and adaptations (often not acknowledged)—is rich in the sort of novel play-forms in which Molnar has achieved his most striking successes.

Plays

"The Attorney-at-Law" (1902)
"Jozsi" (1904)
"The Devil" (1907)
"Liliom" (1909)
"The Guardsman" (1911)
"The Wolf" (1912)
"The Swan" (1914)
"Fashions for Men" (1915)
"White Cloud" (1915)
"Carnival" (1916)
"Lent" (1917)
"Violette" (1921)
"Prologue to King Lear" (1921)
"Marshal" (1921)
"Earthly and Heavenly Love" (1922)
"The Red Mill" (1923)
"The Glass Slipper" (1924)
"Riviera" (1925)
"Still Life" (1925)
"The Play in the Castle" (1926)
"Olympia" (1927)
"If Napoleon ——" (1927)
"The Good Fairy" (1932)

Editions.—The Plays of Ferenc Molnar (N. Y. 1929), include practically all the plays of Molnar, with a few variations of title, as: "The Lawyer" [*i.e.* "The Attorney-at-Law"]; "The Tale of the Wolf" [*i.e.* "The Wolf"]; "The Violet" [*i.e.* "Violette"]; "Mima" [*i.e.* "The Red Mill"]; "The Play's the Thing" [*i.e.* "The Play in the Castle"]; *Fashions for Men and The Swan,* trans. by B. F. Glazer (N. Y. 1922); *Husbands and Lovers,* trans. by Benjamin Glazer (N. Y. 1924), includes nineteen dialogues.

Separate Plays—"The Devil," adapted by Oliver Herford (N. Y. 1908); "Liliom," trans. by B. F. Glazer (N. Y. 1921); "The Guardsman," trans. by G. I. Colbron, H. Bartsch, and P. Moeller (N. Y. 1924); "The Play's the Thing" ["The Play in the Castle"], adapted by P. G. Wodehouse (N. Y. 1927); "The Good Fairy," trans. by J. Hinton (N. Y. 1932); "The Swan," trans. by B. F. Glazer (N. Y. 1929); "Olympia," adapted by S. Howard (N. Y. 1928).

References

W. P. Eaton, *Plays and Players* (Cincinnati, 1916); Ludwig Lewisohn, *The Drama and the Stage* (N. Y. 1922); Isaac Goldberg, *The Drama of Transition* (Cincinnati, 1922); T. H. Dickinson, *The Theater in a Changing Europe* (N. Y. 1937).

Liliom

Legend in 7 scenes and a prologue (1909). Text: translation by B. F. Glazer (N. Y. 1921).

Since its initial performance in Budapest "Liliom" has been acted in many countries, including the United States. It is often revived, and is warmly received by audiences of varying tastes. It is, in its essence, a love-story, and in spite of the supernatural element introduced into the last part of it, an easily understandable play.

1. Certain questions naturally arise in connection with any consideration of this fantastic drama. It is obvious that the dramatist, in adopting the form he does, was actuated by a desire to emphasize his theme, which was simply the power of love, *through and beyond death.* The love of Julie for Liliom is instinctive, without afterthought, and Liliom's affection for her (such as it was, quite as free from reflection. The child Louise, at the end of the last scene, asks her mother to tell her about the "strange man":

JULIE. What is there to tell you, child? Nothing has happened. We were peacefully eating, and a beggar came who talked of bygone days, and then I thought of your father. . . .

LOUISE. Mother—tell me—has it ever happened to you—has anyone ever hit you—without hurting you in the least?

JULIE. Yes, my child. It has happened to me, too. . . .

LOUISE. Is it possible for someone to hit you—hard like that—real loud and hard—and not hurt you at all?

JULIE. It is possible, dear—that someone may beat you and beat you and beat you—and not hurt you at all. . . .

Liliom has been dead fifteen years, and he returns for a day to see his wife and child. To Julie he is only a beggar who reminds her of her husband. What is he supposed to be? It is necessary, before considering this question, to return to the preceding scene, a presentment of Liliom's conception of heaven. Why, indeed, after his death, should the dramatist show us Liliom floating up to the Bar of Judgment? Certainly, this scene prepares us for the last: we understand it—at least from Liliom's point of view; but what does it mean?

It means first that the scene in heaven offered the dramatist a wonderful opportunity for (shall we call it?) poetic comedy. It is not just heaven, but Liliom's conception of heaven. The last scene is shown from Liliom's point of view: we see Julie and Louise through his eyes; but at the same time we return to earth. Julie is, as it were, not "in on" the supernatural business. She is still in life: she cares not for the bodily return of Liliom, she still lives through the love of the "roughneck" whom she loved when he was alive. She knows all she need know, that "it is possible . . . that someone may beat you . . . and not hurt you at all."

The difficulty arises when we try to explain rationally the supernatural scenes. Why does not Julie recognize Liliom? Why, indeed, are we concerned at all with Liliom after his death? Well, the playwright simply asks us to accept the scenes as they stand. Why not, he would urge, write a scene from two points of view? The one from that of a character who is dead, the other from that of a living being? He adopts much the same sort of convention which the old painters adopted (see Veronese's "Rape of Europa") when they pictured three or four episodes of the same story in a single canvas. As a matter of fact, there is no rational explanation of the last scenes, but does that make a particle of difference? Is it necessary to rationalize "Faust"?

2. The play is called "Liliom," but, after all, is it not Julie's play? Molnar goes to particular pains throughout the drama to emphasize the character of the woman, and to render it unmistakably clear that Liliom is in no sense a hero. Indeed he has not one redeeming virtue. He is the same at the end of the play as he was at the beginning: he is the inspirer, not the inspired, the instrument through which Julie learns—though all unconsciously—the meaning of love. Most dramatists develop their characters, who are shown changing because of what happens to them: recall the scene in the park where Julie is first attracted to Liliom. She is an ignorant servant-girl who never had a fellow, and understands nothing of love or lovemaking. (See pp. 39-46, a charming scene.) But Julie develops; we see her changing from scene to scene: she learns all—it seems—that can be learned, of the cruelty and beauty of life.

3. Take the scene in Scene V, where Liliom is brought back dead. Julie is passive—stunned, it is true, but none the less (so far as her words are concerned) apparently apathetic. Wolf refers to Liliom as a bad man, and Julie assents. She even admits that it was "lucky" it happened—that is, Liliom's

death. Marie breaks down as she embraces Julie, and the latter turns to her with the superb line, "Don't cry, Marie." Then (p. 141) she is alone with Liliom's body, and her heart speaks:

> Sleep, Liliom, sleep. . . . You bad, quick-tempered, rough, unhappy, wicked—*dear* boy—sleep peacefully, Liliom—they can't understand how I feel—I can't even explain to you. . . . You treated me badly—that was wicked of you—but sleep peacefully, Liliom. . . . I love you.

A long speech, one which in life would never have been uttered, because such women as Julie can only feel. But this long speech is the artist's way of illuminating the soul of the girl. The soliloquy is here inevitable. Besides, it throws a new light on Julie, and the rest of the play is but a gradual revelation of what Liliom *has* meant to her in the past.

4. We now come to an especially difficult question. If you accept my theory (and I set it forth only as my personal opinion) that this is Julie's play and not Liliom's, why drag in the heaven scene? It is delightful, but what has it to do with the story? Of course, if this is the tale of Liliom's adventures, then it is justified. If it is not, the scene is superfluous. And what is superfluous is bad. Life—looking at it from the artist's angle—is full of superfluities, but art curtails what is not vital; this in spite of the fact that it is sometimes the artist's business to express the superfluities themselves. That is another matter.

I am not sure that Scene VI *is* superfluous. Think it over.

5. When "Liliom" was produced in New York the title rôle was played by a handsome and attractive actor, and Julie by a no less handsome but more or less sophisticated actress. Any woman would have been glad to have this Liliom, and any man would hold himself lucky to have this Julie. When the play was performed (1923) in Berlin, Liliom was played by one of the homeliest (if most gifted) actors on the German stage, Max Pallenberg, and Julie by the wonderful Lucie Höflich, a buxom lady of about fifty, who weighs not an ounce under

two hundred. Pallenberg was rough, dirty, ill-tempered, and Höflich was just such a stupid simple girl as you will find in any middle-class German home. The Berlin production was infinitely more effective than the New York production. Why?

THE FRENCH DRAMA

THE FRENCH DRAMA

Compared with the total number of plays written, the number of French plays available in English is small. Rostand is known to us through several translations of his best work. The best plays of Brieux and Hervieu are now accessible, though the majority must be read in the original. Lavedan and Lemaître, Porto-Riche and Bernstein and Capus must be estimated by English readers through one play each (not counting one-act trifles); Pierre Wolff's long plays have not been translated at all, nor those of Bataille, nor Descaves. Flers and Caillavet, Romain Coolus, Abel Hermant, Alfred Hennequin, Paul Gavault, Emile Fabre, Jean Richepin, Francis de Croisset, Henry Kistemaeckers, have all been translated or adapted, and certain of their plays produced both in England and America, though none have been published in English. Curel and Maurice Donnay are accessible, though so far only three or four of their plays have found translators, while Georges Ancey, Léon Hennique and Jean Jullien are represented by only one play each. Of Albert Guinon, Gustave Guiches, Marie Lenéru, the novelist Paul Bourget and the poet Jean Aicard, not one play has been published in translation. Virginia and Frank Vernon's volume, *Modern One-Act Plays from the French,* includes twenty-two plays. Two or three of Sacha Guitry's clever plays are also available in English, and of Lenormand, Vildrac, Savoir, Deval, and Bourdet.

Certain of the exceptional dramatists are far better known to us than their more illustrious fellow-craftsmen: Romain Rolland, several of whose historical dramas have been translated; Paul Hyacinthe-Loyson, author of "The Apostle"; Jacques Copeau; the poet Claudel, of whom several plays have been turned into beautiful English; Georges Duhamel, the poet and story-writer; and H. F. Lenormand, whose "Failures" was performed in New York.

Matthews' *French Dramatists of the Nineteenth Century* is a record that ends with the establishment of the Free Theater. My *Contemporary French Dramatists* contains a dozen chapters on the playwrights of the past forty years; Chandler's *Contemporary Drama of France* is a pretty complete record of the contemporary theater. The latest work on the subject is Hugh Allison Smith's *Main Currents of Modern French Drama.*

A chapter on the drama is to be found in Cunliffe and Bacourt's

French Literature During the Last Half-Century, and more or less material is included in the few general books on the drama.

Henry Becque

Henry Becque, the father of the modern French Naturalistic school, was born at Paris in 1837. His early works were produced in the sixties, but "The Parisian Woman" and "The Vultures," his most important plays, were peddled about for years before they were performed. During the last years of his life, Becque was recognized as the master, the founder of one of the most important movements of modern times. He died in 1899.

The production of "The Vultures" in 1882 and "The Parisian Woman" in 1885 marked the beginning of the new school which, in 1887, under the leadership of André Antoine, had a theater of its own, the famous Free Theater.

Becque is termed a Naturalist because his characters were held to be living beings, because they give the illusion of reality, and because his technique is subordinate to and of less importance than his characterization. He writes because he wishes to present to us a "slice of life"; he has no lesson to teach, no sermon to pronounce, no thesis to prove. His plays, in the words of a French critic, "are life" itself. Huneker says, "Becque's major quality is his gift of lifelike characterization. Character with him is of prime importance. He did not tear down the structure of the drama, but merely removed much of the scaffolding which time had allowed to disfigure its façade."

Through the perspective of years we are now able to realize that the Naturalism of the 80's and 90's was only a phase, one of many methods of interpreting life. Becque, after all, came no closer to "reality" than many so-called Romantics. He was instrumental in bringing about a reaction against the clever artificialities of the facile technicians.

Plays

"The Prodigal Son" (1868)
"Michel Pauper" (1870)
"The Elopement" (1871)
"The Merry-Go-Round" (1878)
"The Virtuous Women" (1880)
"The Vultures" (1882)
"The Woman of Paris" (1885)
"The Start" (1898)
"Madeleine" (1898)
"Widowed" (1898)
"A Four-Handed Game" (1898)
"An Execution" (1898)
"The Puppets" [unfinished] (1910)

("Sardanapalus," 1867, is the libretto of an opera.)

Editions.—The Vultures, The Woman of Paris, The Merry-Go-Round, translated, with introduction, by Freeman Tilden (N. Y. 1913).

Separate Plays.—"The Crows" [*i.e.* "The Vultures"], by Bénédict Papot (*Drama,* Chicago, 1912); "The Shuttle" [*i.e.* "The Merry-Go-Round"], by L. A. Loiseaux (N. Y. no date); "A Quiet Game" [*i.e.* "A Four-Handed Game"], by Sheba Harris (*Play Book,* Madison, Wis 1913).

Reprint in Collection.—"The Vultures" (Tilden translation) in Moses' *Representative Continental Dramas* (Boston, 1924).

References

James Huneker, *Iconoclasts* (N. Y. 1905); A. Filon, *Modern French Drama,* trans. by C. J. Hogarth (N. Y. 1898); Ashley Dukes, *Modern Dramatists* (Chicago, 1912); Brander Matthews, *French Dramatists of the 19th Century* (N. Y. 1910); Barrett H. Clark, *Four Plays of the Free Theater* (Cincinnati, 1914), and *Contemporary French Dramatists* (Cincinnati, 1915); F. W. Chandler, *The Contemporary Drama of France* (Boston, 1920); and *Aspects of Modern Drama* (N. Y. 1914); Arnold Bennett, *Books and Persons* (N. Y. 1917); George Moore, *Impressions and Opinions* (N. Y. 1913); H. A. Smith, *Main Currents of Modern French Drama* (N. Y. 1925); S. M. Waxman, *Antoine and the Théâtre Libre* (Cambridge, Mass., 1926).

The Vultures

Play in 4 acts (1882). Texts: translation, as "The Crows," by B. Papot (*Drama,* Chicago, 1912); by F. Tilden, in *The Vultures, The Woman of Paris, The Merry-Go-Round* (N. Y. 1913); reprint of the same in Moses' *Representative Continental Dramas* (Boston, 1924).

"The Vultures" was one of the numerous attempts made by the Naturalists to do for the drama what Zola and the Goncourts, Maupassant, and Daudet, were doing for the novel. The novelists all wrote plays; it was reserved for Becque to write "The Vultures" and "The Woman of Paris," examples of the best that Naturalism had to offer. "It was Becque," says Dr. F. W. Chandler, "who in practice pointed the way to stage naturalism, achieving far more for that cause than did Zola."

1. The first act is given over almost altogether to exposition. With its long speeches, asides and soliloquies, we should to-day call it very old-fashioned. A glance at Pinero's "Thunderbolt" or Maugham's "Circle" will show the distance covered in the development of sheer technique since 1882. Yet in

this play the French dramatist appears deliberately to avoid the facile expedients of his successful contemporaries: he will have none of the suave prattle of Sardou or Bisson; he prefers to attend to the chief business before him, which is the presentation of character—in huge slices, as it were.

Do you think that he was really unable to conduct his opening scenes as Sardou conducts, say, the opening scenes of "Divorçons" or "Patrie!"?

One important thing does happen in the first act: the death of Vigneron, announced just before the curtain falls, was hardly expected. The playwright of the "well-made" play school would call it "unprepared." So it is. It comes as a shock. But then the dramatist intended that it should shock. "This is life," he would say. "Don't people die suddenly in the midst of life, despite MM. Sardou and Bisson? Then why not show things in a play as they happen in life, which aims to reproduce, or at least to reflect, life?

This is also exposition, in that it prepares for the important business of the play, which has not yet begun; the play does not actually begin until the early part of the second act. As a matter of fact, the whole first act *could* be put into a page or two of exposition and placed at the beginning of what is now the second. But Becque, knowing what he was about, wished to prepare his background with all possible care. The home-life of the Vignerons, their ideas and tastes, their physical surroundings, are all elements in the picture.

2. There is one basic difference in treatment between this play and the usual French play of the present time. Such playwrights as Lavedan, Donnay, Capus, and above all Sacha Guitry, are "finished" writers, as to style and construction; Becque is brutal and direct, unpolished, and since the people he usually portrays are not "society," they are more "lifelike" than if they were.

The transition from scene to scene is abrupt, especially in the first act, too much so to give the illusion even of that rhythm which is so great an asset in all representations of life. Read pages 49 and 50 (*The Drama* edition); there are parts of three distinct episodes, and yet there are no modulation, no blending, no "bridging sections." More skilled, though perhaps less inspired dramatists, would have welded these incidents together, blended them into a harmonious whole.

3. The second act is typical of Becque's manner at its best; although it shows the influence of Molière, it has a savage note of satire, a brusque and peremptory movement. The three "vultures" scene is one of the most bitterly ironical in all modern drama. Here we have none of the suavity of a Capus, the brilliant charm of a Guitry; the dramatist seems almost to have forgotten that he was writing a play—for which we are grateful. His instinct has served him well.

4. It is in the third act that we find a good deal of the sort of material that was to be developed later by Hervieu and Brieux. Becque throws out a suggestion—the injustice of the law, for instance, a thesis which Hervieu was later to develop in "The Nippers"; or he shows the impossibility of an unmarried woman's making an honest living, which Brieux used in "Blanchette" and "The Independent Woman." François de Curel, Emile Fabre, Léon Hennique and a score of others, following the trail blazed by Becque, were quick to perceive the dramatic possibilities inherent in a play like "The Vultures," which came to be regarded as the "Bible of the Naturalists."

5. The play has what is known as an unemphatic ending. Conventional plays of the school of Scribe and Sardou end almost invariably with what in America is called a "punch,"—a "big" scene. This is pointed, but the other method is no less so, often because of its very unobtrusiveness. The unemphatic ending contains a sting, a satirical touch that sums up the act, or, in some instances, illustrates the theme of the entire play. Galsworthy's "Strife," for instance. Tench says to Harness, "D'you know, sir—these terms, they're the *very same* we drew up together, you and I, and put to both sides before the fight began? All this—all this—and—what for?" Harness then answers, "That's where the fun comes in!", and the curtain drops. In Louis N. Parker's "Disraeli," the first act "curtain" is another example. This is, as we have already seen (p. 48),

a common practice nowadays, and the reason for it is chiefly because it heightens illusion. In life, the exciting is mingled with the commonplace; one of the most interesting and dramatic things in life is the strange contrast between the sublime and the commonplace, the tragic and the comic. Therefore, instead of ending his act or play with a scene of great tension or high emotion, the dramatist seeks to reproduce a still more "lifelike" scene, placing one of these contrasted moments at the most critical point in his act, that is, in the last part of it. One of the quietest endings is in Wedekind's "Music." "At the end, when Klara, after undergoing imprisonment, exile, poverty, public disgrace and the loss of her beloved child, finds herself bereft of even Reissner's regard, she is led away in a stupor from the miserable attic. It is then, in reply to a wish of the physician that she will suffer no lasting mental disturbance, that Lindekuh preludes the fall of the curtain by the caustic remark: 'She'll be able to sing a song.'"[1]

On the other hand, need it be said that not *all* of life is unemphatic? Is there not danger in overemphasizing the unemphatic? Galsworthy has been blamed for his cautious "curtains" on the grounds that life is seldom so tense and undramatic as he shows it.

Take, as an example of the emphatic ending, Echegaray's rather melodramatic play "Madman or Saint" (also translated as "Folly or Saintliness"). Is the strong scene with which this drama ends esthetically justifiable?

FRANCOIS DE CUREL

Viscount François de Curel was born at Metz, in Lorraine, in 1854. He was an eager and precocious reader. "In my early youth," he says, . . . "I felt that the writing of books was an enviable and honorable profession. . . . At the age of five I read all the *Robinsons* I could lay hand on: *Crusoe, Swiss Family,* etc. I devoured them and pondered upon them." He was first educated

[1] From F. J. Ziegler's preface to his translation of Wedekind's "Awakening of Spring."

(against his wishes) in the sciences, but as he was a man of large fortune he was soon able to devote himself to writing. At the age of thirty-one he published his first novel which, curiously enough, revealed certain qualities that caused a critic to advise the author to write plays.

This he proceeded to do, but found no manager willing to produce his first efforts until, in 1891, he sent three MSS. to Antoine, director of the Free Theater. Each play was signed by a different pseudonym, and all were accepted at the same time. These early plays and their immediate successors—"A False Saint," "The Fossils," "Love Embellishes," etc.—were characteristic Free Theater dramas: it was through Antoine that Curel was encouraged to write plays, and although Antoine has long since ceased to exercise any influence in the theater, Curel remains the most austere and highly respected dramatist in France.

Curel is not only a psychologist—most Frenchmen are that—he is able to write moving drama. His primary interest is always in human beings, particularly men and women under the stress of extraordinary and abnormal circumstances. "He seeks out the strange occurrences in life" (see my *Contemporary French Dramatists*), "shapes the facts into a simple story, and then proceeds to analyze motives. Situations are for him only excuses for soul and mind analysis."

Curel told me (in an interview, 1913) that he still considered himself only an amateur. That is, he was not one of the "regular" professionals who supply the theaters with a new play every season. Curel wrote when the spirit moved him. "Why need I bother to write," he said, "just because I can? I prefer to have something to say." Curel died in 1929.

The Free Theater

The Free Theater, or Théâtre Libre, was founded at Paris by an amateur, André Antoine, early in the spring of 1887. In a small improvised playhouse on Montmartre the young man formed a company of actors for the purpose of producing four one-act plays; these were written by some of the more prominent members of the Naturalist school. The only successful number on that bill was a play by Léon Hennique, founded on a story by Zola. Two months later Antoine offered another bill, to which the Naturalist Oscar Méténier contributed a one-acter. Villiers de l'Isle Adam, the

Brothers Goncourt, and Jean Jullien were the next native writers to be produced. The following season saw performances of Tolstoy's "Power of Darkness," and plays of Ibsen and Strindberg. During the seven years' life of the Theater, such foreign writers as Hauptmann, Björnson, Heijermans, and Verga, were for the first time produced in France. But it was largely due to Antoine that many French dramatists were permitted to experiment as they chose, and among the men who owe their first opportunity to it are Curel, Brieux, Porto-Riche, Hennique, Georges Ancey, Jean Aicard, Pierre Wolff, George Courteline, Romain Coolus, and Albert Guinon. There were, however, others who used the Theater more or less as a place for experiment, dramatists who have done little or nothing since its close, but whose work is none the less interesting as exemplifying the more extreme theories of Antoine. Such are Henry Céard, Jean Jullien, Emile Zola, Paul Alexis, Oscar Méténier and the Goncourts.

"It is Antoine's chief glory," says Brieux,[2] "to have felt this desire [for something new], to have been the first to bring it to its full fruition. From the moment he made his first appearance in the obscure little theater in the Passage de l'Elysée des Beaux-arts, dramatists brought him plays in which they, too, had endeavored to do away with the old conventions, and in which they tried to affect the men and women of their day through sincere work reflecting more clearly than ever before the life of their time. All these authors *existed,* no doubt, but their works were not produced, their manuscripts were not even read."

It was due to the Free Theater that Brahm founded the Free Stage in Berlin, and Grein the London Independent Theater.

PLAYS

"A False Saint" (1892)
"The Fossils" (1892)
"The Guest" (1893)
"Love Embellishes" (1893)
"The Dancer" (1896)
"The Lion's Feast" (1898)
"The New Idol" (1899)
"The Savage Girl" (1902)
"The Beat of the Wing" (1906)
"The Dance Before the Mirror" (1914)
"The Genius' Comedy" (1918)
"The Soul Gone Mad" (1920)
"The Wise Man's Folly" (1922)

---

[2] Quoted from Brieux's Preface to my *Four Plays of the Free Theater* (Cincinnati, 1915). This book contains an essay on the Theater, a list of plays produced, and four typical examples of the repertory: plays by Curel, Ancey, Jullien, and Porto-Riche. See also my *Contemporary French Dramatists* (Cincinnati, 1915).

Editions.—Four Plays of the Free Theater, trans., with introduction, by Barrett H. Clark, and preface by Brieux (Cincinnati, 1914), includes "The Fossils."

Separate Plays.—"A False Saint," trans. by Barrett H. Clark, preface by Archibald Henderson (Garden City, 1916); "The Beat of the Wing," trans. by Alice Van Kaathoven (*Poet Lore,* Boston, 1909).

References

F. W. Chandler, *The Contemporary Drama of France* (Boston, 1920); Barrett H. Clark, *Contemporary French Dramatists* (Cincinnati, 1915); Augustin Filon, *Modern French Drama,* trans. by C. J. Hogarth (N. Y. 1898); Ludwig Lewisohn, *The Modern Drama* (N. Y. 1915).

See also prefaces to "A False Saint" and *Four Plays of the Free Theater;* H. A. Smith, *Main Currents of Modern French Drama* (N. Y. 1925); S. M. Waxman, *Antoine and the Théâtre Libre* (Cambridge, Mass., 1926).

The Fossils

Play in 4 acts (1892; revised 1900). Text: translation by Barrett H. Clark, in *Four Plays of the Free Theater* (Cincinnati, 1915.

Like Lavedan's "Prince d'Aurec," this play is concerned with the old French aristocracy—of which, incidentally, the dramatist is himself a member. Since the founding of the latest French Republic in 1871 the nobility have found themselves in a difficult position. Those among them who are unable to bow to the inevitable, must live their lives in obscurity and often in poverty. It is such a family that Curel portrays in "The Fossils."

1. It has been stated that Curel was one of the Free Theater group. He was enabled to write the sort of "unpopular" plays he wished to write because Antoine offered him a stage, a public, sympathetic understanding, and a company of actors. The critic Adolphe Thalasso (in his book *Le Théâtre libre*) has thus expressed the ideal and achievement of the Free Theater dramatists: "Plays in which life supplies movement begin to take the place of those in which movement supplies life. Complicated plots give way to simple stories; the play of intrigue is offset by the study of reality; characters become natural, classic; the tragic and comic are no longer mingled. . . ." The plays in which "movement supplies life" are, we may assume,

the "well-made" plays of Sardou, Bisson, and their many contemporaries.

In what fundamental respects does "The Fossils" differ from Sardou's "Patrie"? Does "life" supply "movement"? What is meant by this expression?

2. The situation around which the dramatist has built his play is by no means an ordinary one. It is not only unusual, it is almost unheard of. The abnormal is generally not very effective in any work of art, not because it is abnormal or "unpleasant," but because it does not appeal, as a rule, to the human (hence, the normal) sympathies of mankind. There is in all art a *general* appeal. In a play, for instance, it is not enough to portray a character known to or imagined by the dramatist; the character must possess what we call human elements. We generalize—in spite of ourselves—from what we see in art. Hamlet is universal because the Hamlet in each of us responds to the Hamlet of the poet. Although characters in plays often become mad, a madman is an almost impossible character on the stage: he is at most a curiosity, although his *becoming* mad may be tragic and capable of arousing our sympathies. The mad Ophelia is pathetic because we have seen her before she became mad. If she had been brought on the stage in that state she would not have been anywhere near so pathetic.

The Chantemelle family are all more or less unusual people, placed in an unusual situation. By what means is the author able to arouse our sympathy for them?

3. Hélène is obviously used for purposes of dramatic contrast. Is there any other technical reason for introducing her into the story?

4. Is "The Fossils" a tragedy? We have often (pp. 142, 297) raised the question of the meaning of tragedy. It is not a matter of arbitrary classification—or we should not return to the subject so often. Tragedy is rather a state of mind or soul than a "form." The "tragic" plays of modern times are not based upon the themes that used to be regarded as tragic: the characters are not kings and princes, for instance. Society is

infinitely more complicated than it used to be, and the tremendous problems of economics, industry, over-population, war and the like, have wiped out old systems and for the most part old standards of ethics. And yet life is no less tragic than it was in the days of Æschylus.

In his "Note on Tragedy" (in *The Drama and the Stage*), Ludwig Lewisohn says: "It has been said many times . . . that there is no tragedy in modern drama." The reason for this is that certain critics—and, after them, a large part of the public—"are aware that tragedy cuts to the quick of life and springs from the innermost depth of human thinking because it must always seek to deal in some intelligible way with the problem of evil. But since it is most comfortable to believe that problem to have been solved, they avert their faces from a reopening of the eternal question and declare that the answer of the Greeks and the Elizabethans is final. . . ." The conventional critic is inclined to "deny the character of tragedy to every action in which disaster does not follow upon crime. Yet, rightly looked upon, man in every tragic situation is a Job, incapable and unconscious of any degree of voluntary guilt that can justify a suffering as sharp and constant as his own."

Compare this statement with Hervieu's (p. 142) and Masefield's words on the same subject (p. 297). Then turn to Aristotle (*Poetics,* Butcher translation, p. 23):

"Tragedy, then, is an imitation of an action that is serious, complete, and of a certain magnitude; in language embellished with each kind of artistic ornament, the several kinds being found in separate parts of the play; in the form of action, not of narrative; through pity and fear effecting the proper purgation of these emotions." The hero should not be a "virtuous man brought from prosperity to adversity," nor "a bad man passing from adversity to prosperity," nor should the "downfall of the utter villain be exhibited." He should rather be one "who is highly renowned and prosperous,—a personage like Œdipus, Thyestes, or other illustrious men of such families." [3]

[3] For the development of all theories of drama, and especially the influence of Aristotle from his day to our own, see my anthology, *European Theories of the Drama* (New York, revised 1929).

To return to Lewisohn: "Thus modern tragedy does not deal with wrong and just vengeance, which are both, if conceived absolutely, pure fictions of our deep-rooted desire for superiority and violence. It is inspired by compassion." "Compassion" and "pity"—where is the difference? Is the hero of Sophocles' "Œdipus the King" visited with "just vengeance"? Is Orestes, in Æschylus' "Libation Pourers" and "Furies"? And what of Hamlet? Is he not as much the victim of circumstances as Job, or—to take one of Lewisohn's modern instances—Mrs. Alving in "Ghosts"? Wherein does Lewisohn's theory differ from Aristotle's? Lewisohn further states that modern tragedy "cannot deal with guilt in the older sense." What is guilt in the older sense? He means the violation of "the inscrutable will of the gods," or "a breach of the universal moral law sanctioned and set forth by God." But is all great tragedy the spectacle of "guilt" punished by violence? Surely the greatest heroes of tragedy are the victims of forces over which they have no control.

In what respects is "The Fossils" tragic? Does it "seek to deal in some intelligible way with the problem of evil"? Does it inspire compassion?

For an illuminating discussion of tragedy, see Allardyce Nicoll's *Introduction to Dramatic Theory*.

Henri Lavedan

Henri Lavedan, born of a middle-class family at Orléans in 1859, went to school at first in the neighborhood of Orléans, then at Paris, and was graduated soon after the close of the Franco-Prussian War, in 1871. He studied law for a year, and then gave it up, feeling that he was not suited for the profession. He made his literary début with a number of clever and cynical dialogues, picturing for the most part the idle classes of Parisian society. His first long play was "A Family," produced at the Comédie Française in the early nineties. Before this, a few of his short satirical dialogues had made their appearance at Antoine's Free Theater in 1888. This was followed by what is probably his finest play, "The Prince d'Aurec." Lavedan excels in his character work, the best examples of which are to be found in the play mentioned, as well as in "The Latest Fad," "The Marquis de Priola," and "The Duel."

PLAYS

"A Family" (1891)
"The Prince d'Aurec" (1892)
"Criticism of the Prince d'Aurec" (1892)
"The Two Nobilities" (1894)
"High Life" (1895)
"Catherine" (1898)
"The Latest Fad" (1898)
"The Old Sport" (1899)
"The Medici" (1901)
"The Marquis de Priola" (1902)
"Varennes" [with G. Lenôtre] (1904)
"The Duel" (1905)
"Sire" (1909)
"The Taste for Vice" (1911)
"The King's Dog" (1913)
"To Serve" (1913)
"Pétard" (1914)
"Sacrificed" [with M. Zamacoïs] (1917)

Editions.—The only long play translated is "The Prince d'Aurec," by Barrett H. Clark in *Three Modern Plays From the French* (N. Y. 1914); of the many little dialogues, seven are translated: "Along the Quays," "For Ever and Ever," "Where Shall We Go?" "The Afternoon Walk," and "Not at Home," trans. by Sibyl Collar Holbrook (*Poet Lore,* Boston, 1917), and reprinted in Moses' *Representative One-Act Plays by Continental Authors* (Boston, 1923); "Their Heart," by W. V. Silverberg (*Poet Lore,* Boston, 1919); "Two Husbands," by R. T. House (*Poet Lore,* Boston, 1908); "The King's Pet" [*i.e.* "The King's Dog"], trans. by Virginia and Frank Vernon, in Vernons' *Modern One-Act Plays from the French* (N. Y. 1934).

REFERENCES

Barrett H. Clark, *Contemporary French Dramatists* (Cincinnati, 1915); F. W. Chandler, *The Contemporary Drama of France* (Boston, 1920), and *Aspects of Modern Drama* (N. Y. 1914); Augustin Filon, *Modern French Drama,* trans. by C. J. Hogarth (N. Y. 1898); Clayton Hamilton, *Seen on the Stage* (N. Y. 1920); Otis Skinner, *Footlights and Spotlights* (N. Y. 1924); Ludwig Lewisohn, *The Modern Drama* (N. Y. 1915); H. A. Smith, *Main Currents of Modern French Drama* (N. Y. 1925).

THE PRINCE D'AUREC

Comedy in 3 acts (1892). Text: translation by Barrett H. Clark, in *Three Modern Plays From the French* (N. Y. 1914).

Many modern French writers have dealt with the question of the aristocracy of to-day; among the dramatists are notably François de Curel ("The Fossils"), Paul Bourget ("L'Emigré"), and finally Lavedan ("Catherine" and "The Two Nobilities"). The present play, by reason of its detailed characterization, its wit, its truth to life, is probably the best work of its kind written during the past quarter-century.

1. Dumas *fils* once said that a play should comprise "A painting, an ideal, a judgment." This comedy of Lavedan's certainly comprises "a painting." Does it have "an ideal" and "a judgment"? As a painting compare it with Ibsen's "Hedda Gabler." In what respects does each of these plays fall under any of the headings mentioned above? Were the purposes of the authors, so far as they had purposes, in any way comparable?

2. "The Prince d'Aurec" is an admirable example of the creation of dramatic background. The Prince himself is the chief object of interest, but he cannot always occupy the center of the stage; the audience would weary of him. The dramatist must therefore provide relief. His problem was how to divert us and yet tell something important about the Prince. This difficult feat of keeping us amused is so well accomplished that we are scarcely aware that in those scenes from which the Prince is absent, we are, however, witnessing the influences which have helped to make him what he is. If we are shown members of the *bourgeoisie,* like De Horn and Montade, it is only that we may be better able to contrast the born aristocrat with the born bourgeois; if we are amused at Jojo's sallies and the Duchess' "breaks," it is that the dramatist is furnishing us legitimate amusement and at the same moment directing sidelights on the Prince's character.

3. The play opens with a significant scene: creditors are pressing the Prince. Though we have not yet seen the man himself, we already know something of him. The scene likewise serves to arouse our curiosity: how will D'Aurec extricate himself from his pecuniary difficulties? When he finally enters, he is at once an object of interest. He is himself not long in arousing further interest. His summary disposal of the creditors we know will result in disaster later on. Throughout the play the author, with great skill, alternates scene with

scene, with the hero and without him, but in each we learn something about him.

Are there any scenes in which the character of the Prince ceases to develop? Is there a single superfluous scene in the play?

4. Why are Montade and De Horn so carefully elaborated? What is the purpose of the little scene between the Duchess and the lawyer who years before had asked her to become his wife?

5. Like most French writers, Lavedan is interested in the theory of his art. Several years ago he wrote a short dissertation on dramatic technique.

A dramatist [he said] takes a short trip. One evening he is witness, quite accidentally, of a very dramatic conjugal explanation in the next room [at the hotel]. . . . The dramatist hears everything. The keyhole tempts him; he succumbs and sees all. . . . The scene he witnesses is a terrific one, palpitating with emotion. The dramatist is delighted. What a magnificent scene—ready-made! Here is truth . . . if I could only remember it, write it exactly as it took place, without altering a word, without bothering my head about "style." . . . Thereupon our dramatist . . . puts down on paper . . . without changing a syllable . . . the marvelous scene. . . . Next day he reads over the throbbing words, and something strange happens: As he reads over the fiery passages, it seems to him that they are not quite so ardent, that the dialogue lapses and lags. . . . Why does that scene, which had been lived, . . . fail to stand the test of reading? . . . Here, he says, is the first reason: when, yesterday, I was the fortunate though somewhat culpable witness of that terrible explanation, I knew that it was in earnest . . . that I was beholding life and not a drama. . . . If that same drama were transferred to the stage it ought of course to appeal to me as life appeals to me, because drama is a representation of life (notice, I say "a" representation, not "the" representation). . . . Now, if I wish nothing but life itself, I need not shut myself up in a theater, I have only to look about me and observe. . . . I now begin to understand why my scene in the hotel, so beautiful until it was put upon the stage, becomes cold and wearisome. . . . It lasts, even when read at white heat, one hour and three-quarters. Do you know any scene that long? . . . Ten to twelve minutes are as a rule all that are allowed a dramatist to develop and bring to a climax his "big scene." . . . The actors in any scene from life speak at random . . . without regard for order, form, composition, rules. . . . They never tried to be amusing, . . . they were acting a scene from life itself, . . . there were a thousand incoherent remarks, mistakes of all sorts, of no importance to them, but which, if reproduced in a play, would at once become evident, because *that* is a matter of art, which is subject to necessary rules and regulations. And yet art, if it is to be any but a pretty or futile plaything, must respect life, and not falsify it; it must be rooted in and derived from nothing but life. . . . The dramatist's problem is now so to combine these excellent but diverse elements within the time at his disposal . . . as to form a scene with a beginning, a middle, and an end, rising to a well-defined climax, and falling to a logical close. . . . Life may, in a big dramatic situation, indulge in the luxury of being stupidly irrelevant, the drama may not. . . . Now, in operating upon but not deforming this bit of life, the dramatist . . . has had recourse to technique, that delicate, respect-compelling, difficult and noble process without which he could not have produced a work of art.

Technique, declares Lavedan, is a rearrangement of life. Listen to a conversation—in life—and try to imagine it transferred *direct* to the pages of a novel or a scene in a play. Watch a fight in the street. In both the conversation and the fight you will perceive *elements* of drama, but after pondering the words of the French dramatist you will perceive that technique is—among other things—the art and science of condensation and elimination. The best dialogue (whether in a novel or a play) *sounds* like life, but it is *directed* every moment of the time by the dramatist.

One of the best recent examples of casual-sounding dialogue is in George Kelly's "Show-Off." Read the first ten pages; it is hard to know just where the dialogue is leading us—until some time after it is spoken. Then we see the meaning of every speech and perceive the reason for every line of it.

Maurice Donnay

Maurice Donnay was born in 1854 at Paris, of a well-to-do middle-class family. Although at an early age the young man displayed a liking and some talent for literature, his parents wished him to become a civil engineer. Educated in his native city, he entered a contractor's office in 1885, where he remained for six years. Because he recited some verses of his own in a cabaret on Montmartre, he was forced to resign his position. For two years he appeared at the "Chat Noir," where his graceful and satirical "saynètes"—little verses and dialogues—brought him considerable local popularity. In 1892, "Lysistrata," his first play, was produced at the Grand Théâtre. This adaptation of Aristophanes enjoyed some success, but "Lovers," the play that followed it, immediately gave him national fame. It has remained his best-known and best-loved play. Among Donnay's numerous other plays, all of which deal in one way or another with the relations of the sexes, the most typical are "The Other Danger," "The Return From Jerusalem," and "The Free Woman."

Plays

"They!" (1889)
"Elsewhere" (1891)
"Phryne" (1891)
"Lysistrata" (1892)
"Family Boarding-House" (1894)
"A Mad Enterprise" (1894)
"Accomplices" [with W. Grosclaude] (1895)
"Lovers" (1895)
"The Sad Woman" (1897)
"The Free Woman" (1898)
"Georgette Lemeunier" (1898)
"The Torrent" (1899)
"A Prince's Education" (1900)
"The Clearing" [with L. Descaves] (1900)
"The See-Saw" (1901)
"The Gimlet" (1902)
"The Other Danger" (1902)
"The Return From Jerusalem" (1903)
"The Escalade" (1904)
"Birds of Passage" [with L. Descaves] (1904)
"Appearances" (1906)
"His Guardian Angel" (1908)
"Molière's Household" (1912)
"The Women Scouts" (1913)
"The Impromptu" (1915)
"The Theater With the Armies" (1916)
"The Man-Hunt" (1920)
"The Fair One of Anjou" [with A. Rivoire] (1922)

("Telemachus' Marriage," with J. Lemaître, and "King Candaule," are light opera librettos.)

Editions.—*Lovers, The Free Woman, They!,* trans., with introduction, by Barrett H. Clark (N. Y. 1915), includes the plays mentioned.

Separate Plays.—"The Gimlet," trans. by Barrett H. Clark (*Stratford Journal,* Boston, 1918); "Lysistrata," trans. by H. D. Gibbons (Paris, 1919).

Reprints in Collections and Anthologies.—"The Other Danger" (appears only in this edition, translation by Charlotte T. David) in Clark's *Three Modern Plays From the French* (N. Y. 1914); "Lovers" (Clark translation) in Moses' *Representative Continental Dramas* (Boston, 1924).

REFERENCES

Barrett H. Clark, *Contemporary French Dramatists* (Cincinnati, 1915); F. W. Chandler, *The Contemporary Drama of France* (Boston, 1920); Ludwig Lewisohn, *The Modern Drama* (N. Y. 1915); H. A. Smith, *Main Currents of Modern French Drama* (N. Y. 1925).

See also introductions to the two volumes of translated plays, and biographical material in Moses' *Representative Continental Dramas.*

LOVERS

Comedy in 5 acts (1895). Texts: in *Lovers, The Free Woman, They!* translated by Barrett H. Clark (N. Y. 1915), and same in Moses' *Representative Continental Dramas* (Boston, 1924).

In his Dedication to Molière (affixed to the play "Molière's Household") Donnay writes: "Reassure yourself, Monsieur, we of to-day are far from the old French tellers of tales with their jokes on the subject of infidelity, which you yourself have often retold with so much brightness. . . . The conjugal accident no longer diverts us; it appears to us as a social necessity, yes, a shameful but logical consequence of marriage as it is most frequently practised in the society of our day." "Lovers" is based upon the thesis here enunciated by the author. But it is not a thesis-play: the philosophic undercurrent is no more than what most French writers are apparently unable to avoid in their lightest productions, for (as Donnay once said) "A play is a love-story."

1. Donnay considers a play a love-story. To this brief statement he adds that "since that story is laid in various places we are led to believe that plays differ one from another." An epigram, not a truth of universal application, but interesting as a statement of Donnay's own conception of the drama form. To him the love-story is of supreme importance.

In collecting material for an early book of mine on the French dramatists I had occasion to meet many of the veteran playwrights of the pre-war period:

Scarcely one of them could understand the attitude of the average Anglo-Saxon (toward themselves and their work). When I asked Maurice Donnay which play he would prefer to have translated as a typical example of his work, he replied at once: *"Amants."* I said that the play would not be accepted on the stage . . . and told him that it ran the risk of being criticized on the ground of its immorality. "Why?" he inquired. . . . On another occasion I asked François de Curel why most of his plays were caviar to the French public, and he said that with the exception of his latest play . . . sex played but a minor part in his works. He then added: "The French dramatists treat of love, because it is the only subject which every member of the audience understands, and a dramatist must of course appeal to the masses." I then asked why practically *all* the (French) dramatists kept insisting on the old theme, the triangle, and he repeated what he had said before—and shrugged his shoulders. (From *Contemporary French Dramatists,* 1915.)

"Lovers" is a sophisticated play: situations are taken for granted, an ethical viewpoint indicated, that would require detailed explanations from an English or American playwright. Donnay wrote for audiences that are better trained to accept his situations and viewpoint than are we; but can you imagine the story of "Lovers" handled by Pinero, George M. Cohan, or Booth Tarkington? In what respects does this play differ from "The Second Mrs. Tanqueray"?

2. There are certain works of art that seem to have sprung naturally from the sources of life itself, without the intervention of the hand of man. To many critics—and not alone to Donnay's contemporaries of thirty years ago—"Lovers" has appealed as an example of this sort of work. Ludwig Lewisohn writes: "M. Donnay has found it possible to dispense wholly with plot, with artificial rearrangement of events, with mere cleverness of combination. Like the Germanic playwrights, he simply lets life unfold itself." Mr. Lewisohn's contention is clear, but by implication he seems to condemn "plot" as something artificial, an obstacle, perhaps, to prevent life from unfolding itself. "Plot" is a term open to many interpretations; "story" is almost synonymous. Professor George P. Baker, however (in his *Dramatic Technique*), differentiates "plot" from "story." The latter is "what a play boils down to when you try to tell a friend as briefly as possible what it is

about . . ." but "plot, dramatically speaking, is the story so molded by the dramatist as to gain for him in the theater the emotional response he desires." In other words, "plot" is the theatrical form into which a "story" is put by the dramatist.

Now, "Lovers" certainly has a story, but what does Mr. Lewisohn mean by saying that Donnay dispenses with plot? His statement, it is true, was not applied to this particular play, but "Lovers" has even less "story" than most of the same dramatist's other plays. Can any dramatist altogether "dispense with plot"?

3. Compare "Lovers" with Chekhov's "Seagull" and "The Cherry Orchard." What of the plots in these Russian plays? Has O'Neill's "Emperor Jones" a clearly-defined plot? Do you know any play without a plot?

4. Must a novel have a plot—or story? How about Meredith's "Egoist"?

5. Has "Lovers" any resemblance to the so-called "novelistic" plays of Galdós, especially to his "Duchess of San Quentín"? (*See* pp. 210-211.)

Paul Hervieu

Paul Hervieu was born in 1857 at Neuilly, near Paris. He studied for the Bar, passing his examinations at the age of twenty. After a few years' practice and after refusing a diplomatic post, he began writing short stories and novels, which appeared in the early eighties. His first play was produced in 1890, and five years later "The Nippers" appeared, firmly establishing his reputation. He continued to write for the stage, at the rate of one play about every two years. He was elected to the French Academy in 1900. He died in 1915.

The plays of Hervieu are the most clear-cut examples of the thesis play in the modern theater. With his faultless logic, clear and direct methods of writing, and admirable sincerity, Hervieu comments on and criticizes those phases of life that seem to need correcting—the law, chiefly, and its relation to man and woman in the married state. "The Nippers" is the story of a woman who tries to leave her husband and get a divorce; the husband refuses, until some years later his wife tells him, in a dispute, that he is not the father of the child. Whereupon she refuses to be divorced, in spite of her husband's insistence. The child binds them together. "We are only two miserable beings," she says, "and misery knows none but equals." "The Passing of the Torch" shows the sacrifice of one generation for the next; "The Labyrinth" is an attempt to prove the thesis that the child is the everlasting bond between man and wife. Huneker, one of the first Americans to write about Hervieu, called him "the present master-psychologist of the French stage." But Hervieu's psychology was applied rather to "cases"—hypothetical oftener than not—than to human beings, and to-day his plays leave us rather cold.

Plays

"Point de Lendemain"[4] (1890)
"Words Remain" (1892)
"The Nippers" (1895)
"The Law of Man" (1897)
"The Enigma" (1901)
"The Passing of the Torch" (1901)
"Théroigne de Méricourt" (1902)
"The Labyrinth" (1903)
"The Awakening" (1905)
"Modesty" (1908)
"Know Thyself" (1909)
"Bagatelle" (1912)
"Destiny is Master" (1914)

Editions [*separate plays only*].—"In Chains" [*i.e.* "The Nippers"], translated by Y. Asckenasy (*Poet Lore,* Boston, 1909); same by same translator as "Enchained" (*Dramatist,* Easton, Pa. 1910); "The Trail of the Torch" [*i.e.* "The Passing of the Torch"], introduction by Brander Matthews, trans. by J. A. Haughton (Garden City, 1915); "Modesty," by Barrett H. Clark (N. Y. 1913); "The Labyrinth," by Barrett H. Clark and L. MacClintock (N. Y. 1913).

Reprints in Collections and Anthologies.—"Know Thyself" [appears only in this edition, translation by B. Cerf] in Dickinson's *Chief Contemporary Dramatists* (Boston, 1915); "Modesty" (Clark translation) in Lewis' *Contemporary One-Act Plays* (N. Y. 1922).

References

James Huneker, *Iconoclasts* (N. Y. 1905); William Archer, *Playmaking* (Boston, 1912); F. W. Chandler, *Aspects of Modern Drama* (N. Y. 1914), and *The Contemporary Drama of France* (Boston, 1920); Arthur Symons, *Plays, Acting, and Music* (N. Y. 1909); B. Roland Lewis, *The Technique of the One-Act Play* (Boston, 1918); Ludwig Lewisohn, *The Modern Drama* (N. Y. 1915); Archibald Henderson, *The Changing Drama* (Cincinnati, 1919); H. A. Smith, *Main Currents of Modern French Drama* (N. Y. 1925).

---

[4] A proverbial expression meaning "without consequence," or "with no afterthought."

The Labyrinth

Drama in 5 acts (1903). Text: translation by B. H. Clark and L. MacClintock (N. Y. 1913).

"The Labyrinth" is probably the best specimen of the work of Paul Hervieu. It is obviously the work of a thinker, so scientifically built as to allow the student an exceptional opportunity of understanding this dramatist's methods.

1. "What is a tragedy? It is a play every part of which aims to create suspense, deep thinking, and pity. It is accompanied no longer, as of old, with magnificent draperies; it is a thing of the day, logical, prosaic, no longer bloody . . . the ways of Fate are no longer manifested, as with the Greeks, in dreams, visions, or presentiments. Nowadays we try to show how the struggle for existence bears down inexorably upon those who are imprudent, too weak to defend themselves, those whose passions are stronger than their will power." This is what Hervieu says about tragedy. "The Labyrinth" is considered a good example. Why? What is the tragic element in the "Labyrinth"? With the author's own text as a basis, we may infer that it is tragic because (1) there was imprudence in the making of the divorce laws of France, (2) because the people concerned are, being human, too weak to defend themselves, and (3) "their passions are stronger than their will power." The child inevitably forms the binding link between Max and Marianne, in spite of the fact that the two are incompatible; circumstances arise making it impossible for these parents to live as man and wife. What is to become of the child? The tragedy is the child's tragedy, yet the mother is the greater sufferer.

2. Francisque Sarcey, a famous French critic of the last century, brought into current use a phrase which is quite untranslatable, though the meaning is clear; *Scène à faire.* Literally, a "scene which is made necessary by the exigencies of the plot." Archer (in *Playmaking*) calls it the "obligatory scene," a good equivalent. He says, "An obligatory scene is

one which the audience (more or less clearly and consciously) foresees and desires, and the absence of which it may with reason resent." In Henry Arthur Jones' "Mrs. Dane's Defence," the examination scene in the third act is the obligatory scene; in the "Doll's House," it is the final conversation between Nora and Torvald; in "A Gauntlet" (second version), it is the last scene. In "The Labyrinth," the obligatory scene is that between Max and Marianne, which ends the third act. This seems inevitable; it is, moreover, vital, logical, and, from what had gone before, expected. Not perhaps the outcome, but the clash, the culminating point in the struggle. One interesting question arises at this juncture: Where is the climax? At the end of the third act, or the fourth?

This may be answered by studying the last two acts. If these (the fourth, at least) preserve the suspense, and contain new material, and if, beginning only with the fifth act, the *dénouement* begins, then the climax is at the end of the fourth. Does the fourth act rise or fall? Does it show the result of the foregoing action, or does it carry the unresolved action to a still higher point? Determine that, and you will find the climax.

Returning to the matter of the obligatory scene, look for such scenes in the following plays: Pinero's "His House in Order," Dunsany's "Gods of the Mountain," Tarkington's "Clarence," Maugham's "Circle." There are clearly defined *scènes à faire* in all these plays.

3. We have said that the *dénouement,* in most cases the last act of a play, is the most difficult for the dramatist. The weakest part of the "Labyrinth" is the last two acts. Most French critics are not satisfied with the solution, and blame the dramatist for summarily disposing of Max and Guillaume as he does. Their deaths seem at first a rather facile dramatic expedient. One critic (Paul Flat) thinks it would be best to omit the last act. But this would be inconclusive; the audience ought to have some notion of the fate of the persons in whom they have interested themselves. To leave Marianne in her unbearable "labyrinth," and the two men at each other's throats, would be

unsatisfactory; yet it would be impossible for Marianne to return either to Max or Guillaume. It would be equally bad art and bad psychology to kill Marianne, leaving the child to Max. The men must be got out of the way, both of them. That being the only possible solution of the problem, Hervieu has accomplished his task in a masterly fashion. If you will conceive the situation, you will see that Max and Guillaume are bound, sooner or later, to meet, and that one will kill the other. But that would be worse still; for either the husband or the father of the child would survive. Therefore, by killing both, the author has merely compressed into a conclusive incident what is possible, probable, and logically inevitable.

Thus reason the few sympathetic critics. There is no doubt that the problem set by Hervieu is satisfactorily solved by the double death, but plays ought to do more than satisfy the authors' desire to prove theses. Perhaps the "labyrinth" woven by the French dramatist is one from which no escape was possible? In that event, ought it to have been treated at all?

Eugène Brieux

Eugène Brieux, the son of a carpenter, was born in Paris in 1858. He showed an early liking for literature, and soon took up journalism. He was for some years editor of the *Nouvelliste* at Rouen. It was there that he wrote his earlier plays, sending them to Paris for production. "Artists' Families," one of the first, was accepted and produced by Antoine at the Free Theater (1890) and two years later the same manager brought forth the dramatist's first important success, "Blanchette." Returning to Paris he married and devoted himself to the writing of that series of plays to which he now owes his fame. In 1910 he was elected to membership in the French Academy.

Brieux and Hervieu are among the best exponents of the thesis play in France. Hervieu, we have seen, attacks certain phases of the law, especially those regarding the marriage relation. He attacks, however, in a cold and logical way, proving each step in his argument. Brieux attacks various institutions and prejudices, but always from the standpoint of the sentimentalist and humanitarian, rarely as a psychologist. He declares [5] himself the enemy of every "abuse of power" and all authority, for he believes that men are too fallible to sit in judgment over their fellow-beings. He attacks society because it will not give young girls an opportunity of earning a living by teaching ("Blanchette"); he lays bare the evils of the political "system" ("The Machine"); of charity and its abuses ("The Philanthropists"); of science and its abuse ("The Evasion"); of marriage arrangements ("The Three Daughters of M. Dupont"); of the attitude of secrecy concerning the nature, effects, and cure of the so-called "unmentionable" (venereal) diseases ("Damaged Goods"); in "The Red Robe" he shows how parts of the legal system are inherently evil and corrupt. In "Maternity" he declares war on those who fail to regard motherhood as sacred. In each play, he criticizes some aspect of a living question. He says: [6] "We [the dramatists] must have an idea in our plays . . . taken from the life about us, from among the sufferings of our fellow-beings." Brieux died in 1932.

Plays

"Bernard Palissy" [with G. Salandri] (1880)
"The Divorce Office" [with G. Salandri] (1880)
"Artists' Families" (1890)
"Duramé's Daughter" (1890)
"M. de Réboval" (1892)
"Blanchette" (1892)
"The Brood" (1893)
"The Machine" (1894)
"The Blue Rose" (1895)
"The Philanthropists" (1896)
"The Escape" (1896)
"The Three Daughters of M. Dupont" (1897)
"The School for Mothers-in-Law" [from "The Brood"] (1898)
"Racing Results" (1898)
"The Cradle" (1898)
"The Red Robe" (1900)
"The Substitutes" (1901)
"Damaged Goods" (1902)
"The Little Friend" (1902)
"Maternity" (1903)
"The Deserter" [with Jean Sigaux] (1904)
"The May Beetles" (1906)
"The Frenchwoman" (1907)
"Simone" (1908)
"Suzette" (1909)
"Faith" (1909)
"The Independent Woman" (1912)
"The Bourgeois in the Country" (1914)
"The Americans in France" (1920)
"Three Good Friends" (1921)
"The Lawyer" (1922)
"The Child" ["Pierrette and Galaor"] (1923)
"The Lavolette Family" (1926)

(Brieux dramatized Hervieu's novel *L'Armature*, 1905.)

---

[5] ". . . My method—if such it can be called—consists of crying out against every abuse of power. It is a fact that all forms of power, all authority, arouse my indignation, because in human hands they develop sooner or later into tyranny." Extract from a letter to me, Jan. 5, 1912.

[6] In the *Revue Bleue*, quoted by Bertrand in *E. Brieux* (Paris, 1910).

Editions.—Three Plays by Brieux, trans. by Mrs. Bernard Shaw, St. John Hankin, and John Pollock, with preface by Bernard Shaw (N. Y. 1911), includes "Maternity," 1st version, "The Three Daughters of M. Dupont," "Damaged Goods," and 2nd version of "Maternity"; *Blanchette and The Escape,* by F. Eisemann, preface by H. L. Mencken (Boston, 1913), includes the plays mentioned; *Woman on Her Own, False Gods, and The Red Robe,* by Mrs. Bernard Shaw, J. B. Fagan, and A. B. Miall, with introduction by Brieux (N. Y. 1916), includes the plays mentioned ["Woman on Her Own" is "The Independent Woman," and "False Gods" is "Faith"].

Separate Plays.—"The School for Mothers-in-Law," by W. H. Wright (*Smart Set,* N. Y. 1913), and by E. Goodman (*The International,* N. Y. 1911); "Artists' Families," by B. H. Clark, preface by J. R. Crawford (Garden City, 1918); "Damaged Goods," by John Pollock, preface by Mrs. Bernard Shaw (London, 1914).

Reprint in an Anthology.—"The Red Robe" (translation by F. O. Reed) in Dickinson's *Chief Contemporary Dramatists* (Boston, 1915).

References

P. V. Thomas, *The Plays of Eugène Brieux* (Boston, 1915); W. H. Scheifley, *Brieux and Contemporary French Society* (N. Y. 1917); F. W. Chandler, *Aspects of Modern Drama* (N. Y. 1914), and *The Contemporary Drama of France* (Boston, 1920); Emma Goldmann, *The Social Significance of the Modern Drama* (Boston, 1914); B. H. Clark, *Contemporary French Dramatists* (Cincinnati, 1915), and *Four Plays of the Free Theater* (Cincinnati, 1914); Ashley Dukes, *Modern Dramatists* (Chicago, 1912), and *The Youngest Drama* (Chicago, 1924); William Archer, *Study and Stage* (London, 1899); Archibald Henderson, *The Changing Drama* (Cincinnati, 1919); William Winter, *The Wallet of Time,* Vol. II (N. Y. 1913); A. B. Walkley, *Drama and Life* (N. Y. 1908); Ludwig Lewisohn, *The Modern Drama* (N. Y. 1915); C. Lewis Hind, *More Authors and I* (N. Y. 1922); Arnold Bennett, *Books and Persons* (N. Y. 1917); W. L. Courtney, *Old Saws and Modern Instances* (N. Y. 1918); J. W. Cunliffe and P. de Bacourt, *French Literature During the Last Half-Century* (N. Y. 1923); H. A. Smith, *Main Currents of Modern French Drama* (N. Y. 1925).

See also.—Brieux's prefaces to Clark's *Four Plays of the Free Theater* (Cincinnati, 1914); Clark's *Four Plays by Emile Augier* (N. Y. 1915), and "Woman on Her Own," etc., listed above.

The Three Daughters of M. Dupont

A comedy in 4 acts (1899). Text: translation by St. John Hankin in *Three Plays by Brieux* (N. Y. 1911).

"The Three Daughters of M. Dupont" is not Brieux's best play, but it is representative. The good and bad qualities of this dramatist are more apparent here than in any other of his plays.

This is a thesis play par excellence. The dramatist wishes to expose the evils of the French system of marriage in its bearing upon women. There are three points to be made, and he creates three characters, each illustrating one point. Let us see how every side of the question is handled, and whether the author chooses to suggest any solution to his problem, or merely to show a state of affairs.

1. The exposition is concerned first with the case of Caroline, and when we have received sufficient information to enable us to distinguish her and be ready for the unfolding of her story later on, Julie enters. Notice how clearly (p. 82) these characters are drawn, and differentiated one from the other. Caroline believes that Courthezon has succeeded in his invention "because she prayed for it," and Julie, we learn, has been to see Mme. Leseigneur, for she only goes "to houses where there are children." These indications are supplemented by others (pp. 82, 83), until there is no possibility of the audience forgetting what it is needful they should have in mind. The next character introduced is not the other daughter, but M. Dupont. Brieux might have brought Angèle in as a subject of conversation, but there are two reasons against this procedure: (1) Angèle is not usually mentioned within the family circle, and (2) the scene required variety. The introduction or even the mention of a third daughter so early in the act, would tend to make the play even more diagrammatic than it is. Therefore we learn of the project to marry off Julie, and that the "intended's" parents, the Mairauts, are coming to arrange the marriage. Then (p. 90) Angèle is spoken of, quite naturally, and her story told. The formal proposal for Julie's hand occupies the rest of the first act.

2. When Bernard Shaw says that "in that great comedy which Balzac calls the 'comedy of humanity,' to be played for the amusement of the gods rather than that of the French public, there is no summit in the barren plain that stretches from Mount Molière to our times until we reach Brieux," he must refer to such scenes as that (pp. 97-107) in which the Mairauts and the Duponts make arrangements for their children's union.

This particular scene recalls Molière and Labiche, and, if he had written no others, would entitle Brieux to rank as a writer of true comedy. But can you understand Shaw's absurd statement?

Compare this with scenes similarly treated, in Molière's "Miser" and Labiche's "Dust in the Eyes," and the best plays of Augier, Beaumarchais, and Meilhac and Halévy. But if Shaw, usually a keen and careful critic, really means what he says, read Beaumarchais' "Marriage of Figaro" or Augier and Sandeau's "M. Poirier's Son-in-Law." Do the occasionally comic scenes of Brieux (even in his genuine comedies, like "The Bourgeois in the Country") measure up to the standards of Beaumarchais and Augier?

3. The second act brings us into the presence of Julie's tragedy; this is *her* act. When she says to her husband, "The real evil is that our parents married us as they did marry us. . . . And here we are chained to one another," the case of Julie is nearly disposed of. And when, later on, it is clear that because of the selfishness and sensuality of her husband she is not permitted to have children, her tragedy is complete.

4. The following acts are concerned with the cases of Angèle, who was forced to leave the family because of a "youthful slip"; and of Caroline, who, because of the dowry system, has lost her chances of marriage. The last act brings the story to a close. The lives of the two elder sisters are over, their fate sealed. Julie at least had a chance, and we are given to understand that she will leave her husband later on, when she has an opportunity. "And since to pay for bread to eat and clothes to wear and a roof to cover me I must either give myself to a husband I hate or to a lover whom, perhaps, I may love, I choose the lover." With these words, Julie's chapter closes. The "happy ending," Julie's reconciliation with her husband, is the bitterest part of the play; Julie ostensibly returns to "duty," but she is determined to escape as soon as she can.

The end of one of Brieux's earliest plays, "Blanchette," contains a similarly "happy" catastrophe: the eager young girl who refuses to marry a peasant in the first act is, in the last, owing to circumstances over which she has no control, forced to do so.

5. The trouble with most thesis plays is not the thesis, but the play. There seems to be no valid reason why a play about woman's suffrage or the injustice of the law should not be a good play, but the fact remains that in most cases it is not. This is usually because the dramatist cares more about proving his point than telling the truth about life. Shakespeare teaches; he shows the injustice of the law; he even endeavors to make men better; but his chief concern is with men and women. "It is my nature to preach," says Brieux (quoted in Henderson's *Changing Drama*). . . . "I have always to preach. My plays all have a purpose. That is why I write them. . . . The theater is what attracts people; there you can get them. . . . I want them to think about some of the problems of life. . . ." A frank statement: Brieux brings people into the theater because there he can "get them" to see that "all evil comes from a lack of feeling of responsibility." Which is all very well, only humanity will not always sit in the theater to listen to sermons, because it is particularly hard to be a good preacher and a good artist at the same time.

Edmond Rostand

Edmond Rostand was born in 1868, at Marseilles. His early schooling was received in his native city. He came to Paris and entered the Lycée Stanislas; after his graduation he studied law and received a degree. His first work of any note was a volume of poems, "Les Musardises," which appeared in 1890. Although these refined and skillfully written verses attracted some attention, the poet did not become well known until a few years later. In 1894 his first important play was produced at the Comédie Française; "The Romancers," with its charm and delicate satire, captivated the public and such conservative critics as Sarcey and Lemaître. This little comedy was followed by "The Princess Faraway," which Sarah Bernhardt played in 1895; the same actress also produced "The Woman of Samaria" two years later. In 1897, "Cyrano de Bergerac," with Constant Coquelin in the title rôle, was produced in Paris. "Cyrano" was the greatest theatrical success of modern times. The critics were unanimous in their praise; Emile Faguet, a careful and in some ways conservative critic, writes: "Mon Dieu! M. Rostand, how deeply I appreciate the fact that you exist!" "L'Aiglon," played by Bernhardt, appeared in 1900. The following year the poet was elected to the French Academy. Owing to ill health he left soon after for the South; there, near the Spanish border, he built his villa, where he resided until his death in 1918. "Chantecler," his next play, did not appear until 1910. The play had been too much advertised, and in consequence the audience on the first night was disappointed and not a little puzzled. The production was not a great success, though most of the critics thought it in no way inferior to the earlier works. A little later Bernhardt produced "The Sacred Wood," a pantomime acted to the accompaniment of a poem. Rostand's last work, left unfinished, was "Don Juan's Last Night," produced in 1922.

Rostand has been hailed as the prophet of a great Romantic revival, but since he has no important followers, it is as well to consider his work independently. He is, like Maeterlinck, a more or less isolated phenomenon. His plays are poetic, romantic, charming, and witty; but despite his genuine gift for delightful verse, he is regarded by the more conservative critics as an exceedingly deft craftsman rather than a great poet or a great dramatist. His success in "Cyrano" came at a time when playgoers had forgotten the Romantic traditions, and were beginning to tire of the lifeless "slices of life" served by the earnest followers of Antoine.

Plays

"The Red Glove" (1888)
"The Two Pierrots" (1891)
"The Romancers" (1894)
"The Princess Faraway" (1895)
"The Woman of Samaria" (1897)
"Cyrano de Bergerac" (1897)
"L'Aiglon" (1900)
"Chantecler" (1910)
"The Sacred Wood" (1910)
"Don Juan's Last Night" (1921)

Editions.—Plays of Edmond Rostand, trans. by H. D. Norman, 2 vols. (N. Y. 1921), includes "The Romantics" [*i.e.* "The Romancers"], "The Princess Faraway," "The Woman of Samaria, "Cyrano de Bergerac," "The Eaglet" [*i.e.* "L'Aiglon"], and "Chantecler."

Separate Plays.—"The Romancers," trans. by Mary Hendee (N. Y. 1899, and reprints, Boston, no date), by Barrett H. Clark (N. Y. 1915), and by George Fleming as "The Fantasticks" (N. Y. 1900); "La Princesse Lointaine" ["The Princess Faraway"], by Charles Renauld (N. Y. 1899), and by A. E. Bagstad (Boston, 1921); "Cyrano de Bergerac," by Gertrude Hall (N. Y. 1898), by Gladys Thomas and M. F. Guillemard (N. Y. 1900), by Charles Renauld (N. Y. 1898), by H. T. Kingsbury (Boston, 1898), by Helen B. Dole (N. Y. no date), and by Brian

Hooker (N. Y. 1923); "L'Aiglon," by L. N. Parker (N. Y. 1900); "Chantecler," by Gertrude Hall (N. Y. 1910); "Weeping Pierrot and Laughing Pierrot" [*i.e.* "The Two Pierrots"], by Amy Lowell (N. Y. 1914); same, as "The Two Pierrots," by V. and F. Vernon, in *Modern One-Act Plays From the French* (N. Y. 1934); "The Last Night of Don Juan," by T. L. Riggs (Yellow Springs, O., 1929).

Reprints in Collections and Anthologies.—"Cyrano de Bergerac" (Hall trans.) in Dickinson's *Chief Contemporary Dramatists, II* (Boston, 1921), the same in Moses' *Representative Continental Dramas* (Boston, 1924); "The Romancers" (Clark trans.) in Smith's *Short Plays* (N. Y. 1924).

References

Barrett H. Clark, *Contemporary French Dramatists* (Cincinnati, 1915); F. W. Chandler, *The Contemporary Drama of France* (Boston, 1920), and *Aspects of Modern Drama* (N. Y. 1914); G. K. Chesterton, *Varied Types* (N. Y. 1905); Augustin Filon, *Modern French Drama,* trans. by C. J. Hogarth (N. Y. 1898); E. E. Hale, Jr., *Dramatists of To-day* (N. Y. 1905); Norman Hapgood, *The Stage in America* (N. Y. 1899); Ludwig Lewisohn, *The Modern Drama* (N. Y. 1915); C. F. Nirdlinger, *Masques and Mummers* (N. Y. 1899); George Jean Nathan, *The World in Falseface* (N. Y. 1923); W. L. Phelps, *Essays on Modern Dramatists* (N. Y. 1921); J. T. Grein, *Premières of the Year* (London, 1900), *Dramatic Criticism* (London, 1899), and *Dramatic Criticism,* Vol. III (London, 1902); Clayton Hamilton, *Seen on the Stage* (N. Y. 1920); T. S. Eliot, *The Sacred Wood* (N. Y. 1921); William Winter, *The Wallet of Time,* 2 vols. (N. Y. 1913); H. A. Smith, *Main Currents of Modern French Drama* (N. Y. 1925).

Cyrano de Bergerac

Heroic comedy in 5 acts (1897). Texts: translation by Gertrude Hall (N. Y. 1898); by Gladys Thomas and M. F. Guillemard (N. Y. 1900); by Chas. Renauld (N. Y. 1898); by H. T. Kingsbury (Boston, 1898); by Helen B. Dole (N. Y. no date); by Brian Hooker (N. Y. 1923); and by H. D. Norman, in *Plays of Edmond Rostand,* 2 volumes (N. Y. 1921); Hall translation reprinted in Dickinson's *Chief Contemporary Dramatists,* second series (Boston, 1921), and in Moses' *Representative Continental Dramas* (Boston, 1924).

"Cyrano de Bergerac" is one of the most celebrated modern plays. Its success throughout Europe and America is attributable to the sympathetic and ingratiating Cyrano himself, to its embodiment of the spirit of romance, and its inexhaustible wit. The poetry is not of much importance, for the play succeeds in poor translations.

1. The exposition is exceptionally brilliant; it would be difficult to name another play in which the historical atmosphere is

so admirably created. Compare, by way of contrast, the wholly adequate but direct and businesslike exposition of "Hedda Gabler."

About the first entrance of the principal character: this usually comes some minutes *after* the rise of the curtain, because (1) the attention required to grasp the main facts of the exposition must not be diverted by the appearance of the "star," (2) the "star" is especially anxious to have the audience know who he (or she) is, in order that he (or she) may not be bothered by explaining the matter; and (3) he—or she—must appear at an effective moment.[7] Avoiding the conventional entrance—as, for instance, a dramatic appearance at the back of the stage—Rostand brings in Cyrano unperceived and finally, when it is feared that he is absent, a voice from the multitude shouts, "Rascal, have I not forbidden you to appear for a month?" Soon "a hand holding a cane rises up over the heads of the spectators," then "the cane is shaken," and at length Cyrano "stands up suddenly, standing on a chair, his arms crossed, his beaver cocked fiercely, his moustache bristling, his nose terrible to see." A novel entrance and very effective because of its utter unexpectedness, both to the audience on the stage and to that in the theater.

2. In all Rostand's plays we find long and elaborate speeches, tirades of a kind dear to the heart of every actor: the best of these are in "Cyrano," "L'Aiglon" and "Chantecler." These speeches were written for Coquelin and Bernhardt. That is to say, they were deliberately intended for these actors because of their ability to declaim them in a highly dramatic manner.

Every theatrical production is a collaboration.[8] Rostand, like most dramatists, writes for his actors, and Coquelin in par-

[7] Compare the opening acts of Dumas *fils*' "Lady With the Camellias" (Camille), Pinero's "Second Mrs. Tanqueray," and Tarkington's "Clarence."

[8] There is no use in arguing here the long controversy as to whether a play is a play if it is not acted. I am here referring to acted plays. It is nonsense to declare that a play in MS. or a book is not a play, and that the mere fact of production—*any* production—gives it life and being. (See my pamphlet, *The Modern Drama,* and Ashley Dukes' *Drama.*

ticular was of invaluable service to him. Coquelin was perfectly aware of his own powers and shortcomings, and the poet wrote more or less to order; Coquelin could deliver long speeches full of bravado, humorous and pathetic, and such speeches Rostand wrote for him. In "Cyrano," Coquelin wanted a death scene, and a death scene was prepared for him. This collaboration is extremely helpful for author and actor, and in the cases we are now considering, justifiable and successful. Shakespeare did the same thing, and most modern dramatists have at least the actor or actress in view whom they wish to interpret the principal characters in their plays. In certain plays of Henry Arthur Jones—"Mrs. Dane's Defence," "The Liars," "The Case of Rebellious Susan"—there are rôles known as "Wyndham" rôles, written especially for Sir Charles; many of Sardou's plays—"La Tosca," "Theodora," "Gismonda," "Cleopatra," "The Sorceress"—were written to order for Bernhardt; most of Clyde Fitch's plays were written for particular actresses—"The Truth" for Clara Bloodgood, "Her Own Way" for Maxine Elliott, and "The Stubbornness of Geraldine" for Mary Mannering. Owing to the "star" system in America, the public often speaks of "Mrs. Fiske's play" or "Otis Skinner's" rather than that of the author. But collaboration may have a disastrous effect on both collaborators: the play may suffer from over-emphasis on the principal character, and the actor place too much importance upon himself and his rôle. Sardou was a poorer dramatist because of his association with Bernhardt, while that actress often sacrificed the play to her own individuality, to the detriment of both the play and her own art. Richard Mansfield ruined many good plays—"Julius Cæsar" among them—because he considered Mansfield of greater importance than the work he was ostensibly interpreting.

3. "Cyrano" is a richly varied and highly elaborated work; the numerous scenes and large cast constitute a broad canvas. But there is unity throughout, in the figure of Cyrano. When he is not on the stage the memory of him remains (a speech or a "gesture," perhaps), and if we are not thinking of what he did

last we are looking forward to what he will do next. Analyze a few scenes taken at random and see just how the poet does this.

4. We have already spoken of the "rule" about keeping a secret from the audience. If a secret is long withheld from them,[9] they become impatient. Paul Hervieu's "Enigma" keeps a secret to the end, and when it is known, there is nothing but the solution to satisfy us; the time spent in wondering who is guilty (one of two women is unfaithful to her husband) might much better have been devoted to the enjoyment of character analysis. Charles Lamb's play, "Mr. H.," preserves the mystery of the hero's name until the very last, and when the revelation is made—the name is Hogsflesh—there is little satisfaction. Further, when once an audience learns the secret—as they did in the case of Lamb's play on the first night—the element of surprise, upon which the play is based, is gone.

Little surprises and unforeseen events, however, are legitimate; the long-lost relative, the discovery of a forgotten letter, may be used with impunity—if any one should dare to employ such relics of "Sardoodledom" in this sophisticated age—were unquestionably dramatic in their day—as they often are in ours. The point is that these surprises are pleasant and legitimate so long as they do not interfere with the more serious business of plot or characterization. In the dramatization of Jules Verne's "Tour of the World in Eighty Days" there is a splendid instance of surprise: the eighty days are up, and Fogg has apparently lost his wager that he could make the trip in that time. But at the last moment he learns that he has gained a day in his tour, because of his race "with the sun"—a fact forgotten by him and by the audience; the surprise is genuine and the pleasure spontaneous. In "Cyrano" (Act IV) Roxane's entrance is indeed unexpected, but as her coming is not of prime importance, and as her identity is not long hidden, there is practically no suspense, only a momentary surprise. These are instances where the audience are kept in ignorance,

[9] *See* Archer, *Playmaking,* and the same critic's article, "The God-like Playgoer," *Morning Leader* (London, September 24, 1910).

and are genuinely surprised; their attention is not diverted from the play itself, and consequently the play does not suffer. If, however, a secret is kept from the *characters*, but is known to the audience, our enjoyment is usually greater. We in the audience know that Hamlet is going to fail: it is foreordained; and we know that Œdipus will struggle in vain against the decrees of Fate—but neither Hamlet nor Œdipus is aware of his impending tragedy. That knowledge on the part of the audience gives them the feeling of superiority of which Archer speaks, and makes of each individual a "God-like Spectator."

5. Why should Cyrano die? The play is called a "heroic comedy," yet it ends in death. Now, it may be urged that Coquelin wished to have a death scene; but Rostand was too much an artist to spoil his play for the sake of his desire to please even so distinguished an actor as his friend Coquelin. Further, the death of Cyrano is hardly an ordinary death; it is rather the crowning event of his heroic life. He was ever unlucky, it was his fate to "be the prompter—and be forgotten," and his death is a fitting end to his life; yet—and this consoles us for his death—he bears away "unsmirched" his plume: the symbol of his honor.

Still, is the death of Cyrano logical? If there had been no Coquelin and the play were written for no actor in particular, do you think Rostand would have killed off his hero?

When he came to write "Chantecler," and portray a character similar to that of Cyrano, he let him live and triumph.

Chantecler

Play in 4 acts (1910). Texts: translation by Gertrude Hall (N. Y. 1910); and by H. D. Norman in *Plays of Edmond Rostand,* 2 volumes (N. Y. 1921).

When "Chantecler" appeared, the earliest verdict seemed to be that it was not up to the author's standard, and it was not so great a stage success as the earlier plays. To the public the play was confusing. This was largely due to the symbolism and partly to the very brilliant quality of its style, more involved and much more difficult than the poet's other plays. "Chantecler" is a more mature work, deeper in its spiritual implication than either "Cyrano" or "L'Aiglon"; it deals with human aspirations and struggles, and is not primarily concerned with a story. It is a modern play, the only one Rostand ever wrote, and marks a turning point in his artistic development; it proves that during the ten years between the production "L'Aiglon" and that of "Chantecler" he was not content with the ephemeral celebrity to be won by the manufacture of popular successes.

"Chantecler" is, in the author's own words, the "drama of human endeavor grappling with life."

1. Has the poet selected the best medium of expression for his theme? Rostand has answered this question and explained his intentions himself in the following words:[10]

> I wished to write a modern play in verse. Now the lyrical qualities of a poetic production do not go well with the modern suit and the commonplace frock coat. It needs the additional costume. One must turn back for this two or three centuries, at least, or be obliged to set the play in countries of which the customs, language, and interests are very far from our own. But a poet may have the desire to express modern ideas with a modern vocabulary, to allude to happenings of the day the most Parisian, to laugh as one laughs on the boulevard in 1910, and to think as one thinks in France in the twentieth century. A problem difficult to solve! The sight of my barnyard at Cambo immediately offered me a solution. Why, here was the costume dreamt of—if one can say so!—here indeed was the means of remaining modern, and at the same time that of being picturesque and lyrical. Characters garbed in animal dress, expressing themselves like human beings—like the Parisians of the day. What a find! And furthermore, what an opportunity to speak of things in nature, to be deeply moved by flowers, birds, the bits of grass, or the insect—and what a setting!—No, really, the poet could not wish for a more beautiful theme!

But was it "a find"? Do you feel that the undoubtedly clever device of putting characters "in animal dress" is entirely successful?

---

[10] In *The Story of Chantecler,* by M. F. Liberma.

Let us see how Rostand has succeeded. The play contains nothing very novel in the way of technical treatment; its merits are largely lyrical and poetic. As we are concerned here mainly with the technical side of the question, we shall inquire into how the author has built his play, and developed his ideas.

The exposition is somewhat helped by the Prelude, or prologue, which creates the atmosphere. It is indeed almost wholly atmospheric. The exposition proper merely intensifies the atmosphere and then introduces the characters. There is practically nothing of the past that needs to be known; the action starts on the stage, before our eyes. The Turkey and the Blackbird are soon sketched in, then Chantecler comes, singing his Hymn to the Sun: Patou sounds a note of warning and foreshadows Chantecler's struggle, sowing seeds of doubt in his mind. The Pheasant Hen arrives, Chantecler is captivated by her brilliant plumage, and the love motif has begun. There remains only the setting in motion of the wheels of action and the placing of the opposing forces; these are the birds of the night, and the Blackbird, all conspiring against Chantecler. What will happen to him?

2. Of the themes announced in the first act, two are developed in the second: the conspiracy against Chantecler and the love of Chantecler and the Pheasant Hen. Chantecler voices his profession of faith, and is eventually prevailed upon to tell her his secret.

How are these themes developed?

3. The third act is an elaborate exposition of the fatuousness of the enemies of Chantecler. Chantecler is the poet, the worker, the embodiment of all that is best in the French character. His enemies are the "Blagueurs," the faddists, the philistines. The "Guinea-hen's Reception" is a satire on faddism; into the midst of this scene comes the real enemy of Chantecler, the mercenary who will overcome him by physical force. The fight between the two is the climax of the play, and Chantecler's moment of triumph—when he protects the barnyard against the Hawk—its culminating point. But he must leave his old barnyard, "to save his soul." The struggle is over, and the opposing forces,

chief among them the fighting cock who in a fury cut one claw with the other, are vanquished.

There remains only the *dénouement*. What will Chantecler do? How will his love for the Pheasant Hen end? In the last act we know these questions will be answered.

4. The Pheasant Hen's jealousy of Chantecler's power, and his own idea that his song causes the sun to rise, induce her to put Chantecler's faith to the test. The momentary disillusion is a bitter disappointment, for the sun rises independently of Chantecler's "Cocorico!"; it is also cruel for him to hear a voice sweeter than his own, the Nightingale's, but his faith in himself and his own small mission renews his self-confidence, and leaves him bigger and stronger than he was in his earlier parochial surroundings, that unquestioned lord of the little barnyard that was after all only a small and unimportant corner of the world.

5. Could the story, the characters and theme, have been set in a modern framework without the loss of a great deal that now charms us in this play?

THE BELGIAN DRAMA

THE BELGIAN DRAMA

There is no such continuous and dramatic tradition in Belgium as there is, for instance, in France, and in classifying Maeterlinck as a Belgian I am doing so largely because of the spirit of his work, although he writes in the French language.

"Properly speaking, while there has existed a Belgian theater for many years, there are few signs of a truly native Belgian drama. The Belgian theater has to a great extent depended upon traveling companies from Paris, or else produced Parisian plays with its own native troupes.... To such dramatists as sought a livelihood through their art, Belgium had little to offer. Gustave Vanzype . . . says that he who writes in Belgium, especially for the theater (where he can hope for nothing except the satisfaction of having created and of having at great cost deserved the esteem of the very small public interested in such things), is inspired by the ambition to be an artist himself."[1]

Many Belgian writers have written plays for the theater, but the most successful of them—like Crommelynck, Maeterlinck, and the authors of "The Marriage of Mlle. Beulemans"—have not remained in their own country.

Most of the Belgian playwrights are unknown to readers of English: Charles Van Lerberghe, whose "On the Scent" offers a striking parallel to Maeterlinck's early work; Henri Maubel, Edmond Picard, poets and novelists who have tried their hands at the drama—have not been translated. François Léonard and François-Charles Morisseaux, Henri Liebrecht, who have all written plays, are unknown save to Belgians and a few others who read French. Sylvain Bonmariage is well known in Paris, while Fernand Wicheler and Franz Fonson became famous there over a decade ago through their amusing comedy, "The Marriage of Mlle. Beulemans." Henri Davignon has written patriotic

---

[1] Excerpts from my article on "Belgian Drama," in the New York *Evening Post*, 1918.

plays that are none the less distinctive. The well-known novelists Georges Eckhoud and Eugène Demolder have likewise experimented, but their plays are the products of literary rather than dramatic impulses.

The poet Emile Verhaeren has been exceptionally fortunate in having Arthur Symons as a translator. "The Dawn" and "The Cloister" are his best-known plays; these and two others are available in English.

But the two most interesting of the professional playwrights are Fernand Crommelynck—whose plays have recently achieved popular success in Paris—and Gustave Vanzype. Nothing of Crommelynck has yet been translated, and of Vanzype only two plays—"Mother Nature" and "Progress"; of Rodenbach only "The Veil."

Horace Van Offel and Paul Spaak were some years ago known as the "promising" young men of the theater. Van Offel's "Intellectuals" and "Victory" are good examples of Belgian dramaturgy. Spaak's "Kaatje" is a powerful peasant tragedy.

There is no book in English on the Belgian drama. Jethro Bithell's *Belgian Literature* and Turquet Milne's work on *Belgian Writers* contain brief chapters on the drama.

Maurice Maeterlinck

Maurice Maeterlinck was born of a Flemish family of ancient descent, at Ghent, Belgium, in 1862. In accordance with the wishes of his parents he studied law, and even practiced for some time in his native city. But in 1886 he left Belgium for Paris, and there made the acquaintance of writers who were later to exercise considerable influence over him; among these was Villiers de l'Isle Adam. It was he who, according to Maeterlinck, directed him "toward the spiritual, poetic and mysterious side of things." In 1889, after his return to Belgium on the death of his father, he published his first work, a volume of poems—*Serres Chaudes*—and the "Princess Maleine," the play that called forth the extravagant praise of Octave Mirbeau, who called Maeterlinck "A Belgian Shakespeare." Until 1896 he spent most of his time in Belgium writing plays, a few poems, and making translations from the English. In that year he returned to Paris. From that time forward he devoted himself to his life work, which comprises a number of philosophical works.

Although Maeterlinck writes in French, he does not belong to what is loosely termed the French school of dramatists. He is in some respects the disciple of Poe and Emerson, both of whom played an important part in his development. As playwright, mystic, symbolist, and philosopher, he has exerted an enormous influence over a host of other writers, some of whom have made good use of his theories, while others have reduced them to absurdity. Briefly, he has tried to express moods, subconscious and half-realized feelings, and in order to do so he has created the so-called "Static" drama, the drama of situation and atmosphere.

In *The Treasure of the Humble* he makes clear his position regarding this new form: "I have grown to believe that an old man, seated in his arm-chair, waiting patiently, with his lamp beside him; giving unconscious ear to all the eternal laws that reign about his house, interpreting, without comprehending, the silence of doors and windows and the quivering voice of the light, submitting with bent head to the presence of his soul and his destiny—an old man who conceives not that all the powers of this world, like so many heedful servants, are mingling and keeping vigil in his room, who suspects not that the very sun itself is supporting in space the little table against which he leans, or that every star in heaven and every fiber of the soul are directly concerned in the movement of an eyelid that closes, or a thought that springs to birth—I have grown to believe that he, motionless as he is, does yet live in reality a deeper, more human, and more universal, life than the lover who strangles his mistress, the captain who conquers in battle, or 'the husband who avenges his honor.'"

Maeterlinck's later development has made necessary a modification of the statement that his chief contribution to the modern drama is the invention of the Static play. He himself realizes the futility of arbitrary classifications and, in a letter to me, makes clear his own ideas on the subject: "You must not attach too great importance to the expression 'Static'; it was an invention, a theory of my youth, worth what most literary theories are worth—that is, almost nothing. Whether a play be *static,* or *dynamic, symbolistic,* or *realistic,* is of little consequence. What matters is that it be well written, well thought out, human and, if possible, superhuman, in the deepest significance of the term. The rest is mere rhetoric."

Plays

"The Princess Maleine" (1889)
"The Blind" (1890)
"The Intruder" (1890)
"The Seven Princesses" (1891)
"Pelléas and Mélisande" (1892)
"Alladine and Palomides" (1894)
"Interior" (1894)
"The Death of Tintagiles" (1894)
"Aglavaine and Sélysette" (1896)
"Sister Beatrice" (1900)
"Ardiane and Barbe-bleue" (1901)
"Monna Vanna" (1903)
"Joyzelle" (1903)
"The Miracle of St. Anthony" (1903)
"The Blue Bird" (1908)
"Mary Magdalene" (1913)
"The Betrothal" (1918)
"The Burgomaster of Stilemonde" (1918)
"The Cloud That Lifted" (1923)
"The Power of the Dead" (1923)
"Berniquel" (1923)
"Marie Victoire" (1929)
"Juda de Kerioth" (1929)

Editions.—The Plays of Maurice Maeterlinck, 2 vols. (Chicago, 1894-1896), trans. by Richard Hovey and later reprinted in various editions as below, includes "Princess Maleine," "The Intruder," "The Blind," "The Seven Princesses," "Alladine and Palomides," "Pelléas and Mélisande," "Home" [*i.e.* "Interior"] and "The Death of Tintagiles." *Pelléas and Mélisande, Alladine and Palomides, Home* [*i.e. Interior*], by Richard Hovey, includes the plays mentioned (N. Y. 1911); *The Intruder, The Blind, The Seven Princesses, The Death of Tintagiles,* by Richard Hovey (N. Y. 1911), includes the plays mentioned; *Joyzelle, Monna Vanna,* trans. by A. T. de Mattos and Alfred Sutro (N. Y. 1907), includes the plays mentioned; *Sister Beatrice and Ardiane and Barbe-bleue,* by Bernard Miall (N. Y. 1902), includes the plays mentioned; *The Princess Maleine and The Intruder,* by Gérard Harry and William Wilson (London, 1892), includes the plays mentioned; *Pelleas and Melisanda and The Sightless* [*i.e. The Blind*], by Laurence Alma-Tadema (London, no date), includes the plays mentioned; *The Blind, The Intruder,* by Mary Vielé (Washington, 1891), includes the plays mentioned; *Three Little Dramas for Marionettes,* trans. by Alfred Sutro and William Archer (London, 1899), includes "Interior," "The Death of Tintagiles," and "Alladine and Palomides"; the same with preface by Granville Barker (London and N. Y. 1911); *A Miracle of St. Anthony and Five Other Plays,* anonymous translation (N. Y. 1917), includes the play mentioned, "Pelléas and Mélisande," "The Death of Tintagiles," "Alladine and Palomides," "Interior," and "The Intruder"; *The Cloud That Lifted and The Power of the Dead,* by F. M. Atkinson (N. Y. 1923), includes the plays mentioned.

Separate Plays.—"Princess Maleine," trans. by Richard Hovey (N. Y. 1911); "The Sightless" [*i.e.* "The Blind"], by Charlotte Porter and Helen Clarke (*Poet Lore,* Boston, 1893); "The Seven Princesses," by William Metcalfe (London, no date), and by Charlotte Porter and Helen Clarke (*Poet Lore,* Boston, 1894); "Pelléas and Mélisande," by E. Winslow, with preface by M. J. Moses (N. Y. 1908), and by Charlotte Porter and Helen Clarke (*Poet Lore,* Boston, 1894); "Alladine and Palomides," by the same (*Poet Lore,* Boston, 1895), by R. R. Johnson and N. Erichson (Chicago, 1899), and by Alfred Sutro (London, 1907); "Interior," by William Archer (London, 1908); "The Death of Tintagiles," by Alfred Sutro (London, 1908); "Aglavaine and Sélysette," by Alfred Sutro (N. Y. 1911)—in earlier editions, to 1904, with introduction by J. W. Mackail, later by Sutro—and by Charlotte Porter and Helen Clarke (*Poet Lore,* Boston, 1903); "The Intruder," anonymously (London, 1892; revised edition, 1913); "Monna Vanna," by Alfred Sutro (N. Y. 1907), by A. I. du P. Coleman (N. Y. 1903), and by Charlotte Porter (*Poet Lore,* Boston, 1904); "Joyzelle," by C. Stratton (*Poet Lore,* Boston, 1905); "The Blue Bird," by A. T. de Mattos (N. Y. 1909, and with a new act, 1912); "Mary Magdalene," by the same (N. Y. 1910); "The Betrothal," by the same (N. Y. 1918); "The Miracle of Saint Anthony," by the same (N. Y. 1918); "The Burgomaster of Stilemonde," by the same (N. Y. 1918); "Sister Beatrice," anonymous translation (*Anglo-Saxon Review,* London, 1900).

Reprints in Collections and Anthologies.—"Pelléas and Mélisande" (Hovey translation) in Dickinson's *Chief Contemporary Dramatists* (Boston, 1915); "The Intruder" (anonymous translation, London, 1892) in Shay and Loving's *Fifty Contemporary One-Act Plays* (Cincinnati, 1920), and (anonymous translation) in Cohen's *One-Act Plays by Modern Authors* (N. Y. 1921); "The Blind" (Hovey translation) in Moses' *Representative One-Act Plays by Continental Authors* (Boston, 1923); "The Death of Tintagiles" (anonymous translation), in Shay's *Treasury of Plays for Women* (Boston, 1923); "Interior" (Archer translation) in Shay's *Twenty-Five Short Plays (International)* (N. Y. 1925).

References

Jethro Bithell, *Life and Writings of Maurice Maeterlinck* (N. Y. 1913); Gérard Harry, *Maurice Maeterlinck,* trans. by A. Allinson (London, 1910); Montrose J. Moses, *Maurice Maeterlinck, a Study* (N. Y. 1911); Edward Thomas, *Maurice Maeterlinck* (N. Y. 1911); Macdonald Clark, *Maurice Maeterlinck, Poet and Philosopher* (N. Y. 1916); Una Taylor, *Maurice Maeterlinck, a Critical Study* (N. Y. 1915); Henry Rose, *On Maeterlinck: or Notes on the Study of Symbols* (London, 1911), and *Maeterlinck's Symbolism* (N. Y. 1911); W. L. Courtney, *The Development of Maurice Maeterlinck,* etc. (London, 1904); E. E. Hale, Jr., *Dramatists of To-day* (N. Y. 1905); James Huneker, *Iconoclasts* (N. Y. 1905); Ashley Dukes, *Modern Dramatists* (Chicago, 1912); Arthur Symons, *The Symbolist Movement in Literature* (N. Y. 1917), *Plays, Acting and Music* (N. Y. 1909), and *Dramatis Personæ* (Indianapolis, 1923); Edwin Björkman, *Voices of Tomorrow* (N. Y. 1913); Archibald Henderson, *European Dramatists* (Cincinnati, 1913), and *The Changing Drama* (Cincinnati, 1919); G. K. Chesterton, *Varied Types* (N. Y. 1905); Holbrook Jackson, *Romance and Reality* (London, 1911); A. Thorold *Six Masters in Disillusion* (N. Y. 1909); A. B. Walkley, *Frames of Mind* (London, 1899); B. H. Clark, *European Theories of the Drama* (Cincinnati, 1918); C. Lewis Hind, *Authors and I* (N. Y. 1921); Percival Wilde, *The Craftsman-*

ship of the One-Act Play (Boston, 1923); R. de Gourmont, *The Book of Masks* (Boston, 1921); William Lyon Phelps, *Essays on Modern Dramatists* (N. Y. 1921); Otto Heller, *Prophets of Dissent* (N. Y. 1918); Ludwig Lewisohn, *The Modern Drama* (N. Y. 1915); F. W. Chandler, *Aspects of Modern Drama* (N. Y. 1914), and *The Contemporary Drama of France* (Boston, 1920); H. M. Walbrook, *Nights at the Play* (London, 1911); John Freeman, *The Moderns* (N. Y. 1917); George Jean Nathan, *Comedians All* (N. Y. 1919); Solomon Eagle, *Books in General,* third series (N. Y. no date); Frank Harris, *Contemporary Portraits,* I (N. Y. 1915); Mrs. Patrick Campbell, *My Life and Some Letters* (N. Y. 1922); Vance Thompson, *French Portraits* (N. Y. 1913); H. A. Smith, *Main Currents of Modern French Drama* (N. Y. 1925); Georgette Leblanc, *Souvenirs, My Life with Maeterlinck* (N. Y. 1932); T. H. Dickinson, *The Theater in a Changing Europe* (N. Y. 1937).

See also.—Maeterlinck's *Treasure of the Humble* (N. Y. 1897), *Wisdom and Destiny* (N. Y. 1898), *The Buried Temple* (N. Y. 1902), *The Measure of the Hours* (N. Y. 1907), *The Double Garden* (N. Y. 1904), and Clark's *European Theories of the Drama* (Cincinnati, 1918).

Pelléas and Mélisande

Play in 5 acts (1892). Texts: Hovey translation in the *Plays,* 2 vols. (Chicago, 1894-1896), and reprinted in *Pelléas and Mélisande, etc.* (N. Y. 1911); Alma-Tadema translation in *Pelleas and Melisanda, etc.* (London, no date); E. Winslow translation (N. Y. 1908); Porter and Clarke translation (*Poet Lore,* Boston, 1894); and reprint of Hovey translation in Dickinson's *Chief Contemporary Dramatists* (Boston, 1915) and in Dickinson's *Continental Plays,* I (Boston, 1935).

"Pelléas and Mélisande" is the first of Maeterlinck's plays with a simple and conventionally well-developed plot. "The Princess Maleine" was a phantasmagoria, disjointed and obscure; "The Intruder," "The Blind," and "The Seven Princesses," were "Static" mood-pictures without stories. "Pelléas and Mélisande," besides showing a great advance in plot construction, contains unmistakable indications of the development of the poet's power to delineate character. What were mere marionettes in the earlier plays, so strange and far-away that they could evince little else than wonder, become in this play flesh and blood. Mélisande is a human being, capable of arousing our sympathies.

1. "Pelléas" was, then, a new departure for Maeterlinck. He realizes that the drama cannot be static and living at once, he feels the shortcomings of his earlier efforts.

In order fully to understand this progress the student must note carefully what parts of "Pelléas and Mélisande" belong to the "early" period, and what are new. Compare "The Intruder" with the present play, and determine in what respects the later play differs from it. Then, in connection with "Monna Vanna," notice how the dramatist, having emerged from the shadowy dream-world of "Pelléas," is at pains to humanize and vitalize his characters.

In "The Intruder" do you find any external incident, important in itself, which would be visible in a stage representation, rather than as a mere indication of what is going on in the mind of the character? What scenes in "Pelléas" are independent of the rest of the play, yet interesting and effective in themselves?

In "The Blue Bird" do you notice any technical advance over "Pelléas and Mélisande"? Over "Monna Vanna"?

2. This play is so evanescent in mood, so saturated with romance, that it must necessarily suffer from technical analysis. The suggestions here given should therefore be carried out only after a sympathetic reading. Like most of Maeterlinck's plays, it is more interesting as a study of atmosphere, an evocation of the subconscious self, than as acted drama.

Charles Lamb once remarked that "King Lear" was too great to be played; an old man in a false beard, his ravings accompanied by rumblings of thunder made by beating upon a sheet of tin, could not but spoil the effect of transcendent greatness produced by a reading of the play. The case of Maeterlinck is somewhat analogous. Many scenes in "The Blue Bird," even in the pseudo-intelligent productions in America and France, were nearly ruined; the moment "The Land of Memory" is put on the stage (and the "set" designed for the Moscow Art Theater was thoroughly adequate) Maeterlinck's "Land of Memory," created in the imagination of the sensitive reader, vanishes. "The Kingdom of the Future," as played by children and women acting as children, often verges on the ridiculous.

If certain plays are less beautiful, or less dramatic, on the stage than when they are read, are they, then, plays? According to the theories and definitions of critics, a play must be presented by actors on a stage, before an audience.

In one of the books on which the present volume is based, the names of Gordon Craig and two or three others were mentioned among the pioneers in stagecraft. In that illuminating magazine, *The Mask,* my book was reviewed and I was taken to task because I had dared assert (with Lamb and Maeterlinck) that some plays were either too great or too delicate for stage performance, and that the problems involving their proper production were as yet unsolved. "We should like," so runs the criticism, "to know what 'problems' Mr. Clark can have in mind or could propose with which the competent stage manager is unable to cope. There might certainly be some which would scare the mere 'impresario,' but the *practical* stage director can always be relied upon to 'find a way or make one,' and Mr. Clark, if he feels doubtful of this, might propose some of his 'problems,' and 'let the end try the man.'"

Such "problems" *were* proposed, and my point elucidated, but as my letter was neither answered nor printed, I have forgotten the details of the argument. However, I am perfectly willing to "let the end try the man," the only man capable of encompassing it, Gordon Craig himself, a distinguished artist and prophet. I wonder if Mr. Craig has yet realized all his wonderful dreams? If he can honestly say he has, then he is not the artist I think him. Are not the greatest emotions inexpressible, the greatest pictures unpainted, the greatest plays not only unproduced, but unwritten?

After all, my point was not that these particular plays of Maeterlinck are so great that they ought not to be seen on the stage, but that what is most suggestive and elusive is either altogether lost or hopelessly vulgarized in a theater. When in "The Blue Bird" the lilies spring from the graves of the dead, who can sit in the theater and not agree that the scene was infinitely more effective between the covers of the book?

Monna Vanna

Play in 3 acts (1903). Texts: translation by Alfred Sutro (N. Y. 1907); by A. I. du P. Coleman (N. Y. 1903); by Charlotte Porter (*Poet Lore*, Boston, 1904); reprint of the Sutro translation in *Joyzelle, Monna Vanna* (N. Y. 1907).

With "Monna Vanna" Maeterlinck wrote a play that was intended for the usual sort of production in a regular theater. The characters are human beings presented to us in the flesh, and not etherealized abstractions or mystical symbols. He had before this time maintained that action, in the ordinary sense, was not essential in drama, but "Monna Vanna" is made up not only of action but of struggle and violent contrasts. He says, and his words should be compared with what he said at an earlier date, that there "are no words so profound, so noble and admirable, but they will soon weary us if they leave the situation unchanged, if they lead to no action, bring about no decisive conflict, or hasten no definite solution."[2]

1. In this play, then, there is a very definite struggle, one of the eternal struggles, between love and duty. But the interest lies largely in the central figure, in the character of Monna Vanna. She is the first complete full-length portrait in Maeterlinck's gallery. The plot, background, and struggle are therefore employed chiefly to enable us to know more of her, to bring to light further and deeper knowledge of the inmost recesses of her spiritual being. The sacrifice she is called upon to make, for instance, reveals what may be termed her "civic conscience," her renunciation of personal happiness for the good of her people; each act will be found to test her mind and heart, and each scene in which she appears to add to our knowledge of her. It is she who interests us, more even than the situations in which she figures. There is what seems perhaps a contradiction of this in the tent scene of the second act. Suspense adds greatly to the interest of the scene; we are of course anxious to see how it will end, but we are more anxious to see how Monna Vanna will act, and what effect Prinzivalle will produce upon her, and what effect she upon him. The

[2] In Moses, *Maurice Maeterlinck: A Study*.

scene is skillfully managed; dramatic suspense and the delineation of character are so subtly interwoven that we hardly realize which is which. This is, of course, as it should be, for it is only after we begin to analyze our reactions that we can distinguish the means which occasioned them.

2. The climax comes, as we should expect, at the end of the second act. The third, however, is remarkably well sustained throughout. The tension is by no means released as the curtain rises for the last time, for we must know how Guido will receive his wife on her return. The scene we expect is not *the* "scène à faire," but it is *a* "scène à faire." The big scene was in the second act. The meeting of husband and wife is going to show us the result of what has happened, and it is incumbent upon the playwright to show us the two together.

And now see how suspense is created and sustained: the crowd is in a fever of excitement as their savior enters the city, and this excitement is communicated to the audience through Marco. This retailing of incidents at second hand is a common expedient, often used in plays where races or fights occurring off-stage are told of by some one visible to the audience. It is a step beyond the messenger in Greek drama, who tells what has happened rather than, as a present spectator, what is actually happening. The latter method is more vivid, it is certainly convenient, as well as stimulating to the imagination. After the crowd is admitted, the tension is still maintained, as Guido sends the populace home preparatory to his questioning of Vanna. Then comes the (secondary) obligatory scene, full of surprises, full of the subtle interplay of character upon character, tense and throbbing. Then the scene between Vanna and her husband. Guido persists in believing his wife "guilty." The action rises to the point where Guido condemns Prinzivalle to prison; Monna Vanna, realizing the futility of trying to persuade her husband of the truth, lies, declaring that "he [Prinzivalle] belongs to her," and finally begs that she also may be incarcerated. The action has taken another turn, with no flagging of the interest, but rather a tightening of the tension; the outcome becomes more and more problematical. But when Vanna tells Marco, "Father, he is mine; you shall answer for him . . . (*She looks fixedly at him.*) You understand," the play is over. Guido, incapable of believing in a virtue that is not dictated by convention, has lost his wife: she has gone to one who can better love and understand her. "Yes," she says, "it has been a bad dream . . . but the beautiful one will begin again. The beautiful one will begin——"

3. Read one of the early Maeterlinck plays—say, "Interior" or "The Intruder"—and compare the characters with those in "Monna Vanna." Do you see the difference between the dramatist's "first" manner and his "second"? Not that "manners" and "periods" are of the slightest importance; the point is, do you recognize the development of the poet's power to construct and work out a dramatic story?

A Note on Marionettes

Maeterlinck put on the title page of an early volume the words *Three Plays for Marionettes.* He states that "Princess Maleine" was written for production in the same manner. He says (Preface to "Pélleas and Mélisande," etc., N. Y. 1911): "I have been asked more than once whether my dramas from 'Princess Maleine' to 'The Death of Tintagiles' were really written for a marionette theater, as I had declared them to be. . . . As a matter of fact, they were not written for ordinary actors. . . . At that time I sincerely believed, as I now do, that these poems die by the introduction of living beings. . . . Is it not evident that the Macbeth or Hamlet that we see on the stage bears no resemblance to the Macbeth or Hamlet of the text? . . . That a great part of the efforts of the poet to create above all a superior existence, a life closer to our soul, has been nullified by the introduction of an enemy substance which cannot manifest itself save in dragging down this superior existence to the level of everyday life? . . . Art always employs roundabout means, it never goes direct. . . . Representation [by actors] brings everything back to the point where it was before the poet came. . . . The theater is a place where most masterpieces die, because the acting of a masterpiece by means of accidental and human elements is antinomian. . . . The poem retires as man comes forth. . . . It is for these reasons . . . that I have dedicated my little dramas to beings that are sympathetic . . . which for want of a better term, I call, 'marionettes.'"

A consideration of the art of the marionette show is outside the scope of the present work, but the subject is full of fascination, offering suggestions that cannot fail to interest. Many dramatists and other artists feel that the theater is inadequate for the performance of certain kinds of plays. Thomas Hardy, in the preface to "The Dynasts," says that his play ("an epic-drama of the war with Napoleon, in three parts, nineteen acts, and one hundred and thirty scenes") is "intended simply for mental performance, and not for the stage. Some critics have averred that to declare a drama as being not for the stage is to make an announcement whose subject and predicate cancel each other. The question seems to be an unimportant matter of terminology. . . . By dispensing with the theater altogether, a freedom of treatment was attainable in this form that was denied where the material possibilities of stagery had to be rigorously remembered. . . . Whether mental performance alone may not eventually be the fate of all drama other than that of contemporary or frivolous life, is a kindred question not without interest."

It sets you thinking. Truly, most of the world's great plays *are* for "mental performance alone": either the plays of the Greeks are "not plays at all" (if we follow the critics who declare that performance is the *sine qua non* of the drama form), or we must consider them as fit only for the theater of the mind.

But there are, as I say, those who would adopt the convention of the puppet-stage. A. B. Walkley (*Pastiche and Prejudice*) writes: "I ventured, when Mr. Hardy first published 'The Dynasts,' to suggest that the perfect performance of that work would be as a puppet show, with Mr. Hardy reading out his own blank verse. . . . The puppet presentation would . . . clarify, simplify, attenuate the medium through which the poem reaches the audience. The poet and his public would be in close contact. . . . A puppet-show 'Hamlet' might be an exquisite experiment in that highest art whose secret is suggestion."

But, if we would be logical, does not the puppet (like the actor) come between poet and audience? Is not the highly conventionalized doll only another kind of actor? Does not *it* introduce "accidental" elements, though of a different kind, as well as the actor?

A good deal has been written about marionettes in English, though the best authorities are the untranslated French writers Maindron and Magnin. For references in English, see Gordon Craig, *On the Art of the Theater* (Chicago, 1911), *Towards a New Theater* (N. Y. 1913), *The Theater—Advancing* (Boston, 1917); all the numbers of his magazines *The Mask* (Florence, 1908-1924), and *The Marionette* (Florence, 1918); Helen H. Joseph, *A Book of Marionettes* (N. Y. 1920); Arthur Symons, *Plays, Acting and Music* (N. Y. 1909); A. B. Walkley, *Drama and Life* (N. Y. 1908), *Pastiche and Prejudice* (N. Y. 1921); D. C. Calthrop, *Punch and Judy* (London, 1926); and Madge Anderson, *The Heroes of the Puppet Stage* (N. Y. 1923); Edith F. Ackley, *Marionettes—Easy to Make, Fun to Use* (N. Y. 1929); W. Mills and L. Dunn, *Marionettes, Masks and Shadows* (N. Y. 1927); Remo Bufano, *Be a Puppet Showman* (N. Y. 1933); W. S. Lanchester, *Hand Puppets and String Puppets* (London, 1937).

THE DUTCH DRAMA

THE DUTCH DRAMA

Of the many dramatists who have written and are still writing original plays in Holland, there are scarcely half a dozen who have been mentioned in English books, nor over half a dozen of their plays translated. But there are several serious playwrights in Holland. Heijermans is the undisputed master of them all, although until recent years the distinguished Marcellus Emants was called the Dean of Dutch Literature—including drama. Of his few plays, "The Power of Stupidity" is considered the best. Willem Schürmann, author of "The Vrolier Family," "The Double Life," and "Toadstools," is rather more of a dramatist; Jan Fabricius, a Dutch Colonial journalist, is the author of at least one powerful and successful drama, "On the Straight Path." Frederik Van Eeden, the novelist, wrote one effective play, "Ysbrand." This was translated by Harry Kemp and produced privately in America. "The Promised Land" and "The Gateway" have enjoyed a certain popularity in Holland. The women have done notable work. Chief among these is Mrs. J. A. Simons-Mees, who has for over a generation been writing social dramas, the best of which have held the stage since the nineties. "Disillusioned," "A Mother," "Agatha's Marriage," "Life's Currents," "The Paladin," and "The Conqueror," are her most successful. The last-named was translated into English. Mrs. Roland Holst is known only in her own country; Marie Metz-Koning is known to readers of English through her short play, "The White Lie." Herman C. J. Roelvink's "Stormbird" is published in translation by Arthur Davison Ficke. J. H. Speenhof, well known as a critic, is represented only by his one-act play "Louise," in Shay and Loving's *Fifty Contemporary One-Act Plays.* Geert Teis, pen name of Geert W. Spitzen, has written a number of peasant plays ("Dizzepie Dizzepu," "The Soil," and "A Master Finds His Master") and has achieved popularity in the neighboring districts of Germany as well as in Holland.

There is very little material on the Dutch drama in English. The only article in any of the drama books is in Ashley Dukes' *Modern Dramatists,* and that is devoted almost exclusively to Heijermans.

HERMAN HEIJERMANS

Herman Heijermans was born at Rotterdam in 1864. His life was spent largely in the literary and journalistic world, though he was for some years the director of his own theater in Amsterdam. As novelist and critic, short story writer and dramatist, he led various advance-guard movements of his day, and made his influence felt beyond the borders of his own land. In Holland he is recognized as the most gifted of many dramatists. He began writing plays in the early nineties. It was with "Ghetto" that he won distinction, a powerful picture of sordid life in the Jewish quarter of Amsterdam. "The Good Hope" is his most successful play.

Says Dr. Huizinga: "Heijermans is unquestionably a born playwright. Sure-footed, he has steadily progressed in his art to greater perfection and success. His daring realism seemed often a hindrance in the way of his success, even in the Netherlands, the 'cradle of liberty.'" It is as a painter of character that Heijermans excels, and in his half dozen really successful plays he is able to combine a gift for characterization with a firm grasp of the dramatic medium. Heijermans died in 1924.

PLAYS

"Ahasuerus" (1893)
"Dora Kremer" (1893)
"Neighbors" (1893)
"A Jewish Trick" (1894)
"Ghetto" (1898)
"Number Eighty" (1898)
"The Machine" (1899)
"The Seventh Commandment" (1899)
"The Good Hope" (1900)
"May Day" (1900)
"The Coat of Mail" (1901)
"Ora et Labora" (1902)
"The Child" (1903)
"The Screened Bed" (1903)
"At the Young Jan" (1903)
"Shackles" (1903)
"All Souls" (1904)
"May Time" (1904)
"Saltimbank" (1904)
"The Maid" (1905)
"Jubilee" (1906)
"Strange Chase" (1907)
"The Great Flight" (1908)
"The Rising Sun" (1908)
"The Sleeping Beauty" (1909)
"The Heir" (1910)
"Good Luck" (1911)
"Robert, Bertram & Co." (1914)
"Daybreak" (1916)
"Eva Bonheur" (1916)
"The Wise Tomcat" (1919)

Editions.—"The Good Hope," trans. by Harriet G. Higgins (*Drama,* Chicago, 1912, and by L. Saunders and C. Heijermans-Houwink (N. Y. 1928); "The Ghetto," adapted by C. B. Fernald (London, 1899); "Jubilee," trans. by Lilian Saunders and Caroline Heijermans-Houwink (*Drama,* Chicago, 1923); "Saltimbank," by the same (*Drama,* Chicago, 1923); "The Rising Sun," trans. by C. St. John (London, 1925); "Links" ["Shackles"] by Howard Peacey and W. R. Brandt (*Poet Lore,* Boston, 1927).

References

Ashley Dukes, *Modern Dramatists* (Chicago, 1912); J. T. Grein, *Premières of the Year* (London, 1900); C. St. John, *Introduction* to "The Rising Sun" (London, 1925); B. H. Clark and M. Lieber, *Great Short Stories of the World* (N. Y. 1925).

The Good Hope

Drama of the sea in 4 acts (1900). Texts: translation by Harriet G. Higgins (*Drama,* Chicago, 1912), and by L. Saunders and C. Heijermans-Houwink (N. Y. 1928).

"The Good Hope" has been performed more than a thousand times in Holland alone. It is probably the best play written by any modern Dutch dramatist. Its popularity is accounted for primarily because of its passionate character: every personage in the play is thrillingly alive. It is also a virile revolutionary document setting forth the doctrine of social freedom.

1. This play, like "The Cherry Orchard" and "The Weavers," is a picture: it depicts in detail a group of human beings. In order to show many aspects of the character of each of them, the dramatist has set them in the midst of a series of crises which will test them to the utmost.

It is difficult to exhibit a person's character when he is living under ordinary circumstances, because people don't show very much of their essential selves in everyday life; unless, that is, one has unlimited time and opportunity to observe them. A hero is heroic as a rule only once or twice in a lifetime; the coward will not show his cowardice until he is forced to do so. No character can be made very interesting if he is shown during *any* two or three hours of his existence. Even the novelist, who has so much more time at his disposal and can also describe mental processes, must select critical moments, though it may often seem that he is at considerable pains to show his people under ordinary conditions. Jane Austen *appears* often to avoid dramatic situations and critical moments, but actually she is always selecting crises for her characters, though these may seem, compared with the situations in Ibsen, to be far from important. She gives us the impression of describing year after year in the lives of her heroines, but as a matter of fact she shows only samples, short excerpts from the records of their existence.

In the Heijermans play the crisis is very clearly marked. But the crisis is not an unusual one: he is writing of fisherfolk whose life is passed on and by the sea.

The first act is solid exposition: the terms of the struggle must be laid down, the persons who are to engage in it introduced, and the specific instance whereby the tragedy is to arise and develop, carefully elaborated.

Compare this act with the first act of Hauptmann's "Weavers." By what means is the atmosphere created in each of these plays?

2. The theme is twofold: that the sea is victor in man's struggle to snatch a living from it, and that man is cruel to man in the eternal struggle for gold. In Synge's "Riders to the Sea" the same struggle between man and the sea is the basis of the action, but the Dutch playwright has introduced another element. Is "The Good Hope" based upon a social thesis? Is it a problem play? If so, then how important is the struggle with the sea? Is it necessary to drag in the cruelty of employers, adding that to the impersonal cruelty of fate?

3. Geert is a revolutionary. Is there any reason for believing that he voices the opinions of the author? If he is simply put into the play to preach revolution, does this fact weaken it? There are many other dramas in which such characters play important rôles; sometimes they are only too obviously lay figures, but often they are integral parts of the play itself. See, for purposes of comparison, Pinski's "Isaac Scheftel," Hauptmann's "Weavers," and Galsworthy's "Strife."

4. In connection with "Riders to the Sea" the question was raised whether it was possible to achieve authentic tragic effects within the compass of the one-act form. "The Good Hope," so far as length is concerned, is of course long enough for the development of a tragic theme, but is it a tragedy? The point here, as always, with plays as with any other form of art, is *not* whether any particular play is a tragedy, a tragi-comedy,

a melodrama, or a farce; but whether it is what it ought to be, what the artist intended that it should be. "Hamlet" might just as well be called a farce-comedy so long as we know what it is and understand it. The discussion, for instance, of whether the last act of "Hamlet" is melodramatic or not, is worth discussing, because it may throw light on Shakespeare's intentions and methods.

Is "The Good Hope" a tragedy? Suppose the struggle with the sea is a hopeless struggle, that nothing can be done about it? Is the death of sailors proper material for tragedy? Or, suppose the evil to a certain extent remediable, that the employers, for instance, could be forced to make their ships safe? The fact that they do not certainly causes the death of sailors. But is this tragic?

Can a tragedy be based upon the accidental? Suppose Hamlet had tripped when he was about to kill Polonius, fallen on his own sword, and killed himself? Suppose Lear had toppled off the cliff? Suppose Iago had overreached himself early in the play and Othello had discovered the villain's machinations in time? Suppose, in the Heijermans play, that the employers were to reform and Geert and the rest be given paying positions in some office? There is no doubt that the true tragedy is based upon something inevitable in the character of the protagonist, something that comes up against another character, or fate, or facts, that are too much for him. Accident, naturally, enters into the artist's scheme of things, but accident that is *not* accidental. There is the accidental accidental (in the instances I have just suggested) and there is the inevitable accidental, as in the last act of "Hamlet."

In his *Introduction to Dramatic Theory* Professor Allardyce Nicoll says: "Whenever a tragedy lacks the feeling of universality, whenever it presents merely the temporary and the topical, the detached in time and in place, then it becomes simply sordid. The cardinal element in high tragedy is universality." How about this? Is "The Good Hope" universal in its appeal? Is it merely sordid?

THE ITALIAN DRAMA

THE ITALIAN DRAMA

Gabriele D'Annunzio's best plays have been translated by Arthur Symons. With the exception of this dramatist, Giacosa, and Pirandello, the great mass of Italian plays await English translators. Our record of a dozen plays in English is very brief. Marco Praga is known to us through one work; likewise Giovanni Verga, Ercole Luigi Morselli, Sabatino Lopez, Tommaso Gallarati-Scotti, Luigi Chiarelli, Rosso di San Secondo, and Gerolamo Rovetta; there are three of Roberto Bracco, and three very short scenes of Francesco Marinetti. And that is about all. There are no published English translations of Sem Benelli, Camillo and Giannino Antona-Traversi, E. A. Butti, or Augusto Novelli.

There are just two books in English on the modern Italians: Addison McLeod's *Plays and Players of Modern Italy,* and Lander MacClintock's full and authoritative study, *The Contemporary Drama of Italy.* Most of the books on modern drama contain very little on the Italians; Isaac Goldberg's *Drama of Transition* is, however, especially useful on the newer dramatists.

Since the establishment of the Fascist state there has been, so far as I can see, no activity among Italian playwrights worth our consideration.

GABRIELE D'ANNUNZIO

Gabriele D'Annunzio was born in 1863 at Pescara in the Abruzzi, Italy. He showed an early predilection for poetry, and while still at school published his first verses, at the age of sixteen. After a short period of schooling in Tuscany, he went to Rome where he began writing poetry and short stories. His first novel appeared in 1889; this was soon followed by others which spread his fame abroad. The best plays date from the late nineties and early nineteen-hundreds, the "Dream of a Spring Morning" appearing in 1897. With Sarah Bernhardt's production of "The Dead City," D'Annunzio's power as a dramatist began to be recognized. He was classed as a "decadent" to be sure, yet a powerful one. His spectacular exploits during and just after the war, as aviator, orator, and political freebooter, have brought him once again—as in the nineties—into the limelight.

D'Annunzio is recognized as the greatest force in modern Italian literature. He is the perfect type of esthete, his is the religion of beauty. In "Gioconda" Cosimo Dalbo says ". . . so much sorrow shall not have been suffered in vain, so much evil shall not have been useless, if one thing so beautiful remains over, to be added to the ornament of life." And Lucio Settala replies, "It is true. I sometimes think of the fate of one whose ship and all that was in it went down in a storm. On a day as calm as this, he took a boat and a net, and he returned to the place of the shipwreck, hoping to draw something out of the depths. And, after much labor, he drew on shore a statue. And the statue was so beautiful that he wept for joy to see it again; and he sat down on the sea-shore to gaze upon it, and was content with that gain, and would seek nothing more: . . . I forgot the rest!"—The man on the sea-shore is D'Annunzio himself; he sees what is beautiful, in character, in setting, in style. The critic Croce says of him: "Is he a constructive thinker and a sage? Is he a profound and coherent philosopher? A good counselor? No. But he is a poet and that ought to suffice; the more so that this species of poets by divine right is rarer than that of the sages, the reasoners, and the good counselors."

Plays

"The Parable of the Foolish Virgins and the Wise Virgins" (1897)
"The Dream of a Spring Morning" (1897)
"The Parable of the Rich Man and Poor Lazarus" (1898)
"The Parable of the Prodigal Son" (1898)
"The Dream of an Autumn Sunset" (1898)
"The Dead City" (1898)
"Gioconda" (1898)
"Glory" (1899)
"Francesca da Rimini" (1902)
"The Daughter of Jorio" (1904)
"The Light Under the Bushel" (1905)
"More Than Love" (1907)
"The Ship" (1908)
"Phædra" (1909)
"The Martyrdom of St. Sebastian" (1911)
"The Pisan Woman" (1913)
"The Honeysuckle" (1913)
"Parisina" (1913)
"The Piave" (1918)

(D'Annunzio has also written a moving picture scenario, "Cabiria," 1914. "The Martyrdom of St. Sebastian" was written for the musical accompaniment of Claude Debussy; "Parisina" for the music of Pietro Mascagni; "The Piave" for the music of Italo Montemezzi.)

Editions (*separate plays*).—"The Dream of a Spring Morning," translated by Anna Schenck (*Poet Lore,* Boston, 1902); "The Dream of an Autumn Sunset," by the same (*Poet Lore,* Boston, 1904);

"Gioconda," by Arthur Symons (N. Y. 1902, reprint, Chicago, 1913); "The Dead City," by G. Mantellini (Chicago, 1902), and by Arthur Symons (N. Y. 1902); "Francesca da Rimini," by Arthur Symons (N. Y. 1902); "The Daughter of Jorio," by C. Porter, P. Isola, and A. Henry (*Poet Lore,* Boston, 1907, and in book form, Boston, 1911); "The Ship," anonymously (*Poet Lore,* Boston, 1909); "The Honeysuckle," by C. Sartoris and G. Enthoven (N. Y. 1915).

Reprints in Collections and Anthologies.—"Gioconda" (Symons translation) in Dickinson's *Chief Contemporary Dramatists* (second series, Boston, 1921); "The Daughter of Jorio" (translation by Porter, Isola, and Henry) in Moses' *Representative Continental Dramas* (Boston, 1924); and Symons' trans. of "Francesca" in Dickinson's *Continental Plays, I* (Boston, 1935).

References

James Huneker, *Iconoclasts* (N. Y. 1905); Addison McLeod, *Plays and Players of Modern Italy* (Chicago, 1912); Lander MacClintock, *The Contemporary Drama of Italy* (Boston, 1920); Ashley Dukes, *Modern Dramatists* (Chicago, 1912), and *The Youngest Drama* (Chicago, 1924); Arthur Symons, *Studies in Prose and Verse* (N. Y. 1904); W. L. Courtney, *The Development of Maurice Maeterlinck,* etc. (London, 1904); Oscar Heermann (ed.), *Living Dramatists* (article on D'Annunzio by J. M. Sheehan, N. Y. 1905); William Sharp, *Studies and Appreciations* (N. Y. 1912); F. W. Chandler, *Aspects of Modern Drama* (N. Y. 1914) and *Modern Continental Playwrights* (N. Y. 1931); C. Lewis Hind, *Authors and I* (N. Y. 1921); C. H. Herford, *Shakespeare's Treatment of Love and Marriage* (London, 1921); A. B. Walkley, *Drama and Life* (N. Y. 1908); J. T. Grein, *Premières of the Year* (London, 1900); Archibald Henderson, *The Changing Drama* (Cincinnati, 1919).

Gioconda

Tragedy in 4 acts (1898). Texts: translation by Arthur Symons (N. Y. 1913); reprint of same in Dickinson's *Chief Contemporary Dramatists* (second series, Boston, 1921).

"Gioconda" exemplifies the kind of theme that forms the basis of practically every play, novel, and poem written by D'Annunzio: it is a revelation of the artist at odds with a practical world. Dr. MacClintock (in *The Contemporary Drama of Italy*) declares that the play "poses the problem" as to whether the artist is to be bound "by the trammels of conventional morality, to submit himself to the laws which govern the rest of humanity, or is he to create a world for himself?" It is not likely that the poet cared in the least about oughts or shoulds: it is his business (at least it is his wish) to state the terms of this struggle and to portray the actors in it. "Gioconda" is simply a picture of a situation, and the characters are, as it were, set loose in it to work out their several destinies as best they may.

1. The first act is leisurely: the dramatist seems not in the least anxious about coming to the point. He insists upon setting the stage for his drama, and in order that the characters may be perfectly familiar to the audience, he permits them to say a great deal. But in the course of this leisurely exposition we are, almost unawares, allowed to lift the many veils between us and the pasts of these people. The play has begun in earnest just before the fall of the curtain.

The first act of a play rarely leaves the reader or spectator in doubt as to what sort of play he is seeing; it should let him know whether he is to see comedy or tragedy, farce or melodrama. Such indications are made nearly always early in the course of the action or exposition of the first act. In "Gioconda," Silvia Settala's words foreshadow the serious nature of events to come: "Then, do you know, a breath passed, a vapor, a mere nothing, and cast down everything, and the anxiety came back, and the dread and the tremor!" These lines forebode evil; the more so as everything is so apparently calm for the remainder of the act. We feel instinctively that this is the calm before a tempest. Were the play to turn out well, complications would have immediately set in, and a happy event been foreshadowed; instead, all is apparently serene, and this we may take as foreshadowing evil.

This indication is necessary, as the audience must know where to place their sympathies, and in what frame of mind to listen to the play; otherwise, they risk losing the thread, and what is more to the point, are unable to take sides with or against the personages. A play in a theater, like music that is being executed, unfolds itself but once: the spectator, unlike the reader of a book, cannot turn back the pages or read a passage twice.

2. Although the first act is a unit in itself, it leaves us curious to know the precise direction that the action will take; a trained reader or listener will vaguely anticipate a struggle

between Silvia and the forces in opposition to her: in this case, the object of Lucio's former love. The second act should unmistakably reveal this struggle, present to our view the contending parties, and show us at least the probable direction of the plot. As we are told (in the original edition, not the translation) that the play is a tragedy, it is not difficult to surmise that the peaceful relations between Silvia and Lucio, as seen in the first act, will be broken off in tragic fashion—just how, the next three acts will disclose.

The second act opens with a note of warning. Gioconda, the model, is heard from, and Lucio's "No, no, no," preceded by the stage direction "with a shudder of dread" (p. 44, separate ed.), leaves little room for doubt. Lucio will return to Gioconda. With great rapidity the struggle becomes clearly defined. The conversation between Lucio and Cosimo, culminating in the former's long speech (pp. 54-59), shows us the inevitability of Lucio's relapse, and leads us to believe that Gioconda is still his "ideal." Lucio's love for her is the result of his personality, it is deeply imbedded in his soul; because of this fatal attraction, and in spite of his resolutions, Lucio will bring suffering upon himself, his wife, and his family.—Another element in the struggle is introduced (p. 70) as Silvia resolves to meet Gioconda and try to get the key of Lucio's studio from her; the obligatory scene is now foreseen, the struggle in its culmination, the climax. The next act must be concerned with the contest.

3. The scene is laid—where but in the studio? Gioconda is not introduced at once; the scene begins at low tension and works up to a big "situation." Silvia states the case (p. 93) to her rival, "One of us two is the intruder. Which?"—and the scene begins. Silvia argues eloquently, passionately, but Gioconda is confident of her strength, until Silvia tells her to go; that precipitates the actual struggle, ending with the attempted destruction of the statue, and the "lacerating cry from Silvia, torn by agony from her very vitals" (p. 109). This is the climax. A short staccato scene, with Lucio and Francesco, ends the act. Again the actual outcome is uncertain.

4. The struggle is over; between the third and fourth acts Lucio has succumbed and gone away with Gioconda. D'Annunzio's description of Silvia (p. 113) tells the story: "Silvia Settala appears on the threshold, from the inner room; she pauses; takes several steps towards the window; looks into the distance, looks about her with infinitely sad eyes." And we know at once what has happened.

"Silvia may make her home a haven of peace; she may tend and nurse her husband when the other woman drives him to attempt self-destruction; she may fondle him with caresses and words of love as beautiful as ever flowed from woman's lips; she may lie for his sake; she may sacrifice her beautiful hands to save his statue from the violence of her rival—she may do all this and more, yet the other conquers all along the line, for she is the mate of his being, his body, his ego, and Silvia's love is but the placid affection which neither satisfies nor inspires the high-strung, insatiable soul of the creative artist" (J. T. Grein, in *Premières of the Year*).

This last act is in many ways a masterpiece of dramatic art. First, it carries the story to its logical conclusion; second, it sustains the interest up to the end; third, it gradually brings us back to the "level of life" whence it began; and finally, it contains that gentle chastening or cleansing element—in this case, the tragedy and sweetness of mother-love—that gives to tragedy a lasting quality. The scene that closes the play is terrible, but its terror inspires pity, not revulsion: this is true tragic beauty.

Compare the theatrically unemphatic ending of "Gioconda" with the tense and decidedly emphatic last act of Echegaray's "Folly or Saintliness?"

GIUSEPPE GIACOSA

Giuseppe Giacosa was born at Colleretto Parella, Italy, in 1847. After studying law in Turin, he began his career as a man of letters; this was early in the seventies. He "resided during the first part of his literary career in Turin and later at Milan. He came to America in 1891." . . . During the last years of his life he was director of the magazine *La Lettura.* He died in the town where he was born in 1906.

Dr. MacClintock, whose *Contemporary Drama of Italy* is the chief and only comprehensive work in English on the modern Italian drama, makes clear the position of this playwright in the following terms: "The work of Giuseppe Giacosa links together in a very interesting way the old and the new manners in Italian drama: . . . he reflects to a nicety the varying dramatic taste of his time. . . . In each of the dramatic genres he essayed Giacosa has left a work . . . of genuine significance even when not absolutely vital and enduring. His gift to the Italian stage was a body of new themes, a corpus of new subject-matter; he renovated the drama with his fresh and clean ideas and clear style. He co-operated nobly in the creation of the national theater."

It was Giacosa who, more than any other, infused a true Italian element into his best plays; he did much to free the stage of his country from French adaptations and pseudo-French "triangle" plays.

PLAYS

"A Game of Chess" (1871)
"An Old Story" (1871)
"To a Dog That Licks Ashes Do Not Confide Flour" (1871) [1]
"Don't Say Flour Unless You Have It in the Sack" [1] (1871)
"The Triumph of Love" (1872)
"Bank Affairs" (1873)
"The Sons of the Marquis Arturo" (1874)
"Sad Doubts" (1874)
"Gallant Intrigues" (1874)
"Nocturnal Surprises" (1875)
"A Candidate" (1875)
"Teresa" (1875)
"Mountain Torrents" (1876)
"At the Piano" (1877)
"The Husband in Love With His Wife" (1877)
"The Brother-in-Arms" (1877)
"The Red Count" (1880)
"Luisa" (1881)
"The Thread" (1883)
"The Siren" (1883)
"Surrender at Discretion" (1885)
"The Honorable Ercole Mallardi" (1885)
"Sad Loves" (1888)
"The Cat's Claw" (1888)
"The Belated Repentance" (1888).
"The Lady of Challont" (1891)
"The Rights of the Soul" (1894)
"As the Leaves" (1900)
"The Stronger" (1904)

(In collaboration with Luigi Illica, Giacosa wrote the librettos of the following Puccini operas: "Madam Butterfly," "La Bohème," and "La Tosca.")

Editions.—The Stronger, Like Falling Leaves [*i.e.* "As the Leaves"], *Sacred Ground* [*i.e.* "Rights of the Soul"], trans., with introduction, by E. and A. Updegraff (N. Y. 1915), includes the plays mentioned.

[1] Italian proverbs.

Separate Plays.—"As the Leaves," trans. anonymously. (*Drama*, Chicago, 1911); "The Stronger," anonymously (*Drama*, Chicago, 1913); "Unhappy Love" [*i.e.* "Sad Loves"], by E. A. Trombly (*Poet Lore*, Boston, 1917); "The Wager" [*i.e.* "A Game of Chess"], adapted by Barrett H. Clark (N. Y. 1914); "The Rights of the Soul," by Isaac Goldberg (*Stratford Review*, Boston, 1918).

Reprints in Collections and Anthologies.—"Sacred Ground" [*i.e.* "The Rights of the Soul"] (Updegraff translation), in Moses' *Representative One-Act Plays by Continental Authors* (Boston, 1923); "The Rights of the Soul" (translation by Theodora Marcone) in Shay and Loving's *Fifty Contemporary One-Act Plays* (Cincinnati, 1920); "Like Falling Leaves" [*i.e.* "As the Leaves"] (Updegraff translation), in Moses' *Representative Continental Dramas* (Boston, 1924).

References

Lander MacClintock, *The Contemporary Drama of Italy* (Boston, 1920); Addison McLeod, *Plays and Players of Modern Italy* (Chicago, 1914).

As the Leaves

Comedy in 4 acts (1900). Texts: anonymous translation (*Drama*, Chicago, 1911); and as "Like Falling Leaves," by E. and A. Updegraff in *The Stronger, Like Falling Leaves, Sacred Ground* (Boston, 1915).

"As the Leaves" is an exceptionally good example of the modern social comedy. Its essential veracity, its strong yet sympathetic treatment of phases of life that are common to most of humanity, and its masterly construction, all combine to create the illusion that we are participating in an actual family struggle. Starting at a level with life, the action gradually mounts from crisis to crisis, and ultimately seems to recede back to life again.

1. In studying the play, notice the natural and skillful manner in which incident follows incident, how one situation grows out of the preceding, and how the entire work appears to spring into existence like life itself, and not as if conjured into being at the will of a clever craftsman. The skill of the dramatist is hardly noticed, so admirably has he managed to convey a sense of the casualness of everyday existence.

2. The play is so well constructed, that a too detailed analysis of its component parts might prevent our enjoying it as a

whole—for a *first reading,* however. Read it for the pure enjoyment of the story, and afterwards analyze it and inquire into the methods utilized to give it consistency and charm.

A word as to the characterization. As in life, no character is essentially bad or good, and in his treatment of all the personages Giacosa's warm-hearted sympathy and interest in humanity are keenly felt. We feel sorry for Tommy and Giulia, for Rosani and Nennele; and if Tommy is snobbish, Nennele is stubborn; if Giulia is frivolous, Giovanni is at times weak; while even the delightful Massimo has a too pronounced tendency to preach.

The situation, too, is admirable—this reversal of the family fortunes; it serves to bring out the essential characteristics of each of the persons involved. Since action of some sort seems an unavoidable necessity in a play, each of these persons must *do* something, and since all are acting under unusual stress, we see new aspects and a further development of their characters.

3. Every act in a play ought to advance (1) either the story or (2) the development of the characters, or both.

In life, we cannot remain altogether unaffected either by what we see or hear, and so must it be, of course, in a play, only there (because all art, and particularly the drama, is a compression and a synthesis, an exaggeration of the significant) the effect produced upon the audience is usually more emphatic than it is in life. We therefore expect each act in a play to carry us appreciably in advance of the preceding act. It is the playwright's business to see to it that his plot and characters —either simultaneously or one after the other—carry on the development.

In "As the Leaves" the end of each act leaves the audience on a higher emotional level than the beginning: they know more of the motives of the characters, of their doings and thoughts, than at the rise of the curtain. The first act, for example, shows the family preparing to go away; we know nothing of them. Before the end of the act, the characteristics of Tommy, Nennele, Giulia and, to a certain extent, of Rosani, are clearly outlined.

Trace this development in each of the succeeding acts.

4. The last act is short. Why is this? First, there is little material, and the author, it seems, has a wholesome aversion to "stringing out" the story. Second, a short scene, if it have movement and suspense, is very effective on the stage. Nennele, discouraged at the apparent loss of Massimo and the weakness of Tommy and her stepmother, has determined to take her own life. Her suicide would have been too tragic an outcome, especially as the father is not so weak as Nennele thought him, and as Massimo "did understand," and did come back to her. Nor is the "happy" ending a concession to the sentimental members of the audience; in this case, it is almost as inevitable as are the suicides in "Mid-Channel" and "Hedda Gabler." After Tommy and Giulia drift off "as the leaves," something definite is required to end the play. A "slice of life," in order to be a work of art, must be secure at each end, so to speak, and not left suspended in mid-air.

5. Why is "As the Leaves" called a "comedy"?

LUIGI PIRANDELLO

Luigi Pirandello was born at Girgenti, Sicily, in 1867. After a thorough education in Italy, he "went to the University of Bonn, where he was graduated in philosophy and philology. His subsequent career has been devoted to professorship, but has permitted him enough leisure in which to produce a veritable library of books. . . . From poetry he progressed to the novel, to criticism, to the theater." (Isaac Goldberg, in *Plays of the Italian Theater.*)

But it is as a dramatist that Pirandello is best known. As such, he is a distinguished member of the new generation of Italians, in which Luigi Chiarelli, Enrico Cavacchioli, F. Maria Martini, Sabatino Lopez, and Rosso di San Secondo, have all made their mark. These men have continued the pioneer work of Giacosa in freeing the Italian stage of the French tradition. Like them, Pirandello has sought more or less to intellectualize the drama, and in some of his most sophisticated work he has adopted the extreme methods of the so-called "Grotesque" school.

In Dr. Goldberg's opinion, Pirandello "ventilates issues, shifts personages over the chessboard of his fancy, forms new combinations with the colored glass of his dramatic kaleidoscope. . . . What has he written? Are they plays at all? I leave such questions to the pedagogues. Pirandello's best productions are a welcome addition to the modern stage; if no category exists for them, why, some one will have to invent one for them, that is all."

Mention should be made (though Pirandello is not of the movement) of the Futurists. Francesco Marinetti is interesting not so much for his Futurist plays, as for his curious manifestoes. These are "mad pronouncements in the manner of the Dadaists, but serve to reveal the state of mind of the young generation." In the Synthetic Futurist Theater the play is to be "atechnical, dynamic, simultaneous, autonomous, alogical, and unreal." Revolt, as everywhere—in Germany and Russia especially—against the past. The actual accomplishments of the Futurists are almost negligible; they are symptomatic, but the men of talent (like Pirandello) cannot remain unaffected by them. Pirandello, a recent recipient of the Nobel Prize, died in 1936.

PLAYS

"Scamandra" (1910)
"Sicilian Limes" (1911)
"Cece" (1911)
"The Doctor's Duty" (1911)
"The Vise" (1912)
"At the Door" (1914)
"If Not Thus" (1915)
"Liola" (1916)
"Just Think, Giacomino!" (1916)
"Right You Are (If You Think So)" (1916)
"The Pleasure of Honesty" (1917)
"Cap and Bells" (1917)
"The Patent" (1918)
"It's Nothing Serious" (1919)
"Man, Beast and Virtue" (1919)
"Signora Morli" (1920)
"All For the Good" (1920)
"As Before, and Better" (1920)
"Six Characters in Search of an Author" (1921)
"The Rights of Others" (1921)
"And Ye Clothed Me" (1922)
"Henry IV" (1922)
"The Man with a Flower in His Mouth" (1923)
"The Life I Gave Thee" (1923)
"Each in His Own Way" (1924)
"Our Lord of the Ship" (1925)
"The Other Son" (1925)
"The Jar" (1925)
"The New Colony" (1926)
"The Husbands' Friend" (1927)
"Diana" (1927)
"Tonight We Improvise" (1930)
"Lazarus" (1930)
"As You Desire Me" (1931)
"Fantasms" (1931)

Editions.—Three Plays, first two trans. by Edward Storer, the last by Arthur Livingston, with "Prefatory Note" by the latter (N. Y. 1922), includes "Six Characters in Search of an Author," "Henry IV," and "Right You Are (If You Think So)"; *Each in His Own Way and Two Other Plays,* trans., with a "Note," by Arthur Livingston (N. Y. 1923), includes "Each in His Own Way," "The Pleasure of Honesty," and "Naked" [*i.e.* "And Ye Clothed Me"]; *Plays of the Italian Theater,* trans. by Isaac Goldberg (Boston, 1921), includes "Sicilian Limes." *The One-Act Plays of Luigi Pirandello,* trans. by various hands (N. Y. 1932), includes "The Imbecile"; "By Judgment of Court" [*i.e.* "The Patent"]; "Our Lord of the Ship"; "The Doctor's Duty"; "The Man With the Flower in His Mouth"; "At the Gate" [*i.e.* "At the Door"]; "The Vise"; "The House with the Columns" [*i.e.* "The Other Son"]; "Sicilian Limes"; and "The Jar."

Separate Plays.—"Sicilian Limes," trans. by Isaac Goldberg (*Theater Arts,* N. Y. 1922); "As You Desire Me" (N. Y. 1931); "Tonight We Improvise," trans. by S. Putnam (N. Y. 1932).

References

Lander MacClintock, *Contemporary Drama of Italy* (Boston, 1920); Isaac Goldberg, *The Drama of Transition* (Cincinnati, 1922); Ashley Dukes, *The Youngest Drama* (Chicago, 1924); Clayton Hamilton, *Conversations on Contemporary Drama* (N. Y. 1924); Walter Starkie, *Luigi Pirandello* (N. Y. 1937); John Palmer, *Studies in the Contemporary Theater* (Boston, 1926); Barrett H. Clark, *Great Short Novels of the World* (N. Y. 1922); D. Vittorini, *The Drama of Luigi Pirandello* (N. Y. 1935); T. H. Dickinson, *The Theater in a Changing Europe* (N. Y. 1937).

Six Characters in Search of an Author

Comedy in the making, in 3 acts (1921). Text: translation by Edward Storer, in *Three Plays by Luigi Pirandello* (N. Y. 1922).

"Six Characters" is primarily interesting because of its technical form. The playwright simply picks to pieces before the audience all the elements of a play, and then proceeds to put them together again. No doubt he performed this trick for the purpose of emphasizing certain dramatic points, but largely by reason of the devices by which he succeeds, are we interested in the drama.

1. Pirandello did not actually invent a new method of writing plays. What he has done is simply to expand the device employed by novelists—Fielding, for instance, in *Tom Jones,* and Thackeray in *Vanity Fair*—by means of which the artist takes the public into his confidence. So sure is the artist of the vitality of his puppets that he can safely call our attention to the artifices whereby they are set in motion. By stripping from the artistic medium all that is likely to lend a color of actuality, the artist is performing a trick on the one hand, and on the other (if he succeeds), creating life after his own fashion.

A. E. Thomas and Clayton Hamilton went further than this

in their "unusual play," "The Big Idea." Here the play itself consists of the plot that is being used by the principal characters *as a plot* for their own play. In the last act the two plots (of the play itself and of the piece that is being written) converge and intermingle. "The Big Idea" is a remarkably clever work, but its chief virtue lies in its ingenuity. How far is this true of the Pirandello play?

2. Pirandello has been called an "intellectual" dramatist. The term is, of course, relative: Shaw and Ibsen are "intellectual." Such dramatists are supposed to be guided in their treatment of situations and characters by mental rather than emotional considerations. "Romeo and Juliet" is certainly not the product of a philosopher, but "The Tempest," on the other hand (with all its magnificent poetry), *is* a philosophical work as well as a play. So are Goethe's "Faust," and Shaw's "Man and Superman." How about "Six Characters"? Turn to the second act (p. 51). We are here in the midst of a dramatic scene. The Stepdaughter is "acting" her scene, but so naturally that we are not sure whether we ought to be amused or touched:

THE MANAGER (*running his hands through his hair*). For Heaven's sake! What are you saying?

THE STEPDAUGHTER (*crying out*). The truth! The truth!

THE MANAGER. It may be. I don't deny it, and I can understand all your horror; but you must surely see that you can't have this kind of thing on the stage. It won't go.

THE STEPDAUGHTER. Not possible, eh? Very well! I'm much obliged to you—but I'm off!

THE MANAGER. Now be reasonable! Don't lose your temper!

THE STEPDAUGHTER. I won't stop here! I won't! I can see you've fixed it all up with him in your office. All this talk about what is possible for the stage . . . I understand! He wants to get at his complicated "cerebral drama," to have his famous remorses and torments acted; but I want to act my part, *my part!*

And here we have the dramatist as if speaking aloud of his own aspirations as a writer: what *will* go on the stage, what will not? He is playing with, dramatizing his mental processes.

In this sense, Pirandello may be called an "intellectual." But compare this play with "Man and Superman," or better still, with "Getting Married." The Shaw plays are "intellectual" because you feel the dramatist behind the characters, expressing *ideas*.

Pirandello is evidently impatient over the restrictions of form: he would not only understand all the mental and emotional processes of his characters, he would show these on the stage, and show himself showing them. Says The Father in "Six Characters": "For man never reasons so much and becomes so introspective as when he suffers; since he is anxious to get at the cause of his sufferings, to learn who has produced them, and whether it is just or unjust that he should have to bear them." The dramatist (like Henry James in his later works) is not content merely to show a part of the sufferings of his personages: he must show all, and the why and wherefore, the justice or the injustice of their lot. But "Drama is action, sir, action and not confounded philosophy," declares The Manager. "I am not so sure," replies Pirandello in effect, "for is not philosophy a sort of action?" (Recall Andreyev's remarks on Nietzsche, p. 67.)

3. Read Pirandello's "Right You Are! (If You Think So)," another play in which the dramatist has succeeded in turning inside out the ordinary processes of playwriting. Here he not only keeps a secret from his audience, but from his characters, and indeed from himself, to the very last. The play is concerned with the guesses of a number of people as to the identity of a certain woman. She is either one person or another: and yet at the end it turns out that she is neither one. "I am nobody," she says. In other words, you—the characters—are a lot of curiosity-mongers—and, says Pirandello to the audience, so are you! He was asked recently to solve the mystery, and in reply he said, with a shrug: "How do I know?" The underlying idea of the play is that the truth is not absolute but relative, that every thing and every person is different in each new relationship. Life is a kaleidoscope, never twice the same. Why should not this idea be dramatized?

In "Six Characters" we literally *see* life—multiple, kaleidoscopic, inscrutable—trying to fit itself into an art form. Is the idea susceptible of dramatic treatment? This question can only be answered by determining whether Pirandello has written an effective play. It is said Einstein reached his conclusions about Relativity by first "challenging an axiom." In a small way, this is what the Italian dramatist is doing. No rule, no law, no theory is valid to the artist who can successfully break it. The whole question now is whether Pirandello has successfully accomplished what he tried to do.

4. Pirandello's plays, whatever else they may be, offer us the keenest sort of intellectual sport. There is scarcely a scene in the best of his plays that fails to challenge our ideas on life or art. If they had no artistic merit at all, they would at least be worth reading as mental exercises. Mr. M. L. Malevinsky, a brilliant New York lawyer, who has for some years engaged in lawsuits involving questions of plagiarism, has recently written a challenging book on dramatic technique. *The Science of Playwriting*—like the plays of Pirandello—provokes discussion and argument. See especially the author's discussion of "theme" and "motive." How much of his theory can be applied to a study of Pirandello's plays?

THE SPANISH DRAMA

THE SPANISH DRAMA

Except for Benavente (of whom John Garrett Underhill has given us a score of fastidious and charming translations), the modern Spaniards are not easily accessible. Gregorio Martinez-Sierra, however, is one more exception: two volumes of his plays, translated by Mr. Underhill, Helen and Harley Granville-Barker, include nine dramas. Of Echegaray's eighty-odd plays scarcely a dozen are translated; of Galdós' only three. The Brothers Serafín and Joaquín Alvarez-Quintéro are known through four long plays and two or three one-acters; Manuel Linares Rivas, Eduardo Marquina, Joaquín Dicenta, Ramon del Valle-Inclán and Eduardo Zamacoïs, through one play each.

Of the Catalan Angel Guimerá two plays are translated, and of his compatriot Santiago Rusiñol, only one sketch.

At least one play (however slight) of each of the important modern Spaniards has been turned into English.

There is no book in English on the modern Spanish drama. Such material as exists must be sought in the introductions and prefaces of the translations of plays, in Storm Jameson's *Modern Drama in Europe,* Isaac Goldberg's *Drama of Transition,* Frank W. Chandler's *Modern Continental Playwrights,* and Thomas H. Dickinson's *Theater in a Changing Europe.*

José Echegaray

José Echegaray was born at Madrid in 1832. Always an apt pupil, at an early age he showed exceptional ability in mathematics and the exact sciences, but although he never lost his interest in these subjects, he became interested in literature and the theater, and in later years made an intensive study of the European drama. He was graduated with honors in 1853 from the Escuela de Caminos and became a tutor in mathematics. Not long afterward he was appointed to a professorship in that subject in the same school from which he graduated. From that time on the field of his interests widened; he studied political economy, philosophy, and geology. He was also engaged in engineering and chemical pursuits. At the age of thirty-two he wrote a play, but laid it aside. In 1868 he was appointed Minister for the Colonies, but five years later was exiled for political reasons. It was in France that he wrote "The Check Book," his first produced play. On his return to Spain in 1874 it was performed, but not until the following year was he firmly established as a dramatist. From the middle seventies until 1908 he wrote two or three plays a year. He died in 1916.

"Spaniards declare that for more than 200 years their drama has not brought forth a serious rival to this man. And there can hardly be a doubt that, in any selection of names of the great dramatists, Lope de Vega and Calderon de la Barca will find the place nearest to themselves occupied by José Echegaray." (John Graham, in the Introduction to his translation of "The Son of Don Juan.")

But since the advent of the younger dramatists—Benavente in particular—the fame of Echegaray is somewhat dimmed. Dr. Goldberg (in *The Drama of Transition*) says:

"To say that Echegaray, on the whole, is a bad playwright because he is a belated romantic is as futile a toying with terms as to pronounce any other writer great because he happens to be an opportune realist. Echegaray, in general, is an inferior dramatist because the plays themselves are vitiated at their source. They do not develop from a core of passion, produced inevitably by the clash of character and circumstance. They are the artificial result of a passion that they do not contain." Exception is made by Dr. Goldberg of "The Great Galeoto," which he declares to be "with justice recognized . . . as an addition to world-literature."

Plays

"The Check Book" (1874)
"The Wife of the Avenger" (1874)
"The Last Night" (1875)
"At the Hilt of the Sword" (1875)
"A Sun That Rises and a Sun That Sets" (1875)
"The Gladiator of Ravenna" (1876)
"The Beginning and the End" (1876)
"Folly or Saintliness?" (1877)
"The Peacemaker" (1877)
"A Fault and a Punishment" (1877)
"What Cannot Be Told" (1877)
"Before the Pillar and the Cross" (1878)
"In Pursuit of an Ideal" (1878)
"Sometimes Below" (1878)
"In the Bosom of Death" (1879)
"The Tragic Wedding" (1879)
"The Shoreless Sea" (1879)
"Death on the Lips" (1880)
"The Great Galeoto" (1881)
"Harold the Norman" (1881)

"The Two Curious Impertinents" (1882)
"Conflict Between Two Duties" (1882)
"A Miracle in Egypt" (1883)
"In Supposing Evil. . . . Will You Guess?" (1884)
"The Pest of Otranto" (1884)
"Happy Life, Sad Death" (1885)
"Lysander the Bandit" (1886)
"Evil Race" (1886)
"Two Fanaticisms" (1887)
"Count Lothario" (1887)
"Reality and Delirium" (1887)
"The Son of Steel and the Son of Flesh" (1888)
"The Sublime in the Commonplace" (1888)
"Everlasting Source of Troubles" (1889)
"The Extremists" (1889)
"The Prologue to a Drama" (1890)
"Always Ridiculous" (1890)
"Irene de Otranto" (1891)
"The Embryo Critic" (1891)
"Comedy Without Dénouement" (1891)
"The Son of Don Juan" (1892)
"Sic vos, non vobis, or The Last Alms" (1892)
"Mariana" (1892)
"The Power of Impotence" (1893)
"At the Sea-Shore" (1893)
"The Enraged Lady" (1894)
"The Cleansing Stain" (1895)
"The First Act of a Drama" (1895)
"The Stigma" (1895)
"Wild Love" (1896)
"The Street Singer" (1896)
"Calumny as a Chastisement" (1897)
"The Doubt" (1898)
"The Man in Black" (1898)
"The Silence of Death" (1898)
"The Madman Divine" (1900)
"Accursed Heritages" (1902)
"The Steps of a Throne" (1903)
"The Unstable One" (1903)
"Letting Oneself Be Dragged Along" (1905)
"Hero and Clown" (1908)

Edition.—The Great Galeoto, Folly or Saintliness, trans., with introduction, by Hannah Lynch (Boston, 1895), includes the plays mentioned.

Separate Plays.—"The Great Galeoto" (Lynch translation), preface by E. R. Hunt (Garden City, 1914); by Jacob S. Fassett, Jr. (Boston, 1914); "Madman or Saint" [*i.e.* "Folly or Saintliness?"], by Ruth Lansing (*Poet Lore,* Boston, 1912); "Mariana," by James Graham (Boston, 1895), and by F. Sarda and C. D. S. Wuppermann (N. Y. 1909); "The Son of Don Juan," by James Graham (Boston, 1895); "The Madman Divine," by E. H. West (*Poet Lore,* Boston, 1908); "The Street Singer," by J. G. Underhill (*Drama,* Chicago, 1917); "Always Ridiculous," by T. W. Gilkyson (*Poet Lore,* Boston, 1916).

Reprints in Collections and Anthologies.—"The Man in Black" [printed only in this edition], by Ellen Watson in the *Universal Anthology,* Vol. XXVII (London, 1899); "The Great Galeoto" (translation by Eleanor Bontecou), in Clark's *Masterpieces of Modern Spanish Drama* (Cincinnati, 1922); "The Street Singer" (Underhill translation), in Shay's *Twenty-five Short Plays* (*International*) N. Y. 1925).

[An American adaptation of "The Great Galeoto," called "The World and His Wife," by C. F. Nirdlinger, was published in 1908 at New York. This is reprinted in Moses' *Representative Continental Dramas* (Boston, 1924).]

References

J. D. M. Ford, *Main Currents of Spanish Literature* (N. Y. 1919); Storm Jameson, *The Modern Drama in Europe* (N. Y. 1920); Isaac Goldberg, *The Drama of Transition* (Cincinnati, 1922); William Archer, *The Theatrical World,* Vol. V (London, 1898); C. F. Nirdlinger, *Masques and Mummers* (N. Y. 1899); Bernard Shaw, *Dramatic Opinions and Essays,* 2 vols. (N. Y. 1907); J. T. Grein, *Dramatic Criticism,* Vol. III (London, 1902); F. W. Chandler, *Aspects of Modern Drama* (N. Y. 1914).

The Great Galeoto

Play in 3 acts and a prologue (1874). Texts: translation by Hannah Lynch, Garden City, 1914; same in *The Great Galeoto, Folly or Saintliness* (Boston, 1895); by J. S. Fassett, Jr. (Boston, 1914); by Eleanor Bontecou in Clark's *Masterpieces of Modern Spanish Drama* (Cincinnati, 1922).

"The Great Galeoto" is an especially notable example of the thesis play. The thesis is made clear in the prologue and during the course of the play, and is never lost sight of; yet seldom are the situations or characters in any way falsified or exaggerated at the cost of verisimilitude. Theme and plot go hand in hand, and are so admirably fused that if either were developed more than it is, the play would suffer. The skill with which the thesis is handled is the more remarkable when we consider that Echegaray had little experience at the time he was writing. Augier and Dumas *fils,* the originators of the modern thesis play, were still at work, and were both to write some of their best plays, while Ibsen had hardly begun his social dramas.

1. Compare the prologue of "The Great Galeoto" with that of Andreyev's "Anathema" and Rostand's "Chantecler." Of what use is the introductory scene? Why does not the author either call it the first act or, omitting it entirely, introduce the material into the exposition of his next (and consequently first) act?

2. For psychological and artistic reasons, we are now aware, a dramatist must vary his scenes. Study Echegaray's methods in the second act.

3. In the Nirdlinger Americanized version of this play called "The World and His Wife," new characters are introduced, and the time of the play has been changed. Compare the original with this stage version. Which is the better, and why?

4. When this play was written, the soliloquy and aside had not gone out of style. What use does Echegaray make of these rather cumbersome devices? Had Pinero, for instance, been writing the play, in what way could he have modified the dialogue in order to do away with these "outworn conventions"?

5. The essence of the tragedy lies in the impersonal agency which brings about the situation treated by the dramatist. Here lies the secret of the artist's skill: Echegaray has managed throughout to "dramatize" society—"They," the city of Madrid. This has been accomplished by very definite means. Can you detect them?

6. Echegaray's theme is universal: the tongue of gossip does incomparable harm. In her little comedy, "Spreading the News," Lady Gregory treats a like theme, but from its comic side. In what other respects are the plays similar?

7. If some characters had of necessity to be eliminated from the play, which would go first, with the least injury to the whole? Has Echegaray practiced that economy in the number of characters which is essential not only in the drama, but in all art, since what is not strictly necessary is actually detrimental?

8. Just after the first performance of "The Great Galeoto" in 1881, a Spanish critic wrote: "Here your treatment of a social problem had the good fortune to run on lines that in all eyes seemed elevated and humane. . . ." Another critic wrote: "He has treated a great social question in a masterly manner. . . . Everybody recognized the truth of the picture, though none cared to accept it as personal: . . . the social moral avenged by the creative genius of Señor Echegaray owes him a reward and satisfaction . . . for the lesson received."

Echegaray *was* interested in the social problem, there is no denying that, but we may ask ourselves how far he has allowed his feelings as a citizen (a man interested in the well-being of his fellowmen) to influence his work as an artist? Was "The Great Galeoto" written *in order to* demonstrate the evil effects of gossip? Or did the dramatist use the Galeoto theme for the purpose of making a dramatic play? Perhaps his motives were mixed. Echegaray has told us that he is interested in morals. In the preface to "The Son of Don Juan" he declares that he never defends his dramas, either "materially or morally," but in explaining why he used Oswald's phrase ("Mother, give me the sun!") from Ibsen's "Ghosts," he cannot resist saying just a little more: "And this phrase . . . enfolds a world of ideas, an ocean of sentiments, a hell of sorrows, a cruel lesson, a supreme warning to society and to the family circle. Thus I look at it. A generation devoured by vice . . . ," etc.

We have often had occasion in this book to ask ourselves how far the artist may go in formulating moral lessons and still remain an artist. The question cannot be settled by the application of any rule or formula. There is no doubt, however, that it lies with the artist to use whatever materials he can turn to advantage. The great artist will always universalize his moralizings, and allow the "lesson" to apply itself. Ibsen said that he never answered questions, he only asked them. Dumas fils, on the other hand, and Brieux, not only ask, but answer their questions.

Compare Echegaray's "Great Galeoto" with his "Son of Don Juan." How far is the first a "lesson"? And how far is the second?

Benito Pérez-Galdós

Benito Pérez-Galdós was born at Las Palmas, in the Canary Islands, in 1845. At an early age he went to Madrid to study law, but finding this unsuited to his tastes, he turned to journalism and soon began writing fiction, which was to be his life-work. In two vast series of novels, the so-called *National Episodes,* he described and analyzed the Spain of the nineteenth century. Over half a century ago he made an unsuccessful effort to become a dramatist, but it was not until late in his career that he turned seriously to the theater.

Galdós died at Madrid in 1920.

As a dramatist Galdós offers a particularly interesting study. His chief importance is rightly claimed to consist in his refusal to allow himself to be dominated by the traditional technique. His plays are to a certain extent "novelistic." He has himself said that there "are those who aver that there is a natural antagonism between the means and ends of the novel form and the drama form; they start, however, at the same source, and are two fraternal rivers, each intermingling with the other." His first play, "Reality," was based upon two of his own novels; "Doña Perfecta" and "The Grandfather" are based upon the novels bearing the same names. Galdós' plays, says Dr. Goldberg, "reveal a healthy disregard for the conventions of stage technique. They do not yield readily to the arrogant confines of the proscenium, and tend to overflow the banks of the accepted form."

Plays

"Reality" (1892)
"Gerona" (1893)
"The Life of the House" (1893)
"The Duchess of San Quentín" (1894)
"The Condemned" (1894)
"Will" (1895)
"Doña Perfecta" (1896)
"The Dragon" (1896)
"Electra" (1901)
"Life and Spirit" (1902)
"Mariucha" (1903)
"The Grandfather" (1904)
"Barbara" (1905)
"Love and Science" (1905)
"Pedro Minio" (1908)
"Celia in the Slums" (1913)
"Alcestes" (1914)
"Sister Simona" (1915)
"Reason in Unreason" (1915)
"Solomon the Miser" (1916)
"Saint Joanna of Castile" (1918)

Editions (separate plays).—"Electra," trans. anonymously (*Drama*, Chicago, 1911); "The Grandfather," by Elizabeth Wallace (*Poet Lore*, Boston, 1911).

Reprints in Collections and Anthologies.—"The Duchess of San Quentín" (appears only in this edition; translation by P. M. Hayden), in Clark's *Masterpieces of Modern Spanish Drama* (Cincinnati, 1922); "Electra" (translation by C. A. Turrell) in Turrell's *Contemporary Spanish Dramatists* (Boston, 1919).

References

J. Fitzmaurice-Kelly, *History of Spanish Literature* (N. Y. 1898); J. D. M. Ford, *Main Currents of Spanish Literature* (N. Y. 1919); Isaac Goldberg, *The Drama of Transition* (Cincinnati, 1922).

See also.—Prefaces to *Masterpieces of Modern Spanish Drama*, *Contemporary Spanish Dramatists*, and translation of "Electra" (in *Drama*).

The Duchess of San Quentín

Comedy in 3 acts (1894). Text: translation by P. M. Hayden in Clark's *Masterpieces of Modern Spanish Drama* (Cincinnati, 1922).

Although Galdós wrote his first play in 1850, his career as a dramatist did not open until the nineties. "The Duchess of San Quentín" was one of his earliest successes. Although it is not, like several of the other works, a dramatization of a novel, it exemplifies the writer's so-called "novelistic" theories of playwriting.

1. Well, what *is* the difference between a play and a novel? The followers of Benedetto Croce—notably J. E. Spingarn in America—maintain that "the theater simply does not exist," that there is essentially, and theoretically, only an accidental difference between one work of art and another. A play has usually been regarded as something that must be *performed before an audience,* but to Croce the audience is non-existent. He says: ". . . all these external conditions [that is, the theater, the stage, the mob] are merely dead material which has no æsthetic significance outside the poet's soul; and only in the poet's art should we seek to find them."

The views of Croce and Spingarn, and of those whose views they combat, are set forth at some length in the introductory chapter of Dr. Goldberg's *Drama of Transition.* That chapter gives the student an adequate idea of the different theories. But without going too deep into the subject, we are here confronted with the problem of inquiring into the difference (granted its existence) between a play and a novel.

A play, at least, is *usually,* if not necessarily, performed before an audience, and for that very reason it is shorter than a novel; and because many persons who have come together for such a performance usually demand emotional excitement or stimulation in the form of action (rather than description, let us say) the play is *usually* a combination of exciting events so arranged as to arouse the emotion of the audience. Let us, without too readily accepting one theory or another, consider the matter open-mindedly: after all, the most ardent Crocean would not deny that most plays *are* theater-pieces intended to be exhibited to crowds of people, and that most novels are narrative fictions printed in book form. The heart of the question is really this: whether or not there is a necessary and fundamental difference between one *genre* or form and another. This cannot, of course, be determined off-hand, but it is worth thinking about. Perhaps we shall never find a completely satisfactory solution. After all, life itself has not yet been completely and satisfactorily explained, has it?

2. What is meant by the "novelistic" qualities in Galdós' plays is doubtless their lack of (conventional) theatric form, the long and seemingly casual passages of dialogue, and the author's leisurely manner in developing his story. Compared with the usually melodramatic tension of Echegaray, Galdós saw "what Echegaray may never have imagined," says Dr. Goldberg, "that there is a place upon the stage for calmness, for passion that does not tear itself to pieces."

Can you point to a scene in "The Duchess of San Quentín" which is "novelistic"?

3. The first act is full of exposition; some of it is concerned with the events of sixty years ago. See Don José's speech on page 116. A good deal of ground is covered here and in other speeches like it; it is almost as though the dramatist were writing an introductory chapter to a novel. But does he successfully "put over" the act? That is the principal consideration. It makes not a jot of difference how "novelistic" any play is, so long as it is successful—successful, that is, as a work of art. In other words, it is quite absurd to declare that such a work is "All very well, but it isn't a play."

Call "The Duchess of San Quentín" a novel, if you wish, or "The Cherry Orchard" a story, or "Hedda Gabler" a picture; it makes no difference. It is only worth discussing if the Galdós play had been *better* as a novel, the Chekhov play *better* as a story, or the Ibsen play better as a picture.

4. Do you think "The Duchess" would prove more effective as a novel than it is as a play?

Jacinto Benavente

Jacinto Benavente was born at Madrid in 1866. After studying law for a time he relinquished any intentions he may ever have had of finishing his course. After leaving the University he joined a traveling circus and later a theatrical troupe. Though his first published work was a volume of poems (1893), he essayed playwriting, making his début a year later with "Thy Brother's House." This was followed in 1896 by "In Society," recognized, says John Garrett Underhill, as the work of "an extraordinary talent." For the past generation Benavente has exercised a wide and beneficent influence upon the Spanish drama.

> Benavente has tried his hand at almost every *genre,* and he has been successful in them all—peasant drama and the tragedy of blood, so long associated with Spain in the minds of foreigners, satires of provincial and metropolitan society, of the aristocracy, dramas of the middle class, court comedy in the most subtle and refined of forms. . . . He has written romantic comedies and dramas, rococo spectacles, imaginative fairy plays. . . . In all these different *genres* he has moved with consummate ease, without the suggestion of effort, until the drama of character has seemed the most facile and casual of arts (Underhill).

Benavente belonged to the so-called Generation of '98, whose appearance marked the end of the old tradition-ridden Spanish art and the rise of the "school" that boasted that they based their art not upon tradition but upon "observation." The awakening of the younger generation was one of the results of the national upheaval following the disaster of the Spanish-American War. Echegaray, who was considered to belong to the age that had just closed, was Spanish to the core; Benavente, though he remained firmly rooted in the best traditions of his country, belongs to the world.

The Generation of '98

The new movement—like most new movements in all countries—was the result of a desire for novelty, and a natural reaction against the past. Pio Baroja, the novelist, himself a member of the '98 group, writes of it as follows: "During the years 1898 to 1900 a number of young men suddenly found themselves thrown together in Madrid, whose only rule was the principle that the immediate past did not exist for them. This aggregation of authors and artists might have seemed to have been brought together under some leadership, and to have been directed to some purpose; yet one who entertained such an assumption would have been mistaken. . . . Doubtless such gatherings of new men, eager to interfere in and influence the operations of the social system . . . are common upon a larger scale in all revolutions." (In *Youth and Egolatry,* quoted by Goldberg.)

"The revolt against the theater," says Dr. Goldberg, "was crystallized in the manifesto issued against Echegaray at the time when the rest of the nation was celebrating his reception of the Nobel Prize." (An honor recently conferred upon Benavente himself.)

PLAYS

"In the Place of Don Juan" (1892)
"Thy Brother's House" (1894)
"In Society" (1896)
"Husband to La Tellez" (1897)
"Pure Farce" (1897)
"The Banquet of Wild Beasts" (1898)
"The Woman's Theater" (1898)
"A Lover's Tale" (1899)
"A Surgical Operation" (1899)
"A Long Farewell" (1899)
"The Angora Cat" (1900)
"Acquiring an Education" (1900)
"The Open Wound" (1900)
"Modes" (1901)
"The Taint of Vulgarity" (1901)
"In Perfect Innocence" (1901)
"Sacrifice" (1901)
"The Governor's Wife" (1901)
"Cousin Roman" (1901)
"Love of Loving" (1902)
"The Husband's Train" (1902)
"The Victor Soul" (1902)
"The Automobile" (1902)
"Saturday Night" (1903)
"The Favorites" (1903)
"The Perfect Man" (1903)
"Why Women Love" (1903)
"Broad Daylight" (1903)
"The House of Good Fortune" (1903)
"The Fire Dragon" (1904)
"No Smoking" (1904)
"Princess Bébé" (1904)
"Autumnal Roses" (1905)
"A Surprise for the Countess" (1905)
"An Added Attraction" (1905)
"The Evil Doers of Good" (1905)
"Crickets and Ants" (1905)
"Manon Lescaut" (1906)
"Stronger Than Love" (1906)
"The Owls" (1907)
"Grandmother and Grandchild" (1907)
"Love Shocks" (1907)
"The Enchanted Cup" (1907)
"The Eyes of the Dead" (1907)
"Othello's Tale" (1907)
"One Touch of Nature" (1907)
"The Bonds of Interest" (1907)
"The Princess Without a Heart" (1907)
"The Last Minuet" (1907)
"The Living Truth" (1908)
"The Smile of Mona Lisa" (1908)
"Señora Ama" (1908)
"His Widow's Husband" (1908)
"Brute Force" (1908)
"Trifles" (1908)
"The Magic of an Hour" (1909)
"In the Clouds" (1909)
"At Close Range" (1909)
"The Devil! What Next?" (1909)
"The School of Princesses" (1909)
"The Prince Who Learned Everything Out of Books" (1909)

"A Retreat for My Lady" (1909)
"Earning a Living" (1909)
"The Grandson" (1910)
"The Graveyard of Dreams" (1911)
"La Malquerida" ["The Passion Flower"] (1913)
"The Collar of Stars" (1915)
"The Truth" (1915)
"His Proper Self" (1915)
"Field of Ermine" (1916)
"The City of Gaiety and Confidence" (1916)
"The Evil That Men Do" (1917)
"Young Lions" (1918)
"Mephistophela" (1918)
"Our Lady of Sorrows" (1918)
"The Law of the Children" (1918)
"A Traitor to All, To All Be Ye Loyal" (1919)
"Man's Honor" (1919)
"The Vestal of the West" (1919)
"Devil May Care" (1919)
"Cinderella" (1919)
"Once Upon a Time" (1919)
"A Lady" (1920)
"A Poor Woman" (1920)
"Beyond Death" (1922)
"A Lesson in Love" (1924)

(In addition to the above, Benavente has published nineteen short sketches, not intended for production, a "sequence" in six scenes, and a fantasy; these are included in two volumes: *Plays of the Imagination* (1892), and *Figurines* (1898). He is also the author of four monologues and eight translations.

Editions.—Plays by Jacinto Benavente, trans., with introduction, by J. G. Underhill (N. Y. 1917), includes "His Widow's Husband," "The Bonds of Interest," "The Evil Doers of Good," and "La Malquerida"; 2nd series, translated, with introduction, by the same (N. Y. 1919), includes "No Smoking," "Princess Bebé," "The Governor's Wife," and "Autumnal Roses"; 3rd series, translated, with introduction, by the same (N. Y. 1924), includes "The Prince Who Learned Everything Out of Books," "Saturday Night," "In the Clouds," and "The Truth"; 4th series, translated, with introduction, by the same (N. Y. 1924), includes "The School of Princesses," "A Lady," "The Magic of an Hour," and "The Field of Ermine."

Separate Plays.—"No Smoking," trans. by J. G. Underhill (*Drama,* Chicago, 1917); "The Smile of Mona Lisa," by J. A. Herman (Boston, 1915); "The Bonds of Interest," by J. G. Underhill (*Drama,* Chicago, 1915); "Saturday Night," by the same (*Poet Lore,* Boston, 1918); "Brute Force," trans. by J. G. Underhill (N. Y. 1935).

Reprints in Collections and Anthologies.—"The Bonds of Interest" (Underhill translation) in Dickinson's *Chief Contemporary Dramatists,* 2nd series (Boston, 1921), and Moses' *Representative Continental Dramas* (Boston, 1924); "His Widow's Husband" (Underhill translation) in Shay and Loving's *Fifty Contemporary One-Act Plays* (Cincinnati, 1920).

References

Isaac Goldberg, *The Drama of Transition* (Cincinnati, 1922); Storm Jameson, *The Modern Drama in Europe* (N. Y. 1920); Clayton Hamilton, *Seen on the Stage* (N. Y. 1920); Walter Starkie, *Jacinto Benavente* (N. Y. 1925); F. W. Chandler, *Modern Continental Playwrights* (N. Y. 1931); and T. H. Dickinson, *The Theater in a Changing Europe* (N. Y. 1937).

The Bonds of Interest

Comedy in a prologue and 3 acts (1907). Texts: translation by J. G. Underhill (*Drama,* Chicago, 1915); and in *Plays* (N. Y. 1917); reprinted in Dickinson's *Chief Contemporary Dramatists,* 2nd series (Boston, 1921).

A play of exquisite charm, and an especially good example of one of the many moods of this inventive and versatile dramatist. "The Bonds of Interest" is a striking proof of the fact that a man of genius can use the oldest and most hackneyed forms provided he has something to say and can say it well.

1. "Here," writes Dr. Goldberg, "we have a sort of anti-technique; an art that seeks not so much to conceal itself as to invite attention to its operation. It is one of the many signs of the reaction against realism that stirs upon the stage of every nation. . . ." By "anti-technique" is meant the method whereby the playwright quite frankly asks his audience to observe the means by which he creates his effects. In the prologue we are offered "a little play of puppets, impossible in theme, without any reality at all. You will soon see how everything happens in it that could never happen, how its personages are not real men and women, nor the shadows of them, but dolls or marionettes of paste and cardboard, moving upon wires which are visible even in a little light and to the dimmest eye."

In "The Yellow Jacket" (by George C. Hazelton and Harry Benrimo) a more or less similar method is adopted. The "Chorus" explains the action and occasionally comments upon the purely mechanical elements which serve to develop the plot. It is almost as though the dramatist were poking fun at his own work. Does Benavente, in "The Bonds of Interest," destroy your illusion? Do the prologue and the final speech (virtually an epilogue) seem an integral part of the play? Would you feel you were missing anything essential if they were left out?

The Italian dramatist Pirandello (see p. 196) has gone much

further than the Spaniard in exposing the skeleton of his technique to public scrutiny. Many novelists seem to enjoy showing their readers how the trick is done, and instead of pretending that their story is life, they take peculiar pleasure in telling you that it is not; Molnar's recent comedy, "The Play's the Thing," is a good example. Another instance comes to mind, in a story by O. Henry, "Springtime à la Carte." Here is the passage:

> On the previous summer Sarah had gone into the country and loved a farmer.
>
> (In writing your story never hark back thus. It is bad art, and cripples interest. Let it march, march.)
>
> Sarah stayed two weeks at Sunnybrook. . . .

2. "The Bonds of Interest," like most good plays, is sufficiently interesting in itself to hold the average audience, but there is running through it a philosophic theme. As a matter of fact the play is simply an exposition of that. The dramatist goes to the trouble of making that unmistakably clear: Crispin's long speech to Columbine in Act II ("We have all within ourselves," etc.) is a brief statement of what this theme is. Mr. Underhill is even more definite. He says that "Leander typifies the untutored best in man, which is good intention. He is unsullied by a life of hardship and defeat, of flight from a heartless justice, of cheats and deceptions and lies. Crispin is the slave, the servant. . . . In the end he changes places with Leander . . . who drifts upon the fortunes of others, for out of experience springs the knowledge of the true values of life, which is redeemed only by disinterested love, which is always service and sacrifice."

Is it absolutely necessary to accept this interpretation, true as it is, in order to enjoy the play? By the way, was "Hamlet" written in order to expose a philosophy of life, or to supply the actors with a good show? If it was intended merely as a show, this does not prevent its being a great philosophical play, but the question is worth debating.

3. The Benavente play is a satire on human nature. Why did the dramatist change his men and women into the conven-

tional figures of the Italian Improvised Comedy, or Commedia dell'Arte? Everyone knows (even if it were not so stated in the prologue) that the device is only a trick, and the moment the curtain rises on the play itself we proceed to change the puppets into real men and women. We say to the dramatist: "We understand: you have conceived real human beings and then told us they were not real. Why did you not either say nothing about it, or else give us these persons as they are?"

4. A big scene, dramatically, occurs off-stage between the first and second acts: the fight between Leander and the supposed desperadoes. Is there any valid reason why this scene, which would surely be diverting and dramatic on the stage, should be omitted? The same sort of thing was done between the first and second acts in Rostand's "Cyrano de Bergerac." Why not show the fight? It is often done—in the last act of "Macbeth," for instance. Is it because what happens off-stage is said to be more stirring than what transpires before our eyes? Surely the torture scene in Sardou's "La Tosca" is more horrible because we can *imagine* what is going on in the room off-stage; and when Magda goes into her father's room we thrill with the knowledge that something momentous is about to occur. The French critic Jules Lemaître (quoted in Matthews' *Principles of Playmaking*) declares that "often what is set before our eyes, strikes us more forcibly than what is merely told; yes, action is ordinarily more moving than narrative. But what is infinitely more pathetic than an action told or seen, is an action which is divined. Victor Hugo has said that nothing is more interesting than a wall behind which something is taking place."

5. "A good play," says Mr. Underhill in explaining the work of Benavente, "cannot really be read. Although a performance may be visualized from the printed page, the effect of the performance cannot be felt: too many imaginative and constructive processes intervene. Yet these effects of the unwritten action are precisely those in which true drama lies. The dramatic action, the unwritten action which lies behind the plane of language, is taken by Benavente to be the vehicle

of his under plot—an unwritten action for an unwritten plot. The action in its purest form thus becomes the instrument of the subjective plot, which is the heart of the play." A fruitful matter for meditation, and a problem not easily solved. But Mr. Underhill here refers to the implicational fourth dimension of all art; his contention is at least applicable to the other arts. There is, of course, the overtone, the suggestion, in a picture, a novel, a symphony, or a play. It is quite true that "Hamlet" means more to us than the actual words printed on a hundred pages of paper, or three hours' performance on a stage. But after all, is it not arguing in a circle to declare that certain artists create (consciously or otherwise) implicational values by subtle processes, while others do not achieve them at all? Life can be expressed or interpreted in a thousand ways, and so long as it is expressed truthfully the presentment, in whatever form, is provocative, evocative, suggestive. The great picture is to the sensitive beholder only a point of departure for the discovery of "meanings" or emotions, and every great play has "an unwritten action." Benavente himself has said that the best of the artist's genius "is not in what is explained in his works, but what escapes from them."

The difference between Benavente and the mediocre dramatist is that the Spaniard is able, by more or less simple means, to suggest the inexpressible. That is why he is an artist.

Do you believe that "a good play cannot really be read?" That no great play can reveal its full greatness except in the theater before an audience? Is there magic in the actor or the producer or the scene-painter? Can a company of actors—granting intelligence, sympathy, a knowledge of acting—endow Shakespeare with greater beauty, greater dramatic power, and deeper implications, than can be realized by the imaginative reader sitting alone in his library?

Meantime, having touched upon a few rather essential matters and a few of the dramatic virtues of "The Bonds of Interest," let us forget our theories and read the play through again.

THE ENGLISH DRAMA

THE ENGLISH DRAMA

It was largely due to the practice of Henry Arthur Jones and Sir Arthur Pinero that English dramatists began to publish their plays; Shaw, a little later, had recourse to publication at first because he could find no producer for his plays.

There are several works devoted entirely or largely to the modern English drama. Of these the most comprehensive are (for the early days) William Archer's *English Dramatists of To-day* and *About the Theater,* Augustin Filon's *The English Stage,* Allardyce Nicoll's *British Drama,* and Mario Borsa's *English Stage of To-day.* Thomas H. Dickinson's *Contemporary Drama of England,* J. W. Cunliffe's *Modern English Playwrights,* A. E. Morgan's *Tendencies of Modern English Drama,* St. John Ervine's *The Theater in My Time,* and Camillo Pellizzi's *English Drama* cover all of modern English drama until recent times.

Most books on the modern drama in general contain chapters on the English dramatists. This does not apply to the post-war drama. A number of young writers have printed plays some of which—owing to difficult economic conditions—have not had a fair chance of production.

More recently some of these younger playwrights, R. C. Sheriff, A. A. Milne, Noel Coward, Dodie Smith ("C. L. Anthony"), in particular have become popular figures in the modern English theater.

Sir Arthur Pinero

Arthur Wing Pinero—later Sir Arthur Pinero—was born at London in 1855. Trained at first for the law, he remained in his father's law office until he was nineteen, when he became an actor, and for a year played minor rôles with the Wyndhams in Edinburgh. In 1876 he came to London, and soon after entered Irving's company and remained at the Lyceum for five years. During this time the young actor had been trying his hand at plays, the first of which, "£200 a Year," was produced at the Globe in 1877. "Daisy's Escape" and "Bygones" followed soon after at the Lyceum. The success of "Daisy's Escape" and the conviction that he was not destined to become a great actor, induced Pinero to devote himself altogether to the writing of plays.

"The Squire" (1881) was the first to show real promise. The year after its production William Archer described the dramatist as a "thoughtful and conscientious writer with artistic aims, if not yet with full command of his artistic means." The artistic means quickly developed in the farces, "Dandy Dick," "The Schoolmistress," and "The Magistrate." "Sweet Lavender" and "The Profligate," more serious in tone, followed in the late eighties. "The Second Mrs. Tanqueray" (1893) more than justified the high hopes aroused by "The Profligate." Throughout the nineties Pinero shared with Jones the supremacy of the English theater, and to this day he is regarded by certain critics as the best-equipped and most skillful playwright of the English-speaking world.

Pinero is master of the dramatic forms he has chosen to develop, and though others (most of them more or less influenced by his example) have had much more to say about life and have said it more subtly, he will be remembered for his achievements as a master craftsman. He died in 1934.

Plays

"£200 a Year" (1877)
"Two Can Play at That Game" (1877)
"The Comet" (1878)
"Daisy's Escape" (1879)
"Hester's Mystery" (1880)
"Bygones" (1880)
"The Money-Spinner" (1880)
"Imprudence" (1881)
"The Squire" (1881)
"Girls and Boys" (1882)
"The Rector" (1883)
"Lords and Commons" (1883)
"The Rocket" (1883)
"Low Water" (1884)
"In Chancery" (1884)
"The Magistrate" (1885)
"The Schoolmistress" (1886)
"The Hobby-Horse" (1886)
"Dandy Dick" (1887)
"Sweet Lavender" (1888)
"The Weaker Sex" (1888)
"The Profligate" (1889)
"The Cabinet Minister" (1890)
"Lady Bountiful" (1891)
"The Times" (1891)
"The Amazons" (1893)
"The Second Mrs. Tanqueray" (1893)
"The Notorious Mrs. Ebbsmith" (1895)
"The Benefit of the Doubt" (1895)
"The Princess and the Butterfly" (1897)
"Trelawney of the 'Wells'" (1898)
"The Gay Lord Quex" (1899)
"Iris" (1901)
"Letty" (1903)
"A Wife Without a Smile" (1904)
"His House in Order" (1906)
"The Thunderbolt" (1908)
"Mid-Channel" (1909)
"Preserving Mr. Panmure" (1911)
"The 'Mind-the-Paint' Girl" (1912)

"The Widow of Wasdale Head" (1912)
"Playgoers" (1913)
"The Big Drum" (1915)
"The Freaks" (1917)
"Mr. Livermore's Dream" (1917)
"Monica's Blue Boy" [wordless play to music] (1918)
"Quick Work" (1919)
"The Enchanted Cottage" (1922)
"A Seat in the Park" (1922)
"A Private Room" (1928)
"Doctor Harmer's Holiday" (1930)
"Child Man" (1930)
"A Cold June" (1932)

(This list does not include translations from the French: "The Ironmaster" (1884), and "Mayfair" (1885); nor librettos for light operas.)

Editions.—The Social Plays of Arthur Wing Pinero, 4 vols., with prefaces by Clayton Hamilton (N. Y. 1917-1922), includes "The Second Mrs. Tanqueray," "The Notorious Mrs. Ebbsmith," "The Gay Lord Quex," "Iris," "Letty," "His House in Order," "The Thunderbolt," and "Mid-Channel." *Two Plays* (London, 1930) includes "Doctor Harmer's Holiday" and "Child Man."

Separate Plays.—"The Magistrate" (Boston, no date); "The Cabinet Minister" (Boston, no date); "Dandy Dick" (Boston, no date); "The Amazons" (Boston, no date); "The Gay Lord Quex" (N. Y. 1900, Boston, no date); "His House in Order" (Boston, 1907); "The Hobby-Horse" (Boston, no date); "Iris" (N. Y. 1902, Boston, 1905); "Lady Bountiful" (Boston, no date); "Letty" (Boston, 1905); "The Notorious Mrs. Ebbsmith" (Boston, no date); "The Profligate" (Boston, no date); "The Schoolmistress" (Boston, no date); "The Second Mrs. Tanqueray" (Boston, no date); "Sweet Lavender" (Boston, no date); "The Times" (Boston, no date); "The Weaker Sex" (Boston, no date); "A Wife Without a Smile" (Boston, 1905); "The Big Drum" (Boston, 1915); "The Enchanted Cottage" (Boston, 1922); "The Freaks" (Boston, 1922); "Preserving Mrs. Panmure" (Boston, 1912); "The 'Mind-the-Paint' Girl" (London, 1913); "The Thunderbolt" (Boston, 1909); "Mid-Channel" (Boston, 1910); "The Benefit of the Doubt" (London, 1896); "Trelawney of the 'Wells'" (N. Y. 1898, Chicago, no date); "The Money-Spinner" (N. Y. 1900); "The Squire" (N. Y. 1905); "The Rocket" (N. Y. 1905); "In Chancery" (N. Y. 1905); "Hester's Mystery" (London, no date); "The Princess and the Butterfly" (N. Y. 1897); "Playgoers" (N. Y. 1913); "A Seat in the Park" (N. Y. 1922).

Reprints in Collections and Anthologies.—"The Second Mrs. Tanqueray" in Dickinson's *Chief Contemporary Dramatists* (Boston, 1915); "The Widow of Wasdale Head" in Clark's *Representative One-Act Plays by British and Irish Authors* (Boston, 1921).

References

Hamilton Fyfe, *Arthur Wing Pinero* (London, 1902) and *Sir Arthur Pinero's Plays and Players* (London, 1930); William Archer, *Poets of the Younger Generation* (London, 1902), *Real Conversations* (London, 1904), *About the Theatre* (London, 1886), *English Dramatists of To-day* (London, 1882), *The Theatrical World,* 5 vols. (London, 1894-1898), *Playmaking* (Boston, 1912), and *The Old Drama and the New* (Boston, 1923); Augustin Filon, *The English Stage,* translated by F. Whyte (N. Y. 1897); Mario Borsa, *The English Stage of To-day,* translated by S. Brinton (N. Y. 1908); Oscar Heermann (ed.), [article on Pinero by W. M. Massee] *Living Dramatists* (N. Y. 1905); E. E. Hale, Jr., *Dramatists of To-day* (N. Y. 1905); T. H. Dickinson, *The Contemporary Drama of England* (Boston, 1917); George Moore, *Impressions and Opinions* (N. Y. 1913); P. P. Howe, *Dramatic Portraits* (N. Y. 1913); Bernard Shaw, *Dramatic Opinions and Essays,* 2 vols. (N. Y. 1907); Ashley Dukes, *Modern Dramatists* (Chicago, 1912), and *The Youngest Drama* (Chicago, 1924); A. B. Walkley, *Drama and Life* (N. Y. 1908), *Frames of Mind* (London, 1899), and *Playhouse Impressions* (London, 1892); Ludwig Lewisohn, *The Modern Drama* (N. Y. 1915); F. W. Chandler, *Aspects of Modern Drama* (N. Y. 1914); C. F. Armstrong, *From Shakespere to Shaw* (London, 1913); H. M. Walbrook, *Nights at the Play* (London, 1911); Brander Matthews, *A Study of the Drama* (Boston, 1910), *Inquiries and Opinions* (N. Y. 1907), and *The Principles of Playmaking* (N. Y. 1919); Clayton Hamilton, *The Theory of the Theater* (N. Y. 1910), *Studies in Stagecraft* (N. Y. 1914), *Problems of the Playwright* (N. Y. 1917), and *Seen on the Stage* (N. Y. 1920); J. T. Grein, *Dramatic Criticism* (London, 1899), *Dramatic Criticism,* Vol. III (London, 1902), *Premieres of the Year* (London, 1900); C. F. Nirdlinger, *Masques and Mummers* (N. Y. 1899); Daniel Frohman, *Memories of a Manager* (Garden City, 1911); W. P. Eaton, *At the New Theater and Others* (Boston, 1910); Norman Hapgood, *The Stage in America* (N. Y. 1901); Hesketh Pearson, *Modern Men and Mummers* (London, 1922); William Winter, *The Wallet of Time,* 2 vols. (N. Y. 1913); James Agate, *At Half-Past Eight* (N. Y. 1923); Weedon Grossmith, *From Studio to Stage* (N. Y. 1913); Mrs. Patrick Campbell, *My Life and Some Letters* (N. Y. 1922); A. E. Morgan, *Tendencies of Modern English Drama* (N. Y. 1924); A. Nicoll, *British Drama* (N. Y. 1933); J. W. Cunliffe, *Modern English Playwrights* (N. Y. 1927); St. J. Ervine, *The Theater in My Time* (London, 1933).

See also.—Pinero's *Robert Louis Stevenson as a Dramatist* (N. Y. 1914), *Browning as a Dramatist* (London, 1912), and "Prefatory Note" to Courtney's *Idea of Tragedy* (N. Y. 1900).

The Second Mrs. Tanqueray

Play in 4 acts (1893). Texts: Boston, no date; in *The Social Plays* (Vol. I, N. Y. 1917); and reprinted in Dickinson's *Chief Contemporary Dramatists* (Boston, 1915).

This play was acclaimed with tremendous enthusiasm when it was first produced. One critic spoke of it as "epoch-making," while William Archer (it was a compliment in those days) declared that it was a work "which Dumas might sign without a blush." The play's importance lies in the fact that it was the best conceived and most logically developed serious play of its generation. The only plays that could be compared with it were Pinero's own "Profligate" and Jones' "Saints and Sinners." It was during the nineties that such plays as this (together with Wilde's "Woman of No Importance," Jones' "Michael and His Lost Angel," and Shaw's "Mrs. Warren's Profession") brought the English stage into the European dramatic movement, with which it had had no relation a short time before.

1. The exposition has been highly praised.[1] Each step is prepared with skill, the story of Aubrey's venture being unfolded in a manner that is both interesting and amusing. There is no trace of the stilted and obvious dialogue that is found in most of the plays of the time. Compare the opening scene of "Mrs. Tanqueray" with Pinero's "Sweet Lavender." The dramatist is no longer under the necessity of introducing such awkward speeches as ". . . I, Edmund Bulger, widower, have loved you, Mrs. Ruth Rolt, widow, ever since you fust set foot in the Temple, fifteen years ago, a-bearing your two-year-old baby in your arms, ma'am." In "The Second Mrs. Tanqueray," by means of an apparently casual conversation, occurring at a natural meeting of Aubrey's friends, his past, his intentions, his relationships, are all made unmistakably clear.

But the business of putting over an exposition has been far better done since 1893. Look at the masterly first act of "The Thunderbolt," or the first act of Barrie's "What Every Woman Knows" and Galsworthy's "Justice."

Compare the expositions in these plays with that of "The

---

[1] Shaw's opinion should, however, be noted. He said: ". . . but when one turns over the pages of 'The Second Mrs. Tanqueray,' and notes the naïve machinery of the exposition of the first act, in which two whole actors are wasted on sham parts, and the hero, at his own dinner party, is compelled to get up and go ignominiously into the next room 'to write some letters' when something has to be said behind his back. . . . When one counts the number of doors which Mr. Pinero needs to get his characters on and off stage . . . it is impossible to avoid the conclusion that what most of our critics mean by mastery of stagecraft is recklessness in the substitution of dead machinery and lay figures for vital action and real characters."

Second Mrs. Tanqueray." Galsworthy's play has scarcely any, but is it required? Could that of "The Second Mrs. Tanqueray" be as summarily disposed of as that of "Mid-Channel"?

2. Pinero has always kept well abreast of the fluctuations in popular tastes and habits of mind. A severe but usually just critic (P. P. Howe, in *Dramatic Portraits*) says of him: "No other hand . . . could supply so efficiently the actual demand. When in the fullness of time and honors, Sir Arthur Pinero has need of an epitaph, it may well be this: 'He kept the theaters open.' He did. As a playwright that was his business. He doubtless thought that an open theater was better than a closed theater. What the critic insinuates is that he did nothing else. But is this true? Read Tom Robertson's 'Caste,' or W. S. Gilbert's 'Sweethearts,' and you will begin to realize that Pinero (at least during his early career) not only kept the theaters open, but thereby deserved the gratitude both of the theatergoers and of the dramatists who were just beginning to write their own plays. Henry Arthur Jones once said to me: 'Don't forget that when I began it was the day of Robertson and H. J. Byron. They were my only models!'" Both Jones and Pinero knew what was going on in Europe; they read Ibsen and were not slow to realize that the ideas then stirring the Continent could be utilized for the English stage. It was not, of course, until the advent of Shaw and Barker that these ideas were finally and convincingly introduced into England (so far as the drama was concerned), but it was Pinero and Jones who paved the way. Howe proceeds: ". . . Perhaps it would not have been possible . . . to have achieved the first act of 'The Thunderbolt' if the third act of 'The Voysey Inheritance' had not shown him the way." And perhaps "The Voysey Inheritance" would never have been written if Pinero and Jones had not shown Barker the way.

Timeliness (of theme, of character, and of dialogue) is an important element in the writing of plays that are intended, as most plays are, for immediate success on the stage. The dramatist of the early nineties was not on the job who failed to perceive that he was living in an age of unrest. Ibsen was a new name: the Independent Theater had produced "Ghosts" in 1891, and English Puritanism had let loose all its hatred and horror upon the heads of Grein and his associates. "Mrs. Warren's Profession" was censored. Wilde was scandalizing the bourgeoisie. George Moore was fighting the libraries. William Morris and Edward Carpenter, H. G. Wells, and Bernard Shaw were dangerous radicals. Suffrage agitation was in the air. Pinero, who doubtless cared little about anything except his art, was none the less on the alert to make use of such themes as were susceptible of dramatic treatment. Jones based his "Michael" upon what was considered by many to be a daring idea. Pinero wrote a "revolutionary" play about that dreadful type, a "woman with a past." The time was ripe, and the dramatist knew it.

3. In his lecture on "R. L. Stevenson: the Dramatist," Pinero says:

> "What is dramatic talent? Is it not the power to project characters, and to cause them to tell an interesting story through the medium of dialogue? This is *dramatic* talent; and dramatic talent, if I may so express it, is the raw material of *theatrical* talent. Dramatic, like poetic, talent is born, not made; if it is to achieve success on the stage, it must be developed into theatrical talent by hard study, and generally by long practice. For theatrical talent consists in the power of making your characters not only tell a story by means of dialogue, but to tell it in such skillfully devised form and order as shall, within the limits of an ordinary theatrical representation, give rise to the greatest possible amount of that peculiar kind of emotional effect the production of which is the one great function of the theater."

Pinero is a dramatist who has developed his dramatic into a thoroughly theatrical talent, by "hard study" and by "long practice." The transition may be best observed by comparing the "dramatic" "Sweet Lavender" with the "theatrical" "Second Mrs. Tanqueray."

4. Pinero's distinction between "theatrical" and "dramatic" is of course arbitrary, but his meaning is clear: he differentiates

the naturally effective ("dramatic") from the artistically effective ("theatrical"). Do you recall any play that is largely "dramatic," a play, so to speak, that has not been submitted to the finer processes of art? Most of the old-fashioned melodramas, like "The Two Orphans" and "The Streets of New York," are undoubtedly "dramatic." Do they possess "theatrical" qualities?

Iris

Drama in 5 acts (1901). Texts: N. Y. 1902, Boston, 1905; reprint in *The Social Plays,* Vol. II (N. Y. 1918).

In "The Second Mrs. Tanqueray" Pinero is content to place before his audience a situation, and by choosing a group of characters, allow the situation, as it were, to work itself out. In "Iris," although there is a situation, the author wished to draw the picture of a woman, struggling in that situation, rather than a situation from which people struggle to extricate themselves. The earlier play was more a story, the later, a painting. "Iris" is justly considered one of the best technical feats accomplished by Pinero; the story is simply and interestingly told, the character of the heroine carefully portrayed.

1. The exposition here is of especial importance. Every step Iris takes in her downward course throughout the play is dependent upon (1) the conditions of the will, and (2) her character. These two points must be indelibly impressed upon the audience, or what follows is bound to be unconvincing. Take careful note of the many references to Iris' temperament; the opening scene, between Miss Pinsent and Kane, is full of them, and when Iris herself enters she adds to our knowledge of the facts. Kane's ". . . It is only fair to assume that your husband, *knowing how greatly your happiness depends upon personal comfort,* was actuated by a desire to safeguard you" (the italics are mine), is especially significant. Iris even goes so far as to quote from the will.

Does Pinero succeed in convincing you of the probability of these conditions? Does he prepare a sufficiently firm foundation upon which to build the rest of the structure? Is the exposition of "Iris" more economical or less so than that of "The Second Mrs. Tanqueray"? Compare it with the exposition of "Mid-Channel."

Do not forget, by the way, that "exposition," like every other purely technical device, is only a means to an end, and that the successful work of art makes you forget, or never directs your attention to, the means. The Latin epigram about art concealing art is another way of putting it.

2. Pinero has selected a character more subtle and difficult to portray than Mrs. Tanqueray: Iris, a weak woman, taxes the dramatist's powers far more than Paula, whose very strength offers a point of resistance upon which to build situations. Positive wills, active agents, are the stuff of which most drama is made; passive or negative wills present obstacles. In "The Second Mrs. Tanqueray" the conflict of wills furnishes ready-made material, in "Iris" the lack of will, the drifting of the heroine, forces the dramatist at every turn to devise situations; he is called upon to exert all his ingenuity in order to keep the story moving.

Compare the two plays from this viewpoint. Notice how carefully Pinero has built up his situations, and how each reveals some new aspect of the heroine's character.

3. The curtain falls nine times during this play. Why? Does this division in any way detract from the effectiveness or unity of the play? Is it a technical weakness? Could the dramatist have managed as well without these frequent interruptions? Does the process add to the interest or intensify the suspense?

4. Pinero is said to be a master of dramaturgic devices. One example will here suffice: shortly after the opening of the fourth act we find the following stage direction:

(After some hesitation, he produces a bunch of keys and removes from it a latchkey. Weighing the key in his hand meditatively, he walks towards the settee; then he turns and tosses the key upon the table. . . . She picks up the key and, rising, drops it into a vase which stands upon the mantelpiece. The key strikes the bottom of the vase with a sharp sound. Having done this, she resumes her seat and sips her tea.)

The significance of the incident is doubly impressed upon the audience; first Maldonado's detaching the key and throwing it upon the table, and second Iris' dropping it, "with a sharp sound," into the vase. This is a clever if not altogether novel trick: it advances the plot and reveals character. What other instances are to be found in "Iris"?

5. In the last act Pinero has the courage which he lacked in "Sweet Lavender," and which some critics declare he lacked when he made Paula Tanqueray commit suicide in order to escape from an intolerable situation. Trenwith's return is a bitter stroke, as it should be; and Iris' confession is wrung from the depths of her being. There is an element of tragedy in her final effort to retain Trenwith, in her query, "Would the home have been ready for me?," and his answer, "Yes." Then comes Maldonado's denunciation; Iris must leave. This, too, savors of tragedy, but after she leaves,

"MALDONADO *utters a fierce cry and, with one movement of his arm, sweeps the china and bric-à-brac from the mantelpiece . . . overturns the table with a savage kick; then, raising a chair high in the air, he dashes it to the floor and breaks it into splinters.*"

Is this in keeping with the spirit of the last scene? Of the whole play. (Remember, Pinero was not writing for the movies.)

6. Eugene Walter's "Easiest Way" is in many respects similar to "Iris." Compare the two plays. Take, for instance, the first acts of each play. Assuming that you know nothing of either, how far could you reconstruct the ensuing action?

This suggests an interesting problem—certain aspects of which have already been discussed, the problem of where to begin a play. This is an exceedingly important matter for the dramatist who cannot (as the novelist can) describe in detail the critical events in the lives of his characters over a long period of years.

Compare "Iris" and "The Easiest Way." Why did Pinero open his story where he did, and why did Walter choose to open his play where *he* did?

MID-CHANNEL

Play in 4 acts (1909). Texts: Boston, 1910; reprinted in *The Social Plays,* Vol. IV (N. Y. 1922).

"Mid-Channel" is one of the most successful of Pinero's serious social studies. Though it was written late in the author's career it is technically superior to any of the plays that preceded it. In spite of an exceptionally good cast it was not particularly successful in England, though in America (where it was acted by Ethel Barrymore) it had a year's run.

1. In his critical preface to "Mid-Channel" (in *The Social Plays*) Clayton Hamilton raises an interesting question regarding the technique of exposition:

> The first act of "Mid-Channel" opens with a conventional series of questions and answers between Ethel Pierpoint and her mother. In 1910 I accused the author of having adopted a labor-saving device in this respect. Sir Arthur answered with his customary frankness. "After the elaborate exposition of 'The Thunderbolt,'" he said to me, "it no longer seemed worth while to begin 'Mid-Channel' with a clever passage. It is difficult to be clever, but it is not impossible. There are certain things that must be told to the audience, as quickly and conveniently as possible, at the outset of any play. Why not tell these things quite frankly and get them over with?"

Why not? Could the same method have been successfully employed with the exposition of "The Thunderbolt"?

Granting that the exposition of "Mid-Channel" is rather conventional, compact, obvious, would the play have gained by having a long and more detailed exposition? In other words, what is gained by the method here adopted? And what is lost?

2. Though the student is again warned of the danger of attempting to set up too rigid standards of classification, it is always interesting and sometimes useful to speculate on the difference between one type of play and another; comedy and tragedy, for instance; even if it is not possible to arrive at satisfactory conclusions, the effort will prove stimulating and add

to the intelligent enjoyment of drama as a whole. What, we again ask, is tragedy? Paul Hervieu says:

> It is a play every part of which aims to create suspense, deep thinking, and pity. It is accompanied no longer, as of old, with magnificent draperies; it is a thing of the day, logical, prosaic, no longer bloody . . . the ways of fate are no longer manifested, as with the Greeks, in dreams, visions, or presentiments. Nowadays we try to show how the struggle for existence bears down inexorably upon those who are imprudent, too weak to defend themselves, those whose passions are stronger than their will power.

This, of course, is peculiarly applicable to the plays of Hervieu himself, who has written tragedies according to his own formula. The French dramatist, as a rule, makes plays out of the human passions; with him the passions are usually sufficient in themselves to explain failure and tragedy. With the Anglo-Saxon this is not enough: if passions do work havoc with human lives, he is unwilling to accept that as the sole reason for failure; he must add external circumstances. In "Iris," however, Pinero accounts for the woman's ruin by her passion and her weakness, chiefly the latter, but he is careful to furnish a convenient Maldonado, the personification of an external force. The French dramatist can make his character declare, "C'est plus fort que moi!" ("I can't help it!"), and proceed with the happy assurance that his motivation is sufficient. Pinero is not an emotional dramatist, as Donnay and D'Annunzio are emotional; he must account for his tragic failures in some other way. In "Mid-Channel," Zoe gives us the reason for her tragedy and her husband's. She says: "It was doomed from the moment we agreed that we'd never be encumbered in our career with any—brats of children."

Pinero's "dramas" are practically tearless: they are dramatic and effective, but only in the rarest instances do they move us to tears. Perhaps this is the result of his English environment, and possibly the fear that the British public dislikes any display of the deeper emotions. Pinero prefers to be intellectual, rather than emotional, and wishes his plays to rest upon logic rather than upon passion. It must be remembered that his characters are nearly all English.

3. The "Raisonneur" (literally, the "Reasoner") is a stock figure in many of the plays of the nineteenth century, and in the plays of Dumas *fils* serves simply as a mouthpiece for the author. He is often a dull and prosy individual. In England, especially in the plays of Pinero and Jones, we find him as a middle-aged, kindly man-of-the-world, the adviser who invariably sets matters straight and administers doses of good advice, ostensibly to the characters of the play, but actually to the audience. He is at once a dramatic expedient, a foil, and a preacher. In the hands of the actor for whom the part is written, he becomes a link, as it were, between the audience and the author. Some striking instances of the use of the "Raisonneur" are found in "The Liars," "Mrs. Dane's Defence," "The Case of Rebellious Susan," and "Dolly Reforming Herself," of Jones. In "Mid-Channel" it is Peter Mottram. Here, besides bringing about the temporary reconciliation between man and wife, he announces the theme of the play, and offers a pleasant relief to the sordidness of the rest of the piece.

Is there a character corresponding to Peter in "The Second Mrs. Tanqueray"? In "The Thunderbolt"?

4. The suicide in "Mid-Channel" is as inevitable as the suicides in "Hedda Gabler" and "Justice." The dramatist has left no possible escape for the unfortunate woman. Trace the steps leading up to the catastrophe. Is there a point where matters could have been satisfactorily arranged? Might a logical change of heart have taken place in Theodore? Zoe being as she was, and Theodore remaining obdurate—in strict accordance with his character as we know it—could a reconciliation have been made plausible?

HENRY ARTHUR JONES

Henry Arthur Jones was born at Grandborough, Bucks, in 1851. He attended school in his native town, and at an early age entered business at Bradford. He was for several years a commercial traveler. Before he was thirty, however, he wrote his first play, "Only 'Round the Corner," which was produced at Exeter in 1878. During the next four years he wrote several short plays. In 1882 he won his first brilliant success, with the famous melodrama "The Silver King," written in collaboration with Henry Herman. "Saints and Sinners" appeared two years later, and marked an epoch in the development of modern English drama. Like Pinero, he wrote some of his best plays during the busy nineties, including "Michael and His Lost Angel," "The Liars" and "The Case of Rebellious Susan," the first a tragic drama, the others social satires. Until 1917, Jones continued writing plays of varying merit; since then he has devoted most of his energies to political pamphleteering.

Aside from his sixty plays, Jones has contributed a considerable mass of theory and propagandist literature on the modern drama, setting high standards in dramatic art both for the dramatist and the public. To him is due in part that impetus which has resulted in what he himself calls the Renascence of the English Drama. His work is doubly significant. It marks the return of the best English traditions to the modern stage, for in spite of the innovations for which he has so ardently pleaded, he remains at his best a dramatist of the school of Goldsmith and Sheridan. Jones died in 1929.

Plays

"Only 'Round the Corner" (1878)
"Hearts of Oak" (1879)
"Harmony" (1879)
"Elopement" (1879)
"A Clerical Error" (1879)
"An Old Master" (1881)
"His Wife" (1881)
"Home Again" (1881)
"A Bed of Roses" (1881)
"The Silver King" [with Henry Herman] (1882)
"Chatterton" [with Henry Herman] (1884)
"Saints and Sinners" (1884)
"Hoodman Blind" [with Wilson Barrett] (1885)
"The Lord Harry" [with Wilson Barrett] (1886)
"The Noble Vagabond" (1886)
"Hard Hit" (1887)
"Heart of Hearts" (1887)
"Wealth" (1889)
"The Middleman" (1889)
"Judah" (1890)
"Sweet Will" (1890)
"The Deacon" (1890)
"The Dancing Girl" (1891)
"The Crusaders" (1891)
"The Bauble Shop" (1893)
"The Tempter" (1893)
"The Masqueraders" (1894)
"The Case of Rebellious Susan" (1894)
"The Triumph of the Philistines" (1895)
"Michael and His Lost Angel" (1896)
"The Rogue's Comedy" (1896)
"The Physician" (1897)
"The Liars" (1897)

"Grace Mary" (1898)
"The Manœuvres of Jane" (1898)
"Carnac Sahib" (1899)
"The Lackey's Carnival" (1900)
"Mrs. Dane's Defence" (1900)
"The Princess's Nose" (1902)
"Chance the Idol" (1902)
"Whitewashing Julia" (1903)
"Joseph Entangled" (1904)
"The Chevaleer" (1904)
"The Heroic Stubbs" (1906)
"The Hypocrites" (1906)
"The Goal" (1907)
"The Evangelist" (1907)
"Dolly Reforming Herself" (1908)
"Fall In, Rookies!" (1910)
"We Can't Be as Bad as All That" (1910)
"The Knife" (1910)
"The Ogre" (1911)
"Lydia Gilmore" (1912)
"The Divine Gift" (1912)
"Mary Goes First" (1913)
"The Lie" (1914)
"Cock o' the Walk" (1915)
"Her Tongue" (1915)
"The Pacifists" (1917)

Editions.—The Selected Plays of Henry Arthur Jones, 4 vols., edited, with introductions, by Clayton Hamilton (Boston, 1924), includes "The Silver King," "The Middleman," "Judah," "The Dancing Girl," "Michael and His Lost Angel," "The Liars," "Mrs. Dane's Defence," "The Hypocrites," "The Crusaders," "The Tempter," "The Masqueraders," "The Case of Rebellious Susan," "Dolly Reforming Herself," "The Divine Gift," "Mary Goes First," "Grace Mary," and "The Goal"; *The Theater of Ideas* (N. Y. 1915) includes "The Goal," "Her Tongue," and "Grace Mary."

Separate Plays.—"Harmony" (N. Y. no date); "Elopement" (N. Y. no date); "Hearts of Oak" (N. Y. no date); "A Clerical Error" (N. Y. 1906), "An Old Master" (N. Y. no date); "A Bed of Roses" (N. Y. no date); "The Deacon" (N. Y. no date); "Sweet Will" (N. Y. no date); "Joseph Entangled" (N. Y. 1906); "The Silver King" (N. Y. 1907); "The Dancing Girl" (N. Y. 1907); "The Middleman" (N. Y. 1907); "The Hypocrites" (N. Y. 1908); "Mrs. Dane's Defence" (N. Y. 1905); "The Case of Rebellious Susan" (N. Y. 1909); "The Liars" (N. Y. 1901); "The Masqueraders" (N. Y. 1909); "Dolly Reforming Herself" (N. Y. 1910); "The Manœuvres of Jane" (N. Y. 1905); "Judah" (N. Y. 1894); "The Physician" (N. Y. 1899); "The Rogue's Comedy" (N. Y. 1898); "The Triumph of the Philistines" (N. Y. 1899); "The Crusaders" (N. Y. 1893); "Whitewashing Julia" (N. Y. 1905); "The Tempter" (N. Y. 1905); "Carnac Sahib" (London, 1899); "Michael and His Lost Angel" (N. Y. 1896); "Saints and Sinners" (London, 1891); "The Divine Gift" (N. Y. 1913); "Mary Goes First," preface by Clayton Hamilton (Garden City, 1914); "The Lie" (N. Y. 1915).

Reprints in Collections and Anthologies.—"Michael and His Lost Angel" in Dickinson's *Chief Contemporary Dramatists* (Boston, 1915); "The Masqueraders" in Moses' *Representative British Dramas* (Boston, 1918); "The Goal" in Clark's *Representative One-Act Plays by British and Irish Authors* (Boston, 1921); "Dolly's Little Bills" in *One-Act Plays for Stage and Study* (N. Y. 1924) [this last an arrangement of a scene, by the author, from "Dolly Reforming Herself"].

References

William Archer, *The Theatrical World,* 5 vols. (London, 1894-1898), *About the Theater* (London, 1886), *English Dramatists of To-day* (London, 1882), *Playmaking* (Boston, 1912), *Study and Stage* (London, 1899), and *The Old Drama and the New* (Boston, 1923) ; A. B. Walkley, *Drama and Life* (N. Y. 1908), and *Playhouse Impressions* (London, 1892) ; T. H. Dickinson, *The Contemporary Drama of England* (Boston, 1917) ; F. W. Chandler, *Aspects of Modern Drama* (N. Y. 1915) ; Mario Borsa, *The English Stage of To-day,* trans. by S. Brinton (N. Y. 1908) ; Augustin Filon, *The English Stage,* trans. by F. Whyte, introduction by Jones (N. Y. 1897) ; Daniel Frohman, *Memories of a Manager* (Garden City, 1911) ; P. P. Howe, *Dramatic Portraits* (N. Y. 1913) ; D. E. Oliver, *The English Stage* (London, 1912) ; Clement Scott, *The Drama of Yesterday and To-day,* 2 vols. (N. Y. 1899) ; George Moore, *Inquiries and Opinions* (N. Y. 1913) ; Bernard Shaw, *Dramatic Opinions and Essays,* 2 vols. (N. Y. 1907) ; Ludwig Lewisohn, *The Modern Drama* (N. Y. 1915) ; Barrett H. Clark, *European Theories of the Drama* (N. Y. 1929) ; W. P. Eaton, *The American Stage of To-day* (Boston, 1908) ; Clayton Hamilton, *The Theory of the Theater* (N. Y. 1910), and *Studies in Stagecraft* (N. Y. 1914) ; J. T. Grein, *Dramatic Criticism* (London, 1899), *Dramatic Criticism,* III (London, 1902) ; Brander Matthews, *A Study of the Drama* (Boston, 1910) ; William Winter, *The Wallet of Time* (N. Y. 1913) ; A. E. Morgan, *Tendencies of Modern English Drama* (N. Y. 1924) ; Allardyce Nicoll, *British Drama* (N. Y. 1933) ; J. W. Cunliffe, *Modern English Playwrights* (N. Y. 1927) ; Doris Arthur Jones, *Taking the Curtain Call* (N. Y. 1930) ; Richard A. Cordell, *Henry Arthur Jones and the Modern Drama* (N. Y. 1932).

See also.—Jones' *The Renascence of the English Drama* (N. Y. 1895), *The Foundations of a National Drama* (N. Y. 1913) ; Introduction to Brunetière's *Law of the Drama* (N. Y. 1914), to *The Theater of Ideas* (N. Y. 1915), and prefaces to "The Divine Gift," "The Case of Rebellious Susan," and "The Triumph of the Philistines."

Michael and His Lost Angel

Play in 5 acts (1896). Texts: N. Y. 1896 in Dickinson's *Chief Contemporary Dramatists* (Boston, 1915), and in *The Selected Plays* (Boston, 1924).

"Michael and His Lost Angel" is Jones' most ambitious play. It is remarkable as the most sincerely outspoken drama of passion of its time. Bernard Shaw said of it: "It seems . . . to me to be a genuinely sincere and moving play, feelingly imagined, written with knowledge as to the man and insight as to the woman by an author equipped not only with the experience of an adept playwright, and a kindlv and humorous observer's sense of contemporary manners, but with that knowledge of spiritual history in which Mr. Jones' nearest competitors seem so stupendously deficient." The play was not a success, owing to difficulties in casting, it was said, but Shaw has hit the nail on the head in the following sentence: "The melancholy truth of the matter is that the English stage got a good play, and was completely and ignominiously beaten by it."

1. Measuring "Michael and His Lost Angel" by the definitions of tragedy set forth by Hervieu, and those considered in connection with Pinero's "Iris," in what category does this play belong?

2. In his *Dramatic Opinions and Essays* Shaw remarks:

As to the first two acts, I ask nothing better; but at the beginning of the third comes the parting of our ways; and I can point out the exact place where the roads fork. In the first act, Michael, a clergyman, compels a girl who has committed what he believes to be a deadly sin, to confess it publicly in church. In the second act he commits that sin himself. At the beginning of the third act he meets the lady who has been his accomplice; and the following words pass between them:

AUDRIE. You're sorry?
MICHAEL. No. And you?
AUDRIE. No.

Now, after this, what does the clergyman do? Without giving another thought to the all-significant fact that he is not sorry—that at the very point where, if his code and creed were valid, his conscience would be aching with remorse, he is not only impenitent, but positively glad, he proceeds to act as if he really were penitent, and not only puts on a hair shirt, but actually makes a confession to his congregation in the false character of a contrite sinner, and goes out from among them with bowed head to exile and disgrace, only waiting in the neighborhood until the church is empty to steal back and privily contradict his pious imposture by picking up and hiding a flower which the woman has thrown on the steps of the altar.

Shaw blames Michael for not being true to his own conviction: he should either have been sorry, and told Audrie so—in which case there would have been no play—or else not have confessed himself wrong. In this case, the play would have been tragic in every sense of the word, for society would have prevented the couple from living as they thought it right to live. But as it is, we have nothing but a weakling, at most a pathetic, not a tragic figure.

How far is Shaw's criticism just? Does Jones intend Michael to be contrite? Is he really "not sorry," as he declares to Audrie? Is the play a true tragedy? And if it is not, what is it? In any event, does it make any difference what it is or is not called?

3. Jones has repeatedly asserted that literature and the drama should be inseparable; a play must stand the test of time, and to do this, it must stand the test of print. In his essay on "Literature and the Modern Drama" (*The Foundations of a National Drama*) he says:

> If your drama is truly alive, it will necessarily be literature. If you have faithfully and searchingly studied your fellow citizens; if you have selected from amongst them those characters that are interesting in themselves, and that also possess an enduring human interest; if in studying these interesting personalities, you have severely selected from the mass of their sayings and doings and impulses, those words and deeds and tendencies which mark them at once as individuals and types; if you have then recast and re-imagined all the materials; if you have cunningly shaped them into a story of progressive and cumulative action; if you have done all this, though you may not have used a single word but what is spoken in ordinary American intercourse to-day, I will venture to say that you have written a piece of live American literature—that is, you have written something that will not only be interesting on the boards of the theater, but can be read with pleasure in your library, can be discussed, argued about, tasted, and digested as literature.

Literature in the drama, then, is not altogether a matter of style. Style is first "dramatic," and afterwards, if need be, "literary" in the non-dramatic sense. Novelists and poets have from time immemorial written literary plays without possessing any sense of dramatic form. The Roman Seneca wrote "plays" which were probably never produced, even in antiquity. The great poets of the nineteenth century—Shelley, Keats, Browning, Tennyson, Swinburne—all wrote "plays" which, if produced, would bore most audiences. These fail not because they happen to be literature, but because they happen to be poor drama. In most cases (though Shelley declares he wrote for the stage) the poets failed because they were intent upon style rather than plot. Aristotle knew far better than they that plot is the first requisite of tragedy. Modern novelists like Galsworthy and Barrie have written plays of literary distinction, but it will be seen that the style of their dialogue is far different from the style of their novels and stories. On the other hand, masters of English prose like Stevenson and George Moore have written dramas all of which, though written in a style which would for the most part look well in a novel, is out of place in their undramatic plays. Moore knows a good deal about the theater, but such plays as "The Strike at Arlingford," "The Coming of Gabrielle," and "The Bending of the Bough" are full of "fine writing" which would, in a novel, be admirable, but which on the stage is usually tedious.

We are confronted with a curious anomaly: it is only great literature that survives in drama: Sophocles is read to-day and will be read a thousand years hence, because he was a literary artist; but some of the most successful dramatists of the nineteenth century (Scribe, for instance) are to-day no more than curiosities. Suppose (for the sake of argument) we conceive a play as great as "Hamlet," but written (so far as the language alone is concerned) as it would be written by the popular novelist A. Would it survive? Or suppose a poor play to be written as Shakespeare (were he only the author of the "Sonnets") would write it? Would it survive? It assuredly would survive, *as literature,* but the *play* would die because it was not drama.

Perhaps the test is not a fair one, but the issue is clear, is it not?

4. What of the style in "Michael and His Lost Angel"?

The Liars

Comedy in 4 acts (1897). Texts: N. Y. 1901; and in *The Selected Plays* (Boston, 1924).

"The Liars" is as fine an example of the English comedy of manners as any written during the past quarter century. Skillful plot construction, clever dialogue, and good-natured satire combine to make it a masterpiece. Behind all the amusement is the eternal "lesson": that society in order to exist must adhere to a set of regulations, and that any infringement of its laws invariably brings social ruin. Needless to say, the idea is not forced upon us; it is allowed, as it should be, to evolve out of the story.

1. In the third act of J. O. Francis' Welsh play, "Change," the dramatist eliminates all the characters except the mother and Lizzie Ann, directing his attention upon these two. He does this in order to make his climax, which occurs at the end of the third act, a unified and striking scene. More than this, he must select from among his characters those to whom the sympathy of the audience is most naturally attracted. An audience usually has their attention directed, as the play approaches its climax, to one person or one small group of persons; or else to one situation or crisis in which these characters are involved; when the plot becomes tense there can be no scattering of attention. In Jones' "Mrs. Dane's Defence" there is a similar narrowing down of the interest, until the climax begins in the cross-examination scene, where Mrs. Dane and her interlocutor occupy, figuratively as well as actually, the center of the stage. If the action were to be diagrammed it might be represented by a pyramid, of which the apex is the climax.

In "The Liars," the dramatist adopts an entirely different method: instead of eliminating characters, he adds to their number from moment to moment. From the very beginning of the third act, he begins building up for the climax. First, there is the letter from George, which Lady Jessica reads to

Lady Rosamund; then Freddie's entrance, adding a further complication; then Sir Christopher's, which seems to promise a way out of the disagreeable predicament. Then enter Mrs. Crispen and Mrs. Coke, and finally George. Most inopportunely of all, comes Archibald Coke, who precipitates the final downfall, and not long after, Gilbert, followed by Falkner.

Study in detail the methods by which the cumulative effect is made. If, in "Change" and "Mrs. Dane's Defence," the rise in tension and the elimination of characters can be represented by a pyramid, might not that of "The Liars" be represented by an inverted pyramid? In what does the unity of the act consist?

2. The play is virtually over with the fall of the curtain on the third act. What function does the last act fulfill? To what means does the dramatist resort to make his final act interesting? Is it really superfluous?

3. "The Liars," like all authentic comedies, is a comedy of character. Congreve's "Way of the World," one of the greatest English comedies, is almost devoid of story. "A plot," says Meredith in his *Essay on Comedy,* was "an afterthought with Congreve." We have said that great drama—especially great comedy—has little need of plot, because the characters will almost take care of themselves. And yet "The Liars" has a very distinct and carefully developed plot. Is it, therefore, of necessity an inferior comedy?

Meredith says, in the essay just referred to, that "one excellent test of the civilization of a country . . . I take to be the flourishing of the comic idea and comedy; and the test of fine comedy is that it shall awaken thoughtful laughter."

What is "thoughtful laughter"? Does "The Liars" awaken it? Does the comedy arise from the plot, or from the characters?

Oscar Wilde

Born in Dublin in 1854, of cultured and well-to-do Irish parents, Oscar Wilde spent his early youth in his native country. For three years he attended Trinity College in Dublin, but completed his university education at Oxford, where he specialized in the classical studies. After traveling in Italy and Greece, he came to London. His first book was a volume of poems (1881); these were followed by the play, "Vera, or the Nihilists," performed in the United States in 1883. "The Duchess of Padua," a verse tragedy, was acted in 1891. Meantime Wilde had been in Paris, there making the acquaintance of many of the literary men of the period. In 1884 he married, and was enabled, through his wife's fortune, to devote his time to lecturing and writing. The important plays—"Lady Windermere's Fan," "A Woman of No Importance," "An Ideal Husband," and "The Importance of Being Earnest"—were produced between 1892 and 1895. In 1895, Wilde was sentenced to two years' imprisonment with hard labor as the result of a notorious trial instigated against him by the Marquess of Queensberry. (For details of the trial, which are beyond the scope of the present work, see Arthur Ransome's *Oscar Wilde,* original edition, and Wilde's own *De Profundis.*) On leaving prison he went to France; there, and at Naples, where he went later and wrote "The Ballad of Reading Gaol," he dragged out the few remaining years of his life. He died at Paris in 1900.

In *De Profundis* Wilde said: "I took the drama, the most objective form known to art, and made of it as personal a mode of expression as the lyric or the sonnet; at the same time I widened its range and enriched its characterization." He refers to his "social" plays, and speaks rather of what he intended to do than of his actual accomplishment. In his poetic plays and fragments—"The Duchess of Padua," "A Florentine Tragedy," and "Salomé"—he wrote imitative pieces and some picturesque pseudo-Elizabethan poetry; his other plays, except "Vera," are comedies whose cleverness, ingenuity, and wit earned for them the admiration of contemporary audiences.

Wilde, more than any other man of his day, recognized the "necessity of style." Although his plays occasionally contain specimens of artificial and stilted language, a farce like "The Importance of Being Earnest" is a triumph of artificiality, a work intended simply as a display piece. Wilde could invent plots and develop an intrigue with great skill. Henry Arthur Jones, Sir James Barrie, Somerset Maugham, Bernard Shaw, and Granville Barker owe much to their brilliant predecessor.

Plays

"Vera, or the Nihilists" (1883)
"The Duchess of Padua" (1883)
"Lady Windermere's Fan" (1892)
"A Woman of No Importance" (1893)
"An Ideal Husband" (1895)
"The Importance of Being Earnest" (1895)
"Salomé" (1896)

(There are, besides, two fragments of plays: "A Florentine Tragedy" and "La Sainte Courtisane." "For Love of the King" is a Burmese Masque. This last is published in London, 1922.)

Editions.—There are many editions, more or less complete, of the works of Wilde. Among these the best are the Patrons' Edition, 12 vols. (Garden City, no date), and the Ravenna Edition, 15 vols. (N. Y. no date). *The Plays of Oscar Wilde,* 4 vols. (Boston, 1905-1907), includes all the plays and fragments; Vol. XII of the Patrons' Ed. includes "A Florentine Tragedy," "Salomé," and "La Sainte Courtisane"; *The Plays of Oscar Wilde,* 1 vol. (N. Y. 1914), includes all the complete plays.

Separate Plays.—"The Duchess of Padua" (N. Y. 1906, London, 1909); "A Florentine Tragedy" (N. Y. 1908); "An Ideal Husband" (Boston, 1906, 2 eds., one in paper; London, 1899*ff.*); "The Importance of Being Earnest" (London, no date, and several reprints; N. Y. no date, and reprints; Boston, 1906); "Lady Windermere's Fan" (London, 1893, and reprints; N. Y. 1907, and reprints); "A Woman of No Importance" (London, 1899, and reprints; Boston, 1906, 2 eds., one in paper; N. Y. no date, and reprints); "Vera" (London, 1880); "Salomé" (in French, Paris, 1893; in English trans., London, 1894, and reprints; N. Y. 1906-1911, and reprints, and in *Poet Lore*, Boston, 1907).

Reprints in Collections and Anthologies.—"Lady Windermere's Fan" in Dickinson's *Chief Contemporary Dramatists* (Boston, 1915), and in Tatlock and Martin's *Representative English Plays* (N. Y. 1917); "The Importance of Being Earnest" in Moses' *Representative British Dramas* (Boston, 1918); "Salomé" in Clark's *Representative One-Act Plays by British and Irish Authors* (Boston, 1921).

References

Frank Harris, *Oscar Wilde, His Life and Confessions,* 2 vols. (N. Y. 1918); L. C. Ingleby, *Oscar Wilde* (London, 1907); Arthur Ransome, *Oscar Wilde* (N. Y. 1912); Lord Alfred Douglas, *Oscar Wilde and Myself* (N. Y. 1914); Anna Comtesse de Brémont, *Oscar Wilde and His Mother* (London, no date); Stuart Mason, *Oscar Wilde, Art and Morality* (London, 1912), and *Bibliography of Oscar Wilde* (London, no date); W. W. Kenilworth, *A Study of Oscar Wilde* (N. Y. 1912); André Gide, *Oscar Wilde, a Study,* trans. by S. Mason (N. Y. 1905); R. H. Sherard, *The Real Oscar Wilde* (London, 1915), and *Oscar Wilde: the Story of an Unhappy Friendship* (London, 1902), and *The Life of Oscar Wilde* (N. Y. 1906); R. T. Hopkins, *Oscar Wilde, A Study of the Man and His Work* (London, 1913); E. La Jeunesse, A. Gide and F. Blei, *Recollections of Oscar Wilde,* trans. by P. Pollard (London, 1906); Bernard Shaw, *Dramatic Opinions and Essays,* 2 vols. (N. Y. 1907); Holbrook Jackson, *The Eighteen-Nineties* (N. Y. 1923); Frank Harris, *Contemporary Portraits,* Vol. I (N. Y. 1915); P. P. Howe, *Dramatic Portraits* (N. Y. 1913); St. John Hankin, *Dramatic Works,* Vol. III (N. Y. 1912); C. E. Montague, *Dramatic Values* (N. Y. 1911); Archibald Henderson, *European Dramatists* (Cincinnati, 1913); William Archer, *The Theatrical World,* 5 vols. (London, 1894-1898), *Playmaking* (Boston, 1912), and *The Old Drama and the New* (Boston, 1923); Mario Borsa, *The English Stage of To-day,* (N. Y. 1908); A. Filon, *The English Stage* (N. Y. 1897); F. W. Chandler, *Aspects of Modern Drama* (N. Y. 1914); T. H. Dickinson, *The Contemporary Drama of England* (Boston, 1917); W. B. Yeats, *The Trembling of the Veil* (London, 1922); Ludwig Lewisohn, *The Modern Drama* (N. Y. 1915); J. T. Grein, *Dramatic Criticism,* III (London, 1902); Robert Lynd, *The Art of Letters* (London, 1920); J. C. Powys, *Suspended Judgments* (N. Y. 1923); Vincent O'Sullivan, *Aspects of Wilde* (N. Y. 1936); G. J. Renier, *Oscar Wilde* (N. Y. 1933); Arthur Symons, *A Study of Oscar Wilde* (London, 1933).

See also.—Wilde's *De Profundis* (in various eds.); *Decorative Art in America* (N. Y. 1906); *A Critic in Pall Mall* (N. Y. 1919); "Reviews," in *The Writings,* Vol. IV (N. Y. 1909).

Salomé

Play in 1 act. Written in 1892, prohibited in Paris the same year. (First produced in that city in 1896. Originally written in French, translated by Lord Alfred Douglas). Texts: in French (Paris, 1893); in English (London, 1894), (N. Y. 1896 and reprints); in Patrons' Edition (Garden City, no date); in Ravenna Edition (N. Y. no date); in *Plays,* 4 vol. ed. (Boston, 1905-1907), and *Plays,* 1 vol. (N. Y. 1914); reprinted in Clark's *Representative One-Act Plays by British and Irish Authors* (Boston, 1921).

"Salomé," like most of Wilde's plays, is a rich and ornate picture: it was written for the purpose of displaying a neat and well-balanced plot, but more especially to exhibit the poet's virtuosity in the writing of a colored and rhythmic if somewhat monotonous language. The figured style of the dialogue is the work of a writer who delights in the sound of mere words. In the original French the style is something of a patchwork: there are speeches reminiscent of Maeterlinck's early manner, and occasional purple patches in the manner of Baudelaire and Flaubert. The play is, however, remarkable for its well-handled plot: it is thoroughly dramatic and holds the attention of the audience to the end.

"In 1901, within a year of the author's death, it was produced in Berlin; from that moment it has held the European stage. It has run for a longer consecutive period in Germany than any play by any Englishman, not excluding Shakespeare. Its popularity has extended to all countries where it is not prohibited. It is performed throughout Europe, Asia, and America. It is played even in Yiddish" (Robert Ross, quoted in Ransome's *Oscar Wilde*).

1. Since the dramatist in writing a one-act play cannot afford much space for lengthy exposition, he often sums it up in a few pages or even a few lines. He is forced to concern himself with the story or incident he has set out to tell. The exposition of "Salomé" is not in the usual form: it is largely the revelation of facts at second-hand, and is done in a more or less summary fashion. The first eight or ten pages are taken up with conversation carried on by the Nubian, the Cappadocian, Herodias' Page, First and Second Soldiers, and the Young Syrian. This is once interrupted by the Voice of Jokanaan. This sort of exposition is doubtless "talky"; it retards the action, yet in a poetic play some allowance may be made for the decorative aspect of the piece, the inherent beauty of the words, and we are willing to have the atmosphere created and wait for the entrance of Salomé herself before the story is appreciably advanced.

Compare the opening scene of "Salomé" with the opening scenes of Galsworthy's "Strife" and Thomas' "Arizona."

2. And now for a further consideration of the one-act play as an independent form. It differs from the full-length play (see p. 314) not altogether in the matter of brevity; it is not a miniature long play, but generally a single incident, episode, or situation. Its technique differs from that of the long play because, as a rule, the dramatist must cover more ground within a shorter space of time. A certain amount of exposition is needful in every play, in the one-act as well as the long, and if anything is going to happen in the one-acter, the dramatist can afford little time in getting under way. Inasmuch as there is rarely time enough to expose and develop more than a single subject, there is rarely very much characterization in

the one-acter: characterization takes time. But the one-act play is a very effective vehicle for the exposition of striking situations; it is rarely used for purposes of showing in detail what human beings are like and why they behave as they do.

Percival Wilde has written an interesting volume on the *Craftsmanship of the One-Act Play*. His definition runs as follows: "A one-act play is an orderly representation of life, arousing emotion in an audience. It is characterized by superior unity and economy; it is playable in a comparatively short space of time; and it is intended to be assimilated as a whole." It is far easier to analyze and destroy such definitions than to make them, but except for the last part of this definition, Mr. Wilde's words apply with equal force to all plays. Superior unity and economy are indeed relative terms: the best one-act play in the world cannot be considered superior either in unity or economy to the best five-act play. The phrase "comparatively short space of time" means anywhere from ten minutes, let us say, to about an hour; "assimilated as a whole" refers, as the author explains, to the fact that there are no long waits between scenes, or no drop of the curtain at all during the performance. A long play is "assimilated part by part"; the one-acter is not, and this it is that differentiates one form from the other. The curtain may actually drop once or even ten times, "provided that by doing so it does not destroy" the unity.

Clayton Hamilton's definition is elsewhere quoted (p. 352). Other theories may be read and pondered, but in the final analysis it is impossible to offer any definition of a living form that is altogether satisfactory; we may generalize, and generalization is often interesting and useful, but theory comes after the fact.

The point now is whether "Salomé" is essentially different in form from Shaw's "Getting Married," which has no act divisions; from Barrie's "The Will," which has; from Shakespeare's "Hamlet," which had no act divisions when it was first performed (or possibly one), and which now has four.

3. As in most tragic plays—and in many others—there is here a continual repetition of the fate motif. The Witches'

scenes in "Macbeth" is a classic example. This is a device used by the dramatist in order to warn the audience that the outcome is to be tragic. How does Wilde make use of it in this play?

4. Contrast is a basic principle of all art. In Richard Strauss's opera of "Salomé," the composer makes use of the interruptions of Jokanaan in order to introduce striking musical contrast. In the play, the first interruption—"After me will come another greater than I," etc.—is a good example of Wilde's use of contrast. The First Soldier and the Cappadocian have been conversing in short sentences:

FIRST SOLDIER. The Jews worship a God they cannot see.

THE CAPPADOCIAN. I cannot understand that.

FIRST SOLDIER. Indeed they believe only in those things they cannot see.

THE CAPPADOCIAN. That seems absolutely ridiculous to me.

Then comes the Voice of Jokanaan. Again: Salomé speaks of the moon:

SALOMÉ. How good it is to see the moon! She resembles a small coin. One might say she was a little flower of silver. She is cold and chaste, the moon—I am sure she is a virgin. She has a virgin's beauty—yes, she is a virgin. She has never soiled herself. She has never given herself to men, as the other goddesses have.

THE VOICE OF JOKANAAN. He is come, the Lord! He is come, the Son of Man. The centaurs have hid themselves, and the sirens have quitted the streams and lie under the leaves in the forests.

Find other examples of dramatic contrast. Is contrast effected here by other methods?

5. "Salomé" is one of the most theatrical of its author's dramatic works. Its success must not be attributed to the accessory qualities—the literary style, etc.—but to its inherent theatrical appeal. Few other one-act plays move so surely, so rhythmically, straight up to a climax so well-devised and thrilling.

Simplicity is the keynote of the action: from Salomé's first inquiries about Jokanaan—"Is he an old man, the prophet?"—there is a steady procession of climaxes, or crises, each leading to another and a greater one. Salomé's curiosity, then her strange love for the uncouth prophet, Herod's entrance, the momentary pause in the tension, then the upward flight of the action, Herod's demand for Salomé to dance, then another moment of suspense, and the rapid climax—here are the things which combine to make "Salomé" an effective theater piece.

LADY WINDERMERE'S FAN

Comedy in 4 acts (1892). Texts: London, 1893, and reprints; N. Y. 1907, and reprints, N. Y. and Boston, no date; in various eds. of *Works;* in *Plays,* 4 vols. (Boston, 1905-1907), and *Plays,* 1 vol. (N. Y. 1914); reprinted in Dickinson's *Chief Contemporary Dramatists* (Boston, 1915), and in Tatlock and Martin's *Representative English Plays* (N. Y. 1917).

It has been said that the form of this play, its wit, its decorative pattern "were of more importance to Wilde than the theme or the characters." We may expect therefore that this "play about a good woman" is rather a clever excuse for a theatrically effective drama and verbal pyrotechnics, than a sympathetic study of the protagonist. The play has stood the test of time, however, fairly well, and in spite of the brilliancy of the plays of such men as Maugham and Davies, it is not yet entirely outmoded.

1. The first act—in the earlier version—ends with the following speech of Lord Windermere:

(*Calling after her.*) Margaret! Margaret! (*A pause.*) My God! What shall I do? I dare not tell her who this woman really is. The shame would kill her. (*Sinks down into a chair and buries his face in his hands.*)

In later editions this speech is altered to:

My God! What shall I do? I dare not tell her that this woman is her mother!

Why was the change made? How does it affect the attitude of the audience in the succeeding acts?[2]

2. Every play necessarily challenges comparison with life, and provided we are ready to accept the artist's conditions—his æsthetic viewpoint—we have a right to measure his work by the standard of truth to life. Some pages from the end of the first act, Lady Windermere speaks the following lines:

How horrible! I understand now what Lord Darlington meant by the imaginary instance of the couple not two years married. Oh! It can't be true—she spoke of enormous sums of money paid to this woman. I know where Arthur keeps his bank book—in one of the drawers of that desk. I might find out by that. I *will* find out. (*Opens drawer.*) No, it is some hideous mistake. (*Rises and goes C.*) Some silly scandal! He loves *me!* He loves *me!* But why should I not look? I am his wife, I have a right to look! (*Returns to bureau, takes out book and examines it, page by page, smiles and gives a sigh of relief.*) I knew it, there is not a word of truth in this stupid story. (*Puts book back in drawer. As she does so, starts and takes out another book.*) A second book—private—locked! (*Tries to open it, but fails. Sees paper knife on bureau, and with it cuts cover from book. Begins to start at the first page.*) Mrs. Erlynne—600—Mrs. Erlynne—700—Mrs. Erlynne—400. Oh! it is true! it is true! How horrible! (*Throws book on floor.*)

(*Enter* LORD WINDERMERE, *C.*)

---

[2] The following is taken from a letter of Wilde written to a London newspaper in 1892: "Allow me to correct a statement put forward in your issue of this evening to the effect that I have made a certain alteration in my play in consequence of the criticism of some journalists who write very recklessly and very foolishly in the papers about dramatic art. . . . I am bound to state that all my friends, without exception, were of opinion that the psychological interest of the second act would be greatly increased by the disclosure of the actual relationship existing between Lady Windermere and Mrs. Erlynne—an opinion, I may add, that had previously been strongly held and urged by Mr. Alexander. As to those of us who do not look on a play as a mere question of pantomime and clowning, psychological interest is everything. I determined, consequently, to make a change in the precise moment of revelation. . . ."

This rhetorical outburst, reduced here to cold type, can be made convincing on the lips of an emotional actress, but we are now considering the text—the skeleton of the play—and we perceive that the dramatic effect is too easily achieved, it is too obvious, and consequently a little discrimination will prevent our believing what we hear. The improbability of the situation is too apparent. Further, Lord Windermere's poor excuse that "the shame would kill" Lady Windermere, is quite insufficient motive. Had Wilde really cared to make his audience believe, he would have taken the trouble to base his plot on a more secure foundation. It is such carelessness as this that doubtless called forth Shaw's accusation that Wilde was "lazy." Wilde was concerned chiefly with externals; he knew that he was telling an interesting if improbable story; he had a number of choice epigrams and some good dramatic material for the ensuing acts—and besides, had Lord Windermere told Lady Windermere the truth, there would have been no play!

The fundamental mistake just pointed out in the first act weakens the story, and Lord Windermere's keeping the secret results in his wife's attempted elopement with Lord Darlington. There is no need multiplying instances of this sort: as the plot proceeds, the weak motivation becomes more and more apparent. By the time the "big" scene comes, with its heavy tirade, we doubt the sincerity of the characters. The "Believe what you choose about me" speech in the third act does not ring true.

3. Wilde's skill in preparing for a big scene has been already observed in "Salomé." In "The Importance of Being Earnest" there is an even better example. What instances can you find in the present play?

Bernard Shaw

George Bernard Shaw was born at Dublin in 1856. Forced at an early age to earn his own living, he entered a land-agent's office in his native city. But his interest in other things—chiefly music and political science—made him restless, and in 1876 he went to London, where for several years he subsisted on a small allowance from his mother, studying and doing hack literary work. Between

1880 and 1883 he wrote four novels, which were failures from a financial viewpoint. But during this time the young man formed valuable associations in Socialistic and literary circles, making friends with William Morris, Sidney Webb, William Archer, Edward Carpenter, and others. In the early nineties he became dramatic critic of the *Saturday Review.* In 1892 his first play, "Widowers' Houses," was performed. This was followed by "The Philanderer" (1893), and "Mrs. Warren's Profession," which was forbidden by the censor. Meantime he was busy lecturing, propagandizing, writing, and participating in the activities of the Fabian Society. Besides, at various times in the nineties, he was both musical and art critic.

Shaw's contribution to the drama is many-sided: first, his own brilliant plays, satires for the most part on contemporary prejudices; second, his five years' work as dramatic critic; and finally, his ideas as an economist and sociologist. It is rather as a philosopher (and popularizer of the philosophies of others) than an artist that his work has penetrated to every corner of Europe. Both in theory and practice he has always favored the thesis play, or play of ideas. To him the theater is a means and not an end. "I am convinced," he says, "that fine art is the subtlest, the most seductive, the most effective means of propagandism in the world, excepting only the example of personal conduct; and I waive even this exception in favor of the art of the stage, because it works by exhibiting examples of personal conduct made intelligible and moving to crowds of unobservant, unreflecting people to whom real life means nothing."

But Shaw happens at the same time to be an artist, and the artist in him occasionally overshadows the moralist, and we get a "Candida" or a "Saint Joan."

The Independent Theater

The Independent Theater, founded in 1891 by J. T. Grein and a few associates, was one of those symptomatic movements that grow out of a desire on the part of small groups of theater lovers to produce plays that are different from the usual run. In France Antoine began the revolt; in Germany two years later Brahm and his fellows opened the Free Stage Society; in 1891 came the London venture. Ibsen and Shaw were the dramatists whom it most helped to establish. In a letter to Grein which forms part of the latter's preface to a recent volume of criticism (1921), Shaw writes:

"It is now very close on thirty years since you madly began an apparently hopeless attempt to bring the English theater into some sort of relation with contemporary culture. Matthew Arnold had suggested that step; but nobody in the theater took the slightest notice of him, because nobody in the theater knew of the existence of such a person as Matthew Arnold. . . . When you first desperately stuck an advertisement into the papers to say that unheard-of enterprise called the Independent Theater would on a certain Sunday night and Monday afternoon perform an unheard-of play . . . when the papers thereon declared that the manager of the theater ought to be prosecuted for keeping a disorderly house, and that you and the foreign blackguard named Ibsen who was your accomplice, should be deported as obvious undesirables, you made a hole in the dyke; and the weight of the flood outside did the rest. When you declared that you would bring to light treasures of unacted English drama grossly suppressed by the managers of that day, you found that there was not any unacted English drama except two acts of an unfinished play (begun and laid aside eight years before) by me; but it was the existence of the Independent Theater that made me finish that play. . . . Everything followed from that: the production of 'Arms and the Man,' . . . Miss Horniman's establishment of Repertory Theaters in Dublin and Manchester, the Stage Society, Granville Barker's tentative matinées of 'Candida' at the Court Theater, the full-blown management of Vedreene and Barker, Edie Craig's Pioneers, and the final relegation of the nineteenth century London theater to the dust-bin by Barrie. . . ."

Plays

"Widowers' Houses" (1892)
"Arms and the Man" (1894)
"Candida" (1895)
"The Devil's Disciple" (1897)
"The Man of Destiny" (1897)
"The Philanderer" (1898)
"Mrs. Warren's Profession" (1898)
"You Never Can Tell" (1899)
"Cæsar and Cleopatra" (1899)
"Captain Brassbound's Conversion" (1900)
"The Admirable Bashville" (1901)
"Man and Superman" (1903)
"John Bull's Other Island" (1904)
"How He Lied to Her Husband" (1904)
"Passion, Poison, and Petrifaction" (1905)
"Major Barbara" (1905)
"The Doctor's Dilemma" (1906)
"The Interlude at the Playhouse" (1907)
"Getting Married" (1908)
"The Shewing-up of Blanco Posnet" (1909)
"Press Cuttings" (1909)
"Misalliance" (1910)
"The Dark Lady of the Sonnets" (1910)

"Fanny's First Play" (1911)
"Overruled" (1912)
"Androcles and the Lion" (1913)
"Pygmalion" (1913)
"Great Catherine" (1913)
"The Music Cure" (1914)
"Augustus Does His Bit" (1917)
"The Inca of Perusalem" (1917)
"O'Flaherty V. C." (1918)
"Annajanska, the Bolshevik Empress" (1918)
"Heartbreak House" (1919)
"Back to Methuselah" (1921)
"Saint Joan" (1923)
"The Glimpse of Reality" (1926)
"The Fascinating Foundling" (1926)
"The Apple Cart" (1930)
"Too True to be Good" (1932)
"On the Rocks" (1933)
"The Six of Calais" (1934)
"The Simpleton of the Unexpected Isles" (1934)
"The Millionairess" (1936)

Editions.—Plays, Pleasant and Unpleasant, 2 vols. (London and Chicago, 1898; N. Y. 1906), includes "Widowers' Houses," "The Philanderer," "Mrs. Warren's Profession," "You Never Can Tell," "Arms and the Man," "Candida," and "The Man of Destiny"; *Three Plays for Puritans* (London and Chicago, 1898, N. Y. 1906) includes "The Devil's Disciple," "Cæsar and Cleopatra," and "Captain Brassbound's Conversion"; *John Bull's Other Island and Major Barbara* (N. Y. 1910) includes also "How He Lied to Her Husband"; *The Doctor's Dilemma, Getting Married, and The Shewing-up of Blanco Posnet* (N. Y. 1911); *Misalliance, The Dark Lady of the Sonnets, and Fanny's First Play* (N. Y. 1914); *Androcles and the Lion, Overruled, and Pygmalion* (N. Y. 1916); *Heartbreak House, Great Catherine, etc.* (N. Y. 1919) includes also three sketches; *Fanny's First Play and The Dark Lady of the Sonnets* (N. Y. no date); *The Man of Destiny and How He Lied to Her Husband* (N. Y. no date); *Translations and Tomfooleries* (N. Y. 1926) includes "The Admirable Bashville," "Press Cuttings," "The Glimpse of Reality," "Passion, Poison, and Petrifaction," "The Fascinating Foundling," and "The Music Cure." *Three Plays* (N. Y. 1934) includes "Too True to be Good," "Village Wooing," and "On the Rocks"; *Three New Plays* (N. Y. 1936) includes "The Simpleton of the Unexpected Isles," "The Millionairess," and "The Six of Calais"; *Nine Plays of Bernard Shaw* (N. Y. 1935) is a selection.

Separate Plays.—"Man and Superman" (N. Y. 1904); "Widowers' Houses" (N. Y. no date); "Press Cuttings" (London, 1909); "Back to Methuselah" (N. Y. 1921); "Saint Joan" (N. Y. 1924); "The Philanderer" (N. Y. no date); "Mrs. Warren's Profession" (N. Y. no date); "Arms and the Man" (N. Y. no date); "Candida" (N. Y. no date); "You Never Can Tell" (N. Y. no date); "The Admirable Bashville" (N. Y. 1909); "The Devil's Disciple" (N. Y. no date); "Cæsar and Cleopatra" (N. Y. no date); "Captain Brassbound's Conversion" (N. Y. no date); "John Bull's Other Island" (N. Y. no date); "Major Barbara" (N. Y. no date); "The Doctor's Dilemma" (N. Y. no date); "Getting Married" (N. Y. no date); "The Shewing-up of Blanco Posnet" (N. Y. no date); "Misalliance" (N.Y. no date); "The Apple Cart" (N. Y. 1931).

References

G. K. Chesterton, *George Bernard Shaw* (N. Y. 1909); Archibald Henderson, *George Bernard Shaw* (N. Y. 1918), *Table-Talk of G. B. S.* (N. Y. 1925) and *Bernard Shaw, Playboy and Prophet* (N. Y. 1932); Holbrook Jackson, *Bernard Shaw* (London, 1907); H. L. Mencken, *George Bernard Shaw* (Boston, 1905); Edward Shanks, *Bernard Shaw* (London, 1924); Renee M. Deacon, *Bernard Shaw as Artist-Philosopher* (N. Y. 1910); Joseph McCabe, *George Bernard Shaw* (N. Y. 1914); John Palmer, *George Bernard Shaw: Harlequin or Patriot?* (N. Y. 1915); P. P. Howe, *Bernard Shaw* (N. Y. 1915); A. Hamon, *The Twentieth Century Molière: Bernard Shaw* (N. Y. 1916); Richard Burton, *Bernard Shaw, the Man and the Mask* (N. Y. 1916); Herbert Skimpole, *Bernard Shaw* (London, 1918); D. A. Lord, *George Bernard Shaw* (N. Y. 1916); Thomas H. Dickinson, *The Contemporary Drama of England* (Boston, 1917); Gilbert Norwood, *Euripides and Shaw* (Boston, 1921); E. E. Hale, Jr., *Dramatists of To-day* (N. Y. 1905); Dixon Scott, *Men of Letters* (N. Y. 1923); Archibald Henderson, *European Dramatists* (N. Y. 1926), and *The Changing Drama* (Cincinnati, 1919); P. P. Howe, *Dramatic Portraits* (N. Y. 1913); James Huneker, *Iconoclasts* (N. Y. 1905); C. E. Montague, *Dramatic Values* (N. Y. 1911); Francis Grierson, *The Invincible Alliance* (N. Y. 1913); Ashley Dukes, *Modern Dramatists* (Chicago, 1912), and *The Youngest Drama* (Chicago, 1924); D. E. Oliver, *The English Stage* (London, 1912); William Archer, *Playmaking* (Boston, 1912), *The Old Drama and the New* (Boston, 1923), and *The Theatrical World,* 5 vols. (London, 1894-1898); C. Lewis Hind, *Authors and I* (N. Y. 1921); Robert Lynd, *Old and New Masters* (N. Y. 1919); Daniel Frohman, *Memories of a Manager* (Garden City, 1911); William Lyon Phelps, *Essays on Modern Dramatists* (N. Y. 1921); A. B. Walkley, *Drama and Life* (N. Y. 1908), and *Frames of Mind* (London, 1899); John Palmer, *The Future of the Theater* (London, 1913), and *The Censor and the Theaters* (N. Y. 1913); Barrett H. Clark, *European Theories of the Drama* (Cincinnati, 1918); W. L. George, *Dramatic Actualities* (London, 1914); C. F. Armstrong, *From Shakespeare to Shaw* (London, 1913); F. W. Chandler, *Aspects of Modern Drama* (N. Y. 1914); Ludwig Lewisohn, *The Modern Drama* (N. Y. 1915), and *The Drama and the Stage* (N. Y. 1922); H. M. Wallbrook, *Nights at the Play* (London, 1911); St. John Ervine, *Some Impressions of My Elders* (N. Y. 1923); D. MacCarthy, *The Court Theater* (London, 1907), and *Remnants* (London, 1918); Francis Hackett, *Horizons* (N. Y. 1919); Hesketh Pearson, *Modern Men and Mummers* (London, 1922), and *A Persian Critic* (London, 1923); J. T. Grein, *Premières of the Year* (London, 1900); *Dramatic Criticism,* III (London, 1902), and *The World of the Theater* (London, 1921); James Agate, *The Contemporary Theater, 1923* (London, 1924), and *Alarums and Excursions* (N. Y. 1922); *Ellen Terry and Bernard Shaw, A Correspondence* (N. Y. 1931); Holbrook Jackson, *The Eighteen-Nineties* (N. Y. 1923); Norman Hapgood, *The Stage in America* (N. Y. 1901); Edward Shanks, *First Essays on Litera-*

ture (London, 1923); A. Hamon, *The Technique of Bernard Shaw's Plays* (London, 1912); Mrs. Patrick Campbell, *My Life and Some Letters* (N. Y. 1922); Allardyce Nicoll, *British Drama* (N. Y. 1933); C. L. & V. M. Broad, *A Dictionary to . . . Bernard Shaw* (N. Y. 1929); S. C. Sen Gupta, *The Art of Bernard Shaw* (N. Y. 1936); Frank Vernon, *The Twentieth-Century Theater* (Boston, 1924); J. S. Collis, *Shaw* (N. Y. 1925). See also, by Shaw: *Dramatic Opinions and Essays* (N. Y. 1907), *The Quintessence of Ibsenism* (N. Y. 1915); *The Perfect Wagnerite* (N. Y. 1901), the essay on Wilde in Harris's *Oscar Wilde* (N. Y. 1918); essays reprinted in Clark's *European Theories of the Drama* (N. Y. 1929); "Preface" and "Appendices" to the Independent Theater edition of "Widowers' Houses" (London, 1893), "Preface" to *Three Plays by Brieux* (N. Y. 1911), *The Sanity of Art* (N. Y. 1908), *The Author's Apology* (N. Y. 1905), "Preface" to *Dramatic Opinions and Essays* (N. Y. 1907); *The Art of Rehearsal* (N. Y. 1928).

Candida

A mystery in 3 acts (1897). Texts: N. Y. no date, and in *Plays Pleasant and Unpleasant,* Vol. II (Chicago, 1898, N. Y. 1906); and in *Nine Plays of Bernard Shaw* (N. Y. 1935).

"Candida" is a shaft aimed at current conceptions of what is moral, right, and fitting. It has always been accepted as a commonplace that the father is the respected head of the family, yet Crampton in "You Never Can Tell" indicates that all fathers are not and should not be such. In "Candida" Shaw attempts to shatter the ideals of the "sanctity of the family," and shows a weak man and a strong man—each at first appearing to be the reverse—with a woman between them. The woman finally clings to the weaker, as he needs her most; not, Shaw implies, because she happens to be his wife.

As an acting play "Candida" is one of Shaw's best works. Not radically different in form from the "Well-made" play, it takes the old conventions and turns them into new channels, and promulgates ideas which are for the most part strictly germane to the story, and sets forth characters with vividness in a highly entertaining manner. Shaw had not as yet freed himself from those elements of "Sardoodledom" against which he had so vigorously protested in his early days as a critic. As will be seen, "Man and Superman" marked a great advance toward technical freedom, while "Getting Married" and "Misalliance" at length bridged the gap.

1. The plays of the past fifty years differ strikingly from those of earlier times in the matter of stage directions. The

Greeks, the Latins, and the Elizabethans wrote primarily for the simplest of stages, so that the merest suggestion (Entrances, Exits, and so on) sufficed for the director. There are few indications of "business." Since it has become the fashion to issue plays in book form, certain dramatists feel the need of amplifying and expounding. Ibsen was among the first to do this, and Shaw has followed in his steps. With the development of the drama, which has been extraordinarily rapid since Ibsen's day, has come the need of commenting upon the more complex settings and subtler characters, which are comparatively new. In general, the earlier plays were simpler, they treated characters more as types. With the advent of Ibsen, stock actors found that such indications as "First Lead," "Villain," and "Ingénue" were not sufficient. Therefore Ibsen told something about his characters in stage-directions. Not satisfied with this, Shaw told a great deal.[3] He carried the practice almost to an extreme, but he was practically forced to do so. Shaw has said that when he published his first two volumes of plays "nobody dreamed of reading plays, which were usually printed in acting editions only, with frankly technical stage-directions, very useful to producers, but utterly destructive to the imagination of a reader." Nobody "would touch" his plays, so that he was compelled to "make people read them."

Determine, after a careful reading of the stage-directions in this play, which among them can be utilized by the actor, manager, and stage-carpenter, and which are for the reader alone.

---

[3] "It is astonishing to me," says Shaw in his preface to *Plays, Pleasant and Unpleasant,* Vol. I, "that Ibsen, who devotes two years to the production of a three-act play, the extraordinary quality of which depends on a mastery of characterization and situation which can only be achieved by working out a good deal of the family and personal history of the individuals represented, should nevertheless give the reading public very little more than the technical memorandum required by the carpenter, the gasman, and the prompter. Who will deny that the resultant occasional mysteriousness of effect, enchanting though it may be, is produced at the cost of intellectual obscurity? Ibsen, interrogated as to his meaning, replies, 'What I have said I have said.' Precisely, but the point is that what he hasn't said he hasn't said."

Compare the stage-directions of Granville Barker in "The Voysey Inheritance" or "The Madras House," and of Barrie in "The Twelve-pound Look," with those in "Candida."

2. It is often said that the characters in Shaw's plays are merely puppets, without life and emotions, set in action by a clever thinker and craftsman. In his *Dramatic Portraits,* P. P. Howe states of the characters in "Mrs. Warren's Profession," and makes the remark applicable to Shaw's characters in general: ". . . They are puppets at the end of wires, and the wires are attached to a battery, and Mr. Shaw is in charge of the current." Usually, Shaw is so much in earnest, so "full of his message," that he cannot adopt an aloof attitude such as, for instance, is found throughout the work of Galsworthy, and allow his personages to speak and act in accordance with their own thoughts, passions, and beliefs. Still, how far does Mr. Howe's criticism apply to "Candida"? To Lady Cecily Waynfleete in "Captain Brassbound's Conversion"? To Dick Dudgeon in "The Devil's Disciple"? Are these people human beings, or are they only puppets?

3. Shaw speaks of the occasional obscurity in Ibsen's plays resulting from a lack of proper stage-directions. What is the value of Shaw's own stage-directions in "Candida"? Especially in the latter part of the first act? Would that scene between Marchbanks and Morrell be quite intelligible without them? Could the dramatist have made it so without them? Has he failed, using the novelist's method in default of dramatic dialogue? What, at the end of the final act, was "The secret in the poet's heart"?

4. During his early days Shaw waged a merciless war against the conventions of the "Well-made" play; and yet he not infrequently made use of those same conventions in his own plays. As one critic put it, he fell in love with his own medium, and it finally mastered him.

Determine in what respects "Candida" is "well-made." Are the "curtains" effective? What of the exposition? Is it sufficient? Obvious? And the development? Compare this play, structurally, with Sudermann's "Magda" and Björnson's "Gauntlet."

A still more "old-fashioned" play of Shaw's is his first, "Widowers' Houses." Notice the "asides," the soliloquy, and the numerous stilted speeches in that play.

Man and Superman

A comedy and a philosophy; a play in 4 acts (1903). Texts: N. Y. 1904; and reprints.

We have seen how in the best of Shaw's work up to the production of "Man and Superman" the thinker and preacher, while always endeavoring to assert himself, was somehow subordinated to the dramatist. In this comedy—and a philosophy—the play itself is used chiefly as a vehicle for the exposition of a thesis. In the preface to the popular edition the author writes: "As I have not been sparing of such lighter qualities as I could endow the book with for the sake of those who ask nothing from a play but agreeable pastime, I think it well to affirm plainly that the third act, however fantastic its legendary framework may appear, is a careful attempt to write a new Book of Genesis for the Bible of the Evolutionists. . . ." Not content with a long prefatory letter, he added a seventy-five-page "Revolutionist's Handbook" to his 190-page play, in order to expound what of his philosophy he was unable to crowd into the comedy.

As a brilliant achievement, an amusing collection of pamphlets, a piece of sustained clear thinking, the volume is a noteworthy achievement, yet "Man and Superman," as a play in the ordinary sense of the word, is pretty feeble: there is so much dissertation that the play—what there is of it—occasionally appears as an impertinent intrusion. Still, there is enough left when it is presented—minus the third act, which has never been played with the rest—to allow one to see how good it might have been.

1. In his protest against the "incorrigibly romantic" Englishman, Shaw has written good plays according to the old dramatic formulas, and equally good ones after he threw them aside. In his revolt against what he considers false in art and life he has been consistent. In "Arms and the Man" his message was the

destruction of the conventional conception of the "heroic" soldier; in "Widowers' Houses" he made of Blanche a cold and unsympathetic girl, largely because he felt that Pinero and G. R. Sims would have made her a little friend of the poor. And so, in "Man and Superman" the love scenes are reversed: the aggressive Ann Whitefield pursues the unwilling Jack Tanner. Conventional dramatists of all times have pictured the lover at the feet of his haughty and distant mistress. Not content with telling the mere truth, and unwilling to utter half-truths about poverty and war and sex, Shaw has stated what appears to his normal eyes to be the truth, from what seems to the average reader and playgoer a decidedly oblique angle. This he has done for the sake of emphasis.

Shaw's "love scenes" are characteristic of his methods. Take the lovers in "Widowers' Houses," in "Mrs. Warren's Profession," "Arms and the Man," "You Never Can Tell," "The Doctor's Dilemma," and "Pygmalion"; compare them with the lovers in Pinero's "Iris," Jones' "Michael and His Lost Angel," and Sheldon's "Romance." Shaw seems mortally afraid of anything touching upon the romantic, yet in "Candida," "The Doctor's Dilemma," and "The Shewing-up of Blanco Posnet," he is not altogether untouched by the universal failing. He never approaches the Latin method, where lovers express in words and gestures every breath in the whirlwind of passion. It should not be too hastily concluded that Shaw is averse from the depiction of true passion—Mrs. Dubedat in "The Doctor's Dilemma" is intended as a deep-feeling woman—but rather that he was dissatisfied with the conventional treatment which too often masqueraded as such; not that he was, in the words of Vaughn in his own "Fanny's First Play," "psychologically incapable of the note of passion." Shaw is too much an artist not to try to use such powers as he possesses.

2. The first act is as good a first act as Shaw ever wrote: there is little discursiveness, the plot is carefully, amusingly, and interestingly begun. But is it quite clear? Is, for instance, the mistake as to Violet's position—the scene occupying the last few pages of the act—made quite plain? The act closes on

this scene, and great importance is attached to the episode. Technique or no technique, the end of an act is a conspicuous point, and what is put there is bound to attract attention.

3. The second act is on the whole good drama, concerned for the most part with the Ann-Tanner story; it progresses straight up to the little climax. The starting of the motor, visible to the audience, is a clever device for advancing the plot. Straker is possibly a little puzzling, but he is so amusing that we may excuse his actual or apparent superfluity. We do not yet know whither his philosophizing is to lead us. So far, then, so good.

4. The third act is never played—except independently, as "Don Juan in Hell"—the reason given being that the entire play would prove too long for a single representation.[4] But Shaw is always so scrupulous and uncompromising when it comes to the performance of his plays, that this excuse must be taken as a confession of failure: the act is practically negligible so far as the play is concerned. Fortunately, there was scarcely any preparation in the two preceding acts for this one, nor does the third contain much that concerns the fourth. Only a very few minor changes are made for the stage version.

Read the third act, and try to determine what relation it has with the rest of the play.

5. The last act is good and bad, dramatically. In nearly every Shaw play the dramatic qualities should, if possible, be differentiated from the intellectual, the didactic. The earlier pages of this fourth act are interesting and amusing, but Malone's talk about Ireland properly belongs in "John Bull's Other Island." "Man and Superman" is only resumed when Tanner and Ann take the stage again, and Ann, summoning up all her power in order to fulfill her mission, finally captures Tanner.

---

[4] I have before me a printed note which the author wrote at the request of the management of some society which performed "Don Juan in Hell." Toward the end of the note G. B. S. says: "A discussion arises . . . as to the merits of the heavenly and hellish states, and the future of the world. The discussion lasts more than an hour, as the parties, with eternity before them, are in no hurry." The playgoer, however, has not eternity before him, and Shaw knew this.

Some of the more striking difficulties under which the dramatist labored in trying to weld together many utterly foreign elements in this play, have been touched upon. Can you discover others? There is little need to indicate the redeeming features of "Man and Superman": the intellectual agility, the wit, the good humor. These are evident, but only because Shaw is so nearly a great dramatist is it worth while to observe his shortcomings.

Getting Married

Comedy in 1 scene (1908). Texts: N. Y. no date; and in *The Doctor's Dilemma, Getting Married, and The Shewing Up of Blanco Posnet* (N. Y. 1911).

If Shaw's plays are considered in chronological order, from "Widowers' Houses" to "Misalliance," it will be observed that they evolve, in the matter of technical form, from what is a more or less close approximation to the old-fashioned "Well-made" play to the loosest sort of "conversation" play. In studying the two works already outlined, we have seen how "Candida" was in many respects "well-made," and how "Man and Superman" departed to a great extent from the formulas. In "Getting Married" a radical departure will be observed; here we find a complete neglect of technical canons.

1. Nowadays it is more difficult to classify plays than it used to be: there are comedies which end with the death of the principal character (Rostand's "Cyrano de Bergerac" and Lemaître's "Bertrade"), nondescript pieces in which the hero dies and his wife remarries (Shaw's "The Doctor's Dilemma"); and others which defy classification (Andreyev's "Anathema" and Wedekind's "Such is Life"). For example, the term "play of ideas" may be applied to many of Ibsen's later works, yet "The Wild Duck" and "Rosmersholm" are much more than this. Chekhov's "The Seagull" is certainly a play of ideas, but it is at the same time a comedy of conversation, and a tragedy. Yet, if we attempt to use the term in a narrower sense we may call most of Brieux's plays, most of Hervieu's, all of Paul-Hyacinthe Loyson's, many of Shaw's, and some of Galsworthy's,

plays of ideas.[5] It has already been pointed out that good plays are based upon some idea, but the particular kind of play to which we now refer is that in which the dramatist's purpose is to furnish, discuss, and evolve ideas. In this sense, then, "Getting Married" is a play of ideas.

The form is not fixed, yet one of its characteristics is a good deal of conversation: the easiest and, in many cases, most direct method of conveying ideas on the stage is through dialogue. Yet the moment an audience is asked to listen to talk, the talk must be superlatively interesting or otherwise attractive, for action is necessarily either lacking or of small importance. But Shaw is a consummate dialectician and a master of speech. Were it not for this cleverness and the sheer interest aroused by the discussion, "Getting Married" would be a very dull pamphlet. Nothing occurs; a number of characters sit round and talk.

2. In the introductory note to the printed play, the author says:

N. B. There is a point of some technical interest to be noted in this play. The customary division into acts and scenes has been disused, and a return made to unity of time and place as observed in the ancient Greek drama. In "The Doctor's Dilemma," there are five acts; the place is altered five times; and the time is spread over an undetermined period of more than a year. No doubt the strain on the attention of the audience and on the ingenuity of the playwright is much less; but I find in practice that the Greek form is inevitable when drama reaches a certain point in poetic and intellectual evolution. Its adoption was not, on my part, a deliberate display of virtuosity in form, but simply the spontaneous falling of a play of ideas into the form most suitable to it, which turned out to be the classical form. "Getting Married," in several acts and scenes, with the time spread over a long period, would be impossible.[6]

---

[5] "Les âmes ennemies," "L'evangile du sang," and "L'apôtre" (the last-named is translated as "The Apostle"), Brieux's "Damaged Goods," Hervieu's "Law of Man," and Galsworthy's "Justice," are plays of ideas.

[6] See Strindberg's "Author's Preface" to "Miss Julia," from which these few sentences are taken: " . . . I have tried to abolish the division into acts. And I have done so because I have come to fear that

3. With the above explanation as a basis, and with what of the long preface the reader cares to peruse, let him see how the dramatist has managed to present his characters and his ideas in order to interest his audience.

First, the theme is of interest to the greater part of the audience; second, a great number and variety of characters are introduced; third, the details, the odds and ends of what would be action in an ordinary play, are allowed especial prominence.

In what other ways does Shaw attract and hold the attention? What are his methods for supplying an equivalent of action, story, suspense, etc.?

4. Every work of art that is radically different from others is at first condemned as false art, and there are those who hold that "Getting Married" is not a play at all. But the question is, what has Shaw done and how has he succeeded? Anything that "goes" in the theater is a play, but it must eventually "go."

After all, is there any basis for the assertion that because "Getting Married" has no action, it is therefore merely a series of dialogues on marriage? Has not Shaw rather helped to broaden the field of drama?

5. In what respects, if any, is this "comedy" a play, in the accepted conventional sense of the term?

6. Do you see any reason why Shaw, after writing "Getting Married" and "Misalliance," returned to the more conventional forms in "The Shewing-up of Blanco Posnet," "Fanny's First Play," and "Pygmalion"? Or why, after writing these, he should adopt in turn such varying forms as he uses in his latest plays, like "Heartbreak House," "Back to Methusaleh," or "Saint Joan"?

---

our decreasing capacity for illusion might be unfavorably affected by intermissions during which the spectator would have time to reflect and to get away from the suggestive influence of the author-hypnotist. My play will probably last an hour and a half, and as it is possible to listen that length of time, or longer, to a lecture, a sermon, or a debate, I have imagined that a theatrical performance would not become fatiguing in the same time."

C. Haddon Chambers

Charles Haddon Chambers was born at Stanmore, New South Wales, in 1860. He was educated privately at home and later at Sydney. In 1875 he entered the Civil Service. Five years later he visited England. In 1882 he settled there and became a journalist, writer of stories, and dramatist.

Chambers is one of the popular playwrights who have written a number of amusing, sentimental, and satirical comedies for the English and American stages. His technique differs little from that of Pinero, except that it is not so highly developed. Besides writing three or four plays of some value as contemporary pictures of manners, he has adapted a number of French plays, taking from them the flavor of the original and substituting a British atmosphere in order to render them acceptable to a public, in America as well as in England, which was not ready to judge works of art according to European standards.

Chambers died in 1921.

Plays

"One of Them" (1886)
"The Open Gate" (1887)
"Captain Swift" (1888)
"The Idler" (1891)
"The Honorable Herbert" (1891)
"The Queen of Manoa" [with W. O. Tristram] (1892)
"The Old Lady" (1892)
"The Pipe of Peace" (1892)
"The Fatal Card" [with B. C. Stephenson] (1894)
"John-a-Dreams" (1894)
"Boys Together" [with J. Comyns Carr] (1896)
"The Days of the Duke" (1897)
"The Tyranny of Tears" (1899)
"The Golden Silence" (1903)
"Sir Anthony" (1908)
"Passers-By" (1911)
"The Saving Grace" (1917)

("The Awakening" and two or three others are adapted from the French; "Devil Caresfoot," written with J. Stanley Little, is a dramatization from Rider Haggard.)

Editions (separate plays).—"The Idler" (N. Y. 1902); "Captain Swift" (N. Y. 1902); "The Open Gate" (N. Y. no date); "Sir Anthony" (N. Y. 1909); "The Tyranny of Tears," with preface by Alice Brown (Boston, 1902); "Passers-By" (N. Y. 1919); "The Saving Grace" (N. Y. 1919).

References

Mario Borsa, *The English Stage of To-day,* trans. by S. Brinton (N. Y. 1908); J. T. Grein, *Premières of the Year* (London, 1900), and

Dramatic Criticism, Vol. III (London, 1902); C. F. Nirdlinger, *Masques and Mummers* (N. Y. 1899); Norman Hapgood, *The Stage in America* (N. Y. 1901); G. J. Nathan, *Comedians All* (N. Y. 1919); A. E. Morgan, *Tendencies of Modern English Drama* (N. Y. 1924).

The Tyranny of Tears

Comedy in 4 acts (1899). Text: Boston, 1902.

The play is technically of the Pinero-Jones school; still, it has a freshness which is sometimes lacking in more ambitious plays. There are no surprises, there is little to astound or arouse deep reflection. Based upon one of those inherent human qualities easily recognized by an average audience, it pursues its agreeable way through four pleasing acts.

1. In dealing with a conventional comedy of this sort, it is fitting that conventional standards be applied to it. It will be seen that such plays as Elizabeth Baker's "Chains" and certain pieces of Granville Barker cannot be so easily measured by the older standards, but practically all the works of Jones, Pinero, Chambers, Davies, and Somerset Maugham, are easy to classify. Nor need this imply any detraction from their merits; technical originality in itself is little enough. While there is nothing new under the sun there may be new angles of vision, but a dramatist who chooses to view life from his new-found angle may be able to lay no better claim upon our admiration than that he has discovered a new *manner.*

The dramatist who writes conventional plays has his form ready to hand, and may proceed at once to attack the matter. A play by Pinero or Jones is almost invariably well put together, and we may, as Bernard Shaw once said of the latter's plays, attack the matter without troubling about the manner.

"The Tyranny of Tears" is a conventional comedy of character and sentiment. Determine whether the dramatist has wished his audience to be interested rather in the story, or in the characters. What foundation is there for your opinion? Did Chambers aim to write a play showing how a man may be tyrannized over by a loving wife, or is he rather concerned with a story, into which he has allowed an idea, as it were, to wander?

2. Few more striking instances of the basic difference between the French and the English temperaments can be found than by comparing the treatment of a similar theme in this play and in Porto-Riche's "Loving Wife" ("Amoureuse"). The Frenchman is concerned chiefly with the sexual side of marriage, and insists that Etienne is forced to remain with his wife because she is still attractive to him. Chambers calls this attraction "tears" and uses the situation as a basis for a pleasant and innocuous comedy. Porto-Riche goes straight to the heart of the question. In Anglo-Saxon countries the problem would appear much as Chambers has related it, while in Latin lands it would more closely resemble Porto-Riche's treatment. Chambers could not have written "Amoureuse" because he doubtless lacked the insight necessary for that task and would not have written it, even had the censor passed it. On the other hand, Porto-Riche would not have wasted his time on what he would doubtless consider a prudish and trivial piece of work like "The Tyranny of Tears."

3. In Brander Matthews' *Study of the Drama,* the author divides certain sorts of dialogue, after the manner of the French critics, into three kinds: *mots de caractère, mots de situation,* and *mots d'esprit.* He says (p. 126):

The French, among whom the critical faculty is more acutely developed than among other peoples, have a larger vocabulary of critical terms than there is in any other language; and they have devised a classification of certain of the effects of dialogue which are common to every type of comic play. They call a jest which evokes laughter a *mot,* and they make a distinction which is not easy to render in English between *mots d'esprit, mots de situation,* and *mots de caractère.* The *mot d'esprit* is the witticism pure and simple, existing for its own sake, and detachable from its context—like the remark of one of the characters in "Lady Windermere's Fan": "I can resist everything—except temptation." The *mot de situation* is the phrase which is funny solely because it is spoken at that particular moment in the setting forth of the story, like the "What the devil was he doing in that galley?" which is not laughter-provoking in itself and apart from the incident calling it forth, but which arouses peals of merriment in its proper place in Molière's "Scapin." And the *mot de caractère* is the phrase which makes us laugh because it is the intense expression, at the moment, of the individuality of the person who speaks it—like the retort of the wife to her sister in the "Comedy of Errors," when she has been roundly abusing her husband. Luciana satirically comments that a man no better than this is no great loss to be bewailed. Whereupon Adriana, smiling through her tears, returns: "Ah, but I think him better than I say—" a line which gets its laugh, of course, but which lingers in the memory as a sudden revelation of the underlying character of the speaker.

All plays contain examples of one or more of these kinds of *mots*. The *mot de situation* is perhaps the commonest, while *mots de caractère* are, though they may be interesting and amusing, and *mots d'esprit* laughter-provoking, more or less in the nature of accessories. The least necessary of all are the *mots d'esprit*: it is a regrettable fact that Oscar Wilde occasionally marred scenes in his best comedies by introducing far too many. The second act of "Lady Windermere's Fan," the first part of the third act of the same play, and the first act of "A Woman of No Importance," are outstanding examples.

In the present play find examples of the three kinds of *mots*; what do they add to your enjoyment? Are there any superfluous *mots*: phrases, repartees, or epigrams which, if omitted, would in no way mar the general effect?

4. Study the "curtains" throughout. Is the rise of the action, the tension in plot, increased, crisis by crisis, as in Sudermann's "Magda" and Pinero's "Second Mrs. Tanqueray," or is it disjointed and sudden as in Becque's "Vultures" and Wedekind's "Spring's Awakening"?

Hubert Henry Davies

Hubert Henry Davies was born at Woodley, in Cheshire, in 1869. He first entered the field of journalism, and pursued his profession in the United States for a number of years. Since 1899, when his first play, "A Dream of Love," was produced, until the year of his death, he devoted all his time to the writing of plays, most of which have been successful in England and America. He died in France, in 1917, as a result of nervous breakdown occasioned by strenuous work in a military hospital.

Davies possessed a fastidious sense of form and a pleasant literary style. He was not an innovator; he was content to accept the dramatic conventions as he found them, and did not venture abroad in quest of new methods or new ideas. He is always pleasantly conventional, although in his best plays—"The Mollusc," "Mrs. Gorringe's Necklace," "Doormats," and "Captain Drew on Leave"—there is ever some original treatment of character, some interesting underlying idea.

Says Hugh Walpole, in his Introduction to Davies' collected plays: "He could see nothing, hear nothing, share in nothing without finding something that made life more entertaining, more whimsical, more delicately absurd than it had been before. . . . His wit was quick, clean, darting, always sure of its aim, always knowing when to stop, always kindly and, best of all, original. . . . He was able to say the obvious things about people and places without ever being obvious at all. . . ." In his last play, "Outcast," he showed indications of what he might have achieved.

Plays

"A Dream of Love" (1898)
"The Weldons" (1900)
"Fifty Years Ago" (1900)
"Cousin Kate" (1903)
"Mrs. Gorringe's Necklace" (1903)
"Cynthia" (1903)
"Captain Drew on Leave" (1905)
"The Mollusc" (1907)
"Lady Epping's Lawsuit" (1908)
"Bevis" (1909)
"A Single Man" (1910)
"Doormats" (1912)
"Outcast" (1914)

Editions.—The Plays of Hubert Henry Davies, with introduction by Hugh Walpole, 2 vols. (London, 1921), includes "Mrs. Gorringe's Necklace," "Cousin Kate," "Lady Epping's Lawsuit," "Captain Drew on Leave," "The Mollusc," "A Single Man," "Doormats," and "Outcast."

Separate Plays.—"Cousin Kate" (Boston, 1910); "Mrs. Gorringe's Necklace" (Boston, 1910); "The Mollusc" (Boston, 1914); "Lady Epping's Lawsuit" (Boston, 1914); "A Single Man" (Boston, 1914); and "Captain Drew on Leave" (Boston, 1924).

Reprint in an Anthology.—"The Mollusc" in Dickinson and Crawford's *Contemporary Drama: English and American* (Boston, 1925).

References

P. P. Howe, *Dramatic Portraits* (N. Y. 1913); T. H. Dickinson, *The Contemporary Drama of England* (Boston, 1917); W. A. Darlington, *Through the Fourth Wall* (N. Y. no date); Frank Vernon, *The Twentieth-Century Theater* (Boston, 1924); A. E. Morgan, *Tendencies of Modern English Drama* (N. Y. 1924).

The Mollusc

Comedy in 3 acts (1907). Texts: Boston, 1914; in *The Plays* (London, 1921); reprinted in Dickinson and Crawford's *Contemporary Drama: English and American* (Boston, 1925).

There are few modern plays so neatly constructed and so pleasantly written as "The Mollusc." It is unquestionably Davies' finest achievement.

1. For two thousand years dramatists and critics have been reading and discussing (principally discussing) the celebrated fragment of Aristotle, known in English as the *Poetics.*[7] To this day it remains the best statement of dramatic theory in the world. But for several reasons, some of them good and most of them stupid, there is a widespread impression that the Greek scholar laid down as immutable laws the doctrine of the three Unities, of time, place, and action. The *Poetics* should be read by every student. It will be seen that Aristotle not only does not enjoin the three Unities, he mentions no more than one, that of action. As to time, the following passage has been construed to mean that the time covered by the action of a play should not exceed one day. This passage reads as follows: "Epic poetry and tragedy differ, again, in their length: for tragedy endeavors, as far as possible, to confine itself to a single revolution of the sun, or but slightly to exceed this limit." This is not, of course, a law, and the Greeks often failed to

---

[7] For the best translation of the *Poetics,* together with a commentary, see S. H. Butcher's *Aristotle's Theory of Poetry and Fine Art, with a Critical Text and Translation,* 4th ed. (London, 1911). For another translation of the sections on drama, see my *European Theories of the Drama* (Cincinnati, 1918).

observe it. The unity of place is "nowhere even hinted at in the *Poetics*," says Butcher, and throughout Greek drama the principle was not adhered to. Unity of action is, of course, no more than the unity demanded of all art, for psychological reasons. There are several passages referring to this, of which the following is characteristic: " . . . The plot, being an imitation of an action, must imitate one action and that a whole, the structural union of the parts being such that, if any one of them is displaced or removed, the whole will be disjointed and disturbed. For a thing whose presence or absence makes no visible difference, is not an organic part of the whole."

For centuries dramatists have troubled themselves by attempting to adhere to non-existent "rules": Corneille spent years arguing the matter out, and the Italians of the Renaissance (it was Castelvetro who in the sixteenth century *deduced* the unity of place) doubtless discouraged the writing of plays because of their formal insistence on the alleged Aristotelian maxims. Occasionally an independent genius like Molière or Lope de Vega would brave the scorn of the critics and write as he chose, but it was not until the last century that Aristotle can be said to have lost his influence.

Occasionally, even nowadays, a dramatist will write a play according to the so-called three Unities. Charles Rann Kennedy has done so in "The Servant in the House," Bernard Shaw in "Getting Married," and Davies in "The Mollusc."

The last act of the Davies play takes place one week later than the third, but this is really a detail. The place is "Mrs. Baxter's sitting-room," the action is Tom's "education of a mollusc."

What is gained by this (conscious or unconscious) adherence to the pseudo-Aristotelian rules?

2. During the past twenty-five years or so there has been a tendency to lessen the number of characters in plays. The artist loves his limitations; Davies took pleasure in restricting himself to the use of but four personages, the French dramatist Jules Lemaître, in "The Pardon," enjoyed the game of making only three carry the plot of a full-length play.

The young German, Walter Hasenclever, has written a full-length play in five acts ("Beyond") in which there are only *two* characters. This is vastly more difficult than it used to be. Many classical plays, from Æschylus to Sheridan, show a striking disregard for the time-scheme; Shakespeare was often careless in this respect: a character might enter a room or a street from nowhere and go nowhere, and might return in an impossibly short time. While it is of course necessary on the stage to accept the convention of the foreshortening of time, we are unwilling—nowadays at least—to accept unmotivated and otherwise improbable entrances and exits. Now we insist on knowing where a character comes from, how he happens to be where he is; if he leaves, his errand must be clear; if we are given to understand that he will return in half an hour, he must not come in two minutes later. (This, by the way, is the reason why very few clocks ever run on the stage.) In "The Mollusc," the comings and goings of each person are satisfactorily accounted for.

Work out the time-scheme of "Macbeth" or "Hamlet"—if you can!

3. Why do people behave as they do? In life and on the stage. The difference between the conventional dramatist and one who attempts to create new forms and treat human beings from a new view-point, is that with the former the characters act according to set ideas, or as they have acted in other plays. A good dramatist will inform us exactly why A behaved as he did under the circumstances; a psychologist, like François de Curel or Ibsen, will delve still deeper and reveal hidden corners of human character from the intuition which is genius. Dramatists like Molière or Shakespeare will draw a synthetic picture of life: the characters *are*, they behave as they do because they are what they are. In "Hamlet," the Prince reveals his thoughts and feelings in speech and action: he simply speaks his mind. If Hamlet were a conventional sort of man he would have killed his uncle, if "Hamlet" were a conventional play, the Prince would kill the murderer because the facts known to Hamlet would be sufficient to motivate the

revenge. But Shakespeare knew Hamlet's mind and revealed it to us through the man's actions and words.

If we are made to feel that Zoe Blundell's suicide is natural—that is, if the events which led up to it allowed her to do nothing else, she being what she was—then Pinero's "Mid-Channel" is well motivated; if Cyrano's compliance with Roxane's request that he protect her lover is in accordance with Cyrano's character, then that act on his part is well motivated.

Study the motivation in "The Mollusc," in Shaw's "Man and Superman," and in Jones' "The Liars."

4. "The Mollusc" is a comedy of manners. This type of play is not easily defined, but the necessity for scientific definitions we have by now, I hope, shown to be more imaginary than real. We can point to certain plays and say: These are comedies of manners: to Congreve's "Way of the World," Sheridan's "School for Scandal," Molière's "Learned Ladies," Jones' "Dolly Reforming Herself." The form, says Clayton Hamilton in the Introduction to Jones' "Mary Goes First" (1914), "requires for its inspiration a social tradition that has been handed down for centuries. . . . Manners do not become a theme for satire until they have been crystallized into a code; and, to laugh politely, a playwright must have an aristocracy to laugh at."

The "manners" are, then, those of the members of a particular social class, and the comedy is the result of the dramatist's satirical viewpoint.

Can you think of other modern examples of the comedy of manners? Are there any American plays that can be properly so designated? Is there any reason why the form should not be cultivated in this country? See, in this connection, S. N. Behrman's play, "The Second Man."

John Galsworthy

John Galsworthy was born at Coombe, Surrey, in 1867. He received his education first at Harrow, and later at Oxford, from which he was graduated in 1889. His first intention was to practice law. and in 1890 he was called to the bar. He says: "I read in various chambers, practiced almost not at all, and disliked my profession thoroughly." As he was not under the necessity of earning a living, he traveled abroad for some years. It was in the early nineties that he began writing, and in 1899 he published his first work, the novel "Jocelyn." This was followed by a short novel and a volume of stories. Before the production of his first play he wrote four other novels. Since 1906, the date of "The Silver Box," Galsworthy has continued to publish novels, stories, essays, and to write plays, some of which—like "The Skin Game" and "Loyalties" —have enjoyed long runs both in England and in America.

In such stories as "The Country House" and such plays as "Strife," Galsworthy shows extraordinary skill in revealing the inherent absurdity of man-made institutions and conventions. It is largely with the social conventions of marriage and the general relation of man to man that Galsworthy is concerned; in plays and novels and essays he has exposed, in his emphatic unemphatic manner, the *irony* of *things*.

Galsworthy died in 1933.

PLAYS

"The Silver Box" (1906)
"Joy" (1907)
"Strife" (1909)
"Justice" (1910)
"The Little Dream" (1911)
"The Pigeon" (1912)
"The Eldest Son" (1912)
"The Fugitive" (1913)
"The Mob" (1914)
"Hall-Marked" (1914)
"A Bit o' Love" (1915)
"The Little Man" (1915)
"The Foundations" (1917)
"The Skin Game" (1920)
"The First and the Last" (1920)
"Defeat" (1921)
"Punch and Go" (1921)
"A Family Man" (1921)
"The Sun" (1921)
"Windows" (1922)
"Loyalties" (1922)
"The Forest" (1924)
"Old English" (1924)
"The Show" (1925)
"Escape" (1926)
"Exiled" (1929)
"The Roof" (1929)

Editions.—Plays (N. Y. 1909) includes "The Silver Box," "Joy," and "Strife"; *Plays,* 2nd series (N. Y. 1913), includes "The Eldest Son," "The Little Dream," and "Justice"; *Plays,* 3rd series (N. Y. 1914), includes "The Fugitive," "The Mob," and "The Pigeon"; *Plays,* 4th series (N. Y. 1920), includes "A Bit o' Love," "The Skin Game," and "The Foundations"; *Plays,* 5th series (N. Y. 1923), includes "Loyalties," "Windows," and "A Family Man"; *Six Short Plays* (N. Y. 1921) includes "The First and the Last," "The Little Man," "Hall-Marked," "Defeat," "Punch and Go," and "The Sun"; *The Little Man and Other Satires* (N. Y. 1915) includes that play and "Hall-Marked," "The First and the Last" [with stories] (London, 1920). *The Plays of John Galsworthy* (London, 1929) contains the 27 plays published to date; same (N. Y. 1934) does not include "Exiled" and "The Roof"; *The Winter Garden* (London, 1935) includes four short plays, "The Winter Garden," "The Golden Egg," "Similes," and "Exiled" (an unused episode from longer play of same title).

Separate Plays.—"The Silver Box" (N. Y. 1916); "Strife" (N. Y. 1916); "Joy" (N. Y. 1916); "The Eldest Son" (N. Y. 1912); "Justice" (N. Y. 1910); "The Fugitive" (N. Y. 1913); "The Mob" (N. Y. 1914); "The Pigeon" (N. Y. 1912); "A Bit o' Love" (N. Y. 1915); "The Skin Game" (N. Y. 1920); "The Little Dream" (N. Y. 1911); "The Foundations" (N. Y. 1920); "Loyalties" (N. Y. 1922); "Windows" (N. Y. 1922); "A Family Man" (N. Y. 1922); "The Forest" (N. Y. 1924); "Old English" (N. Y. 1925); "The Show" (N. Y. 1925); "Escape" (N. Y. 1927); "The Roof" (N. Y. 1929); "Exiled" (London, 1929).

Reprints in Collections and Anthologies.—"Strife," in Dickinson's *Chief Contemporary Dramatists* (Boston, 1915); "The Silver Box," in Moses' *Representative British Dramas* (Boston, 1918); "The Sun," in Leonard's *Atlantic Book of Modern Plays* (Boston, 1921); "The Little Man," in Cohen's *One-Act Plays* (N. Y. 1921), in A. D. Dickinson's *One-Act Plays* (Garden City, 1922), and in J. W. Marriott's *One-Act Plays of To-day* (Boston, 1924); *Six Selected Plays of John Galsworthy* (N. Y. 1924) includes "The Silver Box," "Strife," "Justice," "A Bit o' Love," "The Pigeon," and "Loyalties."

References

Sheila Kaye-Smith, *John Galsworthy* (N. Y. 1916); P. P. Howe, *Dramatic Portraits* (N. Y. 1913), and *The Repertory Theater* (N. Y. 1911); John Palmer, *The Censor and the Theaters* (N. Y. 1913), and *The Future of the Theater* (N. Y. 1913); Edwin Björkman, *Is There Anything New Under the Sun?* (N. Y. 1911); Charlton Andrews, *The Drama To-day* (Philadelphia, 1913); Ashley Dukes, *Modern Dramatists* (Chicago, 1912), and *The Youngest Drama* (Chicago, 1924); Emma Goldman, *The Social Significance of the Modern Drama* (Boston, 1914); C. H. Herford, in *Essays and Studies by Members of the English Association* (Oxford, 1914); T. H. Dickinson, *The Contemporary Drama of England* (Boston, 1917); William Archer, *Playmaking* (Boston, 1912), and *The Old Drama and the New* (Boston, 1923); F. W. Chandler, *Aspects of Modern Drama* (N. Y. 1914); Clayton Hamilton, *Studies in Stagecraft* (N. Y. 1914), *Problems of the Playwright* (N. Y. 1917), and *Seen on the Stage* (N. Y. 1920); Frank Vernon, *The Twentieth-Century Theater* (Boston, 1924); Archibald Henderson, *The Changing Drama* (Cincinnati, 1919); Ludwig Lewisohn, *The Modern Drama* (N. Y. 1915), and *The Drama and the Stage* (N. Y. 1922); H. M. Walbrook, *Nights at the Play* (London, 1911); A. B. Walkley, *Pastiche and Prejudice* (N. Y. 1921); J. T. Grein, *The World and the Theater* (London, 1921); C. Lewis Hind, *Authors and I* (N. Y. 1921); A. E. Morgan, *Tendencies of Modern English Drama*

(N. Y. 1924); St. John Ervine, *Some Impressions of My Elders* (N. Y. 1923); W. P. Eaton, *At the New Theater and Others* (Boston, 1910), and *Plays and Players* (Cincinnati, 1916); J. W. Cunliffe, *English Literature During the Last Half-Century* (N. Y. 1923); F. T. Cooper, *Some English Story-Tellers* (N. Y. 1912); Gilbert Norwood, *Euripides and Shaw* (Boston, 1921); Philip Guedalla, *A Gallery* (London, 1924); A. Chevrillon, *Three Studies in English Literature* (London, 1923); Allardyce Nicoll, *British Drama* (N. Y. 1925); James Agate, *A Short View of the English Stage* (London, 1926); J. W. Cunliffe, *Modern English Playwrights* (N. Y. 1927); R. H. Coats, *John Galsworthy as a Dramatic Artist* (N. Y. 1926); H. V. Marrot, *The Life and Letters of John Galsworthy* (N. Y. 1936); Leon Schalit, *John Galsworthy* (N. Y. 1929).

See also.—Galsworthy's *The Inn of Tranquillity* (N. Y. 1912), and *Another Sheaf* (N. Y. 1919).

Strife

Drama in 3 acts (1909). Texts: N. Y. 1916; in *Plays* (N. Y. 1909); in Dickinson's *Chief Contemporary Dramatists* (Boston, 1915), Baker's *Six Selected Plays of John Galsworthy* (N. Y. 1924), and in *The Plays of John Galsworthy* (N. Y. 1934).

In his essay, "Some Platitudes Concerning Drama," Galsworthy says: "A Drama must be shaped so as to have a spire of meaning. Every grouping of life and character has its inherent moral; and the business of the dramatist is so to pose the group as to bring that moral poignantly to the light of day. Such is the moral that exhales from plays like 'Lear,' 'Hamlet,' and 'Macbeth.'"

1. "Strife" is an austere and just arrangement of acts, facts, motives, and opinions, building up to "a spire of meaning" and concerned with the struggle between capital and labor. Galsworthy's first care was to set before his audience a clear statement, without taking sides with one party or the other. He mentions in the above quoted essay three courses open to the dramatist: (1) to give the public what it wants; (2) to give it what it thinks it ought to have, and (3) "to set before the public no cut-and-dried codes, but the phenomena of life and character, selected and combined, *but not distorted* by the dramatist's outlook, set down without fear, favor, or prejudice, leaving the public to draw such poor moral as nature may afford. This third method requires a certain detachment; it requires a sympathy with, a love for, and a curiosity as to, things for their

own sake; it requires a far view, together with patient industry, for no immediately practical result."

This is theory, and, as far as it goes, very good theory. Probably the first question that occurs to us is how far Galsworthy has applied his theory to his own work.

2. A "certain detachment" is to be observed throughout "Strife." The dramatist's "sympathy with . . . things for their own sake" is felt in his desire to look at his situation from many points of view: one scene is balanced against another, the first showing the thoughts and feelings of the under-dog, the next exhibiting the attitude of the capitalists. For example, we are first made to see the representatives of capital, then Harness is introduced, and, a moment later, "the men." First the capitalist's side is heard, then the workingmen's. Within a few pages of the end of the act there is a deadlock between the contending parties; then Enid is brought in. Enid presents another aspect of the question; she, the daughter of Anthony, the head of the capitalists, may be termed the "human element." "We see *all* the distress," she says. "You remember my maid Annie, who married Roberts? It's so wretched, her heart's weak; since the strike began, she hasn't even been getting proper food." In the second act Enid is in the Roberts' cottage. Again the author's detachment is evident: he does not sentimentalize upon the workingmen any more than he overemphasizes the obduracy of the Board. If he feels that some human element is necessary, for the sake of truth and dramatic contrast, he allows the gentle and very human Enid (even the name is indicative of her character) to do the sentimentalizing. And again Galsworthy the practical dramatist follows the rules of Galsworthy the theorist:

> The art of writing true dramatic dialogue is an austere art, denying itself all license, grudging every sentence devoted to the mere machinery of the play, suppressing all jokes and epigrams severed from character, relying for fun and pathos on the fun and tears of life. From start to finish good dialogue is hand-made, like good lace; clear, of fine texture, furthering with each thread the harmony and strength of a design to which all must be subordinated.

Throughout the first scene of the second act the characters are laid bare with admirable clear-sightedness and detachment of vision. If the poor are in a bad condition, it is to a certain extent the fault of their pride and dogged tenacity. Madge Thomas' reply, "What suffering? . . . Who said there was suffering?" reveals a person very near to actual life.

In brief, then, Galsworthy shows that if the rich are hard, they have a modicum of the milk of human kindness, and that if the poor are miserable, they are at times stubborn and haughty.

3. Elsewhere in the same essay the author remarks: "Now, true dramatic action is what characters do, at once contrary, as it were, to expectation and yet because they have already done other things." Galsworthy means that the dramatist should not invent situations and adhere to a fixed plan when he is dealing with units which are intended to represent human beings. When, therefore, a character acts "contrary, as it were, to expectation," it is because we, the audience, do not know their true character. It is by means of unexpected turns and the revelation of motives hitherto unknown to the audience, that a dramatist paints character: he unrolls it, and the personages *develop*. Again this author's sympathy with life urges him to state that it is pretty difficult to determine just what a human being *will* do next.

Follow carefully the scenes in which the principal characters appear, bearing in mind the remarks just quoted.

4. In "Strife," what is the "spire of meaning"? What is the "inherent moral"? Was Galsworthy more interested in the moral than the characters? Or did he wish merely to exhibit a certain "grouping of life and characters"?

The Pigeon

Fantasy in 3 acts (1912). Texts: N. Y. 1912, and in *Plays*, 3rd series (N. Y. 1914).

In a little poem ("A Prayer") Galsworthy, the poet, asks that he may be given "to understand." All of Galsworthy's plays are written by a man who wishes to dig beneath the surface, to learn to understand and to help others to do so. We have already seen how a dramatist should hold himself somewhat aloof from life in order to see it fairly: "Strife" is the best of this dramatist's plays to exemplify his attitude and his workmanship. "The Pigeon," "a fantasy in conception and a realistic play in execution," in Galsworthy's own words, is much less a cold expression of facts than "Strife." Its very theme is human charity. If one seeks some definite preachment of philanthropy—such as Brieux gave in "The Philanthropists"—the play will puzzle: the author shows only a "grouping of life and character," and allows us to seek out the "inherent moral." At the end, Wellwyn is as hopeless as he was at first, the flower-girl and her miserable companions are no nearer to a solution of the problem than before the curtain rose. Had Brieux or Hervieu written the play they would undoubtedly have offered some sort of moral, suggested some remedy; Galsworthy is content with giving us some insight into the thoughts and feelings of three hopeless waifs.

1. The first act is a work of art: Galsworthy never wrote a better act. The tag-end of a scene supposed to have passed just before the curtain rose, opens it: then Wellwyn and his daughter are briefly introduced. There is no "exposition" in the ordinary sense: the characters evolve through the medium of dialogue that is "spiritual action." There is no superfluous word: each syllable counts. This is truly "austere art."

Let us consider another passage from the author's theoretical writings:

> The aim of the dramatist in employing it [naturalistic technique] is obviously to create such an illusion of actual life passing on the stage as to compel the spectator to pass through an experience of his own, to think, and talk, and move with the people he sees, thinking, talking, and moving in front of him. A false phrase, a single word out of tune or time, will destroy that illusion and spoil the surface as surely as a stone heaved into a still pond shatters the image seen there. . . . It is easy enough to *reproduce* the exact conversation and movements of persons in a room; it is desperately hard to *produce* the perfectly natural conversation and movements of those persons, when each natural phrase spoken and each natural

movement made has not only to contribute toward the growth and perfection of a drama's soul, but also to be a revelation, phrase by phrase, movement by movement, of essential traits of character. To put it another way, naturalistic art, when alive, indeed to be alive at all, is simply the art of manipulating a procession of most delicate symbols.

2. If the writer of "Strife" and "The Pigeon" has succeeded in adhering to his principles, it might be well to look into the validity of these principles. One final quotation:

> We want no more bastard drama; no more attempts to dress out the simple dignity of everyday life in the peacock's feathers of false lyricism; no more straw-stuffed heroes or heroines; no more rabbits and goldfish from the conjurer's pockets, nor any limelight. Let us have starlight, moonlight, sunlight, and the light of our own self-respect.

Galsworthy, in a word, is the enemy of all that is false in the theater of "theatricality." In his plays, there is ever a conscious effort to avoid effects, "big scenes," hackneyed dialogue and situations. Galsworthy seems afraid of a "curtain"; it has been aptly said of him that the " 'curtains' seemed to hesitate to come down on anything that could possibly be mistaken for a climax." Yet it should be remembered that Galsworthy, disgusted with the falsity and triviality of a vast amount of present-day drama, was forced into his austere and reticent attitude. He has at least shown that plays do not necessarily have to be built according to time-worn formulas; he has also proved that one of the surest methods of obtaining emphasis is—up to a certain point—to under-emphasize. Mrs. Jones' "Oh! Sir!" which closes "The Silver Box" is an admirable example of this sort of thing.

In "The Pigeon" notice how the "curtains" are managed. What elements of the usual "well-made" play are observable in these? Compare the second act of this play—as to its plot development—with the second act of "Candida."

3. In *The Future of the Theater* John Palmer states:

Their [the characters in Galsworthy's plays] merit consists in all the commonplaces they do not utter, in all the obvious things they do not do, in all the fine speeches they do not make. In "The Eldest Son" Freda says "Oh, Bill!" and Bill makes the three following speeches: (1) "Freda!"; (2) "Good God!"; (3) "By Jove! This is——" Whereupon the curtain saves him from committing his author any further. These are tactics of masterly inactivity. The scene is suggested by the players; and the audience supplies the emotion. Mr. Galsworthy has done nothing, except to suggest very clearly that he has avoided doing anything wrong.

The last sentence here is an evident exaggeration, but how much of the entire criticism applies to "Strife" and "The Pigeon"? Has Galsworthy in detaching himself, in his attempt to be scrupulously exact and fair in his presentation of the grouping of life he chose to exhibit, gone too far, stood too far aloof, and lost that personal element, that touch of humanity, without which no art can exist?

4. The following letter to the writer touching upon the play now under consideration, may throw some light on the "fantastic" element:

. . . About those dates in "The Pigeon." Christmas Eve because of Ferrand's remark: "He is come, Monsieur!" and the general tenor of Wellwyn's acceptance of every kind of outcast. New Year's Day because of Ferrand's remark: "'Appy New Year!" which marks the disappearance of casual charity in favor of Institutionalism, of the era of outcasts in favor of the era of reformers. April first because of the joke at the end on the Humblemen which symbolizes the fact, or rather the essence, of the play, that, while Wellwyn (representing sympathy and understanding) is being "plucked" all through the play, he comes out and knows he does, on top at the end, as the only possible helper of the unhelpable. [The author adds: "I hope this is sufficiently obscure!"]

H. Granville-Barker

Harley Granville-Barker was born at London in 1877. At an early age he became an actor in a provincial company. He first appeared on the London stage in 1892. Playing under Lewis Waller and Ben Greet, then with the Elizabethan Stage Society, and finally with Mrs. Campbell, he soon became known in the theatrical world. During many years he produced plays and acted for the Stage Society, where he mounted many of Shaw's works for the first time. In 1904, together with J. E. Vedrenne, he managed the Court Theater, where he made known to theater-goers new plays by Shaw, Hankin, Barrie, Galsworthy, and himself. He continued his managerial activities at the Duke of York's Theater, the Savoy—where he inaugurated a series of Shakespearian revivals—the St. James' and the Kingsway.

Shortly after the outbreak of the War he brought his Company to America, where he made a tour with a small repertory of plays. He then engaged in war work, after which he gave up his managerial career. He has often lectured in America. During the past five or six years he has written only one play, and translated and adapted works from the French and Spanish.

Granville-Barker's plays are, in the best sense of the word, experiments in form. They are much more than technical feats, to be sure, but one feels that they are primarily quests after a newer and more flexible medium than that which the workers in the traditional form habitually use. "The Madras House," for example, judged by the standards of Pinero, is hardly a play at all; its artistic unity lies rather in the theme than in the actual plot. In "Waste," the theme again—more concrete than in "The Madras House"—dominates the form. "The Voysey Inheritance," a study of upper middle-class English life, comes nearer to the traditional dramatic form. It is the author's most successful play.

Plays

"The Weather Hen" [with Berte Thomas] (1899)
"The Marrying of Ann Leete" (1902)
"A Miracle" (1902)
"Prunella" [with Laurence Housman] (1904)
"The Voysey Inheritance" (1905)
"Waste" (1907)
"The Madras House" (1910)
"Rococo" (1911)
"The Harlequinade" [with D. C. Calthrop] (1914)
"Vote by Ballot" (1914)
"Farewell to the Theater" (1916)
"The Secret Life" (1923)
"His Majesty" (1929)

("The Morris Dance" is a dramatization of Stevenson and Osbourne's "The Wrong Box." Granville-Barker has translated plays of Martinez-Sierra, Schnitzler, and the "Deburau" of Sacha Guitry.)

Editions.—Three Plays (N. Y. 1909) includes "The Marrying of Ann Leete," "The Voysey Inheritance," and "Waste"; *Three Short Plays* (Boston, 1917) includes "Rococo," "Vote by Ballot," and "Farewell to the Theater."

Separate Plays.—"The Marrying of Ann Leete" (N. Y. 1909); "The Voysey Inheritance" (N. Y. 1909); "Waste" (N. Y. 1909); "The Madras House" (N. Y. 1911); "The Harlequinade" (Boston, 1918); "Prunella" (N. Y. 1913, Boston, 1920); "The Secret Life" (Boston, 1923); "His Majesty" (N. Y. 1929).

Reprints in Collections and Anthologies.—"The Madras House," in Dickinson's *Chief Contemporary Dramatists* (Boston, 1915), and in Moses' *Representative British Dramas* (Boston, 1918); "Rococo," in Clark's *Representative One-Act Plays by British and Irish Authors* (Boston, 1921).

References

T. H. Dickinson, *The Contemporary Drama of England* (Boston, 1917); Desmond MacCarthy, *The Court Theater* (London, 1907); Ashley Dukes, *Modern Dramatists* (Chicago, 1912), and *The Youngest Drama* (Chicago, 1924); Archibald Henderson, *European Dramatists* (N. Y. 1926), and *The Changing Drama* (Cincinnati, 1919); John Palmer, *The Future of the Theater* (N. Y. 1913), and *The Censor and the Theaters* (N. Y. 1913); Ludwig Lewisohn, *The Modern Drama* (N. Y. 1915); William Archer, *Playmaking* (Boston, 1912), and *The Old Drama and the New* (Boston, 1923); A. B. Walkley, *Drama and Life* (N. Y. 1908), and *More Prejudice* (N. Y. 1923); P. P. Howe, *The Repertory Theater* (N. Y. 1911), and *Dramatic Portraits* (N. Y. 1913); F. W. Chandler, *Aspects of Modern Drama* (N. Y. 1914); M. Borsa, *The English Stage of To-day* (N. Y. 1908); Gilbert Norwood, *Euripides and Shaw* (Boston, 1921); A. E. Morgan, *Tendencies of Modern English Drama* (N. Y. 1924); Allardyce Nicoll, *British Drama* (N. Y. 1933); James Agate, *A Short View of the English Stage* (London, 1920); J. W. Cunliffe, *Modern English Playwrights* (N. Y. 1927); St. John Ervine, *The Theater in My Time* (London, 1933); Elizabeth Drew, *Discovering Drama* (N. Y. 1937).

See also by William Archer and Granville-Barker, *Schemes and Estimates for a National Theater* (N. Y. 1908); Barker's *Prefaces to Shakespeare,* 3 series (London, 1933-37) and to *Three Plays of Maeterlinck* (N. Y. 1915), and his books, *The Exemplary Theater* (Boston, 1922); *A National Theater* (London, 1930); *Study of Drama* (N. Y. 1934); *On Dramatic Method* (London, 1931); and *On Poetry in Drama* (London, 1937).

The Voysey Inheritance

Play in 5 acts (1905). Texts: N. Y. 1909; in *Three Plays* (N. Y. 1909).

Unlike the didactic plays of Shaw, unlike the fantasies of Barrie, or the well-balanced pieces of Galsworthy, "The Voysey Inheritance" is essentially a character study. It has been only moderately successful on the stage.

1. In the Shaw outlines (pp. 255-257) some attention was given to the matter of stage directions. In the English theater of to-day there are three dramatists who use this method of affording their readers a greater insight into the characters than could be afforded in actual stage presentation: Shaw, Barrie, and Barker. Shaw refused to rely upon the actors; Barrie, who has until recently refused to allow his plays to be printed, felt that without the actors the reader could not possibly re-create the necessary atmosphere; Barker probably felt that owing to the failure of most of his plays (from a practical viewpoint), it was imperative to reconstruct the *milieu* by means of words.

Such directions as the following must be very annoying to the average manager:

> . . . *Relieved of his coat, Mr. Voysey carries to his table the bunch of beautiful roses he is accustomed to bring to the office three times a week, and places them for a moment only, near the bowl of water there ready to receive them, while he takes up his letters.*

A play intended only for the manager would, of course, have no reference to the fact that Voysey *"is accustomed to bring"* the flowers *"to the office three times a week,"* as this cannot be *shown* on the stage. Such directions are for the reader, or for such exceptional managers as are willing to study the manuscript and endeavor to reproduce the atmosphere which the dramatist has striven to create.

Turn to the opening of the second act of this play. Speaking of the dining room at Chislehurst, the author says: *"It has the usual red-papered walls (like a reflection, they are, of the underdone beef so much consumed within them),"* etc. While this is outside the province of what can be done by the stage carpenter, it should be advantageous to an imaginative director.

Compare the stage directions of "Man and Superman," "The Voysey Inheritance," and "The Twelve-Pound Look."

2. This play is a character-comedy, a play of ideas, and a

conversation piece. There are long scenes which, strictly speaking, have little or nothing to do with the story, but are they necessarily superfluous?

Has Barker's "Waste" any superfluous scenes?

3. One of the results of the "commercialization" of the stage is the reduction of the number of characters in a play. The theater is almost everywhere a business affair. Each character added to the cast means another actor, and another twenty-five to two thousand dollars a week increase in the pay-roll. This is of course not invariably the reason for the existence of small casts in many modern plays: often the dramatist needs but three, four, five, or six characters, and takes pride in the fact that he can construct a full-length piece without having recourse to the rather facile Shakespearean method of bringing in a character every time he thinks he needs one. Jules Lemaître in "The Pardon," Hubert Henry Davies in "The Mollusc," have written skillful and artistic plays with—in the case of the former three, and—in the latter—four characters only, while in Walter Hasenclever's "Beyond"—a full-length play—there are only two. However, a manager will try his best to cut down the cast as much as possible.

Can this be done to "The Voysey Inheritance"? Take the character you consider the least important from the play. Would the play suffer?

Do you think that Barker required all the characters he put into his play? If so, in what way? That is, did he prefer to paint a picture of life, regardless of the artistic arrangement of its component elements, or did he imagine that the more characters he introduced the more interesting would the play be? Briefly, did he adopt the dramatist's viewpoint, or the novelist's?

See the discussion on novel and drama under Galdós, p. 211.

STEPHEN PHILLIPS

Stephen Phillips was born at Somertown, England, in 1867. After receiving his primary education at Peterborough, he joined F. R.

Benson's company, in which he acted for some years. For a while he adopted the profession of army tutor, then devoted himself entirely to the writing of plays and poetry. During the last years of his life he was editor of the *Poetry Review*. He died in 1915.

Stephen Phillips is included in this book because he is the one English poet of his time whose verse plays have had any considerable success in the theater. But he was not a professional dramatist: he was a poet with a certain talent for writing plays. The poetic drama (or should we say the verse-drama) remains in England for the most part a literary form, and has little or nothing to do with the stage, but there is no fundamental reason why there should not be a revival of poetic drama—granted the poetry and the drama. Thomas Hardy's "Dynasts" is not written for the stage (see p. 172), but a day may come when the stage will adapt itself to "The Dynasts." Robert Bridges, Laurence Binyon, Comyns Carr, Rudolph Besier, Laurence Housman, and John Masefield, have all written verse plays.

Plays

"Paolo and Francesca" (1899)
"Herod" (1900)
"Ulysses" (1902)
"The Sin of David" (1904)
"Aylmer's Secret" (1905)
"Nero" (1906)
"Faust" [with J. Comyns Carr] (1908)
"The Last Heir" (1908)
"Pietro of Siena" (1910)
"The King" (1910)
"Nero's Mother" (1913)
"The Adversary" (1913)
"Armageddon" (1915)
"Harold" (1916)

Editions.—The Collected Plays (N. Y. 1920) includes "Aylmer's Secret," "Ulysses," "The Sin of David," "Nero," "Faust," and "Pietro of Siena"; *Lyrics and Dramas* (N. Y. 1913) includes "Nero's Mother," "The Adversary," and "The King."

Separate Plays.—"Paolo and Francesca" (N. Y. 1901); "Herod" (N. Y. 1901); "Ulysses" (N. Y. 1902); "The Sin of David" (N. Y. 1904); "Nero" (N. Y. 1906); "Faust" (N. Y. 1908); "Pietro of Siena" (N. Y. 1910); "Armageddon" (N. Y. 1915); "The King" (N. Y. 1912); "Harold" (N. Y. 1916).

Reprint in Anthology.—"Paolo and Francesca," in Dickinson and Crawford's *Contemporary Drama: English and American* (Boston, 1925).

References

William Archer, *Real Conversations* (London, 1904), *Poets of the Younger Generation* (London, 1902); A. E. Morgan, *Tendencies of Modern English Drama* (N. Y. 1924); E. E. Hale, Jr., *Dramatists of To-day* (N. Y. 1905); Arthur Symons, *Studies in Prose and Verse* (N. Y. 1904), and *Studies in Seven Arts* (N. Y. 1906); Brander Matthews, *Inquiries and Opinions* (N. Y. 1907), and *A Study of the Drama* (Boston, 1910); Thomas H. Dickinson, *The Contemporary Drama of England* (Boston, 1917); F. W. Chandler, *Aspects of Modern Drama* (N. Y. 1914); Ludwig Lewisohn, *The Modern Drama* (N. Y. 1915); Clayton Hamilton, *The Theory of the Theater* (N. Y. 1910); Solomon Eagle, *Books in General* (N. Y. 1919); J. T. Grein, *Dramatic Criticism*, Vol. III (London, 1902); C. Lewis Hind, *Authors and I* (N. Y. 1921); W. P. Eaton, *At the New Theater and Others* (Boston, 1910); Coulson Kernahan, *In Good Company* (N. Y. 1917); Hesketh Pearson, *Modern Men and Mummers* (London, 1922).

Paolo and Francesca

Tragedy in 4 acts (1899). Texts: N. Y. 1901; reprinted in Dickinson and Crawford's *Contemporary Drama: English and American* (Boston, 1925).

"Paolo and Francesca" belongs to the category of the so-called "poetic drama," a form that has fallen more or less intc disrepute among the English-speaking peoples. Most of the world's great plays are poetic dramas; but they are great first as drama and second as poetry. There is nothing reprehensible in writing poetic drama; the chief trouble nowadays seems to be a lack of poets and dramatists to write them.

1. When the great Victorian poets, Tennyson, Browning, Swinburne, and Matthew Arnold, wrote plays, they had only the vaguest notion of the exigencies of the stage: "Queen Mary," "A Blot in the 'Scutcheon," "Atalanta in Calydon," and "Empedocles on Ætna," are written to appeal rather to the ear and the intellect than to the eye and the emotions. These poets were either unaware that the dramatic form was different from the lyric or epic, or they did not care to write plays for the stage, preferring the "dramatic poem." For the most part they failed to distinguish dramatic dialogue from lyric and epic verse. Browning's lines in "A Blot in the 'Scutcheon" reveal character, but they are undramatic because they are not written to be *seen* and *heard*. The play gives one the impression of reading a number of the poet's "Dramatic Monologues,"

strung together upon a thread of story: the poet gains nothing by putting his thoughts in what appears to be play form. It is not alone through failure to grasp the essentials of dialogue that the poets have not succeeded in writing plays: they were unable to execute their conceptions in a way that could "get over" in the theater.

As usual, we must turn to Shakespeare for outstanding examples of genuine dramatic dialogue. He reveals character, creates atmosphere, indicates spiritual action, and advances the story. The following quotation from "Macbeth" will illustrate the point:

> . . . The raven himself is hoarse
> That croaks the fatal entrance of Duncan
> Under my battlements. Come, you spirits
> That tend on mortal thoughts, unsex me here,
> And fill me, from the crown to the toe, top-full
> Of direst cruelty! make thick my blood,
> Stop up the access and passage to remorse,
> That no compunctious visitings of nature
> Shake my fell purpose, nor keep peace between
> The effect and it! Come to my woman's breasts,
> And take my milk for gall, you murdering ministers,
> Wherever in your sightless substances
> You wait on nature's mischief! Come, thick night,
> And pall thee in the dunnest smoke of hell,
> That my keen knife see not the wound it makes,
> Nor heaven peep through the blanket of the dark,
> To cry, "Hold, hold!"
>
> *Enter* MACBETH.
>
> Great Glamis! worthy Cawdor!
> Greater than both, by the all-hail hereafter!
> Thy letters have transported me beyond
> This ignorant present, and I feel now
> The future in the instant.

Stephen Phillips, in "Ulysses," "Herod," and "Paolo and Francesca," has shown a gift for dramatic dialogue; and as a dramatist, many scenes from these plays show a sense of the theater and skill in developing a plot. Still "Paolo and Francesca," in many ways this poet's finest effort, is far from a good play—in any sense of the term—chiefly because Phillips the poet too often forgets Phillips the dramatist.

2. Most poetic plays are modeled, with certain modifications, upon the plays of ancient Greece or those of the age of Elizabeth; Stephen Phillips, being an Englishman, follows—even in "Ulysses"—Elizabethan models.

As the story of Paolo and Francesca is well known—it is told in Dante's "Divine Comedy"—we are prepared for such mystic forebodings as occupy the greater part of the brief first act. First, Paolo's desire to leave, his brother's anxiety, then the scene (pp. 22-26) with Lucrezia, and that immediately following, with the blind Angela. There is no doubt as to what the story is to relate: Angela's words supply the necessary warning:

> His face was dim: a twilight struggles back.
> I see two lying dead upon a bier—
> Slain suddenly, and in each other's arms. . . .
> . . . He shall be
> Not far to seek: yet perilous to find.
> Unwillingly he comes a wooing: she
> Unwillingly is wooed: yet shall they woo.
> His kiss was on her lips ere she was born.

And Phillips, the dramatist, adds the stage direction: "*Francesca, in passing, pauses and offers trinket to Angela, who shudders, letting it fall. Exeunt all but Angela, who remains staring before her.*" If there was the least doubt in the mind of the audience as to the truth of Angela's words, her action would dispel it.

3. So far, the story is compact and moving. The second act is well developed up to the second scene (p. 51), which takes up the plot where it was left in the first act. Giovanni learns the identity of Francesca's fated lover. Then the scene changes—Shakespeare's method again—to a more or less "comic relief" scene, written in prose. This interlude is followed by Paolo's soliloquy (pp. 59-61).

The soliloquy in modern plays is often considered to be a confession of weakness on the part of the dramatist. It had hitherto been used largely as a makeshift by the dramatist who was unwilling or unable to reveal character or advance his plot by other and more "natural" means. Yet in the poetic drama it does not seem so artificial as it does in the more "realistic" prose plays, largely, no doubt, because the poetic drama is considered a traditional form, in which the quaint practices of the past ought to be preserved. In other words, what is one ridiculous convention more or less, in a tissue of ridiculous conventions? Obviously, Paolo's speech reveals character, but as a dramatic expedient its insertion at this critical point looks very much like a makeshift. The dramatist's problem was, how to get Paolo to return to Francesca? The struggle goes on in Paolo's mind, and the poet has only to give words to the lover's thoughts and emotions. But in a play that is not sufficient. Just how this end was to be accomplished is not our business or intention to determine; yet the fact remains that here a monologue is not sufficiently convincing, especially as the monologue leaves us in doubt as to the character's immediate intentions. Here is the end of the speech:

I cannot go; thrilling from Rimini,
A tender voice makes all the trumpets mute.
I cannot go from her: may not return.
O God! what is thy will upon me? Ah!
One path there is, a straight path to the dark.
There, in the ground, I can betray no more,
And there forever am I pure and cold.
The means! No dagger blow, nor violence shown
Upon my body to distress her eyes.
Under some potion gently will I die;
And they that find me dead shall lay me down
Beautiful as a sleeper at her feet.

Take the last two lines: lovely verses, it is true, but do they "belong" to the character and the situation? Is this an instance where the poet asserts his rights and leaves the dramatist to his own devices?

4. The break in the middle of Act II was justifiable because of the contrast it afforded. The third act, however, should intensify the plot, concentrate our attention upon the central idea, not because of any arbitrary "laws" of dramatic technique, but because the human mind demands this sort of synthesis. To start a story, develop it a little, then stop it, then play *around* it, is not only bad art but bad psychology: we demand a logical continuation of the story once it is started. Instead of this we have another contrast scene, which opens the act, then Giovanni's entrance (p. 70), and his rather unconvincing errand; the coincidence of his overhearing Paolo, then Paolo's soliloquy (p. 78), and finally Giovanni's scene with the messenger (pp. 80-81.) Then, Scene 3, there is a good dramatic scene. Note the atmospheric lines:

> FRANCESCA. I cannot sleep, Nita; I will read here.
> Is it dawn yet? (NITA *sets lamp down.*)
> NITA. No, lady: yet I see
> A flushing in the east.
> FRANCESCA. How still it is!
> NITA. This is the stillest time of night or day!

Toward the end of the act, the poet's mistake in crowding too many incidents into a small space becomes apparent; not only does the crowding confuse, it occupies space which should, we feel, be given to the love scene. We are told, it is true, that the two "have to each other moved all night," but how much more convincing would have been a longer scene between the lovers, such as D'Annunzio gave in his "Francesca da Rimini"! Compare the two plays and see just how the Italian developed this part of the story.

5. That admirable love scene which should have supported the third act is placed instead in the otherwise admirable fourth. But does it belong here? Do you feel that its postponement has weakened the plot? The poet evidently did not. Why?

6. There are lyrical passages throughout, passages written

altogether for their own sake, which do not contribute to the story. Can you pick these out? On the other hand, there are dramatic lines and passages which are peculiarly apt and effective. Among these latter are:

> Henceforward let no woman have two sons, (p. 51)
>
> So still it is that we might almost hear
> The sigh of all the sleepers in the world. (p. 85)
>
> . . . You then that huddle all together
> Like cattle against thunder—what hath chanced? (p. 92)
>
> PAOLO. Why did you shiver and turn sudden cold?
> FRANCESCA. I felt a wind pass over me. (p. 111)
>
> I did not know the dead could have such hair.
> Hide them. They look like children fast asleep. (p. 120)

These are lines that could not be so effective were they not spoken by the right person under the right circumstances. Find further examples.

Is a dramatist ever justified in writing lines or whole speeches simply because they are beautiful or striking, whether or not they contribute to his play as drama? Are there such lines or speeches in "Romeo and Juliet," or "Hamlet"?

ST. JOHN HANKIN

St. John Emile Clavering Hankin was born in 1860 at Southampton. His early education was received in his native city, but he later attended Malvern College, and then Merton College at Oxford. After his graduation in 1890, he went to London, and took up journalism. Four years later, he went to Calcutta, where he continued his journalistic career. The following year he returned and began writing for *The Times* and *Punch*. In 1909, in a fit of depression as a result of his neurasthenic condition, he drowned himself.

Hankin allied himself with the pioneers of the Court Theater and the Stage Society, where innovations and attempts to break loose from the conventionalities of the theater were readily welcomed. John Drinkwater, in his introduction to the *Dramatic Works,* says: "St. John Hankin lived and wrote at the beginning of a new movement, and his permanent distinction in drama will be rather that of right endeavor and the recapture of just instincts than of full-bodied achievement . . . that he was one of the few who first sought to bring back sincerity and a fit dignity of form to the great art is a distinction of which he will not easily be deprived." Hankin was more a symptom than a finished product; yet his efforts to interpret life in an artistic and pleasing framework entitle him to a place among the less important members of the advance-guard of his day.

Plays

"The Two Mr. Wetherbys" (1903)
"The Return of the Prodigal" (1905)
"The Charity That Began at Home" (1906)
"The Cassilis Engagement" (1907)
"The Last of the De Mullins" (1908)
"The Burglar Who Failed" (1908)
"The Constant Lover" (1912)
"Thompson" [finished by George Calderon] (1913)

Editions.—The Dramatic Works of St. John Hankin, with introduction by John Drinkwater, 3 vols. (N. Y. 1912), includes all the plays except "Thompson", the same (exclusive of essays), 2 vols. (N. Y. 1923); *Three Plays with Happy Endings* (London, 1907), includes "The Return of the Prodigal," "The Charity That Began at Home," and "The Cassilis Engagement"; *Dramatic Sequels* (N. Y. 1926) contains several satirical sketches.

Separate Plays.—"The Two Mr. Wetherbys" (N. Y. 1907); "The Return of the Prodigal" (N. Y. 1907); "The Charity That Began at Home" (N. Y. 1907); "The Cassilis Engagement" (N. Y. 1907); "The Constant Lover" (*Theater Arts,* N. Y. 1919, and in paper, N. Y. 1912); "The Last of the De Mullins" (London, 1909); "Thompson" (Boston, 1918).

Reprints in Collections and Anthologies.—"The Cassilis Engagement" in Moses' *Representative British Dramas* (Boston, 1918), and in Dickinson and Crawford's *Contemporary Drama: English and American* (Boston, 1925); "The Constant Lover," in Shay and Loving's *Fifty Contemporary Oue-Act Plays* (Cincinnati, 1920).

References

P. P. Howe, *Dramatic Portraits* (N. Y. 1913), and *The Repertory Theater* (N. Y. 1911); J. M. Kennedy, *English Literature, 1880-1905* (N. Y. 1913); Charlton Andrews, *The Drama To-day* (Philadelphia, 1913); T. H. Dickinson, *The Contemporary Drama of England* (Boston, 1917); Mario Borsa, *The English Stage of To-day,* trans. by S. Brinton (N. Y. 1908); A. E. Morgan, "Tendencies of Modern English Drama" (N. Y. 1924); D. MacCarthy, *The Court Theater* (London, 1907); Archibald Henderson, *The Changing Drama* (Cincinnati, 1919); John

Drinkwater, *Prose Papers,* including revised introduction to *Dramatic Works* (London, 1917); Arnold Bennett, *Books and Persons* (N. Y. 1917); James Agate, *The Contemporary Theater, 1923* (London, 1924); Gilbert Norwood, *Euripides and Shaw* (Boston, 1921); J. W. Cunliffe, *Modern English Playwrights* (N. Y. 1927); Allardyce Nicoll, *British Drama* (N. Y. 1933); C. Pellizzi, *English Drama* (N. Y. 1935).

See also.—Hankin's Essays, *A Note on Happy Endings, Puritanism and the English Stage, Mr. Bernard Shaw as Critic, How to Run an Art Theater for London, The Collected Plays of Oscar Wilde,* and *The Need for an Endowed Theater,* in Vol. III of the *Dramatic Works.*

The Cassilis Engagement

Comedy in 4 acts (1907). Texts: N. Y. 1907; in *Dramatic Works,* 1912, and same, 1923; reprinted in Moses' *Representative British Dramas* (Boston, 1918), and in Dickinson and Crawford's *Contemporary Drama: English and American* (Boston, 1925).

The influence of Oscar Wilde is evident. Lady Remenham's "Engagements are such troublesome things. They sometimes even lead to marriage. But we'll hope it won't be as bad as that in this case," is decidedly reminiscent. The characters are mostly types; still, in most of Hankin's plays there is an effort to develop the occasionally impersonal types of Wilde and infuse into them the breath of life. The prodigal in "The Return of the Prodigal," Ethel and Mrs. Cassilis in the comedy under discussion, are human beings, even if Lady Remenham, Mrs. Borridge, and Geoffrey are time-worn types.

1. Hankin has theorized on the writing of plays, and his words possess interest and value in connection with the study of "The Cassilis Engagement." He says: "I select an episode in the life of one of my characters or a group of characters, when something of importance to their future has to be decided, and I ring up my curtain. Having shown how it was decided, and why it was so decided, I ring it down again." This comedy is clear and unified, quite in accordance with the dramatist's theory, but we might inquire into the exact methods by which he has attained the desired end.

What is the "episode" round which the play is built? Where is it first referred to? Is the theme explained through a "raisonneur," is it evolved in action, or in apparently casual conversation? Are we asked to interest ourselves in a "character," or a "group of characters"? Which character, or which group of characters?

Could the author have advantageously begun his play at an earlier or later time than he did? That is, was his curtain "rung up" at the most interesting and opportune moment of the episode?

How was the "something of importance to their future" decided? By what means has the dramatist worked out his central idea?

2. The "curtains" in this play deserve especial attention: a crisp and pregnant phrase, an incident, a mysterious word—will cause the audience to await impatiently the opening of the next act. Notice with what apparently artless care the first act is terminated. Mrs. Cassilis' "Marry her!—Nonsense, my dear Margaret," instantly attracts our attention and directs our interest to the speaker. We wish to know precisely how Geoffrey and Ethel are to be "cured," and are anxious to see how the (evidently) clever Mrs. Cassilis is to effect the cure. Plot interest, as distinguished from character interest, is here introduced.

Can you detect the point where plot and character interests merge?

3. It is as important to close a play without arousing further interest as to close each of the preceding acts by stimulating it. There should be an air of finality that precludes further curiosity; we should have no wish to inquire into the future. To lead an audience to expect more, after the play is over, is as fatal as to deprive it of sufficient curiosity after the first act. The dramatist must know where to end his play. In a tragedy this particular point is not difficult to determine, for a tragedy usually ends in the failure of the protagonist, in most instances, his death. For centuries comedies have ended with the union of lover and sweetheart, who had, during one, two, three, four, or five acts, been kept apart more or less skillfully by the hand of the dramatist. Of recent years, writers, even of comedy, have begun to discard the conventional notion that the united lovers married and lived happy ever after, and have sought

what they deem a closer approximation to the facts of life. They have come to realize that, as Emile Faguet once remarked, marriage is not the end but the beginning of trouble. To mention two instances, Maurice Donnay's "Lovers" and Henry Bataille's "Poliche" end with a scene where the lovers separate; they do this because only by an amicable breaking-off can they assure themselves of true and lasting happiness. Here the dramatists have repudiated marriage as the balm for wounded hearts. *Their* serious dramas usually begin *after* the happy union of the happy pair.

Hankin disliked "happy endings." (See his article on this subject in the third volume of the *Dramatic Works.*) Is the ending of "The Cassilis Engagement" satisfactory, psychologically and artistically? Is it "happy"? Find instances of technically "happy" endings which are in reality quite the reverse. There are many of these, particularly in the plays of dramatists who had originally carried their characters through to logical endings, but were forced by practical considerations to "send the audience away from the theater smiling." It is as if the playwright said: "Very well, if the public *will* insist on a wedding, a wedding they shall have, but you just wait and see how it will turn out!"

4. Analyze the third act, and determine, so far as possible, the following questions: How much of the story is carried on in pantomime through the stage-directions? Could, for example, the *"Bye-play for Ethel's song,"* etc. (N. Y. edition, p. 193, Vol II, *Dramatic Works*) have been worked out in dialogue? Is the dumb-show more effective than ordinary dialogue would be? Is Ethel's change of attitude convincing?

Compare "The Cassilis Engagement" as a study in character and technique with the same author's "Return of the Prodigal."

John Masefield

John Masefield was born at Ledbury, England, in 1875. At the age of fourteen he ran away from home and went to sea. But a sailor's life was not altogether what he wanted, and on a later voyage, bound for America, he decided that he would write. He landed in New York with only "a whole suit of clothes, a sound pair of shoes, and the unquenchable spirit which still burns from the depths of his blue eyes." He remained in America for some time, working in factories and on farms and often without food or shelter, and it is related that he was assistant to a Sixth Avenue bartender in New York City. Returning at last to London, he began writing.

He has written novels, ballads, lyrics, small epics, and plays. The plays were formed, to a certain extent, under the influence of his friends Yeats and Synge. His early short plays and his "Nan" were produced by the special "new" theaters of the day, Barker's Court Theater and Frohman's Repertory at the Duke of York's somewhat later. Masefield is an austere artist, and in his few dramas he has exemplified his belief that "tragedy . . . is a vision of the heart of life."

Plays

"The Campden Wonder" (1907)
"The Tragedy of Nan" (1908)
"Mrs. Harrison" (1909)
"The Tragedy of Pompey the Great" (1910)
"Philip the King" (1914)
"The Faithful" (1915)
"The Sweeps of Ninety-Eight" (1916)
"The Locked Chest" (1916)
"Good Friday" (1916)
"A King's Daughter" (1923)
"Melloney Holtspur" (1923)
"The Trial of Jesus" (1925)
"Tristan and Isolt" (1927)
"The Coming of Christ" (1928)
"End and Beginning" (1933)

"Anne Pedersdotter" (Boston, 1917) is an English version of a play by H. Wiers-Jensen; "Esther" and "Berenice," 1 vol. (N. Y. 1922), are translations from Racine.)

Editions.—The Poems and Plays of John Masefield, 2 vols. (N. Y. 1918), includes in Vol. II: "The Campden Wonder," "Mrs. Harrison," "The Locked Chest," "The Sweeps of Ninety-Eight," "The Tragedy of Nan," "The Tragedy of Pompey the Great," "The Faithful," "Philip the King," and "Good Friday"; *The Tragedy of Nan and Other Plays* (N. Y. 1910) includes "The Tragedy of Nan," "The Campden Wonder," and "Mrs. Harrison"; *Philip the King and Other Poems* (N. Y. 1914) includes only "Philip the King"; *The Locked Chest, The Sweeps of Ninety-Eight* (N. Y. 1917) includes the two plays mentioned; *Good Friday and Other Poems* (N. Y. 1916) includes only "Good Friday"; *The Collected Poems* (London, 1923) includes "Philip the King" and "Good Friday"; *A Poem and Two Plays* (London, 1919) includes "The Locked Chest" and "The Sweeps of Ninety-Eight."

Separate Plays.—"The Tragedy of Nan" (N. Y. 1909); "Melloney Hotspur" (N. Y. 1923); "A King's Daughter" (N. Y. 1923); "The

Tragedy of Pompey the Great" (N. Y. 1914); "The Faithful" (N. Y. 1915); "Good Friday" (London, 1916); "Tristan and Isolt" (N. Y. 1927); "The Coming of Christ" (N. Y. 1928); "End and Beginning" (N. Y. 1933).

Reprints in Collections and Anthologies.—"The Tragedy of Pompey the Great" in Moses' *Representative British Dramas* (Boston, 1918); "The Locked Chest" in Smith's *Short Plays by Representative Authors* (N. Y. 1922).

REFERENCES

W. H. Hamilton, *John Masefield, a Study* (London, 1922); A. E. Morgan, *Tendencies of Modern English Drama* (N. Y. 1924); Cecil Biggane, *John Masefield, a Study* (Cambridge, England, 1924); A. Williams, *Bibliographies of Modern Authors. No. 2, John Masefield* (N. Y. 1921); John Galsworthy, *The Inn of Tranquillity* (N. Y. 1912); C. E. Montague, *Dramatic Values* (N. Y. 1911); T. H. Dickinson, *The Contemporary Drama of England* (Boston, 1917); Desmond MacCarthy, *The Court Theater* (London, 1907); C. Lewis Hind, *Authors and I* (N. Y. 1921); Arnold Bennett, *Books and Persons* (N. Y. 1917); Robert Lynd, *Old and New Masters* (N. Y. 1919); William Archer, *The Old Drama and the New* (Boston, 1923); Edward Shanks, *First Essays on Literature* (London, 1923); H. M. Walbrook, *Nights at the Play* (London, 1911); S. P. B. Mais, *From Shakespeare to O. Henry* (N. Y. 1923); Coulson Kernahan, *Six Famous Living Poets* (London, 1922); J. M. Murry, *Aspects of Literature* (London, 1920); Dixon Scott, *Men of Letters* (N. Y. 1923); Allardyce Nicoll, *British Drama* (N. Y. 1933); J. W. Cunliffe, *Modern English Playwrights* (N. Y. 1927); C. Pellizzi, *English Drama* (N. Y. 1935).

See also.—Masefield's preface to "Nan" (*Poems and Plays,* Vol. II); his *William Shakespeare* (N. Y. no date), *John M. Synge* (N. Y. 1915); preface to Gordon Craig's *Scene* (N. Y. 1923), and *The Taking of Helen and Other Prose Selections* (N. Y. 1924). *Recent Prose* (London, 1924) includes everything in *The Taking of Helen,* and the essay on Synge as well.

THE TRAGEDY OF NAN

Play in 3 acts (1908). Texts: N. Y. 1909; in *Poems and Plays,* Vol. II (N. Y. 1918); in *The Tragedy of Nan and Other Plays* (N. Y. 1910).

"Tragedy," says Masefield in a note prefixed to a late edition of this play, "at its best is a vision of the heart of life. The heart of life can only be laid bare in the agony and exaltation of dreadful acts. The vision of agony, or spiritual contest, pushed beyond the limits of dying personality, is exalting and cleansing. It is only by such vision that a multitude can be brought to the passionate knowledge of things exalting and eternal." "The Tragedy of Nan" is an attempt "towards the achieving of that power" which "helps the genius of a race to obtain it, though the obtaining may be fifty years after the strivers are dead."

1. The above quotation shows a conception of tragedy different from what is commonly held. The exalting and cleansing element is Greek; the "passionate knowledge of things exalting and eternal" with the insistence on "dreadful acts" as a necessary premise to the laying bare of the heart of life, is in a manner Masefield's own twist to a well-known theory. The story of "Œdipus" is a series of "dreadful acts," and it would seem that Masefield—if we are to take his words literally—demands that the "dreadful acts" be shown. Is this the correct interpretation? Few dramatists would risk such a "dreadful" scene as that in which Nan forces Jenny to eat the tainted mutton pie. The word "dreadful" is curious. Just what does it mean? "The heart of life," it is held, "can only be laid bare" through "dreadful acts." True, it is not claimed that dreadful acts in themselves are exalting and cleansing. Ordinarily, there is nothing inspiring in murder, or in one person's forcing another to eat poisoned meat. It is the artist's business to utilize the raw material of life by surrounding each fact or deed with a set of significant circumstances.

Open any newspaper. A man murders a woman. The facts are horrible, and we read the sordid details with disgust. The same story is written by a novelist or a dramatist, and the *same facts* are so presented as to exalt and cleanse the soul. The act is given a meaning: the complex motives of human beings under the stress of passion are made clear, and the story becomes actually beautiful. François de Curel, to name one writer in a hundred, found most of the plots for his plays in the newspapers.

2. As art is a synthesis of life, all that is unessential must be omitted in order that the typical, the characteristic, may be brought into emphatic relief. In a play, where the incidents are ordinarily supposed to cover a space of many hours, days, or even years, those that the dramatist chooses must be condensed into about two hours: he cannot waste a word or a

gesture. This necessitates an acceptance on the part of the audience of the convention of foreshortening: incidents, psychological changes, development of character, occupy much less time on the stage than they would in life or in the more leisurely art-form, the novel. An hour may be assumed to pass in ten minutes; in a moment a character reaches a decision which in life might require days or months; young men and women fall in love at first sight with little or no regard to verisimilitude. Needless to say, there must be sufficient motivation to account for these sudden changes, or the audience will refuse to believe the playwright. In Shakespeare's "Richard III," the Queen, who is accompanying her husband's bier to the church, is met by Richard, her husband's known murderer, and is wooed in less than ten minutes—and successfully wooed. This is too great a strain upon the credulity of the audience, in spite of the fact that the play is obviously melodrama. In Ibsen's "Doll's House," Nora's change of mind covers less than a week, but Ibsen takes good care to support her final act by credible motivation.

In "Nan" is Dick's change of heart well motivated? Notice what reasons the dramatist sets forth; that is his defense, as it were. Still, is his change acceptable?

3. The last act in a play is often the shortest. The reason for this is that the climax, which in ninety-nine cases out of a hundred comes at the end of the penultimate act, brings the play to its highest pitch of interest and suspense, and there remains little to be accomplished in the last. *Dénouement* is not, as a rule, so interesting as development. Many plays fail because of an uninteresting or anti-climactic final act. It is the business of the dramatist to hold over some absorbing revelation, or some long-expected turn of affairs, in order that his audience may await with impatience the rise of the last curtain. In W. C. De Mille's "The Woman," this has been skillfully accomplished.

How has Masefield succeeded? His last act is the longest in the play. What does he do to make it interesting?

It is well to ask one's self, as the curtain is falling on the penultimate act of a play, whether there is much more worth waiting for.

4. Masefield's paper on "Play-writing" (in *The Taking of Helen and Other Prose Selections,* 1924) is decidedly worth reading. He says little that has not already been said by one or other of the wise men—Aristotle, or Lessing or Goethe—but he says it in new and interesting ways. "The foundation of drama," he writes, "is this, that human action is hypnotic; if you do something, you will hold the attention of men." A good reason is here given for the dictum that action rather than words is the basis of drama. And here again is the Brunetière theory of conflict: "When you have two men earnestly intent on opposite sides of some issue vital to themselves, you have a contest or play, interesting, exciting, or absorbing to watch. A play is a contest between opposed wills, or a contest between a human will and the fate which surrounds him."

And now to consider these simple statements in connection with "Nan." Wherein lies the contest between opposed wills? Why is this contest interesting, exciting, or absorbing?

Simplicity, says Masefield, is demanded of the dramatic form; when the contest is not presented "simply, the play ceases to hold the attention of men." One way to attain simplicity is by observing "those guides to all simple construction, the Unities of Time, of Place, and of Action." (For just what Aristotle has said on that matter, see p. 269.)

In what respects is "Nan" unified, in the strict sense of adhering to the pseudo-Aristotelian unities?

Stanley Houghton

Stanley Houghton was born at Ashton-upon-Mersey in 1881. At the age of sixteen he entered his father's law office in Manchester, where he worked until 1912, when his play "Hindle Wakes" was produced. From that year until the end of his short life, he devoted most of his time to the writing of plays. Early in 1913 he left England and toward the end of the year he died in Venice.

At the time of his death Houghton was probably the best-known dramatist of the so-called Manchester School, a group of young people whose plays were produced under the direction of Miss Horniman at the Gaiety Theater. Houghton possessed a real sense of the theater, and though he was largely concerned with social and ethical problems, his plays never degenerated into what has been termed the lowest form of literature, the purely didactic.

The Manchester School

This name was more or less loosely applied to Houghton and several other young dramatists, most of whose plays were produced at the Gaiety Theater in Manchester under the direction of Miss A. E. F. Horniman. In the Introduction to Houghton's *Works,* Harold Brighouse, himself one of the "group," writes as follows: "In the autumn of 1907 Miss A. E. F. Horniman initiated at the Midland Theater, Manchester, the first Repertory Theater in Great Britain. By the spring of 1908 she had acquired the Gaiety Theater, and established it upon the lines which made it famous. The plays, selected by Miss Horniman and produced with more than a touch of genius by Mr. Iden Payne, set up at once a new dramatic standard for the provinces. . . . Watching her early plays, Houghton discovered his medium with his opportunity. . . ." Besides offering a wide variety of modern plays, Miss Horniman encouraged new writers to produce plays portraying the life of the Midlands. Among the dramatists whose work has become identified with the Manchester group are Harold Brighouse, Allan Monkhouse, Basil Dean, and Charles McEvoy. Not all these men were as closely identified with the movements as, say Synge was with the Abbey Theater movement, but they were undoubtedly enabled to write the sort of plays they wished to write with the assurance of intelligent production.

Plays

"The Dear Departed" (1908)
"Independent Means" (1909)
"The Master of the House" (1910)
"The Younger Generation" (1910)
"Fancy Free" (1911)
"Hindle Wakes" (1912)
"Phipps" (1912)
"Pearls" (1912)
"The Perfect Cure" (1913)
"The Fifth Commandment" (1913)
"Ginger" (1913)
"Trust the People" (1913)
"The Old Testament and the New" (1914)
"Partners" (1914)
"Marriages in the Making" (1914)
"The Hillarys" [with Harold Brighouse] (1915)

Editions.—The Works of Stanley Houghton, 3 vols. (London, 1914), includes all the plays (except "Trust the People," "Ginger," "Pearls," and "The Hillarys," which are unpublished) together with an Introduction by Harold Brighouse, and a number of Houghton's criticisms; *Five One-Act Plays* (N. Y. 1912) contains "The Dear Departed," "The Master of the House," "Fancy Free," "Phipps," and "The Fifth Commandment."

Separate Plays.—"The Dear Departed" (N. Y. 1910); "The Younger Generation" (N. Y. 1910); "Hindle Wakes" (N. Y. 1912, Boston, 1913); "Independent Means" (N. Y. 1911); "Fancy Free" (London, 1912).

Reprints in Collections and Anthologies.—"Fancy Free" in Clark's *Representive One-Act Plays by British and Irish Authors* (Boston, 1921); "Hindle Wakes" in Dickinson and Crawford's *Contemporary Drama: English and American* (Boston, 1925); "Phipps" in *One-Act Plays for Stage and Study* (N. Y. 1924).

References

T. H. Dickinson, *The Contemporary Drama of England* (Boston, 1917); John Palmer, *The Future of the Theater* (London, 1913); Gerald Cumberland, *Set Down in Malice* (N. Y. 1909); F. W. Chandler, *Aspects of Modern Drama* (N. Y. 1914); William Archer, *The Old Drama and the New* (Boston, 1923); Clayton Hamilton, *Studies in Stagecraft* (N. Y. 1914); W. P. Eaton, *Plays and Players* (Cincinnati, 1916); Dixon Scott, *Men of Letters* (N. Y. 1923); G. J. Nathan, *Another Book on the Theater* (N. Y. 1915); Frank Vernon, *The Twentieth-Century Theater* (Boston, 1924); A. E. Morgan, *Tendencies of Modern English Drama* (N. Y. 1924); J. W. Marriott, *Modern Drama* (London, n. d.); Allardyce Nicoll, *British Drama* (N. Y. 1933).

See also.—Houghton's "Dramatic Criticism" (4 essays) in Vol. III of the *Works.*

Hindle Wakes

Play in 3 acts (1912). Texts: N. Y. 1912, and in *Works,* Vol. II (London, 1914); reprinted in Dickinson and Crawford's *Contemporary Drama: English and American* (Boston, 1925).

"Hindle Wakes" is original by reason of the manner in which a difficult thesis is treated; of its theme (the same, by the way, as that treated in St. John Ervine's "The Magnanimous Lover" and Galsworthy's "The Eldest Son"), its telling dialogue, and its construction. The characters are well drawn, lifelike, thoroughly human.

1. It is only by comparison with such plays as "Sweet Lavender" that one can appreciate the progress made in the art of dialogue during the past generation. The early Pinero play shows the influence of the stilted style of Robertson and H. J. Byron; still, it purported to be realistic in treatment. Read the first five pages of "Sweet Lavender," then the first five of "Hindle Wakes." Then the first five of "The Second Mrs. Tanqueray," and finally read five more of the Houghton play. Again, read a scene from Pinero's "Thunderbolt," one of the few frankly realistic pictures of English middle-class society which Pinero has attempted, and read another scene from "Hindle Wakes." Pinero cannot escape from the shackles of his predecessors; Houghton came to the theater with a fresh outlook on life, and few ideas about the "literary" style of dialogue.

Bearing in mind Henry Arthur Jones' remarks (p. 238) on literature and the stage, determine in what respects this play is literature.

2. "Hindle Wakes," besides being a "slice of life" and an interesting story, is a "thesis play." This does not mean that the author wrote it solely to exploit an idea, or that he was so interested in the moral that he neglected anything to make it an interesting spectacle: the idea serves only to increase the interest. Up to the very last of the play (p. 97, Boston edition) the author's solution is not made clear. This was Ibsen's method in the "Doll's House," where, up to the middle of the last act, Nora's sudden resolution was not even hinted at. It is likely that if these dramatists had been more interested in the propagandist side of their work they would doubtless have foreshadowed the end earlier in the play: their enthusiasm would inevitably have led them into argument and discussion. But both Ibsen and Houghton allowed their plays to develop naturally up to what in a conventional play would have been the beginning of the usual end, and then—by a sudden turn—changed the whole *dénouement*.

What indications are there that Houghton was less concerned than Ibsen with the idea, as distinct from the play as a dramatic entertainment? Does Houghton adopt a moral attitude? An immoral attitude?

3. What is the advantage of dividing the first act into three scenes? Is there any necessity for combining these three parts into one act? Why should not the author have made each of these into a separate act? Why did he not divide the second and third acts into scenes?

4. In the thesis play there is a danger that characters may speak a good deal more logically and with much more penetration than they would in life: the dramatist puts his own arguments into their mouths, and often distorts them as characters. What would ordinarily be the logic of their actions he often makes them reason out in a way that would be out of the question in any other place. The logical explanation of Fanny's conduct occurs in the last scene of this play (pp. 97-104). Notice the following dialogue.

ALAN. . . . you'd damage my prospects, and all that sort of thing. You can see that, can't you?

FANNY. Ay! I can see it now you point it out. I hadn't thought of it before.

ALAN. Then, that isn't why you refused me?

FANNY. Sorry to disappoint you, but it's not.

ALAN. I didn't see what else it could be.

FANNY. Don't kid yourself, my lad! It isn't because I'm afraid of spoiling *your* life that I'm refusing you, but because I'm afraid of spoiling *mine!* That didn't occur to you?

ALAN. It didn't.

FANNY. You never thought that anybody else could be as selfish as yourself.

ALAN. I may be very conceited, but I don't see how you can hurt yourself by wedding me. You'd come in for plenty of brass, anyhow.

FANNY. I don't know as money's much to go by when it comes to a job of this sort. It's more important to get the right chap.

ALAN. You like me well enough?

FANNY. Suppose it didn't last? Weddings brought about this road have a knack of turning out badly. Would you ever forget it was your father bade you marry me? No fear! You'd bear me a grudge all my life for that.

And again,

ALAN. But you didn't ever really love me?

FANNY. Love you? Good Heavens, of course not! Why on earth should I love you? You were just some one to have a bit of fun with. You were an amusement—a lark.

ALAN (*shocked*). Fanny! Is that all you cared for me?

FANNY. How much more did you care for me?

ALAN. But it's not the same. I'm a man.

FANNY. You're a man, and I was your little fancy. Well, I'm a woman, and *you* were *my* little fancy. You wouldn't prevent a woman enjoying herself as well as a man, if she takes it into her head?

ALAN. But do you mean to say that you didn't care any more for me than a fellow cares for any girl he happens to pick up?

FANNY. Yes. Are you shocked?

ALAN. It's a bit thick; it is really!

FANNY. You're a beauty to talk!

ALAN. It sounds so jolly immoral. I never thought of a girl looking on a chap just like that! I made sure you wanted to marry me if you got the chance. . . .

Is the dramatist forcing his characters to utter ideas which they would as a matter of fact scarcely be able to formulate, merely in order that the theme may be clear?

How far has an author the right to do this?

5. The play involves not only a statement of an ethical problem, but very clearly a judgment. "Hindle Wakes," it need hardly be said, was not written for the purpose of propounding ethical problems; and yet the moral issue is made the basis of the plot. One reason why such plays are easier to discuss than plays like "Salomé" is that most questions of human conduct are decided according to conventional codes of ethics, whereas the delineation of character and the presentation of situations must be decided largely on the basis of æsthetics and psychology. That is why most people prefer to discuss the "problem" of Nora Helmer and her husband rather than Nora herself and the man she leaves.

But it will have been observed, during the course of our study, that it is really impossible to discuss technique apart from human psychology. For practical purposes we try to do so, and, roughly speaking, we consider various aspects of a play separately. Alan and Fanny are, however, human beings placed in a certain predicament by Stanley Houghton, and their problem, their motives, their *technical* position in the play, are all parts of a whole. Technique is only the means by which the artist has succeeded—more or less well—in presenting to us a group of persons.

ELIZABETH BAKER

Elizabeth Baker was born in London. She began her professional life as a cashier, but soon after took up shorthand and stenography; the latest available record of her activities states that she is a private secretary. She declared (in a letter written some years ago) that she writes plays in her leisure hours. Her first play, "Beastly Pride," was produced at the Croyden Repertory Theater, and was so well received that she was encouraged to write a full-length play. This was "Chains," produced first by the Play Actors, then at Charles Frohman's Repertory Theater. It has since been seen at most of the repertory theaters of Great Britain. An adaptation was played in New York. "The Price of Thomas Scott" was produced by Miss Horniman's Company in London and Manchester in 1913.

Like Githa Sowerby, author of "Rutherford and Son," Miss Baker is an amateur—in the true sense: she writes plays because she likes to write them. Both these women have gone to everyday life for their material, both have cared and dared to write about dull, ordinary people. In Miss Baker's case this is especially true. "Chains" is a simple picture of the clerk class. Her sincerity, her simplicity, her power of analysis, her penetration, entitle her to a position of honor among what was, before the War, the "young" Naturalistic group.

PLAYS

"Beastly Pride" (1907)
"Chains" (1909)
"Miss Tassey" (1910)
"Cupid in Clapham" (1910)
"Edith" (1912)
"The Price of Thomas Scott" (1913)
"Over a Garden Wall" (1915)
"Miss Robinson" (1918)
"Partnership" (1921)
"Bert's Girl" (1925)
"Umbrellas" (1927)
"Faithful Admirer" (1927)

Editions (separate plays).—"Chains" (Boston, 1911); "Miss Tassey" (London, 1913); "The Price of Thomas Scott" (London, 1913); "Miss Robinson" (London, 1920); "Partnership" (London, 1921); "Umbrellas" (London, 1927); "Edith" (London, 1927); "Bert's Girl" (London, 1927).

Reprints in Collections and Anthologies.—"Miss Tassey" in Clark's *Representative One-Act Plays by British and Irish Authors* (Boston, 1921); "Chains" in Dickinson and Crawford's *Contemporary Drama* (Boston, 1925); "Cupid in Clapham" in *One-Act Plays for Stage and Study,* Vol. III (N. Y. 1927); "Faithful Admirer" in Shay's *Fifty More Contemporary One-Act Plays* (N. Y. 1928).

References

William Archer, *Playmaking* (Boston, 1912); G. P. Baker, *Dramatic Technique* (Boston, 1919); T. H. Dickinson, *The Contemporary Drama of England* (Boston, 1917); Clayton Hamilton, *Studies in Stagecraft* (N. Y. 1914); A. E. Morgan, *Tendencies of Modern English Drama* (N. Y. 1924).

Chains

Play in 4 acts (1909). Texts: Boston, 1911; and in Dickinson and Crawford's *Contemporary Drama: English and American* (Boston, 1925).

Miss Baker's quiet unpretentious picture is the antithesis of the color, movement, and intrigue of Pinero's "The Gay Lord Quex." If Pinero was limited, as to execution and theme, so is Miss Baker, but each has fulfilled an important function: Pinero brought the artificial comedy of his predecessors to its height, while Miss Baker has shown that it was possible to write a successful play without utilizing the ordinary and time-worn conventions.

1. In William Archer's *Playmaking* (pp. 48-49) the author, in speaking of what is dramatic and what undramatic, refers to the present play:

> We have already seen, indeed, that in a certain type of play—the broad picture of a social phenomenon or environment—it is preferable that no attempt should be made to depict a marked crisis. There should be just enough story to afford a plausible excuse for raising and for lowering the curtain. . . . As a specimen, and a successful specimen, of this new technique, I may cite Miss Elizabeth Baker's very interesting play, "Chains." There is absolutely no "story" in it, no complication of incidents, not even any emotional

tension worth speaking of. . . . A city clerk, oppressed by the deadly monotony and narrowness of his life, thinks of going to Australia—and doesn't go: that is the sum and substance of the action. Also, by way of underplot, a shopgirl, oppressed by the deadly monotony and narrowness of her life, thinks of escaping it by marrying a middle-aged widower—and doesn't do it. If any one had told the late Francisque Sarcey or the late Clement Scott, that a play could be made out of this slender material, which should hold an audience absorbed through four acts, and stir them to real enthusiasm, these eminent critics would have thought him a madman. Yet Miss Baker has achieved this feat, by the simple process of supplementing competent observation with a fair share of dramatic instinct.

First of all, let us ask ourselves, does Archer's description fit the case? *Is* "Chains" as deficient in action as the critic would have us believe? Then let us see what the dramatist does offer in place of the usual more or less violent action? Does the struggle take place entirely within the minds of the characters? Is "Chains" in any way a "well-made" play? How?

2. The Russian dramatist Andreyev is another who believes that external incidents—"action"—are not necessary for a play. In his *Letter on the Theater* (quoted, p. 67) he asks the question: "Is action, in the accepted sense of movements and visible achievements on the stage, necessary to the theater?" Andreyev's plays for the greater part depict mental and spiritual struggles, but Andreyev makes use of the soliloquy and even has recourse to the *Deus ex machina* device of the ancients, by using such characters as "The Being in Grey" (in "The Life of Man") to explain the thoughts of his characters. Miss Baker, who doubtless has no definite theories, allows her "ordinary" characters to work out their own destiny, without the aid of explanation.

Compare the "static" plays, "The Intruder" of Maeterlinck and "The Life of Man" of Andreyev, with "Chains."

3. Miss Baker is one of only two women dramatists considered in this volume. The question may well be asked, Why

are there no great or even near-great women playwrights? In the European countries there is scarcely a name that emerges above the rank and file. Marie Lenéru, a Frenchwoman, wrote two or three powerful dramas several years ago; Mme. Rostand has written two or three light fantasies; Judith Gautier has perhaps half-a-dozen poetic plays to her credit. In Germany and Austria and Russia I can think of no woman who has written a really big play. In Holland there are a number of women playwrights, none of whom, however, is claimed as a peer of the first of the Dutch writers. And Italy and Spain? I cannot say, but I have neither seen nor read a single play by a Spanish or Italian woman. In England and the United States, the number of women dramatists is larger than elsewhere. Besides Miss Baker, there are Githa Sowerby (with her one play), Cicely Hamilton, Gertrude Robins (whose one-acters are creditable products); Lady Gregory; and a few others.

In the United States, there is a host of clever women, who have, on the whole, written just as good plays as all but two or three of the men: Margaret Mayo, Mary Roberts Rinehart, Rachel Crothers, Clare Kummer, "Bosworth Crocker," Susan Glaspell, Josephine Preston Peabody, and Eleanor Gates.

And yet, with the exception of the always exceptional Lady Gregory, there is none among them who has approached the tragic irony of a Galsworthy, the poetic and imaginative power of a Benavente, the satiric irony of a Shaw.

A general question, of course, but worth discussing. Consider a few of the best plays by women (Githa Sowerby's "Rutherford and Son," Elizabeth Baker's "Chains," Gertrude Robins' "Realties," Rachel Crothers' "The Three of Us," Clare Kummer's "Rollo's Wild Oat," Susan Glaspell's "Bernice"). Do you discover in any of these the feminine note? If so, what is it?

Is there any reason why a woman should not be as good a playwright as a man?

In Brander Matthews' *A Book About the Theater* there is an article on "Women Dramatists." Women, it is said, are not lacking in powers of observation; they can write well and with great charm, but they are deficient in the sense of structure, without which no dramatist can succeed. Professor Matthews sums up his argument by declaring first that "women are likely to have only a definitely limited knowledge of life, and, second, . . . that they are likely also to be more or less deficient in the faculty of construction." Henry James is quoted in support of the contention that women *can* succeed in the novel form because it demands little or no definite structure, while the play must have it or cease to be. Says James: "The novel, as practiced in English, is the perfect paradise of the loose end, . . ." whereas the "play consents to the logic of but one way, mathematically right, and with the loose end as gross an impertinence on its surface and as grave a dishonor as the dangle of a snippet of silk or wool on the right side of a tapestry."

SIR JAMES BARRIE

James Matthew—now Sir James—Barrie was born at Kirriemuir, Scotland, in 1860. He was educated first at Dumfries and then at Edinburgh University. After his graduation he did newspaper work for a time, first at Nottingham and later at London. He began his literary career as a writer of novels and sketches, but in the early nineties he tried his hand at plays—one-acters, farces, musical comedies for the most part, works of no particular merit. "The Professor's Love-Story" (1894) was the first to show anything of his dramatic ability. With "The Little Minister," three years later, he became firmly established as a playwright. "Quality Street" and "The Admirable Crichton" (1902) were recognized as masterpieces. During the past twenty years Barrie has devoted himself almost entirely to the writing of plays.

The dramatic work of this popular and beloved Scottish writer has aroused a vast amount of critical controversy. There are few who deny that he is thoroughly familiar with the craft of playwriting; the trouble—with the dissenters—seems to lie in the philosophical basis upon which the plays are built. Ludwig Lewisohn and George Jean Nathan have no use for a man who, as they declare, is simply a purveyor of maudlin sentimentality. A. B. Walkley in England, however, and William Lyon Phelps and Clayton Hamilton in America, have difficulty in finding superlatives to sing his praises.

In the best of Barrie's plays there is exquisite sensibility and delicate art. Among his contemporaries, Barrie has no rival as a writer of sentimental comedy, nor has anyone surpassed him as a technician for the revelation upon the stage of his time of a delicately sentimental personality. Barrie died in 1937.

Plays

"Becky Sharp" (1891)
"Ibsen's Ghost" (1891)
"Richard Savage" [with H. B. Marriott-Watson] (1891)
"Walker, London" (1892)
"The Professor's Love Story" (1894)
"The Little Minister" (1897)
"The Wedding Guest" (1900)
"Quality Street" (1902)
"The Admirable Crichton" (1902)
"Little Mary" (1903)
"Peter Pan" (1904)
"Pantaloon" (1905)
"Alice-Sit-by-the-Fire" (1905)
"Josephine" (1906)
"Punch" (1906)
"What Every Woman Knows" (1908)
"Old Friends" (1910)
"The Twelve-Pound Look" (1910)
"A Slice of Life" (1910)
"Rosalind" (1912)
"The Legend of Leonora" ["The Adored One"] (1913)
"Half-an-Hour" (1913)
"The Will" (1913)
"Der Tag," (1914)
"Rosy Rapture, the Pride of the Beauty Chorus" (1915)
"The New Word" (1915)
"A Kiss for Cinderella" (1916)
"The Old Lady Shows Her Medals" (1917)
"Dear Brutus" (1917)
"Barbara's Wedding" (1918)
"A Well-Remembered Voice" (1918)
"The Truth About the Russian Dancers" (1920)
"Mary Rose" (1920)
"Shall We Join the Ladies?" (1922)
"The Boy David" (1937)

("Jane Annie," 1893, is the libretto of a comic opera, written with Conan Doyle; London, 1893.)

Editions.—Half-Hours (N. Y. 1914) includes "The Twelve-Pound Look," "Pantaloon," "Rosalind," and "The Will" [one edition also includes "Der Tag"]; *Echoes of the War* (N. Y. 1918) includes "The Old Lady Shows Her Medals," "The New Word," "Barbara's Wedding," and "A Well-Remembered Voice." *Shall We Join the Ladies?* (N. Y. 1929) includes also "Half-an-Hour," "Seven Women," and "Old Friends." *Representative Plays of Barrie* (N. Y. 1926) includes "Quality Street," "The Admirable Crichton," "What Every Woman Knows," "Dear Brutus," "The Twelve-Pound Look," and "The Old Lady Shows Her Medals." *The Plays of J. M. Barrie* (1 volume, N. Y. 1928) contains 20 plays, of which "Seven Women" and "Old Friends" are published for the first time.

Separate Plays.—"Richard Savage" (London, 1891); "The Wedding Guest" (London and N. Y. 1900); "Quality Street," illustrated (N. Y. 1913); "The Admirable Crichton," illustrated (N. Y. no date); "Quality Street" ("Uniform Edition") (N. Y. 1918); "The Admirable Crichton," same ed. (N. Y. 1918); "What Every Woman Knows," same ed. (N. Y. 1918); "Alice-Sit-by-the-Fire," same ed. (N. Y. 1919); "A Kiss for Cinderella," same ed. (N. Y. 1920); "Dear Brutus," same ed. (N. Y. 1922); "Mary Rose," same ed. (N. Y. 1924); "Walker, London" (London, 1907; N. Y. no date); "Der Tag" (N. Y. 1914).

Reprint in Collection.—"The Twelve-Pound Look" in Lewis' *Contemporary One-Act Plays* (N. Y. 1922).

References

P. P. Howe, *Dramatic Portraits* (N. Y. 1913) and *The Repertory Theater* (N. Y. 1911); Brander Matthews, *A Study of the Drama* (Boston, 1910); George Jean Nathan, *The World in Falseface* (N. Y. 1923), and *Comedians All* (N. Y. 1919); H. M. Walbrook, *Nights at the Play* (London, 1911); Clayton Hamilton, *Studies in Stagecraft* (N. Y. 1914), *Seen on the Stage* (N. Y. 1920), and *Problems of the Playwright* (N. Y. 1917); Ludwig Lewisohn, *The Drama and the Stage* (N. Y. 1922); William Archer, *Playmaking* (Boston, 1912), and *The Old Drama and the New* (Boston, 1923); A. B. Walkley, *Drama and Life* (N. Y. 1908); W. P. Eaton, *Plays and Players* (Cincinnati, 1916); Daniel Frohman, *Memories of a Manager* (Garden City, 1911); J. T. Grein, *Dramatic Criticism,* III (London, 1902); Percival Wilde, *The Craftsmanship of the One-Act Play* (Boston, 1923); C. Lewis Hind, *Authors and I* (N. Y. 1921); Alexander Woollcott, *Shouts and Murmurs* (N. Y. 1922), and *Enchanted Aisles* (N. Y. 1924); H. Granville-Barker, *The Exemplary Theater* (Boston, 1922); Dixon Scott, *Men of Letters* (N. Y. 1923); James Agate, *At Half-Past Eight* (N. Y. 1923); A. E. Morgan, *Tendencies of Modern English Drama* (N. Y. 1924); Allardyce Nicoll, *British Drama* (N. Y. 1933); H. M. Walbrook, *J. M. Barrie and the Theater* (London, 1922); P. Braybrooke, *J. M. Barrie* (Phila., no date); J. W. Cunliffe, *Modern English Playwrights* (N. Y. 1927); Thomas Moult, *Barrie* (N. Y. 1928); F. J. Harvey Darton, *J. M. Barrie* (N. Y. 1929); J. A. Hamerton, *Barrie* (N. Y. 1930).

The Twelve-Pound Look

Play in 1 act (1910). Texts: in *Half-Hours* (N. Y. 1914), in Lewis' *Contemporary One-Act Plays* (N. Y. 1922), in *Representative Plays* (N. Y. 1926), and in *The Plays of J. M. Barrie* (N. Y. 1928).

Perhaps the best way to test the ability of the novelist who is at the same time a dramatist is to ask whether his plays are better as drama than they would be as novels or stories. "The Twelve-Pound Look" might have been a story, but it is assuredly better as a play, because the dramatist has, as a result of his own process of visualization, made points which could not have been so effectively made had the story been cast into narrative form. This is his justification. This little piece is not a novelized story: it is a play.

1. The question of stage directions, as we have already seen (pp. 256, 287), is an interesting and a curious one. Bernard Shaw incorporates long and detailed descriptions not only of settings, but of states of mind; he occasionally adds irrelevant suggestions and explanations, it must be admitted, quite outside the province of the *mere* dramatist.

Until very recently, Barrie has refused to print his plays; one reason for this was that, since they were written to be produced, much of the charm and atmosphere would be lost if the dialogue were reduced to cold type. Finally, however, he has found a way of creating this necessary atmosphere: the stage directions in his printed plays supply the deficiency, and it is to be doubted whether the imaginative reader loses much by not seeing the plays on the stage. Because of their whimsical charm, their personal intimacy, and literary merit, the stage directions of Barrie surpass those of Shaw and Barker. Take, for example, the opening of "The Admirable Crichton":

A moment before the curtain rises the Hon. Ernest Woolley drives up to the door of Loam House in Mayfair. There is a happy smile on his pleasant, insignificant face, which presumably means that he is thinking of himself. He is too busy over nothing, this man about town, to be always thinking of himself, but, on the other hand, he almost never thinks of any other person. Probably Ernest's great moment is when he wakes of a morning and realizes that he really is Ernest, for we must all wish to be that which is our ideal. We can conceive him springing out of bed light-heartedly and waiting for his man to do the rest. He is dressed in excellent taste, with just the little bit more which shows that he is not without a sense of humor: the dandiacal are often saved by carrying a smile at the whole thing in their spats, let us say. . . .

Throughout the play now under discussion there is a great deal of such intimate detail, but it will be noticed that, even if the dramatist describes something which cannot actually be seen on the stage, there is little or no irrelevancy. Every word makes for unity—in the reader's mind, if not for the spectator's physical eye. Can as much be said, for instance, of Shaw's "Getting Married"?

2. Barrie is one of the few English dramatists who have taken the one-act form seriously. Like Synge and Schnitzler, he has been equally successful in the full-length and the one-act play. Clayton Hamilton and Percival Wilde have already (pp. 352, 246) been quoted on the theory of the one-acter. Says George Middleton:

> In spite of the difficulties of the one-act play—with its obligatory swiftness of exposition and economy of means—the author is confident, too, that it presents peculiar advantages in dealing tersely with the sharp contrasts of character and with the conflicts in social points of view, which, after all, cause most of the vital drama of life (Preface to *Tradition*).

In another preface Mr. Middleton says that his plays "make no pretence save to show character in action, and, in several instances, to picture its different reactions from the same stimulus. They are studies in consequences and readjustments, being, in fact, a further expression of some preceding situation. Each play is, therefore, the epitome of a larger drama which is suggested in the background." The word "epitome" is significant. It suggests economy of means and brevity of treatment. In the prefatory notes of Augustus Thomas' *Witching Hour* the dramatist relates this incident:

> About that time, Mr. Henry Loomis Nelson . . . showed me a letter from Mark Twain, refusing to write a short story for *Harper's* because Mark Twain had found "that a short story was a novel in the cradle which, if taken out occasionally and fondled, would grow into a full-sized book." Partly on that hint, my one-act play was occasionally taken from its cradle and caressed.

Is there any good reason why a one-act play should not be so caressed and developed into a three- or four-act play? Many good "sketches" have made bad plays, but is that the fault of the process, or the dramatist?

Read, for purposes of comparison, half a dozen widely different one-act plays, let us say the following: Schnitzler's "Green Cockatoo," A. A. Milne's "The Man in the Bowler Hat," Evreinov's "Merry Death," Paul Green's "White Dresses," George Middleton's "The Groove," and Philip Moeller's "Helena's Husband." Do these plays conform to the theories of the writers we have quoted? And what if they do not? Are they good drama?

And "The Twelve-Pound Look"? Is it a long play in embryo? How would the dramatist go about it if he wished to make a three-act play of it? Can you discover any place where the author economized in his exposition? In other words, do you detect any essential difference between the opening of this play and that of "The Admirable Crichton" or "Dear Brutus"?

Evidently Barrie looks upon the one-act form, among other things, as a means of training young authors. In a recent number of an English magazine he suggests that encouragement be given to playwrights under thirty years of age, in the writing of one-acters. Without much hope that it will be accepted, he outlines a plan by which theaters shall receive a small state subsidy which shall be spent in producing the works of unknown writers, who should in this way be enabled "to break out into the longer play and its emoluments," after being "fortified by their new knowledge of 'technique.'"

Do you believe that the knowledge of "technique" to be learned by writing one-acters is useful in writing full-length plays?

3. The closing half-minute of the play is full of implications. Barrie does not tell the audience that Lady Sims is going to buy one of "those machines," but it is clear that she is thinking about it. "Are they very expensive?" she asks, and her question is not answered, but it echoes in our ears after the fall of the curtain, which hides Sir Harry from us. Here

is a great deal "suggested in the background," for "we may be sure that he will soon be bland again. We have a comfortable feeling, you and I, that there is nothing of Harry Sims in us."

4. At the risk of breaking some rule of unity, we shall here quote a few lines from Barrie's Introduction to *The Comedies of Harold Chapin* (1921), because Barrie happens to have something interesting to say about technique and rules. He begins:

> When I agreed, very gladly, to write a few words of introduction to this volume, I cautiously bought a book about how to write plays (there are many of them), in order to see whether Mr. Chapin wrote his properly. But the book was so learned, and the author knew so much, and the subject when studied grew so difficult, that I hurriedly abandoned my inquiry. Thus one of us at least missed his last chance of discovering what that mysterious thing, "stage technique," really is, which after all does not greatly matter as nearly every one else seems to know.

He goes on to say that "plays ought undoubtedly to be 42 by 36, which is the real reason why writing them should be so difficult." Here we have the artist who knows that all the technique in the world is as nothing in the hands of him who cannot use it almost as though it never existed.

The Admirable Crichton

Comedy in 4 acts (1902). Texts: N. Y. no date, N. Y. 1918, and *Representative Plays* (N. Y. 1926).

This is an exceptionally good example of what may be termed "pure" comedy. It marks no radical departure in technique, it sets forth no very original ideas, but it is an ingratiating, pleasant, witty play, in which characters are clearly and relevantly developed in an amusing story. Few will refuse to accept the verdict of the English critic A. B. Walkley, who declared it to be "as delightful a play as the English stage has produced in our generation," though there are some who may not agree with Professor Phelps' "greatest English drama of modern times."

1. William Lyon Phelps (in *Essays on Modern Dramatists*), while fully appreciating the comedy elements in "Crichton," goes to some pains to elucidate the underlying philosophy of the play:

> It is clear [he says] that the play is a tragedy, not only for Crichton, but for Lady Mary—yes, perhaps for Lord Loam when the change from open air, exercise, simple food, to their opposites, brings on some horrible disease of the liver. . . . And the reason why this comedy is a tragedy is not because either Crichton or Lady Mary falters at the essential moment, but because the conditions of life make their mutual happiness impossible.

This raises an interesting point. "Tragic" and "comic," as applied to plays, are relative terms: it all depends on the point of view. Most farces are funny to the audience as well as to certain characters in the play; but to *someone* the situation is, if not actually tragic, at least serious. Shylock, in the first part of "The Merchant of Venice," was probably intended as a comedy part; the murder of Polonius—to us who regard Hamlet as a sympathetic character and Ophelia's father as a prosy old fool, is, if not comic, at least not a serious matter; but suppose Shakespeare (using the same characters and the same situation) had written from Polonius' point of view! The small boy who was stung by a wasp reproved his parents for blaming the wasp: "From the wasp's point of view," he answered, "he was perfectly justified: I was breaking up his home!"

Now, in "Crichton," Professor Phelps sees tragedy in the circumstances which forced the hero and Lady Mary to separate. Do you think that Barrie intended this as tragedy? It is a question largely of proportion: was the emphasis placed upon this point? Suppose (and this is quite possible) there had developed no other than purely amicable feelings between the two? Would the essential thesis of the play remain unchanged? Imagine it for a moment, and then imagine the tragic element of "Hamlet" or "Othello" left out.

2. It is difficult to study or discuss this play (and really not half so amusing as to read or see it) without discussing the

author's ideas. A. B. Walkley has made one serious criticism against it. He says (in *Drama and Life*):

> The most cruel thing is the dwindling of Crichton to his original proportions; and, what is more serious, it is an incredible thing. Dramatically, I admit, it must so befall; Mr. Barrie's scheme involves symmetry and contrast, the return of all concerned to their precise starting-point . . . while it was "natural" for Crichton to develop into the hero, or "overman" of Acts II and III, it was not "natural" for him to shrink back into his old self. For "nature" . . . never forgets. . . .

What does Walkley mean by "dramatically, I admit, it must so befall"? That the drama, in order to be symmetrical, must falsify "nature"? Is his criticism valid? Would Crichton be different? Barrie's thesis is evidently based on the assumption that circumstances alter cases, and with the logic of mathematics he seems to take it for granted that if A is in such and such circumstances he will react thus and so, no matter how often A is taken out of one environment and then put back. Walkley ("Nature . . . never forgets") puts in a plea for the element of change, for the lapse of time and the development of A under new circumstances.

But *is* Crichton the same in Act IV as he was in Act I? Turn to the last page of the text. Lady Mary, very evidently, *is* changed: "Then there's something wrong with England," she tells Crichton, and to this he replies:

> CRICHTON. My lady, not even from you can I listen to a word against England.
>
> LADY MARY. Tell me one thing: you have not lost your courage?
>
> CRICHTON. No, my lady.

Does this suggest a change? "England," obviously, stands for "civilization," the social system that made possible the situation round which "The Admirable Crichton" was written.

3. Yeats is said to have given Dunsany his first, and only, lesson in playwriting. "Surprise . . . is what is necessary. Surprise, and then more surprise, and that is all." This advice was given in reference to a one-act play, but it is applicable, after a fashion, to plays of every sort, and indeed to all art. Poe said something about "continual slight variety" being one of the elements of art. Whatever else the drama is or may become, it is nothing if it fails to interest, and surprise is one of the many ways of arousing interest. In itself it may be no more than a trick, but in the hands of a capable dramatist it may be utilized for various purposes. Is there not in the greatest poetry a "continual slight variety," an element of surprise, that gives it its everlasting freshness? There is scarcely a scene in "Crichton" that has no surprise: it is oftenest a repartee, amusing in itself. These surprises come not like the crude revelations at the end of an ordinary mystery-novel nor even like the "twist" in an O. Henry tale, but like flashes of momentary inspiration, illuminating the heart or mind of a person, or explaining a situation.

One obvious instance is the entrance of Lord Loam in Act II. The lost peer might have turned up in any of a hundred different ways, but Barrie describes him *"crawling on his hands and knees, a very exhausted and dishevelled peer, wondrously attired in rags."* Had it been Tweeny or any ordinary mortal it would have been a good entrance, but Lord Loam is a peer, he has been given up as lost; we remember the dignified appearance of the nobleman at home, and—how are the mighty fallen!

Two minutes later the Lord sees the pot hanging from its tripod:

LORD LOAM (*gazing at the pot as ladies are said to gaze on precious stones*). Is that—but I suppose I'm dreaming again. (*Timidly*) It isn't by any chance a pot on top of a fire, is it?

LADY MARY. Indeed, it is, dearest. It is our supper.

LORD LOAM. I have been dreaming of a pot on a fire for two days. (*Quivering*) There's nothing in it, is there?

ERNEST. Sniff, uncle. (LORD LOAM *sniffs.*)
LORD LOAM (*reverently*). It smells of onions!

This may not be the greatest art: but it is the quintessence of dramatic skill.

It has been said—with what justice I am well aware—that masterpieces cannot be analyzed, that art appeals or it does not appeal. It is possible, however, to study, consider—yes, analyze—works of art, though it is impossible to dissect the life and soul of art, as it is the life and soul of man. But art, being an expression of life, can be studied and analyzed just as life itself is studied and analyzed. A man reveals himself in words and deeds. It is thus that plays reveal their characters, and thus that this play—like any other—can be profitably scrutinized scene for scene and act for act.

SOMERSET MAUGHAM

William Somerset Maugham was born at Paris in 1874. He was educated at Canterbury and later at Heidelberg, where he studied medicine. His career as a dramatist began in the early years of the century with his more or less serious plays. Then came the lighter plays and farces, which brought the young dramatist a certain measure of fame. Meantime he was busy writing novels. "The Moon and Sixpence," one of his latest, is by all odds the best known. Then, after the outbreak of the war (in which he served with the medical corps) he wrote a number of satirical comedies, including "Our Betters" and "The Circle" in the traditional style of the best English comedy. "The Circle" is one of the most distinguished specimens of the modern comedy of manners.

Somerset Maugham is of the classic line. In none of his plays does he depart very far from the beaten path; he is not a thesis playwright, he is not interested in politics or "ideas"; he is content to write about the upper middle classes, to satirize their weaknesses and vanities, observing them in the rôle of a casual bystander. His best work is therefore his characterization, though his technique is almost faultless. "Our Betters" and "The Circle," though they are neither revolutionary nor novel, are bitter satires of modern life.

PLAYS

"Schiffbrüchig" (1902)
"A Man of Honor" (1903)
"Lady Frederick" (1907)
"The Explorer" (1908)
"Jack Straw" (1908)
"Mrs. Dot" (1908)
"Penelope" (1909)
"Smith" (1909)
"The Tenth Man" (1910)
"Landed Gentry" ["Grace"] (1910)
"Loaves and Fishes" (1911)
"The Land of Promise" (1914)
"The Unattainable" ["Caroline"] (1916)
"Our Betters" (1917)
"Love in a Cottage" (1918)
"Cæsar's Wife" (1919)
"Home and Beauty" ["Too Many Husbands"] (1919)
"The Unknown" (1920)
"The Circle" (1921)
"East of Suez" (1922)
"The Camel's Back" (1924)
"The Constant Wife" (1927)
"The Letter" (1927)
"The Sacred Flame" (1934)
"The Breadwinner" (1937)
"Sheppey" (1933)
"For Services Rendered" (1933)

Editions.—(In England most of the plays have been republished in a set of several volumes.) *Six Comedies* (N. Y. 1937) includes "The Unattainable," "Home and Beauty," "The Constant Wife," "The Breadwinner," "The Circle," and "Our Betters."

Separate plays.—"Landed Gentry" (Chicago, no date); "A Man of Honor" (Chicago, no date); "Mrs. Dot" (Chicago, no date); "Penelope" (Chicago, no date); "Smith" (Chicago, no date); "The Tenth Man" (Chicago, no date); "The Explorer" (Chicago, no date); "Jack Straw" (Chicago, no date); "Lady Frederick" (Chicago, no date); "The Unattainable" (London, 1923); "Our Betters" (N. Y. no date); "The Circle" (N. Y. 1921); "East of Suez" (N. Y. 1922); "The Unknown" (London, 1922); "Home and Beauty" (London, 1923); "The Constant Wife" (N. Y. 1927); "The Letter" (N. Y. 1927); "The Breadwinner" (N. Y. 1931); "For Services Rendered" (N. Y. 1933); "Sheppey" (London, 1933).

Reprints in Anthologies.—"Our Betters" in Dickinson's *Chief Contemporary Dramatists, II* (Boston, 1921); "The Circle" in Dickinson and Crawford's *Contemporary Drama* (Boston, 1925).

REFERENCES

T. H. Dickinson, *The Contemporary Drama of England* (Boston, 1917); Ludwig Lewisohn, *The Drama and the Stage* (N. Y. 1922); A. B. Walkley, *More Prejudice* (N. Y. 1923); James Agate, *At Half-Past Eight* (N. Y. 1923) and *First Nights* (London, 1934); Frank Vernon, *The Twentieth-Century Theater* (Boston, 1924); A. E. Morgan, *Tendencies of Modern English Drama* (N. Y. 1924); C. H. Towne, etc., *W. Somerset Maugham* (N. Y. no date); J. W. Cunliffe, *Modern English Playwrights* (N. Y. 1927); C. Pellizzi, *English Drama* (N. Y. 1935).

THE CIRCLE

Comedy in 3 acts (1921). Texts: N. Y. 1921; reprinted in Dickinson and Crawford's *Contemporary Drama* (Boston, 1925).

You may regard this comedy in two ways: as a social document, which shatters (in Dr. Lewisohn's words) the tradition that "the eloping couple who drag out hopeless lives because their particular social group will have none of them," or else as a dramatic entertainment. It is, of course, both a document and an entertainment. But Somerset Maugham is an artist, and only incidentally a sociologist. The *subject* possesses a certain interest, but the treatment of the characters is what holds us. "The Circle" is one of Maugham's two absolutely logical and fearless plays: he is in these no longer the writer of light comedies. He has dared to carry through to the bitter end the logic of his theme.

1. The best comedies, as we have seen (p. 140), have plots which in the final analysis are simply the thread utilized by the dramatist to hold together his gallery of portraits. What the people do in such comedies is not of supreme importance in itself. The dramatist takes his time in coming to the point, but that is of no consequence, for we are held by what each person says, how he looks, why he does one thing and not another—in a word, what he is, and why. In "The Circle," even after the hint is thrown out that Elizabeth and Teddie are in love with each other, we are not greatly interested to know whether or not they are going to elope. We remain in the theater in order to see more of Porteous and Lady Kitty, of Elizabeth and Teddie and the others. If we were swayed entirely by motives of curiosity, we should have only to read the end of the play or to ask someone who had seen it performed, but curiosity has little to do with our interest in this play and others of its kind. It is the how and not the what, that we must know. Curiosity is, however, a legitimate motive in theater-going. Walkley (*Pastiche and Prejudice*) says that certain forms of melodrama (the "thriller" at the Grand Guignol, for example) satisfies one's curiosity about an "experience which in real life it is rare or difficult to obtain." This form of curiosity is universal, but it is not altogether satisfying, for the simple reason that it is easily satisfied. There is no food for speculation, no opportunity given to the imagination. The ordinary mystery play is often very amusing: "The Bat," by Mary

Roberts Rhinehart and Avery Hopwood, is an extraordinarily clever piece of construction, but who would care to go twice to see it?

"The Circle" neither arouses nor satisfies crude curiosity. Whereas you would seriously object to anyone's telling you the plot of "The Bat" before you had seen it, you rather enjoy hearing the story of "The Circle." Lessing (in his *Hamburg Dramaturgy,* that storehouse of wisdom) says that the dramatic interest is "all the stronger and keener the longer and more certainly we have been allowed to foresee everything. . . . I don't think the enterprise would be a task beyond my strength were I to undertake a play of which the end should be announced in advance, from the very first scene." Playwrights have done this, and novelists and the writers of epics, but then they were not writing "Sherlock Holmes" stories.

The tales of O. Henry present an interesting point in this connection. Many of them are written almost exclusively for the "kick" in the closing sentence, and once the point is known we seldom care to re-read the story. They are elaborate jokes, consummately told, it is true, but still jokes. Such is "The Gift of the Magi." But there is a far finer kind of story in which the writer need not exercise his ingenuity in order not to give away his point until the last line. Such is "The Skylight Room," in which one remembers long afterward, not the point (that I have forgotten), but the image of the tired little girl in her garret room looking up through the skylight at Gamma, which she has christened Billy Jackson. In "The Romance of a Busy Broker" you recall the last line, where the broker's secretary, who has just been proposed to, turns to her employer with tears in her eyes, and says, "We were married last evening at eight o'clock in the Little Church Around the Corner."

Do you remember the end of "The School for Scandal"? But you do recall the famous quarrel scene between Sir Peter and Lady Teazle.

To return to "The Circle." Some sort of plot there must be. What is it, and just where does it begin?

2. In Maugham's earlier plays, in "Lady Frederick," for

instance, there is a bewildering display of wit. It is said that when these plays were first put into rehearsal, the director found it necessary to delete many lines which would be sure to arouse laughter, and too many laughs in quick succession might destroy the continuity of the action. Whether or not the anecdote is true, it illustrates an interesting point. The bright speeches, epigrams, repartees in "The Circle" are exceptionally good. The best of them arouse what Meredith declared to be the chief function of great comedy, thoughtful laughter. When Arnold (N. Y. edition, p. 11) says: "I'm always willing to stand by anything I've said. There *are* no synonyms in the English language," Elizabeth replies, "In that case I shall be regretfully forced to continue to say 'Damn' whenever I feel like it." Her retort is not howlingly funny: it would probably not precipitate what is technically known as a laugh, but it does arouse a silent laugh—thoughtful laughter. Why? Arnold has scolded his wife for saying Damn, and she has replied that he once said in public that there were no synonyms in the language, and to that Arnold in defense maintained that "it's very unfair to expect a politician to live in private up to the statements he makes in public." We smile at this little dialogue because it shows character; we feel the essential humanity of each of the speakers.

In "The Circle" there are few if any examples of the epigram pure and simple (the *mot d'esprit*), the things that people can quote as they do bright speeches in the Wilde plays. Such lines are usually pasted, as it were, upon the lips of certain personages, and are not in keeping with the characters of the persons who speak them. In his introduction to Harold Chapin's comedies, Barrie has this to say: "His people very seldom indeed talk 'out of their parts.' You never find B saying something good that might have been said more legitimately by C, who, however, happened not to be in the scene at the time."

Can you find any instances in "The Circle" of "something good" being said by the wrong person? See Maugham's "Jack Straw" and "Our Betters." How many detachable epigrams can you find in those plays? The lines in "The Circle" are rarely amusing apart from the context. How often have we all tried to repeat the funny speeches in a play heard the night before, to one who has not seen it? The joke falls flat, and we take refuge in the excuse that really you have to see the play to get the fun. One of the funniest and most famous lines in all literature is this: "But what the devil was he doing in that galley?" It means nothing—unless you happen to have seen or read Molière's "Rogueries of Scapin," and then you understand. One of the best quiet laughs is in the last act of "Cyrano de Bergerac," where reference is made to this line, but to American audiences, unfamiliar with the Molière play, it meant nothing.

Porteous' line (p. 29), "These new teeth of mine are so damned uncomfortable" is in itself a statement at most prosaic; the fact stated is neither pleasant nor important, but the line tells volumes about the speaker, his temperament, his pathetic decay, and at the same time gives Lady Kitty the cue for her delightful speech, beginning "Men are extraordinary."

But why is it necessary to epigrammatize character in this way, by a few incisive lines or speeches? Simply because the dramatist has not twenty or fifty or a hundred pages in which to describe at leisure his men and women. Lady Kitty is plumped down into our midst at a single stroke (p. 28):

> Lady Kitty. . . . I think it's a beautiful chair. Hepplewhite?
> Arnold. No. Sheraton.
> Lady Kitty. Oh, I know. "The School for Scandal."

Henry James might have shown a hundred aspects of the lady's character in a hundred pages, but who shall say that one method of presentation is necessarily superior to the other? There are those who decry the theater because plays are shorter than novels. Hear Miss Rebecca West:

> Detestable to the mind that can make a copy of the dawn in exquisite words to have to hand the job over to the scene-painter; cramping for one who has been accustomed to trail a story through the four seasons and round the globe to have to cabin it on the

smallness of the stage; infuriating to the mind that can tell exactly in a single phrase how Mabel gave away the secret of her soul when she cast down her eyes, to have to see Miss Mary Smith wrestling through weeks of rehearsal to get that effect with an unsuitable personality and kohled eyelashes; humiliating to the mind that would demonstrate that it, too, was a creator and omniscient about its creatures by writing superhumanly intuitive pages about what passed in the heart of the young girl as she broke from the room and ran into the darkness, to have to bite it all back and set down, "Exit Mabel, L."! . . . In view of these real differences, it is hard to understand why any author who is capable of writing a good novel should ever write a play. . . .

Well, well. No sculptor can make a statue with canvas, and the writer of sonnets will turn out a very poor specimen if he uses many more than fourteen lines.

Compared with Wells' "New Macchiavelli," this little play of Somerset Maugham's is slight: for one thing, it can be seen in two hours and read in one; the novel demands about ten to fifteen times as many hours. The themes are not dissimilar. But is the novel immeasurably finer than the play?

3. The technique of the Maugham play is admirable. It is precisely what is needed. The speeches are stripped to the essentials; there is no decoration; the playwright knows where he is going and how to go. There is not a moment lost. One of the longest and most sustained scenes is the love scene between Teddie and Elizabeth (pp. 42-47). Novelists would surely give a long chapter to such a situation. Can you imagine it in the hands of Meredith? Not that the scene in this or any play is superior, as such, to what the novelist writes; it is different, that is all.

The whole play is built up of such brief scenes.

4. The end of the play is, in "The Circle," a matter of considerable interest. We have already seen, in the case of most of the other plays considered in this volume, that the principal struggle is over, or nearly over, at the end of the penultimate act. But here the question is: Will Elizabeth and Teddie elope, or will they not? Not that the decision is so very vital,

however, for we are still interested in the people and not so much in their doings; still, it will be interesting to see whether the example of the elder couple will influence the younger.

It is precisely in the ending of this play that Maugham's philosophy of life is shown. It would have been easy, and by no means unnatural, to have the young people perceive the error of their ways and return to their respective folds, but no—the playwright, who is a man of the world as well, knows that we do not learn from experience, because every human being is just a little different from every other. Other people's experience does not, therefore, apply to our case. We are not other people.

5. "The Circle" can hardly be described as a problem play, though the author shows us men and women engaged in a situation that presents a problem in ethics. Very much the same problem is offered in "The Constant Wife," a later play by Maugham. In this, a woman is shown deliberately breaking her marriage vow of fidelity, after making herself economically independent of her husband. Here the dramatist deliberately depicts a sympathetic character whose actions are shown to be at variance with the accepted moral code as applied to marriage.

Have we any right to assume that Maugham advocates the adoption of the "constant" wife's ethics in general? Is his play "immoral?"

For a general discussion of this question (one-sided, it is true) see my pamphlet *Œdipus or Pollyanna.*

THE IRISH DRAMA

THE IRISH DRAMA

Practically, without exception, all the plays written and produced by the Irish dramatists are procurable in book or pamphlet form.

There are several books on the Irish drama; chief among these are Ernest Boyd's *Contemporary Drama of Ireland* and *Ireland's Literary Renaissance,* Lady Gregory's *Our Irish Theater,* Cornelius Weygandt's *Irish Plays and Playwrights,* Andrew E. Malone's *The Irish Drama,* and W. G. Fay and Catherine Carswell's *The Fays of the Abbey Theater.* The books of Krans and Reid on Yeats, of Bourgeois and Howe on Synge, and of Bierstadt on Dunsany, are also full of material on the movement in general. See also, for texts and editorial matter, Curtis Canfield's volumes, *Plays of Changing Ireland* and *Plays of the Irish Renaissance.*

William Butler Yeats

William Butler Yeats was born at Dublin in 1865. Educated in his native city and later in London, he was identified at an early age with the movement known as the Irish Literary Revival or Renaissance. In this connection, his chief activity was the founding—in company with Lady Gregory, George Moore, and Edward Martyn—of the Irish Literary Theater. This venture later developed into the Abbey Theater, toward the success of which Yeats and Lady Gregory have largely contributed.

Most of Yeats' own plays were written for production at the Abbey. Besides writing plays, however, he has for over thirty years participated in politics, in the management of various artistic and educational ventures, and been able at the same time to write poetry. Besides which he was chiefly instrumental in encouraging certain writers to furnish the Abbey Theater with plays: it was he who "discovered" Synge and first taught Dunsany some few essentials of the art of playwriting. "The future," says H. S. Krans, "will look back to Mr. Yeats as to a landmark in the literary history of Ireland, both because of his artistic achievement and because he has been a leader in a remarkable movement. Through his poetry the Celtic spirit moves like a fresh wind."

In 1923 Yeats received the Nobel Prize for literature. He is still actively engaged in writing and interested in politics.

Plays

"The Countess Cathleen" (1892)
"The Land of Heart's Desire" (1894)
"The Shadowy Waters" (1900)
"Diarmuid and Grania" [with George Moore] (1901)
"Cathleen ni Houlihan" (1902)
"The Pot of Broth" [with Lady Gregory] (1902)
"The Hour-Glass" (1903)
"On Baile's Strand" (1903)
"Where There is Nothing" (1903)
"The King's Threshold" (1903)
"Deirdre" (1906)
"The Unicorn From the Stars" [with Lady Gregory] (1907)
"The Golden Helmet" (1908)
"The Green Helmet" (1910)
"The Player Queen" (1916)
"At the Hawk's Well" (1916)
"The Dreaming of the Bones" (1919)
"The Only Jealousy of Emer" (1919)
"Calvary" (1921)
"The Cat and the Moon" (1935)
"The Resurrection" (1935)
"The Words Upon the Window-Pane" (1934)
"Fighting the Waves" (1935)
"The King of the Great Clock Tower" (1935)

Editions.—[Most of Yeats' plays have appeared in several editions and in several revised forms. Following are only the principal editions.] *The Collected Works of William Butler Yeats,* 8 vols. (Stratford, 1908), include, in Vol. II, "The King's Threshold," "On Baile's Strand," "Deirdre," and "The Shadowy Waters" [Appendix I is the "acting version" of "The Shadowy Waters"]; in Vol. III, "The Countess Cathleen," "The Land of Heart's Desire," and "The Unicorn From the Stars"; in Vol. IV, "The Hour-Glass," "Cathleen ni Houlihan," and "The Golden Helmet"; *Plays for an Irish Theater* (London and Stratford-on-Avon, 1911) includes "Deirdre," "The Green Helmet," "On Baile's Strand," "The King's Threshold," "The Shadowy Waters," "The Hour-Glass," and "Cathleen ni Houlihan" (together with the "acting version" of "The Shadowy Waters"); *The Poetical Works of William B. Yeats,* Vol. II, *Dramatical Poems* (N. Y. 1906), includes "The Countess Cathleen," "The Land of Heart's Desire," "The Shadowy Waters" [new version], "On Baile's Strand" [new version], "The King's Threshold" [new version], and "Deirdre" (also an "acting version" of "The Shadowy Waters"); the same volume, now called *Dramatic Poems,* was reissued (N. Y. 1912) with the same titles, but "The Land of Heart's Desire" and "The Countess Cathleen" are entirely rewritten; *The Hour-Glass and Other Plays* (N. Y. 1904) includes that play, "The Pot of Broth," and "Cathleen ni Houlihan"; *The Unicorn From the Stars and Other Plays* (N. Y. 1908) includes that play, "Cathleen ni Houlihan," and "The Hour Glass"; Vol. III of *Plays for an Irish Theater* (London, 1904) includes "The King's Threshold," and "On Baile's Strand"; *The Green Helmet and Other Poems* (N. Y. 1912) contains "The Green Helmet"; *The Seven Woods* (N. Y. 1903) contains "On Baile's Strand"; *Two Plays for Dancers* (Dundrum, 1919) includes "The Dreaming of the

Bones" and "The Only Jealousy of Emer"; *The Wild Swans at Coole* (N. Y. 1917) contains "At the Hawk's Well"; *Four Plays for Dancers* (N. Y. 1921) includes "At the Hawk's Well," "The Only Jealousy of Emer," "The Dreaming of the Bones," and "Calvary"; *Responsibilities* (N. Y. 1916) includes "The Hour-Glass." Another collected edition is the *Works,* 6 vols. (N. Y. 1924 and later) : the two volumes of plays include the latest versions of all the plays. In 1935 still another *Collected Plays* appeared (N. Y.). This includes the new plays, "The Cat and the Moon," "The Resurrection," and "The Words Upon the Window-Pane."

Separate Plays.—"The Countess Kathleen," etc. (Boston, 1892) ; "The Land of Heart's Desire" (Chicago, 1894, Boston, 1903, several reprints) ; "The Shadowy Waters" (N. Y. 1901) ; different version (London, 1907) ; "Where There is Nothing" (N. Y. 1902, revised 1903) ; "The Hour-Glass" (London, 1903) ; "Deirdre" (London and Dublin, 1907) ; "The Words Upon the Window-Pane" (Dublin, 1934) ; "The King of the Great Clock Tower" (N. Y. 1935).

Reprints in Collections and Anthologies.—"The Hour-Glass" in Dickinson's *Chief Contemporary Dramatists* (Boston, 1915) ; same in Moses' *Representative British Dramas* (Boston, 1918) ; "The Land of Heart's Desire" in Clark's *Representative One-Act Plays by British and Irish Authors* (Boston, 1921) ; the same in Leonard's *Atlantic Book of Modern Plays* (Boston, 1921) ; "The Words Upon the Window-Pane" in Curtis Canfield's *Plays of Changing Ireland* (N. Y. 1936).

References

H. S. Krans, *William Butler Yeats and the Irish Literary Revival* (N. Y. 1904) ; J. M. Hone, *W. B. Yeats* (N. Y. 1916) ; Forrest Reid, *W. B. Yeats: A Critical Study* (N. Y. 1915) ; Jethro Bithell, *W. B. Yeats* (Paris, 1913) ; Ernest A. Boyd, *Ireland's Literary Renaissance* (N. Y. 1916), and *The Contemporary Drama in Ireland* (Boston, 1917) ; C. Weygandt, *Irish Plays and Playwrights* (Boston, 1913) ; George Moore, *Hail and Farewell,* 3 vols. (N. Y. 1911-1914) ; Lady Gregory, *Our Irish Theater* (N. Y. 1913) ; F. W. Chandler, *Aspects of Modern Drama* (N. Y. 1914) ; Lloyd R. Morris, *The Celtic Dawn* (N. Y. 1917) ; Ludwig Lewisohn, *The Modern Drama* (N. Y. 1915) ; Katharine Tynan, *Twenty-five Years: Reminiscences* (London, 1913), and *The Middle Years* (London, 1916) ; Robert Lynd, *Old and New Masters* (N. Y. 1919) ; C. Lewis Hind, *Authors and I* (N. Y. 1921) ; St. John Ervine, *Some Impressions of My Elders* (N. Y. 1923) ; Thomas McDonough, *Literature in Ireland* (N. Y. 1916) ; W. G. Fay and Catherine Carswell, *The Fays of the Abbey Theater* (N. Y. 1935), A. E. Malone, *The Irish Drama* (N. Y. 1929). See also Yeats' prefaces and notes in the various collected editions, and his books, *The Cutting of an Agate* (N. Y. 1912), and *Reveries Over Childhood and Youth* (N. Y. 1920), *The Trembling of the Veil* (London, 1922) ; *Essays* (N. Y. 1924), *Plays and Controversies* (N. Y. 1924) ; *Dramatis Personæ* (N. Y. 1936).

The Countess Cathleen

Play in 5 scenes (1892). Texts: Boston, 1892; in *Collected Works* (Stratford, 1908); in *Works* (N. Y. 1924); in *Poetical Works*, Vol. II (N. Y. 1906).

Yeats' plays deserve consideration as attempts toward the creation of a new style of drama, not as to form but as to the treatment of subject-matter. In his preface to the second volume of the *Poetical Works* he says: "I have chosen all of my themes from Irish legend or Irish history, and my friends have made joyous, extravagant, and, as I am certain, distinguished comedy out of the common life of the villages, or out of a fantasy trained by the contemplation of that life and of the tales told by its firesides. This theater cannot but be more interesting to people of other races because it is Irish, and, therefore, to some extent, stirred by emotions and thoughts not hitherto expressed in dramatic form. . . ."

1. There is a mystical atmosphere in "The Countess Cathleen" comparable to the earlier plays of Maeterlinck. In what respects is this play similar in technique to "The Intruder" or "Pelléas and Mélisande"? Are there any indications that Yeats was influenced by the Belgian?

2. In a note to his "Deirdre" (*Collected Works*) Yeats says:

> The principal difficulty with the form of dramatic literature I have adopted is that, unlike the loose Elizabethan form, it continually forces one by its rigor of logic away from one's capacities, experiences, and desires, until, if one have not patience to wait till it comes, there is rhetoric and logic and dry circumstance where there should be life.

In this play are there evidences of this struggle of which the poet speaks? Where and of what sort are they? Does Yeats fall into conventional grooves?

Is there any special reason why the play should be divided into five scenes? Are there well-defined divisions in the play: exposition, development, climax, etc.?

3. As in Phillips' "Paolo and Francesca," there are many lyrical passages and short speeches which are of striking beauty, apart from the dramatic context. Is

> You shall at last dry like dry leaves, and hang
> Nailed like dead vermin to the doors of God,

more effective because it is spoken by Maire at a certain moment in this play, than it would be if it stood alone? Are the superb lines,

> The years like great black oxen tread the world,
> And God the herdsman goads them on behind,
> And I am broken by their passing feet,

epic or dramatic?

4. Read Yeats' "Cathleen ni Houlihan," a prose play which is always successful on the stage. Compare it carefully with "The Countess Cathleen." In what respects do the two plays differ? Why is the prose piece more "theatrical"? In "Cathleen ni Houlihan" are there any passages, as there are in "The Countess Cathleen," which might stand alone by reason of their intrinsic beauty?

5. Notice the stage directions. They are simple, but they indicate the poet's sense of action and dramatic effect. The play closes with: *"A sound of far-off horns seems to come from the heart of the Light. The vision melts away, and the forms of the kneeling* PEASANTS *appear faintly in the darkness."* Often a dramatist throws out a hint, which the stage-manager is intended to act upon, filling in the necessary "business." How much leeway has the manager in the present play?

6. In this play—and indeed in all Yeats' plays—there is very little of what we call "character": the shadowy figures in "Deirdre" and "The Land of Heart's Desire" do not force themselves upon our attention because of their humanity. It may be that the poet is deficient in the power to create living beings and makes a virtue of his defect by bringing other gifts to the theater; but he realizes, at any rate, that his Cathleen

and the others are not men and women such as we are accustomed to see in modern plays. In his essay on *The Tragic Theater,* he writes:

> In poetical drama there is, it is held, an antithesis between character and lyric poetry, for lyric poetry—however much it move you when you read it out of a book—can, as these critics think, but encumber the action. Yet when we go back a few centuries and enter the great periods of drama, character grows less and sometimes disappears, and there is much lyric feeling. . . . Suddenly it strikes us that character is continuously present in comedy alone, and that there is much tragedy . . . where its place is taken by passions and motives. . . .

The tragic poet, it seems, has little to do with what we ordinarily term character, which is *usually* idiosyncratic, accidental, realistic; it is his business to idealize character through poetry, divesting it of those personal details which differentiate one person from the other. We may say that comedy is the presentation of men, that tragedy is the presentation of man. Yeats goes on to say that there is "an art that we call real, because character can only express itself perfectly in a real world . . . ," and again, "When we look at the faces of the old tragic paintings, whether it is in Titian or in some painter of medieval China, we find there sadness and gravity, a certain emptiness even, as of a mind that waited the supreme crisis. . . . Whereas in modern art . . . 'vitality' . . . the energy, that is to say, which is under the command of our common moments, sings, laughs, chatters or looks its busy thoughts."

Does this explain the art of Yeats as a dramatist?

JOHN M. SYNGE

Edmund John Millington Synge was born at Newtown Little, near Dublin, in 1871. Little is recorded of his early life, except that he remained at home until he was nearly twenty, and that he graduated from Trinity College, Dublin, in 1892. Endowed with a natural taste for music and a desire for travel, he wandered through Europe —with his violin—for two or three years. He first went to Germany, intending to study music, but returned to Paris, where he tried to make a living by writing book reviews and essays. But it was not until he was "discovered" by Yeats, who persuaded him to return to Ireland (1898) and study the primitive folk in the unfrequented districts, that he began to turn his thoughts to Irish themes. Yeats induced the young man to write for the new Irish Theater. In the Aran Islands, in Kerry and Wicklow and Connemara, Synge wandered, and out of a rich fund of folklore, speech, and character he created his plays.

He died of cancer in 1909, at Dublin.

"He loves," writes Yeats, "all that has edge, all that is salt in the mouth, all that is rough to the hand, all that heightens the emotions by contest, all that stings into life the sense of tragedy. . . . The food of the spiritual-minded is sweet, an Indian scripture says, but passionate minds love bitter food."

Synge was by all odds the greatest of the dramatists who wrote for the Irish Theater.

Plays

"The Shadow of the Glen" [originally "In the Shadow of the Glen"] (1903)
"Riders to the Sea" (1904)
"The Well of the Saints" (1905)
"The Playboy of the Western World" (1907)
"The Tinker's Wedding" (1909)
"Deirdre of the Sorrows" (1910)

Editions.—The Works of John M. Synge, 4 vols. (Boston, 1912), includes all the plays; *Plays* (Dublin and London, 1922) includes all the plays; *Complete Works,* 4 vols. (Dublin, 1910) includes all the plays; Library Ed. of the *Works,* 5 vols. (Dublin, 1911), includes all the plays in the last 2 vols.; *The Tinker's Wedding, Riders to the Sea, and The Shadow of the Glen* (Dublin, 1911) includes the plays mentioned; *The Shadow of the Glen and Riders to the Sea* (London, 1905) includes the plays mentioned.

Separate Plays.—"Riders to the Sea" (*Samhain,* Dublin, 1903, *Poet Lore,* Boston, 1905); in book form, with preface by E. J. O'Brien (Boston, 1911); "The Shadow of the Glen" [originally "In the Shadow of the Glen"] (*Samhain,* Dublin, 1904); in book form (Boston, 1911); "The Well of the Saints" (Dublin, 1905), later eds. with preface by W. B. Yeats (London, 1905 and after); pocket ed. (Dublin, 1911, and Boston, 1911); "The Playboy of the Western World" (Dublin, 1907, and reprints with Synge's preface); pocket ed. (Dublin, 1911, and Boston, 1911); "Deirdre of the Sorrows," preface by W. B. Yeats (Dundrum, 1910, and reprints, Dublin); pocket ed. (Dublin, 1911, and Boston, 1911).

Reprints in Collections and Anthologies.—"Riders to the Sea" in Dickinson's *Chief Contemporary Dramatists* (Boston, 1915), in Leonard's *Atlantic Book of Modern Plays* (Boston, 1921), in Cohen's *One-Act Plays by Modern Authors* (N. Y. 1921), in Moses' *Representative British Dramas* (Boston, 1918), in Clark's *Representative One-Act Plays by British and Irish Authors* (Boston, 1921), and in Hubbell and Beaty's *An Introduction to Drama* (N. Y. 1927).

References

Francis Bickley, *J. M. Synge and the Irish Dramatic Movement* (Boston, 1912); Maurice Bourgeois, *John Millington Synge and the Irish Theater* (N. Y. 1913); P. P. Howe, *J. M. Synge* (N. Y. 1912); C. Weygandt, *Irish Plays and Playwrights* (Boston, 1912); E. A. Boyd, *Ireland's Literary Renaissance* (N. Y. 1916), and *The Contemporary Drama of Ireland* (Boston, 1917); George Moore, *Hail and Farewell*, 3 vols. (N. Y. 1911-1914); Lady Gregory, *Our Irish Theater* (N. Y. 1913); John Masefield, *John M. Synge; a Few Personal Recollections* (N. Y. 1915); W. B. Yeats, *The Cutting of an Agate* (N. Y. 1913), *The Trembling of the Veil* (London, 1922), and *Essays* (London, 1924); Darrell Figgis, *Studies and Appreciations* (London, 1912); Lloyd R. Morris, *The Celtic Dawn* (N. Y. 1917); Ludwig Lewisohn, *The Modern Drama* (N. Y. 1915); Clayton Hamilton, *Studies in Stagecraft* (N. Y. 1914); C. E. Montague, *Dramatic Values* (N. Y. 1911); Mario Borsa, *The English Stage of To-day*, trans. by S. Brinton (N. Y. 1908); F. W. Chandler, *Aspects of Modern Drama* (N. Y. 1914); James Huneker, *The Pathos of Distance* (N. Y. 1913); William Archer, *Playmaking* (Boston, 1912); Holbrook Jackson, *All Manner of Folk* (N. Y. 1912); C. Lewis Hind, *More Authors and I* (N. Y. 1922); Francis Hackett, *Horizons* (N. Y. 1919); Robert Lynd, *Old and New Masters* (N. Y. 1919); H. M. Walbrook, *Nights at the Play* (London, 1911); John B. Yeats, *Essays, Irish and American* (Dublin, 1918); A. E. Morgan, *Tendencies of Modern English Drama* (N. Y. 1924); Stuart P. Sherman, *On Contemporary Literature* (N. Y. 1917); Allardyce Nicoll, *British Drama* (N. Y. 1933); W. G. Fay and Catherine Carswell, *The Fays of the Abbey Theater* (N. Y. 1935); A. E. Malone, *The Irish Drama* (N. Y. 1929). See also Synge's prefaces to "The Playboy of the Western World," and "The Tinker's Wedding," and *The Aran Islands, and In Kerry and Wicklow* (Boston, 1912).

Riders to the Sea

Play in 1 act (1904). Texts: Boston, 1911; in *Works* (Boston, 1912); in *Plays* (London, 1922); in *The Tinker's Wedding*, etc.

(Dublin, 1911); reprinted in Dickinson's *Chief Contemporary Dramatists* (Boston, 1915); in Leonard's *Atlantic Book of Modern Plays* (Boston, 1921); in Cohen's *One-Act Plays by Modern Authors* (N. Y. 1921); in Moses' *Representative British Dramas* (Boston, 1918); in Clark's *Representative One-Act Plays by British and Irish Authors* (Boston, 1921), and in Hubbell and Beaty's *An Introduction to Drama* (N. Y. 1927).

This little drama, with none of the uproarious "romping" of "The Playboy," is still an unmistakable proof of Synge's keen enthusiasm for all that concerns human life. If he can take pleasure in the vitality and animal spirits of a Christy Mahon, he can likewise savor the dumb tragedy of a Maurya.

1. Synge's mastery of words is one of his greatest assets. Like Shakespeare, he can at once suggest environment by purely verbal means. Beautiful words and sentences are not necessarily an integral part of drama, but dramatic language that is beautiful in itself means much. The sharp contrast between the homely and everyday in life, and the gruesomeness of death, is clearly drawn in "Riders to the Sea." Bartley says: "Where is the bit of new rope, Cathleen, was bought in Connemara?" and Cathleen replies: "Give it to him, Nora, it's on a nail by the white boards. I hung it up this morning, for the pig with the black feet was eating it." This is what Yeats means when he speaks of Synge's loving "all that has edge." The words themselves are here almost a part of the action: for one thing, they suggest atmosphere better than half-a-dozen scene-painters could hope to do.

2. In his *Hail and Farewell* (last volume, *Vale*), George Moore writes of "Riders to the Sea": " . . . When I heard this one-act play, it seemed very little more than the contents of Synge's notebook, an experiment in language rather than a work of art, a preparatory essay; he seemed to me to have contented himself with relating a painful rather than a dramatic story, his preoccupation being to discover a style, a vehicle of expression. . . ." And the incident *is* painful rather than dramatic, for the struggle must be imagined, it cannot be seen

and apprehended by the audience. Consequently, we might almost feel that the struggle here depicted was so hopeless as to leave no room for anything but dumb submission. Tragedy is usually the spectacle of man in conflict with other men, or with circumstances against which he has, or seems to have, at least a fighting chance. Synge's play, however, is little more than a spectacle showing the result of a conflict in which man has no chance at all. We, the audience, must sit as mute witnesses of a disaster before which we are powerless.

"Riders to the Sea" serves to illustrate the essential difference between the one-act play and the full-length play. Since the former is almost always concerned with but a single incident, it is capable of very little development. Now a tragedy is not a fact or an event; it shows great and strong characters—at least characters in which there is potential greatness or strength—struggling with forces which are finally too great to be overcome. And *we must see the struggle*. A tragic figure must have the opportunity to fail honorably; we wish to see him trying to evade or at least struggle with his fate. "Hamlet" would be ordinary melodrama if we were deprived of the Prince's soul-revealing soliloquies; "Œdipus," too, if we could not follow the King's efforts to escape what was decreed. A one-act play can scarcely do more than indicate the consequences of a struggle. The last act of "Hamlet" is not a tragedy in itself, and "Riders to the Sea," like that last act, is only the result of what has gone on for a long time before. At the end we feel something of the great sorrow of the old woman as expressed in her last words: "Michael has a clean burial in the far north, by the grace of the Almighty God. Bartley will have a fine coffin out of the white boards, and a deep grave surely. What more can we want than that? No man at all can be living forever, and we must be satisfied."

This is almost like standing at a shaft of a coal mine and watching a party of rescuers bring up the bodies of miners who have been killed below. It is tragic, we say, and we are horrified, but is such "tragedy" a fit subject for drama? Is

"Riders of the Sea" a genuine tragedy? Is it possible to write a tragedy in one act? What of Strindberg's "Miss Julia" and O'Neill's "The Rope," and Paul Green's "The End of the Row"?

This play, like every work of art, should be judged on its own merits, but we are enabled to pass judgment only by comparison with other works. In asking the question, "Is it possible to write a tragedy in one act?" it is not our intention to measure "Riders to the Sea" by any arbitrary rules, but to see whether or not the one-act form happens to be the best medium for the expression of what the playwright wished to convey. Aristotle's words in the *Poetics* are always suggestive, and in this connection they are especially interesting. He says that "Tragedy is an imitation of an action that is complete, and whole, and of a certain magnitude; for there may be a whole that is wanting in magnitude." What does he mean by magnitude? Again: "a beautiful object . . . must not only have an orderly arrangement of parts, but must also be of a certain magnitude; for beauty depends on magnitude and order. Hence a very small animal organism cannot be beautiful; for the view of it is confused, the object being seen in an almost imperceptible moment of time. . . . So in the plot, a certain length is necessary, and a length which can be easily embraced by the memory. . . . We may say that the proper magnitude is comprised within such limits, that the sequence of events, according to the law of probability or necessity, will admit of a change from bad fortune to good, or from good fortune to bad."

It is here suggested that a certain development is necessary, and development in the one-act play is what the dramatist can scarcely show, because the one-act play is a single scene, incident, or situation, and we cannot see more than one stage in the development of a person or a situation. It might also be said that the most momentous developments in tragedy occur between the acts: what we see is almost entirely the critical points during the period of development.

The Playboy of the Western World

Comedy in 3 acts (1907). Texts: Boston, 1911; in *Works* (Boston, 1912); in *Plays* (London, 1922).

In the preface to "The Playboy" Synge writes: ". . . In countries where the imagination of the people, and the language they use, is rich and living, it is possible for a writer to be rich and copious in his words, and at the same time give the reality, which is the root of all poetry, in a comprehensive and natural form." This play is the living embodiment of Synge's ideas on the combination of reality and poetry in the drama. "The Playboy," like all of Synge's plays, is outside the realm of literary "movements" and coteries; his plays are not plays of ideas. Theses and problems die. "Ideas" are for a generation. Again the dramatist says (in the preface to "The Tinker's Wedding"): "The drama is made serious—in the French sense of the word—not by the degree in which it is taken up with problems that are serious in themselves, but by the degree in which it gives the nourishment, not very easy to define, on which our imaginations live. . . . The drama, like the symphony, does not teach or prove anything. . . ."

1. In his travel-book, *The Aran Islands,* we find the following passage:

. . . He often tells me about a Connaught man who killed his father with the blow of a spade when he was in a passion, and then fled to this island and threw himself on the mercy of some of the natives. . . . They hid him in a hole . . . and kept him safe for weeks, though the police came and searched for him, and he could hear their boots grinding on the stones over his head. In spite of a reward which was offered, the island was incorruptible, and after much trouble the man was safely shipped to America.

This impulse to protect the criminal is universal in the west. It seems partly due to the association between justice and the hated English jurisdiction, but more directly to the primitive feeling of these people, who are never criminals yet always capable of crime, that a man will not do wrong unless he is under the influence of a passion which is as irresistible as a storm on the sea. If a man has killed his father, and is already sick and broken with remorse, they can see no reason why he should be dragged away and killed by the law.

Such a man, they say, will be quiet all the rest of his life, and if you suggest that punishment is needed as an example, they ask, "Would any one kill his father if he was able to help it?"

Out of his sympathy and enthusiasm for life, its humor, its bite, its contradictions, its exhilaration, Synge wrote this play. The dramatist's aim was "reality" and "joy." He had no purpose but that of allowing his living creatures to revel in life, and express themselves in the rich and sensuous poetry which he created. But this apparently spontaneous comedy was the result of arduous labor: George Moore relates that the last act was rewritten thirteen times. Like all plays that are serious and beautiful and true, "The Playboy" has been attacked because of the very qualities that are its chief glory. Synge is still blamed because of what he tried to "teach" and "prove." Are there any evidences of the poet's didactic intentions?

2. Many plays, of all ages and periods, have first acts with very little in them but the exposition of a few facts and the creation of the environment, or *milieu*. The opening of "The Playboy" is full of atmosphere, and strikes the keynote of the action that is to follow; but there is no such conscious preparation as there is, say, in the expository act of Pinero's "Thunderbolt." Pegeen Mike, in Synge's play, opens the act with: "Six yards of stuff for to make a yellow gown. A pair of lace boots with lengthy heels on them and brassy eyes. A hat is suited for a wedding-day. A fine tooth comb. To be sent with three barrels of porter in Jimmy Farrell's creel cart on the evening of the coming Fair to Mister Michael James Flaherty. With the best compliments of this season. Margaret Flaherty." Compare this simple paragraph with the elaborate preparatory openings of "The Second Mrs. Tanqueray" and "Iris." What is there, besides this short speech, that may be called pure exposition? Is the "Playboy" well-made in the sense that "Magda" or "The Thunderbolt" are well-made?

3. Throughout the play the development of the plot goes hand in hand with the development of Christy's character.

Beginning with Christy's "I had it in my mind it was a different word and a bigger" (just after his entrance in the first act), trace, by reference to his speeches, how, in his own estimation and in that of his audience, he grows from "a slight young man . . . very tired and frightened and dirty" to a "likely gaffer in the end of all." There is a certain similarity between the growth of Hamlet's character and Christy's.

4. "The Playboy" is literary in the dramatic sense of the word. Can the same be said of Phillips' "Paolo and Francesca"?

See the discussion of literature and drama on page 238.

Lady Augusta Gregory

Lady Augusta Gregory was born at Roxborough, County Galway, Ireland, in 1859. Unlike most successful dramatists, she began writing plays late in life. Before 1904, when her first play was performed, her literary work was confined largely to the translation and rewriting of the early Irish legends.

Together with Yeats, Edward Martyn, and George Moore she founded The Irish Literary Theater in Dublin, which later became the Abbey Theater. She is one of the outstanding figures of the Irish Renascence. With her collections of folklore—*Cuchulain of Muirthemne, Gods and Fighting Men,* etc.—her many plays, her lectures, writings and practical managerial ability, she has contributed more than anyone else, except Yeats, to the success of the Irish dramatic movement.

Her comedies were written to furnish relief to the more somber pieces which at one time threatened to overbalance the repertory of the Abbey Theater. Comedies were scarce, and Lady Gregory set to work on "Spreading the News." Of this she says: "The idea of this play first came to me as a tragedy. . . . But comedy and not tragedy was wanted at our theater to put beside the high poetic work, 'The King's Threshold,' 'The Shadowy Waters,' 'On Baile's Strand,' 'The Well of the Saints,' and I let laughter have its way with the little play."

Lady Gregory's genius is for comedy: the best of her little folk-plays are among the few genuine comedies of modern times. Lady Gregory died in 1932.

Plays

"Spreading the News" (1904)
"Kincora" (1905)
"The White Cockade" (1905)
"Hyacinth Halvey" (1906)
"The Gaol Gate" (1906)
"The Canavans" (1906)
"The Jackdaw" (1907)
"The Rising of the Moon" (1907)
"Dervorgilla" (1907)
"The Unicorn from the Stars" [with W. B. Yeats] (1907)
"The Workhouse Ward" (1908)
"The Image" (1909)
"The Traveling Man" (1910)
"The Full Moon" (1910)
"Coats" (1910)
"The Deliverer" (1911)
"McDarragh's Wife" [later "McDonough's Wife"] (1912)
"The Bogie Men" (1912)
"Damer's Gold" (1912)
"Shanwalla" (1915)
"Hanrahan's Oath" (1915)
"The Wrens" (1915)
"The Golden Apple" (1916)
"The Dragon" (1919)
"The Jester" (1921)
"Aristotle's Bellows" (1921)
"The Story Brought by Brigit" (1924)
"On the Racecourse" (1925)
"Dave" (1926)
"Sancho's Master" (1928)
"Colman and Guaire" (1931)

(Translations and adaptations: Molière's "The Miser," "The Doctor in Spite of Himself," "The Would-be Gentleman," and "The Rogueries of Scapin"; Goldoni's "Locandiera"; and three of Douglas Hyde's plays from the Gaelic.)

Editions.—Seven Short Plays (Dublin, 1909) includes "Spreading the News," "Hyacinth Halvey," "The Gaol Gate," "The Jackdaw," "The Rising of the Moon," "The Workhouse Ward," and "The Traveling Man"; *Folk History Plays* (N. Y. 1912), includes "Grania," "Kincora," "Dervorgilla," "The Canavans," "The White Cockade," "The Deliverer"; *New Comedies* (N. Y. 1913) includes "The Full Moon," "Coats," "McDonough's Wife," "The Bogie Men," and "Damer's Gold"; *Three Wonder Plays* (N. Y. 1922) includes "The Dragon," "Aristotle's Bellows," and "The Jester"; *The Image and Other Plays* (N. Y. 1922) includes "The Image," "The Wrens," "Shanwalla," and "Hanrahan's Oath"; *Three Last Plays* (N. Y. 1928) includes "Sancho's Master," "Dave," and "The Would-be Gentleman."

Separate Plays.—"The Dragon" (N. Y. 1920); "The Golden Apple" (N. Y. 1916); "The Image" (Boston, 1910). All the other plays, except the six in *Folk History Plays,* published separately (N. Y. no date); *My First Play* [*i.e.* "Colman and Guaire"] (London, 1930).

The Molière translations are in *The Kiltartan Molière* (Dublin, 1910); Goldoni's "La Locandiera" (as "Mirandolina"), separately (N. Y. 1924); translations of Douglas Hyde's "The Twisting of the Rope" (in *Samhain,* Dublin, 1901), "The Lost Saint" (in *Samhain,* 1902), and "The Poorhouse" (*Samhain,* 1903). "The Unicorn From the Stars" is printed with the works of Yeats.

Reprints in Collections and Anthologies.—"The Rising of the Moon" in Dickinson's *Chief Contemporary Dramatists* (Boston, 1915), and in Webber and Webster's *One-Act Plays* (Boston, 1923); "Spreading the News" in Clark's *Representative One-Act Plays by British and Irish*

Authors (Boston, 1921), in Leonard's *Atlantic Book of Modern Plays* (Boston, 1921), in Cohen's *One-Act Plays by Modern Authors* (N. Y. 1921), in Knickerbocker's *Plays for Classroom Interpretation* (N. Y. 1924), in Smith's *Short Plays* (N. Y. 1922), and in *One-Act Plays for Stage and Study* (N. Y. 1924); "The Workhouse Ward" in Moses' *Representative British Dramas* (Boston, 1918), and in Shay and Loving's *Fifty Contemporary One-Act Plays* (Cincinnati, 1920); "Hyacinth Halvey" in Lewis' *Contemporary One-Act Plays* (N. Y. 1922).

References

C. Weygandt, *Irish Plays and Playwrights* (Boston, 1913); Ernest A. Boyd, *Ireland's Literary Renaissance* (N. Y. 1916), and *The Contemporary Drama in Ireland* (Boston, 1917); Thomas MacDonagh, *Literature in Ireland* (N. Y. 1916); Maurice Bourgeois, *John Millington Synge and the Irish Theater* (N. Y. 1913); Clayton Hamilton, *Studies in Stagecraft* (N. Y. 1915); Ludwig Lewisohn, *The Modern Drama* (N. Y. 1915); George Moore, *Hail and Farewell* (N. Y. 1911-1914); Mario Borsa, *The English Stage of To-day,* (N. Y. 1908); Percival Wilde, *The Craftsmanship of the One-Act Play* (Boston, 1923); W. B. Yeats, *Essays* (N. Y. 1924); and *Dramatis Personæ* (N. Y. 1936); W. G. Fay and Catherine Carswell, *The Fays of the Abbey Theater* (N. Y. 1935); H. M. Walbrook, *Nights at the Play* (London, 1911); A. E. Morgan, *Tendencies of Modern English Drama* (N. Y. 1924).

See also.—Lady Gregory, *Our Irish Theater* (N. Y. 1913).

Hyacinth Halvey

Comedy in 1 act (1906). Texts: N. Y. no date; in *Seven Short Plays* (Dublin, 1909); reprinted in Lewis' *Contemporary One-Act Plays* (N. Y. 1922).

Lady Gregory speaks as follows (in the "Notes" to *Seven Short Plays*) on the origin of this little play: "I was pointed out one evening a well-brushed, well-dressed man in the stalls, and was told gossip about him, perhaps not all true, which made me wonder if that appearance and behavior as of extreme respectability might not now and again be felt a burden. After a while he translated himself in my mind into Hyacinth; and as one must set one's original a little way off to get a translation rather than a tracing, he found himself in Cloon, where, as in other parts of our country, 'character' is built up or destroyed by a password or an emotion, rather than by experience or deliberation. The idea was more of a universal one than I knew at the first, and I have had but uneasy appreciation from some apparently blameless friends."

Like most of Lady Gregory's comedies, "Hyacinth Halvey" is

based upon a simple and universal philosophical truth: that reputation is in a great measure a matter of "a password or an emotion."

1. "Hyacinth Halvey" is a comedy, but with a continual tendency to become farce. One of the many definitions of farce is that it is a play in which possible persons are shown in impossible situations. The characters are undoubtedly "possible," and the situation likewise, yet somehow Hyacinth's unbroken series of failures to lose his good reputation, and Fardy Farrell's unparalleled failures to lose his bad one, border upon farce. Possibly the Irish setting and the good simple people render the episodes sufficiently foreign to enable us to accept the facts, yet these characters are so delightfully human that they must be taken as universal types.

2. This play, together with "Spreading the News," "The Jackdaw," and "The Workhouse Ward," raises again the question of comedy and tragedy. At the risk of being paradoxical, one might say that a tragedy is a play the closing of which is its goal, the spire of its meaning; a comedy is one that stands in and by itself, for the sake of its characters, and *has no end.* Tragedy shows the struggles of strong individuals against fate ("Œdipus") or circumstances ("Romeo and Juliet"); against themselves ("Hamlet") or against others ("Julius Cæsar" and "Othello"), and *must end* in defeat. Comedy is not concerned with the outcome; it amuses us from moment to moment: the outcome never seriously matters. Usually the end is the union of lovers, the merest convention. Had "Hamlet" ended in any other way than as it does, the play would have been spoiled; had "As You Like It" not ended with a series of unions, the play would still have had meaning in itself, intrinsic dramatic value. Tragedy points forward to the catastrophe—it is not a tragedy until the tragic outcome occurs, while comedy is usually sufficient unto itself.

Lady Gregory has recognized this fact, and left three or four of her comedies with "hanging" ends. The best examples are "Hyacinth Halvey" and "The Jackdaw." In the former, we are shown Hyacinth trying in vain to undeceive the people as to his "charácter"; a series of incidents demonstrates the utter futility of the attempt. There is no *dénouement*; "Let us therefore ring down the curtain," says Lady Gregory.

Similarly, in "The Jackdaw," there is no solution: the police are coming, there will doubtless be an explanation, but that will not interest us. Therefore the dramatist says: *"Sounds of feet and talking and knock at the door.* COONEY *hides under counter.* NESTOR *lies down on top of bench, spreads his newspaper over him.* MRS. BRODERICK *goes behind counter."* Then Nestor says: "(*raising paper from his face and looking out*) Tommy Nally, I will give you five shillings if you will draw 'Tit-Bits' over my feet." That is the end.

3. Notice by way of comparison the elaborate *dénouements* of "Sweet Lavender" and "The Liars."

4. See pp. 245, 352 for a discussion and theories on the one-act play. Does "Hyacinth Halvey" conform to the theories of the critics and dramatists? Here, by the way, is another theory; it is by the Englishman, W. R. Titterton (*From Theater to Music Hall,* 1912). He says:

> A one-act play must give a thrill or an impression; must convey a mood, an emotion, or picture an atmosphere. It has no development. Time does not exist for it—save that eternal shifting thing, the present. As the curtain rises, the hour strikes. . . . A one-act play is an epigram, a lyric, a blow, a sparkle in the dark.

No development. See our discussion of Synge's "Riders to the Sea" (p. 339). Has "Hyacinth Halvey" no development? Has Pinero's "Widow of Wasdale Head"? O'Neill's " 'Ile"? Has Shaw's "Man of Destiny," which Titterton says "could be turned into a fine one-act play"?

LORD DUNSANY

Edward John Moreton Drax Plunkett, known as Lord Dunsany, was born in 1878. He was, according to his biographer, Edward Hale Bierstadt, "educated at Eton and Sandhurst, and then entered the army. He saw active service . . . during the South African war." He was first heard of in connection with the Irish literary movement in 1902 or 1903, while the first book was published in 1905. His first play was not, however, produced until 1909: that was "The Glittering Gate," at the Abbey Theater. "King Argimenes and the Unknown Warrior" followed in 1911 at the same theater, and not long after came "The Gods of the Mountain," produced at the London Haymarket.

Dunsany is, in the best and exact sense of the word, an amateur: he writes his plays for the sheer fun of the thing.

"Something must be wrong," he says in his *Romance and the Modern Stage,* "with an age whose drama deserts romance." This is Dunsany's attitude toward playwriting. He continues: "Romance is so inseparable from life that all we need to obtain romantic drama is for the dramatist to find any age and any country where life is not too thickly veiled and cloaked with puzzles and conventions, in fact to find a people that is not in the agonies of self-consciousness."

PLAYS

"The Glittering Gate" (1909)
"King Argimenes and the Unknown Warrior" (1911)
"The Gods of the Mountain" (1911)
"The Golden Doom" (1912)
"The Lost Silk Hat" (1913)
"The Tents of the Arabs" (1914)
"A Night at an Inn" (1916)
"The Queen's Enemies" (1916)
"Fame and the Poet" (1918)
"The Prince of Stamboul" (1918)
"The Laughter of the Gods" (1919)
"The Murderers" (1919)
"A Good Bargain" (1920)
"If Shakespeare Lived To-day" (1920)
"The Compromise of the King of the Golden Isles" (1920)
"If" (1921)
"The Flight of the Queen" (1923)
"Cheezo" (1923)
"Alexander" (1925)
"The Old King's Tale" (1925)
"The Evil Kettle" (1925)
"The Amusement of Khan Kharuda" (1925)
"Atalanta in Wimbledon" (1929)
"The Raffle" (1929)
"The Journey of the Soul" (1929)
"In Holy Russia" (1929)
"His Sainted Grandmother" (1929)
"The Hopeless Passion of Mr. Bunyon" (1929)
"The Jest of Hahalaba" (1929)
"The Old Folk of the Centuries"
"Mr. Faithful" (1935)

Editions.—Five Plays (London, no date, N. Y. 1914) includes "The Gods of the Mountain," "The Golden Doom," "King Argimenes and the Unknown Warrior," "The Glittering Gate," and "The Lost Silk Hat"; *Plays of Gods and Men* (Boston, 1917) includes "The Tents of the Arabs," "The Laughter of the Gods," "The Queen's Enemies," and

"A Night at an Inn"; *Plays of Far and Near* (N. Y. 1923) includes "The Compromise of the King of the Golden Isles," "The Flight of the Queen," "Cheezo," "A Good Bargain," "If Shakespeare Lived To-day," and "Fame and the Poet"; *Alexander and Three Small Plays* (N. Y. 1926) includes "Alexander," "The Old King's Tale," "The Evil Kettle," and "The Amusements of Khan Kharuda"; *Seven Modern Comedies* (N. Y. 1929) contains "Atalanta in Wimbledon," "The Raffle," "The Journey of the Soul," "In Holy Russia," "His Sainted Grandmother," "The Hopeless Passion of Mr. Bunyon," and "The Jest of Hahalaba."

Separate Plays.—"A Night at an Inn" (N. Y. 1916); "If" (N. Y. 1922); "The Tents of the Arabs" (N. Y. no date); "The Laughter of the Gods" (N. Y. no date); "The Queen's Enemies" (N. Y. no date); "A Night at an Inn" (N. Y. no date); "The Compromise of the King" (N. Y. no date); "The Flight of the Queen" (N. Y. no date); "Cheezo" (N. Y. no date); "A Good Bargain" (N. Y. no date); "If Shakespeare Lived To-day" (N. Y. no date); "Fame and the Poet" (N. Y. no date); also all plays in *Five Plays and Alexander; Seven Modern Comedies; The Old Folk of the Centuries* (London, n. d.); *Mr. Faithful* (N. Y. 1935).

Reprints in Collections and Anthologies.—"King Argimenes" in Dickinson's *Chief Contemporary Dramatists, II* (Boston, 1921); "The Golden Doom" in Clark's *Representative One-Act Plays, etc.* (Boston, 1921), and in Knickerbocker's *Plays for Classroom Interpretation* (N. Y. 1924); "The Gods of the Mountain" in Moses' *Representative British Dramas* (Boston, 1918); "Fame and the Poet" in Leonard's *Atlantic Book of Modern Plays* (Boston, 1921); "A Night at an Inn" in Marriott's *One-Act Plays of To-day* (Boston, 1924); in Cohen's *One Act Plays* (N. Y. 1921), and in Hubbell and Beaty's *An Introduction to Drama* (N. Y. 1927).

References

E. H. Bierstadt, *Dunsany the Dramatist* (Boston, 1919); E. A. Boyd, *Ireland's Literary Renaissance* (N. Y. 1916), *The Contemporary Drama of Ireland* (Boston, 1917); Clayton Hamilton, *Seen on the Stage* (N. Y. 1920); W. A. Darlington, *Through the Fourth Wall* (N. Y. no date); Percival Wilde, *The Craftsmanship of the One-Act Play* (Boston, 1923); C. Pellizzi, *English Drama* (N. Y. 1935); A. E. Malone, *The Irish Drama* (N. Y. 1929).

See also.—Dunsany's *Nowadays* (Boston, 1918), and Preface to *Plays of Near and Far. Nowadays* and *Romance and the Modern Stage* reprinted in revised edition (1919) of Bierstadt's *Dunsany.*

The Gods of the Mountain

Play in 3 acts (1911). Texts: London, no date; in *Five Plays* (N. Y. 1914); reprinted in Moses' *Representative British Dramatists* (Boston, 1918).

This play is a typical product of Dunsany's work; a play written for its own sake, in order to show an interesting and dramatic situation, and to give the actors an opportunity to speak limpid and beautiful lines. In a letter (to Mrs. Emma Garrett Boyd, quoted in Bierstadt's book) Dunsany writes: "I will say first that in my plays I tell very simple stories—so simple that sometimes people of this complex age, being brought up in intricacies, even fail to understand them. Second, no man ever wrote a simple story yet, because he is bound to color it with his own experience. Take my 'Gods of the Mountain.' Some beggars, being hard up, pretend to be gods. Then they get all that they want. But Destiny, Nemesis, the Gods, punish them by turning them into the very idols they desire to be."

1. "The Gods of the Mountain" is divided into three "acts." The printed text runs to about twenty-five pages. Certain critics have pointed out that this drama is really a one-act play. We have already said that the one-act form is not distinguished from the full-length play by its brevity alone: there are Greek plays—in the exact sense of the word "full-length"—that are shorter than many one-acters.

Turn to Clayton Hamilton's *Seen on the Stage,* and consider the following sentences:

> . . . Enthusiastic students of the plays of Lord Dunsany should be warned against the error of being led astray by the unimportant fact that, in the published text of "The Gods of the Mountain," the three successive episodes are headed by the captions "The First Act," "The Second Act," and "The Third Act." . . . The momentary pauses in the action must be considered technically as the same sort of pauses, for the sake of emphasis, that were customarily marked with asterisks by Guy de Maupassant during the course of many of his most notable short stories.

Now, supposing that "The Gods of the Mountain" is *not* a "play in three acts"? What difference does it make what the author calls it? With this particular play, perhaps it makes no difference at all, but as a rule it makes a great deal of difference what the dramatist intended to do. Take Dunsany's

"King Argimenes." He told Mr. Hamilton (reported in *Seen on the Stage*) that sometimes he thinks his plot out before he begins writing, "but at other times, I just get started and follow a mood as a hunter follows the hounds. I will give you an example—'King Argimenes.' . . . I started the play with no idea whatever of its subsequent development. I merely wrote along, to find out what would happen."

Every writer has, of course, his own way of working, and this way is usually the best for him, but "King Argimenes" is a play that seems not to know what it ought to be: it is an overgrown episode and an undeveloped "full-length" play. Dunsany goes on to say that "I didn't know the end when I started the beginning. . . . Of course it is better to have things planned . . . and not to trust entirely to the impulsion of a mood." It is. Returning to "The Gods of the Mountain," do you agree with Mr. Hamilton?[1]

Barrie's "The Will" is in three scenes: Strindberg's "Miss Julia" in one act; Shaw's "Getting Married" has no act division at all; Æschylus' "Suppliants" likewise. Compare these plays one with the other. Which are one-acters and which "full-length"?

2. "The Gods of the Mountain" is, as Dunsany has said, a simple story, still "no man ever wrote a simple story yet, because he is bound to color it with his own experience." Experience is perhaps not the right word: philosophy or personality would surely express more clearly what is meant. This play is a parable, just as every artistic expression of life is a parable: a compression of human existence. Some people find in such compressed versions of life a symbol (which is

---

[1] Here is Mr. Hamilton's definition of the one-act play: "The one-act play is distinguished technically from the full-length play, not by the time required for its presentation, nor by the number of its pauses, marked naturally by the dropping of the curtain, but by its purpose and its mood. The purpose of the one-act play is to produce a single dramatic effect with the greatest economy of means that is consistent with the utmost emphasis; and its mood is derived reasonably from a central insistence upon that factor which was finely phrased by Poe as 'totality of impression'" (*Seen on the Stage*).

only another way of achieving compression); they "read into" the author's words meanings that lie below the surface. This is almost inevitable, and so long as the critic is not fanatical, he is ordinarily a trustworthy guide in discovering and explaining the symbols. But with Dunsany symbolism does not mean what it means with Maeterlinck: his plays can be understood without seeking for "hidden" meanings. The "overtones" that we hear in this little play are only the elements that are inseparable from all true expressions of life. Dunsany (in the letter above quoted) says further:

> First of all you have a simple tale told dramatically, and along that you have hung, without any deliberate intention of mine—so far as I know—a truth, not true to London only or to New York or to one municipal party but to the experience of man. That is the kind of way that man does get hit by destiny. But mind you, that is all unconscious, though inevitable. I am not trying to teach anybody anything. I merely set out to make a work of art out of a simple theme, and God knows we want works of art in this age of corrugated iron. How many people hold the error that Shakespeare was of the school room! Whereas he was of the playground, as all artists are.

Interesting comparisons may be made with Pirandello's "Henry IV," Benavente's "Princess Bébé," Maeterlinck's "Seven Princesses," Georg Kaiser's "From Morn to Midnight," and Ernst Toller's "Masses and Mankind."

3. Dunsany has written one genuine "full-length" play. Compare this play, "If," with the longer of his short plays: "The Laughter of the Gods," "The Tents of the Arabs," and "The Gods of the Mountain."

St. John Ervine

St. John G. Ervine was born at Belfast, in 1883. He first entered the insurance business, and then became dramatic critic of the *Daily Citizen.* Since his residence in London he has written a number of miscellaneous essays, plays, and several novels. During the earlier years of the war he directed the Abbey Theater. After serving in France, he came to America on a lecture tour. He now lives in London.

Ervine began as one of the younger group in the Irish movement, who, together with T. C. Murray and Lennox Robinson, turned their attention to the realistic depiction of life in the cities and small towns. His later plays include examples of fantasy, satire, and conventional drawing-room comedy.

Plays

"Mixed Marriage" (1911)
"The Magnanimous Lover" (1912)
"The Orangeman" (1913)
"The Critics" (1913)
"Jane Clegg" (1913)
"John Ferguson" (1915)
"The Island of Saints; and How to Get Out of It" (1921)
"The Ship" (1922)
"Mary, Mary, Quite Contrary" (1922)
"The Lady of Belmont" (1924)
"Anthony and Anna" (1925)
"The First Mrs. Fraser" (1930)
"Boyd's Shop" (1936)
"People of Our Class" (1936)
"Robert's Wife" (1937)

("The Wonderful Visit," written with H. G. Wells, is founded upon Wells' story of the same name.)

Editions.—Four Irish Plays (Dublin, 1914) includes "Mixed Marriage," "The Magnanimous Lover," "The Critics," and "The Orangeman"; *Four One-Act Plays* (N. Y. 1929) includes "The Magnanimous Lover," "Progress," "Ole George Comes to Tea," and "She Was No Lady."

Separate Plays.—"Mixed Marriage" (Boston, 1911); "The Magnanimous Lover" (Boston, 1912); "Jane Clegg" (N. Y. 1915); "John Ferguson" (N. Y. 1916); "The Ship" (N. Y. 1922); "Mary, Mary, Quite Contrary" (N. Y. 1923); "The Lady of Belmont" (N. Y. 1924); "Anthony and Anna" (N. Y. 1925); "The First Mrs. Fraser" (Boston, 1930); "Boyd's Shop" (N. Y. 1936); "People of Our Class" (London, 1936).

Reprints in Collections and Anthologies.—"Mixed Marriage" in Dickinson's *Chief Contemporary Dramatists, II* (Boston, 1921); "The Magnanimous Lover" in Clark's *Representative One-Act Plays* (Boston, 1921).

See also.—Ervine's preface to "John Ferguson" (N. Y. 1921), *Some Impressions of My Elders* (N. Y. 1923), *The Organized Theater* (N. Y. 1924), *How to Write a Play* (N. Y. 1928), and *The Theater in My Time* (London, 1933).

References

Ernest A. Boyd, *Ireland's Literary Renaissance* (N. Y. 1916), and *The Contemporary Drama of Ireland* (Boston, 1917); Cornelius Weygandt, *Irish Plays and Playwrights* (Boston, 1912); Lady Gregory,

Our Irish Theater (N. Y. 1913); Clayton Hamilton, *Seen on the Stage* (N. Y. 1920); C. Lewis Hind, *More Authors and I* (N. Y. 1922); L. R. Morris, *The Celtic Dawn* (N. Y. 1917); Alexander Woollcott, *Enchanted Aisles* (N. Y. 1924); Gerald Cumberland, *Set Down in Malice* (N. Y. 1919); A. E. Morgan, *Tendencies of Modern English Drama* (N. Y. 1924); Graham Sutton, *Some Contemporary Dramatists* (N. Y. 1926); A. E. Malone, *The Irish Drama* (N. Y. 1929); Allardyce Nicoll, *British Drama* (N. Y. 1933).

Mixed Marriage

Play in 4 acts (1911). Texts: Boston, 1911; in *Four Irish Plays* (Dublin, 1914); reprinted in Dickinson's *Chief Contemporary Dramatists,* 2nd series (Boston, 1921).

"Mixed Marriage" is one of the best examples of the more or less Naturalistic type of play written by the younger dramatists of the Irish movement. T. C. Murray, Lennox Robinson and St. John Ervine have evolved, each in his own way, certain types of family drama in which the depiction of country and city people of the lower middle classes is of greater interest than the story. "Mixed Marriage" is one of these.

1. In order the better to exhibit his characters the author has introduced a thesis, which is clearly stated in the first act. Rainey says: "A wudden have a son o' mine marry a Cathlik fur all the wurl. A've nathin' agin the girl, but A believe in stickin' t'yer religion. A Cathlik's a Cathlik, and a Prodesan's a Prodesan. Ye can't get over that." Tom replies: "Och, sure, they're all the same. Ye cudden tell the differs atween a Cathlik 'an a Prodesan if ye met them in the street an' didden know what their religion wus. A'm not one fur marryin' out o' my religion meself, but A'm no bigot. Nora Murray's a fine wumman." After this plain statement of theme we might expect a thesis play, pure and simple, but the next speech shows that the dramatist is not altogether concerned with the thesis. When Rainey declares, "Fine or no fine, she's a Cathlik an' A'll niver consent til a son o' mine marryin' her," it is reasonable to assume that the play will be one of "conflicting wills." This is, in fact, what it is, and the wills conflict over a question which is after all of only secondary *artistic* importance. The "theme," as will be seen, is used

really as a dramatic expedient, just as the quarrel between the Capulets and the Montagues was only an excuse for the story of the love of Romeo and Juliet. Rainey and Mrs. Rainey, Nora Murray and Hugh, must have something to struggle about, something which will develop and show their characters.

This first act, like the succeeding acts, is well balanced: character against character, with sufficient plot and sufficient background to form a harmonious whole.

2. Struggle, it has been frequently observed, is one of the basic principles of the drama, but whether or not struggle or conflict of some sort can be made the basis of a "law" as Brunetière has tried to make it, is open to question; it is true, however, that most plays are based upon struggle of some kind. "Mixed Marriage" is clearly a struggle of conflicting wills. First we are shown that Hugh is in love with Nora Murray, a Catholic. But the dramatist does not consider it sufficient to confine the struggle to these few people: he introduces external forces. Michael's words are ominous: "It mightn't be again you on'y though?" Notice how the struggle develops from the particular to the general.

3. The "general" just referred to does not mean the "general" question of religion; Michael's words reveal character in that he forces upon Hugh a realization of the general effects that must follow upon the son's marriage. Ervine is a dramatist and an artist, and the question of religion is only of relative importance. The conflict between Protestant and Catholic is a ready-made situation, full of theatrical possibilities. Notice throughout the play how the dramatist utilizes this ready-made situation to exhibit his characters in action.

4. Take two other Irish plays written at about the same time by Ervine's contemporaries—T. C. Murray's "Birthright" and Lennox Robinson's "Harvest"—both of them likewise based upon problems of the day, and see how these writers have utilized their themes. Is there any trace of a desire on the part of these men to inculcate a "lesson" or prove a point? Suppose Ervine had been more concerned with dissuading the

young people of his country from intermarrying than he was with writing an effective play; in what respects would "Mixed Marriage" have differed from the play it now is?

5. Why should not a dramatist teach a "moral"? Who says a play should not be a "lesson"? Clergymen—and others—have from time immemorial referred to certain plays as "uplifting," "incitements to right living" and the like. Channing Pollock's "The Fool" is assuredly a "helpful" play, and "Pollyanna" has no doubt brought happiness into the lives of thousands.

Read the following (which you probably won't agree with), and then ponder over the high-minded committee that recently offered a prize to the dramatist who should most effectively present life in such a way as to persuade young college men bent on suicide to desist: "Do you read a book or go to the theater in order to escape from life, to forget your sorrows? Golly, what a life you must lead! Personally, I read books and go to the theater for more and ever more of life. I for one don't know anything more fascinating than mankind; having only one life to live I know I can't possibly crowd very much actual experience into it, but I can enjoy other people's experiences. . . . I may recoil here and there before the spectacle of misery, violence, or bloodshed, I may be sickened by the tragic failure of human beings who might but for the grace of God be I, but I want it all. I would exclude nothing, not one thing whatsoever, provided it belongs to life."

To this shocking statement of mine (in *Œdipus or Pollyanna*) are opposed Don Marquis' preface to the Nugents' play, "The Poor Nut," and Booth Tarkington's preface to Connelly and Kaufman's comedy, "Dulcy." Take your choice.

THE AMERICAN DRAMA

THE AMERICAN DRAMA

Professor Quinn's *History of the American Drama*, in three volumes (lately revised), is the only complete work on the subject. Among the more or less complete works on the drama (as distinct from the theater) are Montrose J. Moses' *American Dramatist*, Richard Burton's *New American Drama*, Oliver M. Sayler's *Our American Theater*, Thomas H. Dickinson's *Playwrights of the New American Theater*, and Burns Mantle's *American Playwrights of Today*.

Since the very recent plays of the best of our younger dramatists cannot be adequately treated in a volume of this kind, the reader is referred to newspapers and magazines. Were it not necessary to preserve some sort of historical perspective, the following pages would be devoted mostly to the plays of Paul Green, Maxwell Anderson, Sidney Howard, George Kelly, George S. Kaufman, Marc Connelly, Lynn Riggs, Philip Barry, and Clifford Odets.

A great deal of data is to be found in books of dramatic and miscellaneous material, particularly in the various collections of plays, edited by Montrose J. Moses, Arthur Hobson Quinn, Margaret Mayorga, George P. Baker, S. M. Tucker, Thomas H. Dickinson, and Richard A. Cordell.

Bronson Howard

Bronson Croker Howard was born at Detroit, in 1842. After receiving his primary education in Detroit, he prepared himself for Yale at an eastern preparatory school, but was prevented from entering college because of an affection of the eyes. He then returned to Detroit, and joined the staff of the *Free Press*, to which he made numerous contributions. His first play was a dramatization from "Les Misérables," called "Fantine"; this was produced in Detroit in 1864. The following year Howard came to New York, wrote for the *Tribune* and the *Post*, carried plays from manager to manager during a period of five years, until in 1870 Augustin Daly produced "Saratoga," which proved immensely successful. From that time forward, Howard's success was assured; "The Banker's Daughter," "Young Mrs. Winthrop," "The Henrietta," "Shenandoah," and "Aristocracy" were among the most popular American plays of their time. Howard died at Avon-by-the-Sea, New Jersey, in 1908.

Brander Matthews (in *An Appreciation*) says: "Bronson Howard's career as a dramatist covered the transition period of the modern drama when it was changing from the platform-stage to the picture-frame-stage. His immediate predecessor, Dion Boucicault, worked in accordance with the conditions of the platform-stage, with its rhetorical emphasis, its confidential soliloquies to the audience, and its frequent changes of scene in the course of the act. . . . When Bronson Howard began to write for the stage he accepted the convenient traditions of the time, although he followed T. W. Robertson in giving only a single scene to each act. As a result of this utilization of conventions soon to seem outworn, certain of his earlier plays appeared to him late in life incapable of being brought down to date, as they had been composed in accordance with a method now discarded. . . . He moved with his time; and his latest plays, 'Aristocracy' for one, and 'Kate' for another, are in perfect accord with the most modern formula [written twenty years ago]. Yet he did not go as far as some other playwrights of to-day. He knew that the art of the theater, like every other art, can live only by the conventions which allow it to depart from the mere facts of life." Howard was among the first to realize that in the America of his day there was material for an indigenous drama, and he did his best, in spite of French influences, to abandon the conventions of the past and point a way to the future.

Plays

"Saratoga" (1870)
"Diamonds" (1872)
"Moorcroft" (1874)
"Lilian's Last Love" (1877)
"The Banker's Daughter" [revised version of "Lilian's Last Love"] (1878)
"Old Love Letters" (1878)
"Hurricanes" (1878)
"Fun in the Green-Room" (1882)
"Young Mrs. Winthrop" (1882)
"One of Our Girls" (1885)
"Met by Chance" (1887)
"The Henrietta" (1887)
"Baron Rudolph" (1887)
"Shenandoah" (1889)
"Aristocracy" (1892)
"Peter Stuyvesant" [with Brander Matthews] (1899)
"Kate" (1906)

("Fantine," 1864, is based on Hugo's "Les Misérables"; "Wives," 1879, on a play of Molière; "Knave and Queen," written with Sir Charles Young, was never acted, and is not printed; "Kate," though published, was never acted.)

Editions.—"Saratoga" (N. Y. 1870); "Young Mrs. Winthrop" (N. Y. 1899); "Kate" (N. Y. 1906); "Shenandoah" (*see below*); "Old Love Letters," adapted by G. H. Leverton (N. Y. 1936). *The following are privately printed, and may be found in two or three of the large libraries:* "Aristocracy" (N. Y. 1898); "Old Love Letters" (N. Y. 1897); "One of Our Girls" (N. Y. 1897); "Shenandoah" (N. Y. 1897); "The Henrietta" (N. Y. 1901); "The Banker's Daughter" (N. Y. 1878).

Reprints in Collections and Anthologies.—"Shenandoah" in Moses' *Representative Plays by American Dramatists,* III (N. Y. 1921).

References

In Memoriam: Bronson Howard (N. Y. 1910); Brander Matthews, *A Study of the Drama* (Boston, 1910), *Gateways to Literature* (N. Y. 1912), and *The Principles of Playmaking* (N. Y. 1919); Richard Burton, *The New American Drama* (N. Y. 1913); Charlton Andrews, *The Drama To-day* (Philadelphia, 1913); Montrose J. Moses, *The American Dramatist* (Boston, 1925); Daniel Frohman, *Memories of a Manager* (Garden City, 1911) and *Daniel Frohman Presents* (N. Y. 1935); Augustus Thomas, *The Print of My Remembrance* (N. Y. 1922); A. H. Quinn, *A History of the American Drama, From the Civil War to the Present Day* (N. Y. 1927).

See also.—Bronson Howard, *The Autobiography of a Play,* with introduction by Augustus Thomas (N. Y. 1914).

Young Mrs. Winthrop

Play in 4 acts (1882). Text: N. Y. 1899.

Of the three published plays of Howard, "Young Mrs. Winthrop" is the best example of his work as a playwright. The dramatist's best and worst qualities are easily discernible. Like some of his contemporaries and many of his followers, Howard possessed a great deal of that essential kindliness, sympathy with the weaknesses of human nature, and sentiment, which characterize the American writer of plays. "Young Mrs. Winthrop" is a kindly sermon on the dangers and blessings of matrimony, besides being an ingratiating and human comedy.

1. Any play written in 1882 is likely to bristle with "asides," soliloquies, and other conventions which have since fallen into disfavor. This play opens with a soliloquy:

Mrs. Ruth (*L.*). There, Miss Dolly! (*tying ribbon on the doll and holding it up*) you will have a beautiful mother to-morrow, and I shall be your grand-grandmother. Your name is to be "Ruth"—after me—how do you like it? Your little mother has a very large family already, but I am sure she will love you more than any of the rest (*crosses to R. by fire, kisses the doll*). Lie here, my pet (*holding the doll to her breast*). You must go to sleep at once, for mother Rosie will be up very early in the morning. (*Enter* Douglas), etc.

A great deal of labor is spared the dramatist by allowing his audience to know (1) who the character present is, (2) what she is like, (3) a little of the situation. The first "aside" occurs on the next page (p. 4):

Douglas (*stopping, aside*). I asked Constance not to go to-night.

Again, an easy device. Then (p. 25) there is another soliloquy:

Enter Constance, *up L.*

Constance. Back again! (*with a weary air, throwing aside her cloak. Pause.*) How quiet the house is! It's no use going to bed; I cannot sleep. I wish these "social gaieties," as they call them, could go on forever. No matter how much I go out, or how bright the company is, it always ends in this; I am alone again, and I—I can't stop thinking. Oh!—I wish I *could!* I wish I could! Mr. Chetwyn was at the reception this evening. Douglas sent him word he could not meet him at the club. He sent the message after receiving that note from Mrs. Dunbar—*she* was *not* there to-night! Oh!—why must I keep thinking—thinking? (*Starting to her feet and moving C. Pauses.*) Perhaps I am wronging him. Yes. No—no—I will *not* believe it—I *have* not lost his love! There is something I do not understand? I will speak to Douglas about it in the morning. (*Smiling.*) It will all come right. I must get to sleep as soon as I can, to be up bright and early with Rosie. I will peep in at my little darling before I go to sleep. (*Going toward door, R. 2 E.*)

It has often been said in defense of the "aside" and the soliloquy that since the drama is a series of conventions, why not accept these as well as the others? For hundreds of years certain conventions have been accepted, why then should we cast them aside at this late date? The drama has changed radically during the past century, and is still developing at a rapid rate. With the change in subject matter has come a corresponding change in the manner of treatment: realistic subjects, for instance, demanded realistic treatment. The "aside" is not natural, because it does not *seem* natural: people seldom or never turn their heads aside and utter words not intended to be heard by any one else; and when these words are spoken loud enough to be overheard by a large audience, while the characters who must not hear them are within whispering distance of the speaker, the falsity of the situation becomes too apparent. The uselessness of this particular convention is proved by the fact that almost every aside in a play can be deleted and the audience be none the less well informed as to what is going on. Test this in the present play.

On the other hand, the soliloquy is legitimate. Ibsen in "A Doll's House" has made generous use of it. People *do* soliloquize, often aloud; even if they did not, it is not unnatural to hear a character, when he is alone on the stage, give voice to thoughts which must be near the surface. Do Hamlet's soliloquies seem unnatural? Do Nora's in the Ibsen play just mentioned?

Brander Matthews, who collaborated with Howard in "Peter Stuyvesant," says that Howard once said, "half jokingly that, if he happened to write a play without a single soliloquy, he would be tempted to insert one, simply to retain the right to employ it when it was required. It may be noted, however, that he did not carry this out, since his last comedy, 'Kate,' is free from any soliloquy."

Stage conventions are, of course, merely agreements (as the word indicates) between the dramatist and the audience. "Make believe with me," he says, "that this is something which it actually is not, and then forget all about it." The convention is not intended to be a deception. Coleridge, wisest of critics, has said that the "true stage illusion . . . consists not in the mind's judging it [that is, the scenery] to be a forest, but, in its remission of the judgment that it is not a forest." Stage presentations, he says, "are to produce a sort of temporary half-faith, which the spectator encourages in himself and supports by a voluntary contribution on his own part, because he knows that it is at all times possible to see the thing as it really is." And finally: "For not only are we never absolutely deluded . . . but the attempt to cause the highest delusion possible to beings in their senses in a theater, is a gross fault, incident only to low minds. . . ." (*Lectures,* 1836). That Mr. A, the actor, is King Lear (represents him, that is, for a couple of hours) is the first convention; that the stage is a room, or a street, or a blasted heath, is another. We know that Mr. A is not King Lear, and that the stage is only a stage, but we agree to pretend that each is not what it really is. That an hour elapses during a scene which lasts only ten minutes, is still another convention, while in Barrie's "Mary Rose" we are asked to assume that for certain persons a score of years has passed, and for one other person, no time at all.

One of the most curious conventions has arisen since the stage became what is known as the picture-frame or (to some critics) the peep-hole stage. Now, a room has four walls, at least in theory,[1] and yet one of these must be removed if the audience are to see and hear what happens in that room. Generally, we forget that the fourth wall has been removed, but occasionally some over-ingenious or literal-minded dramatist or producer reminds us that it is supposed to exist. In Jerome K. Jerome's "Passing of the Third Floor Back" andirons were set just behind the center of the row of footlights and the actors during the play would come, one after the other, to warm their hands at the rosy glow. The device was at most

---

[1] A friend of mine, a dramatic critic, once contested this, and his argument is, I think, valid. His point is that only an imaginary room has four walls: if you are *in* a room, you cannot see more than three; if you stand at the door and *look* in, you still cannot see more than three, and if you are in a theater, the case is similar. If people are not in rooms, or looking into them from the door or from the auditorium of a theater, then the four walls exist only as a concept. Why, therefore, bother with four walls?

ingenious; Coleridge would doubtless have called this a "gross fault," as he would also have called Belasco's successful attempt to reproduce the interior of a Childs' Restaurant, in "The Governor's Lady."

In a suggestive essay in his book *Through the Fourth Wall,* the English critic W. A. Darlington discusses the point in question:

> My thoughts have now been set running on the subject by a play I saw quite recently, in which one of the characters suddenly fixed a basilisk eye above my head and began to praise pictures which he seemed to spy either floating in the air or pinned to the rail of the balcony. I found myself worried and disturbed. . . . The effect of this touch of ruthless realism, so far as I was concerned, was the instant destruction of all sense of reality. (This is the invariable result of overdoing realism, by the way.) I had no objection whatever to the subconscious knowledge that the stage room before me must possess a fourth wall, which had to be taken bodily out like the front of a doll's house—and for the same excellent reason, that otherwise there could be no play. . . . There is no surer way of bringing home the fact that the fourth wall doesn't exist than by pretending it does.

In 1887, when Antoine opened his Free Theater in Paris the audience laughed when he turned his back on them! It *may* be that the dramatists of the future will find it to their advantage to remind us of the fourth wall, and in that case we shall become used to the convention, just as we are used to a thousand conventions to-day which we scarcely notice: the painted back-drop, the lapse of time, etc.

2. Howard's up-to-dateness—considering the time in which he wrote—his vision of the path to be taken by the play of the future was greater than his actual achievement: he pointed out the way for those who were to be technically more efficient than he. Augustus Thomas says of him (in *The Autobiography of a Play*):

> Some philosopher tells us that a factor of greatness in any field is the power to generalize, the ability to discover the principle underlying apparently discordant facts. Bronson Howard's plays are

notable for their evidence of this power. He saw causes, tendencies, results. His plays are expositions of this chemistry. "Shenandoah" dealt broadly with the forces and feelings behind the Civil War; "The Henrietta" with the American passion for speculation —the money-madness that was dividing families. "Aristocracy" was a very accurate, although satirical, seizure of the disposition, then in its strongest manifestation, of a newly-rich and Western family of native force to break into the exclusive social set of New York and to do so through a preparatory European alliance.

What is the generalization in "Young Mrs. Winthrop"? Wherein lies its modernity?

3. Often—too often in the American drama—the child is brought into the action of a play in order to appeal to the sympathy of the audience. David Belasco has done this in "The Return of Peter Grimm" with notable effect. How has Howard utilized the child-motif in his play?

4. How far may an artist go in his presentation of the crude violence of life? Life itself is full of incidents that arouse every sort of emotion; the drama at its best arouses deep emotions; the drama is a certain kind of presentment of life. Tolstoy's "Power of Darkness" contains terrible scenes, so do Galsworthy's "Justice" and Wedekind's "Earth Spirit." Is there a point beyond which the dramatist may not go? Are there any subjects that should not or cannot be treated?

Augustus Thomas

Augustus Thomas was born at St. Louis in 1859. The following short autobiographical sketch is furnished by Mr. Thomas himself (1912). "After Farragut ran the New Orleans blockade my father took direction of the St. Charles Theater in New Orleans, then owned by Ben DeBar. When he returned to St. Louis in 1865, I was in my seventh year, and my earliest recollections are tinged with his stories of Matilda Herron, John Wilkes Booth, and others who played in that theater. Father was an orator of considerable ability, and I remember him reciting long speeches from Kotzebue, Schiller, and Shakespeare. In his associations with the theater he took me very early to plays, and I have always been an attendant; consequently dialogue seemed the most natural literary vehicle. I found later that this impression was justified when I discovered that the most telling things in Homer and later Greek poets and philosophers were in dialogue—that this was true of Confucius and Christ. I began writing plays when I was about fourteen years of age. When I was sixteen and seventeen, an amateur company that I organized played in certain railway centers on the old North Missouri Railway for the benefit of local unions of the workingmen. In 1882 I made a dramatization of Mrs. Burnett's 'Editha's Burglar.' With this as a curtain-raiser and a rather slap-stick farce called 'Combustion,' I made a tour of the country with a company that I organized, and with which I ran in debt several thousand dollars. In 1889 a four-act version of 'The Burglar,' arranged by me, was played in New York and was successful, and since that time my royalties have enabled me to give my attention on the business side exclusively to playwriting."

Thomas was one of the most successful American dramatists. "Arizona," a melodrama of the West, is one of his typical works; even "The Witching Hour," a later play, is notable for the very qualities which were evident in the earlier melodrama. Thomas is ingenious, he thoroughly understands the art of contriving moving stories, he knows the taste of the public and the requirements of the actor. He is the chief American exponent of the "well-made" play. He died in 1934.

PLAYS

"Alone" (1875)
"The Big Rise" (1882)
"Editha's Burglar" [from a story by Mrs. Burnett] (1883)
"A Man of the World" (1883)
"A Studio Picture" (1883)
"A New Year's Call" (1883)
"A Leaf from the Woods" (1883)
"Combustion" (1884)
"The Burglar" (1889)
"Reckless Temple" (1890)
"Afterthoughts" (1890)
"A Woman of the World" (1890)
"A Night's Frolic" (1891)
"Alabama" (1891)
"For Money" (1891)
"The Holly Tree Inn" (1892)
"Colonel Carter of Cartersville" (1892)
"Surrender" (1892)
"A Proper Impropriety" (1893)
"In Mizzoura" (1893)
"The Music Box" (1894)
"New Blood" (1894)
"The Capitol" (1895)
"The Man Upstairs" (1895)
"The Hoosier Doctor" (1897)
"Colonel George of Mount Vernon" (1898)
"That Overcoat" (1898)
"The Meddler" (1898)
"Oliver Goldsmith" (1899)
"Arizona" (1899)
"Champagne Charley" (1901)

"On the Quiet" (1901)
"Colorado" (1901)
"The Earl of Pawtucket" (1903)
"The Other Girl" (1903)
"The Education of Mr. Pipp" (1905)
"Mrs. Leffingwell's Boots" (1905)
"De Lancey" (1905)
"The Embassy Ball" (1905)
"The Ranger" (1907)
"The Witching Hour" (1907)
"The Member from Ozark" (1907)
"The Harvest Moon" (1909)
"The Matinee Idol" (1909)
"As a Man Thinks" (1911)
"The Model" (1912)
"Mere Man" (1912)
"Indian Summer" (1913)
"At Bay" [with George Scarborough] (1913)
"Three of Hearts" (1913)
"The Battle Cry" (1914)
"The Nightingale" (1914)
"Rio Grande" (1916)
"The Copperhead" (1918)
"Palmy Days" (1919)
"The Tent of Pompey" (1920)
"Speak of the Devil" (1920)
"Nemesis" (1921)
"The Vanishing Lady" (1922)
"Still Waters" (1925)

("Chimmie Fadden" (1897), "The Jucklins" (1896), and "Soldiers of Fortune" (1900), are dramatized from novels.)

Editions (separate plays.)—"Alabama" (Chicago, 1898); "Arizona" (N. Y. 1899); "As a Man Thinks" (N. Y. 1911); "The Man Upstairs" (Washington, 1918). Following have prefaces by author: "The Witching Hour" (N. Y. 1916); "Oliver Goldsmith" (N. Y. 1916); "The Earl of Pawtucket" (N. Y. 1915); "In Mizzoura" (N. Y. 1916); "The Other Girl" (N. Y. 1917); "Mrs. Leffingwell's Boots" (N. Y. 1916); "The Harvest Moon" (N. Y. 1922); "The Copperhead" (N. Y. 1922); "Still Waters" (1926); "Colonel George of Mount Vernon" (N. Y. 1931); "A Constitutional Point" (N. Y. 1932); "A Proper Impropriety" (N. Y. 1932); "Editha's Burglar" (N. Y. 1932); "The Cricket of Palmy Days" [*i.e.* "Palmy Days"] (N. Y. 1929).

Reprints in Collections and Anthologies.—"The Witching Hour" in Dickinson's *Chief Contemporary Dramatists* (Boston, 1915); in Quinn's *Representative American Plays* (N. Y. 1925), and in Moses' *Representative American Dramas* (Boston, 1925); "As a Man Thinks" in Baker's *Modern American Plays* (N. Y. 1920); "In Mizzoura" in Moses' *Representative Plays by American Authors,* III (N. Y. 1921); "The Copperhead" in Cohen's *Longer Plays* (N. Y. 1922); "The Man Upstairs" (Washington, 1918, and N. Y. 1924).

References

Montrose J. Moses, *The American Dramatist* (Boston, 1925); Richard Burton, *The New American Drama* (N. Y. 1913); William Winter, *The Wallet of Time,* II (N. Y. 1913); W. P. Eaton, *The American Stage of To-day* (Boston, 1908), *At the New Theater and Others* (Boston, 1910), and *Plays and Players* (Cincinnati, 1916); George Jean Nathan, *Comedians All* (N. Y. 1919); Clayton Hamilton, *Problems of the Playwright* (N. Y. 1917); A. H. Quinn, *A History of the American Drama* (N. Y. 1936); Burns Mantle, *American Playwrights of Today* (N. Y. 1930).

See also.—Thomas' prefaces to plays indicated above; his introduction to Bronson Howard's *Autobiography of a Play* (N. Y. 1914), and his own book, *The Print of My Remembrance* (N. Y. 1922), and preface to *One-Act Plays for Stage and Study* (N. Y. 1924).

The Witching Hour

Play in 4 acts (1907). Texts: N. Y. 1916; reprinted in Dickinson's *Chief Contemporary Dramatists* (Boston, 1915); in Quinn's *Representative American Plays* (N. Y. 1917); and in Moses' *Representative American Dramas* (Boston, 1925).

In common with Clyde Fitch, Alfred Capus, Sir Arthur Pinero and several hundred other successful playwrights, Augustus Thomas has always kept abreast of the times in the matter of modes, customs, and ideas. Probably his early journalistic career taught him the value of being "alive," for he has always recognized the advantage of producing a play the basic idea of which is in the public mind. It is said that "The Witching Hour" was kept for ten years "until the time was opportune." Montrose J. Moses in his *American Dramatist* quotes Thomas as saying: " 'The Witching Hour' is a seizure of the general attention that is given to telepathy and allied topics. And under all that, lies my own theory, expressed on more than one occasion, that the theater is a place for the visualizing of ideas—that the theater is vital only when it is visualizing some idea then and at the time in the public mind. The theater is a vital part of everyday life; it is an institution, and as an institution it has a claim upon the popular attention principally in that fact. When it becomes a thing preservative, a museum for certain literary forms, or a laboratory for galvanizing archaic ideas, it is almost useless, and seldom successful as a business enterprise."

1. For some years Thomas refused to allow the present play to appear in print; apart from certain practical reasons, he feared that a vehicle intended for production on the stage by actors, supported by scenery and "props" and lights, in which there was no attempt at "galvanizing archaic ideas," would not well survive the ordeal of reading. Very often good dialogue will suffer when perused in the library—dialogue that is interesting and dramatic on the boards; it is very doubtful

whether "Charley's Aunt" would be half so amusing between the covers of a book as it is in the theater.[2]

Note the opening lines of the play:

Jo. Massar Brookfield.
JACK (*outside, left*). Well, Jo?
Jo. Mr. Denning, sah.
JACK. Ask Mr. Denning to come up.
Jo. Yes, sah.
(*Exit center. More talk and laughter, left.*)
(JACK *enters left. . . .*)
JACK (*at door, left*). Lew! I say—Lew—you ladies excuse Mr. Ellinger a moment?
HELEN, ALICE, VIOLA (*outside*). Oh—yes. Certainly.

Nothing could seem more casual, yet here is an underlying art, skillfully concealing itself, which is typical of Thomas' best work. Compare this dialogue with that of "Young Mrs. Winthrop" and of "The Liars."

2. Thomas wished to write a play about telepathic phenomena and superstition; and the exact form into which he was to cast his play must have suggested itself to him when he was thinking of the incidents to illustrate his ideas.

In his preface to the acting edition (N. Y. 1916), the author says that "The Witching Hour" was originally written as a one-act play over thirty years ago. It was refused at first by the managers, but during a considerable period of years it was being expanded.

---

[2] In an interview Augustus Thomas once said: "On the choice of words will depend very much the effectiveness of a play. The tone of them must change to suit the scene, the emotion. One way of creating humor is to use pompous or grandiloquent words. Emotion, on the other hand, keeps the words simple, very near the ground. Part of an audience might, perhaps, get deep feeling from unusual and very precise words, but the audience is made up for the greater part of people who are not thus trained. And when you write for the audience you must write for the great average. You will then use the simple, passionate words such as fire, stars, hand, heart, root, rock, grave. In the same way you may simplify your words by omitting many. For instance, note the increase in emphasis and force between, 'I wish you to go,' 'You must go,' 'Go!' and finally the simple opening of the door."

If [he says] the story was to expand into four acts, these hints and gropings [telepathic communication, etc.] must take on a firmer fiber along with the structural strength of the story: in addition to theory, there must be some substantial and tangible performances; telepathy must *do something;* hypnotism must *dominate* some important situation. This something must be done, and this situation to be dominated, must be devised by the dramatist.

Finally, since the play must convince—if not intellectually at least emotionally, for the time being—it was incumbent upon the playwright to *demonstrate,* during the action, the truth of his thesis.

Couldn't something be found [he continues] to still the foreseen objections of the public? Couldn't the press agent stand up in a private box and present a few arguments? . . . The public at the play where there must be a contest is always itself a third point of a triangle. Why not give the public a representative in the cast of characters—a person who should doubt and disbelieve and deny to the very finish? Of course! . . . And in that setting to doubt and to deny would be to be comic; but standing for the public, our representative must be made good-hearted and likable and so, last of all, Lew Ellinger was invented, or, at least, he stepped out from the convivial chafing-dish group around Brookfield.

If "The Witching Hour" had been held by the author until the season of 1923-1924, would it have been necessary to "prove" so much? Why, indeed, must the dramatist prove his thesis? But, as a matter of fact, is this what Thomas wishes to do?

Can you think of other plays in which the audience are, as it were, given a representative, someone who can voice their feelings or ideas?

3. This play is, in many respects, thoroughly American. The dialogue (or most of it) resembles the speech of everyday life; the characters, what we see of them, remind us of the men and women we see in the street, the office, and the home. The playwright is not especially interested in their philosophy of love, their sex instincts, or their ideas about God and the

universe. That is his business; it is not ours to quarrel with him for not looking at life the way Hauptmann looks at it, or D'Annunzio. He was concerned chiefly with a group of persons and with "visualizing" an idea. The question is, how has he accomplished what he set out to do?

4. In connection with our consideration of the plays of George M. Cohan (p. 398) it is stated that American dramatists are seemingly afraid of sentiment. This is, of course, not true of all (there is Belasco to prove the contrary), but it is certain that a large part of our contemporary dramatic literature is not conspicuous for its emotional appeal. Here is one of the short "love scenes" in "The Witching Hour":

CLAY. Always you when I think about a real house, you bet—a house for *me*—and you'll be there, won't you? (*Takes her in his arms.*)

VIOLA. Will I?

CLAY. Yes—say, "I will."

VIOLA. I will.

(*Reënter* ALICE *and* HELEN.)

ALICE (*astonished*). Viola!

(ALICE *goes left.*)

CLAY. I've asked her—mother.

ALICE. Helen, you knew?

HELEN. Yes.

CLAY (*to* ALICE). And I asked Jack, too.

ALICE. You mean——

CLAY. We're engaged—if you say it's all right.

ALICE. And you—Viola?

VIOLA (*nodding*). Yes——

Here are the barest outlines; not a trace of passion, and what feeling there is must be expressed by the actors. How different from the long pages of Donnay's "Lovers" or Schnitzler's "Light-o'-Love"! and yet, occasionally the American *can* write serious scenes of genuine passion, as witness O'Neill's "The Straw." If the love-making of the average American on the stage is strange, the other sort of sentimentalizing is no less so. On page 44, where there should be none of the poetry and passion of youth, we find another proposal—twenty years after the first—where the lover appears to be retrospectively sentimental:

JACK. Wouldn't it be a pretty finish if you took my hand and I could walk right up to the camera and say, "I told you so"—? You know I always felt that you were coming back.

HELEN. Oh, did you?

JACK (*playfully, and going right center*). Had a candle burning in the window every night.

HELEN. You're sure it wasn't a red light?

JACK (*remonstrating*). Dear Helen! have some poetry in your composition. Literally "red light," of course—but the real flame was here—(*hand on breast*)—a flickering hope that somewhere—somehow—somewhen I should be at rest—with the proud Helen that loved and—rode away.

HELEN (*almost accusingly*). I—believe—you.

JACK. Of course you believe me.

5. There are many episodes and incidents introduced and threads of plot begun in the first act. Study this act carefully and trace each of the important references to superstition and telepathy, each of the "love-scenes," the murder, etc., and notice how each is further developed in the play. Is the first act too crowded?

CLYDE FITCH

William Clyde Fitch was born at Elmira, New York, in 1865. He attended college at Amherst, and immediately after graduation began writing—verse, stories and sketches. In 1890 he began his career as playwright with "Beau Brummell," written for the actor Richard Mansfield. For twenty years he wrote plays, many of which were enormously successful, and in 1909 died at Châlons-sur-marne in France.

Fitch was a clever and ingenious writer of comedies and dramas, the best of which pictured the life of the middle and upper classes in New York. At a time when the American stage was largely dependent upon importations from abroad, Fitch distinguished himself by writing about American people in America. His best plays were his light comedies of character, some of them well-constructed, many of them brilliant only in parts, but all of them sprightly and amusing. He labored under the disadvantage of writing for actors, managers, and audiences that could or would have little use for the sort of satire he could turn out when he wished to. There is no doubt that he wanted to develop his talents more fully than he had been able to, and that his last play, "The City," indicated the direction in which he was moving. His ideas on the drama are thus expressed in his own words: "I feel myself very strongly the particular value—a value which, rightly or wrongly, I can't help feeling inestimable—in a modern play, of reflecting absolutely and truthfully the life and environment about us; every class, every kind, every emotion, every motive, every occupation, every business, every idleness! Life was never so varied, so complex. . . . Take what strikes you most, in the hope it will interest others; take what suits you most to do—what perhaps you can do best, and then do it better. Be truthful, and then nothing can be too big, nothing should be too small, so long as it is here and there. . . . If you inculcate an idea into your play, so much the better for your play and for you and for your audience. . . . One should write what one sees, but observe under the surface. It is a mistake to look at the reflection of the sky in the water of theatrical convention; instead, look up and into the sky of real life itself."

Fitch's practice rarely conformed to his theory: he was, on the whole, too ready to look at the reflection in the water of theatrical convention.

Plays

"Beau Brummell" (1890)
"Betty's Finish" (1890)
"Frédéric Lemaître" (1890)
"A Modern Match" ["Marriage"] (1891)
"Pamela's Prodigy" (1891)
"The Social Swim" (1893)
"Harvest" (1893)
"His Grace de Grammont" (1894)
"April Weather" (1894)
"Mistress Betty" (1895)
"Nathan Hale" (1898)
"The Moth and the Flame" [Re-writing of "Harvest"] (1898)
"The Cowboy and the Lady" (1899)
"Barbara Frietchie" (1899)
"The Climbers" (1901)
"Captain Jinks of the Horse Marines" (1901)
"Lovers' Lane" (1901)
"The Last of the Dandies" (1901)
"The Way of the World" (1901)
"The Girl and the Judge" (1901)
"The Stubbornness of Geraldine" (1902)
"The Girl with the Green Eyes" (1902)

"The Bird in the Cage" (1903)
"Her Own Way" (1903)
"The Frisky Mrs. Johnson" (1903)
"Algy" (1903)
"Glad of It" (1903)
"Major André" (1903)
"The Coronet of a Duchess" (1904)
"Granny" (1904)
"The Woman in the Case" (1904)
"Her Great Match" (1905)
"The Toast of the Town" [rewriting of "Mistress Betty"] (1905)
"Wolfville" (1905)
"The Girl Who Has Everything" (1906)
"The Truth" (1906)
"The Straight Road" (1906)
"Her Sister" [with C. Gordon-Lennox] (1907)
"Miss McCobb, Manicuriste" (1907)
"Girls" (1908)
"A Happy Marriage" (1909)
"The Bachelor" (1909)
"The City" (1910)

(This list does not include the translations and adaptations.)

Editions.—*Plays by Clyde Fitch,* 4 vols., edited by Montrose J. Moses and Virginia Gerson (Boston, 1915), includes "Beau Brummell," "Lovers' Lane," "Nathan Hale," "Barbara Frietchie," "Captain Jinks of the Horse Marines," "The Climbers," "The Stubbornness of Geraldine," "The Girl With the Green Eyes," "Her Own Way," "The Woman in the Case," "The Truth," and "The City."

Separate Plays.—"Pamela's Prodigy" (N. Y. 1893); "Nathan Hale" (N. Y. 1897); "Barbara Frietchie" (N. Y. 1900); "The Climbers" (N. Y. 1906); "The Girl With the Green Eyes" (N. Y. 1905); "Her Own Way" (N. Y. 1907); "The Stubbornness of Geraldine" (N. Y. 1906); "The Truth" (N. Y. 1907); "Captain Jinks" (N. Y. 1902); "Beau Brummell" (N. Y. 1899); "The Cowboy and the Lady" (N. Y. 1923).

Reprints in Collections and Anthologies.—"The Truth" in Dickinson's *Chief Contemporary Dramatists* (Boston, 1915), and in Stauffer's *Progress of Drama* (N. Y. 1927); "Her Great Match" [printed only in this ed.] in Quinn's *Representative American Plays* (N. Y. 1917); "The Moth and the Flame" [printed only in this ed.] in Moses' *Representative Plays by American Authors,* Vol. III (N. Y. 1921); "Beau Brummell" in Cohen's *Longer Plays by Modern Authors* (N. Y. 1922); "The City" in Moses' *Representative American Dramas* (Boston, (1925).

See also.—Fitch's "Play and the Public," in Vol. IV of the *Plays by Clyde Fitch* (Boston, 1915).

References

Archie Bell, *The Clyde Fitch I Knew* (N. Y. 1909); Montrose J. Moses, *The American Dramatist* (Boston, 1925), and Moses and Virginia Gerson, *Clyde Fitch and His Letters* (Boston, 1924); Richard Burton, *The New American Drama* (N. Y. 1913); L. W. Strang, *Plays and Players of the Last Quarter-Century,* 2 vols. (Boston, 1902); Charlton Andrews, *The Drama To-day* (Philadelphia, 1913); William Archer, *Playmaking* (Boston, 1912); Brander Matthews, *A Study of the Drama* (Boston, 1910); Archibald Henderson, *The Changing Drama* (Cincinnati,

1919); W. P. Eaton, *At the New Theater and Others* (Boston, 1910); Arthur Ruhl, *Second Nights* (N. Y. 1914); Norman Hapgood, *The Stage in America* (N. Y. 1901); anonymous, *Clyde Fitch: A Tribute*, in Fitch's *A Wave of Life* (N. Y. no date); W. L. Phelps, *Essays on Modern Dramatists* (N. Y. 1921); J. T. Grein, *Premières of the Year* (London, 1900); William Winter, *The Wallet of Time*, 2 vols. (N. Y. 1913), and *The Life of David Belasco*, 2 vols. (N. Y. 1918); Elisabeth Marbury, *My Crystal Ball* (N. Y. 1923); Augustus Thomas, *The Print of My Remembrance* (N. Y. 1922); Otis Skinner, *Footlights and Spotlights* (N. Y. 1924); A. H. Quinn, *A History of the American Drama, From the Civil War to the Present Day* (N. Y. 1927).

The Truth

Play in 4 acts (1906). Texts: N. Y. 1907; in *Plays* (Boston, 1915); reprinted in Dickinson's *Chief Contemporary Dramatists* (Boston, 1915).

"The Truth" is Fitch's most consistent and best-sustained play. There is in it less of the amusingly irrelevant, and more study and observation of character than in even "The Girl with the Green Eyes" or "The Climbers." It is one of the very few American plays of its time to be successfully produced abroad. The theme is of course universally interesting, and the construction on the whole unusually sound. "The Truth" is one of the few genuine American comedies of manners.

1. Fitch's cleverness as a craftsman is manifested on p. 4:

MRS. LINDON. . . . Becky! One of my oldest friends! One of my bridesmaids!

MAURA. What!

MRS. LINDON. No, she wasn't, but she might have been; she was my next choice if any one had backed out.

This is amusing, and it tells something about the speaker. It is a *mot de caractère*. In the first act is there any notable bit of information given about any of the characters? What of Becky herself?

As the play progresses, notice by what means Becky's character is built up. Is it in situations, by dialogue, or through the conversation of others?

2. The lie has always offered good dramatic material; Ibsen has dramatized it in most of his social plays; Jones, in "The Liars" and "The Lie," and Donnay in "The Free Woman," have written plays about men and women who lie to attain certain ends, and fail. Has this play of Fitch's points in common with any of the plays referred to? What is the dramatic, the "theatrical," essence of "The Truth"? How has the author extracted what is most interesting and appealing from his story?

Fitch's words (quoted on p. 376 of the present volume) regarding underlying ideas in plays are peculiarly apt: "If you inculcate an idea into your play so much the better for your play and for you and for your audience. . . . It is sometimes better for you if it is hidden, but it must of course be integral. . . ." Is Fitch's idea hidden? Is it integral? Just what does he mean by an "idea"? A thesis such as Shaw develops in "Back to Methuselah," a philosophy such as underlies the plays of Andreyev, a purpose such as Brieux promulgates in all his work?

3. The average American audience has not yet come to the point where it will unflinchingly accept the logical consequences of a situation.[1] Eugene Walter in "The Easiest Way" has dared to bring his tragic play to its only possible close, but he succeeded only in spite of this fact, by reason of deft craftsmanship. No one objects to the happy ending of a happy play; the fault lies with the dramatist who begins with a situation and characters from which only evil or tragedy can come. Veiller's "Within the Law," Broadhurst's "Bought and Paid For," and Charles Kenyon's "Kindling," began with interesting ideas, but these were lost sight of before the plays were brought to a fitting close.

If a dramatist introduces a certain character early in the play with the idea of changing the mind and spirit of that

[1] An extreme statement. Where the tone and intention of the play are tragic, a tragic ending will be accepted. Several of our newer dramatists have written plays so absorbingly interesting that audiences listened perforce and were glad to remain to the end. For a discussion of the subject see my *Œdipus or Pollyanna* (Seattle, 1927).

character, he must motivate each action and account for the character at the end of the play. If Ibsen wished to show Nora as a doll in the first act of "A Doll's House," and a mature and thinking woman in the last, he must adduce convincing proofs that the change *would* occur. Jones, in "The Crusaders" and "Dolly Reforming Herself," ridicules the attempts of would-be reformers to accomplish their ends overnight: the "crusaders," in the one, and Dolly and her friends in the other, are sadder and wiser at last, but they are no nearer to reformation than when the curtain first rose. In Bahr's "Concert" the philandering artist will, we are positive, continue to give "concerts" as long as he is so inclined; in Leo Dietrichstein's American version of the Austrian comedy, the amiable pianist assures his wife that he will "give no more concerts." Very often a dramatist will throw a sop to his audience, but at the same time add a "tag" showing that the "lived happily ever after" is the merest convention. Davies' "The Mollusc" is a case in question: Tom's words, which close the play, are: "Were those miracles permanent cures? (*Shakes his head.*) We're never told! We're never told!" This is legitimate, like the happy ending to a fairy story, but when the inexorable logic of life demands truth, and the dramatist deliberately distorts it, the play is, of course, false.

Study carefully the last act of "The Truth," determining exactly how genuine Becky's "conversion" seems, whether the author intended his audience to accept the *dénouement,* or whether he introduced the closing lines simply in order that the audience might feel that all had ended happily:

BECKY. You can't forgive me!
WARDER. We don't love people because they are perfect.
(*He takes her two trembling hands in his, and she rises.*)
BECKY. Tom!
WARDER. We love them because they are themselves.

PERCY MACKAYE

Percy MacKaye, son of Steele MacKaye, the dramatist, was born at New York City in 1875. After his graduation from

Harvard University, he began writing plays. During nearly a quarter of a century he has striven to awaken in the American people a sense of civic consciousness, and through his plays, operas and pageants, has shown the way to a realization of his own high ideals. He has likewise written books and delivered lectures throughout the country and participated in every sort of community festival. Though few of his plays have been commercially successful, MacKaye's influence has, on the whole, been wide and beneficial. In his fantasies and pageants and plays, nearly all dealing with various aspects of American life, he has remained consistently an experimental artist, and in his best work (like "The Scarecrow" and "Washington") brought to the stage a fund of indigenous material.

Plays

"Kinfolk of Robin Hood" (1901)
"The Canterbury Pilgrims" (1903)
"Fenris the Wolf" (1905)
"Jeanne D'Arc" (1906)
"Sappho and Phaon" (1907)
"Mater" (1908)
"The Scarecrow" (1908)
"Anti-Matrimony" (1909)
"A Garland to Sylvia" (1910)
"Chuck" (1912)
"Gettysburg" (1912)
"The Antick" (1912)
"The Cat-Boat" (1912)
"Sam Average" (1912)
"To-morrow" (1913)
"A Thousand Years Ago" (1913)
"Washington" (1919)
"This Fine-Pretty World" (1924)
"Napoleon Crossing the Rockies" (1924)
"The Funeralizing of Crickneck" (1928)
"Timber" (1928)
"The Sphinx" (1929)
"Wakefield" (1932)

(This list does not include the masques, operas, pageants and festival pieces: "Caliban" (1916), "Saint Louis" (1914), "A Masque of Labor" (1912), "Sanctuary" (1913), "The New Citizenship" (1915), "The Evergreen Tree" (1917), "The Roll Call" (1918), "The Will of Song" (1919), "Sinbad the Sailor" (1917), "The Immigrants" (1915), "Rip Van Winkle" (1919). "The Canterbury Pilgrims" was set to music as an opera by Reginald DeKoven.)

Editions.—Poems and Plays by Percy MacKaye, Vol. II (N. Y. 1916), includes "The Canterbury Pilgrims," "Jeanne D'Arc," "Sappho and Phaon," "The Scarecrow," and "Mater." *Yankee Fantasies* (N. Y. 1912) includes "Chuck," "Gettysburg," "The Antick," "The Cat-Boat," and "Sam Average." *Kentucky Mountain Fantasies* (N. Y. 1928) includes "The Funeralizing of Crickneck," "Timber" and "Napoleon Crossing the Rockies."

Separate Plays.—"The Canterbury Pilgrims" (N. Y. 1903); "Jeanne D'Arc" (N. Y. 1911); "Sappho and Phaon" (N. Y. 1907); "Fenris the Wolf" (N. Y. 1905); "A Garland to Sylvia" (N. Y. 1910); "The

Scarecrow" (N. Y. 1908); "Mater" (N. Y. 1908); "Anti-Matrimony" (N. Y. 1910); "To-morrow" N. Y. (1912); "A Thousand Years Ago" (Garden City, 1914); "Washington" (N. Y. 1919); and one scene, same title (N. Y. 1920), also "Washington at the Delaware," one scene separately (N. Y. 1920); "Washington and Betsy Ross," and "Young Washington at Mount Vernon" separately (N. Y. 1926), from "Washington"; "This Fine-Pretty World" (N. Y. 1924); "Kinfolk of Robin Hood" (N. Y. 1926); "Gettysburg" (N. Y. 1934); "The Sphinx" (Evanston, 1929); "Wakefield" (Washington, 1932).

Reprints in Collections and Anthologies.—"The Scarecrow" in Dickinson's *Chief Contemporary Dramatists* (Boston, 1915), and in Quinn's *Representative American Plays* (N. Y. 1925), and in Moses' *Representative American Dramas* (Boston, 1925); "Gettysburg" in Leonard's *Atlantic Book of Modern Plays* (Boston, 1921), and in Cohen's *One-Act Plays* (N. Y. 1921); "Kinfolk of Robin Hood" in Thomas' *Atlantic Book of Junior Plays* (Boston, 1924); "Sam Average" in Lewis' *Contemporary One-Act Plays* (N. Y. 1922), and in Mayorga's *Representative One-Act Plays by American Authors* (Boston, 1919); "Napoleon Crossing the Rockies" in *One-Act Plays for Stage and Study,* III (N. Y. 1927).

Mr. MacKaye collaborated with Evelyn G. Sutherland in "A Song at the Castle," in *Po' White Trash* (Chicago, 1900).

References

Montrose J. Moses, *The American Dramatist* (Boston, 1925); Richard Burton, *The New American Drama* (N. Y. 1913); Brander Matthews, *A Study of the Drama* (Boston, 1910); F. W. Chandler, *Aspects of Modern Drama* (N. Y. 1914); Oliver M. Sayler, *Our American Theater* (N. Y. 1923); Kenneth Macgowan, *The Theater of To-morrow* (N. Y. 1921); T. H. Dickinson, *Playwrights of the New American Theater* (N. Y. 1925); A. H. Quinn, *A History of the American Drama* (N. Y. 1936); *Percy MacKaye, a Symposium* (Hanover, 1928); E. O. Grover, ed., and others, *Annals of an Era* (Washington, 1932).

See also.—MacKaye's *Community Drama* (Boston, 1917), *The Playhouse and the Play* (N. Y. 1909), *The Civic Theater* (N. Y. 1912), and *A Substitute for War* (N. Y. 1915); *Epoch* (N. Y. 1927).

The Scarecrow

"A Tragedy of the Ludicrous." Play in 4 acts (1908). Texts: N. Y. 1908; reprinted in Dickinson's *Chief Contemporary Dramatists* (Boston, 1915).

"The Scarecrow" is founded upon Hawthorne's *Feathertop.* The play is by no means a dramatization, but an independent work of which only the idea and chief characters were taken from Hawthorne.

1. MacKaye was wise in making a direct and visible appeal

in his first act: the mysterious blacksmith shop, the "horned and tailed" devil, the suggestion of witchcraft, these create an atmosphere suited to the plot. The poet does not actually begin his play until this external appeal has been definitely made.

What dramatic, as distinct from literary, expedients are used in this first act to accomplish the ends just mentioned?

2. The idea of the play is not easy to define: there is first the "mirror of truth" episode, then the Justice Merton and Goody Rickby story, and so on. These finally mold themselves into a harmonious whole, which eventually reveals the theme of the play. But each individual thread of action is developed in a leisurely manner. In the second act, for example, there is none of the usual American haste—no "punch," no purely theatrical situations: the poet has found a suitable vehicle for drama as well as for poetic prose. Does he ever allow his theme or his liking for the purely literary to interfere with the dramatic development of the story? If so, where?

3. The climax at the end of the third act is built up according to the formulas of the Well-made play. From the somewhat loose beginning of the second act, trace the process whereby the dramatist has brought his play to the usual climactic point. Does he eliminate or relegate to the background threads of interest which are not so important as the main one, or does he temporarily thrust the important ones into the foreground, asking the audience to accept them for the time being?

4. Consider the last act in the light of its effectiveness as a stage play; is there too much of the theme, and insufficient action?

Why does Ravensbane die at the end? The last two speeches are:

RICHARD (*bending over him*). Dead!
RACHEL (*with an exalted look*). But a man!

Is this the "Tragedy of the Ludicrous"?

5. "The Scarecrow" was well acted and produced with great care and understanding, but it failed. This means that the

number of persons willing to buy seats was not sufficient to enable the producer to meet expenses. Failure in the theater does not of necessity mean that a dramatist cannot write good plays: Congreve's "Way of the World," one of the great comedies of all times, never succeeded on the stage. But failure usually means that some element is lacking, and not necessarily the most important, except from the point of view of the commercial producer.

We can always learn much from failures. Why, in your opinion, was "The Scarecrow" not a box-office success? What element of popular appeal does it lack?

EUGENE WALTER

Eugene Walter was born at Cleveland in 1876. He did reporting on a Cleveland newspaper, then joined the New York *Sun,* and later served in the army. For some years he was advance agent for theatrical managers. For the past twenty years he has devoted himself exclusively to the writing of plays.

Walter is a man of the theater. His plays are for the most part melodramatic situations à la Bernstein, well developed and skillfully constructed. He is journalistic, violent, but nearly always interesting. His violence leads him at times to excess, but it sometimes drives him relentlessly into powerful and gripping situations. "Paid in Full" and "The Easiest Way," in particular, are fearless in their logic, and the author has fortunately not succumbed to the temptation of making happy endings.

PLAYS

"Sergeant James" (1901)
"The Undertow" (1907)
"Paid in Full" (1907)
"The Wolf" (1908)
"The Easiest Way" (1908)
"Boots and Saddles" (1909)
"Just a Wife" (1909)
"Fine Feathers" (1913)
"The Knife" (1917)
"The Heritage" (1917)
"Nancy Lee" (1918)
"The Challenge" (1919)
"Jealousy" (1932)

("The Trail of the Lonesome Pine" and "The Little Shepherd of Kingdom Come" are dramatized from the novels of the same name. Most of Walter's plays have been produced, in various versions, under various titles.)

Editions and Reprints.—"The Easiest Way" (Garden City, 1917), reprinted in Dickinson's *Chief Contemporary Dramatists,* 2nd series (Boston, 1921), and in Moses' *Representative Plays by American Authors,* Vol. III, (N. Y. 1921); also separately as pamphlet in Walter's *How to Write a Play* (N. Y. 1925); "Jealousy" (N. Y. 1932).

REFERENCES

Montrose J. Moses, *The American Dramatist* (Boston, 1925); Richard Burton, *The New American Drama* (N. Y. 1911); Archibald Henderson, *The Changing Drama* (Cincinnati, 1919); George Jean Nathan, *Comedians All* (N. Y. 1919); H. M. Walbrook, *Nights at the Play* (London, 1911); Arthur Ruhl, *Second Nights* (N. Y. 1914); W. P. Eaton, *The American Stage of To-day* (Boston, 1908), and *At the New Theater and Others* (Boston, 1910); Oliver M. Sayler, *Our American Theater* (N. Y. 1923); T. H. Dickinson, *Playwrights of the New American Theater* (N. Y. 1925); A. H. Quinn, *A History of the American Drama, From the Civil War to the Present Day* (N. Y. 1927).

See also.—Walter's *How to Write a Play* (N. Y. 1925).

The Easiest Way

Play in 4 acts (1908). Texts: Garden City, 1917; reprinted in Dickinson's *Chief Contemporary Dramatists,* 2nd series (Boston, 1921), and in Moses' *Representative Plays by American Authors,* Vol. III (N. Y. 1921).

Like William Vaughn Moody's "Great Divide," in America, and Pinero's "Second Mrs. Tanqueray," in England, Walter's "Easiest Way" proved that a serious and "unpleasant" study of contemporary life was possible in theaters not used to anything as a rule but conventional optimistic plays. "The Easiest Way" was really a landmark in the American theater. For the first time a dramatist dared to write simply and truthfully of certain "painful" aspects of life in New York. Here were no false glamour and no conventional presentment of "sin" in the usual sense of the word.

1. The first act is admirably put together. There is no artificial suspense, and the plot appears to develop of its own accord. We feel throughout the casualness of life. The keynote is struck at the very rise of the curtain:

WILL. Blue?
LAURA. No.

WILL. What's up?

LAURA. Nothing.

WILL. A little preoccupied?

LAURA. Perhaps.

WILL. What's up that way?

LAURA. Which way?

WILL. The way you are looking.

LAURA. The road from Manitou Springs. They call it the trail out here.

WILL. I know that. You know I've done a lot of business west of the Missouri.

What could be more casual? And yet see how much ground is covered. Analyze these few words; what information is conveyed to us?

Here is another scene, in which the longest speech contains exactly eight words, all but one of one syllable each:

JOHN. Well, dear?

LAURA. Are you going to be cross with me?

JOHN. Why?

LAURA. Because he came?

JOHN. Brockton?

LAURA. Yes.

JOHN. You didn't know, did you?

LAURA. Yes, I did.

JOHN. That he was coming?

LAURA. He wired me when he reached Kansas City.

JOHN. Does he know?

LAURA. About us?

JOHN. Yes.

LAURA. I've told him.

JOHN. When?

LAURA. To-day.

JOHN. Here?

LAURA. Yes.

JOHN. With what result?

LAURA. I think it hurt him.

JOHN. Naturally.

LAURA. More than I had any idea it would.

JOHN. I'm sorry.

Compression can surely go no further. This is like the ticking of a telegraph instrument. But the words convey meaning, and each speech helps the scene to "march." There is no marking time, no trifling. The dramatist has serious work ahead of him, and these preliminaries must be got out of the way before the play actually begins.

And where does it begin?

2. We have often stressed the point that in a play we must believe. Not, perhaps, in the theme, but certainly in the characters, and that belief is based upon what they say and do. If any word or act destroys our belief we are less likely to follow the action with interest and sympathy. At the end of the first act in this play John and Will make a pact, and the result of Laura's subsequent actions is what we are asked to witness. Is this pact credible? Will says, "If she leaves you first, you are to tell me, and if she comes to me, I'll make her let you know just when and why." And John agrees. Would Will make this offer, and would John accept it?

3. Pinero's "Iris" and Walter's "Easiest Way" offer many points in common. Compare the two plays, especially the characters of Iris and Laura. Are the situations in which they are placed exactly alike?

Pinero has introduced a villain—Maldonado. It is he who precipitates Iris' downfall. Is there a villain in the American play? What is it that brings about Laura's "fall"? Compare, now, the endings of the two plays. Which is truer to life?

4. Toward the end of the second act (p. 198, Dickinson ed.) Laura gives up the fight. "Will," she says, "we'll always be frank. I said I was ready to go. It's up to you—when and where?" Is this step well motivated?

Why, at the end of the same act (p. 200), does Laura first start to send her letter, and then burn it? Why, also, is this incident given an important position in the act just before the fall of the curtain?

5. The play, evidently, is not over when Laura returns to Will. We are doubly anxious to know now what will happen when John returns. The first inkling of his existence is hinted

at by Will himself (p. 203): "I don't suppose, Laura, that you'd be interested now in knowing anything about that young fellow out in Colorado? What was his name—Madison?" It is just such masculine tactlessness (here assuming the guise of Fate) that precipitates tragedy.

Notice (p. 204) a curious fact: the stage directions include the text of John's telegram. Laura reads the dispatch *to herself* (in the older plays such things are read to the audience, in the more modern the recipient has forgotten her glasses and asks the maid to read it), and it is only in the ensuing scenes that we are made familiar with the contents of the message. Was it necessary to print the wire at all?

6. Tragedy often seems the result of coincidence: the last act of "Hamlet" is a tissue of improbabilities. But then coincidences are always occurring in life, and it is the tragedy of life that coincidences are always happening to bring about tragedy. For instance, Laura's tragedy consists of her inability to wait for John. *If* John had only told her he was coming there would have been no tragedy. *If* Juliet had only known a little sooner! *If* Cordelia had only said a few words to her doddering old father! But the seed of tragedy lies in the character of the chief personage, faced by certain facts. Fate is always ready to intervene with coincidences. In "The Easiest Way" the playwright's concern is not to show that Laura just missed happiness and "virtue," but that she is the sort of person who is always missing them; if John had saved her by writing, then the catastrophe would only have been deferred. She is throughout depicted as a creature of circumstances.

7. Eugene Walter is reported by Montrose J. Moses as saying of "The Easiest Way":

> . . . I do not think much of it. To my mind a good play must have a tremendous uplift in thought and purpose. "The Easiest Way" has none of this. There is not a character in the play really worth while, with the exception of the old agent. . . . As it is more or less purely photographic, I do not think it should be given the credit of an inspiration—it is rather devilishly clever, but a great work it certainly is not.

Whether or not it is a great work we need not here discuss. Authors are generally poor judges of their own work, and Walter is no exception to the rule. What does he mean by "uplift"? And why should a "more or less purely photographic" work be poor art? Must the characters in a play be "worth while"?

EDWARD SHELDON

Edward Sheldon was born at Chicago in 1886. He attended Harvard, where he was a member of Professor Baker's class in dramatic technique, and was graduated in 1907. After the production of his first play, "Salvation Nell," by Mrs. Fiske, he was for some time an important figure in the native theater.

Sheldon is a man with true dramatic instinct. His first play, "Salvation Nell," is notable for its minute observation; "The Nigger" came near being a significant play; "The Boss" and "The High Road" are less interesting pictures of various phases of contemporaneous American life; "Romance," as a story pure and simple, is one of the best-made plays of our time. Sheldon is enterprising, and in each of his plays he experiments with form. He has a constant tendency toward the melodramatic, the conventional and the sentimental, but in his later work he has shown greater restraint and a surer mastery over his materials.

PLAYS

"Salvation Nell" (1908)
"The Nigger" (1909)
"The Boss" (1911)
"Princess Zim-Zim" (1911)
"Egypt" (1912)
"The High Road" (1912)
"Romance" (1913)
"The Lonely Heart" (1914)
"The Garden of Paradise" (1914)
"Bewitched" [with Sidney Howard] (1924)
"Lulu Belle" [with Charles MacArthur] (1926)
"Jenny" [with Margaret Ayer Barnes] (1929)
"Dishonored Lady" [with Margaret Ayer Barnes] (1930)

("The Song of Songs," "The Jest," and "Lady of the Camellias," adapted from Sudermann, Benelli, and Dumas, not published.)

Editions (separate plays).—"The Nigger" (N. Y. 1910); "Romance" (N. Y. 1914); "The Garden of Paradise" (N. Y. 1915); "The Boss" appears only in Quinn's *Representative American Plays* (N. Y. 1917).

Reprint.—"Romance" in Baker's *Modern American Plays* (N. Y. 1920).

References

Montrose J. Moses, *The American Dramatist* (Boston, 1925); Richard Burton, *The New American Drama* (N. Y. 1911); William Archer, *Playmaking* (Boston, 1912); Clayton Hamilton, *Studies in Stagecraft* (N. Y. 1914); W. P. Eaton, *At the New Theater and Others* (Boston, 1910), and *Plays and Players* (Cincinnati, 1916); G. J. Nathan, *Comedians All* (N. Y. 1919), and *Another Book on the Theater* (N. Y. 1915); Oliver M. Sayler, *Our American Theater* (N. Y. 1923); T. H. Dickinson, *Playwrights of the New American Theater* (N. Y. 1925); A. H. Quinn, *A History of the American Drama, From the Civil War to the Present Day* (N. Y. 1927).

Romance

Play in 3 acts, a prologue, and an epilogue (1913). Texts: N. Y. 1914, and reprinted in Baker's *Modern American Plays* (N. Y. 1920).

"Romance" is the most close-knit and best constructed of this dramatist's plays. While the subject-matter is not distinctively American, the details, the development, and the point of view are unquestionably indigenous.

1. From time to time, during the past, and of recent years especially, a dramatist has set a play within a play, or in some other manner arranged the time-scheme of his play, in order to achieve some novelty of effect. "Milestones" by Bennett and Knoblauch [now Knoblock] has three acts, the first of which takes place in the sixties, the second in the eighties, and the last in the year 1912. Sheldon's "The High Road" is in five acts, which cover a period of about twenty-five years; George Cohan's "Seven Keys to Baldpate" is a play within a play; "The Big Idea," by A. E. Thomas and Clayton Hamilton, is still another novelty in stagecraft; while "On Trial," by Elmer Reizenstein [now Rice], tells a story backward. Pirandello's "Six Characters in Search of an Author" (see p. 196) is another example of novelty, and in George Kelly's "Torch-Bearers," in which an amateur performance is supposed to be in progress, the stage represents the *back* of the stage on which the amateurs are acting. For other examples of novelty I suggest, at random, Sutton Vane's "Outward Bound." Rolland's

"Danton," Evreinov's "Theater of the Soul," Guitry's "Pasteur." All these are published.

The value of this transposition of the time-scheme usually lies in the novelty, but—and this is especially true in the case of "On Trial"—the novelty soon wears off. There a commonplace melodramatic incident is made interesting because it is told backward; the pleasure is felt only in seeing *how* it is done. Like a clever acrobatic feat, once it is over there is no desire to see it repeated. Where, as in "Milestones," the device is not so novel and involved, or where it is more legitimately used, as in the plays of Cohan, A. E. Thomas, and Clayton Hamilton, more attention may be paid to the play itself. But as a matter of fact, the unfolding of the past has been much more skillfully and naturally accomplished in many of the plays of Ibsen, and especially in Bergström's "Karen Borneman." "Ghosts" and "Rosmersholm" accomplish practically the same ends as does "On Trial," only there is no *visible* return to the past: it is unfolded by means of dialogue and its results are made manifest in the present. "On Trial" interests us only when the past is visibly returned to, with the result that it is made too vivid, and the proper perspective lost. The past cannot be so vivid as the present. In "Karen Borneman" it rises up gradually; in fact, there is a great deal of exposition in the last act, but as the facts are made known as they would be in life itself as a result of certain other facts, the audience keep pace with the characters, and are never perplexed. The only criticism to be made against such plays as "On Trial" is that their very novelty is soon outworn.

"Romance" is the visualization of a story of the past. But as that story *is* the play, the prologue may be taken as incidental: as a frame for the principal action. However, had the story in the prologue been made more important, the intrusion of the old man's story would have thrown into exaggerated relief what should have been only a detail.

2. It has already been remarked that one of the limitations of the American dramatist is his love of easy optimism and sentimentality. Edward Sheldon is not always able to avoid

these failings. The very title of this play implies sentiment, and its theme demands vigorous treatment. Yet, on the stage or off, sentimentality is sentimentality, and all exaggeration is false. In the third act we find the following speech of Tom:

> . . . Don't you hear the midnight cry: "Behold The Bridegroom cometh. Go ye out to meet Him!" Don't you see Him coming from the wilderness like a pillar of smoke, perfumed with myrrh and frankincense? His eyes are as a flame of fire, and on His head are many crowns. He wears a garment dipped in blood and on it a name is written, Lord of Lords and King of Kings! Hark! He is outside knocking at your door! Rose of Sharon, Lily of the Valley, cease your slumber, for the hour has come!

These words, to be sure, are put into the mouth of the passionate young rector, but it is open to question whether the author was not striving to attain an effect independent of what the logic of the situation required. In "The High Road" he attempted this, to the detriment of the truth of the situation.

Sheldon has always been lavish in the use of crowds, brass bands, and the like. These are of course always dramatic, but their constant use tends to weaken the effect of the play. At the end of "The Nigger," in the big act of "The Boss," and at the end of "The High Road," there are "mobs outside"; what of these devices in "Romance"? The touch of melodrama which often nearly spoils an otherwise dramatic scene is evident in the last act of the present play:

> (*Pause. They are both breathing deeply.* Tom, *biting his underlip and never taking his eyes off her face, is crawling softly up on her other side, crouched like a beast prepared to spring upon her unaware. Then, in the silence, just as he is ready to leap, is heard the first note of the midnight bell. The full, deep tones strike solemnly and slowly up to twelve. Then, as it continues, the sound of a choir of men's voices, sturdy and sweet, is heard from far away, gradually growing nearer. They are playing and singing the old Lutheran hymn "Ein' feste Burg." As* Tom *hears them, he gradually straightens and his old look and manner come back to him. He goes rather unsteadily. He stands for a moment look-*

ing out; then turns to RITA, *passing his hand over his forehead as one recovering from a dream.*)

3. Sheldon is rarely mistaken as to the effect he wishes to produce, and his plays are full of minor points which are admirably done: the quaint incident in "The Boss" where the principal character buys the brooch and examines it; the scene in the Governor's office in "The High Road"; most of the first act of "Salvation Nell," are peculiarly Sheldonian. These touches go far to create charm and build up character. What examples are there in "Romance"? How far is the dramatist dependent upon them for the creation of his larger effects?

4. "Romance" is a love-story. So is Molnar's "Liliom." Compare the two plays.

GEORGE M. COHAN

George M. Cohan was born at Providence in 1878. Both his parents were actors, and he himself made his first appearance before the public at the age of ten. Two years later he toured in the title-rôle of "Peck's Bad Boy." In 1904 he achieved popularity in his own musical show "Little Johnny Jones." Then followed a series of successful musical comedies. During the past fifteen years Cohan has acted, sung, and danced in his own plays, and won renown as a skillful producer and manager. He has written a few original plays, but for the most part he has adapted the plays of others, and dramatized novels and stories. However, he has managed to impart his own peculiar style to whatever he has touched, so that a "Cohan" play may be either an original work, the result of collaboration, a dramatization, a rewriting, or even the work of someone else, produced by Cohan.

Cohan's best plays are "Broadway Jones," "Get-Rich-Quick Wallingford," and "Seven Keys to Baldpate," of which only the first is "original." Like the best native playwrights, he is a master of observation in the surface details of life. He has evolved a highly personal method of playwriting essentially of the theater; there is not a trace of "literature" in any of his plays, but there is a fund of humor and a fundamental optimism altogether American.

PLAYS (EXCLUSIVE OF MUSICAL SHOWS)

"Money to Burn" (1895)
"On the Road" (1895)
"A Tip on the Derby" (1897)
"The Dangerous Mrs. Delaney" (1898)
"A Game of Golf" (1898)
"Hogan of the Hansom" (1899)
"To Boston on Business" (1899)
"The Wise Guy" (1899)
"The Town Clown" [with F. Tannehill, Jr.] (1899)
"The Governor's Son" (1901)
"Running for Office" (1903)
"Popularity" (1906)
"The Young Napoleon" (1907)
"The Belle of the Barbers' Ball" (1909)
"Hogan's Millions" (1911)
"Get-Rich-Quick Wallingford" (1910)
"Broadway Jones" (1912)
"Seven Keys to Baldpate" (1913)
"The Miracle Man" (1914)
"The House of Glass" [with M. Marcin] (1915)
"Hit-the-Trail Holliday" (1915)
"A Prince There Was" (1918)
"The Meanest Man in the World" (1920)
"The Farrell Case" (1920)
"The Tavern" (1920)
"The Song-and-Dance Man" (1923)
"American Born" (1925)
"The Home Towners" (1926)
"The Baby Cyclone" (1927)
"Billie" (1928)
"Gambling" (1929)
"Rhapsody" [with Louis K. Anspacher] (1930)
"Friendship" (1931)
"Pigeons and People" (1933)
"Dear Old Darling" (1936)
"Fulton of Oak Falls" (1937)

Editions (separate plays).—"Broadway Jones" (N. Y. 1923); "Seven Keys to Baldpate" (N. Y. 1923); "The Fireman's Picnic" (Washington, 1918); "The Farrell Case" (*Smart Set,* N. Y. 1920); "A Prince There Was" (N. Y. 1927); "The Baby Cyclone" (N. Y. 1928).

REFERENCES

W. P. Eaton, *Plays and Players* (Cincinnati, 1916), and *The American Stage of To-day* (Boston, 1908); Clayton Hamilton, *Problems of the Playwright* (N. Y. 1917); Oliver M. Sayler, *Our American Theater* (N. Y. 1923); N. C. Goodwin, *Nat Goodwin's Book* (Boston, 1914); G. J. Nathan, *Mr. George Jean Nathan Presents* (N. Y. 1917); T. H. Dickinson, *Playwrights of the New American Theater* (N. Y. 1925); A. H. Quinn, *A History of the American Drama* (N. Y. 1936); Burns Mantle, *American Playwrights of Today* (N. Y. 1930). *See also:* Cohan's *Twenty Years on Broadway* (N. Y. 1925).

BROADWAY JONES

Comedy in 4 acts (1912). Text: N. Y. 1923.

"Broadway Jones" is a typical Cohan play. It is unpretentious amusement, intended solely for performance in the theater. You feel that it was built, not written; that it came into being on the stage and not in the study.

1. It has already been observed (p. 372) that the American playwright is a believer in action and movement rather than words. The dialogue in the plays of such men as Cohan, James Montgomery, Augustin McHugh, Charles Klein, and a hundred others, is "snappy," bright, amusing, clever; never literary, except when an effort is made to poke fun at Maeterlinck or college professors. The actors do not use sentences, they talk just enough to carry the plot along. Indeed, the dialogue in American plays of this type is very much like the explanations in a motion picture, a necessary evil. The "business" in American farces and light comedies is of especial importance. "Broadway Jones" opens with pantomime:

> RANKIN, *the man servant, comes on from R., goes up to window C., looks out, C.L., then comes down L. and as he hears* JACKSON *coming in from L. he goes over C.R. of piano and stands until* JACKSON *sits at table L.C.* JACKSON *enters, staggering R., goes up to window C, waves his handkerchief to men outside, then comes down to L. of piano and turns on piano lamp. He sees a photograph on piano, picks it up, looks at it intently for a moment, and then puts it down and bows to it very solemnly. He then comes down and sits R. of table L.C., and is just about to fall asleep when* RANKIN *comes forward from R. and taps him on the shoulder.*

The stage is almost dark, and outside "Lohengrin" is being whistled by a number of "drunks." This is what we gather from the opening scene before a word has been spoken. We now infer much besides: there has been a party, and one of the men has just entered. He is evidently well-to-do. What else do we learn?

Why are these facts not *told?* How much of the play could be shown without the use of words? Pantomime, it need hardly be said, can be made to tell the most complicated stories. Could the playwright have accomplished more by this means than he has?

2. Turn to the opening dialogue. What was just hinted at in the business is now for the most part confirmed by the lines. The scene comes to an end after perhaps five minutes, counting

the pantomime. The curtain is lowered for a few seconds to denote the passage of a few hours.

Why the short scene? Would it have been possible (and advisable) to refer to this incident the next day, and begin the play with the entrance of Wallace?

3. Even snappy American farce-comedies have to have expositions, and in this play the exposition is especially long and complicated. It begins on p. 20 and runs for over ten pages: solid history, every line of it. How is it put over? And why is there so much of it? Does it drag? Why is Mrs. Gerrard an elderly lady? And not particularly attractive? What means are used to make Jackson's proposal to the unprepossessing lady at all plausible?

4. The first act, though it is almost altogether devoid of action, is first-rate comedy. Observe the skill, for instance, with which Jackson is shown first as a ruined man, then on the verge of marrying an unattractive woman for her money, and then—all within the space of a very short time—freed from financial responsibilities as he learns he is heir to his uncle's valuable chewing-gum factory. The most interesting complication is the problem before Jackson at the end of the act: having deliberately and before a witness promised to marry Mrs. Gerrard, he must face the issue, and yet his one reason for proposing to her is suddenly (by the hand of fate and Mr. Cohan) taken away. The problem, notice, does not bother Jackson, he has too much else to think of. There is still another matter to be settled, though this is of less importance: what is Jackson going to do about Pembroke's offer to buy the factory?

The plot is finally started, and we await the rise of the curtain on the second act.

5. George Cohan has evolved a particular style of unemphatic acting that seems to consist in avoiding every possible exhibition of strong feeling or passion. In most of his plays he has written the principal rôle for himself, and his "heroes" have naturally resembled George Cohan. "The Meanest Man in the World" was a triumph of skill in avoiding crises, and yet the play held the audience from first to last. "A Prince There Was" has a

first act in which Cohan holds the audience for nearly an hour while he acts the part of a man who is trying to decide what to do with himself. The audience received the impression of listening to a skilled teller of tales who was preparing the ground for the big situation. Cohan begins the story, then drops the thread of the narration, and takes up another, only to drop that as he approaches a climax.

This can be practiced only by a skilled craftsman. Great novelists have used the same method, notably Balzac in his tragic story of "Pierrette." It is not until you lay down the book that you realize it is almost entirely a study in preparations. The novelist wrote it from many different angles; it is as if he were never able to come to the point and relate the facts in ordered array. A still more striking instance of this indirect mode of telling a story is found in Joseph Conrad's "Chance," where the narrative is thrown about like a ball and told from at least half a dozen different points of view. Henry James was also a master of the indirect method.

Now, George Cohan, I have no doubt, has read little Balzac and probably less Conrad and James, but he understands the fine art of preparation. He appears to be playing with his audience, taking his time with the assurance born of certainty; he *can,* whenever he likes, thrill his audience, but he likes to keep them waiting. "Make 'em wait," was one of Wilkie Collins' maxims for the writing of a successful story. But even when he at last arrives at a dramatic crisis, Cohan keeps cool. Indeed, our pleasure in such a scene is heightened by the nonchalance of the principal character.

One of the minor crises in the succession of crises which constitutes the action of "Broadway Jones" is found in the third act, on p. 78. Jackson has at last found a motive for keeping the gum factory, and that is his affection (in a Cohan play we dare use no stronger word) for Josie. His speech to her begins in a matter-of-fact way, and ends thus:

What I've needed all along—what I've needed all along—was an incentive—that's what I've needed, an incentive, something to inspire me, something to spur me on—to bring me to a realization of—to bring me to a realization of—can you beat that? (*Takes written speech from his pocket and hands it to* Josie.) I knew that thing by heart when I left the hotel. Read the rest of it, will you? (Josie *laughs and starts reading it.*) Wallace wrote that. He thought I could learn it. Not a chance in the world!

The speech shows two things: first, that the playwright is able to preserve the unemphatic tone of the scene without retarding the development of the plot, and second, his extraordinary timidity when faced with the necessity of writing a sentimental scene. The Cohan plays are full of this sort of thing. They abound in situations that would not only permit, but actually require, the display of serious emotions. Never, however, does any man express by word or gesture any emotion for a woman stronger than what may be inferred by such remarks as "You're the little lady for me." The repression of emotion in the Cohan plays is doubtless the result of the author's own temperament; it is also due to the type of acting evolved by him; it is, finally, a reaction against the plays of earlier days in which actors and actresses made it a business to display their talents by wringing tears from the audience.

A certain kind of American and Englishman is never quite comfortable during the sentimental scenes in such plays as "Camille": he wishes that people would keep their feelings within bounds. This is precisely what Cohan has done. The moment anyone in his plays begins to get sentimental he is interrupted. (See the entrance of Mrs. Gerrard, or at least its announcement, on p. 96 of "Broadway Jones").

But does this mean that there is no emotional appeal in the Cohan plays? Love is not the only emotion; does Cohan offer alternatives? Most of the dramatic theorists agree that emotion lies at the root of all drama. George P. Baker (in *Dramatic Technique*) has said that it is the aim of drama to "move an audience to responsive emotion."

What emotional appeal do you find in "Broadway Jones"? What in "Seven Keys to Baldpate"?

6. Is "Broadway Jones" a farce? What impossible or highly improbable situations are we asked to accept?

7. Compare this play with such "Cohan type" plays as McHugh's "Officer 666," Montgomery's "Ready Money," and Roi Cooper Megrue and Walter Hackett's "It Pays to Advertise."

Booth Tarkington

Newton Booth Tarkington was born at Indianapolis in 1869. He grew up in his native town, went to "prep" school at Phillips Exeter, attended college first at Purdue in his own state, and later at Princeton. "After leaving Princeton," says Grant Overton (in *American Nights' Entertainment*), "he returned to Indianapolis and pursued the busy social life possible to a young man of the town while at the same time he read a good deal and tried various styles of writing." After a period abroad, he returned to Indianapolis, now his home.

Tarkington is best known as a novelist. His novels of midwestern life are notable contributions to our own peculiar brand of naturalism: his best novels, that is, like "The Magnificent Ambersons." In "Seventeen" and the lighter works he has achieved success in the depiction of young people, their sorrows and joys, above all their pathetic attempts to grow up.

But the theater has always attracted this enormously successful novelist, and for nearly twenty years he has sought—either alone or in collaboration—to win success in the theater. The truth of the matter seems to be that he never took playwriting seriously: he appears, in all his early plays, to have learned the tricks, but none of the art of playwriting. Says Clayton Hamilton: "Stimulated to renewed activity by the huge success of this initial effort [*The Man from Home*] Messrs. Tarkington and Wilson —if one may judge the matter solely on the basis of the evidence—proceeded, for several seasons, to regard the theater as a joke. At any rate, these exceptionally able novelists turned out a subsequent series of bad plays in quick succession and seemed to be surprised when these left-handed pieces went down, one by one, to speedy failure." But with "Clarence," in 1920, it was evident that Tarkington could write as distinguished a work for the stage as he ever wrote in narrative form, and the plays he has since written are, if not as well-sustained as "Clarence," at least skillful examples of playwriting.

PLAYS

"The Man from Home" [with Harry Leon Wilson] (1906)
"Cameo Kirby" [with Harry Leon Wilson] (1907)
"Your Humble Servant" [with Harry Leon Wilson] (1908)
"Springtime" [with Harry Leon Wilson] (1908)
"Getting a Polish" [with Harry Leon Wilson] (1909)
"Beauty and the Jacobin" (1912)
"Mister Antonio" [with Harry Leon Wilson] (1916)
"The Country Cousin" [with Julian Street] (1917)
"The Gibson Upright" [with Harry Leon Wilson] (1919)
"Up from Nowhere" [with Harry Leon Wilson] (1919)
"Clarence" (1919)
"Poldekin" (1920)
"The Wren" (1921)
"The Intimate Strangers" (1921)
"The Ghost Story" (1922)
"Magnolia" (1922)
"The Trysting Place" (1923)
"Tweedles" [with Harry Leon Wilson] (1923)
"Bimbo the Pirate" (1925)
"The Travellers" (1926)
"Station YYYY" (1926)
"Colonel Satan" (1931)
"How's Your Health?" [with Harry Leon Wilson] (1930)
"Help Each Other Club" (1934)

Editions (separate plays).—"The Man from Home" (N. Y. 1908); "Clarence" (N. Y. 1921); "The Gibson Upright" (Garden City, 1919); "The Country Cousin" (N. Y. 1921); "The Intimate Strangers" (N. Y. 1921); "The Wren" (N. Y. 1922); "Tweedles" (N. Y. 1924); "The Ghost Story" (Cincinnati, 1922); "The Trysting Place" (Cincinnati, 1923); "Beauty and the Jacobin" (N. Y. 1912); "Bimbo the Pirate" (N. Y. 1925); "The Travellers" (N. Y. 1927); "Station YYYY" (N. Y. 1927); "How's Your Health?" (N. Y. 1930); "Help Each Other Club" (N. Y. 1934).

Reprints in Collections and Anthologies.—"The Intimate Strangers" in Cohen's *Longer Plays by Modern Authors* (N. Y. 1922); "Beauty and the Jacobin" in Cohen's *One-Act Plays* (N. Y. 1921); "Monsieur Beaucaire" in *Dramas by Present-Day Writers* (N. Y. 1927).

REFERENCES

R. C. Holliday, *Booth Tarkington* (Garden City, 1918); D. Dickinson, *Booth Tarkington, A Gentleman from Indiana* (Garden City, no date); Grant Overton, *American Nights' Entertainment* (N. Y. 1923); Clayton Hamilton, *Seen on the Stage* (N. Y. 1920); W. P. Eaton, *At the New Theater and Others* (Boston, 1910); Alexander Woollcott, *Enchanted Aisles* (N. Y. 1924); Barrett H. Clark, *Œdipus or Pollyanna* (Seattle, 1927); A. H. Quinn, *A History of the American Drama, etc.* (N. Y. 1936); Burns Mantle, *American Playwrights of Today* (N. Y. 1930).

See also.—Tarkington's "A Prologue," to "Dulcy" (N. Y. 1921).

Clarence

Comedy in 4 acts (1919). Text: N. Y. 1921.

"Clarence" is (with one exception) the first play written by the author without the aid of a collaborator, and it is by all odds his best. In playwriting—as in many other things—it is by no means true that two minds are better than one. Tarkington and Wilson are both first-rate novelists, but the plays they have written together are, with perhaps one exception, in no way comparable to their novels. George Moore and W. B. Yeats once collaborated in writing a play: "Diarmuid and Grania" is one of their few works that has never even been printed.

"Clarence" is a true comedy of character. Tarkington has discarded most of the stage tricks he evidently thought indispensable in his early work, and produced a play that is well-written, amusing, and a real revelation of character.

1. Let me quote a passage from an article [3] (in dialogue) which I wrote when "Clarence" was first published. It raises two or three interesting points:

The Reviewer. . . . You saw the performance [of "Clarence"]?

The Friend. Yes, and very good entertainment it was. But nothing more.

The Reviewer. Nothing more! Good heavens, what do you want? Surely you are not one of those people who insist that a play shall be "as good as a sermon"? You don't expect to be uplifted and all that?

The Friend. No, but I demand something besides entertainment.

The Reviewer. It all depends on what you mean by "entertainment." "Hamlet" is "mere entertainment" for me; I am interested and excited by "Hamlet," but I surely don't go to see it in order to learn philosophy. "Clarence," I grant you, does not "entertain" me as does "Hamlet," but—like "Hamlet," remember—it shows human beings in interesting and critical situations. And that is why we go to the theater.

The Friend. Granted. But "Clarence" is trivial. It does not grapple with human problems; it fails even to reveal a pale re-

[3] "The Outlook," Oct. 4, 1922.

flection of life. The characters are puppets who do nothing, think nothing, and say nothing of exceptional significance.

THE REVIEWER. Look at "Clarence" as you would at a spectacle. Without unriddling the secret of life, Booth Tarkington has managed to throw together a number of genuinely American people. Isn't it interesting to see ourselves on the stage? . . . The humor is quaint, it is quiet, it is not forced; above all, it emerges from the situations and is not gratuitously grafted upon the play, as conventional humor is apt to be. . . . Tarkington gets his laughs, not by bright lines and last-moment inspirations, but by allowing his people to reveal themselves at the right time and under the right circumstances. . . .

The "Friend's" point of view is not uncommon, especially among people who are conversant either with the best European drama or the best American fiction. American audiences are not yet ready for the sort of "ingoing" studies of life which Henry James has, for example, effected in his finest stories. "Clarence" is, *of its kind,* a brilliant comedy of pure character; but there is little use in comparing it with the mature work of Hauptmann. The most we can say is that it is not so full of overtones, it is not so deeply impregnated with the sense of life, as certain other plays are.

"Of its kind." What is its "kind"? A comedy of character. Are not all comedies comedies of character? The more character the less plot is not an immutable rule, but it is generally a fact. In great comedy — Aristophanes, Molière, Shakespeare, Congreve, Sheridan—the plot is of little importance: it is at best a thread which binds the characters together. It may be conventional. It usually is. When we see a Molière play, it is not the story but the people that we remember: "The Merchant Gentleman" ("Le Bourgeois Gentilhomme") is pretty thin so far as the story is concerned; "The Misanthrope" has so little plot that for the life of me I cannot remember what it is. As for Sheridan, what does "The School for Scandal" amount to? And that great comedy of the mid-nineteenth century, "M. Poirier's Son-in-law," has rather less plot than most plays of its kind.

What makes "Clarence" a play? In what respects is it a character play?

2. Once again we may ask ourselves the old question about keeping secrets from the audience. In this play the identity of the chief character is a mystery: his very name is not revealed until the end. Another instance is found in the recent farce produced by George M. Cohan, "The Tavern," in which the hero turns out to be an escaped lunatic; this is not told until just before the last curtain.

If "The Tavern" (not published) is unknown to you, consider the question only in connection with the Tarkington play. Ought the secret to have been revealed earlier in the play? Suppose it had been?

3. In the introductory "Prologue" to "Dulcy," Tarkington writes:

> There is no "sex" in it, no "surge of passion," no approach of death, no "conflict of big primal forces," there is nothing in it imitated from the Russian, nor even from the Russian imitation of the French; moreover there is no author-person gesturing in any phrase of it: never does ink splatter in a word spoken by one of its people. It is just a brilliantly expressed gay thought about some kinds of human foolishness, and since a gay thought about anything can be as true as a gloomy thought about the same thing, and since the gay thought is worth ten times as much as the gloomy one . . . nothing could have been more certain . . . than that "Dulcy" would be called . . . etc.

Tarkington does not, it would seem, care much for Gorky or Shaw or Wedekind. He expresses the "happy" viewpoint that is characteristic of most healthy Americans. Grant Overton relates that in his novels, Tarkington sees no use in delving down into the sex-life of his characters.

We go, and ought to go, to the theater for pleasure, and if "sex" and "gloomy thoughts" do not give you pleasure, then you have only to keep away from theaters where the plays of Chekhov and O'Neill and Hauptmann are performed. Still, sex and gloomy thoughts are part of life, and any artist who makes up his mind to have absolutely nothing to do with them will (to say the least) find himself very limited in his subject-matter.

If this attitude were confined to Booth Tarkington alone, we might consider it simply as an idiosyncrasy. But the doctrine of "happiness" is essentially American. O. Henry rarely allowed the shadow of tragedy to obscure the silver lining of his clouds: but O. Henry must have known much about his world that never found its way into print; the "happy" stories of this genial and lovable writer will be forgotten when the "gloomy" Maupassant is as "alive" as he was a generation ago and is to-day.

The contention is not that there is no place for a "happy" literature, but that the "happy" writer closes his eyes to a large part of life.

Consider "Clarence"; does the author's optimistic view of life prevent his telling anything essential about his characters? Certainly, he *could* have revealed many "unpleasant" aspects of temperament and character in all the personages. Was it necessary, however?

Can you imagine "Clarence" written by Wedekind, or Chekhov, or Andreyev?

4. There are, of course, a number of younger American playwrights (many of them known either among the Little Theater groups or other more or less private ventures) who are well able to handle serious themes in a not altogether optimistic way. See, especially, Mark O'Dea's one-act plays under the title of *Red-Bud Women,* Bosworth Crocker's "Last Straw," Susan Glaspell's "Bernice," J. W. Rogers' "Judge Lynch," Allan Davis' "On Vengeance Height," and Paul Green's "The Hot Iron."

EUGENE O'NEILL

Eugene G. O'Neill, son of the actor James O'Neill, was born at New York in 1888. Before he began writing plays he spent some years at sea, and knocked about this country, consciously or unconsciously accumulating material he was to use later on. In 1909 he went with a mining engineer on a gold prospecting trip to Spanish Honduras. A few months later he was "invalided" home. On his recovery he entered the theatrical world as assistant manager of a traveling company, touring the East and the Middle West. His next venture was his first sea-voyage—"sixty-five days on a Norwegian barque, Boston to Buenos Ayres." The following passage is from a letter to me:[1] "In Argentina I worked at various occupations—in the draughting department of the Westinghouse Electrical Company, in a wool house of a packing plant at La Plata, in the office of the Singer Sewing Machine Company at Buenos Ayres. Followed another voyage at sea, tending mules on a cattle-steamer, Buenos Ayres to Durban, South Africa, and return. After that a lengthy period of complete destitution in Buenos Ayres—'on the beach'—terminated by my signing on as ordinary seaman on a British tramp steamer bound home for New York. My final experience at sea followed soon after this—able seaman on the American Line, New York-Southampton. The next winter I played a part in my father's version of 'Monte Cristo,' touring the Far West. Then I worked as reporter. . . . My health broke down, my lungs being affected, and I spent six months in a sanatorium thinking it over. It was in this enforced period of reflection that the urge to write first came to me. The next fall—I was twenty-four—I began my first play—'The Web.' In 1914-15 I was a student in Prof. Baker's English 47 at Harvard. The summer of 1916 I spent at Provincetown. It was during that summer the Provincetown Players, who have made the original productions of nearly all my short plays in New York, were first organized."

The short plays—produced first by the Provincetown troupe and later by the Washington Square Players—were followed by the long play, "Beyond the Horizon." For nearly twenty years O'Neill has steadily contributed to the theaters of the world a series of original works that have established him as the foremost playwright of our time. In 1936 he received a Nobel Prize.

---

[1] Printed in my book, *Eugene O'Neill.*

PLAYS

"The Web" (1914)
"Thirst" (1914)
"Recklessness" (1914)
"Warnings" (1914)
"Fog" (1914)
"Bound East for Cardiff" (1916)
"Before Breakfast" (1916)
"The Long Voyage Home" (1917)
"The Sniper" (1917)
"In the Zone" (1917)
"'Ile" (1917)
"Where the Cross Is Made" (1918)
"The Rope" (1918)
"The Moon of the Caribbees" (1918)
"The Dreamy Kid" (1919)
"Beyond the Horizon" (1920)
"Chris Christopherson" (1920)
"Exorcism" (1920)
"Gold" (1920)
"The Emperor Jones" (1920)
"Diff'rent" (1920)
"Anna Christie" (1921)
"The Straw" (1921)
"The First Man" (1922)
"The Hairy Ape" (1922)
"Welded" (1924)
"All God's Chillun Got Wings" (1924)
"The Ancient Mariner" (1924)
"Desire Under the Elms" (1924)
"The Fountain" (1925)
"The Great God Brown" (1925)
"Marco Millions" (1927)
"Lazarus Laughed" (1927)
"Strange Interlude" (1928)
"Dynamo" (1929)
"Mourning Becomes Electra" (1931)
"Ah, Wilderness!" (1933)
"Days Without End" (1934)

Editions.—*Thirst,* etc. (Boston, 1914) includes also "The Web," "Warnings," "Fog," and "Recklessness"; *The Moon of the Caribbees* (N. Y. 1919) includes also "Bound East for Cardiff," "The Long Voyage Home," "In the Zone," "'Ile," "Where the Cross Is Made," and "The Rope"; *The Emperor Jones, Diff'rent, The Straw* (N. Y. 1921); *The Hairy Ape, Anna Christie, The First Man* (N. Y. 1922); *All God's Chillun Got Wings and Welded* (N. Y. 1924); *Beyond the Horizon and Gold* (London, 1924). "The Moon of the Caribbees," etc., in Modern Library (N. Y. 1923). *The Complete Works,* 2 vols. (N. Y. 1924), include plays to and including "Desire Under the Elms," except first five, "The Ancient Mariner," "The Sniper," "Chris Christopherson," and "Exorcism." *The Plays,* 6 vols. N. Y. 1925-27), include titles in *Complete Works,* and plays up to 1927. *Nobel Prize Edition, Nine Plays* (N. Y. 1932) includes "The Emperor Jones," "The Hairy Ape," "All God's Chillun Got Wings," "Desire Under the Elms," "Marco Millions," "The Great God Brown," "Lazarus Laughed," "Strange Interlude," and "Mourning Becomes Electra."

Separate Plays.—"The Emperor Jones" (Cincinnati, 1921); "Beyond the Horizon" (N. Y. 1920); "Gold" (N. Y. 1920); "Desire Under the Elms" (N. Y. 1925); "Marco Millions" (N. Y. 1927); "Lazarus Laughed" (N. Y. 1927); "Strange Interlude" (N. Y. 1928); "Dynamo" (N. Y. 1929); "Mourning Becomes Electra" (N. Y. 1931); "Ah, Wilderness!" (N. Y. 1933); "Days Without End" (N. Y. 1934).

Reprints.—"Bound East for Cardiff" in *Provincetown Plays,* I (N. Y. 1916), and in collection, same title (Cincinnati, 1921); "Before Breakfast" in *Provincetown Plays,* III (N. Y. 1916), Shay's *Twenty Contemporary One-Act Plays* (Cincinnati, 1921), and *Treasury of Plays for Women*

(Boston, 1923); "In the Zone" in Mayorga's *Representative One-Act Plays* (Boston, 1937): "'Ile" in Shay and Loving's *Fifty Contemporary One-Act Plays* (Cincinnati, 1920), and in Leonard's *Atlantic Book of Modern Plays* (Boston, 1921); "The Emperor Jones" in Quinn's *Contemporary American Plays* (N. Y. 1923); and in Moses' *Representative American Dramas* (Boston, 1925). "Beyond the Horizon" in 3rd ed. Quinn's *Representative American Plays* (N. Y. 1925).

REFERENCES

Barrett H. Clark, *An Hour of American Drama* (Phila. 1930); *Eugene O'Neill* (N. Y. 1936); R. D. Skinner, *Eugene O'Neill, a Poet's Quest* (N. Y. 1935), and *Our Changing Theater* (N. Y. 1931); S. K. Winther, *Eugene O'Neill, a Critical Study* (N. Y. 1934); A. D. Mickle, *Studies on Six Plays of Eugene O'Neill* (N. Y. 1929); Burns Mantle, *American Playwrights of Today* (N. Y. 1929); A. H. Quinn, *A History of the American Drama, etc.* (N. Y. 1936); J. M. Brown, *Letters From Greenroom Ghosts* (N. Y. 1935); J. T. Shipley, *The Art of Eugene O'Neill* (Seattle, 1928); V. Geddes, *The Melodramadness of Eugene O'Neill* (Brookfield, Conn., 1934); Isaac Goldberg, *The Drama of Transition* (Cincinnati, 1922); Clayton Hamilton, *Seen on the Stage* (N. Y. 1920), and *Conversations on Contemporary Dramatists* (N. Y. 1924); Percival Wilde, *The Craftsmanship of the One-Act Play* (Boston, 1923); G. J. Nathan, *The World in Falseface* (N. Y. 1923); *Passing Judgments* (N. Y. 1935), and *The Intimate Notebooks* (N. Y. 1932); Kenneth Macgowan, *The Theater of To-morrow* (N. Y. 1921); T. H. Dickinson, *Playwrights of the New American Theater* (N. Y. 1925); Isaac Goldberg, *The Theater of George Jean Nathan* (N. Y. 1926).

THE EMPEROR JONES

Play in 8 scenes (1920). Texts: in *The Emperor Jones, Diff'rent, The Straw* (N. Y. 1921); separately (Cincinnati, 1921), and reprinted in Quinn's *Contemporary American Plays* (N. Y. 1923), and various later collections.

One of the most successful of O'Neill's plays. An effective stage-piece. It is one of his more or less fantastic plays, like "The Hairy Ape," in which he employs a sort of symbolism. By certain critics (notably Kenneth Macgowan) the new manner is called "Expressionistic." Whatever it may be called—I believe that "Expressionism" is only a neat phrase for a passing mode not radically different from any other—it is certain that "The Emperor Jones" is a distinguished example of a highly imaginative type of play.

1. O'Neill has this to say of Strindberg, but his words are applicable to his own theory of writing as well:

Yet it is only by means of some form of "super-naturalism" that we may express in the theater what we comprehend intuitively of that self-obsession which is the particular discount we moderns have to pay for the loan of life. The old "naturalism"—or "realism," if you prefer—no longer applies. It represents our fathers' daring aspirations toward self-recognition by holding the family kodak up to ill-nature. But to us their old audacity is blague, we have taken too many snapshots of each other in every graceless position. We have endured too much from the banality of surfaces. Strindberg knew and suffered with our struggle years before many of us were born. He expresses it by intensifying the method of his time and by foreshadowing both in content and form the methods to come. All that is enduring in what we loosely call "expressionism"—all that is artistically valid and sound theater—can be clearly tracked back through Wedekind to Strindberg's "The Dream Play," "There Are Crimes and Crimes," "The Spook Sonata," etc.

Since "The Emperor Jones" has been called an example of Expressionism, it may be interesting to learn what certain critics have to say of Expressionism.

Sheldon Cheney's *Primer of Modern Art,* Kenneth Macgowan's *Theater of To-morrow,* and Macgowan and Jones' *Continental Stagecraft,* contain clear statements of the theory. It is claimed that Expressionism is the negation of representation, the representation, that is, of *surfaces.* The old Romanticism, the old Naturalism, it seems, are no longer sufficient to convey the complexities of modern life. It is the business of the Expressionist to portray what O'Neill calls the "behind-life." What the Expressionist is seeking is what every serious artist has always sought—a more effective means of expressing life.

Expressionism is a German product: the word, at least, was coined in Germany some twenty years ago.[2] The point is not that the Expressionist drama is or is not a novel form, but what virtues does it possess? The plays of Georg Kaiser ("From Morn to Midnight" and "Gas" are accessible in translation)

---

[2] A number of the best-known German "Expressionists" have told me (1923) either that there was no such thing as "Expressionism," or that they did not know what it was.

have, indeed, shown the way toward a freer development of subject-matter than was possible in the theater of the past; Walter Hasenclever's "Beyond" is a brilliant technical feat in the expression of the "behind-life"; Paul Kornfeld and Rolf Lauckner, Arnolt Bronnen and Berthold Brecht have all sought to "express the inexpressible," but most of them have done little more than employ the "old" device of suggesting through implication, symbols, or by means of silence. Ernest Toller has written poetic and naturalistic plays, but has somehow earned the reputation of being an Expressionist playwright, chiefly because two or three plays have been produced "Expressionistically." "Expressionism," says Macgowan, "may be applied . . . to the whole tendency against Realism, just as Romanticism is applied to the whole tendency against Classicism." Younger dramatists, that is to say, dissatisfied with the formulas of Becque and Ibsen and their followers, have sought different means of expression: it is not enough to record what seems to be the actual words and acts of A; his thoughts, his subconscious soul, and his acts are *summarily* presented by means of a symbolic speech or act—aided by scenery or lighting —and a "new" method has been evolved.

But a close examination of such plays as Toller's "Masses and Mankind," Kaiser's "Gas," and O'Neill's "Emperor Jones" and "The Hairy Ape," will reveal nothing *essentially* different in technique from what is found in the work of many earlier plays.

This somewhat long detour is made largely because there is a great deal of confusion over the term Expressionism. Our own American imitations (Elmer Rice's "Adding Machine," J. H. Lawson's "Roger Bloomer" and Kaufman and Connelly's "Beggar on Horseback") are clever adaptations of the technique of Kaiser and Toller. O'Neill, on the other hand, seems to have written "The Emperor Jones" and "The Hairy Ape" in the form that best suited his requirements as an artist writing for the theater, and not to have bothered to imitate anyone.

In "The Emperor Jones," try to determine what elements in the action are "realistically" and what (shall we say?) "poetically" conceived. For instance, we should say that the first act of the "Doll's House" might be played, as it were, in life, in a thousand modern homes, whereas no one ever spoke as Romeo speaks to Juliet in the balcony scene. Here we see a vital difference in method.

2. This play comprises a number of "scenes," each scene is short, and each is laid in a different place. Is "The Emperor Jones" a "short" or "one-act" play, or a "full-length" play? Does it make any difference which it is?

3. The Austrian poet and dramatist, Hofmannsthal, writes (in an article on O'Neill):

> His first acts impress me as being the strongest; while the last, I shall not say go to pieces but, undoubtedly, are very much weaker than the others. The close of "The Hairy Ape," as well as that of "The Emperor Jones," seems to me to be too direct, too simple, too expected; it is a little disappointing to a European with his complex background, to see the arrow strike the target toward which he has watched it speeding all the while.

Just what does this mean? Why should the end of a play not be "direct," "simple," "expected"?

4. An interesting parallel is suggested elsewhere in Hofmannsthal's article:

> Where Mr. O'Neill reveals the first burst of his emotions in powerful, clean-cut pictures that seem almost like simple ballads in our [European] complex world, Hauptmann applies himself to making his characters plastic; he does this by throwing a half-light over his men and women and allowing the values to appear slowly, to emerge in new and true and wonderful aspects, gradually shown through an accumulation of tiny and seemingly unimportant incidents of everyday life. As a result, Hauptmann's plots do not progress with directness or force.

"Mechanical tension"—plot, that is—can be almost dispensed with, once the characters are firmly conceived and executed. The characters, in other words, carry the plot (what there is of it) and not the plot the characters.

Compare "The Emperor Jones" with Hauptmann's character-play "Drayman Henschel."

THE AMERICAN DRAMA, 1928-1938

This section, like that devoted to the *Drama of Soviet Russia,* is based, for reasons explained in the Preface, on a plan somewhat different from that used elsewhere in this book. It is our purpose here to sketch in the mere outlines of a decade of dramatic history, without concentrating on two or three playwrights, and suggest the reading of a number of plays. The method of study is indicated elsewhere in this volume.

The Playwrights

Since this book was last revised, in 1928, a few new writers have made their appearance, though none have written as continuously or as copiously as the outstanding professional playwrights of earlier decades. Of the men to whom chapters were devoted while they were still alive, Thomas is dead; Walter, MacKaye, Sheldon, and Tarkington have almost dropped out of sight, and Cohan writes very little. O'Neill, on the other hand, is extraordinarily active. The places of these writers as leading playwrights have been taken by Kaufman (and his collaborators), Anderson, Rice, Behrman, and two or three others. Somewhat less prolific during the past decade were Martin Flavin, Sidney Howard, Philip Barry, George Kelly, Robert E. Sherwood, Rachel Crothers, and Owen Davis. These have with more or less regularity gone on writing, adding to the contemporary theater, though not so frequently as in the 1920's, their competent and often brilliant plays to our stock of "dependable" products. Others, like Kenyon Nicholson, Samson Raphaelson, and Dan Totheroh, whose careers had scarcely begun ten years ago, have shown aspects of their talents which were hardly perceptible at that time.

In thus cataloguing certain of our playwrights and disposing of them in a line or two, I am aware that this method would be inadequate if it were not that this is only a brief supplementary section to a book which now covers about three-quarters of a century, and several countries besides our own. It is at most intended simply as a sketch in which an attempt is made to indicate a course of reading and study. But to continue:

Side by side with the more or less "regular" playwrights—the better-known men and women who supplied our theater with its popular and successful plays during the 20's—were a number of others who may be loosely termed "experimental"; these were not only the promising youngsters whose work was declared to be "worth watching," but, on occasion, such established writers as O'Neill and Rice who deliberately experimented with forms and ideas.

O'Neill himself, to a greater or less extent, has always experimented, but he stands apart from most of the others in that he has at the same time been wholly professional, and usually successful—from an economic viewpoint. Paul Green, though his work has usually attracted wide notice and critical respect and enthusiasm, is not yet a "regular," and the same thing is true of Lynn Riggs, Albert Bein, Virgil Geddes, George O'Neil, E. P. Conkle, and Leopold Atlas.

Due in part to the increasing economic difficulties in the way of producing plays on Broadway and keeping them going, these experimenters are neither so prolific nor so numerous as they were before 1930 or 1931; and the disappearance of institutions like the Provincetown Players, the Neighborhood Playhouse, the American Laboratory Theater, has made their problem more acute.

Between the appearance of the last edition of this book and the present, we have had several interesting experiments with Labor, People's, Leftist, Radical Theaters (to use loose and general terms), each of which has brought forth its quota of plays. Often crude and naïve, sometimes effective and convincing, the plays that were written for these theaters, or produced elsewhere but written to a certain extent under their influence, are on the whole evidence of a certain freshness and vitality of which the theater seems always to be in need.

Chief among these theaters (unfortunately, they have been unable to exist very long) were the Theater Union and The Group Theater. Though the latter was recently reorganized, it should be noted that it was never definitely "propaganda" in its aims. Many others have sprung up, one of which, The Actors' Repertory, is still in existence. Some of the playwrights who were associated with one or more of these or earlier similar groups, are Albert Maltz, George Sklar, Claire and Paul Sifton, Virgil Geddes, Paul Peters, Victor Wolfson, Clifford Odets, Francis Faragoh, Melvin Levy, and Irwin Shaw. Among the writers who began elsewhere but had one or more plays produced under their auspices, are John Howard Lawson, Paul Green, Albert Bein, Archibald MacLeish, Michael Blankfort, and Emjo Basshe.

It is now too soon to do more, in a work of this kind, than mention the extraordinary work accomplished by the Federal Theater. Readers are, however, referred to Willson Whitman's *Bread and Circuses,* a history of this movement.

To sum up, then: though our theater in 1938 is neither so varied, nor so prosperous, and possibly not so vigorous as it was ten years ago, the old dependables are writing and attracting audiences: O'Neill, Anderson, Howard, Kaufman and their contemporaries; and in spite of the virtual disappearance of the experimental theater, the experimental playwright is still here and there at work.

Typical American Plays

A Reading List

I offer a list of several typical American plays, produced and published since 1928. These should be regarded merely as reflecting in the aggregate the ideas and technique that have given to the American theater of the last ten years its characteristic qualities. Successful and unsuccessful, popular and unpopular, these are to be taken as a sort of cross section. Except where otherwise noted, each of these plays is published in the United States, in a separate edition, and most of them are now in print.

Eugene O'Neill, "Mourning Becomes Electra"
Paul Green, "The House of Connelly" (in volume with other plays, *The House of Connelly, etc.*)
Lynn Riggs, "Green Grow the Lilacs"
John Howard Lawson, "Marching Song"
John Wexley, "They Shall Not Die"
Moss Hart and George S. Kaufman, "Once in a Lifetime"
Maxwell Anderson, "Winterset"
Philip Barry, "Hotel Universe"
Martin Flavin, "The Criminal Code"
Susan Glaspell, "Alison's House"
Bella and Samuel Spewack, "Boy Meets Girl" (in volume *Boy Meets Girl and Spring Song*)
George Sklar and Albert Maltz, "Peace on Earth"
Irwin Shaw, "Bury the Dead"
Clifford Odets, "Awake and Sing"
Rachel Crothers, "Susan and God"
George O'Neil, "American Dream"
Dan Totheroh, "Distant Drums"
E. P. Conkle, "200 Were Chosen"
Robert Turney, "Daughters of Atreus"
Katharine Dayton and George S. Kaufman, "First Lady"
Leopold Atlas, "Wednesday's Child" (in volume *Wednesday's Child and House We Live In*)
Sidney Howard, "The Silver Cord"
Jack Kirkland, "Tobacco Road"
Kenyon Nicholson and Charles Robinson, "Sailor, Beware!"
Albert Bein, "Little Ol' Boy"
Samson Raphaelson, "Accent on Youth" (in volume *Accent on Youth and White Man*)
Sidney Kingsley, "Dead End"
Owen and Donald Davis, "Ethan Frome"
Paul Peters and George Sklar, "Stevedore"
Elmer Rice, "Street Scene"
Robert E. Sherwood, "The Petrified Forest"
S. N. Behrman, "Rain From Heaven"
Marc Connelly, "The Green Pastures"

It will be noticed that a fairly large number of these writers are new: Moss Hart, George Sklar, Albert Maltz, Irwin Shaw, E. P. Conkle, Clifford Odets, Robert Turney, Katharine Dayton, Leopold Atlas, Jack Kirkland, Sidney Kingsley, Albert Bein, George O'Neil and Paul Peters, had had nothing of theirs produced as early as 1928, and several had scarcely begun writing at that time. Messrs. Hart, Kingsley and Kirkland, and Miss Dayton, belong rather to the main current of our drama than in any of the special categories; the others were more or less directly connected with the "Radical" or other experiments in playwriting.

Though the Theater Union has ceased to function, there are clear indications of a reëmergence of labor theaters, but meantime the more gifted playwrights who were given a chance to try their plays out under its auspices are going on writing.

Turning now from the Leftist writers to those who had either little or nothing to do with the Leftist movement, we find Lynn Riggs, George O'Neil, Virgil Geddes, Dan Totheroh, E. P. Conkle, and Robert Turney, all men of distinctive talent of whom it may be said that they are striving to bring to the theater the color and shape and poetry of American life such as cannot be expressed in terms of photographic realism. As one of these writers once said, "Realism is just not good enough." They are, in varying degrees, the actual or potential poets who believe with Maxwell Anderson that great drama must in the last analysis be poetic drama. Others, too, particularly Paul Green, Eugene O'Neill, Anderson, and Marc Connelly have felt the same need and striven for beauty and magnificence of language.

The American writers of the 1930's have been faced with economic problems far more serious than existed during the period 1920 to 1930: it is today much more difficult to try out plays than it used to be, and a real danger exists that young playwrights, without sufficient income and without a proper chance to see their work produced, will be discouraged from even trying to write for the theater: several (Riggs, Totheroh, Odets, George O'Neil, and Wexley, to mention only a few) spend much of their time in Hollywood, while others (Maltz and Blankfort, for instance) have begun to turn to fiction.

Yet the American drama is very much alive: economic difficulties, the struggles of the various trade unions and similar organizations [1] to establish and maintain their respective rights,

[1] The Dramatists' Guild, a protective organization of great power, should be studied, particularly its minimum Basic Agreement or form contract. It is beyond doubt that the Guild has done much to enable playwrights to occupy a position of great importance in the "show business." The student is referred to the printed text of the Agreement.

the influence (good and evil) exerted by the picture industry, are all determining factors in the growth and development of our native drama, and time alone can show what will happen, yet at this moment we have a large number of competent, and a few extremely gifted writers, and a theater that is on the whole firmly established.

REFERENCES

Aside from the references already given elsewhere in this book, the following works (nearly all of which appeared during the past ten years) deal wholly or in part with the American drama of recent years. Works of a general character, with reading lists, as a rule, and further reference lists, are:

Arthur Hobson Quinn's *A History of the American Drama from the Civil War to the Present Day* (N. Y., revised 1936); Burns Mantle's *Best Plays* Series (N. Y., one volume annually), and the same author's *American Playwrights of Today* (N. Y. 1929); Margaret G. Mayorga's *Short History of the American Drama* (N. Y. 1932); Barrett H. Clark's *An Hour of American Drama* (Philadelphia, 1930); R. Dana Skinner's *Our Changing Theater* (N. Y. 1931); Herschel L. Bricker's *Our Theater Today* (N. Y. 1936); Ben Blake's (pamphlet) *The Awaking of the American Theater* (N. Y. 1935). Of somewhat more general character, including material on the business aspects of the theater and drama are Joseph Verner Reed's *The Curtain Falls* (N. Y. 1935); Lee Simonson's *The Stage is Set* (N. Y. 1933); Owen Davis' *I'd Like to do it Again* (N. Y. 1931); Helen Deutsch and Stella Hanau's *The Provincetown* (N. Y. 1931); Morton Eustis' *B'way Inc.* (N. Y. 1934); John Anderson's *Box Office* (N. Y. 1929); Eva Le Gallienne's *At 33* (N. Y. 1934); and Alfred L. Bernheim's *The Business of the Theater* (N. Y. 1932). Contemporary criticism and general articles may be consulted in the collected volumes of two critics who have issued several of these in book form. See George Jean Nathan's *Art of the Night* (N. Y. 1928), *The Testament of a Critic* (N. Y. 1931), *Passing Judgments* (N. Y. 1935), and *The Theater of the Moment* (N. Y. 1936); and John Mason Brown's *The Modern Theater in Revolt* (N. Y. 1929) and *Upstage* (N. Y. 1930).

Valuable material is also to be found in several anthologies:

Allan G. Halline's *American Plays* (N. Y. 1935); Arthur Hobson Quinn's *Representative American Plays* (N. Y., revised 1930); Thomas H. Dickinson's *Chief Contemporary Dramatists,* 3rd series (Boston, 1932); S. Marion Tucker's *Modern American and British Plays* (N. Y. 1931); Richard A. Cordell's *Representative Modern Plays, British and American* (N. Y. 1929); Frank W. Chandler and Richard A. Cordell's *Twentieth Century Plays, American* (N. Y. 1934); and Montrose J. Moses' *Representative American Dramas* (Boston, revised 1933).

THE YIDDISH DRAMA

THE YIDDISH DRAMA

The Yiddish drama, like Yiddish literature, is a new growth. It is scarcely fifty years old, and most of the initiators are alive, living and working in the United States.

The Jewish Art Theater of New York was founded only in 1919, though before that time Yiddish plays were written and performed. Abraham Goldfaden is "considered the founder of the Yiddish theater." His work covers the period of 1887 to about 1910. His contemporaries, I. Shaikewitz, J. Lateiner, and M. Hurwitch—most of them adapters of European plays—were "practised in their craft" before they came to America. It was due to Jacob Gordin, however (1853-1909), that the Yiddish drama began to assume a more dignified form. Coming to America from Russia in 1892, he "took the Yiddish drama . . . from the realm of the preposterous and put a living soul into it." Other playwrights followed: S. Anski, Leon Kobrin, Z. Levin, I. L. Perez, Sholom Aleikhem, David Pinski, Sholom Asch, Perez Hirschbein; and, latest of all, Fishel Bimko, and H. Leivik, author of "Rags," "Different," and "Beggars."

The best account of the Yiddish drama is found in Isaac Goldberg's *Drama of Transition.* Dr. Goldberg has made known to readers of English not only the historical background, but the best Yiddish plays themselves.

DAVID PINSKI

David Pinski was born at Mobilov, in Russia, in 1872. At an early age he went to Moscow, but was forced to leave in 1892 when the Jews were expelled. "Proceeding to Warsaw," says Dr. Goldberg, "he began to write the stories of proletarian life in the Russian ghetto, which first brought him recognition. Pinski soon went to Berlin for study. In 1899 he came to New York to assume the duties of literary editor upon a Socialist weekly. He has also been a student at Columbia University."

His plays have been frequently performed, both abroad and in the United States. "The Treasure" was produced in Berlin by Reinhardt in 1910.

"Among contemporary Jewish playwrights David Pinski is remarkable for this: that he combines with his sensitive and intimate knowledge of his people's life a thorough familiarity with the dominant forms and moods of western literature."

Pinski has, naturally, been influenced by life and ideas both abroad and in America, and by the theatrical forms in use the world over. He has, however, consistently portrayed the Jews, both the figures of the past and the common people of the present. His work is known in every land where his language is spoken.

PLAYS

"Sufferings" (1899)
"Isaac Sheftel" (1904)
"The Mother" (1905)
"Forgotten Souls" (1905)
"The Zwie Family" (1905)
"The Treasure" (1907)
"The Eternal Jew" (1907)
"With Banners of Victory" (1909)
"Gabriel and the Women" (1909)
"Jacob the Blacksmith" (1909)
"The Dumb Messiah" (1912)
"Mountain Climbers" (1912)
"A Dollar!" (1913)
"Conscience" (1913)
"To Each Man His Own God" (1913)
"Bathsheba" (1913)
"Michal" (1914)
"Abigail" (1914)
"In the Harem" (1914)
"Diplomacy" (1915)
"Abishag" (1915)
"Mary Magdalen" (1915)
"Better Unborn" (1915)
"Little Heroes" (1916)
"Nina Marden's Loves" (1917)
"The Beautiful Nun" (1918)
"Professor Brenner" (1918)
"The Phonograph" (1918)
"Love's Devious Paths" (1918)
"The Inventor and the King's Daughter" (1918)
"The God of the Newly-Rich Wool Merchant" (1918)
"Adonijah" (1919)
"The Cripples" (1919)
"Poland—1919" (1919)
"The Final Balance" (1923)
"Three" (1924)
"The Seed of the Righteous" (1924)
"Sorrows" (1932)
"Laid Off" (1932)

Editions.—Three Plays, trans., with preface, by Isaac Goldberg (N. Y. 1918), includes "Isaac Sheftel," "The Last Jew" [*i.e.* "The Zwie Family"], and "The Dumb Messiah"; *Ten Plays,* trans. by Isaac Goldberg (N. Y. 1920), includes "The Phonograph," "The God of the Newly-Rich Wool Merchant," "A Dollar!" "The Cripples," "The Inventor and the King's Daughter," "Diplomacy," "Little Heroes," "The Beautiful Nun," "Poland—1919" and "The Stranger" [*i.e.* "The Eternal Jew"]; *Six Plays of the Yiddish Theater,* trans., with biographical notes, by Isaac Goldberg (Boston, 1916), includes "Abigail" and "Forgotten Souls"; second series, trans. by the same (Boston, 1918), includes

"Little Heroes" and "The Stranger"; *King David and His Wives,* trans. by Isaac Goldberg (N. Y. 1923), includes "Michal," "Abigail," "Bathsheba," "In the Harem," and "Abishag"; "Sorrows" in *Nine One-Act Plays From the Yiddish* (Boston, 1932).

Separate Editions.—"The Treasure," trans., with introduction, by Ludwig Lewisohn (N. Y. 1915); "Michal" (Goldberg translation, *Stratford Journal,* Boston, 1918); "A Dollar," "Cripples," and "Forgotten Souls," trans. by I. Goldberg, separately (N. Y. n. d.).

Reprints in Collections and Anthologies.—"Forgotten Souls" (Goldberg translation) in Shay and Loving's *Fifty Contemporary One-Act Plays* (Cincinnati, 1920); "A Dollar!" (Goldberg translation) in Lewis' *Contemporary One-Act Plays* (N. Y. 1922); "Laid Off" in *One-Act Plays for Stage and Study* (N. Y. 1932).

References

Leo Wiener, *A History of Yiddish Literature in the Nineteenth Century* (N. Y. 1899); Isaac Goldberg, *The Drama of Transition* (Cincinnati, 1922); *The Cambridge History of American Literature,* Vol. IV, for bibliographies (N. Y. 1921); Oliver M. Sayler, *Our American Theater* (N. Y. 1923).

The Treasure

Drama in 4 acts (1907). Text: translation by Ludwig Lewisohn (N. Y. 1915).

"The Treasure," though written in America, is built upon European models. We are told that Pinski spent some time in Berlin, "where he made a study of German literature and philosophy and established friendships with the leading literary and dramatic spirits of the country." His first important play, "Isaac Sheftel," was conceived "under the influence of the Naturalists." And yet the vital elements of the play lie elsewhere than in the mere form. "The Treasure" is a drama not only of the Jewish people; it is universal.

1. The play offers, on the technical side, a fascinating study of method. The means by which the playwright exhibits his characters may be (more or less accurately) described as Naturalistic. People act and speak more like the people we know than do Antony and Cleopatra, or Romeo and Juliet. And yet, out of a situation built up by realistic details, there emerges a deeply moving spirit of poetry.

As a matter of fact, there is very little *essential* difference between one formula and another, between one medium and another: the Naturalistic Zola, believing he had come closer to the facts of everyday life than the Romantic George Sand, was trifling with terms. The "slice of life" theory is as deceptive as the grandiose theories of Victor Hugo. Most of these theorists confounded subject with conception and treatment. The theme of "The Treasure" is anything you choose to call it; what matters is the effect of the play. A "slice of life," treated by Hauptmann, is bound to be more significant, more nearly universal, than the most romantic plot treated by Sudermann.

Professor George P. Baker, writing about "The Treasure," says:

> "The Treasure" is a comedy—or is it a tragedy? . . . It is a play which oddly combines intense realism of details with broad, imaginative sweep. Though there is an admitted general dramatic principle that to mingle the realism of every day with the supernatural is dangerous except in the hands of a master, so perfectly does Mr. Pinski use the two . . . that I more than suspect he is a master.

Why the doubt as to what kind of play "The Treasure" is? What of the mingling of realism and the supernatural? We find it in several modern plays, including Molnar's "Liliom," and Barrie's "Mary Rose." In what others?

2. One critic suggests that there is perhaps a little too much talk in the play. Do you think so? What could be eliminated?

3. The play closes with a sort of epilogue (beginning on p. 191), in which the dead, in "shrouds and praying shawls appear singly and in groups amid the graves. They whisper and breathe their words." Can you give a reason for this scene? There is no doubt the dramatist wished to drive home his "moral" (see p. 194), but are there not other reasons?

Is the close satisfactory? Does it form a convincing conclusion to the story as unfolded in the play? It is, of course, not the artist's function to answer riddles—even when he makes them; it is enough to have stated the proposition correctly and beautifully, but his work must satisfy.

Compare the close of "The Treasure" with that of Andreyev's "Anathema."

Perez Hirschbein

Perez Hirschbein was born in Russia in 1880. He was first heard of as a writer of plays in the Hebrew language, but he soon joined the group of literary men who made Yiddish a literary idiom. Like Pinski and nearly all the Yiddish dramatists, he lives in America, but unlike the others he is exclusively a dramatist. Not that all his plays are primarily adapted to theatrical production: it is only such works as "The Haunted Inn," "A Forsaken Nook" and some of the one-acters that have met with unqualified success on the boards.

"He has been much influenced," says Dr. Goldberg, "by the French symbolists and mystics, as is attested by the dialogue of his plays and the beauty of his prose-poems. In fact, some of his one-act plays incline so strongly to the mystic that the very element which adds to them, perhaps, as poetry, injures them as actable drama."

Plays

"Down Hill" (1904)
"Where Life Languishes" (1904)
"Carrion" (1905)
"Lonely Worlds" (1905)
"Grave Blossoms" (1906)
"Across the Stream" (1906)
"Between Day and Night" (1906)
"The Pledge" (1907)
"In the Dark" (1907)
"At the Cross-Roads" (1907)
"The Earth" (1907)
"Jael" (1908)
"The Last" (1910)
"On the Verge" (1910)
"The Haunted Inn" (1911)
"The Child of the World" (1913)
"A Forsaken Nook" (1913)
"Sparks" (1913)
"Elijah the Prophet" (1914)
"Raisins and Almonds" (1915)
"On the Threshold" (1915)
"Bebele" (1915)
"A Storm" (1915)
"A Life for a Life" (1915)
"The Blacksmith's Daughters" (1915)
"Green Fields" (1916)

Editions (separate plays).—"The Haunted Inn," trans., with preface, by Isaac Goldberg (Boston, 1921).

Reprints in Collections and Anthologies.—"In the Dark," trans. by Isaac Goldberg in *Six Plays of the Yiddish Theater* (Boston, 1916); "On the Threshold," by the same in *Six Plays of the Yiddish Theater,*

2nd series (Boston, 1918); "The Stranger" [*i.e.* "Raisins and Almonds"], "The Snowstorm" [*i.e.* "A Storm"], and "When the Dew Falleth," by Etta Block in *One-Act Plays from the Yiddish* (Cincinnati, 1923).

References

Isaac Goldberg, *The Drama of Transition* (Cincinnati, 1922), and prefaces of all the Goldberg translations; Oliver M. Sayler, *Our American Theater* (N. Y. 1923).

The Haunted Inn

Drama in 4 acts (1911). Text: translation by Isaac Goldberg (Boston, 1921).

"It was with 'The Haunted Inn' . . . that the Jewish Art Theater of New York, under the direction of Mr. Emanuel Reicher, inaugurated its career in the autumn of 1919; by virtue of the striking production and the remarkable acting of Mr. J. Ben-Ami in the rôle of Itsik, the drama was soon the talk not only of the Yiddish reviewers, but also of the critics of the English press. . . ." (Isaac Goldberg.) This is the most successful and ambitious of Hirschbein's many plays.

1. Whatever else "The Haunted Inn" may be, it is primarily a story of love and passion. Simple in the extreme, it is full of a poetic brooding, suggestive of subconscious emotions and ideas, yet it holds us first of all because it relates a tense story. We are chiefly interested to know precisely what Meta and Itsik will do under the stress of circumstances.

The atmosphere is created early in the play. Atmosphere, as a matter of fact, is being created straight through to the end. The exposition begins at once, when Shakhne (p. 2) mentions the engagement party. There is no time lost and by the time the act is well under way, we know practically everything we need to know. In order that the play may be convincing we must see and know why Meta becomes engaged to Leibush and not to Itsik. The play is written not for Gentiles but for orthodox Jews who know how marriages are arranged, not to suit the convenience of the children, but that of the parents. This much is taken for granted, particularly when Meta says:

"I'm your only daughter. Then perhaps you understand that things will be best as you wish."

Does this make any difference? Are we ready to accept the facts as Meta does, or do we blame her for not protesting?

2. The inn is, of course, symbolic. "It is," says the translator, "a symbol of parental restraint and in the end it is the symbol itself which overpowers the will both of the daughter and the father, each seeking an escape from the obsessions of the symbol." All symbolism, when rightly employed, serves to express what cannot be expressed without it. The dramatist has used the inn in order to create striking dramatic effects, but is it necessary to turn the building into a symbol? Would not the play be as clear and as dramatic without the introduction of symbolism?

3. The second act is well executed. It rises to a thrilling climax and leaves us expectant. The wedding celebration is shown in detail in order to furnish a dramatic contrast to what we know to be the feelings of the two persons with whom we sympathize. The act arouses mixed emotions: we know that something is going to happen, and we are sure that this will precipitate trouble, and perhaps tragedy. The suspense begins at the entrance of Itsik: "PEASANT FOLK, *dressed in their best, come in. Among them is* ITSIK. *His bearing is suspicious. He plainly avoids encountering* BENDET. *The playing ceases.*"

Meta, far from allaying our suspicions, arouses them by her quiet manner: "Papa, why do you keep speaking to Itsik in such an angry voice? To-day is my wedding day. I want you to make up with him." Itsik stands to one side, which is the reason why Bendet speaks to him: "And you, Itsik, what do you mean by standing there like a corpse in the corner? Let bygones be bygones. Don't harbor any feelings against Papa Bendet. . . ." Itsik then asks Meta whether she will drink a health with him, and Meta *"makes no reply. Looks around for help in the matter."* Not long after, Meta begins to dance and Itsik follows her. A great deal is here left to the actors, and no doubt the dance is very dramatic. Actors who could not make this effective have no business playing such rôles. Then again another dance: *"No one notices that* Itsik *and* Meta *are now dancing together, and that they draw nearer and nearer to the door, through which they both disappear into the night."*

Though practically nothing has been said by the lovers, they have drawn close to each other during the last part of the act. As a matter of fact, they have first of all practically no opportunity of conversing; and, second, their not conversing serves only to intensify our conviction that they communicate otherwise than by words. Every good actor knows that often there is far more eloquence in a pause than in a magnificent speech. Maeterlinck dramatized silence; the German Expressionists have suggested silences by means of a peculiar sort of stenographic speech. In one of Eugene O'Neill's late plays, "Welded," the last act is rendered intelligible and dramatic by the silences. What is said in words is intended to convey practically nothing, while the pauses render the act significant. It was probably due to a misunderstanding of this that the play failed.

In "The Haunted Inn," we, the audience, supply what the dramatist omitted, and our pleasure is the greater because we feel we are actively coöperating in the action.

How far any dramatist may go in leaving such points to the intelligence of his actors and the imagination of the audience, cannot be determined. It depends largely on the way the play is written, and, of course, on the imaginative powers of the actors.

THE DRAMA OF SOVIET RUSSIA

The most casual investigation of the plays written in Russia during the past twenty years will show that the theater in that country underwent a change almost as profound as that which marked off the new political structure from the old. True, certain theaters, like the Moscow Art Theater and two or three others, were taken over and more or less quickly induced to conform to the political exigencies and ideas of the time. This change was in certain respects not so revolutionary as it would have been if the playwright had occupied in Russia the position of authority and importance now occupied by the playwright in America; but in Russia (with very few exceptions), both a short time before the Revolution and ever since, the playwright has been largely under the domination of the director, not to mention the government censor. Today he is subjected to the double authority of the director and the State. No matter how orthodox he may be, no matter how disinclined to assert his intellectual independence of the theory and practice of Communism, granted he has any, he is a servant, and not a leader. It is no doubt true that few if any playwrights today have any desire to question the fundamental theories of their totalitarian state, but the fact remains that if they had they would be unable to do so.

There is, of course, room for argument on this point, and we must realize that where the sources of information are rigidly controlled by the State, we too in the final analysis are greatly hampered in reaching final conclusions about the Russian drama and those who make it.

There seems, however, to be little or no doubt that where the State is supreme, and holds such absolute power as it holds in present-day Russia, the artist is not free, as we understand that word. The wonder is not that there should be so many interesting plays as that writers of any talent or originality can be found to turn them out at all. In Germany and Italy it seems (and we must qualify our opinions in this way because we lack untainted information) that either the original writers have been exiled or silenced, or simply that they don't exist there.

Our concern here is with the plays as we have them in English translations, and since there are not many I am suggesting that all of them be read and studied. But in doing this, the student is urged to read at least some of the books on the Soviet Theater, because without the background as furnished there, the drama of recent times in Russia is scarcely understandable. It will at once become clear that in the case of every one of these plays the writer is dramatizing an idea, pleading on behalf of some aspect of that particular brand of Communism that, theoretically at least, is now used by the present Russian government. The authors of these plays are either passionately "sold" on the idea, or are sufficiently skilled to make it seem so. It is not unfair to assume that the author of "Tempo" cares far more about increasing the efficiency of factory workers than he does about revealing the secret springs of human motive.

And yet—the Russian theater is a living thing. It is part and parcel of Russian life: it takes the place there of our community clubs, our libraries, our political and civic meetings, our newspapers, and a good deal besides. As contrasted with a good deal of our own drama, the Russian is strikingly contemporary; it appeals, evidently, to farmers and mechanics, officials and artists; if it is a class theater (which it is) it is one that appeals to an immensely large class. It is popular in the best sense. But so closely is it linked with the State, its wishes and orders and compulsions, and so closely knit into the very fiber of the physical theater, dominated by the director, that the text itself is often felt to be incomplete, which it is.

No matter how valuable the Russian theater may be to the party that now controls the country; no matter how wide its appeal may be, the fact remains that the plays, as we know them, are scarcely more than curious phenomena. No play has appeared that can approach, as a work of art, "The Cherry Orchard" or "The Lower Depths"; no Chekhov or Gorky has risen in Soviet Russia, and in my private opinion, none can arise. The fact that Gorky was allowed to return to Russia during the last years of his life, does not affect the argument: his characteristic work was done long before, and his "Soviet" plays are not important.

Nevertheless, let us examine the Soviet plays. Here is a list of all the outstanding works now available in English translations:

Vsevolod Ivanov, "Armored Train 14-69"
Valentine Katayev, "Squaring the Circle"
Vladimir Kirchon, "Red Rust"
V. V. Mayakovsky, "Mystery-Bouffe"
S. Tretiakov, "Roar China"

Collections.—*Six Soviet Plays* includes Alexander Afinogenyev's "Fear"; Michael Bulgakov's "Days of the Turbins"; Valentine Katayev's "Squaring the Circle"; Vladimir Kirchon's "Bread"; Nikolai Pogodin's "Tempo"; and Anatol Glebov's "Inga."

Four Soviet Plays includes Nikolai Pogodin's "Aristocrats"; Ivan Kocherga's "Masters of Time"; Maxim Gorky's "Yegor Bulichov and Others"; and V. Vishnevsky's "An Optimistic Tragedy."

References.—Magazines and newspapers (especially *Theatre Arts Monthly, New Theater, New Theater and Film,* and *Theater Workshop*) are among the best sources on particular plays, theaters, and playwrights; but there are a few books of outstanding interest. For the earlier period, see Huntley Carter's two books, *The New Theater and Cinema of Soviet Russia,* and *The New Spirit in the Russian Theater.*

Two later books are probably better for the student, first because they are recent, and second because each of them offers a somewhat more reasoned analysis. P. A. Markov's *The Soviet Theater* is informative, particularly since it is written by an official of the Soviet government, but it naturally sets forth, without a shadow of what most of us would consider criticism, the State's viewpoint. Norris Houghton's *Moscow Rehearsals* is a far better book. Although it is on the whole sympathetic toward the Russian idea, it is by no means uncritical.

BIBLIOGRAPHIES

I

GENERAL WORKS ON THE MODERN DRAMA

(Including general works in which the modern drama is considered)

JOHN ANDERSON, *Box Office* (N. Y. 1929).
CHARLTON ANDREWS, *The Drama of Today* (Philadelphia, 1913).
ALFRED BATES [ed.], *The Drama. Its History, Literature and Influence on Civilisation,* 22 vols. (London, 1903-1904).
MARTHA FLETCHER BELLINGER, *A Short History of the Drama* (N. Y. 1927).
IVOR BROWN, *Parties of the Play* (London, 1928).
GILBERT CANNAN, *The Joy of the Theater* (N. Y. 1913).
HUNTLEY CARTER, *The New Spirit in Drama and Art* (N. Y. 1912); *The New Spirit in the European Theater* (N. Y. 1926).
F. W. CHANDLER, *Aspects of Modern Drama* (N. Y. 1914).
BARRETT H. CLARK, *The Modern Drama* (pamphlet, Chicago, 1927).
THOMAS H. DICKINSON, *An Outline of Contemporary Drama* (Boston, 1927).
——— and others, *The Theater in a Changing Europe* (N. Y. 1937).
ELIZABETH DREW, *Discovering Drama* (N. Y. 1937).
ASHLEY DUKES, *Drama* (N. Y. 1926); *Modern Dramatists* (Chicago, 1912); *The Youngest Drama* (Chicago, 1924).
ISAAC GOLDBERG, *The Drama of Transition* (Cincinnati, 1922).
EMMA GOLDMAN, *The Social Significance of the Modern Drama* (Boston, 1914).
E. E. HALE, JR., *Dramatists of To-day* (N. Y. 1905).
CLAYTON HAMILTON, *Conversations on Contemporary Dramatists* (N. Y. 1924).
ARCHIBALD HENDERSON, *The Changing Drama* (Cincinnati, 1919); *European Dramatists* (N. Y. 1926).
STORM JAMESON, *The Modern Drama in Europe* (N. Y. 1920).
ELEANOR JOURDAIN, *The Drama in Europe* (N. Y. 1924).

Ludwig Lewisohn, *The Modern Drama* (N. Y. 1915).
J. W. Marriott, *Modern Drama* (London, no date).
Brander Matthews, *The Development of the Drama* (N. Y. 1903); *A Study of the Drama* (Boston, 1910).
Nellie Burget Miller, *The Living Drama* (N. Y. 1924).
Fred D. Millett, *The Art of the Drama* (N. Y. 1935).
Malcolm Morley, *The Theater* (London, 1935).
H. K. Motherwell, *The Theater of To-day* (N. Y. 1927).
C. K. Munro, *Watching a Play* (London, 1933).
William Lyon Phelps, *The Twentieth Century Theater* (N. Y. 1918); *Essays on Modern Dramatists* (N. Y. 1921).
R. Dana Skinner, *Our Changing Theater* (N. Y. 1931).
Thomas Wood Stevens, *The Theater, From Athens to Broadway* (N. Y. 1933).
L. A. G. Strong, *Common Sense About the Drama* (N. Y. 1937).
Donald Clive Stuart, *The Development of Dramatic Art* (N. Y. 1928).
Frank Vernon, *The Twentieth Century Theater* (Boston, 1924).
N. S. Wilson, *European Drama* (London, 1937).

Technique and Theory

Adult Education Committee, *The Drama in Adult Education* (London, 1926).
James Agate, *Playgoing* (N. Y. 1927).
Charlton Andrews, *The Technique of Playmaking* (Springfield, Mass., 1915).
Frank Archer, *How to Write a Good Play* (London, no date).
William Archer, *Playmaking* (Boston, 1912).
Matthew Arnold, *Letters of an Old Playgoer* (N. Y. 1919).
Charles Aubert, *The Art of Pantomime,* trans. by Edith Sears (N. Y. 1927).
Emile Augier, and Others, *How to Write a Play,* trans. by D. Miles (N. Y. 1916).
Stephen F. Austin, *The Principles of Drama-Therapy* (N. Y. 1917).
George P. Baker, *Dramatic Technique* (Boston, 1919).
Alexander Bakshy, *The Theater Unbound* (London, 1924).
Ramsden Balmforth, *The Ethical and Religious Value of the Drama* (N. Y. 1926).
Herschel L. Bricker [ed.], *Our Theater Today* (N. Y. 1936).

JOHN MASON BROWN, *The Modern Theater in Revolt* (N. Y. 1929); *Upstage* (N. Y. 1930); *Letters From Greenroom Ghosts* (N. Y. 1934); *The Art of Playgoing* (N. Y. 1936).

F. BRUNETIÈRE, *The Law of the Drama* (N. Y. 1914).

RICHARD BURTON, *How to See a Play* (N. Y. 1914).

C. H. CAFFIN, *The Appreciation of the Drama* (N. Y. 1908).

MARTHA CANDLER, *Drama in Religious Service* (N. Y. 1922).

GILBERT CANNAN, *The Joy of the Theater* (N. Y. 1913).

FANNY CANNON, *Writing and Selling a Play* (N. Y. 1915).

CAREL CAPEK, *How a Play is Produced* (London, 1928).

BARRETT H. CLARK, *European Theories of the Drama* (N. Y. 1929); *Modern Drama* (Chicago, 1927); *Œdipus or Pollyana* (Seattle, 1927).

P. J. COOKE, *The Handbook of the Drama* (London, no date).

W. L. COURTNEY, *The Idea of Tragedy* (N. Y. 1900); *Old Saws and Modern Instances* (N. Y. no date).

ELNORA WHITMAN CURTIS, *The Dramatic Instinct in Education* (Boston, 1914).

W. MACNEILE DIXON, *Tragedy* (London, 1924).

BONAMY DOBREE, *Timotheus: The Future of the Theater* (N. Y. 1925).

JOHN DRINKWATER, *The Gentle Art of Theater-going* (Boston, 1927); *Prose Papers* (London, 1917).

LORD DUNSANY, *Nowadays* (Boston, 1918).

ST. JOHN ERVINE, *How to Write a Play* (N. Y. 1928).

C. C. EVERETT, *Poetry, Comedy, and Duty* (N. Y. 1890).

NICOLAS EVREINOFF, *The Theater in Life*, trans. by A. I. Nazaroff (N. Y. 1927).

GUSTAV FREYTAG, *The Technique of the Drama*, trans. by E. J. MacEwan (Chicago, 1895).

PROSSER HALL FRYE, *Romance and Tragedy* (Boston, 1922).

THOMAS WALTON GALLOWAY, *The Dramatic Instinct in Religious Education* (Boston, 1922).

JOHN GALSWORTHY, *Another Sheaf* (N. Y. 1919); *The Inn of Tranquillity* (N. Y. 1912).

ROBT. I. GANNON, *The Technique of the One-Act Play* (N. Y. 1925).

VIRGIL GEDDES, *Beyond Tragedy* (Seattle, 1930).

W. L. GEORGE, *Dramatic Actualities* (London, 1914).

W. S. GILBERT, *A Stage Play* (N. Y. 1916).

HALCOTT GLOVER, *Drama and Mankind* (London, 1923).

H. GRANVILLE-BARKER, *The Exemplary Theater* (Boston, 1922); *On Dramatic Method* (London, 1931).

TERENCE GRAY, *Dance-Drama* (Cambridge, England, 1926).

SYDNEY GRUNDY, *The Play of the Future* (London, 1914).

CLAYTON HAMILTON, *The Theory of the Theater* (N. Y. 1910); *Studies in Stagecraft* (N. Y. 1914); *Problems of the Playwright* (N. Y. 1917); *Seen on the Stage* (N. Y. 1920); *So You're Writing a Play* (Boston, 1935).

ARCHIBALD HENDERSON, *The Changing Drama* (Cincinnati, 1919).

ALFRED HENNEQUIN, *The Art of Playwriting* (Boston, 1890).

H. N. HILLEBRAND, *Writing the One-Act Play* (N. Y. 1925).

E. HILLIARD, etc., *Amateur and Educational Dramatics* (N. Y. 1917).

BRONSON HOWARD, *The Autobiography of a Play* (N. Y. 1914).

JAY B. HUBBELL and JOHN O. BEATY, *An Introduction to Drama* (N. Y. 1927).

ELIZABETH R. HUNT, *The Play of To-day* (N. Y. 1913).

EDITH J. R. ISAACS [ed.], *Theater, etc.* (Boston, 1927).

S. E. JELIFF and L. BRINK, *Psychoanalysis and the Drama* (Washington, 1922).

HENRY ARTHUR JONES, *The Renascence of the English Drama* (N. Y. 1895); *The Foundations of a National Drama* (N. Y. 1913); *The Theater of Ideas* [Preface] (N. Y. 1915).

MRS. KENDAL, *Dramatic Opinions* (Boston, 1890).

ARTHUR E. KROWS, *Playwriting for Profit* (N. Y. 1927).

JOHN HOWARD LAWSON, *Theory and Technique of Playwriting* (N. Y. 1936).

B. ROLAND LEWIS, *The Technique of the One-Act Play* (Boston, 1918).

M. L. MALEVINSKY, *The Science of Playwriting* (N. Y. 1925).

T. L. MARBLE, *How to Appreciate the Drama* (N. Y. 1914).

CHARLES E. MATHER and others, *Behind the Footlights* (N. Y. 1935).

BRANDER MATTHEWS, *The Development of the Drama* (N. Y. 1916); *Playwrights on Playmaking* (N. Y. 1923); *The Principles of Playmaking* (N. Y. 1919); *A Book About the Theater* (N. Y. 1916); *Rip Van Winkle Goes to the Play* (N. Y. 1926).

GEORGE MEREDITH, *An Essay on Comedy* (N. Y. 1918).

GEORGE JEAN NATHAN, *The Popular Theater* (N. Y. 1918); *The Critic and the Drama* (N. Y. 1922).

ALLARDYCE NICOLL, *An Introduction to Dramatic Theory* (N. Y. 1924); Same (revised as *The Theory of Drama* (London, 1931); *Film and Theater* (N. Y. 1936).

GRACE SLOAN OVERTON, *Drama in Education* (N. Y. 1926).

JOHN PALMER, *The Future of the Theater* (London, 1913); *Comedy* (N. Y. no date).

WILLIAM LYON PHELPS, *The Twentieth Century Theater* (N. Y. 1918).

SIR ARTHUR PINERO, *Robert Louis Stevenson as a Dramatist* (N. Y. 1914).

GEORGES POLTI, *The Thirty-Six Dramatic Situations,* trans. by L. Kay (Franklin, O., 1921); *The Art of Inventing Characters,* trans. by L. Kay (Franklin, O., 1922).

W. T. PRICE, *The Technique of the Drama* (N. Y. 1908); *The Analysis of Play-Construction, etc.* (N. Y. 1909).

ENID ROSE, *First Studies in Dramatic Art* (London, 1926).

H. F. RUBINSTEIN, *What Isn't Wrong With the Drama* (London, 1927).

MARY M. RUSSELL, *Drama as a Factor in Social Education* (N. Y. 1924).

FRANCISQUE SARCEY, *A Theory of the Theater,* trans. by H. H. Hughes (N. Y. 1916).

BERNARD SHAW, *The Quintessence of Ibsenism* (N. Y. 1913); *The Author's Apology* (N. Y. 1905); see Prefaces to plays listed under Shaw.

L. E. SHIPMAN, *The True Adventures of a Play* (N. Y. 1914).

LEE SIMONSON, *The Stage is Set* (N. Y. 1932).

E. F. S[PENCE], *Our Stage and Its Critics* (London, 1910).

J. E. SPINGARN, *Creative Criticism* (N. Y. 1917).

G. F. STURGIS, *The Influence of the Drama* (N. Y. 1913).

MARK SWAN, *How You Can Write Plays* (N. Y. 1927).

A. H. THORNDIKE, *Tragedy* (Boston, 1908).

A. B. WALKLEY, *Dramatic Criticism* (London, 1903).

EUGENE WALTER, *How to Write a Play* (N. Y. 1925).

GEOFFREY WHITWORTH, *The Theater of My Heart* (London, 1930).

PERCIVAL WILDE, *The Craftsmanship of the One-Act Play* (Boston, 1923).

ELISABETH WOODBRIDGE, *The Drama, Its Law and Technique* (Boston, 1898).

W. B. Yeats, *The Cutting of an Agate* (N. Y. 1912); *Plays and Controversies* (N. Y. 1924); *Essays* (N. Y. 1924).

Stark Young, *The Theater* (N. Y. 1927); *Theater Practice* (N. Y. 1926); *Glamor* (N. Y. 1925).

Stagecraft and Production

Harry Lee Andrews and Bruce Weirick, *Acting and Play Production* (N. Y. 1925).

Esther W. Bates, *The Art of Producing Pageants* (Boston, 1925).

Hallam Bosworth, *Technique in Dramatic Art* (N. Y. 1926).

Bruce Carpenter, *The Way of the Drama* (N. Y. 1929).

Huntley Carter, *Max Reinhardt* (N. Y. 1914); *The New Spirit in Drama and Art* (N. Y. 1913); *The New Spirit in the European Theater* (N. Y. 1926).

Sheldon Cheney, *The New Movement in the Theater* (N. Y. 1914); *The Art Theater* (N. Y. 1925); *The Open-Air Theater* (N. Y. 1918); *Theater Decoration* (N. Y. 1928).

Barrett H. Clark, *How to Produce Amateur Plays* (Boston, 1926).

Allan Crafton and Jessica Royer, *The Process of Play Production* (N. Y. 1926).

Gordon Craig, *On the Art of the Theater* (Chicago, 1911); *The Theater-Advancing* (Boston, 1921); *Towards a New Theater* (N. Y. 1913); *Scene* (N. Y. 1923); *Books and Theaters* (London, 1926); *Fourteen Notes* (Seattle, 1931).

Alexander Dean, *Little Theater Organization and Management* (N. Y. 1926).

Monica Ewer, *Play Production For Everyone* (London, 1924).

Helen Ferris, *Producing Amateur Entertainments* (N. Y. 1921).

Samuel J. Hume and Lois Foster, *Theater and School* (N. Y. 1931).

Kenneth Macgowan, *The Theater of To-morrow* (N. Y. 1921).

Kenneth Macgowan and R. E. Jones, *Continental Stagecraft* (N. Y. 1922).

Constance D'Arcy Mackay, *How to Produce Children's Plays* (N. Y. 1915); *Costumes and Scenery for Amateurs* (N. Y. 1915); *Children's Theaters and Plays* (N. Y. 1927).

Roy Mitchell, *The School Theater* (N. Y. 1925); *Creative Theater* (N. Y. 1927).

H. K. Motherwell, *The Theater of To-day* (N. Y. 1927).

WILLIAM POEL, *Shakespeare in the Theater* (London, 1913); *What Is Wrong With the Stage* (London, 1920).

C. HAROLD RIDGE, *Stage Lighting for Little Theaters* (Cambridge, England, 1925).

ALBERT RUTHERSTON, *Decoration in the Theater* (Chapbook, London, 1919).

OLIVER M. SAYLER, *Max Reinhardt* (N. Y. 1924).

H. B. SELL, *What Is It All About?* (Chicago, 1914).

FRANK SHAY, *The Practical Theater* (N. Y. 1926).

HORACE SHIPP, *Community Playing* (London, no date).

CONSTANCE SMEDLEY, *Action* (London, no date).

ANDRE SMITH, *The Scenewright* (N. Y. 1926).

MILTON SMITH, *The Book of Play Production* (N. Y. 1926).

CLARENCE STRATTON, *Theatron* (N. Y. 1928).

EMERSON TAYLOR, *Practical Stage Directing for Amateurs* (N. Y. 1916).

H. W. WHANSLAW, *Everybody's Theater* (London, no date).

C. M. WISE, *Dramatics for School and Community* (Cincinnati, 1923).

ESSAYS AND COLLECTED CRITICISM

(Devoted in whole or in part to dramatic criticism or articles on the drama and the theater)

JAMES AGATE, *Buzz! Buzz* (London, 1919); *At Half-Past Eight* (N. Y. 1923); *The Contemporary Theater, 1923* (London, 1924); *The Contemporary Theater, 1924* (London, 1925); *The Contemporary Theater, 1925* (London, 1926); *The Contemporary Theater, 1926* (London, 1927); *Alarums and Excursions* (N. Y. 1923); *First Nights* (London, 1934); *More First Nights* (London, 1937); *My Theater Talks* (London, 1933); *Their Hour Upon the Stage* (Cambridge, 1930).

H. F. ALLEN, *The Play's the Thing* (Cedar Rapids, Ia., 1927).

WILLIAM ARCHER, *The Theatrical World*, 5 vols. (London, 1894-1898); *Study and Stage* (London, 1899); *About the Theater* (London, 1886); *Real Conversations* (London, 1904).

MAX BEERBOHM, *Around the Theaters*, 2 vols. (in *Works, Vol. III*, London, 1923).

EDWIN BJÖRKMAN, *Voices of To-morrow* (N. Y. 1913).

IVOR BROWN, *Masques and Phases* (London, 1926).

SYDNEY W. CARROLL, *Some Dramatic Opinions* (London, no date).

A. K. CHESTERTON, *Adventures in Dramatic Appreciation* (London, no date).

W. L. COURTNEY, *The Development of Maurice Maeterlinck, etc.* (London, 1904); *Old Saws and Modern Instances* (N. Y. no date).

GERALD CUMBERLAND, *Set Down in Malice* (N. Y. 1919).

W. A. DARLINGTON, *Through the Fourth Wall* (N. Y. no date); *Literature in the Theater* (N. Y. 1926).

HUGH S. DAVIES, *Realism in the Drama* (Cambridge, 1934).

JOHN DRINKWATER, *Prose Papers* (London, 1917).

WALTER PRICHARD EATON, *At the New Theater and Others* (Boston, 1910); *The American Stage of To-day* (Boston, 1908); *Plays and Players* (Cincinnati, 1917); *The Actor's Heritage* (Boston, 1924); *The Drama in English* (N. Y. 1930).

T. S. ELIOT, *The Sacred Wood* (N. Y. 1921).

ST. JOHN ERVINE, *Some Impressions of My Elders* (N. Y. 1923).

JOHN FREEMAN, *The Moderns* (N. Y. 1917).

EDWARD FULLER, *The Dramatic Year* (Boston, 1889).

J. T. GREIN, *Dramatic Criticism,* Vols. I-III (London, 1899-1903); *Premières of the Year* (London, 1900); *The Theater and the World* (London, 1921); *The New World of the Theater* (London, 1924).

ARCHIBALD HADDON, *Hullo Playgoers!* (London, 1924).

CLAYTON HAMILTON, *Studies in Stagecraft* (N. Y. 1914); *Problems of the Playwright* (N. Y. 1917); *Seen on the Stage* (N. Y. 1920); *Conversations on Contemporary Drama* (N. Y. 1925).

PERCY HAMMOND, *But Is It Art?* (N. Y. 1927).

ST. JOHN HANKIN, Essays in Vol. III, *Dramatic Works* (N. Y. 1912).

NORMAN HAPGOOD, *The Stage in America* (N. Y. 1901).

FRANK HARRIS, *Contemporary Portraits,* 5 series (N. Y. 1916-27).

OSCAR HEERMANN (ed.), *Living Dramatists* (N. Y. 1905).

C. LEWIS HIND, *Authors and I* (N. Y. 1921); *More Authors and I* (N. Y. 1922).

JAMES HUNEKER, *Iconoclasts* (N. Y. 1905); *Egoists* (N. Y. 1908); *Ivory Apes and Peacocks* (N. Y. 1915); *The Pathos of Distance* (N. Y. 1913).

JOSEPH KNIGHT, *Theatrical Notes* (London, 1893).

LUDWIG LEWISOHN, *The Drama and the Stage* (N. Y. 1922).

ROBERT LYND, *Old and New Masters* (N. Y. 1919).

S. B. P. MAIS, *From Shakespeare to O. Henry* (N. Y. 1923).

BURNS MANTLE, *The Best Plays of 1919-20* (Boston, 1920); Same title, annually (to date); also, *Best Plays 1909-1919* (N. Y. 1934).

ANNIE RUSSELL MARBLE, *The Nobel Prize Winners in Literature* (N. Y. 1925).

C. E. MONTAGUE, *Dramatic Values* (N. Y. 1911).

GEORGE MOORE, *Impressions and Opinions* (N. Y. 1913).

MOWBRAY MORRIS, *Essays in Theatrical Criticism* (London, 1882).

J. M. MURRY, *Aspects of Literature* (London, 1920).

GEORGE JEAN NATHAN, *Another Book on the Theater* (N. Y. 1915); *The World in Falseface* (N. Y. 1923); *The Theater, the Drama, The Girls* (N. Y. 1921); *Comedians All* (N. Y. 1919); *Mr. George Jean Nathan Presents* (N. Y. 1917); *Materia Critica* (N. Y. 1924); *The House of Satan* (N. Y. 1926); *The Autobiography of an Attitude* (N. Y. 1925); *Art of the Night* (N. Y. 1928); *Land of the Pilgrims' Pride* (N. Y. 1927); *Since Ibsen* (N. Y. 1933); *Passing Judgments* (N. Y. 1935); *The Theater of the Moment* (N. Y. 1936); *The Intimate Notebooks* (N. Y. 1932).

EVELYN NEWMAN, *The International Note in Contemporary Drama* (N. Y. 1931).

C. F. NIRDLINGER, *Masques and Mummers* (N. Y. 1899).

GILBERT NORWOOD, *Euripides and Shaw, etc.* (Boston, 1921).

WILLIAM LYON PHELPS, *As I Like It* (N. Y. 1923); Same, 2nd series and 3rd series (N. Y. 1924-1926).

ARTHUR RUHL, *Second Nights* (N. Y. 1914).

H. B. SAMUEL, *Modernities* (N. Y. 1914).

DIXON SCOTT, *Men of Letters* (N. Y. 1923).

BERNARD SHAW, *Dramatic Opinions and Essays*, 2 vols. (N. Y. 1907).

E. F. S[PENCE], *Our Stage and Its Critics* (London, 1910).

GRAHAM SUTTON, *Some Contemporary Dramatists* (N. Y. 1926).

L. D. SYLES, *Essays in Dramatic Criticism* (N. Y. 1898).

ARTHUR SYMONS, *Plays, Acting and Music* (N. Y. 1909); *Studies in Prose and Verse* (N. Y. 1904); *Dramatis Personæ* (Indianapolis, 1924).

H. M. WALBROOK, *Nights at the Play* (London, 1911); *A Playgoer's Wanderings* (London, 1926).

A. B. Walkley, *Frames of Mind* (London, 1899); *Drama and Life* (N. Y. 1908); *Pastiche and Prejudice* (N. Y. 1921); *More Prejudice* (N. Y. 1923); *Still More Prejudice* (N. Y. 1925).

William Winter, *The Wallet of Time* (N. Y. 1913).

Alexander Woollcott, *Shouts and Murmurs* (N. Y. 1922); *Enchanted Aisles* (N. Y. 1924).

Stark Young, *The Flower in Drama* (N. Y. 1923); *Glamor* (N. Y. 1925); *Theater Practice* (N. Y. 1926).

Theaters

(*Miscellaneous*)

Anonymous, *The Truth About the Theater* (Cincinnati, 1916).

William Archer and H. Granville-Barker, *Schemes and Estimates for a National Theater* (N. Y. 1908).

A. G. Arvold, *The Little Country Theater* (N. Y. 1923).

H. R. Barbor, *The Theater, etc.* (London, 1924).

David Belasco, *The Theater Through Its Stage Door* (N. Y. 1919).

Louise Burleigh, *The Community Theater* (Boston, 1917).

Sheldon Cheney, *The Open-Air Theater* (N. Y. 1916); *The Art Theater* (N. Y. 1917); *The Theater* (N. Y. 1929).

Barrett H. Clark, *Œdipus or Pollyanna* (Seattle, 1927).

J. R. Crawford and M. P. Beagle, *Community Drama and Pageantry* (New Haven, 1916).

Basil Dean, *The Repertory Theater* (Liverpool, 1911).

Helen Deutsch and Stella Hanau, *The Provincetown* (N. Y. 1931).

Thomas H. Dickinson, *The Insurgent Theater* (N. Y. 1917).

Ruth C. Dimmick, *Our Theaters To-day and Yesterday* (N. Y. 1913).

Walter Prichard Eaton [ed.], *The Theater Guild* (N. Y. 1929).

Morton Eustis, *B'way Inc.* (N. Y. 1934).

Franklin Fyles, *The Theater and Its People* (N. Y. 1900).

G. M. G., *The Stage Censor* (London, 1908).

Rosamond Gilder, *A Theater Library* (N. Y. 1932); with George Friedley, *Theater Collections* (N. Y. 1936).

C. J. de Goveia, *The Community Playhouse* (N. Y. 1923).

Robert Grau, *Forty Years' Observation of Music and the Drama* (N. Y. 1909).

R. L. Hartt, *The People at Play* (Boston, 1909).

Alice Minnie Herts, *The Children's Educational Theater* (N. Y. 1917).
Oliver Hindsell, *Making the Little Theater Pay* (N. Y. 1925).
Arthur Hopkins, *How's Your Second Act?* (N. Y. 1918).
Arthur Hornblow, *Training for the Stage* (Philadelphia, 1916).
P. P. Howe, *The Repertory Theater* (N. Y. 1911).
Glenn Hughes, *The Story of the Theater* (N. Y. 1928).
Edith J. R. Isaacs, *Theater* (Boston, 1927).
A. E. Krows, *Play Production in America* (N. Y. 1916).
Desmond MacCarthy, *The Court Theater* (London, 1907).
Kenneth Macgowan, *Footlights Across America* (N. Y. 1929).
Constance D'Arcy Mackay, *The Little Theater in the United States* (N. Y. 1917).
Percy MacKaye, *Community Drama* (Boston, 1917).
———, *The Civic Theater* (N. Y. 1912).
———, *The Playhouse and the Play* (N. Y. 1909).
Allardyce Nicoll, *The Development of the Theater* (N. Y. 1927).
John Palmer, *The Censor and the Theaters* (N. Y. 1913).
Irving Pichel, *Modern Theaters* (N. Y. 1925).
Romain Rolland, *The People's Theater,* trans. by B. H. Clark (N. Y. 1918).
J. T. Smith, *The Parish Theater* (N. Y. 1917).
Shepard Traube, *So You Want to Go Into the Theater?* (Boston, 1936).
Frank A. Waugh, *Outdoor Theaters* (Boston, 1917).
Willson Whitman, *Bread and Circuses* (N. Y. 1937).

Reminiscences

(By actors, managers, etc., in which there are references to the drama)

Frank Archer, *An Actor's Note Books* (London, no date).
George Arliss, *Up the Years from Bloomsbury* (N. Y. 1927).
Max Beerbohm, *Herbert Beerbohm Tree* (N. Y. 1921).
William A. Brady, *Showman* (N. Y. 1937).
Mrs. Patrick Campbell, *My Life and Some Letters* (N. Y. 1922).
John Austin Clapp, *Reminiscences of a Dramatic Critic* (Boston, 1902).
Constance Collier, *Harlequinade* (London, 1929).
Noel Coward, *Present Indicative* (N. Y. 1937).

JOHN DREW, *My Years on the Stage* (N. Y. 1922).
DANIEL FROHMAN, *Memories of a Manager* (Garden City, 1911).
———, *Daniel Frohman Presents* (N. Y. 1935).
———, *Encore* (N. Y. 1937).
JOHN GOLDEN and VIOLA B. SHORE, *Stage Struck John Golden* (N. Y. 1930).
WEEDON GROSSMITH, *From Studio to Stage* (N. Y. 1913).
ARTHUR HOPKINS, *Letters to a Lonely Boy* (N. Y. 1937).
EVA LEGALLIENNE, *At 33* (N. Y. 1934).
ELISABETH MARBURY, *My Crystal Ball* (N. Y. 1923).
JOSEPH VERNER REED, *The Curtain Falls* (N. Y. 1935).
CLEMENT SCOTT, *The Drama of Yesterday and To-day,* 2 vols. (N. Y. 1899).
OTIS SKINNER, *Footlights and Spotlights* (N. Y. 1924).
E. H. SOTHERN, *The Melancholy Tale of Me* (N. Y. 1916).
ELLEN TERRY, *The Story of My Life* (N. Y. 1908).
AUGUSTUS THOMAS, *The Print of My Remembrance* (N. Y. 1922).
J. RANKEN TOWSE, *Sixty Years at the Theater* (N. Y. 1916).
GEORGE C. TYLER, *Whatever Goes Up* (Indianapolis, 1934).
WILLIAM WINTER, *Life of David Belasco,* 2 vols. (N. Y. 1918).
———, *Vagrant Memories* (N. Y. 1915).

AMERICAN DRAMA

ALFRED L. BERNHEIM, *The Business of the Theater* (N. Y. 1932).
RICHARD BURTON, *The New American Drama* (N. Y. 1911).
BARRETT H. CLARK, *An Hour of American Drama* (Philadelphia, 1930).
MARY CAROLINE CRAWFORD, *The Romance of the American Theater* (Boston, 1913).
THOMAS H. DICKINSON, *The Case of American Drama* (Boston, 1915); *Dramatists of the New American Theater* (N. Y. 1924).
ARTHUR HORNBLOW, *A History of the Theater in America,* 2 vols. (Philadelphia, 1919).
OTTO H. KAHN, *The American Stage* (pamphlet, N. Y. 1925).
BURNS MANTLE, *American Playwrights of Today* (N. Y. 1929).
MARGARET G. MAYORGA, *A Short History of the American Drama* (N. Y. 1932).
MONTROSE J. MOSES, *The American Dramatist* (Boston, 1925).
——— and JOHN MASON BROWN, *The American Theater as Seen by its Critics, 1752-1934* (N. Y. 1934).

ARTHUR HOBSON QUINN, *A History of the American Drama,* 3 vols., last two on modern drama (N. Y. 1925-37).

OLIVER M. SAYLER, *Our American Theater* (N. Y. 1923).

ENGLISH DRAMA

JAMES AGATE, *A Short View of the English Stage, 1900-1926* (London, 1926).

WILLIAM ARCHER, *English Dramatists of To-day* (London, 1882); *The Old Drama and the New* (Boston, 1923).

MARIO BORSA, *The English Stage of To-day,* trans. by S. Brinton (N. Y. 1908).

J. W. CUNLIFFE, *Modern English Playwrights* (N. Y. 1927).

THOMAS H. DICKINSON, *The Contemporary Drama of England* (Boston, 1931).

WALTER PRICHARD EATON, *The Drama in English* (N. Y. 1930).

ST. JOHN ERVINE, *The Organized Theater* (N. Y. 1924).

AUGUSTIN FILON, *The English Stage,* trans. by F. Whyte (N. Y. 1898).

P. P. HOWE, *Dramatic Portraits* (N. Y. 1913).

HOLBROOK JACKSON, *The Eighteen Nineties* (N. Y. 1923).

HENRY ARTHUR JONES, *The Renascence of the English Drama* (N. Y. 1895); *The Foundations of a National Drama* (N. Y. 1913).

J. M. KENNEDY, *English Literature: 1880-1905* (Boston, 1912).

BACHE MATTHEWS, *A History of the Birmingham Repertory Theater* (London, 1924).

A. E. MORGAN, *Tendencies of Modern English Drama* (N. Y. 1924).

ALLARDYCE NICOLL, *British Drama* (N. Y. 1933).

D. E. OLIVER, *The English Stage* (London, 1912).

C. PELLIZZI, *English Drama* (N. Y. 1935).

NIGEL PLAYFAIR, *The Story of the Lyric Theater, Hammersmith* (London, 1924).

GRAHAM SUTTON, *Some Contemporary Dramatists* (N. Y. 1926).

FRANK VERNON, *The Twentieth Century Theater* (Boston, 1925).

FRENCH DRAMA

F. W. CHANDLER, *The Contemporary Drama of France* (Boston, 1920); *Aspects of Modern Drama* (N. Y. 1914).

BARRETT H. CLARK, *Contemporary French Dramatists* (Cincinnati, 1915).

J. W. Cunliffe and P. de Bacourt, *French Literature During the Past Half Century* (N. Y. 1923).

Augustin Filon, *Modern French Drama,* trans. by C. J. Hogarth (N. Y. 1897).

Sacha Guitry, *If Memory Serves* (N. Y. 1935).

Margaret H. Harrison, *Modern Religious Drama in Germany and France* (Boston, 1936).

Ludwig Lewisohn, *The Modern Drama* (N. Y. 1915).

Brander Matthews, *French Dramatists of the Nineteenth Century* (N. Y. 1910).

John Palmer, *Studies in the Contemporary Theater* (Boston, 1927).

H. A. Smith, *Main Currents of Modern French Drama* (N. Y. 1925).

S. M. Waxman, *Antoine and the Théâtre Libre* (Cambridge, Mass., 1926).

German Drama

F. W. Chandler, *Aspects of Modern Drama* (N. Y. 1914).

J. F. Coar, *Studies in German Literature in the Nineteenth Century* (N. Y. 1903).

Ashley Dukes, *Modern Dramatists* (Chicago, 1912); *The Youngest Drama* (Chicago, 1924).

Kuno Francke (ed.), *German Classics of the Nineteenth Century* (N. Y. 1904-1914).

———, *Glimpses of Modern German Culture* (N. Y. 1898).

———, *German Ideals of To-day* (Boston, 1907).

Isaac Goldberg, *The Drama of Transition* (Cincinnati, 1922).

Margaret H. Harrison, *Modern Religious Drama in Germany and France* (Boston, 1936).

Otto Heller, *Studies in Modern German Literature* (Boston, 1905).

O. E. Lessing, *Masters of Modern German Literature* (Dresden, 1912).

Ludwig Lewisohn, *The Modern Drama* (N. Y. 1915).

Pierre Loving, *Revolt in German Drama* (Girard, Kan., 1925).

Percival Pollard, *Masks and Minstrels of New Germany* (Boston, 1911).

Alfred Stoeckius, *Naturalism in Recent German Drama* (N. Y. 1903).

GEORG WITKOWSKI, *The German Drama of the Nineteenth Century*, trans. by L. E. Horning (N. Y. 1909).

IRISH DRAMA

MAURICE BOURGEOIS, *John Millington Synge and the Irish Dramatic Movement* (N. Y. 1913).
ERNEST BOYD, *Ireland's Literary Renaissance* (N. Y. 1916); *The Contemporary Drama of Ireland* (Boston, 1917).
W. G. FAY and CATHERINE CARSWELL, *The Fays and the Abbey Theater* (N. Y. 1935).
LADY GREGORY, *Our Irish Theater* (N. Y. 1913).
H. S. KRANS, *W. B. Yeats and the Irish Literary Revival* (N. Y. 1904).
THOMAS MACDONAGH, *Literature in Ireland* (N. Y. 1916).
ANDREW E. MALONE, *The Irish Drama* (London, 1929).
GEORGE MOORE, *Hail and Farewell* (N. Y. 1911-1914).
LLOYD R. MORRIS, *The Celtic Dawn* (N. Y. 1917).
L. PAUL-DUBOIS, *Contemporary Ireland* (Dublin, 1911).
W. P. RYAN, *The Irish Literary Revival* (London, 1894).
CORNELIUS WEYGANDT, *Irish Plays and Playwrights* (Boston, 1913).
W. B. YEATS, *The Cutting of an Agate* (N. Y. 1912); *Plays and Controversies* (N. Y. 1924); *Essays* (N. Y. 1924); *Dramatis Personae* (N. Y. 1936).

ITALIAN DRAMA

ISAAC GOLDBERG, *The Drama of Transition* (Cincinnati, 1922).
LANDER MACCLINTOCK, *The Contemporary Drama of Italy* (Boston, 1920).
ADDISON MCLEOD, *Plays and Players of Modern Italy* (Chicago, 1912).

POLISH DRAMA

ROMAN DYBOSKI, *Modern Polish Literature* (London, 1924), contains chapters on "Modern Polish Comedy" and "Modern Polish Drama."

RUSSIAN DRAMA

B. ALPERS, *The Theater of the Social Mask* (N. Y. 1934).
ALEXANDER BAKSHY, *The Path of the Modern Russia Stage* (Boston, 1916).

Maurice Baring, *Landmarks in Russian Literature* (N. Y. 1910).
A. Bruckner, *A Literary History of Russia* (N. Y. 1908).
Huntley Carter, *The New Theater and Cinema of Soviet Russia* (London, 1925); *The New Spirit in the Russian Theater* (N. Y. 1929).
Norris Houghton, *Moscow Rehearsals* (N. Y. 1936).
Alexander Kropotkin, *Ideals and Realities in Russian Literature* (N. Y. 1915).
Kurt London, *The Seven Soviet Arts* (London, 1937).
P. A. Markov, *The First Studio* (N. Y. 1934); *The Soviet Theater* (N. Y. 1935).
V. Nemirovitch-Danchenko, *My Life in the Russian Theater* (Boston, 1936).
Oliver M. Sayler, *The Russian Theater* (N. Y. 1922); *Inside the Moscow Art Theater* (N. Y. 1925).
Constantin Stanislavsky, *My Life in Art* (Boston, 1924).
Leo Wiener, *The Contemporary Drama of Russia* (Boston, 1924).

Scandinavian Drama

(Drama in Denmark, Norway, and Sweden)

H. H. Boyesen, *Essays on Scandinavian Literature* (N. Y. 1911).
C. B. Burchardt, *Norwegian Life and Literature* (Oxford, 1920).
Edmund Gosse, *Northern Studies* (London, 1890).

Spanish Drama

J. D. M. Ford, *Main Currents of Spanish Literature* (N. Y. 1919).
Isaac Goldberg, *The Drama of Transition* (Cincinnati, 1922).
Storm Jameson, *The Modern Drama in Europe* (N. Y. 1920).

Yiddish Drama

N. Buchwald, article in *Cambridge History of American Literature,* IV (N. Y. 1921).
Isaac Goldberg, *The Drama of Transition* (Cincinnati, 1922).
M. J. Landa, *The Jew in Drama* (N. Y. 1927).
Oliver M. Sayler, *Our American Theater* (N. Y. 1923).
Leo Wiener, *A History of Yiddish Literature in the 19th Century* (N. Y. 1899).

II

PUBLISHED PLAYS

A. ANTHOLOGIES AND COLLECTIONS OF MODERN DRAMA

The number of play anthologies has grown to such an extent that it is possible here to indicate only the titles and year of publication, and the number of plays contained in each collection. This list is selective, many school texts being omitted.

GEORGE P. BAKER, *Modern American Plays* (N. Y. 1920), 5 plays.

FRANK W. CHANDLER and RICHARD A. CORDELL, *Twentieth Century Plays* (N. Y. 1934), 18 plays.

BARRETT H. CLARK, *Representative One-Act Plays by British and Irish Authors* (Boston, 1921), 21 plays; *World Drama,* 2 vols. (N. Y. 1933), 20 plays. Vol. II contains modern plays.

——— and THOMAS R. COOK, *One-Act Plays* (Boston, 1929), 12 plays.

——— and KENYON NICHOLSON, *The American Scene* (N. Y. 1930), 34 plays.

KATHRYN COE and WILLIAM H. CORDELL, *The Pulitzer Prize Plays, 1918-1934* (N. Y. 1935), 16 plays.

GEORGE R. COFFMAN, *A Book of Modern Plays* (Chicago, 1925), 7 plays.

HELEN LOUISE COHEN, *Longer Plays by Modern Authors (American)* (N. Y. 1922), 4 plays; *One-Act Plays by Modern Authors* (N. Y. 1927), 21 plays; Same, enlarged edition (N. Y. 1934), 21 plays; *More One-Act Plays* (N. Y. 1927), 14 plays.

THOMAS H. DICKINSON, *Chief Contemporary Dramatists* (Boston, 1915), 20 plays; *Chief Contemporary Dramatists,* 2nd Series (Boston, 1921), 18 plays; *Chief Contemporary Dramatists,* 3rd Series (Boston, 1930), 20 plays; *Continental Plays,* Vol. 1 (Boston, 1935), 10 plays; Same, Vol. 2 (Boston, 1935), 10 plays.

——— and JACK R. CRAWFORD, *Contemporary Drama; English and American* (Boston, 1925), 16 plays.

RANDOLPH EDMONDS, *Six Plays for a Negro Theater* (Boston, 1934).

ALLAN GATES HALLINE, *American Plays* (N. Y. 1935), 17 plays.

JAY B. HUBBELL and JOHN O. BEATY, *An Introduction to Drama* (N. Y. 1927), modern section contains 14 plays.

Glenn Hughes, *Short Plays for Modern Players* (N. Y. 1931), 12 plays.

Edith J. R. Isaacs, *Plays of American Life and Fantasy* (N. Y. 1929), 18 plays.

Winifred Katzin, *Eight European Plays* (N. Y. 1927).

Edwin Van B. Knickerbocker, *Twelve Plays* (N. Y. 1924); *Plays for Classroom Interpretation* (N. Y. 1921), 7 plays.

Frederick Houk Law, *Modern Plays, Short and Long* (N. Y. 1924), 11 plays.

Sterling Andrus Leonard, *The Atlantic Book of Modern Plays* (Boston, 1921), 15 plays.

Garrett H. Leverton, *Plays for the College Theater* (N. Y. 1932), 28 plays.

B. Roland Lewis, *Contemporary One-Act Plays* (N. Y. 1923), 18 plays.

Alain Locke, *Twenty Plays of the Contemporary Negro Theater* (N. Y. 1927), 20 plays.

Burns Mantle and John W. Gassner, *A Treasury of the Theater* (N. Y. 1935), 34 plays.

Constance M. Martin, *50 One-Act Plays* (London, 1934).

Margaret G. Mayorga, *Representative One-Act Plays by American Authors* (Boston, 1919), 24 plays; Same (revised, 1937), 25 plays; *Twenty Short Plays on a Royalty Holiday* (N. Y. 1937).

Montrose J. Moses, *Representative One-Act Plays by Continental Authors* (Boston, 1923), 19 plays; *Dramas of Modernism and Their Forerunners* (Boston, 1931), 16 plays; *Representative Continental Dramas, Revolutionary and Transitional* (Boston, 1924), 15 plays; *Representative British Dramas, Victorian and Modern* (Boston, 1918), 21 plays; *A Treasury of Plays for Children* (Boston, 1921), 14 plays; *Representative Plays by American Dramatists,* 3 vols. Vol. III contains only modern plays (N. Y. 1917-1924), 10 plays; *Another Treasury of Plays for Children* (Boston, 1926), 12 plays; *Ring up the Curtain!* (Boston, 1932), 12 plays; *Representative American Dramas, National and Local* (Boston, 1925), 15 plays; Same (revised, 1933), 19 plays.

Kenyon Nicholson, *The Appleton Book of Short Plays* (N. Y. 1925), 10 plays; *The Appleton Book of Short Plays,* 2nd Series (N. Y. 1927), 12 plays.

Raymond Woodbury Pence, *Dramas by Present-Day Writers* (N. Y. 1927), 15 plays.

Le Roy Phillips and Theodore Johnson, *Baker's Anthology of One-Act Plays* (Boston, 1925), 11 plays.

Arthur Hobson Quinn, *Contemporary American Plays* (N. Y. 1923), 5 plays; *Representative American Plays* (N. Y. 1917), 25 plays; Same, Fifth edition (revised 1930), 28 plays.

Willis Richardson, *Plays and Pageants From the Life of the Negro* (Washington, 1930), 12 plays.

——— and R. Miller, *Negro History in Thirteen Plays* (Washington, 1935).

Frank Shay, *A Treasury of Plays for Women* (Boston, 1922), 18 plays; *A Treasury of Plays for Men* (Boston, 1923), 21 plays; *Twenty-five Short Plays, International* (N. Y. 1925); *Twenty Contemporary One-Act Plays, American* (Cincinnati, 1922); *Fifty More Contemporary One-Act Plays* (N. Y. 1928); *Plays for Strolling Mummers* (N. Y. 1926), 8 plays; *The Appleton Book of Christmas Plays* (N. Y. 1929), 11 plays; *The Appleton Book of Holiday Plays* (N. Y. 1930), 10 plays.

——— and Pierre Loving, *Fifty Contemporary One-Act Plays* (Cincinnati, 1920).

Milton Smith, *Short Plays of Various Types* (N. Y. 1924), 12 plays.

Charles Swain Thomas, *The Atlantic Book of Junior Plays* (Boston, 1924), 14 plays; *The Theater Guild Anthology* (N. Y. 1936), 14 plays.

S. M. Tucker, *Twelve One-Act Plays for Study and Production* (Boston, 1929); *Modern Plays* (N. Y. 1932), 5 plays; *Modern American and British Plays* (N. Y. 1931), 23 plays; *Twenty-Five Modern Plays* (N. Y. 1931); *Modern Continental Plays* (N. Y. 1929), 21 plays.

E. Bradlee Watson and B. Pressey, *Contemporary Drama. American, English, Irish, and Continental Plays,* 6 vols. (N. Y. 1931 ff.).

Charles H. Whitman, *Seven Contemporary Plays* (Boston, 1931); *Representative Modern Dramas* (N. Y. 1936), 20 plays.

Percival Wilde, *Contemporary One-Act Plays From Nine Countries* (Boston, 1936), 16 plays.

[No Editor] *Twelve One-Act Plays.* Introduction by Walter Prichard Eaton (N. Y. 1926).

[No Editor] *One-Act Plays for Stage and Study,* 1st Series. Preface by Augustus Thomas (N. Y. 1924), 25 plays; Same, 2nd Series. Preface by Walter Prichard Eaton (N. Y. 1925), 21 plays; Same,

3rd Series. Preface by Percival Wilde (N. Y. 1927), 21 plays; Same, 4th Series. Preface by Paul Green (N. Y. 1928), 22 plays; Same, 5th Series. Preface by Elmer Rice (N. Y. 1929), 21 plays; Same, 6th Series. Preface by Martin Flavin (N. Y. 1931), 21 plays; Same, 7th Series. Preface by Zona Gale (N. Y. 1933), 21 plays; Same, 8th Series. Preface by Alice Gerstenberg (N. Y. 1934), 20 plays.

B. PLAYS BY DRAMATISTS OTHER THAN THOSE DISCUSSED IN TEXT OF THIS BOOK

The following is a list of several of the more important dramatists and their published plays, which is intended to supplement the lists already furnished in the text of this book. In the case of foreign dramatists, only translations are listed.

American Dramatists

George Ade, "The County Chairman" (N. Y. 1924); "Just Out of College" (N. Y. 1924); "Father and the Boys" (N. Y. 1924); "The College Widow" (N. Y. 1924); "The Mayor and the Manicure" (N. Y. 1924); "Nettie" (N. Y. 1924); "Speaking to Father" (N. Y. 1924); "Marse Covington" (N. Y. 1924); "The Sultan of Sulu" (N. Y. 1903).

Zoë Akins, *Déclassée; Daddy's Gone A-Hunting; and Greatness—A Comedy* (N. Y. 1923); "The Portrait of Tiero," in Isaacs' *Plays of American Life and Fantasy* (N. Y. 1929); "Papa" (N. Y. 1913); "Did It Really Happen?" (*Smart Set,* N. Y. 1917); "The Magical City" (*The Forum,* N. Y. 1916); "Such a Charming Young Man," in *One-Act Plays for Stage and Study,* I (N. Y. 1924); "The Old Maid" (N. Y. 1935); "The Little Miracle" (N. Y. 1936).

Maxwell Anderson, *Three American Plays,* in collaboration with Laurence Stallings (N. Y. 1925), contains "What Price Glory?," "First Flight," and "The Buccaneer"; *Gods of the Lightning and Outside Looking In,* 2 plays (N. Y. 1928); "Saturday's Children" (N. Y. 1927); "Elizabeth the Queen" (N. Y. 1930); "Night Over Taos" (N. Y. 1932); "Both Your Houses" (N. Y. 1932); "Mary of Scotland" (Washington, 1933); "Valley Forge" (Washington 1934); "Winterset" (Washington, 1936); "The Wingless Victory"

(Washington, 1937); "High Tor" (Washington, 1937); "Masque of Kings" (Washington, 1937); "The Star-Wagon" (N. Y. 1937).

LEOPOLD ATLAS, "L," in *Yale One-Act Plays* (N. Y. 1930); "So Long," in *One-Act Plays for Stage and Study,* 8th Series (N. Y. 1934); *Wednesday's Child and House We Live In,* 2 plays (N. Y. 1934); "But For the Grace of God" (N. Y. 1937).

PHILIP BARRY, "You and I" (N. Y. 1923); "The Youngest" (N. Y. 1925); "In a Garden" (N. Y. 1926); "White Wings" (N. Y. 1927); "Paris Bound" (N. Y. 1927); "John" (N. Y. 1928); "Holiday" (N. Y. 1928); "Cock Robin," with Elmer Rice (N. Y. 1929); "Hotel Universe" (N. Y. 1930); "Tomorrow and Tomorrow" (N. Y. 1931); "The Animal Kingdom" (N. Y. 1932); "The Joyous Season" (N. Y. 1934); "Spring Dance" (N. Y. 1936).

LEWIS BEACH, *Four One-Act Plays* (N. Y. 1921) contains "The Clod," "A Guest For Dinner," "Love Among the Lions," "Brothers"; "Let's Get Married" (Boston, 1913); "The Goose Hangs High" (N. Y. 1924); "Ann Vroome" (Boston, 1924); "A Square Peg" (Boston, 1924); "Merry Andrew" (N. Y. 1930).

S. N. BEHRMAN, "Biography" (N. Y. 1933); "Brief Moment" (N. Y. 1931); "End of Summer" (N. Y. 1936); "Meteor" (N. Y. 1930); "The Second Man" (N. Y. 1927); "Rain From Heaven" (N. Y. 1935); *Three Plays,* "Serena Blandish," "Meteor," and "The Second Man" (N. Y. 1934); "Amphitryon 38" (N. Y. 1938).

ALBERT BEIN, "Little Ol' Boy" (N. Y. 1935); "Let Freedom Ring" (N. Y. 1936).

DAVID BELASCO, "May Blossom" (N. Y. no date); "Madam Butterfly," with J. L. Long, in Quinn's *Representative American Plays* (N. Y. 1925), and separately (N. Y. 1935); "The Return of Peter Grimm," in Moses' *Representative American Dramatists,* III (N. Y. 1921) and separately (N. Y. 1933); "The Girl of the Golden West," in Moses' *Representative American Dramatists* (Boston, 1925); "The Rose of the Rancho" (N. Y. 1936); *Six Plays* (Boston, 1929) includes "Madam Butterfly," "Du Barry," "The Darling of the Gods," "Adrea," "The Girl of the Golden West," and "The Return of Peter Grimm."

GEORGE BROADHURST, "The Wrong Mr. Wright" (N. Y. 1918); "Why Smith Left Home" (N. Y. 1912); "What Happened to Jones" (N. Y. 1910); "The Man of the Hour" (N. Y. 1916); "Bought and Paid For" (N. Y. no date).

GEORGE CRAM COOK, "Suppressed Desires," with Susan Glaspell.

Glaspell's *Plays* (Boston, 1920); "Tickless Time," with Susan Glaspell, in Glaspell's *Plays* (Boston, 1920); "The Spring" (N. Y. 1921).

MARC CONNELLY, "The Wisdom Tooth" (N. Y. 1927); "The Green Pastures" (N. Y. 1930); "Little David" (N. Y. 1937).

BOSWORTH CROCKER, *Humble Folk* (Cincinnati, 1923) contains "The Last Straw," "The Baby Carriage," "The Dog," "The First Time," "The Cost of a Hat"; "Pawns of War" (Boston, 1918); "The Last Straw" (N. Y. 1917); "Josephine," in *One-Act Plays for Stage and Study,* VI (N. Y. 1931); "Coquine" (N. Y. 1937).

RACHEL CROTHERS, *Mary the Third, Old Lady 31, A Little Journey* (N. Y. 1923); "A Man's World" (Boston, 1915); "The Three of Us" (N. Y. 1916); "The Rector" (N. Y. 1905), and in *One-Act Plays for Stage and Study,* I (N. Y. 1924); "He and She," in Quinn's *Representative American Plays* (N. Y. 1917), and separately (Boston, 1933); "The Heart of Paddy Whack" (N. Y. 1925); "Once Upon a Time" (N. Y. 1925); "Mother Carey's Chickens," with Kate Douglas Wiggin (N. Y. 1925); *Six One-Act Plays* (Boston, 1925) contains "The Importance of Being Clothed," "The Importance of Being Nice," "The Importance of Being Married," "The Importance of Being a Woman," "What They Think," and "Peggy"; "Nice People," in Quinn's *Contemporary American Plays* (N. Y. 1923); *Expressing Willie, etc.* (N. Y. 1924), includes also "39 East," and "Nice People"; "As Husbands Go" (N. Y. 1931); "Caught Wet" (N. Y. 1932); "Everyday" (N. Y. 1930); "Let Us Be Gay" (N. Y. 1929); "When Ladies Meet" (N. Y. 1932).

OWEN DAVIS, "At Yale" (N. Y. no date); "The Detour" (Boston, 1922); "The Haunted House" (N. Y. 1926); "Easy Come, Easy Go" (N. Y. 1926); "Blow Your Own Horn" (N. Y. 1926); "The Nervous Wreck" (N. Y. 1926); "Icebound" (Boston, 1923); "An Old Sweetheart of Mine" (N. Y. 1911); "Robin Hood" (N. Y. 1923); "The Donovan Affair" (N. Y. 1930); "Ethan Frome," with Donald Davis (N. Y. 1936); "Forever After" (N. Y. 1928); "Just to Remind You" (N. Y. 1931); "Let Him Come and Let Him Look" (London, 1918); "Mile-a-Minute Kendall" (N. Y. 1931); "The Triumphant Bachelor" (Minneapolis, 1935); "The World We Live In" (adapted, N. Y. 1933).

WILLIAM C. DE MILLE, "In 1999" (N. Y. 1914); "Food" (N. Y. 1914); "Deceivers" (N. Y. 1914); "Strongheart" (N. Y. no date); "The Genius," with C. B. De Mille (N. Y. no date); "The Forest

Ring," with C. Bernard (N. Y. 1923); "Poor Old Jim" (N. Y. 1914); *Christmas Spirit and Votes For Fairies,* 2 plays (N. Y. 1913); "My Country—So What?" (N. Y. 1933).

Martin Flavin, "Children of the Moon" (N. Y. 1924); "Caleb Stone's Death Watch" (N. Y. 1925); "Lady of the Rose" (N. Y. 1925); "Service For Two" (N. Y. 1927); *Brains, etc.* (N. Y. 1925), contains also "Casualties," "A Question of Principle," "An Emergency Case," "The Blind Man," and "Caleb Stone's Death Watch"; *Achilles Had a Heel and Tapestry in Gray,* 2 plays (N. Y. 1936); "Amaco" (N. Y. 1933); "Around the Corner" (N. Y. 1937); "Broken Dishes" (N. Y. 1930); "The Criminal Code" (N. Y. 1929); "Cross Roads" (N. Y. 1930); "Spindrift" (N. Y. 1930).

James Forbes, "The Traveling Salesman" (N. Y. 1918); "The Commuters" (N. Y. 1916); "The Famous Mrs. Fair" (N. Y. 1920); "The Chorus Lady" (N. Y. 1920); "The Show Shop" (N. Y. 1922); *The Famous Mrs. Fair, etc.* (N. Y. 1920), contains also "The Chorus Lady," "The Show Shop."

Zona Gale, "The Neighbors" (N. Y. no date); "Miss Lulu Bett" (N. Y. 1923); "Mr. Pitt" (N. Y. 1924); "Uncle Jimmy" (Boston, 1922); "Evening Clothes" (Boston, 1932); "Faint Perfume" (N. Y. 1934).

Virgil Geddes, "The Frog" (Paris, 1926); *The Earth Between and Behind the Night* (N. Y. 1930); "The Stable and the Grove," in *American Caravan,* IV (N. Y.); "Mud on the Hoofs," in *Folk-Say,* IV (Norman, Okla.); *Native Ground,* 3 plays (N. Y. 1932); "Pocahontas and the Elders" (Chapel Hill, 1933); *From the Life of George Emery Blum,* 4 plays (Brookfield, Conn., 1934).

William Gillette, "Electricity" (N. Y. 1924); "Secret Service" (N. Y. no date); "Too Much Johnson" (N. Y. 1912); "Held by the Enemy" (N. Y. no date); "The Red Owl," in *One-Act Plays for Stage and Study,* I (N. Y. 1924); "Esmeralda," with Frances H. Burnett (N. Y. no date); "All the Comforts of Home" (N. Y. no date); "Among Thieves," in *One-Act Plays for Stage and Study,* II (N. Y. 1925); "How Well George Does It" (N. Y. 1936); "Sherlock Holmes" (N. Y. 1935).

Susan Glaspell, "The Inheritors" (Boston, 1921); "The Verge" (Boston, 1922); *Plays* (Boston, 1920) contains "Trifles," "The People," "Close the Book," "The Outside," "Woman's Honor," "Bernice," "Suppressed Desires" (with G. C. Cook), "Tickless

Time" (with G. C. Cook); "Trifles" (N. Y. 1916); *The People and Close the Book* (N. Y. 1918); "Suppressed Desires" (Boston, 1926); "The Comic Artist," with Norman Matson (London, 1927); "Alison's House" (N. Y. 1930).

PAUL GREEN, *The Lord's Will* (N. Y. 1925) contains also "Blackbeard," "The Old Man of Edenton," "The No 'Count Boy," "Fixin's," "The Last of the Lowries," and "Old Wash Lucas"; *Lonesome Road* (N. Y. 1926) contains "In Abraham's Bosom," "The End of the Row," "The Hot Iron," "White Dresses," "The Prayer Meeting," and "Your Fiery Furnace"; "Granny Boling," in *The Drama* (Chicago, 1921); "In Aunt Mahaly's Cabin" (N. Y. 1925); *The Field God and In Abraham's Bosom* (N. Y. 1927); "Unto Such Glory," in *One-Act Plays for Stage and Study,* III (N. Y. 1927); "The Man Who Died at Twelve o'Clock," in *One-Act Plays for Stage and Study,* II (N. Y. 1925), and separately (N. Y. 1927); "Quare Medicine," in Shay's *Fifty More Contemporary One-Act Plays* (N. Y. 1928); *In the Valley, etc.* (N. Y. 1928) contains also "The Picnic," "A Saturday Night," "Supper for the Dead," "The Man on the House," "Unto Such Glory," "Quare Medicine," "In Aunt Mahaly's Cabin," "The Man Who Died at Twelve o'Clock," "The No 'Count Boy," and "The Goodbye"; "Blue Thunder," in *One-Act Plays for Stage and Study,* IV (N. Y. 1928); *The House of Connelly, etc.* (N. Y. 1931) contains "The House of Connelly," "Potter's Field," and "Tread the Green Grass"; "Hymn to the Rising Sun" (N. Y. 1936); "Johnny Johnson" (N. Y. 1937); "Roll Sweet Chariot" (N. Y. 1935); "Shroud My Body Down" (Iowa City, 1935); "The Lost Colony" (Chapel Hill, 1937).

GEORGE C. HAZLETON, JR., and HARRY BENRIMO, "The Yellow Jacket" (Indianapolis, 1913).

SIDNEY HOWARD, "Swords" (N. Y. 1921); "They Knew What They Wanted" (N. Y. 1925); "Lexington" (Lexington, Mass., 1925); "Lucky Sam McCarver" (N. Y. 1925); "Ned McCobb's Daughter" (N. Y. 1927); "The Silver Cord" (N. Y. 1927); "Half Gods" (N. Y. 1929); "Alien Corn" (N. Y. 1931); "Yellow Jack" (N. Y. 1933); "Dodsworth" (N. Y. 1934); "Paths of Glory" (N. Y. 1935); "The Late Christopher Bean" (adapted, N. Y. 1934).

HATCHER HUGHES, "Hell-Bent fer Heaven" (N. Y. 1924); "Ruint" (N. Y. 1925).

GEORGE S. KAUFMAN, "The Butter-and-Egg Man" (N. Y. 1926); "If

Men Played Cards as Women Do" (N. Y. 1926); "The Pride of the Claghornes," in *Blackouts* (N. Y. 1932).

——— and MARC CONNELLY, "Dulcy" (N. Y. 1921); "To the Ladies!" (N. Y. 1923); "Beggar on Horseback" (N. Y. 1924); "Merton of the Movies" (N. Y. 1925).

——— and EDNA FERBER, "Minick" (N. Y. 1924); "The Royal Family" (N. Y. 1927); "Dinner at Eight" (N. Y. 1932); "Stage Door" (N. Y. 1937).

——— and MOSS HART, "Once in a Lifetime" (N. Y. 1930); "Merrily We Roll Along" (N. Y. 1934); "You Can't Take It With You" (N. Y. 1936); "I'd Rather Be Right" (N. Y. 1938).

——— and RING LARDNER, "June Moon" (N. Y. 1929).

CHARLES KENYON, "Kindling" (Garden City, 1914).

GEORGE KELLY, "The Torch Bearers" (N. Y. 1924); "The Show-Off" (Boston, 1924); "Finders-Keepers" (Cincinnati, 1922); *The Flattering Word* (Boston, 1925) contains also "Smarty's Party," "The Weak Spot," and "Poor Aubrey"; "Craig's Wife" (Boston, 1926); "Daisy Mayme" (Boston, 1927); "One of Those Things," in *One-Act Plays for Stage and Study,* III (N. Y. 1927); "Behold—the Bridegroom" (N. Y. 1927); "Philip Goes Forth" (N. Y. 1931); "Reflected Glory" (N. Y. 1937).

SIDNEY KINGSLEY, "Men in White" (N. Y. 1933); "Dead End" (N. Y. 1936).

CHARLES KLEIN, "Maggie Pepper" (N. Y. 1916); "The Daughters of Men" (N. Y. 1917); "The Gamblers" (N. Y. no date); "The Lion and the Mouse" (N. Y. no date); "Heartsease," with J. I. C. Clarke (N. Y. 1916); "The Third Degree" (N. Y. 1917); "The Next of Kin" (N. Y. 1917); "The Music Master" (N. Y. 1935).

EDWARD KNOBLOCK [KNOBLAUCH], "Kismet" (N. Y. 1911); "My Lady's Dress" (Garden City, 1914); "Milestones," with Arnold Bennett (N. Y. 1912); *The Lullaby and Other Plays* (N. Y. 1924) contains also "Marie-Odile," "Tiger! Tiger!"; "The Headmaster," with W. T. Coleby (London, no date).

CLARE KUMMER, "Good Gracious Annabelle" (N. Y. 1922); "A Successful Calamity" (N. Y. 1922); "The Rescuing Angel" (N. Y. 1923); "Be Calm, Camilla" (N. Y. 1922); "Rollo's Wild Oat" (N. Y. 1922); "The Robbery" (N. Y. 1921); "Chinese Love" (N. Y. 1922); "Bridges" (N. Y. 1922); "The Choir Rehearsal" (N. Y. 1922); "Pomeroy's Past" (N. Y. 1927); "Papers," in *One-Act Plays for Stage and Study,* III (N. Y. 1927); "Her Master's

Voice" (N. Y. 1934); "So's Your Old Antique" (N. Y. 1928).

LAWRENCE LANGNER, "The Broken Image" (N. Y. 1918); *Five One-Act Comedies* (Cincinnati, 1922) contains "Matinata," "Another Way Out," "The Family Exit," "Pie," "Licensed"; "Moses" (N. Y. 1925); "Henry, Behave!" (N. Y. 1927).

——— and A. MARSHALL, "The Pursuit of Happiness" (N. Y. 1934); "Accidents Will Happen," in *One-Act Plays for Stage and Study* (N. Y. 1932); "The Sire de Maletroit's Door" (N. Y. 1931).

JOHN HOWARD LAWSON, "Roger Bloomer" (N. Y. 1923); "Processional" (N. Y. 1925); "Loud Speaker" (N. Y. 1927); "The International" (N. Y. 1927); "Success Story" (N. Y. 1932); *With a Reckless Preface,* 2 plays, "Gentlewoman" and "The Pure in Heart" (N. Y. 1934); "Marching Song" (N. Y. 1937).

ROI COOPER MEGRUE, "Under Cover" (N. Y. 1918); "Under Fire" (N. Y. 1918); "It Pays to Advertise," with Walter Hackett (N. Y. 1917); "Seven Chances" (N. Y. 1924); "Tea For Three" (Boston, 1924); "Honors Are Even" (Boston, 1924); "The Same Old Thing," in *One-Act Plays for Stage and Study,* II (N. Y. 1925).

GEORGE MIDDLETON, *Tradition and Other One-Act Plays* (N. Y. 1913); *Possession and Other One-Act Plays* (N. Y. 1915); *Embers and Other One-Act Plays* (N. Y. 1911); *Masks and Other One-Act Plays* (N. Y. 1920); "Back of the Ballot" (N. Y. 1915); "The Road Together" (N. Y. 1916); "Nowadays" (N. Y. 1914); "Criminals" (N. Y. 1915); "The Light of the World," with Guy Bolton (N. Y. 1920); *Polly With a Past and Adam and Eva,* with Guy Bolton (N. Y. 1923), both separately (N. Y. 1924 and 1925); "The Bride," with S. Olivier (N. Y. 1926); "The Cave Girl," with Guy Bolton (N. Y. 1925); "The Big Pond," with A. E. Thomas (N. Y. 1930); "Blood Money" (N. Y. 1929); "Hiss! Boom!! Blah!!!" (N. Y. 1933); "That Was Balzac" (N. Y. 1936).

LANGDON MITCHELL, "The New York Idea" (Boston, 1908).

PHILIP MOELLER, "Sophie" (N. Y. 1919); "Molière" (N. Y. 1919); "Madame Sand" (N. Y. 1917); "Two Blind Beggars and One Less Blind" (N. Y. 1918); *Five Somewhat Historical Plays* (N. Y. 1918) contains "Helena's Husband," "The Little Supper," "Sisters of Susannah," "The Roadhouse in Arden," "Pokey."

JAMES MONTGOMERY, "Ready Money" (N. Y. 1916); "Nothing but the Truth" (N. Y. 1920).

WILLIAM VAUGHN MOODY, "The Fire Bringer" (Boston, 1904); "The Masque of Judgment" (Boston, 1902); "The Great Divide"

(N. Y. 1909); "The Faith Healer" (Boston, 1909); *Poems and Plays* (Boston, 1912), contains above plays.

Kenyon Nicholson, "Honor Bright," with Meredith Nicholson (N. Y. 1923); "Sally and Company" (N. Y. 1925); "The Three Graces," with Dena Reed (N. Y. 1925); "The Meal Ticket" (N. Y. 1926); "The Barker" (N. Y. 1927); "Here's to Your Health" (N. Y. 1927); "Two Weeks Off" (N. Y. 1927); *Garden Varieties* (N. Y. 1924) contains one-act plays; "The Bug Man" (N. Y. 1923); "Meet the Missus," in *One-Act Plays for Stage and Study,* II (N. Y. 1925); "A Night's Work" (N. Y. 1926); "The Organ," with E. Pendray (N. Y. 1926); "Bedside Manners," with S. Behrman (N. Y. 1924); "Wanderlust" (Boston, 1926); "Deliverance" (Boston, 1926); "The Marriage of Little Eva," in Shay's *Fifty More Contemporary One-Act Plays* (N. Y. 1928); "Eva the 5th," with J. Golden (N. Y. 1928); "Sailor Beware!" with C. Robinson (N. Y. 1933); "Shame the Devil," with A. de Sola (N. Y. 1928); "Tell Me Your Troubles" (N. Y. 1928); "Torch Song," (N. Y. 1930); "Words and Music," in *One-Act Plays for Stage and Study,* V (N. Y. 1929); "The Snake Eater," in *One-Act Plays for Stage and Study,* IV (N. Y. 1928).

Clifford Odets, "Awake and Sing!" (N. Y. 1935); "I Can't Sleep" (monologue, *New Theater,* N. Y. 1936); "Paradise Lost" (N. Y. 1936); *Three Plays,* contains "Awake and Sing!", "Waiting for Lefty," and "Till the Day I Die" (N. Y. 1935); *Waiting for Lefty and Till the Day I Die,* 2 plays (N. Y. 1935).

George O'Neil, "American Dream" (N. Y. 1933).

Josephine Preston Peabody, "The Chameleon" (N. Y. 1917); "The Wings" (N. Y. 1915); "Fortune and Men's Eyes" (Boston, 1900); "Marlowe" (Boston, 1901); "The Piper" (Boston, 1909); "The Wolf of Gubbio" (Boston, 1913); "Portrait of Mrs. W." (Boston, 1922).

Channing Pollock, "The Little Gray Lady" (N. Y. 1918); "Such a Little Queen" (N. Y. 1918); "The Fool" (N. Y. 1922); "The Sign on the Door" (N. Y. 1925); "The Enemy" (N. Y. 1925); "The House Beautiful" (N. Y. 1931); "Mr. Moneypenny" (N. Y. 1928); "The Stranglehold" (N. Y. 1934).

Samson Raphaelson, "The Jazz Singer" (N. Y. 1935); "The Wooden Slipper" (Evanston, 1934); "First Love" (N. Y. 1930); *Accent on Youth and White Man* (N. Y. 1935).

Elmer Rice, "On Trial" (N. Y. 1919); "The Passing of Chow-

Chow," in *One-Act Plays for Stage and Study,* II (N. Y. 1925); "The Adding Machine" (Garden City, 1923); "The Home of the Free," in *Morningside Plays* (N. Y. 1917); "Counsellor-at-Law" (N. Y. 1931); "A Diadem of Snow," in *One-Act Plays for Stage and Study,* V (N. Y. 1929); "The House in Blind Alley" (N. Y. 1932); "Judgment Day" (N. Y. 1934); "See Naples and Die" (N. Y. 1930); "Street Scene" (N. Y. 1929); "The Subway" (N. Y. 1929); *Three Plays Without Words* (N. Y. 1934); *Two Plays* contains "Not for Children" and "Between Two Worlds" (N. Y. 1935); "We the People" (N. Y. 1933); "The Left Bank" (N. Y. 1931); "Close Harmony," with D. Parker (N. Y. 1929).

LYNN RIGGS, "Big Lake" (N. Y. 1927); "Knives From Syria," in *One-Act Plays for Stage and Study,* III (N. Y. 1927); "Green Grow the Lilacs" (N. Y. 1931); "Roadside" (N. Y. 1930); *Russet Mantle and the Cherokee Night,* 2 plays (N. Y. 1936); *Sump'n Like Wings and A Lantern to See By,* 2 plays (N. Y. 1928).

IRWIN SHAW, "Bury the Dead" (N. Y. 1936).

ROBERT E. SHERWOOD, "Idiot's Delight" (N. Y. 1936); "The Queen's Husband" (N. Y. 1928); "The Petrified Forest" (N. Y. 1935); "Reunion in Vienna" (N. Y. 1932); "The Road to Rome" (N. Y. 1927); "This Is New York" (N. Y. 1931); "Tovarich" (N. Y. 1937); "Waterloo Bridge" (N. Y. 1930).

LOUIS EVAN SHIPMAN, "Darcy of the Guards" (N. Y. 1915); *Three Comedies* (N. Y. 1923) contains "On Parole," "The Fountain of Youth," "Fools Errant"; "Ben Franklin" (Boston, 1933).

HARRY JAMES SMITH, "A Tailor-Made Man" (N. Y. 1919); "Mrs. Bumpstead-Leigh" (N. Y. 1917); "The Little Teacher" (N. Y. 1919).

WINCHELL SMITH, "The Fortune Hunter" (N. Y. 1909); "The Boomerang," with Victor Mapes (N. Y. 1915); "Turn to the Right," with J. E. Hazzard (N. Y. 1916); "Brewster's Millions," with B. Ongley (N. Y. 1925); "A Holy Terror," with G. Abbott (N. Y. 1926); "The New Henrietta," with V. Mapes (N. Y. 1913); "The Zoo," with M. Arlen (N. Y. 1927). "Thank You," with Tom Cushing (N. Y. 1924); "Lightnin'," with Frank Bacon (N. Y. 1925); "Going Crooked," with William Collier (N. Y. 1926).

BELLA and SAMUEL SPEWACK, "Poppa" (N. Y. 1929); "Clear All Wires" (N. Y. 1932); "Solitaire Man" (N. Y. 1934); *Boy Meets Girl and Spring Song* (N. Y. 1936).

LAURENCE STALLINGS and MAXWELL ANDERSON, *Three American Plays* (N. Y. 1926) contains "What Price Glory?", "First Flight," and "The Buccaneer."

AUSTIN STRONG, "Three Wise Fools" (N. Y. 1919); "The Toymaker of Nuremberg" (N. Y. 1921); "The Little Father of the Wilderness" (N. Y. 1924); "The Drums of Oude" (N. Y. 1926); *The Drums of Oude, etc.* (N. Y. 1926) contains also "The Little Father of the Wilderness" and "Popo"; "Seventh Heaven" (N. Y. 1926).

A. E. THOMAS, "The Rainbow" (N. Y. no date); "Her Husband's Wife" (Garden City, 1914); "Come Out of the Kitchen" (N. Y. 1921); "The Champion," with T. Louden (N. Y. 1922); "Only 38" (N. Y. 1922); "Just Suppose" (N. Y. 1923); "The Big Idea," with Clayton Hamilton (N. Y. 1917); "The Better Understanding," with Clayton Hamilton (Boston, 1924); "Thirty Days," with Clayton Hamilton (N. Y. 1923); "Her Friend the King," with H. Rhodes (N. Y. 1930); "Uncle Tom's Cabin," (adapted, N. Y. 1933).

RIDGELY TORRENCE, *Granny Maumee, The Rider of Dreams, Simon the Cyrenian* (N. Y. 1917); "Abelard and Heloise" (N. Y. 1907); "El Dorado" (N. Y. 1903).

DAN TOTHEROH, "Wild Birds" (N. Y. 1925); *One Act Plays for Everyone* (N. Y. 1931); "Distant Drums" (N. Y. 1932); "Moor Born" (N. Y. 1934).

BAYARD VEILLER, "Within the Law" (N. Y. 1917); "The Thirteenth Chair" (N. Y. 1922); "The Trial of Mary Dugan" (N. Y. 1928).

JOHN WEXLEY, "The Last Mile" (N. Y. 1930); Same, 1 act (N. Y. 1931); "They Shall Not Die" (N. Y. 1934).

JESSE LYNCH WILLIAMS, "Why Marry?" [originally "And So They Were Married"] (N. Y. 1914); "Why Not?" (Boston, 1924).

ARGENTINE DRAMATISTS

JULIO SANCHEZ GARDEL, "The Witches' Mountain," trans. by J. S. Fassett, Jr., in Bierstadt's *Three Plays of the Argentine* (N. Y. 1920).

LUIS BAYON HERRERA, "Santos Vega," trans. by J. S. Fassett, Jr., in Bierstadt's *Three Plays of the Argentine* (N. Y. 1920).

SILVERIO MANCO, "Juan Moreira," trans. by J. S. Fassett, Jr., in Bierstadt's *Three Plays of the Argentine* (N. Y. 1920).

Australian Dramatists

George S. Beeby, *Concerning Ordinary People* (Sydney, 1923) contains "The Banner," "The Point o' View," "Potter and Clay," "Dregs," "One Touch o' Nature," and "Still Waters."

Spencer Brodney, "Rebel Smith" (N. Y. 1925).

Louis Esson, *Dead Timber and Other Plays* (London, 1920) contains "Dead Timber," "The Woman Tamer," "The Drovers," and "The Sacred Place."

Vance Palmer, "The Black Horse" (Melbourne, no date).

Belgian Dramatists

Georges Rodenbach, "The Veil," trans. by H. Harper, in Shay's *Fifty More Contemporary One-Act Plays* (N. Y. 1928).

Gustave Vanzype, *Mother Nature and Progress: Two Belgian Plays*, trans. by B. H. Clark (Boston, 1917).

Emile Verhaeren, *The Plays of Emile Verhaeren* (Boston, 1916) contains "The Dawn," trans. by Arthur Symons; "The Cloister," trans. by Osman Edwards; "Philip II," trans. by F. S. Flint; "Helen of Sparta," trans. by J. Bithell; "The Dawn," trans. by Arthur Symons (Boston, 1915); "The Cloister," trans. by Osman Edwards (London, 1915).

Canadian Dramatists

Martha Allen, "Summer Solstice" (Toronto, 1935).

L. Bullock-Webster, *The Shadow of the Nile* (Toronto, 1935).

J. B. Cowan, "Canuck" (Vancouver, 1931).

Merrill Denison, *The Unheroic North* (Toronto, 1923) contains "Brothers in Arms," "The Weather Breeder," "From Their Own Place," and "Marsh Hay"; "Balm," in *Canadian Plays*, I (Toronto, 1926); "On Christmas Night" (N. Y. 1931); *Henry Hudson and Other Plays*, 6 plays (Toronto, 1931); "The Prize Winner" (N. Y. 1928).

A. M. D. Fairbairn, *Plays of the Pacific Coast* (Toronto, 1935).

R. Edis Fairbairn, "When the King Smiled" (Toronto, 1935).

Rica McLean Farquharson, "Sure of a Fourth" (Toronto, 1935).

James P. Ferguson, "Courage, Mr. Greene," (N. Y. 1936).

Fred Jacobs, *One Third of a Bill* (Toronto, 1925) contains "Autumn Blooming," "The Clever One," "And They Met Again," "Man's World," and "The Basket."

ISABEL ECCLESTONE MACKAY, "The Last Cache" (N. Y. 1927); "Treasure" (N. Y. 1926); "Goblin Gold" (N. Y. 1933); "Two Too Many" (Philadelphia, 1927).

VINCENT MASSEY [ed.], *Canadian Plays from Hart House Theater,* Vol. I (Toronto, 1926) contains "Brothers in Arms," Merrill Denison; "The Weather Breeder," by the same; "Pierre," Duncan Campbell Scott; "The Point of View," Marian Osborne; "Three Weddings of a Hunchback," H. Borsook; "The Second Lie," Isabel Ecclestone Mackay; "Balm," Merrill Denison; "The Translation of John Snaith," Britton Cooke; *Canadian Plays from Hart House Theater,* Vol. II (Toronto, 1927) contains "The God of Gods," Carroll Aikins; "The Freedom of Jean Guichet," L. A. MacKay; and "Trespassers," Leslie Reid.

GEORGE ALFRED PALMER, "Madam Verite at Bath" (Toronto, 1935).

MARJORIE PRICE, "God Caesar" (Toronto, 1935).

ALEXANDER RAMSAY, "Coercion" (Toronto, 1935).

MAZO DE LA ROCHE, "Low Life" (Toronto, 1925); "Whiteoaks" (Boston, 1936); *Low Life and Other Plays,* 3 plays (Boston, 1929).

LYON SHARMAN, "A Somersault to Love" (Toronto, 1926).

LILLIAN BEYNON THOMAS, "Jim Barker's Spite Fence" (Toronto, 1935).

HERMAN H. VOADEN [ed.], *Six Canadian Plays* (Toronto, 1930): B. P. Sandiford's "The Bone Spoon"; A. J. Key's "The Mother Lode"; T. M. Morrow's "Manitou Portage"; J. E. Middleton's "Lake Doré"; C. E. Carruthers' "God-Forsaken"; and D. S. Conover's "Winds of Life."

[NO EDITOR] *One-Act Plays by Canadian Authors* (Montreal, 1926); "The Blue Pitcher," T. M. Morrow; "The Maid," Stuart Armour; "Low Life," Mazo de la Roche; "All Hallows' Eve," Pauline B. Perrigard; "For the Empire," Gregory Doane; "Which?" Frances F. Williams; "The Traitor," Leslie G. Barnard; "The Hardhead," Nancy Rankin; "The Favors of My Lady Leone," Margaret E. Elliott; "A Dead Woman Bites Not," Gregory Doane; "The Happiest Place," Merton S. Threlfall; "The Dream," Mary Wallace Brooks; "Come True," Mazo de la Roche; "The Midnight of Monsieur St. Jean," Leslie G. Barnard; "The King," Pauline B. Perrigard; "Voices," Mary W. Brooks; "The Turn of the Road," Elizabeth J. Church; "The Death of Pierrot," Harry Green; "The Newcomer," Stuart Armour.

Cuban Dramatist

José Antonio Ramos, "When Love Dies," trans. by Isaac Goldberg, in Shay's *Twenty-five Short Plays* (N. Y. 1925).

Czechoslovak Dramatists

(*Bohemian*)

Joseph Capek, "The Land of Many Names," trans. by P. Selver (London, 1926).

Joseph and Karel Capek, "And So ad infinitum," adapted by N. Playfair and C. Bax after the trans. by P. Selver (Oxford, 1923); Same, as "The World We Live In," adapted by Owen Davis (N. Y. 1933); "Adam the Creator," trans. by D. Round (N. Y. no date).

Karel Capek, "The Makropoulos Secret," adapted by R. C. Burrell (Boston, 1925); "R. U. R.," trans. by P. Selver (Garden City, 1923); "The Solstice," trans. by E. D. Schonberger (*Poet Lore,* Boston, 1924); "Pistol of the Beg," trans. by E. D. Schonberger (*Poet Lore,* Boston, 1923).

Victor Dyk, "The Ninth Night," trans. by C. J. Hrbek (*Poet Lore,* Boston, 1918).

Jaroslav Hilbert, "Whom the Gods Destroy," trans. by C. Recht (*Poet Lore,* Boston, 1916).

Alois Jirasek, "Dobromila Rettig," trans. by B. Herman and G. R. Noyes (*Poet Lore,* Boston, 1921).

Jaroslav Kvapil, "The Clouds," trans. by C. Recht (*Poet Lore,* Boston, 1910); "The Will o' the Wisp," trans. by S. Hrbkova (*Poet Lore,* Boston, 1916).

Frana Sramek, "June," trans. anonymously, in Selver's *Anthology of Modern Slavonic Literature* (London, 1919).

Frantisek Subert, "Jan Vyrava," trans. by S. Hrbkova (*Poet Lore,* Boston, 1915); "The Great Freeholder," trans. by B. M. Mekota (*Poet Lore,* Boston, 1924); "The Awakening," trans. by B. M. Mekota (*Poet Lore,* Boston, 1922); "Petr vok Rozmberk," trans. by B. M. Mekota (*Poet Lore,* Boston, 1920); "The Four Bare Walls," trans. by B. M. Mekota and F. H. Snow (*Poet Lore,* Boston, 1917).

Jaroslav Vrchlicky, "At the Chasm," trans. by C. Recht (*Poet Lore,* Boston, 1913); "The Vengeance of Catullus," trans. by C.

Recht (*Poet Lore,* Boston, 1914); "The Witness," trans. by C. Recht (*Poet Lore,* Boston, 1914).

JULIUS ZEYER, "Raduz and Mahulena," trans. by Z. Buben and G. R. Noyes (*Poet Lore,* Boston, 1923).

DANISH DRAMATISTS

HOLGER DRACHMANN, "Renaissance," trans. by L. M. Hollander (*Poet Lore,* Boston, 1908).

ALBERT GNUDTZMANN, "Eyes That Cannot See," trans. by A. Paulson (Cincinnati, 1923); reprinted in Shay's *Twenty-five Short Plays, International* (N. Y. 1925).

GUSTAV WIED, "2 × 2 = 5," trans. by E. Boyd and H. Koppel (N. Y. 1923); "Autumn Fires," in Shay and Loving's *Fifty Contemporary One-Act Plays* (Cincinnati, 1920).

DUTCH DRAMATISTS

MARIE METZ-KONING, "The White Lie," trans. by May Tevis and Pierre Loving, in Loving's *Ten-Minute Plays* (N. Y. 1923).

HERMAN C. J. ROELVINK, "The Stormbird," trans. by A. D. Ficke (*Poet Lore,* Boston, 1913).

J. H. SPEENHOF, "Louise," trans. by A. v. C. P. Huizinga, in Shay and Loving's *Fifty Contemporary One-Act Plays* (Cincinnati, 1920).

ENGLISH DRAMATISTS

RODNEY ACKLAND, "Strange Orchestra" (London, 1932); "Dance With No Music" (London, 1933); "The Old Ladies" (London, 1935); "After October" (London, 1936).

C. L. ANTHONY, "Autumn Crocus" (N. Y. 1931); "Call it a Day" (N. Y. 1936); "Touch Wood" (N. Y. 1934); "Service" (London, 1932); "Bonnet Over the Windmill" (London, 1937).

W. H. AUDEN and CHRISTOPHER ISHERWOOD, "The Dog Beneath the Skin" (N. Y. 1935); "The Ascent of F6" (N. Y. 1937).

ARNOLD BENNETT, *Polite Farces* (N. Y. no date) contains 3 short plays; "The Honeymoon" (N. Y. 1911); "Cupid and Commonsense" (N. Y. no date); "What the Public Wants" (N. Y. 1911); "The Great Adventure" (N. Y. 1913); "Judith" (N. Y. 1919); "The Title" (N. Y. 1918); "Don Juan de Marana" (London, 1923); "Sacred and Profane Love" (N. Y. 1920); "Milestones," with E. Knoblock (N. Y. 1912); "London Life," with E. Knoblock

(N. Y. 1924); "The Bright Island" (N. Y. 1925); "The Ides of March," in *One-Act Plays for Stage and Study,* VIII (N. Y. 1934); "The Snake Charmer," in *One-Act Plays for Stage and Study,* VI (N. Y. 1931).

Rudolf Besier, "Don" (N. Y. 1909); "Lady Patricia" (N. Y. 1911); "The Virgin Goddess" (London, 1907); "The Barretts of Wimpole Street" (Boston, 1936); "Secrets" (London, 1926).

James Bridie, *Three Plays* (London, 1930) includes "The Switchback," "The Pardoner's Tale," and "The Sunlight Sonata"; *The Anatomist and Other Plays* (N. Y. 1931) includes also "Tobias and the Angel," and "The Amazed Evangelist"; *Four Plays* (London, 1934) includes "Colonel Witherspoon," "What It Is to Be Young," "The Dancing Bear," and "The Girl Who Did Not Want to Go to Knala Lumpur"; *Five Plays* (London, 1934) includes "A Sleeping Clergyman," "Tobias and the Angel," "Jonah and the Whale," "The Anatomist," and "The Amazed Evangelist"; "Marriage Is No Joke" (London, 1934); "Mary Read" (London, 1935); "The Black Eye" (London, 1935); "Storm in a Teacup" (London, 1936).

Harold Brighouse, "Garside's Career" (Chicago, 1915); "Dealing in Futures" (London, no date); "Graft" (London, 1913); "The Odd Man Out" (London, 1912); "The Price of Coal" (London, 1911); "Lonesome-Like" (London, 1914); "The Oak Settle" (London, 1911); "Little Red Shoes" (Boston, 1925); "The Apple Tree" (London, 1923); "The Night of 'Mr. H.' " in Cohen's *More One-Act Plays* (N. Y. 1927); "When Did They Meet Again?" in *One-Act Plays for Stage and Study,* III (N. Y. 1927); "The Doorway" (London, 1913); "Spring in Bloomsbury" (London, 1913); "Hobson's Choice" (Garden City, 1916); "Converts" (London, 1920); "Maid of France" (London, 1917); "The Scaring-off of Teddy Dawson" (London, 1911); "Once a Hero" (London, 1922); "Followers" (London, 1922); "The Happy Hangman" (London, 1922); *Three Lancashire Plays* (London, 1920) contains "The Game," "The Northerners," "Zack"; *Plays for the Meadow and Plays for the Lawn,* 4 plays (London, 1921); "Mary's John" (N. Y. 1925); "The Bantam, V. C." (Boston, 1925); *Open-Air Plays,* 5 plays (London, 1926); "The Little Liberty" (N. Y. no date); "New Leisure," in *Tournament Plays* (N. Y. 1936); "When Did They Meet Again?" in *One-Act Plays for Stage and Study,* III (N. Y. 1927); "The Stoker," in *One-Act Plays for Stage and Study,* V (N. Y. 1929); "The Witch's Daughter," in *One-Act Plays for Stage and Study,* IV (N. Y. 1928); "The Wish Shop," in *New Plays for Women and Girls* (N. Y. 1933); "Smoke Screens," in *One-Act Plays for Stage and Study,* VII (N. Y. 1933).

R. C. CARTON, "Bear Leaders" (London, 1913); "Dinner for Two" (London, 1903); "Other People's Worries" (London, 1925); "Lady Huntworth's Experiment" (N. Y. 1904); "Liberty Hall" (London, 1900); "Mr. Hopkinson" (London, 1908); "Mr. Preedy and the Countess" (London, 1910); "The Ninth Waltz" (London, 1904); "Sunlight and Shadow" (London, 1906); "Public Opinion" (London, 1913).

NOEL COWARD, "I'll Leave It To You" (London, 1920); "The Young Idea" (London, 1924); "Hay Fever" (N. Y. 1925); "The Vortex" (N. Y. 1925); "Easy Virtue" (N. Y. 1926); "The Rat Trap" (London, 1924); "Fallen Angels" (London, 1925); "The Marquise" (London, 1927); "The Queen Was In the Parlor" (London, 1926); "This Was a Man" (N. Y. 1926); *Three Plays* (London, 1925) contains "The Rat Trap," "The Vortex," and "Fallen Angels"; "Cavalcade" (N. Y. 1936); "Conversation Piece" (N. Y. 1934); "Design for Living" (N. Y. 1933); "Point Valaine" (N. Y. 1935); "Post Mortem" (N. Y. 1931); "Private Lives" (N. Y. 1933); "Tonight at 8:30" (N. Y. 1936); "Sirocco" (London, 1927); "Bitter Sweet" (N. Y. 1933); *Play Parade* (N. Y. 1933) includes "Hay Fever," "Private Lives," "Design for Living," "Bitter Sweet," "The Vortex," "Cavalcade," and "Post-Mortem"; *Bitter Sweet and Other Plays* (N. Y. 1929) includes also "Easy Virtue" and "Hay Fever."

CLEMENCE DANE, "A Bill of Divorcement" (N. Y. 1921); "Will Shakespeare" (N. Y. 1922); "The Way Things Happen" (N. Y. 1923); "Mr. Fox" (N. Y. 1926); "Shivering Shocks" (London, 1923); "Naboth's Vineyard" (N. Y. 1925); "Granite" (N. Y. 1926); "Mariners" (N. Y. 1927); "Adam's Opera" (N. Y. 1929); "Wild Decembers" (N. Y. 1932); "Come of Age" (N. Y. 1935); "Moonlight Is Silver" (London, 1934).

GORDON DAVIOT, "Richard of Bordeaux" (N. Y. 1935); "Queen of Scots" (London, 1934); "The Laughing Woman" (London, 1934).

JOHN DRINKWATER, "Abraham Lincoln" (Boston, 1919); "Oliver Cromwell" (Boston, 1921); "Mary Stuart" (Boston, 1921); "Robert E. Lee" (Boston, 1923); "Robert Burns" (Boston, 1925); *Pawns* (London, 1917) contains "The Storm," "The God of Quiet," "X = O: A Night of the Trojan War"; *Pawns* (Boston, 1920) contains "Cophetua" in addition to the others: "The Storm" (London, 1915); "The God of Quiet" (London, 1916); "X = O: A Night of the Trojan War" (London, 1917); "Cophetua" (London, 1911); "Rebellion" (London, 1914); *The Collected Plays,* 2 vols. (London, 1925) contains "Cophetua," "Rebellion," "The Storm," "The God of Quiet," "X = O," "Mary Stuart"; four masques: "Abraham Lincoln," "Oliver Cromwell," "Robert E. Lee," and "Little Johnny"; "Bird in Hand" (Boston, 1927); "A Man's House" (London, 1934); "Midsummer Eve" (London, 1932); "Laying the Devil" (London, 1933); "Garibaldi" (London, 1936).

H. V. ESMOND, "When We Were Twenty-One" (N. Y. no date); "Eliza Comes to Stay" (N. Y. 1913); "The Law Divine" (N. Y. 1922); "Her Vote" (N. Y. 1910); "Billie's Little Love Affair" (N. Y. 1904); "One Summer's Day" (N. Y. 1900); "The Wilderness" (N. Y. 1901); "In and Out of a Punt" (London, no date).

JAMES BERNARD FAGAN, "Hawthorne of the U. S. A." (N. Y. 1917); "The Earth" (N. Y. 1910); "The Prayer of the Sword" (London, 1904); "The Wheel of Life" (N. Y. 1922); "And So To Bed" (N. Y. 1927).

HALCOTT GLOVER, "Wat Tyler" (London, 1921); "The King's Jewry" (London, 1921); "Exodus," with H. F. Rubinstein (N. Y. no date); "The Second Round" (London, 1923); "Hail, Cæsar!" (London, 1922); *Wat Tyler and Other Plays* (N. Y. 1926) contains revised versions of "Wat Tyler," "The King's Jewry," and "Hail, Cæsar!"; *Three Comedies* (N. Y. no date).

CYRIL HARCOURT, "The Intruder" (N. Y. 1920); "A Pair of Silk Stockings" (London, 1920); "A Place in the Sun" (London, 1914).

B. MACDONALD HASTINGS, "The New Sin" (London, 1912); "Love—And What Then?" (London, 1912); "The Tide" (London, 1913); "The Angel in the House," with Eden Phillpotts (London, 1915); "Q," with S. Leacock (London, 1915); "The Fourth Act" (London, 1916); "Advertisement" (London, 1916).

LAURENCE HOUSMAN, *False Premises,* 5 plays (N. Y. 1923); *The Wheel,* 3 plays (N. Y. 1920); *Dethronements,* 3 plays (N. Y. 1923); *Little Plays of St. Francis* (Boston, 1922) contains several short scenes, all published separately (London, 1922); *Followers of St. Francis,* 4 plays (Boston, 1924); "Prunella," with Granville Barker (N. Y. 1908); "Pains and Penalties" (London, 1911); "As Good as Gold" (N. Y. 1916); "Bird in Hand" (N. Y. 1916); "The

Return of Alcestis" (N. Y. 1916); "The Lord of the Harvest" (N. Y. 1916); "Nazareth" (N. Y. 1916); "A Likely Story" (N. Y. 1916); "The Snow Man" (N. Y. 1916); "The Chinese Lantern" (N. Y. 1908); "Lysistrata" (London, 1911); "Bethlehem" (N. Y. 1902); "The Death of Orpheus" (London, 1921); "Echo de Paris" (N. Y. 1923); "Possession" (London, 1921); "The Death of Socrates" (Boston, 1925); *The Comments of Juniper,* 6 plays (London, 1926); *Angels and Ministers,* 4 plays (N. Y. 1922); "Victoria Regina" (London, 1935); "Ye Fearful Saints" (London, 1932); *Four Plays of St. Clare* (London, 1934); *Cornered Poets* (London, 1929); "The Golden Sovereign" (N. Y. 1937).

JEROME K. JEROME, "The Master of Mrs. Chilvers" (London, 1911); "The Passing of the Third Floor Back" (London, 1910); "Woodbarrow Farm" (N. Y. 1904); "Fanny and the Servant Problem" (N. Y. 1909); "When Greek Meets Greek" (Chicago, no date); "Barbara" (N. Y. no date); "Sunset" (N. Y. no date); "Miss Hobbs" (N. Y. 1902); "Robina in Search of a Husband" (N. Y. 1913); "The Celebrity" (N. Y. 1927).

CHARLES RANN KENNEDY, "The Idol Breaker" (N. Y. 1914); "The Necessary Evil" (N. Y. 1913); "The Servant in the House" (N. Y. 1908); "The Terrible Meek" (N. Y. 1912); "The Winterfeast" (N. Y. 1908); "The Rib of the Man" (N. Y. 1917); "The Army With Banners" (N. Y. 1919); *Plays for Three Players* (Chicago, 1927) contains "The Chastening," "The Admiral," and "The Salutation"; *Plays for Three Players,* II (Chicago, 1933) contains "Crumbs," "Old Nobody," and "Flaming Ministers."

FREDERICK LONSDALE, "Aren't We All?" (N. Y. 1925); "Spring Cleaning" (N. Y. 1925); "The High Road" (N. Y. 1928); "On Approval" (N. Y. 1928); "The Last of Mrs. Cheyney" (N. Y. 1929); "Canaries Sometimes Sing" (N. Y. 1930).

BENN W. LEVY, "Springtime For Henry" (N. Y. 1932); "Art and Mrs. Bottle" (N. Y. 1934); "Mrs. Moonlight" (N. Y. 1935); "The Devil Passes" (N. Y. 1933); "Hollywood Holiday," with J. van Druten (London, 1931); "The Man With Red Hair" (London, 1928); "This Woman Business" (N. Y. 1925); "Mud and Treacle" (N. Y. 1928); "The Poet's Heart" (London, 1937).

RONALD MACKENZIE, "Musical Chairs" (London, 1932); "The Maitlands" (London, 1934).

J. HARTLEY MANNERS, *Happiness and Other Plays* (N. Y. 1914) contains also "The Day of Dupes," "Just as Well"; "Peg o' My

Heart" (N. Y. 1918); "The House Next Door" (Boston, 1912); "Out There" (N. Y. 1918); "Wreckage" (N. Y. 1916); "The Harp of Life" (N. Y. no date); "The Woman Intervenes" (N. Y. no date); "Queen's Messenger" (N. Y. no date); "The Girl in Waiting" (Boston, 1922); "The National Anthem" (N. Y. 1922); "Hanging and Wiving," in *One-Act Plays for Stage and Study,* I (N. Y. 1924).

A. E. W. MASON, "Green Stockings" (N. Y. 1914); "The Witness for the Defence" (N. Y. 1913).

A. A. MILNE, *First Plays* (N. Y. 1919) contains "Wurzel Flummery," "The Lucky One," "The Boy Comes Home," "Belinda," "The Red Feathers"; *Second Plays* (N. Y. 1921) contains "Make-Believe," "Mr. Pim Passes By," "The Camberly Triangle," "The Romantic Age," "The Stepmother"; *Three Plays* (N. Y. 1922) contains "The Dover Road," "The Truth About Blayds," "The Great Broxopp"; *Four Plays* (London, 1926) contains "To Have the Honor," "Ariadne," "Portrait of a Gentleman in Slippers," and "Success" (all the above are published separately, N. Y. and London, 1919-1927); "Success" (London, 1923); "The Man in the Bowler Hat" (London, 1923); "The Artist" (London, 1923); "The Perfect Alibi" (N. Y. 1928); "Miss Marlow at Play" (N. Y. 1927); "The Ivory Door" (N. Y. 1927); "Michael and Mary" (N. Y. 1932); "Toad of Toad's Hill" (N. Y. 1929); "Miss Elizabeth Bennett" (London, 1936); "Other People's Lives" (London, 1935).

ALLAN MONKHOUSE, *Four Tragedies* (London, 1923) contains "The Hayling Family," "The Stricklands," "Resentment," "Reaping the Whirlwind"; "The Education of Mr. Surrage" (London, 1913); "Mary Broome" (Boston, 1913); "The Conquering Hero" (N. Y. no date); "The Grand Cham's Diamond" (Boston, 1924); "First Blood" (London, 1924); "Sons and Fathers" (London, 1925); "O Death, Where Is Thy Sting?" (London, 1926); *War Plays* (London, 1916) contains "Shamed Wife," "Night Watches," and "Choice"; "Paul Felice" (London, 1930); "Cecilia" (London, 1932); "The Wily One," in *One-Act Plays for Stage and Study,* IV (N. Y. 1928).

C. K. MUNRO, "At Mrs. Beam's" (N. Y. 1923); "The Rumor" (N. Y. 1924); "Storm" (N. Y. 1925); "Progress" (London, 1924); "The Mountain" (London, 1926); "Bluestone Quarry" (London, 1931); *Three Plays* (London, 1932) includes "The Rumor," "At Mrs. Beam's," and "The Birth, Death and Life of Mr. Eno."

LOUIS N. PARKER, "Pomander Walk" (N. Y. 1915); "The Cardinal" (N. Y. 1923); "Disraeli" (N. Y. 1911); "Mavourneen" (N. Y. 1916); "Summer Is A-Comin' In" (London, no date); "Drake" (N. Y. 1912); "A Minuet" (N. Y. 1922); "The Man in the Street" (London, 1912); "The Aristocrat" (N. Y. 1917); "Joseph and His Brethren" (N. Y. 1913); "Beauty and the Barge," with W. W. Jacobs (London, no date); "Rosemary" (N. Y. 1924); "Lourdes" (Boston, 1935).

EDEN PHILLPOTTS, *Three Plays* (London, 1913) contains "The Shadow," "The Mother," "The Secret Woman"; *Curtain Raisers* (London, 1912) contains "The Point of View," "Hiatus," "The Carrier-Pigeon"; "St. George and the Dragons" (London, 1919); "The Angel in the House," with B. M. Hastings (London, 1915); "Devonshire Cream" (N. Y. 1925); "Bed Rock," with B. M. Hastings (London, 1925); "The Market Money" (London, 1919); "The Blue Comet" (N. Y. 1927); "Yellow Sands" (N. Y. 1927); "The Farmer's Wife" (N. Y. 1917); "A Pair of Knickerbockers" (N. Y. no date); "Golden Wedding," with Chas. Groves (N. Y. no date); Jane's Legacy" (N. Y. 1931); "The Runaways" (London, 1928); "Buy a Broom" (London, 1929); "A Cup of Happiness" (London, 1933).

MORDAUNT SHAIRP, "The Offence" (London, 1925); "The Crime at Blossom's" (Boston, 1933); "The Green Bay Tree" (Boston, 1933).

J. B. PRIESTLEY, "Dangerous Corner" (N. Y. 1933); "Laburnum Grove" (N. Y. 1934); "The Roundabout" (N. Y. 1934); "Eden End" (London, 1934); "Cornelius" (London, 1935); "Duet in Floodlight" (London, 1935); "Bees on the Boatdeck" (London, 1935); "Time and the Conways" (London, 1937); "I Have Been There Before" (London, 1937); "Mystery at Greenfingers" (London, 1937); "The Good Companions," with E. Knoblock (London, 1935); "Spring Tide," with E. Billam (London, 1936); *Three Plays, etc.* (London, 1935), includes "Dangerous Corner," "Eden End," and "Cornelius."

R. C. SHERIFF, "Journey's End" (N. Y. 1929); "Badger's Green" (London, 1930); "St. Helena," with J. de Casalis (N. Y. 1935).

ALFRED SUTRO, "The Perplexed Husband" (N. Y. 1913); "Freedom" (N. Y. no date); "John Glayde's Honor" (N. Y. 1907); "The Barrier" (N. Y. 1908); "The Builder of Bridges" (N. Y. 1909); "The Fire-Screen" (N. Y. 1912); "The Walls of Jericho" (N. Y.

1906); "Mollentrave on Women" (N. Y. 1905); "The Cave of Illusion" (London, 1900); "The Choice" (London, no date); "The Two Virtues" (London, 1914); "The Price of Money" ["The Perfect Lover"] (N. Y. 1906); "The Clever Ones" (London, no date); "The Fascinating Mr. Vanderveldt" (N. Y. 1907); "The Great Well" (London, 1923); "The Laughing Lady" (London, 1922); "Far Above Rubies" (London, 1924); "Uncle Anyhow" (London, 1919); "A Man With a Heart" (London, 1925); *Five Little Plays* (N. Y. 1912) contains "The Man in the Stalls," "A Marriage Has Been Arranged," "The Man on the Kerb," "The Open Door," "The Bracelet"; "The Desperate Lovers" (London, 1927); "Living Together" (London, 1929).

JOHN VAN DRUTEN, "There's Always Juliet" (N. Y. 1932); "Young Woodley" (N. Y. 1930); "Most of the Game" (N. Y. 1936); "Flowers of the Forest" (N. Y. 1935); "The Distaff Side" (N. Y. 1935); "Behold We Live" (N. Y. 1935); "After All" (N. Y. 1931); "Return of the Soldier" (London, 1930); "London Wall" (London, 1931); "Somebody Knows" (London, 1932); "Diversion" (London, 1933); "Gertie Maude" (London, 1937).

FRANK VOSPER, "Lucky Dip" (London, 1931); "Murder on the Second Floor" (N. Y. 1930); "Love From a Stranger" (London, 1936); "People Like Us" (London, 1929).

KEITH WINTER, "The Shining Hour" (N. Y. 1934); "The Rats of Norway" (London, 1933); "Worse Things Happen at Sea" (London, 1935); "The Ringmaster" (London, 1936).

EMLYN WILLIAMS, "A Murder Has Been Arranged" (N. Y. 1931); "Night Must Fall" (N. Y. 1937); "He Was Born Gay" (London, 1937).

ISRAEL ZANGWILL, "The Melting Pot" (N. Y. 1909); "The Forcing-House" (N. Y. 1922); "Merely Mary Ann" (N. Y. 1921); "The Next Religion" (N. Y. 1912); "Plaster Saints" (N. Y. 1914); "The War God" (N. Y. 1911); "The Cock Pit" (N. Y. 1921); "Six Persons" (N. Y. no date); "Too Much Money" (N. Y. 1925); "We Moderns" (N. Y. 1926).

FRENCH DRAMATISTS

VILLIERS DE L'ISLE ADAM, *The Revolt and the Escape*, trans. by Theresa Barclay (London, 1910).

GEORGES ANCEY, "Monsieur Lamblin," trans. by B. H. Clark (*Strat-*

ford Journal, Boston, 1918); "The Dupe," trans. by B. H. Clark, in *Four Plays of the Free Theater* (Cincinnati, 1914).

JEAN-JACQUES BERNARD, "Two Men," trans. by B. E. Mason (*One Act Play Magazine,* N. Y., July 1937); "Martine," trans. by Winifred Katzin, in *Eight European Plays* (N. Y. 1927); "Glamor," in Katzin's *Eight European Plays* (N. Y. 1927); "The Poet's Secret," in Vernon's *Modern One-Act Plays from the French* (N. Y. 1934); "The Unquiet Spirit," trans. by J. L. Frith (London, 1932); "Martine," trans. by J. L. Frith (London, 1932); "L'Invitation au Voyage," by E. Boyd, in Dickinson's *Continental Plays* (Boston, 1935).

TRISTAN BERNARD, "French Without a Master," trans. by B. H. Clark (N. Y. 1915); same, as "French as He is Spoke," trans. by G. Mayer (London, 1907); "I'm Going!" trans. by B. H. Clark (N. Y. 1915); "Free Treat," in Vernon's *Modern One-Act Plays from the French* (N. Y. 1934).

HENRI BERNSTEIN, "The Thief," trans. by J. A. Haughton (Garden City, 1915); "Promise," trans. by H. M. Harwood (London, 1937).

THÉODORE BOTREL, "Du Guesclin," trans. by E. S. Dickerman (*Poet Lore,* Boston, 1919).

MAURICE BOUCHOR, "A Christmas Tale," trans. by B. H. Clark (N. Y. 1915).

EDOUARD BOURDET, "The Captive," trans. by Arthur Hornblow, Jr. (N. Y. 1926); "The Sex Fable" (N. Y. 1931).

G. A. DE CAILLAVET, "Choosing a Career," trans. by B. H. Clark (N. Y. 1915).

ALFRED CAPUS, "Brignol and His Daughter," trans. by B. H. Clark (N. Y. 1915); "The Adventurer," trans. by B. Papot (*The Drama,* Chicago, 1914); "My Tailor," trans. by B. H. Clark (*Smart Set,* N. Y. 1918), also in Shay's *Plays for Strolling Mummers* (N. Y. 1926).

L. CHANTEL, "Who Killed Me?" in Vernon's *Modern One-Act Plays from the French* (N. Y. 1934).

PAUL CLAUDEL, "The Hostage," trans. by Pierre Chavannes (New Haven, 1917); "Tête d'Or," trans. by J. S. Newberry (New Haven, 1919); "The Tidings Brought to Mary," trans. by L. M. Sill (New Haven, 1916); "The City," trans. by J. S. Newberry (New Haven, 1920); "The Satin Slipper," trans. by F. J. O'Connor (N. Y. no date); "The Book of Christopher Columbus" (New Haven, 1930).

ROMAIN COOLUS, "Love and Learning," in Vernon's *Modern One-Act Plays from the French* (N. Y. 1934).

JACQUES COPEAU, "The House Into Which We Are Born," trans. anonymously (N. Y. 1924).

GEORGES COURTELINE, "The Pitiless Policeman," trans. by H. J. Williams (*Poet Lore,* Boston, 1917); "Blank Cartridge," trans. by R. W. Sneddon (*International,* N. Y. 1914); "Peace at Home," trans. by J. L. Cook (*Poet Lore,* Boston, 1918); Same, trans. by F. C. Fay (*International,* N. Y. 1913), and in Vernon's *Modern One-Act Plays from the French* (N. Y. 1934).

FRANCIS DE CROISSET, "On With the New," in Vernon's *Modern One-Act Plays from the French* (N. Y. 1934).

GEORGES DUHAMEL, "The Light," trans. by Sasha Best (*Poet Lore,* Boston, 1914); "In the Shadow of Statues," trans. by Sasha Best (*Poet Lore,* Boston, 1914); "The Combat," trans. by Sasha Best (*Poet Lore,* Boston, 1915).

HENRI DUVERNOIS, "The Bronze Lady and the Crystal Gentleman," in Vernon's *Modern One-Act Plays from the French* (N. Y. 1934).

PAUL FERRIER, "The Codicil," trans. by E. L. Mullin (*Poet Lore,* Boston, 1908).

ANATOLE FRANCE, *The Bride of Corinth, etc.* (N. Y. 1921) contains also "Crainquebille," "The Man Who Married a Dumb Wife," "Come What May"; "Crainquebille" trans. by B. H. Clark (N. Y. 1915); "The Man Who Married a Dumb Wife," trans. by C. H. Page (N. Y. 1915).

SIMON GANTILLON, "Maya," trans. by E. Boyd (N. Y. 1928); "Cyclone," trans. by D. L. Orna (*One-Act Play Magazine,* N. Y., Sept. 1937).

HENRI GHÉON, "The Comedian," trans. by A. B. (London, 1927); "The Marriage of St. Francis," trans. by C. C. Martindale (London, no date); "Saint Bernard," trans. by B. V. Jackson (N. Y. 1933); "The Journey of the Three Kings," trans. by C. Martindale (N. Y. 1936).

JEAN GIRAUDOUX, "Siegfried," trans. by P. Carr (N. Y. 1930); "Amphitryon 38," adapted by S. N. Behrman (N. Y. 1938).

MARCEL GIRETTE, "The Weaver of Dreams," in Vernon's *Modern One-Act Plays from the French* (N. Y. 1934).

REMY DE GOURMONT, "Théodat," trans. by Richard Aldington (*The Drama,* Chicago, 1916); "The Old King," trans. by Richard Aldington (*The Drama,* Chicago, 1916).

SACHA GUITRY, "Deburau," trans. by Granville Barker (N. Y. 1922); "Pasteur," in Dickinson's *Chief Contemporary Dramatists,* II (Boston, 1921); "Villa for Sale," in Vernon's *Modern One-Act Plays from the French* (N. Y. 1934).

GYP, "The Little Blue Guinea-Hen," trans. by R. T. House (*Poet Lore,* Boston, 1919).

CHARLES HELLEM, with W. Valcros and P. d'Estoc, "Sabotage," trans. by A. Tridon (*Smart Set,* N. Y. 1913, and in *The Dramatist,* Easton, 1914).

LÉON HENNIQUE, "The Death of the Duc d'Enghien," trans. by F. C. Evans (*Poet Lore,* Boston, 1909).

JEAN JULLIEN, "The Serenade," trans. by B. H. Clark, in *Four Plays of the Free Theater* (Cincinnati, 1914).

JULES LEMAITRE, "The Pardon," trans. by B. H. Clark, in *Three Modern Plays from the French* (N. Y. 1914); Same as "Forgiveness," trans. by F. C. Fay (*Poet Lore,* Boston, 1914).

H.-R. LENORMAND, "Time Is a Dream," in Dickinson's *Chief Contemporary Dramatists,* III (Boston, 1930); "Failures," trans. by W. Katzin, in volume with "Time Is a Dream" (N. Y. 1923); "In Theater Street," adapted by A. Dukes (N. Y. 1937); *Three Plays,* trans. by D. L. Orna (London, 1928), contains "The Dream Doctor," "Man and his Phantoms," and "The Coward."

ANDRÉ DE LORDE, "At the Telephone," anon. trans., in *One-Act Plays for Stage and Study,* II (N. Y. 1925).

PAUL-HYACINTHE LOYSON, "The Apostle," trans. by B. H. Clark (Garden City, 1916).

MAX MAUREY, "Rosalie," trans. by B. H. Clark (N. Y. 1913).

ANDRÉ OBEY, "Noah," adapted by A. Wilmurt (N. Y. 1935); "Lucrèce," adapted by T. Wilder (Boston, 1933).

OCTAVE MIRBEAU, "Scruples," trans. by Clyde Barrett, in Loving's *Ten-Minute Plays* (N. Y. 1923), and separately (N. Y. 1927).

J. PELADAN, "St. Francis of Assisi," trans. by H. J. Massingham (London, 1913).

GEORGES DE PORTO-RICHE, "The Loving Wife," in Dickinson's *Chief Contemporary Dramatists,* II (Boston, 1921); "Françoise' Luck," trans. by B. H. Clark in *Four Plays of the Free Theater* (Cincinnati, 1914).

JULES RENARD, "Carrots," adapted by Alfred Sutro (N. Y. 1904); "Good-Bye," trans. by B. H. Clark (*Smart Set,* N. Y. 1916); "Home-Made Bread," trans. by L. A. Loiseaux (N. Y. no date).

André Rivoire, "The Little Shepherdess," trans. by B. H. Clark (N. Y. 1915).

Romain Rolland, *The Fourteenth of July and Danton,* trans. by B. H. Clark (N. Y. 1918); "The Montespan," trans. by H. V. B. De Kay (N. Y. 1923); "Liluli," anon. trans. (N. Y. 1922); "The Game of Love and Death," trans. by Eleanor S. Brooks (N. Y. 1926); "The Wolves," trans. by B. H. Clark (N. Y. 1937); "Palm Sunday," trans. by E. Löhrke (N. Y. 1928); "Les Leonides," trans. by E. Löhrke (N. Y. 1929).

Jules Romains, "Doctor Knock," trans. by H. Granville-Barker (London, 1925); "The Peach," in Vernon's *Modern One-Act Plays From the French* (N. Y. 1934); "Six Gentlemen in a Row," trans. by H. Granville-Barker (London, 1927).

Maurice Rostand, "He Who Did Not Kill," in Vernon's *Modern One-Act Plays from the French* (N. Y. 1934).

Alfred Savoir, "He," adapted by C. Erskin (N. Y. 1932); "Going to the Dogs," in Vernon's *Modern One-Act Plays from the French* (N. Y. 1934).

Edmond See, "An Old Friend," in Vernon's *Modern One-Act Plays from the French* (N. Y. 1934).

Pierre Veber, "Happiness," in Vernon's *Modern One-Act Plays from the French* (N. Y. 1934).

Charles Vildrac, "The Steamer Tenacity," trans. by J. S. Newberry (*Poet Lore,* Boston, 1921); "Michel Auclair," in Leverton's *Plays for the College Theater* (N. Y. 1929); "The Pilgrim," trans. by R. C. Allen (*One-Act Play Magazine,* N. Y., Oct. 1937).

Pierre Wolff, "Unhoodwinkable," trans. by B. H. Clark (*Smart Set,* N. Y. 1919); "Fidèle," trans. by B. H. Clark (*Drama Reader,* Cleveland, 1917); Same, as "Faithful," in Vernon's *Modern One-Act Plays from the French* (N. Y. 1934).

Miguel Zamacois, "The Jesters," trans. by J. N. Raphael (N. Y. 1908).

German Dramatists

Franz Adam Beyerlein, "Lights Out," trans. by H. Havelock (London, 1905); same, as "Taps," trans. by C. Swickard (Boston, 1915).

Ferdinand Bruckner, "Elizabeth of England," trans. by A. Dukes (London, 1931); "Races," trans. by R. Langner (N. Y. 1934).

Max Dreyer, "On Probation," trans. by Mary Harned (*Poet Lore,* Boston, 1903).

Otto Ernst, "Master Flachsmann," trans. by H. M. Beatty (N. Y. no date).

Marie E. Von Eschenbach, "A Man of the World," trans. by R. T. House (*Poet Lore,* Boston, 1911).

Bruno Frank, "12,000," trans. by W. A. Drake (N. Y. 1928); "Storm in a Teacup," adapted by J. Bridie (London, 1936).

Lion Feuchtwanger, *Three Plays* (N. Y. 1934) includes "Prisoners of War," "1918," and "The Dutch Merchant."

Ludwig Fulda, "By Ourselves," trans. by Haya Wally (*Poet Lore,* Boston, 1912); the same, as "Tête-à-Tête," trans. by E. L. Townsend, in *The German Classics,* XVII (N. Y. 1914).

A. Goetze, "Heights," trans. by Sasha Best (*Poet Lore,* Boston, 1914).

Max Halbe, "The Rosenhagens" trans. by P. H. Grummann (*Poet Lore,* Boston, 1910); "Mother Earth," trans. by P. H. Grummann, in *The German Classics,* XX (N. Y. 1914); "Youth," trans. by S. T. Barrows (Garden City, 1916).

Ernst Hardt, "Tantris the Jester," trans. by J. Heard, Jr. (Boston, 1913).

Walter Harlan, "The Nurnberg Egg," trans. by Winifred Katzin, in *Eight European Plays* (N. Y. 1927).

Otto Erich Hartleben, "Love's Carnival," trans. by R. Bleichmann (London, 1904); "Hanna Jagert," trans. by S. E. Holmes (*Poet Lore,* Boston, 1913); "The Demands of Society," trans. by H. Harper, in Shay's *Fifty More Contemporary One-Act Plays* (N. Y. 1928).

Walter Hasenclever, "Contagion" (*Smart Set,* N. Y. 1918).

Carl Hauptmann, "War, a Te Deum," trans. by A. von Ende (*The Drama,* Chicago, 1916); "Ephraim's Breite," trans. anonymously (*Poet Lore,* Boston, 1900); "The Dead Are Singing," trans. by Mary L. Stephenson (*Texas Review,* 1916).

Paul Heyse, "Mary of Magdala," trans. by William Winter (N. Y. 1903).

George Hirschfeld, "The Mothers," trans. by Ludwig Lewisohn (Garden City, 1916).

Georg Kaiser, "From Morn to Midnight," trans. by Ashley Dukes (N. Y. 1922); "Gas," trans. by Ashley Dukes (London, 1923); "The Fire in the Opera House," trans. by Winifred Katzin, in *Eight*

European Plays (N. Y. 1927); "The Coral," "Gas I," and "Gas II," trans. by W. Katzin and H. Scheffauer, in Tucker's *Modern Continental Plays* (N. Y. 1929); "The Phantom Lover," trans. by H. Bernstein and A. E. Meyer (N. Y. 1928).

HEINRICH MANN, "Madame Legros," trans. by Winifred Katzin, in *Eight European Plays* (N. Y. 1927).

MAX NORDAU, "A Question of Honor," trans. by Mary J. Stafford (Boston, 1907).

ERNST ROSMER [ELSE BERNSTEIN], "John Herkner," trans. by Mary Harned (*Poet Lore,* Boston, 1911); "Twilight," trans. by P. H. Grummann (*Poet Lore,* Boston, 1912).

FELIX SALTEN, "Count Festenberg," trans. by A. B. Kuttner (*International,* N. Y. 1911); "Moral Courage," trans. by H. de Selincourt, in Shay's *Fifty More Contemporary One-Act Plays* (N. Y. 1928).

KARL SCHOENHERR, "Faith and Fireside," trans. by E. von Mach, in *The German Classics,* XVI (N. Y. 1914).

CARL STERNHEIM, "A Place in the World" ["The Snob"], trans. by Winifred Katzin and B. H. Clark, in Katzin's *Eight European Plays* (N. Y. 1927); "The Mask of Virtue," adapted by A. Dukes (N. Y. 1935).

AUGUST STRAMM, "The Bride of the Moor," trans. anonymously (*Poet Lore,* Boston, 1914); "Sancta Susanna," trans. by E. J. O'Brien (*Poet Lore,* Boston, 1914).

LUDWIG THOMA, "Moral," trans. by Charles Recht (N. Y. 1916).

ERNST TOLLER, "The Machine Wreckers," trans. by Ashley Dukes (N. Y. 1922); "Man and the Masses," trans. by Ashley Dukes (N. Y. 1924); "Broken-Brow," trans. by V. Mendel (London, no date); *Seven Plays, etc.* (N. Y. 1936) includes "Masses and Man," "The Machine Wreckers," "Transfiguration," "Mary Baker Eddy," "Draw the Fires," "Hoppla!," "Hinkemann"; No More Peace" (N. Y. 1936).

KARL VOLMOELLER, "Turandot," trans. by J. Bithell (N. Y. no date); "Uncle's Been Dreaming," trans. by Winifred Katzin, in *Eight European Plays* (N. Y. 1927).

FRANZ WERFEL, "Goat Song," trans. by Ruth Langner (N. Y. 1926); "Juarez and Maximilian," trans. by Ruth Langner (N. Y. 1926); "Paul Among the Jews," trans. by P. P. Levertoff (London, 1928); "The Eternal Road," trans. by L. Lewisohn (N. Y. 1936).

J. WIEGAND and W. SCHARRELMANN, "The Wages of War," trans. by A. von Ende (*Poet Lore,* Boston, 1908).

ADOLF WILDBRANDT, "The Master of Palmyra," trans. anonymously (*Poet Lore,* Boston, 1901).

ERNST VON WILDENBRUCH, "Harold," trans. by Otto Heller (*Poet Lore,* Boston, 1891); "King Henry," trans. by R. M. Wernaer, in *The German Classics,* XVII (N. Y. 1914).

CHRISTA WINLOE, "Girls in Uniform," adapted by B. Burnham (Boston, 1936).

FRIEDRICH WOLF, "Sailors of Cattaro," trans. by K. Wallis and M. Blankfort (N. Y. 1934).

STEFAN ZWEIG, "Jeremiah," trans. by E. and C. Paul (N. Y. 1922); "Volpone" adapted by R. Langner (N. Y. 1928).

HUNGARIAN DRAMATISTS

LAJOS BIRO, "The Bridegroom," trans. by Charles Recht (*The Drama,* Chicago, 1918); "The Grandfather," trans. by Charles Recht (*The Drama,* Chicago, 1918).

LADISLAUS FODOR, "A Church Mouse," adapted by C. Erskin (N. Y. 1931).

W. GYALUI, "After the Honeymoon," trans. by B. H. Clark (N. Y. 1915).

MELCHIOR LENGYEL, "Typhoon," English version by Laurence Irving (Chicago, 1913).

¬ELA SZENES, "A Budapest Salesman Should Not Read French Illustrated Magazines," in Shay's *Fifty More Contemporary One-Act Plays* (N. Y. 1928).

ERNÖ SZEP, "In May," trans. by J. Szebenyei (N. Y. 1925).

ERNST VAJDA, "Fata Morgana," trans. by J. L. A. Burrell and P. Moeller (Garden City, 1924).

ICELANDIC DRAMATISTS

INDRIDI EINARSSON, "Sword and Crozier," trans. by L. M. Hollander (*Poet Lore,* Boston, 1912).

GUDMUNDER KAMBAN, "Hadda Padda," trans. by S. L. Peller (N. Y. 1917).

JOHANN SIGURJONSSON, *Modern Icelandic Plays,* trans. by H. K. Schanche (N. Y. 1916), contains "Eyvind of the Hills," and "The Hraun Farm."

Irish Dramatists

William Boyle, "The Eloquent Dempsy" (Dublin, 1911); "The Mineral Workers" (Dublin, 1910); "The Building Fund" (Dublin, 1911); "Family Failing" (Dublin, 1913).

Curtis Canfield [ed.], *Plays of the Irish Renaissance* (N. Y. 1932) includes Yeats' "On Baile's Strand" and "The Only Jealousy of Emer"; Russell's "Deirdre"; Gregory's "Hyacinth Halvey"; Hyde's "Twisting of the Rope"; Fitzmaurice's "The Dandy Dolls"; Synge's "Riders to the Sea"; Colum's "The Land"; Murray's "Birthright"; Pearse's "The Singer"; Martyn's "Mæve"; O'Casey's "Juno and the Paycock"; Robinson's "The Big House."—*Plays of Changing Ireland* (N. Y. 1936) includes Yeats' "Words Upon the Window Pane"; Johnston's "The Old Lady Says No"; Robinson's "Church Street"; Longford's "Yahoo"; Shiels' "The New Gossoon"; Countess of Longford's "Mrs. Jiggins"; Manning's "Youth's the Season"; Mayne's "The Bridge Head."

Padraic Colum, *Three Plays* (Boston, 1916) contains "The Fiddler's House," "The Land" and "Thomas Muskerry"; *The Fiddler's House . . . The Land* (Dublin, 1909); "Thomas Muskerry" (Dublin, 1910); "Mogu the Wanderer" (Boston, 1917); "The Miracle of the Corn," in *Dramatic Legends* (N. Y. 1925); "The Betrayal" (*The Drama,* Chicago, 1920), also in *One-Act Plays for Stage and Study,* III (N. Y. 1927); "Balloon" (N. Y. 1929).

George Fitzmaurice, *Five Plays* (Boston, 1917) contains "The Country Dressmaker," "The Moonlighter," "The Magic Glasses," "The Pie-Dish," "The Dandy Dolls."

Douglas Hyde, "The Twisting of the Rope," "The Marriage," "The Lost Saint," "The Nativity"; the above are translated by Lady Gregory, in her *Saints and Dreamers* (Dublin, 1903); "The Bursting of the Bubble" (Dublin, 1903).

Denis Johnston, "The Moon in the Yellow River" (N. Y. 1933), in volume with "Storm Song," "A Bride for the Unicorn" (London, 1935); "The Old Lady Says No," in Canfield's *Plays of Changing Ireland* (N. Y. 1936).

Edward Martyn, *The Tale of a Town, and The Enchanted Sea,* 1 vol. (London, 1902); *The Heather Field, and Mæve* (London, 1899); "The Dream Physician" (N. Y. 1918); "Grangecolman" (Dublin, 1912).

Rutherford Mayne, *The Drone and Other Plays* (Dublin, 1912) contains also "Red Turf," "The Troth," "The Turn of the Road."

GEORGE MOORE, "The Bending of the Bough" (Chicago, 1900); "The Strike at Arlingford" (London, 1893); "Martin Luther" (London, 1879); "The Apostle" (Boston, 1911); "The Apostle" [different play] (London, 1923); "Elizabeth Cooper" (Boston, 1913); "The Coming of Gabrielle" (N. Y. 1920); "Esther Waters" (Boston, 1913); "The Making of an Immortal" (N. Y. 1928).

T. C. MURRAY, "Birthright" (Dublin, 1911); "Maurice Harte" (Dublin, 1912); *Spring and Other Plays* (Dublin, 1917) contains "Spring," "The Briery Gap," and "Sovereign Love"; "Aftermath" (Dublin, 1922); "Autumn Fire" (Boston, 1926); "The Pipe in the Fields" (*Dublin Magazine,* Dublin, 1927); *A Stag at Bay and Maurice Harte* (London, 1934); "Michaelmas Eve" (London, 1932).

SEUMAS O'BRIEN, *Duty and Other Irish Comedies* (Boston, 1916) contains also "Jurisprudence," "Matchmakers," "Magnanimity," "Retribution"; "The Black Bottle," in *One-Act Plays for Stage and Study, II* (N. Y. 1925); "The Cobbler's Den," in *One-Act Plays for Stage and Study,* III (N. Y. 1927); "Blind" (N. Y. 1918); "The Birdcatcher" in Shay's *Fifty More Contemporary One-Act Plays* (N. Y. 1928); "The Well" (N. Y. 1937); "Christmas Eve," in *One-Act Plays for Stage and Study,* IV (N. Y. 1928).

SEAN O'CASEY, *Two Plays* (N. Y. 1925) contains "Juno and the Paycock," and "The Shadow of a Gunman"; "The Plough and the Stars" (N. Y. 1926); "The Silver Tassie" (N. Y. 1930); "Within the Gates" (N. Y. 1935); *Windfalls* (N. Y. 1934) includes two short plays.

PADRAIC PEARSE, *The Singer and Other Plays* (Dublin, 1918) contains "The Singer," "Iosagan," "The King," and "The Master."

LENNOX ROBINSON, *Two Plays* (Dublin, 1911) contains "Harvest" and "The Clancy Name"; "The Whiteheaded Boy" (N. Y. 1920); "Patriots" (Dublin, 1912); "The Lost Leader" (Dublin, 1918); "The Round Table" (N. Y. 1924); "Never the Time and the Place" (*Dublin Magazine,* Dublin, 1924); "Crabbed Youth and Age" (N. Y. 1924); "The Cross Roads" (Dublin, 1909); "The Dreamers" (Dublin, 1915); *The White Blackbird; Portrait,* 2 plays (Dublin, no date); *Plays* (N. Y. 1926) includes "The Round Table," "Crabbed Age and Youth," "Portrait," "The White Blackbird," "The Big House," and "Give a Dog —"; "The Far off Hills" (N. Y. 1932); "Is Life Worth Living?" (N. Y. 1933); "Ever the

Twain" (London, 1930); *More Plays* (N. Y. 1935) includes "All's Over, Then?" and "Church Street."

George Shiels, *Two Irish Plays* (London, 1930) includes "Mountain Dew" and "Cartney and Kevney"; *Professor Tim and Paul Twyning* (London, 1927); "The New Gossoon" (London, 1936); *The Passing Day and the Jailbird* (London, 1937).

Italian Dramatists

Roberto Bracco, "Phantasms" trans. by Dirce St. Cyr (*Poet Lore,* Boston, 1908); "The Hidden Spring," trans. by Dirce St. Cyr (*Poet Lore,* Boston, 1907); "Night of Snow"; Same, as "A Snowy Night," trans. by Arthur Livingston, in Shay's *Twenty-five Short Plays, International* (N. Y. 1925).

Alberto Cassella, "Death Takes a Holiday," adapted by W. Ferris (N. Y. 1929).

Luigi Chiarelli, "The Mask and the Face," English version by C. B. Fernald (London, no date).

Tommaso Gallarati-Scotti, "Thy Will Be Done," trans. by Valerie Petri (N. Y. 1923).

Cesare Lodovici, "The Idiot," trans. by P. Sombart (*Poet Lore,* Boston, no date).

Sabatino Lopez, "The Sparrow," trans. by Isaac Goldberg, in *Plays of the Italian Theater* (Boston, 1921).

F. T. Marinetti, "Anti-neutrality," trans. by M. Cram (*Vanity Fair,* 1919); "Simultaneity," trans. by M. Cram (*Vanity Fair,* 1919); "Moonlight," trans. by M. Cram (*Vanity Fair,* 1919).

Ercole Luigi Morselli, "Water Upon Fire," trans. by Isaac Goldberg, in *Plays of the Italian Theater* (Boston, 1921); "Gastone, the Animal Trainer," trans. by Isaac Goldberg, in *Plays of the Italian Theater* (Boston, 1921).

Marco Praga, "The Closed Door," trans. by A. S. MacDonald (N. Y. 1923).

Gerolamo Rovetta, "Young Italy, or Romanticism," trans. by A. B. Piddington (Sydney, Australia, 1916).

Rosso Di San Secondo, "The Stairs," trans. anonymously, in Katzin's *Eight European Plays* (N. Y. 1927).

Giovanni Verga, "The Wolf-Hunt," trans. by Isaac Goldberg, in *Plays of the Italian Theater* (Boston, 1921).

Polish Dramatists

Stanislaw Przybyszewski, "For Happiness," trans. by Lucile Baron (*Poet Lore,* Boston, 1912); "Snow," trans. by O. F. Theis (N. Y. 1920).

Bruno Winawer, "The Book of Job," trans. by J. Conrad (London, 1931).

Portuguese Dramatist

Jose de Alencar, "The Jesuit," trans. by E. R. de Britto (*Poet Lore,* Boston, 1920).

Russian Dramatists

Alexander Afinogenyev, "Fear," in Lyons' *Six Soviet Plays* (Boston, 1934).

Michael Artzibashef, "War," trans. by Thomas Seltzer (N. Y. 1916); *Jealousy, Enemies, The Law of the Savage,* 1 vol., trans. anonymously (N. Y. 1923).

Michal Bulgakov, "Days of the Turbins," in Lyons' *Six Soviet Plays* (Boston, 1934).

Nicholas Evreinov, "A Merry Death," trans. by C. E. Bechhofer, in *Five Russian Plays* (N. Y. 1916); "The Beautiful Despot," trans. by C. E. Bechhofer, in *Five Russian Plays* (N. Y. 1916); "The Theater of the Soul," trans. by M. Potapenko and C. St. John (London, 1915); "The Chief Thing," trans. by H. Bernstein and L. Randole (N. Y. 1926).

Anatol Glebov, "Inga," trans. by I. Talmadge, in Lyons' *Six Soviet Plays* (Boston, 1934).

Vsevolod Ivanov, "Armored Train 14-69," trans. by G. Cowan and A. T. K. Grant (N. Y. 1933).

Valentine Katayev, "Squaring the Circle," in Lyons' *Six Soviet Plays* (Boston, 1934), and separately (Boston, 1934, and N. Y. 1934).

Vladimir Kirshon, "Bread," in Lyons' *Six Soviet Plays* (Boston, 1934); "Red Rust," trans. by F. Vernon (N. Y. 1930).

Ivan Kocherga, "Masters of Time," trans. by A. Wixley, in *Four Soviet Plays* (N. Y. 1937).

A. V. Lunacharski, *Three Plays of A. V. Lunacharski* (N. Y., no date) contains "Faust and the City," "The Magi," and "Vasilisa the Wise."

V. V. Mayakovsky, "Mystery-Bouffe," trans. by G. R. Noyes and A. Kaun, in Noyes' *Masterpieces of the Russian Drama* (N. Y. 1933).

Ivan Narodny, "Fortune Favors Fools," trans. by M. O. Mieler (*Poet Lore,* Boston, 1912).

Nikolai Pogodin, "Tempo," in Lyons' *Six Soviet Plays* (Boston, 1934); "Aristocrats," trans. by A. Wixley, in *Four Soviet Plays* (N. Y. 1937).

Mikhail Saltuikoff-Shchedrin, "The Death of Pazukhin," trans. by Julian Leigh (N. Y. 1924).

Ippolit Vasilievich Shpazhinsky, "Madame Major," trans. by F. H. Snow (*Poet Lore,* Boston, 1917).

Feodor Sologub, "The Triumph of Death," trans. by John Cournos (*The Drama,* Chicago, 1916).

Sergei Stepniak, "The New Convert," trans. by T. B. Eyges (Boston, 1917).

Ilya Surguchev, "Autumn," trans. by D. A. Modell (N. Y. 1924).

Alexis Tolstoy, "Tsar Fyodor Ivanovitch," trans. by J. Covan (N. Y. 1922); "The Death of Ivan the Terrible," trans. by G. R. Noyes, in *Masterpieces of the Russian Drama* (N. Y. 1933).

S. Tretiakov, "Roar China," trans. by F. Poliahovska and B. Nixon (N. Y. 1930).

Lesya Ukrainka, "The Babylonian Captivity," trans. by C. E. Bechhofer, in *Five Russian Plays* (N. Y. 1916).

V. Vishnevsky, "An Optimistic Tragedy," trans. by H. G. Scott and R. S. Carr, in *Four Soviet Plays* (N. Y. 1937).

Spanish Dramatists

Joaquín Dicenta, "Juan José," trans. by C. A. Turrell, in *Contemporary Spanish Dramatists* (Boston, 1919).

Angel Guimerá, "Marta of the Lowlands," trans. by Wallace Gillpatrick (Garden City, 1914); "Daniela," trans. by J. G. Underhill in *Masterpieces of Modern Spanish Drama* (Cincinnati, 1922); Same, as "La Pecadora," trans. by Wallace Gillpatrick (N. Y. 1916).

Willis K. Jones, *Spanish One-Act Plays in English* (Dallas, 1934).

Eduardo Marquina, "When the Roses Bloom Again," trans. by C. A. Turrell, in *Contemporary Spanish Dramatists* (Boston, 1919).

Gregorio Martinez-Sierra, *Plays of Gregorio Martinez-Sierra,* 2 vols. (N. Y. 1923). Vol. I contains "The Cradle Song," "The

Lover," "Love Magic," "Poor John," and "Madame Pepita," trans. by J. G. Underhill, the last in collaboration with May Heywood Broun. Vol. II contains "The Kingdom of God," "The Two Shepherds," "Wife to a Famous Man," and "The Romantic Young Lady," trans. by Helen and Harley Granville-Barker; "The Romantic Young Lady," reprinted separately (N. Y. 1926); "Take Two From One," trans. by H. and H. Granville-Barker (N. Y. 1925); "Holy Night," trans. by P. Hereford (N. Y. no date); "A Lily Among Thorns," trans. by H. and H. Granville-Barker, in Dickinson's *Chief Contemporary Dramatists,* III (Boston, 1930).

José Maria Peman, "A Saint in a Hurry," trans. by H. de Blacam (London, 1935).

Joaquín and Serafín Alvarez Quintéro, "The Women's Town," trans. by C. A. Turrell in *Contemporary Spanish Dramatists* (Boston, 1919); "Malvaloca," trans. by J. S. Fassett (Garden City, 1916); "The Fountain of Youth," trans. by S. N. Baker (Cincinnati, 1922); "A Bright Morning," trans. by C. C. Castillo and E. L. Overman (*Poet Lore,* Boston, 1916); "Fortunato," trans. by A. S. MacDonald (N. Y. 1918); "By Their Words Ye Shall Know Them," trans. by J. G. Underhill (*The Drama,* Chicago, 1917); "Papa Juan," trans. by Thomas Walsh (*Poet Lore,* Boston, 1918); *Four Comedies* (N. Y. 1932) trans. by Helen and Harley Granville-Barker, includes "Love Passes By," "Don Abel Wrote a Tragedy," "Peace and Quiet," and "Doña Clarines"; "Four Plays" (London, 1927), trans. by same includes "The Women Have Their Way," "A Hundred Years Old," "Fortunato," and "The Lady From Alfaqueque."

Manuel Linares Rivas, "The Claws," trans. by C. A. Turrell, in *Contemporary Spanish Dramatists* (Boston, 1919).

Santiago Rusiñol, "The Prodigal Doll," trans. by J. G. Underhill (*The Drama,* Chicago, 1917).

Antonio Sotillo and Andres Micho, "The Judgment of Posterity," trans. by J. G. Underhill (N. Y. 1935).

Ramon Del Valle-Inclan, "The Dragon's Head," trans. by May Heywood Broun (*Poet Lore,* Boston, 1918).

José Andres Vazquez, "With Chains of Gold," trans. by W. K. Jones (*Poet Lore,* Boston, 1923).

Eduardo Zamacois, "The Passing of the Magi," trans. by C. A. Turrell, in *Contemporary Spanish Dramatists* (Boston, 1919).

SWEDISH DRAMATISTS

HANS ALIN, "Poverty," trans. by A. Paulson, in Shay's *Twenty-Five Short Plays, International* (N. Y. 1925).

TOR HEDBERG, "Borga Gard," trans. by H. Colquist (*Poet Lore,* Boston, 1921).

VERNER VON HEIDENSTAM, "The Soothsayer," trans. by K. M. Knudson (Boston, 1919); "The Birth of God," trans. by K. M. Knudson (Boston, 1920).

YIDDISH DRAMATISTS

S. ANSKY, "The Dybbuk," trans. by L. Alsberg and Winifred Katzin (N. Y. 1926); "Father and Son," trans. by Bessie F. White (Boston, 1932).

MARC ARNSTEIN, "The Eternal Song," trans. by Etta Block, in *One-Act Plays from the Yiddish* (Cincinnati, 1923).

SHOLOM ASCH, "The God of Vengeance," trans. by Isaac Goldberg (Boston, 1918; revised, Girard, Kan., no date); "The Sinner," trans. by Isaac Goldberg, in *Six Plays of the Yiddish Theater* (Boston, 1916); "Winter," trans. by Isaac Goldberg, in *Six Plays of the Yiddish Theater* (Boston, 1916); "Sabbatai Zevi," trans. by F. Whyte and G. R. Noyes (Philadelphia 1930).

I. D. BERKOWITZ, "Landsleit," trans. by B. F. White, in *Nine One-Act Plays From the Yiddish* (Boston, 1932).

F. BIMKO, "Liars," trans. by E. Block, in *One-Act Plays From the Yiddish,* II (N. Y. 1929).

SOLOMON BLOOMGARDEN ("YEHOASH"), "The Shunamite," trans. by H. T. Schnittkind (*Stratford Journal,* 1919), reprinted in Shay's *Twenty-five Short Plays, International* (N. Y. 1925).

SAMUEL DAIXEL, "After Midnight," trans. by B. F. White in *Nine One-Act Plays From the Yiddish* (Boston, 1932).

J. HALPERN, "Mother and Son," trans. by Etta Block, in *One-Act Plays from the Yiddish* (Cincinnati, 1923).

LEON KOBRIN, "The Black Sheep," trans. by Isaac Goldberg in *Six Plays of the Yiddish Theater,* 2nd Series (Boston, 1918); "The Secret of Life," trans. by Isaac Goldberg in *Six Plays of the Yiddish Theater, 2nd Series* (Boston, 1918).

H. LEIVICK, "The Golem," trans. by J. C. Augenlicht (*Poet Lore,* Boston, 1927); Same [parts], by Bessie F. White in *Nine One-Act Plays From the Yiddish* (Boston, 1932).

Z. Levin, "Poetry and Prose," trans. by Isaac Goldberg in *Six Plays of the Yiddish Theater* (Boston, 1916); "The Doctor's First Operation," trans. by B. F. White, in *Nine One-Act Plays From the Yiddish* (Boston, 1932).

Z. Libin, "Colleagues," trans. by B. F. White, in *Nine One-Act Plays From the Yiddish* (Boston, 1932).

Isaac Loeb Perez, "Champagne," trans. by Etta Block, in *One-Act Plays from the Yiddish* (Cincinnati, 1923); "After the Funeral," "Of an Early Morning," and "The Sisters," trans. by E. Block, in *One-Act Plays from the Yiddish,* II (N. Y. 1929); "The Sewing of the Wedding Gown," trans. by B. F. White, in *Nine One-Act Plays from the Yiddish* (Boston, 1932).

S. J. Rabinowitsch, "She Must Marry a Doctor," trans. by Isaac Goldberg, in *Six Plays of the Yiddish Theater* (Boston, 1916).

Abraham Reisin, "Brothers," in Shay's *Fifty More Contemporary One-Act Plays* (N. Y. 1928), and in Block's *One-Act Plays From the Yiddish,* II (N. Y. 1929).

"Yehoash" (*see* Solomon Bloomgarden).

INDEX

INDEX

(12)

THE END